REPORTS OF CASES

ARGUED AND ADJUDGED IN THE

SUPERIOR COURT OF JUDICATURE

OF THE

PROVINCE OF MASSACHUSETTS BAY,

BETWEEN 1761 AND 1772.

BY JOSIAH QUINCY, JUNIOR.

PRINTED FROM HIS ORIGINAL MANUSCRIPTS IN THE POSSESSION OF HIS SON, JOSIAH QUINCY, AND EDITED BY HIS GREAT-GRANDSON, SAMUEL M. QUINCY.

WITH AN APPENDIX

UPON THE WRITS OF ASSISTANCE.

"Many records have in long procefs of time been loft, and poffibly the things themfelves forgotten at this day; which yet, in or near the times wherein they were made, might caufe many of thofe authoritative alterations in fome things touching the proceedings and decifions in law; the original caufe of which change being otherwife at this day hid and unknown to us." — HALE'S HISTORY OF THE COMMON LAW.

BOSTON:
LITTLE, BROWN, AND COMPANY.
1865.

RIVERSIDE, CAMBRIDGE:
PRINTED BY H. O. HOUGHTON AND COMPANY.

PREFACE.

THE name of JOSIAH QUINCY, JR., as a patriot, is well known to thofe who are familiar with the provincial hiftory of Maffachufetts. But of JOSIAH QUINCY, JR., as a lawyer, of his profeffional labors and acquirements, and his pofition at the bar, nothing can now be known except by his immediate defcendants. He was a jurift as well as a patriot; and his love of his profeffion for its own fake was only furpaffed by his devotion to the caufe of his country.

The manufcripts here publifhed are in the poffeffion of Hon. JOSIAH QUINCY, the fon of the reporter, now in his ninety-third year. It is needlefs to fay that they are now offered to the profeffion merely as matters of legal and hiftorical curiofity and intereft; the only other ante-revolutionary reports which have ever been publifhed in this country being 1 Harris and McHenry, Jefferfon, and 1 Dallas, pp. 1 to 29.

Thefe manufcripts confift of three volumes; one with paper covers, (from the original color of which it is referred to as "Red Reports,") and two others bound in parchment, and numbered "3" and "4." The firft two volumes of this fet are miffing, and were probably deftroyed in a fire by which the reporter's law library was loft. The Middlefex cafes reported between pp. 318 and 340 are contained in the fragment of another volume apparently juft commenced, but not in the

handwriting

handwriting of JOSIAH QUINCY, JR. Whether in ſeſe caſes he employed an amanuenſis, or whether the volume is the work of another reporter, cannot now be known, as the firſt pages were unfortunately deſtroyed by one ignorant of their value. All the others are in QUINCY'S own hand, the reports at the firſt term having been taken while he was yet an undergraduate in college. The firſt ſet of foot-notes, to which reference is made by aſteriſks, &c., are the original notes of the reporter; thoſe referred to by numerals are by the editor, as are alſo the marginals. The "Records" referred to in the margin are thoſe of the Superior Court of Judicature, and are to be found in the Clerk's Office of the preſent Supreme Judicial Court. The notes and Appendix to the celebrated caſe of the "Writs of Aſſiſtance," and the notes relating to Slavery in Maſſachuſetts and in England, are the work of HORACE GRAY, JR., ESQ., of the Boſton Bar.

This volume is printed *verbatim et literatim* from the manuſcript, and, as the reader will ſee, in ſome places partakes more of the nature of a private journal than of that of a volume of law reports. It had been my intention to give an outline of the hiſtory of the Province during the period which it embraces, as well as ſome biographical ſketches of the moſt diſtinguiſhed of thoſe whoſe names are mentioned, but that the breaking out of the war in which the country is ſtill involved has ſuddenly called me from the profeſſion to more engroſſing duties, which allow neither time nor opportunity for the completion of the taſk propoſed. For all other omiſſions of whatever the preface ſhould explain or ſupply, I muſt aſk the reader to accept the ſame excuſe.

SAMUEL M. QUINCY.

PORT HUDSON, LA., Feb. 9th, 1864.

A

TABLE

OF THE

CASES Reported in this VOLUME.

A.

B.

C.

D.

E.

Auguſt Term

II Geórgii Ter. in Sup. Cur.

Preſent:

The Honourable

Thomas Hutchinſon, Eſqr., Chief Juſtice.
Benja: Lynde, John Cuſhing, Peter Oliver, Eſqrs., Juſtices.

1762.

POOR v. DOUGHARTY.

Poor *verſ.* Dougharty.

Rec. 1763. Fol. 105.

A Juſtice of the Peace cannot be admitted to teſtify to any Matter which came before him judicially, although he kept no Record of the Tranſaction.

In an Action for falſe Impriſonment, the Juſtice's Mittimus, on which the Plaintiff was committed,

THE Defendant Dougharty loſt ſome Goods, which he ſuſpected Poor had ſtolen; upon which Complaint was made to a Juſtice of the Peace, who heard their ſeveral Stories, and ordered Poor to Goal for further Examination. Poor was again examined, but Dougharty not appearing, was diſcharged, and ſuffered to go without Day. The Juſtice kept no Record of any Part of the Tranſaction. The preſent Action was commenced by Poor *vs.* Dougharty for falſe Impriſonment. *The Juſtice was offered as a Witneſs* to prove the Facts alledged, and objected to, for that whatever came before him was Matter of Record, for a Juſtice's Court is a Court of Record, and that no Parol Evidence

1762.
POOR
v.
DOUGHARTY.

dence can be given of that which is Matter of Record. For this was cited 2 Lilly, 419; Wood's Inft. Com. Law, 82.

is not Evidence of the Facts therein recited.
But it may go to the Jury as a Mittimus. *Oliver & Cufhing, JJ., diff.*
Whether a Paper fhall go to the Jury or not when the Court is equally divided on that Queftion — *quære.*

Meffrs. Otis & Thacher. It was faid contrary, that though it be Matter of Record, yet, if it is not recorded, then the Juftice may be called. The only Rule being that you fhall produce the beft Evidence you can. Now as Poor is unable to produce Record, not through any Default of his own, he may be allowed to produce Parol Evidence. That if a Record is burnt, they may fwear Witneffes to prove the Fact which had been recorded, and this within the fame Reafon. Authorities cited: 1 Salk. 14; 1 Strange, 691; Viner, Tit. Evid. 56; 7 Mod. 169; 2 Show. 145.

Mr. Gridley. It was faid further, for the Defendant, what is in Court muft be proved by Record, what is *in Pais* by Witneffes; Anything which paffes before a Court is not Matter of Fact, but of Record.

The Court (1) upon this Point *ruled* unanimoufly, that the Juftice fhould not be fworn to Anything that came before him judicially. (2)

Then

---

(1) Under the Provincial Government, the Superior Court of Judicature confifted of five judges, and was held for all purpofes by a full bench. All jury trials were conducted in the prefence of the full Court, and not lefs than three judges were competent to prefide. Anc. Chart. 330. 9 Pick. 569.

(2) S. P. *Sayles* v. *Briggs*, 4 Met. 421. There the juftice was offered to prove facts of which he fhould have made a record. Mr. Juftice Hubbard fays: "It is argued that this teftimony fhould be received from neceffity,

1762.
Poor v. Dougharty.

Then the Juſtice's Mittimus was produced as Evidence. The Mittimus, as a Mittimus, was allowed by the Council for the Defendant. But the Recital of the Fact contained in it was excepted to, and the Exception was *ruled by the Court* to be *good.*

It was then debated whether the Mittimus was to be given to the Jury or not, as one Part of it was legal Evidence and the other not — on which *the Court* was divided. (3)

It was then debated whether it muſt go in, as *the Court* was divided upon it, or be taken out, upon which they were alſo divided, and the Caſe was adjourned for a full Court. (4) At February, A. D. 1763, the Mittimus was admitted: *Oliver & Cuſhing* against; *Ch. Juſt., Lynde, & Ruſſell* for it.

---

neceſſity, as there is no way by which the plaintiff can obtain redreſs; and that this is the beſt teſtimony which now exiſts. But it will be productive of leſs miſchief for an individual to ſuffer from the neglect or misfortune of an officer in not making a judicial record, than to eſtabliſh a precedent that the record itſelf, or a part of it, may be proved by parol. It has been argued that the record may be preſumed to be loſt. The rules which apply to the admiſſion of teſtimony to prove the contents of a loſt record, or to the introduction of minutes by which the record may be extended, have no real bearing on a caſe like the preſent, where no ſuch loſs ever took place, and no ſuch minutes were ever made." See alſo *Kendall* v. *Powers*, 4 Met. 553; *Wells* v. *Stevens*, 2 Gray, 115; *Tillotſon* v. *Warner*, 3 Gray, 574.

(3) In *Commonwealth* v. *Wingate*, 6 Gray, 485, the Court allowed a complaint in evidence to go to the jury, although the record of the conviction of the defendant was upon the ſame paper — the jury being inſtructed that ſuch conviction could not be conſidered as evidence.

(4) The effect of a diviſion is to incapacitate the Court from taking any action whatever on that point. 3 Chit. Prac. 10. 12 Co. 118. 1 Salk. 15. *Goddard* v. *Coffin*, Daveis, 381. And the burden being on the

1762.

BAKER v. FROBISHER.

Baker verſ. Frobiſher.

Rec. 1762. Fol. 387.

On a Sale of Goods, there is an implied Warranty that they are merchantable, unleſs ſold by Sample.

FOR ſelling the Plaintiff unmerchantable Soap.(1) It was ſaid there was no expreſs Warranty at the Time of the Sale. But 2d Lord Raymond, 1120, was cited *contra*. And *the Juſtices* were of the Opinion that every Man is bound to ſee his Goods are merchantable at the Time of Sale. (2) But Evidence being brought to prove that the Plaintiff's Wife, who was the Contractor, ſaw a Sample of the Soap, the Jury were directed to find Coſts for the Defendant.

INGRAHAM v. COOK.

Ingraham verſ. Cook & al.

Rec. 1762. Fol. 288.

A new Indorſer to a Writ will be ordered whenever it can be made to appear that the preſent Indorſer cannot anſwer Coſts.

IN this caſe, Ingraham, the Plaintiff, indorſed the Writ. It was urged by the Council for the Defendant, before the Trial, that Ingraham was gone in

the party offering the paper, it would ſeem that a divided court would have no power to admit it.

(1) The declaration in this caſe alleged that the defendant, a ſoap-boiler, "deceitfully contriving to defraud" the plaintiff, delivered him "unmerchantable ſoap of ſtinking material," and "falſely affirmed the ſame to be good and merchantable."

(2) The oppoſite doctrine now prevails — all ſuch caſes being held to be within the principle of *caveat emptor*. *Winsor* v. *Lombard*, 18 Pick. 60. *Mixer* v. *Coburn*, 11 Met. 559. But the rule intimated above ſeems once to have been aſſumed in Maſſachuſetts. See *Oliver* v. *Sale*, poſt — *Otis, arguendo:* "The rule of merchandiſe which obliges the vendor to anſwer for what he ſells without warranty, is confined to manufactures of the country, which a man muſt be ſuppoſed to know the quality of."

1762. INGRAHAM v. COOK.

in the Army, had no Eftate, and could not anfwer the Cofts. It was faid *contra*, that a new Indorfer is never ordered but in the Cafe of abfconding infolvent Debtors, and that the Plaintiff was in the Pay of the Government. But *the Court ruled*, that a new Indorfer ought to be found in every Cafe where it could be made to appear to the Court that there was Danger the prefent Indorfer could not anfwer Cofts. But a Witnefs was produced who knew the Plaintiff to have a confiderable Sum of Money at Intereft; upon which the Motion was filenced. (1)

NEWMAN v. HOMANS.

Newman *verf.* Homans.

Rec. 1762. Fol. 383.

After a reafonable Time a Factor is liable for Intereft on the Price received for Goods of his Principal. And fuch Intereft may be recovered in an Action of Affumpsit, as well as in Account.

THE Queftion was, whether Intereft or Depretiation ought to be allowed by a Factor after any

(1) The Prov. Sts. of 1 Geo. 1 and 1 Geo. 2 (Anc. Chart. 406, 466) provided for the indorfement of all writs by the plaintiff or attorney, but contained no provifion for finding a new indorfer in any cafe. The St. of 1784, c. 28, provided in addition, that where the plaintiff was not an inhabitant of the State, he fhould procure a fufficient indorfer who was, and alfo that where the writ was indorfed by plaintiff's attorney, if such attorney was fhown to be of infufficient ability, a new indorfer fhould be ordered. This act was repealed by St. 1833, c. 50, which contains the provifions fubftantially reënacted by the Rev. Sts. c. 90, § 10, (Gen. Sts. c. 123, § 20; c. 129, § 29,) viz., making the indorfement a condition precedent only where the plaintiff is not an inhabitant of the State, and giving the Court difcretionary power to require it wherever it appears reafonable. But it feems that mere poverty of the plaintiff will not be confidered fufficient caufe for fuch requirement, in the abfence of vexation or oppreffion. Per *Shaw*, C. J., 21 Pick. 212. An indorfer will be required where the plaintiff removes from the State during the pendency of the action. 8 Mass. 272. 1 Gray, 114. But the removal of a foreign plaintiff into the State does not have the effect to difcharge the indorfer. 8 Met. 149.

1762.

Newman v. Homans.

any Period, otherwiſe than upon an Action of Account, in which he ſhews at what Time he received Pay for the Goods. (1)

The Court was of Opinion, that after a reaſonable Time he ought. (2)

Zuill v. Bradley.

Zuill *verſ.* Bradley.

Rec. 1762. Fol. 388.

Where Father and Son of the ſame Name reſide in the ſame Town, *it ſeems* that the Omiſſion of "junior," in a Writ againſt the Son, is good Cauſe of Abatement. *It ſeems*, that Duplicity is no Objection to a Plea in Abatement.

THE Plaintiff ſues Bradley by the Name of Daniel Bradley, of Haverhill, &c., Trader.

Upon which the Defendant pleads as follows: "And Daniel Bradley, junior, of Haverhill, &c., "Innholder, whoſe Body was attached by this Writ, "comes and ſays he is the ſame Perſon who was ſued "by the ſaid John Zuill by the Name of Daniel "Bradley, of Haverhill, &c., Trader. And the ſaid "Daniel Bradley, junior, ſays this Writ ought to abate, "becauſe he ſays that at the Time of the Purchaſe "thereof *there were* two Men in ſaid Town of Haverhill known by the names of Daniel Bradley and "Daniel Bradley, junior, and that he hath been always

(1) It appears by the record that this was *indebitatus aſſumpſit* for money had and received. The declaration alleged a promiſe to pay, with intereſt, to which the defendant demurred in the Court of Common Pleas, and the demurrer was ſuſtained. In the Superior Court this deciſion was reverſed, and the caſe ſent to a jury.

(2) S. P. *Dodge* v. *Perkins*, 9 Pick. 368. Where a factor, having received money, unreaſonably neglects to inform his principal, he is liable for intereſt for the time of ſuch unreaſonable delay.

1762. Zuill v. Bradley.

"ways called and known by the Name of Daniel "Bradley, junior, and not by the Name of Daniel "Bradley only, as in this Writ is ſuppoſed, and that "the ſaid Daniel Bradley, ſenior, is his the ſaid Dan-"iel Bradley junior's Father, and all this the ſaid "Daniel Bradley, junior, is ready to verify; where-"fore he prays Judgment of this Writ that it abate, "and for his Coſts.

"2. The ſaid Writ ought to abate, for that he the "ſaid Daniel Bradley, junior, was at the Time of the "Purchaſe of this Writ, and ſtill is, an Innholder, and "not a Trader, as in this Writ is ſuppoſed, and this "he alſo is ready to verify; wherefore he prays Judg-"ment of this Writ that it abate, and for his Coſts."

O. Thacher.

To which it was objected, that there was a Duplicity which deſtroyed it, for that he pleaded, that his Name was Daniel Bradley, junior, and not Daniel Bradley only, and alſo that he was an Innholder and not a Trader; and Mod. was cited. But it was overruled. (1)

Upon

---

(1) The Court would ſeem to have held duplicity to be no objection to a plea in abatement. The caſe of *Trevelian* v. *Seccomb*, Carth. 7, 8, ſeems to countenance ſuch a view, but the miſtake is explained in Steph. Pl. note (56). See alſo Bac. Ab. Abatement, (P); and 5 Pick. 223, where the objection of duplicity was overruled on the ground that one of the allegations was ſurpluſage. It has been held in the Superior Court of Suffolk, that under the Practice Act of 1852, an anſwer in abatement may be objected to for duplicity, on motion. 20 Law Rep. 463. And this on the ground that the anſwer is ſubject to the ſame rules againſt duplicity as was formerly the plea. But before the Pracice Act, duplicity could not be taken advantage of. St. 1836, c. 273, § 3. 1 Cuſh. 137. And by § 13 of the act, "different conſiſtent defences may be ſtated in the ſame anſwer."

1762. Zuill v. Bradley.

Upon a full Hearing, it was *ruled*, that as they were in the ſame Town, and Father and Son, it was a Miſnomer sufficient to abate the Writ. (2) *Ch. Juſt.* doubted of the Words "*there were.*" He thinks that the Latin Word "*habentur*" is of greater Extent, but ſuppoſes it is not ſufficient to make it bad. (3)

Blower v. Campbell.

Blower *verſ.* Campbell.

Rec. 1763. Fol. 16.

Whether the Deſcription "Blackſmith" includes a Nailor or not —*quære*.

THE Defendant was named in the Writ, Blackſmith, to which he pleaded he was a Nailor, and not a Blackſmith, and therefore prays Judgment for the Abatement of the Writ.

It was replied that Blackſmith was a general Name, including many Species, of which a Nailor was one.

The Defendant's Council anſwered that they were ſo diſtinct that the one knew Nothing of the other's Buſineſs, and a Forger, Gunſmith, &c., might as well be called Blackſmith.

The

(2) "It ſeems to be only in the caſe of a father and ſon of the ſame names, that the addition is required to be ſtated in a writ where the ſon is made defendant." *Kincaid* v. *Howe*, 10 Maſs. 204. See alſo 5 Dane Ab. 705. To the point that "junior" is no part of a man's name, but an addition uſed to deſcribe and deſignate the perſon, ſee 1 Pick. 388; 15 Pick. 7; 17 Pick. 200.

(3) It appears, however, by the record, that the judgment was finally given "on the ſecond exception," perhaps on account of the Chief Juſtice's doubt on this point.

The Court were unanimously of the Opinion that the Writ was good, but for different Reasons; some because the Defendant had at certain Times done some Articles of Blacksmith's Work; others for the Reason aforesaid.

1762.
BLOWER v. CAMPBELL.

Jones *vers.* Belcher.

JONES v. BELCHER.

Rec. 1762. Fol. 389.

A Bond given here for a Debt due in England to a third Party, draws New England Interest.

DEBT upon a Bond given here, which it was suggested was for a Debt due in England. Moved that English Interest only should be paid. Cases in Eq. 288, cited.

But *the Court* were of Opinion, as the Bond was given to a Person here, (not the Creditor in England,) and the Debt was become his, New England Interest ought to be granted. (1)

Minot *vers.* Prout.

MINOT v. PROUT.

Rec. 1766. Fol. 78.

Suing and entering upon a Mortgage is no Bar to an Action upon the Bond secured thereby.

DEBT upon a Bond. Defendant pleads as follows: "The said Timothy comes and defends

---

(1) This is according to the general rule of computing interest according to the *lex loci contractus*. *Winthrop* v. *Carleton*, 12 Mass. 4. *Von Hemert* v. *Porter*, 11 Met. 210. But where interest is given as damages, the *lex fori* prevails. *Barringer* v. *King*, 5 Gray, 9, 12. *Eaton* v. *Mellus*, 7 Gray, 566.

1762.
Minot
v.
Prout.

"fends, &c., and prays Oyer of the Condition there-"of, and the ſame is read to him in theſe Words:

"The Condition of the aforewritten Obligation, "&c., (this Condition as uſuall,) which being read "and heard, the ſaid Timothy ſaith that the ſaid "Chriſtopher his Action aforeſaid againſt him the "ſaid Timothy ought not to have and maintain, "becauſe he ſaith that the ſaid Timothy, on the "Day of the Date of the ſaid Obligation, and col-"lateral thereto, at Boſton aforeſaid, made and exe-"cuted to the ſaid Chriſtopher a Deed of Mortgage "of a Meſſuage and Land, ſituate, &c., which "Mortgage was executed to the ſaid Chriſtopher "to be a collateral Security for the Payment of the "Sum in the Condition aforecited mentioned and "the Intereſt thereof, and afterwards, viz., at Boſ-"ton aforeſaid, on the 13th of December, 1758, he "the ſaid Chriſtopher by his Deed, ſealed with his "Seal, aſſigned and conveyed the ſaid Mortgage, "as well as the Obligation now ſued on, to one "William Brown, of, &c., and the ſaid William "afterwards, viz., the ſame Day, made his Election, "and for the Non-payment of the ſaid Sum en-"tered on the ſaid mortgaged Premiſes, and became "ſeiſed thereof in his Demeſne as of Fee, and ſtill "holds the ſaid mortgaged Premiſes; and all this "the ſaid Timothy is ready to verify, wherefore he "prays Judgment if the ſaid Chriſtopher his Action "aforeſaid againſt him the ſaid Timothy ſhall have "and maintain.

"*O. Thacher.*"

To

To which the Plaintiff replied: "And the said "Christopher saith, that for Anything above al- "ledged, he the said Christopher ought not to be "barred from having and maintaining his Action "aforesaid, because protesting the said William "Brown never made any Election as he the said "Timothy above supposeth for Plea, the said Chris- "topher saith *that the said William Brown did not* "*enter into or upon the said mortgaged Premises for* "*the Non-payment of the said Sum mentioned in the* "*Condition aforesaid, and the Interest thereof*, as the "said Timothy in his Plea abovesaid hath alledged, "and this the said Christopher prayeth may be in- "quired of by the Country.

"*R. Dana.*"

Upon Demurrer, Exception taken to the Replication, that it was a Negative Pregnant. *Doct. Placitandi*, 256, cited: That either the whole Plea should have been traversed, or he should have set forth the particular Matter. Cro. James, 559.

Contra. They having demurred to our Replication, on that Demurrer we may take Exception to their Plea, which if bad we need not answer their Exception to our Replication. Their Plea is insufficient; for though he had entered upon the Mortgage, yet that is not conclusive that the Bond may not be sued.

Upon this it was largely debated whether a Mortgage being sued and entered upon, the Bond could have Effect, and *e contra.*

Ruled

1762. MINOT v. PROUT.

Ruled unanimouſly, that it could, and that the Plea is bad. (1)

Bond to be chancered next Term. (2)

DUDLEY v. DUDLEY.

Rec. 1762. Fol. 415.

Deviſe as follows: "I give to my Son W. my new Farm in R.," "from whence he ſhall annually ſupply and bring Home to his Mother her Firewood during her Life." "I alſo give him my Farm of 1000 Acres

Dudley *verſ.* Dudley & al. (3)

THE late Governour Dudley, by his Will, deviſed as follows:

"I give my Wife One Hundred Pounds per "Annum, to be paid quarterly during her Life by "Paul Dudley my eldeſt Son, out of the Iſſues and "Rents of my Eſtates herein given him.

"I give to my Son, William Dudley, my new "Farm in the Woods in Roxbury, containing 150 "Acres with the Woodland there, purchaſed of "Devotion Craft, from whence he ſhall annually ſupply

---

(1) S. P. *Amory* v. *Fairbanks*, 3 Maſs. 562. *Ely* v. *Ely*, 6 Gray, 439. See alſo 8 Pick. 336; 5 Cuſh. 231.

(2) A bill in chancery was accordingly filed praying that the penalty "be chancered down to the ſum of one penny." But the Court gave £176 10*s*.

(3) This was a review of a "plea of partition" brought by the younger children of William Dudley, againſt Thomas the eldeſt ſon. The ſpecial verdict found that the premiſes were the ſame called by the teſtator his "farm of a thouſand acres at Manchaug," that William died inteſtate, and that Thomas then entered on the premiſes; "if therefore the ſaid William, by force of the will aforeſaid, took an eſtate in fee ſimple in the thouſand acres aforeſaid, then they find for the defendants coſts; otherwiſe they find for the original defendant and now plaintiff."

"supply and bring Home to his Mother her Fire-"wood during her Life.

1762.

DUDLEY *v.* DUDLEY.

"I also give him my Farm of one 1000 Acres "at Manchaug and Three Hundred Pounds toward "building him an House.

"I have already disposed in Marriage of my "Four Daughters, and paid them what I intended.

"I further give each of them 1000 Acres, to be "taken out of my 6000 Acres in the Town of Ox-"ford; and to my Nephew Daniel Allen, and my "Niece Ann Hilton, 500 Acres, out of the same "Dividend, to be equally divided between them; "all those Lands to descend to the Children sev-"erally, and the *Heirs of their Bodies.*

"To my eldest Son Paul I give the Inheritance "of all my Houses and Lands in Roxbury, Oxford, "Woodstock, Newtown, Brookline, Merrimack, or "elsewhere, all my Stock, Debt, Money, and all "Estate belonging to me whatsoever, except as "above set down. *And my Will is that my Lands "descend after the Manner of England forever; to the "Male Heirs first, and after to the Females. If either "of my Sons die without Male Issue, his Brother and "his Male Issue shall inherit the Lands herein be-"queathed,"* &c.

at M. and £300 toward building him an House." After other Legacies and a Residuary Devise, the following: "And my Will is that my Lands descend after the Manner of England forever; to the Male Heirs first and after to the Females. If either of my Sons die without Male Issue, his Brother and his Male Issue shall inherit the Lands herein bequeathed." *Held*, that W. took a Fee Simple in the "Farm of 1000 Acres at M."

The Question in this Case was, whether William Dudley took a Fee Simple by his Father's Will.

Mr.

1762.
DUDLEY *v.* DUDLEY.

Mr. Otis for the Fee Simple. (4) The Words upon which I ſuppoſe they build their Fee Tail are theſe, "*If either of my Sons die without Male Iſſue, his* "*Brother,*" *&c.* There are no Words precedent to theſe which can be ſuppoſed in the leaſt to favour that Opinion, but on the contrary are inconſiſtent with it; he muſt have intended to have given him a Fee in the 1000 Acres, or his End, which was to build him an Houſe, could not be anſwered, for £300 can't be ſuppoſed any way ſufficient, and therefore we muſt ſuppoſe he deſigned William ſhould ſell the Land; and it is Law and Reaſon that a ſpecial Deviſe ſhould take Effect, which could not otherwiſe, a general Clauſe notwithſtanding, nor is the Law to be wreſted in favor of ſuch Eſtates; for however Eſtates Tail were once favoured and praiſed, as in the Statute *De Donis*, yet Ld. Coke tells us they were convinced of their Miſtake, and exclaims in pretty full Terms. Co. L. 20. Wood, Inſt. And here the Reaſon is greater than in England, for here all Eſtates are partable. (5)

Nay I don't think the Words give even Paul an Eſtate Tail. The Intention of the Teſtator is one of the grand Principles, and ſhall not be counteracted, and it is to be favoured as far as poſſible conſiſtent with the Rules of the Common Law; and unleſs there are ſome operative Words, Fee Simple muſt

---

(4) The MS. report of the arguments in this caſe bears evidence of being the original minutes taken in court. A little confuſion, and an occaſional defect in grammar, are thus accounted for.

(5) See *poſt*, *Baker* v. *Mattocks*.

muſt be ſuppoſed to be given. Now here are no expreſs Words in Favour of a Fee Simple. "And "my Will is that my Land deſcend after the Man-"ner of England forever, to the Male Heirs firſt, "and after to the Females, &c." I think it manifeſt his Intention was, that they ſhould deſcend according to the Common Law, which knows no Eſtate Tail; and that being his Intention, the Law will not admit an Inheritance contrary to the known Law of the Country; and this being contrary to the Law deſcends as a Fee Simple, and the Word "Male Heirs, &c." ſhall be attributed to Unſkillfulneſs.

Mr. Kent for the Tail. Mr. Otis can't ſuppoſe an Eſtate Tail can't be made in this Province, ſo we need only inquire into the Teſtator's Intention. Cites 3 Salk. 394, *Fiſher* vs. *Nichols*, of the favourable Conſtruction of Wills. In Paul's Gift there was nothing enjoined him, but annual Payments which the Profits would ſecure. "To William I give "Manchaug Farm, and £300 towards building him "an Houſe," they are evidently ſeparate. He gives him Manchaug Farm, and moreover I give him £300 towards building him an Houſe. To Paul he gives the *Inheritance* of his Land, &c.; this Word is uſed in Tails. Vid. Caſes in Eq. Abr. 178, 179. 1 Salk. Tit. Deviſe, 234.

The Court aſked, as there had been no Authorities yet produced on the other Side, whether it would not be more regular to have them read now, before the Council in Favour of the Tail cloſed. Upon which *Mr. Gridley* produced his Authorities. 1 Inſt. 9 b, any Eſtate charged is a Fee Simple. 2 Peere Wms.

1762.
DUDLEY *v.* DUDLEY.

Wms. 673. Siderfin, 312. Moore's Rep. 53. Viner, Tit. Deviſe, 82. 3 Mod. 82.

Mr. Trowbridge for the Tail. In his firſt Deviſe to his Wife, he gives her £100, for Paul to pay out of the Rents and Iſſues of his Eſtate, which evidently exclude from his Intention to give Paul a Fee Simple; ſo in the Gift of the Wood it is idle to ſay that is greater or anything near equal to the yearly Rents of the 150 Acres. And as to the Manchaug Farm and £300; it is true £300 would not build him an Houſe at Roxbury, but does it appear that he meant ſo? Perhaps, and moſt probably, he intended on the Farm at Manchaug.

Ch. Juſt. The words are build *him* an Houſe; not an Houſe ſimply, but *him*, one whom he knew was to live at Roxbury.

Trowbridge continues. The firſt Words in a Will may direct, but the laſt ſhall controul, and this is the Difference between Wills and Deeds. The Deviſe to his Couzins is in theſe Words, "*to deſcend to* "*the Children ſeverally, and the Heirs of their Bodies.*" A Fee Tail *may deſcend.* If in the firſt Words he intended a Fee Simple, in the laſt he altered his Mind, and intended to controul the firſt. "If *either* "die without Male Iſſue, then," &c. — *either.* A Deviſe of this Sort is as great an Eſtate Tail as can be given, and the Word Body ſhall be ſupplied. Lilly, Tit. Deviſe. 6 Coke, 16, *Collier's Caſe.* Ventris, 230. Hawk. Abr. 17. Had he deſigned it ſhould deſcend as Fee Simple in England, it would have deſcended

descended to the Daughters of William before the Sons of Paul, &c., but here it is otherwise.

Mr. Gridley for the Fee. The Intent of the Devisor is the only Thing your Honours will govern yourselves by, (Vid. Peere Wms. *ut supra,*) and that Intention is to be spelt out by little Hints, by other Devises, &c. Viner, Tit. Devise, 182. Notwithstanding 'tis a Devise he says 'shall *descend.*' He designed William should sell, and he must sell, and that gives a Fee Simple, as much as express Words. He designed William should live in Roxbury, and £300 is not sufficient to build him an House there, a Dwelling House. The Law takes Notice of the Rule of Grants, Words in the Beginning and End refer to the Whole. Sid. *ut supra.* It is not—I give 1000 Acres, I give him £300 towards building him an House, but they are so coupled as to be the same; I give him 1000 Acres and £300 towards building him an House. Vid. Moore's *ut sup.* (*Ch. Just.* In the Authority you cite, they were each equally applicable to the Purpose, here not: Land does not seem so much so as Money.) In this Country we make our Real Estate almost Personal Estate by Act of Parliament, and our own Acts; besides, Gov. Dudley did not perhaps leave a Sufficiency in Money. The Word *descend* I grant is used in Tails, but when it is used, there we always use the proper express, Words of Tail; here it is—shall descend to him—not the Heirs of the Body, &c. Estates Tail can never be supposed by a Devise after the Manner of England, for being a minor Estate should have been mentioned in express Words. Supposing the Females decease, there is

 no

1762. DUDLEY v. DUDLEY.

no further Deviſe, if it is a Tail. The Law of this Province forbids his giving it as the Law of England: But if he meant ſo, it could not be Tail, for it is the Common Law. I imagine Governor Dudley thought that was the Manner of England, that the Sons of the other ſhould take excluſively of the Daughters of the other, and the Will is inaccurate throughout as to the Daughters. Shall what is underſtood be ſet aſide by one inſenſible Expreſſion?

It was moved by *Mr. Kent*, and ſeconded by *Mr. Trowbridge*, that they might be heard again before Judgment, and *the Court* thinking it a Matter of Nicety and Conſequence, deſired a further Argument, and continued it to the next Term for Judgment. (4)

Mr. Otis. The ſingle Queſtion is, whether theſe Words, "I alſo give him my Farm of 1000 Acres at Manchaug and Three Hundred Pounds to build him an Houſe," compared with the whole Will, make a Fee Simple or a Tail. The Words of Acts executed in the Life are to be "to Heirs forever," in a Fee Simple, "Heirs of the Body" general, Male or Female, in a Fee Tail; greater Indulgence is to be given to Wills.

I ſhall endeavour to ſhow that from this Clauſe by itſelf, or conſidered with Reſpect to the others, it muſt

(4) The report of the caſe accordingly breaks off at this point in the MS., and is reſumed between the caſes of *Gardner* v. *Purrington* and *Rogers* v. *Kenrick*, decided at the next term. For convenience, however, it is printed as a whole.

muſt be the Intention of Dudley to give his Son a Fee Simple; and ſeparately conſidered, there could be no Doubt; but 'tis the Clauſe "after the Manner of England, &c." which cauſes it. The Queſtion will be whether the laſt Words create a Tail in any, even to the Eſtate given Paul, and if it does, whether they extend through the Whole. Ld. Hobart ſays the two great Principles upon which all Deviſes hang, are the Intention of the Teſtator, which ſhall be indulged as far as the Rules of Law admit.

I think the Conſideration of the Intention, is the moſt rational Way of judging of any Will; and I think whoever does that will think any Eſtate Tail remote from the Teſtator's Intention. The firſt Words are only an Inheritance according to the Intent of the Common Law; his Intent was, I allow, to make a Common Law Deſcent, Spite of the Province Law, — to cut off his Daughters only. We ſhall conſider how far this Intent is to be indulged. No Man ſhall create an Eſtate contrary to the Laws of his Country; we know none according to the Courſe of the Common Law. As for the other Words of the Will, Manchaug Farm is given for ſuch a Purpoſe, as could not be anſwered by ſuch an Eſtate as they contend for; he has it given to build an Houſe, which he could not do, if he had only his Life in it. Co. Lit. 9, b. It is an old Principle, that paying is an Argument that the Land ſhall go. It has been ſaid that a Deviſe of Woodland formerly in this Country conveyed a Fee Simple, and that it has been adjudged ſo; any Words that can amount to an Intent that the Deviſee

1762. DUDLEY *v.* DUDLEY.

viſee ſhall have the Advantage of the Whole of it, ſhall have a Fee; it is not the firſt or laſt Part of a Will that ſhall ſtand, but the Whole together. Viner, 324, Tit. Deviſe. If he intended he ſhould reap the ſame Benefit, as he would if it had been a Fee, it ſhall be. Viner, 224, 13. Will to be taken altogether. Ibid. 182, 11, 12, 13. His Intent being contrary to Law, firſt Deviſees take a Fee Simple. Ibid. 229. Swin. 165, 141. Entails diſfavoured.—No Tail unleſs the firſt Words give a Fee Simple; none where it is given in any ſuch Manner. The firſt Words may be controuled, where it is a plain Fee Simple, here it is not; he tries to invent a new Conveyance, his Words are apt to convėy according to the Law of England; he muſt either give it according to the Cuſtom of the Country, or in Fee Tail general or ſpecial. An implied Eſtate Tail has never been raiſed when the firſt Words were to give an Eſtate unknown to the Law of the Country. No Teſtator was ever interpreted to mean to give a Tail becauſe that came neareſt to his Intention.

Mr. Gridley's Authorities: Sid. 312—Rule that firſt and laſt Words relate to the whole; middle to the middle only. Moor, Caſe 153, p. 52. Plowd. Comment. 540. Viner, Tit. Deviſe, 182, 11. 3 Lev. 111. 4 Mod. 154. 3 Lev. 125. 3 Mod. 182. Styles, 276, 392.

Mr. Auchmuty. I ſhall conſider this by looking into the Words of the Will, collect the Intent, and compare it with the Rules of Law.—"His Brother and his Male Iſſue ſhall inherit." Theſe Words are

1762.

DUDLEY *v.* DUDLEY.

are deſcriptive of an Eſtate Tail, and no other. The firſt Words are liable to be reſtrained, controuled, or defeated by the laſt; if a laſt Word contradict the firſt, the laſt ſhall ſtand. 1 Lilly, 449. Co. Lit. 112, b. The Words relate as well to William as Paul. Cro. Ja. 448. This is a Caſe Mr. Otis ſaid could not be found. Cro. Ja. 695, *Chadock* v. *Cowley*. It ſeems abſurd that an expreſs Eſtate may be controuled by latter Words, and yet that where there is no certain Eſtate given by the firſt Words, that they ſhall not; I ſhould think they might *a fortiori*. 9 Coke, 128, *Sonday's Caſe*. 1 Ld. Raymond, 185, *Baker* vs. *Wall*. Ib. 568, *Nottingham* vs. *Jennings*. Comyns, 539, *Brice* vs. *Smith*. I cite theſe to ſhow the firſt Words need not be expreſs, and that the laſt ſhall explain the firſt. I utterly deny that the giving Woodland could by Law give a Fee; but if that be the Caſe, when the Teſtator afterwards explains his Meaning, that muſt cauſe it to be otherwiſe. As to the Practice of the Court, the Rules of Law by being recollected would deſtroy it. I believe no Practice agreeable to that Rule of Woodland can be brought, and if there can, not where there are other ſuch Words as are here.

As to the Houſe, it does not appear that it was to build an Houſe at Roxbury; he was at that Time building an Houſe there, and the Deviſe, which takes no Effect till the Death of the Teſtator, might be ſome Years off. — Could he not have paſſed it by Deed, had that been his Intent? It is much more rational to conclude, that, as he had given him a Farm, he intended he ſhould live there, therefore gave him £300 to build him an Houſe there,

1762. DUDLEY *v.* DUDLEY.

there, to encourage the Settlement: There are two Tracts given William and Paul much in the ſame Words. I can't find any Reaſon why they ſhould be confined to Paul; all the Lands therein bequeathed, in Caſe one died without Iſſue Male, are given to the other; he deſigning to entail all his Lands to the Survivor of his Sons, and his Male Iſſue, he has done it. I agree he intended to exclude the Daughters; could he then think he was giving a Fee Simple, when he expreſsly excludes them? He has not given a general Eſtate Tail, but confined it to Male Iſſue—They ſay he is making a new Eſtate, I ſay he has made an old one. In the Caſe of Raymond, 'tis ſaid he intended an Eſtate Tail, becauſe the Daughters were excluded. Take it as a Tail, all Purpoſes will be anſwered, the Daughters will be excluded, the Heirs Male will have it; and 'tis a Tail with Croſs Remainders, all which he ſeems to have had in View. The Heir-at-Law is favoured—ſo he is here: As to the paying, it is not always denotive of a Fee: The Wood is out of Roxbury, what is that to Manchaug? He has given that Farm, and ordered that Wood to be furniſhed; there is a Difference where a Sum in groſs is ordered, and where an annual Sum not exceeding the Rents. Co. Lit. 9, b. There is an Authority that ſays, where he gives it ſpecially, it is not an Inheritance. 2 Bacon. William could not be a Loſer by ſuch a Payment. Gilbert cites Cro. Eliz. 498. If the Deviſor orders A to pay B a Sum in groſs, this gives a Fee, though not even then, I ſuppoſe, if he afterwards explains it otherwiſe. As to the Authorities of Viner, they relate only to the Conſtruction of Wills, which we agree with them: As

As for the Caſe from Moor, of the Coats, (5) they were to be paid forever: It would be inconſiſtent, but that as the Incumbrance was perpetual, the Eſtate ſhould be perpetual alſo. The other Moor Caſe is only that all Parts of a Will are operative, we agree to it, if they can be reconciled. How can it be ſuppoſed the Land as well as £300 are to go towards building him an Houſe?—the other Words of the Will diſpoſe of the Land otherwiſe, this is in Anſwer to the Grammar Caſe (6); Plowden's Caſe is only the Say of Council. Moor's Caſe of the Item (7) is anſwered by Cro. Ja. 695. The Intention of the Will can be no otherwiſe anſwered than by Tail;—if a Tail not an Iota is loſt.

Mr. Trowbridge. We all agree that the whole Will is to be taken together; that if the firſt Words are doubtful, the laſt may explain them, but if the firſt are expreſs, the latter ſhall not controul them. It muſt be abſurd to ſuppoſe that the Farm as well as Money was given to build an Houſe; in ſome Caſes the *Item* may couple, in ſome not. 5 Co. 7, *Wyndham's Caſe.* 6 Co. 61, *Catesby's Caſe.* That the Word "*and*" is to be governed according to the Subject-Matter.—If there is any particular Eſtate limited, paying does not make a Fee. 1 Vent. 227. Gilb. Law of Deviſes. Comyn's, 539, *Brice* vs. *Smith.* Thoſe Lands which he gives his Daughters, he expreſſly entails, ſo he does what he gives his Couzins, and uſes the Word *deſcend* as he does here; as for the Word Inheritance, an Eſtate Tail is

(5) Erroneouſly cited; the "Caſe of the Coats" is *Smith* v. *Tyndal*, 2 Salk. 685.

(6) Sid. 312.

(7) Moore, caſe 153.

1762.

DUDLEY
v.
DUDLEY.

is as much an Inheritance as a Fee Simple. As for the Manner of England, I deny that he meant Common Law, he only intended it ſhould be partable as here; If his Intent could not be anſwered according to the Rules of Law, the Law will mould it into ſuch one, as is moſt agreeable to his Will and Deſign.

Mr. Gridley. The Intent of the Deviſor ſhall be the Pole Star of the Will, and then every Iota ſhall have its Force, if it can conſiſtent with the reſt. I agree that the Subject-Matter muſt govern in all Caſes; the Subject-Matter here is a Supply to William to build him an Houſe. With Regard to Mr. Trowbridge's Authorities, I ſee not how they are applicable; the firſt is a Common Law Conveyance, to be judged by Common Law Maxims, to be taken moſt ſtrongly againſt the Grantor; here the Intent of the Deviſor is to be purſued;—If the £300 is given for the Houſe, the Lands are given; they are tied by an indiſſoluble Band, and can't be ſeparated, but by a Violence upon Common Senſe. The Moor Caſe has *Item*, here is none. We muſt conſider of our Country and Real Eſtate here: To a Perſon unacquainted with our Eſtate, this might ſeem ſtrange, but to us who know Real Eſtates are liable for the Payment of Debts, and are by Act of Parliament made Chattels Real, for the Payment of Debts, (8) that they are almoſt the only Things we have to trade upon, and that they continue in a Family ſcarce over three Generations, 'tis not ſtrange they ſhould be put upon the ſame Footing with Perſonal Eſtate. In this I take it, both muſt be ſupported

(8) Anc. Chart. 292.

ſuppoſed for the ſame Purpoſe, it is a Conſtruction ariſes from the Neceſſity of the Thing, and the Nature of Real Eſtate here. As for the Objection againſt our Conſtruction, that it is uncertain how long he would live; there was an Houſe for Paul, and one deſigned for William; if there was none erecting, 'twas for one hereafter to be built, if one was built, to finiſh it or to reimburſe him. As for the after Words; whether they ſhall deſtroy the Force of the Firſt — the Words "after the Manner of England," — it being unlimited, it muſt be Common Law; who would ſuppoſe Tail Male to mean the Manner of England?

"The Heirs Male, and after to the Female;" the whole Complexion is to the Creation of a new Eſtate; this laſt ought to be wholly laid aſide, this extraordinary, impoſſible Clauſe.

If this Clauſe operate at all, it can't take to the Manchaug Farm; if that can be ſatisfied elſewhere, it need not be applied here; let it go to the Roxbury Lands. 9 Mod. 154, *Adams* vs. *Clark*.

The Chief Juſtice delivered the Judgment of the Court in Favour of the Fee Simple. (9)

---

(9) This judgment is recorded as of September term at Worceſter, but the entry bears evidence of having been inſerted at a later date. The deciſion was undoubtedly given, as here reported, at February term in Suffolk. It alſo appears that "immediately upon entering up this judgment, the ſaid Thomas moved for an appeal to his Majeſty in Council, which the Court did not allow." The Province Charter provided for an appeal to the King in "perſonal actions" only. Anc. Chart. 32.

It is to be regretted that we have no means of aſcertaining on what ground this deciſion was given. If the Court were ſatisfied that the

 land,

1762.

JACKSON
v.
FOYE.

Rec. 1762.
Fol. 385.

Evidence of Payment of full Rent by a Tenant, for thirty Years, and of the giving a Note of Hand for the Balance found due on a Settlement, is sufficient Proof of a Contract to pay Taxes under the Province Law, which provides that "where no Contract is" the Landlord shall reimburse half the Taxes. *Russell, J., dissentiente.*

Jackson *vers.* Foye.

MRS. JACKSON was upwards of thirty Years a Tenant to Mrs. Foye, paid her Rent without any Deduction but for Repairs, which were often made. A. D. 1758 they settled Accounts, and Mrs. Jackson, owing Mrs. Foye, gave her a Note of Hand on Interest. The present Action was brought by Jackson against Foye for half the Rates for Twenty Years.

The only Question was, whether these Settlements, that Note of Hand given, when, if the Rates had been reckoned, there would have been a Balance due to Jackson, amounted to Evidence of an express Contract.

The

---

land, as well as the money, was given "toward building the house," it was evidently excepted from any operation of the subsequent general clause. But if the effect of that clause became necessary to be considered, a more difficult question must have arisen. The words directing a descent "according to the manner of England," &c., seem clearly to intend a common law descent, in opposition to the law of the Province. But the words which immediately follow, "If either of my sons die," &c., would seem to import an indefinite failure of issue, and to give the brothers estates in tail male general, with cross remainders, also in tail male. *Abbott* v. *Essex Co.* 18 How. 202. *Hall* v. *Priest*, 6 Gray, 18, and cases cited. The question cannot be better stated than in Mr. Otis's words, *ante*, p. 20 — "Can an implied estate tail ever be raised, when the first words give an estate unknown to the laws of the country?" In the case of *Banister* v. *Henderson*, *post*, 131, Mr. Auchmuty says that "the point of charge had weight" in this case. This seems hardly probable, as one was directly on the rents and profits, and the other a charge of wood to be furnished from the land itself. See 24 Pick. 139. And even a personal charge of a sum in gross will not enlarge a clear estate tail, though only arising by implication. 2 Jarman on Wills, (1st Am. ed.) 172. 5 T. R. 535. 2 B. & Ad. 318.

1762. JACKSON v. FOYE.

The Court (*Juſtice Ruſſell diſſentiente*) gave it to the Jury as their Opinion, that it did, and directed them to give the Defendant Coſts, which they did. (1)

Wiſwall *verſ.* Hall.

WISWALL v. HALL.

Rec. 1762. Fol. 385.

Referees cannot be admitted to teſtify that their Award that each Party ſhould bear his own Coſts, was made in Conſideration of a Promiſe by one Party never to enforce a certain Judgment againſt the other.

PLAINTIFF and Defendant had formerly ſubmitted Matters in Controverſy to certain Referees, who had reported thereon. This Action was brought by Wiſwall *vs.* Hall to recover the Coſts upon that former Suit, for though the Referees had reported that they ſhould bear the Coſts between them, yet Wiſwall alledged that it was upon a Promiſe of Hall to bear the whole Coſts. (2) To verify this he offered the Referees as Evidence. But *the Court ruled* unanimouſly that they could not by parol Evidence controul the Report which was of Record. (3)

---

(1) This deciſion was under the following proviſion contained for many years in the annual tax acts of the Province: "Saving all contracts between landlord and tenant, and where no contract is, the landlord to reimburſe one half of the tax ſet upon ſuch houſes and lands." See *poſt*, *Derumple* v. *Clark*. The ſame proviſion in ſubſtance is contained in Rev. Sts. c. 7, § 8, by which the tenant was authorized to retain half the taxes out of his rent, unleſs there was an agreement to the contrary. By Gen. Sts. c. 11, § 9, he may ſo retain the whole taxes or recover the ſame by action.

(2) This is inaccurately ſtated. The declaration alleges that the promiſe by the defendant, but for which "the referees would have awarded the plaintiff coſts," was, never to enforce a certain other judgment for coſts previouſly recovered.

(3) Arbitrators cannot by parol teſtimony contradict their formal award in writing. 10 Met. 433. 4 Cuſh. 317, 399.

1762.
Sayer
v.
Thorp.

Rec. 1763.
Fol. 17.

Whether the Owner and Hirer of a Veſſell can join in an Action of Treſpaſs for running away with the Veſſell — *quære.*

Sayer & al. *verſ.* Thorp & al.

THE only Queſtion of Law in this Caſe was, whether the Owner of a Veſſell and the Perſon who hired and freighted her could join in an Action of Treſpaſs for running away with the Veſſell. (1) It was not doubted that they might both have their Actions, (2) but whether they could join was the Doubt. It was ſaid on one Side, that Tenant

(1) There are ſeveral depoſitions on file in this caſe, from which it appears that the ſloop Proſperous was employed in freighting wood on the Chignecto River, Nova Scotia, for the uſe of Fort Cumberland, and that the party who ran away with her were deſerting ſoldiers of the fort. The defence was, the conſent or connivance of the maſter, who was alleged to have been paid for a ſimilar uſe of the ſloop on a former occaſion, and to have induced the attempt by telling the ſoldiers that there would be no reſiſtance, and that they were fools to ſtay in ſo bad a place after their time was up. And in his own depoſition he acknowledges having found forty-one dollars in his cabin, which he was told the ſoldiers had left, and which he was induced to put in his cheſt. There appears alſo among the papers a printed proclamation by Governor Pownall, bearing date March 17, 1759, and reciting that his Majeſty, having determined to make a general invaſion of Canada, called upon his faithful and brave ſubjects of New England for aſſiſtance; and that the Province, having reſolved to raiſe a number of men, "have made proviſion for the levying and ſupport of ſuch *to the firſt day of November next*, ſaid men to be then diſmiſſed." The words here in Italics are underſcored, ſhowing that the paper was offered to prove that the ſoldiers' term of enliſtment had expired before the running away with the veſſel. See 3 Hutchinſon's Hiſt. Maſs. 79. The verdict was for the defendants.

(2) It was formerly held that both owner and bailee might maintain treſpaſs, but that a recovery by one ſhould ouſt the other of his right ot action. Bac. Ab. Treſpaſs, C. 2. It has been ſince decided, that general ownerſhip, without either poſſeſſion or right to poſſeſſion, is not ſufficient. *Ward* v. *Macauley*, 4 T. R. 488. *Muggridge* v. *Eveleth*, 9 Met. 233.

1762.

SAYER *v.* THORP.

ant and he in Reverſion of a Freehold ſhall never join; and on the other, that it would be a Cauſe of multiplying Actions. The Parties agreeing, this Point was not determined.

Mr. Gridley in this Argument ſaid: Treſpaſs and Debt are the two great Actions on which the Fullneſs of Evidence is required, and are Actions of the higheſt Nature.

Oliver *verſ.* Sale.

OLIVER *v.* SALE.

Rec. 1762. Fol. 385.

A Perſon who ſells a Negro as a Slave, whom he knows to be free, is liable to an Action by the Vendee for the Fraud. *Aliter*, where he tells the Vendee at the Time of Sale that he will not ſell the Negro as a Slave.

A Depoſition which comes up in a Caſe from the Inferiour Court may be read, though the Witneſs is alſo preſent in Court.

OLIVER ſues the Defendant for ſelling him two free Mulattos for Slaves. (1) There was no Bill of Sale, but only ſeveral Receipts of Money for two *Negro Boys ſold & delivered.* It was ſuggeſted on the other Side that the Defendant ſold them not as Slaves, but only his Right, if he had any, in them. (2) — The Caſe was thus argued.

Mr.

(1) The declaration was for deceit, in ſelling the mulattos to the plaintiff as ſlaves, knowing them to be free.

(2) Previouſly to the adoption of the State Conſtitution in 1780, negro ſlavery exiſted to ſome extent in Maſſachuſetts, and negroes held as ſlaves might be ſold; but all children of ſlaves were by law free. Body of Liberties of 1641, art. 91. Maſs. Colony Laws, (ed. 1660,) 5; (ed. 1672,) 10. Prov. Sts. 2 & 4 Anne. Anc. Chart. 52, 53, 745–749. 1 Hutchinſon's Hiſt. Maſs. 444. 2 Hildreth's Hiſt. U. S. 419. 1 John Adams's Works, 51, 55. James Otis's Rights of the Colonies, (1764,) 29, 37. 4 Maſs. Hiſt. Coll. 194 & *ſeq.* 2 Dane Ab. 413, 416, 426, 427. 3 Plym. Col. Rec. 27. 5 Ib. 216. Winſor's Hiſt. of Duxbury, 70, 71, & note. *Cutler* v. *March*, Rec. 1697, fol. 159. *Alliſon* v. *Cockran*, *poſt*, 94. 4 Maſs, 127, 128, & note. 13 Maſs. 551, 552. 16 Maſs. 75, 76. 10 Cuſh. 410. 2 Kent Com. (6th ed.) 252. 2 Palfrey's Hiſt. New England, 30 & note, 280 note, 370.

Slaves

1762.
OLIVER
v.
SALE.

Mr. Thacher, for Plaintiff. I think from the Words of the Receipt it may be learnt what was his Intent. *Sold & delivered* conveys the Property; and as he had really no Right to a Day's Service in the Lads, as they were free, he could not pass any Property

---

Slaves were admitted to be church members at a period when church members had peculiar political privileges. 2 Winthrop, 26, & Savage's note. Anc. Chart. 117. 1 Bancroft's Hist. U. S. 360. Slaves were sometimes required, sometimes prohibited, to serve in the militia. 3 Mass. Col. Rec. 268, 397. 4 Ib. pt. 1, 86, 257. Journals Mass. Prov. Congress, (ed. 1838,) 29, 302, 553. They were enlisted in the army in the Old French War. 4 Mass. Hist. Coll. 199, 203. 98 Mass. Archives, 122. They were competent witnesses, even in capital trials, *e. g.* in the trial of the *British Soldiers* in 1770, (ed. 1770, p. 111,) and in suits of other slaves for freedom, as appears by the files of court.

The right to marry was secured to them in 1705 by Prov. St. 4 Anne. Anc. Chart. 748. The subsequent records of Boston and other towns show that their banns were published like those of white persons. In 1745, a negro slave obtained from the Governor and Council a divorce for his wife's adultery with a white man. *Jethro Boston's Case*, 9 Mass. Archives, 248. In 1758, it was adjudged by the Superior Court of Judicature, that a child of a female slave, "never married according to any of the forms prescribed by the laws of this land," by another slave, who "had kept her company with her master's consent," was not a bastard. *Flora's Case*, Rec. 1758, fol. 296. And the wife of a slave was not allowed to testify against him. MS. note by John Adams of *Cæsar* v. *Taylor*, in Essex, 1772, (Rec. 1772, fol. 91,) in the possession of Hon. Charles Francis Adams; which also shows that the defendant in an action of false imprisonment was not permitted under the general issue to prove that the plaintiff was his slave.

Such actions, called "suits for liberty," were common as early as 1765. 2 John Adams's Works, 200. The latest instance of a verdict for the master is believed to have been in 1768. *Newport* v. *Billing*, Rec. 1768, fol. 284. But the case of *James* v. *Lechmere*, in Middlesex, a year later, which has been often spoken of as having determined the unlawfulness of slavery in Massachusetts, is shown by the records and files of court to have been brought up from the inferior court by sham demurrer, and, after one or two continuances, settled by the parties. Rec. 1769, fol. 196. The case mentioned by Dr. Belknap in 4 Mass. Hist. Coll. 202, as "the first trial of this kind," may have been that of *Margarett* v. *Muzzy*, which was a writ *de homine replegiando*, sued out and tried in Middlesex in 1768, and on review in 1770, in which, as appears by the

1762. OLIVER v. SALE.

Property in them, and therefore must be supposed to have sold them as Slaves, or meant from the first to have defrauded.

Ch. Just. Everything which is bought is sold.

Witnesses were produced who were present at the Time of the Sale, and heard Defendant say they were Slaves.

Mr. Otis, for Defendant. I hold in the Case of a Negro, there should be an express Warranty of their Freedom, and that the Rule of Merchandise which obliges the Vendor to answer for what he sells without Warranty is confined to Manufactures of the Country which a Man must be supposed to know the Quality of; but in this Case it is impossible in most Cases to know whether they are free or not.

Ch.

the depositions on file, there was much conflicting evidence, and the plaintiff prevailed. Rec. 1768, fol. 311; 1770, fol. 216. Slavery was certainly recognized by law in Massachusetts after this; for in May, 1771, Hutchinson wrote to Lord Hillsborough, "Slavery by the Provincial laws gives no right to the life of the servant; and a slave here is considered as a servant would be who had bound himself for a term of years exceeding the ordinary term of human life; and I do not know that it has been determined that he may not have a property in goods, notwithstanding he is called a slave." 27 Mass. Archives, 159, 160.

Slaves convicted of theft were sentenced, like other persons, besides being whipt, to pay treble the value to the owner of the goods stolen, and, if unable to do so, were ordered to be "disposed of in service" for life, or for a term of years, "for payment of the same." *Hercules & Sharper's Cases*, Rec. 1757, fol. 54, 55; Docket of February term, 1757, in Suffolk, *ad finem*. *Jeoffs's Case*, Rec. 1771, fol. 35.

By virtue of the first article of the Declaration of Rights, prefixed to the Constitution of Massachusetts, if not before, slavery was entirely abolished here. 2 Bradford Hist. Mass. 124. 4 Mass. Hist. Coll. 201–203. 31 Ib. 90. 34 Ib. 333. Willard Memoir, 153. 4 Mass. 128. 9 Amer. Jur. 490. 18 Pick. 208–210. 7 Cush. 296. 7 Gray, 478. 5 Leigh, 622, 623. 20 Law Rep. 101, 108, 456.

1762.
Oliver v. Sale.

Ch. Juſt. Is there not as palpable a Fraud, when a Man ſells a Negro as a Slave whom he knows to be free, as when he ſells a Bag of Feathers and aſſures them to be Hops? That he knew them to be free they muſt prove, or do not ſupport their Declaration. (3)

Mr. Otis offered a Depoſition lodged in the Caſe to be read.

Mr. Thacher demanded, as the Witneſs was there in Court, she might be examined orally. (4)

Court ruled, that when Depoſitions come up in the Caſe they may be firſt read. (5)

Mr.

---

(3) According to the rule now ſettled in this country, it ſeems that the *ſcienter* would be unneceſſary — the vendor being liable on the implied warranty of title in the ſale of a chattel. *Coolidge* v. *Brigham*, 1 Met. 547.

(4) Among the papers in this caſe are the depoſitions of Anna Bill and Lydia Whitaker, one of whom was undoubtedly the witneſs "there in Court." The depoſitions are ſubſtantially ſimilar, and the following is an exact copy of that of Lydia Whitaker: —

"Lydia Whitaker of Lawfull age teſtifies & ſays that ſhe was at the "houſe of Capt. John Sale when Mr Nath'l Brown & Mr John Oliver "came to buy two of his negro boys & Capt. Sale told them that he "would not ſell them for Slaves becauſe he underſtood they were to be "free after ſome time, & he would only ſell his right & title in them, "& Mr Oliver ſaid he would run the riſk of their ever getting free.

her
"Lydia X Whitaker
mark

"Sworn before the Court in Oct'r 1761
"Att. Middlecott Cooke *Cler.*"

(5) The cuſtom of uſing the depoſition in addition to oral teſtimony once prevailed in Maſſachuſetts. Compare Colony Law of 1647 and Prov. St. of 7 W. 3, (Anc. Chart. 209, 288,) with the St. of 1797, c. 35, reënacted in Rev. Sts. c. 94, § 25, and Gen. Sts. c. 131, § 28.

1762.

OLIVER *v.* SALE.

Mr. Otis. When the Apprentice's Indentures are aſſigned, he may properly be ſaid to be ſold, but 'tis no Argument of his Slavery.

The Evidence being clear that Sale had ſaid he would not ſell them as Slaves, and told Plaintiff ſo when they were ſold, *the Court* directed the Jury to find Defendant Coſts.

N. B. In Aggravation of Damages, had they found for the Plaintiff, *Mr. Thacher* ſaid: "Oliver by ſelling theſe Boys for Slaves expoſed himſelf to a Writ of Replevin,* upon which if Sheriff returns '*They are Eſloigned*,' there ſhall go a *Capias in Withernam*,† and his own Body ſhall be ſubjected to Confinement till they are produced."

Hallowell *verſ.* Dalton.

HALLOWELL *v.* DALTON.

Rec. 1762. Fol. 390.

After Bond given to review, and before the Service of the Writ, the Depoſition of Witneſſes going to Sea may be taken under the Province Law of 7 W. 3, c. 11.

THIS Caſe was a Review of an Action brought by Dalton againſt Hallowell. The only Queſtion of Law was, whether after Bond given to review, before the Service of the Writ, there can be ſaid to be ſo much of Suit depending, and ſo much of Parties, as that a Juſtice may, out of Court, take the Evidence of Men going to Sea, according to the Province Law 7 W. 3, c. 11. (1) *Ruled*, there is.

* *Homine replegiando.* Vid. F. N. B. 66. New Nat. B. 151, 152.

† If this is returned *non eſt invent.*, a *Capias* ſhall iſſue againſt the Defendant's Goods and Effects.

---

(1) This law provided for the taking of affidavits of "witneſſes in civil

5 cauſes,"

1762.

Gould v. Stevens.

Rec. 1762. Fol. 383.

An Executor of his own Wrong is not liable to an Attachment of his Body or proper Goods on a Debt of the Teſtator.

Gould *verſ.* Stevens.

THIS Action was an Attachment againſt Stevens as Executor of Somebody, a Debtor of the Plaintiff's. Plea in Abatement was made, that by the Law as Executor he ſhould have been ſummoned, and not his Body or proper Goods attached. The Replication to this was, that though he was named Executor in the Writ, he was not appointed by the Teſtator, but was Executor of his own Wrong.

Mr. Thacker. The Province Law 2 Ann. c. 5, (1) directs the Manner of Suits againſt Executors and Adminiſtrators. Executor of his own Wrong takes the Duty and the Burden, he is by Wrong in the ſame Manner as if by Right, and is anſwerable no further than as Effects come to his Hands. The Common Law is the ſame with the Province Law.

Mr. Sewall, contra. An Executor in his own Wrong cannot maintain an Action certain. He is not favoured as Executor by Right. 4 Wm. & Mary, c. 2. 1 Salk. 297. 2 Ventris, 179. The Law knows Nothing of them but to reſtrain and puniſh them.

Judgment that the Writ abate.

---

cauſes," with a "notification to the adverſe party," but ſpecified no time as the commencement of a ſuit. Anc. Chart. 288. But the St. of 1797, c 35, provided for taking depoſitions only "when the writ, original ſummons, or complaint ſhall have been ſerved." This is in ſubſtance reënacted in Rev. Sts. c. 94, § 15, and Gen. Sts. c. 131, § 19.

(1) Anc. Chart. 377. St. 1783, c. 32, § 9. Rev. Sts. c. 110, § 1. Gen. Sts. c. 128, § 5.

1762.

BARRISTERS' HABITS.

Memorandum. (1)

Rec. 1762. Fol. 400.

JAMES OTIS, Edmund Trowbridge, Jeremy Gridley, Richard Dana, Benjamin Kent, Daniel Farnham, John Worthington, James Otis, junr., James Putnam, Joſeph Hawley, John Chipman, Oxenbridge Thacher, Robert Auchmuty, Sam'l White, James Hovey, Samuel Fitch, Jonathan Sewall, William Cuſhing, Robert Treat Paine, William Pynchon, William Read, Samuel Swift, Joſeph Dudley, Benja: Gridley, Samuel Quincy, and John Adams, having been called by the Court to be Barriſters at Law, the following Gentlemen, viz., Edmund Trowbridge, Jeremy Gridley, Benjamin Kent, James Otis, junr., Oxenbridge Thacher, Robert Auchmuty, Samuel Fitch, Jonathan Sewall, Robert Treat Paine, Samuel Swift, Samuel Quincy, and John Adams, Eſquires, appeared accordingly this Term in Barriſters' Habits. (2)

---

(1) As this memorandum cloſes the record of the term on the Suffolk docket, it is here inſerted, although not a part of Mr. Quincy's reports.

(2) John Adams was ſworn on the 14th of November, 1761. Rec. 1761, fol. 239. In a note to his diary at that date he ſays: "About this time the project was conceived, I ſuppoſe by the Chief Juſtice, Mr. Hutchinſon, of clothing the judges and lawyers with robes. Mr. Quincy and I were directed to prepare our gowns and bands and tie wigs, and were admitted barriſters, having practiſed three years at the inferior courts according to our new rules." 2 John Adams's Works, 133. See alſo Adams's Letters to Tudor, 10 Ib. 233, 245.

February Term

III Georgii Ter. in Sup. Cur.

Preſent:

The Honourable

Thomas Hutchinſon, Eſqr., Chief Juſtice.
Benja: Lynde, John Cuſhing, Chambers Ruſſell, Peter Oliver, Eſqrs., Juſtices.

WRENTHAM PROPRIETORS *v.* METCALF.

Rec. 1763. Fol. 17.

Proprietors of common and undivided Lands are incompetent Witneſſes in a Suit where the Corporation is a Party.

Wrentham Proprietors *verſ.* Metcalf. (1)

IT was moved that ſome of the Proprietors ſhould be admitted Witneſſes in this Caſe, who were not of the Committee who brought this Suit. 2 Lev. 231,* was cited, where *Scroggs, Ch. Juſt.*,

* *Quære* of this Caſe. Theory of Evid. 105, 106, and 2 Lilly's Abr. 702. 1 Str. 575, 1069. Vid. 2 Lev. 236. 2 Sid. 109. 1 Vern. 154. 2 Vern. 317. Vid. Cun. Law Dict'y, Will.

(1) This was an action of ejectment, originally brought in the Inferior Court againſt Joſhua Daniels, who ſuggeſted that he held the premiſes by deed of bargain and ſale with warranty from Jonathan Metcalf, whom he prayed might be vouched in to defend the ſuit, and who was ſubſequently admitted for that purpoſe. In the Superior Court the caſe was entitled as above.

Juſt., ſays, "that it ought not to be a general Rule "that Members of Corporations ſhall be admitted "or denied to be Witneſſes in Actions for or againſt "their Corporations: But every Caſe ſtands upon "its own particular Circumſtances, viz., whether "the Intereſt be ſo conſiderable as by Preſumption "to produce Partiality or not."

In this Caſe at Bar it was objected that they were liable to Coſts, and might each Member be taken for the Whole. A Guardian not admitted in Evidence in Favour of his Charge.

Ruled, that they be not admitted in this Caſe. *Ch. Juſt.* doubted whether in any Caſe, where the Intereſt was ever ſo ſmall, if they were direct Plaintiffs they ſhould be admitted. (2)

---

(2) The general rule ſeems to have been that only members of public or municipal, religious, and charitable corporations were competent witneſſes in ſuits where the corporation was a party or intereſted. 1 Greenl. Evid. §§ 331, 333. The St. of 1792, c. 32, provided for the admiſſibility of members of any "town, diſtrict, precinct, pariſh or other religious incorporate ſociety." Counties, ſchool diſtricts and mutual inſurance companies were afterward added to the liſt. Rev. Sts. c. 94, § 54. St. 1850, c. 34. By the practice acts of 1851 and 1852, all incompetency from intereſt was removed, except in caſe of parties to ſuits; and finally, by Sts. 1856, c. 188, and 1857, c. 305, parties themſelves have been admitted. Gen. Sts. c. 131, §§ 13, 14.

1763.
DERUMPLE
v.
CLARK.

Derumple *verſ.* Clark.

Rec. 1763.
Fol. 19.

Evidence of Payment of full Rent by a Tenant for five or ſix Years, without any Claim of Deduction for Taxes, ſuch being alſo the Cuſtom of the Town, is ſufficient Evidence of a Contract to pay Taxes under the Province Law, which provides that "where no Contract is" the Landlord ſhall reimburſe half the Taxes. *Ruſſell, J., diſſentiente.*

THIS Action was brought by the Tenant againſt the Landlord for the Recovery of half the Taxes, upon the Province Law called the Tax Act. (1) This Caſe was ſaid to differ from the Caſe of *Jackſon* v. *Foye*, (2) try'd before this Court in Auguſt Term laſt, as in that Caſe Jackſon had been Tenant to Foye ſo many Years, there had been many Settlements,—whereas here Derumple had been Tenant only five or ſix Years. The Rent had been paid, but there had been no regular methodical Settlement.

Mr. Auchmuty, for Plaintiff, urged, that the Law was very expreſs and particular—"Where no Contract is, the Landlord ſhall reimburſe the Tenant half the Taxes," ſo that the Payment of the whole Rent is no Argument of a Contract to pay half the Taxes, for the Tenant by the Law is not to keep back his Rent, but to have the Taxes reimburſed, which is an Argument that the Whole is firſt to be paid. I can have no Idea of an implied Contract in this Caſe; the Law evidently points out an expreſs one.

Mr. Thacker, for Defendant. It has been the uninterrupted Cuſtom of this Town for the Tenant to pay the whole Taxes, and though this Law is of very

(1) See *ante*, p. 27, note (1). (2) *Ante*, p. 26.

very antient Date, (3) we find no Action on it till 1752; ſo that it always ſuppoſed that ſuch a Contract is made. The Words of the Law are not—where no expreſs,—no written,—no verbal,—but "where *no Contract* is." And I think the continual paying Rent for ſeveral Years without any Demand of a Deduction, and ſeveral Receipts having been given by the Plaintiff to the Defendant in full of all Accounts, are full Evidence that ſuch was the Intention and Meaning of the Parties, which is a ſufficient Contract. To have this Point called in Queſtion would be big with the greateſt Inconveniences. If Landlords who from Year to Year have received their whole Rents, and given Diſcharges for them, are to be called to account for many Years' Taxes, it would be productive of an ample Harveſt of Suits, of which perhaps our Brotherhood might reap the Gleanings.

Mr. Auchmuty. As to the Cuſtom of the Town; if there had been no Law, that might have been an Argument of ſome Weight; but the Law is expreſs, and ſhall any pretended Cuſtom controul it? As for the Conſequences they muſt not be conſidered—if it is Law, it is Law, &c.

Juſtice

(3) The earlieſt ſtatute proviſion that we find on this ſubject is in the Prov. St. of 4 W. & M. in 1692. By this act however, as by the Gen. Sts. of 1860, c. 11, § 9, the landlord was to pay the whole taxes in the abſence of any particular agreement. The first proviſion for a contribution was in the Prov. St. of 6 W. & M. in 1694, and is as follows: "The fermer or occupier of any houſes or lands, being aſſeſſed for the ſame in his occupation, to be reimburſed the one half of what he ſhall ſo pay toward the ſaid aſſeſſment by the landlord or leſſor where there is no particular contract to the contrary, and ſhall be allowed to diſcount the ſame out of his rent." The laſt clauſe was omitted in ſubſequent acts. *Ante*, p. 27, note (1).

1763.
DERUMPLE v. CLARK.

Juſtice Oliver. As for the Cuſtom of the Town, I can't think it of any Weight; but as the Law ſays "where no Contract is," you muſt confine it to an expreſs Contract. I ſee no eſſential difference between this and the Caſe of *Foye & Jackſon*, and can't but think the Evidence you have is a Preſumption of a Contract ſo ſtrong that you muſt find for the Defendant.

Juſtice Ruſſell. I think the Law evidently means an expreſs Agreement. However, I don't think we have here any Evidence of an implied Agreement, or any Agreement at all.

Juſtice Cuſhing. If there be Anything to ſhow the Intention of the Parties, I hold that Evidence of a ſufficient Agreement within the Senſe of the Law; and that the Intention of theſe Parties was that the Tenant ſhould pay the Whole, may be collected from the Evidence joined to the Cuſtom of the Town.

Juſtice Lynde. I always thought that the Intention of this Law was not to affect the Taxes in ſuch Towns as this, but merely where Farms are let to the Halves, where the Benefit of the Eſtate being divided, 'tis but juſt the Charges ſhould be divided too. I think the Cuſtom of the Town is a great Thing, and that the Parties are to be ſuppoſed to intend according to the Cuſtom. I think the Evidence ſufficient to prove a Contract within the Intendment of the Law.

Ch. Juſt. You are to go according to Law and Evidence.

1763. Derumple v. Clark.

Evidence. Where the Law is in any Cafe doubtfull and the Equity of it plain, you fhould verge towards Equity. Cuftom fhall not be placed in Oppofition to Law, but it may be a Circumftance going to interpret the Intention of the Parties. I fee Nothing to diftinguifh this from the Cafe of *Jackfon* v. *Foye*.

Verdict for Defendant.

Daniels *verf.* Bullard.

Daniels v. Bullard.

Rec. 1763. Fol. 106.

The Fact that a Witnefs is immediately about to leave the Country will not authorize the taking his Depofition without Notice to the oppofite Party.

A DEPOSITION was offered; the Caption imported that the Witnefs was immediately going out of the Country, and therefore the oppofite Party not notified. *Ruled* bad.

Barnes *verf.* Greenleaf.

Barnes v. Greenleaf.

Rec. 1763. Fol. 23.

An Officer who difcharges a Defendant from Arreft in Confideration of the Promife of a third Perfon for his Appearance, can

THE Queftion in this Cafe was, whether Mr. Wheelwright fhould be admitted as a Witnefs. The Action was brought againft Greenleaf (Sheriff) for an infufficient Service of a Writ upon which the Return ftood thus: "I have attached the Defendant, and taken Mr. Wheelwright's Word for his Appearance." (1) Mr. Wheelwright was offered

(1) The return as fet forth on record is as follows:
"Suffolk fs. Bofton, June 17, 1762. I attached the body of the within

1763.

BARNES
v.
GREENLEAF.

maintain no Action on ſuch Promiſe; and ſuch Perſon is therefore a competent Witneſs for the Officer in an Action for the inſufficient Service.

offered to prove that at the Plaintiff's Conſent the Priſoner was diſmiſſed. He was objected to, becauſe 'twas ſaid the Sheriff would recur to him, if he loſt in this Action. But 'twas anſwered, there could be no ſuch Recourſe, for the Sheriff deviating from the Path of his Duty muſt expect the Conſequence. (2) He was admitted and ſworn.*

ELWELL
v.
PIERSON.

Rec. 1763.
Fol. 56.

Deviſe of Land as follows: "To my Son S. and his Heirs forever, provided that my ſaid Son ſhall maintain Myſelf and his Mother during our Lives with ſufficient and convenient Maintenance." Afterwards: "Alſo whereas it is expreſſed that my Son ſhall have this my Living to him and his forever, my Will and Meaning is, and I do hereby appoint my Grandſon R.,

Elwell verſ. Pierſon.

(From Eſſex.) (3)

THE Queſtion in this Caſe was, whether Samuel, Son of the original Deviſor, took an Eſtate Tail,

* Vid. 4 Bac. Ab. 462, 463, top. (4)

---

within named Thomas Carnes, and Nathaniel Wheelwright Eſq. gave his word for his appearance at Court.

BENJA: CUDWORTH,
Deputy Sheriff."

(2) S. P. *Denny* v. *Lincoln*, 5 Maſs. 385. In that caſe the officer forbore to arreſt, upon a promiſe by a third party to deliver the debtor to him at a day named. *Parſons*, C. J. "It is to be regretted that officers having a plain path before them will not purſue it. If they deviate from it, it muſt be at their own peril, and they cannot protect themſelves againſt the damages ariſing from a breach of official duty by any collateral ſtipulation for indemnity." See alſo 4 Maſs. 370. But taking receipts for property attached, or notes in conſideration of forbearing to attach, is conſiſtent with the officer's duty. *Foſter* v. *Clark*, 19 Pick. 329. And ſuch receiptor has been held incompetent through intereſt. 23 Pick. 86.

(3) The eſtate ſued for is deſcribed as "a neck of land in Glouceſter Harbour now called Pierſon's Neck."

(4) Bac. Ab. Sheriff, O.

Tail, and if he did, whether the Plaintiff is ſole Heir in Tail of Samuel, being eldeſt Son of eldeſt Son all along.

1763.
ELWELL *v.* PIERSON.

The Words of the Will are theſe: "I give to "Samuel Elwell the Houſe I now live in," &c.

Afterwards: "I give all my ſaid Houſing &c. "expreſſed, to him my ſaid Son Samuel, and *his* "*Heirs forever*, provided that my ſaid Son ſhall "maintain Myſelf and his Mother during our Lives "with ſufficient and convenient Maintenance."

Afterwards: "Alſo whereas it is above expreſſed "that my Son Samuel ſhall have this my Living "above ſaid to him and his forever, my Will and "Meaning is, and I do hereby appoint my Grand-"ſon Robert, Son of ſaid Samuel, to be the next "immediate Heir unto this my Living after his "Father, my ſaid Son Samuel, to enjoy the ſame to "him and his Heirs forever. And in Caſe that ſaid "Robert do die without Heir, it ſhall then fall to "the next eldeſt of my Grandſons ſurviving, and ſo "in like Caſe of Mortality one from another to the "next eldeſt of my Grandſons ſurviving."

Son of ſaid S., to be the next immediate Heir unto this my Living after his Father, to enjoy the ſame to him and his Heirs forever. And in Caſe that ſaid R. do die without Heir, it ſhall then fall to the next eldeſt of my Grandſons ſurviving, and ſo in like Caſe of Mortality, one from another to the next eldeſt of my Grandſons ſurviving." *Held*, that S. took an Eſtate in Fee Simple. *It ſeems*, that but for the Charge of Maintenance, S. would have taken an Eſtate Tail.

Mr. Thacher for the Tail. It is objected that there were but two Witneſſes to the Will. At that Time the Law required but two. The Statute of Frauds was never ſuppoſed to extend here, till we made a like Law here. (5) Vid. Old Colony Laws, 158.

(5) Prov. St. 4 W. & M. Anc. Chart. 233.

1763. Elwell v. Pierson.

158. (6) The Queſtion is, whether Samuel took an Eſtate Tail, by the Words of the Will. Great Condeſcenſion is given to Wills, and Words, which in Acts executed in the Lifetime would not make Eſtates Tail, will make them in Wills, becauſe Teſtators are ſuppoſed to be *inops conſilii*, and Lord Holt obſerves that there were no ſuch Conveyances at Common Law, but by Statute. The Teſtator's Intent is to be the Rule of Conſtruction, if agreeable to Rules of Law. The firſt Deviſe is an Inheritance; then he explains his Grandſon Robert to be the next immediate Heir of his ſaid Son Samuel; he does not retract, but only directs how that Inheritance ſhall go. The Intent appears from this alſo — He ſays, the next eldeſt Brother ſhall inherit for want of Heirs; now he could not die without Heirs, while he had any Brothers, whence it appears he excluded Brothers from his Idea of Heirs in this Caſe, and ſo could only mean Heirs of the Body. There is a Difference between the Remainder over being given to a Stranger, and to one of Kin; in the firſt Caſe it cannot be explanatory of what Heirs are meant; in the laſt it is. 9 Co. 128, *Sonday's Caſe*. Cro. Ja. 415, *Webb & Hearing*. Id. 448, *King* vs. *Rumball*. Id. 695, *Chaddock* vs. *Cowley*. 1 Ld. Raym. 569, *Nottingham* vs. *Jennings*. Comyns, 539, *Brice* vs. *Smith*. Ld. Talbot, 1, *Tyte* vs. *Willis*.

The only Queſtion remaining is, whether this Eſtate Tail firſt veſted in Samuel the Son, or Robert

(6) Col. Laws, ed. of 1672. Anc. Chart. 204, § 2.

ert the Grandſon; I think in Samuel, firſt, becauſe Samuel had an Inheritance by the firſt Words; Secondly, becauſe the Teſtator appoints Robert his next immediate Heir; this is ſurely ſhowing how the Inheritance ſhall be limited, and it is as it would be limited by Law, ſuppoſing it an Eſtate Tail. The Inheritance of Samuel ſhall by no means be taken away, if the Will can be conſtrued otherwiſe, as in this Caſe the Words do not make an Eſtate for Life only, but a Limitation.

Mr. Gridley. The Queſtion is, whether Samuel took a Fee Simple or Tail; the firſt Words of the Will give him a Fee, but afterwards ſay Robert ſhall be his Heir: We all agree as to the Fee — we ſay the other Words ſhew the Intent. If Samuel had a Fee, he could convey it, and Robert would not be his Heir; in the ſecond Place, every Word ſhall be operative if poſſible; whereas on their Suppoſition the laſt Words are of no Force. Robert on their Suppoſition ſhould take only as the Law gave him, and Robert took as a Purchaſer, which he could not do unleſs Samuel took an Eſtate for Life: If a Fee, he could not — if he took a Fee, the laſt Words go for Nothing.

Auchmuty againſt the Tail. Their Authorities do not reach this Caſe, the Intent of the Teſtator is to be followed, but the Intent muſt be clear and muſt be agreeable to the Rules of Law. The Fee is at firſt plainly given; and where an expreſs Eſtate is given, nothing by Implication ſhall take it away. 1 Salk. 236, *Popham* vs. *Banfield.* Cro. Cha. 368, *Spirt* vs. *Bence.* 6 Co. 16, *Wild's Caſe.* Where an

1763. ELWELL *v.* PIERSON.

an Implication affects an Heir at Law, that Implication muft be very ftrong. 2 Bac. 66, Tit. Devife.

I'll confider the Force of the Words in the Will, and whether thofe Words operate fo ftrongly as to turn the plain Fee Simple into a Tail. If Robert died and left Iffue, well — but if not, then to the next eldeft Grandfon, which is not the Courfe of Tails; fo that the Teftator's meaning cannot be collected from thefe Words; and if a Man fhall try to make fuch an Eftate as the Law never made, I take it to be utterly void. I fhall fhew the Words, pointing out the next immediate Heir a meer Nullity. The Grandfon of an younger Son may be an elder Grandfon than thofe of an elder, which is not agreeable to Tail.

Ch. Juft. Quære — Whether the fecond Son of an eldeft Son may not be called an elder Grandfon, than an elder Grandfon of a younger Son?

Mr. Auchmuty. This with vulgar Minds would not be a natural Thought. I think if he has any Eftate, it is a Fee Simple. Cro. Jam. 590, *Pells* vs. *Brown.* (This Cafe he largely compared with the Cafe at Bar.) The ordering him to maintain his Mother amounts to his ordering him to pay her a Sum in grofs, which is allowed to caufe a Fee Simple. 2 Bacon, 54. (7) 3 Rep. 31, a. 1 Lill. 451. The true Diftinction is between a Sum to be paid out

(7) Bac. Ab. Devife, C.

out of the Rents, and a Sum in groſs, which may be greater. But ſuppoſing the Caſe to be doubtful, as they are the Plaintiffs, I take it to be incumbent upon them to make out a clear Title.

Mr. Gridley. 2 Bacon, 62. (8) With Regard to the Diſheriſon of the Heir, that is not in this Caſe to be conſidered — if it is the Mind of the Teſtator, that is the Rule. By the firſt Part Samuel was to have had a Fee Simple, but ſo as not to exclude Robert; 'tis plain he intended Robert ſhould have the Eſtate. Samuel muſt either have a Fee Simple, Tail or an Eſtate for Life: If for Life, how is it to him and his Heirs? — if in Fee, what has Robert? The laſt Clauſe confirms my Opinion, it muſt be ſuppoſed that by eldeſt Grandſon he intended Grandſon by Samuel; this is the natural Courſe, that if Robert died, it ſhould go to the Brothers of Robert, other Children of Samuel.

Ch. Juſt. Is it not better firſt to make it an Eſtate Tail in Samuel, that it ſhould rather go to theſe, than other Grandſons, than becauſe it is thus divided, that therefore it is an Eſtate Tail?

Mr. Gridley. Caſes in Equity, 184, Caſe 28, *Shaw* vs. *Weigh.* Cro. Cha. 57. As for the Caſe *Pells & Brown*, here is nothing like a Limitation; Upon his Suppoſition it tends to ſuch a Perpetuity as the Law abhors, it ſhould have been "if Samuel die without Iſſue;" here it is "if Robert." With

(8) Bac. Ab. Deviſe, D.

1763.
ELWELL v. PIERSON.

With Regard to the Maintenance, if there is a Doubt, what the Eſtate is, it ſhall be a Fee Simple, but never was any Maintenance conſtrued to make a Fee Simple, when a clear Tail was: Maintenance in ſome Tails is good.

The Court choſe to conſult upon the Matter, and ſo Judgment was adjourned to Auguſt Term, where the *Chief Juſtice* delivered the Opinion of the Court, which he ſaid was unanimous that Samuel by the Words would have taken a Tail; but that the Burden and Duty of Maintenance made it a Fee Simple. (9)

Ruſſel *verſ.* Oakes.

RUSSEL v. OAKES.

(From Middleſex.)

Rec. 1763. Fol. 91.

Payment by the Maker to the Promiſee of a Note on Demand is a good Defence againſt a ſubſequent Indorſee for Value without Notice. *Hutchinſon, C. J., diſſ.*

THIS was an Action of the Caſe on a Note of Hand which was indorſed to the Plaintiff, and appeared to have been paid before the Indorſement. The Queſtion was, whether the Plaintiff ſhould recover in this Action or be barred by the Payment. (1)

Mr.

(9) It would ſeem, however, that the Court muſt have conſidered the intent of the teſtator to be doubtful, as otherwiſe it would be difficult to anſwer Mr. Gridley's poſition that "never was any maintenance conſtrued to make a fee-ſimple when a clear tail was." 2 Jarman on Wills, 172.

(1) It appears by the declaration that the note in ſuit bore date, October 19, 1759, and was payable on demand to one James Webber or

1763.

RUSSEL *v.* OAKES.

Mr. Trowbridge for Defendant. Strange, 674. It is always held when Payment is once made, a Promiſe is of no Force. Lucas, 287. (2) After the Promiſee had once received it he could not recover himſelf; he cannot give a greater Power than he has himſelf. Skinner, 410. In a Declaration on inland Bills 'tis ſaid "then wholly unpaid." 2 Show. 495.

Mr. Gridley. This Caſe muſt appear evident on our Side to any Perſon who is at all acquainted with the Nature of Bills of Exchange. To pay him *or* his Order, is there any Intereſt to transfer? Is not the Intereſt gone? The Indorſer is guilty of a Fraud againſt the Indorſee, who has his Action for it. There is an entire Difference between this and in Caſe it had not been paid till after the Indorſement, for by this the Property is changed and in the Indorſee. Trade would be rendered very precarious, if ſuch negotiable Notes can't be diſcharged but by taking up of the Note.

Mr. Kent. Cunningham on Bills of Exchange cites Comyns. It was formerly ſettled Law that the Conſideration ſhould not be called in Queſtion — they are upon the ſame Footing as Inland Bills.

Ch. Juſt. If this Action ſhould be barred, it ſeems

---

order, and by him indorſed to the plaintiff. The queſtion of law was raiſed by a ſpecial verdict, which ſhowed that the plaintiff took the note by indorſement on the 4th of Auguſt, 1761, after it had been paid, but without knowledge of the payment.

(2) —— v. *Ormſton*, 10 Mod. 287.

1763. Russel v. Oakes.

feems to me that one half of the Trade muft be extremely precarious, for it refts upon fuch Bills, whofe Credit muft be deftroyed. It deftroys the Diftinction between Notes negotiable and not.

Juft. Ruffell. There is no Difference between them till the Indorfement.

Judgment was rendered at Cambridge in Auguft Term, 1763, for Defendant.* (3) *Ch. Juft. diffentiente.*

* *Qu.* If the Reafon of the Judgment in Strange, 1155, would not have been pertinent in this Cafe. Vid. Salk. 344; Carth. 356; L'd Raym'd, 87.

(3) S. P. *Baker* v. *Wheaton*, 5 Mafs. 512. *Hemmenway* v. *Stone*, 7 Mafs. 58. But see St. 1839, c. 121, § 1; Gen. Sts. c. 53, § 10.

Report of the fecond Argument upon Writs of Affiftance.

The cafe on the next page, argued and decided at Auguft term, 1761, feems to have been copied into the book here from notes taken at that time. That the notes were Quincy's own appears from the memorandum prefixed to the argument of Otis, *poft*, 55; and at the end of the cafe in the MS. is a reference to "Law File C," which probably contained his original notes, now loft. It feems ftrange that this argument fhould not have been mentioned by the hiftorians. Even John Adams, who was admitted to the bar only four days before, (*ante*, 35,) and to whom we are indebted for a report of the firft argument upon Writs of Affiftance in February 1761, (*poft*, 469,) does not appear to have left any notice of this one, except in a letter of October 4, 1780, to Mr. Calkoen, in which he fays that the queftion "was folemnly and repeatedly argued before the fupreme court by the moft learned counfel in the Province." 7 John Adams's Works, 267. But Adams's diary contains only one entry between his admiffion and June 5, 1762. 2 John Adams's Works, 133, 134. And his autobiography and his letters to William Tudor were written many years afterwards. *Vid. poft*, 409, 417. Hutchinfon, having received his inftructions from England fince the firft argument, (*poft*, 415, note,) probably confidered the fecond argument a mere form. For copies of the papers, and other information about the Writs of Affiftance, fee Appendix I.

August Term (1)

Georgii Ter. in Sup. Cur.

Paxton's Cafe of the Writ of Affiftance.

1761.

PAXTON'S CASE.

Rec. 1761. Fol. 225.

This Court has Power to iffue general Writs of Affiftance to Officers of the Cuftoms.

CHARLES PAXTON, Efq., applied to the Superiour Court for the Writ of Affiftants, as by Act of Parliament to be granted to him.

Upon this, the Court defired the Opinion of the Bar, whether they had a Right and ought to grant it.

Mr. Otis & Mr. Thacher fpoke againft.

Meffrs. Gridley & Auchmuty (2) for granting it.

Mr. Thacher firft read the Acts of 14 Car. 2, ch. 22, and 7 & 8 of Wm. & Mary, upon which the Requeft for this Writ is founded. (3)

Though this Act of Parliament has exifted 60 Years, yet it was never applied for, nor ever granted, till

---

(1) Auguft term 1 Geo. 3, which was adjourned without day on Thurfday, November 19th, 1761. Rec. 1761, fol. 239. The argument and decision, here reported, were made upon Wednefday, the 18th of November. Bofton Gazette of November 23, 1761.

(2) Auchmuty was foon after appointed Advocate General, in the place of Otis, who had refigned to avoid arguing for these Writs. Wafhburn's Jud. Hift. Mafs. 185, 186.

(3) Sts. 13 & 14 Car. 2, c. 11, § 5; 7 & 8 W. 3, c. 22, § 6; quoted in Gridley's firft argument, *poft*, 480, 481.

1761. PAXTON'S CASE.

till 1756;(4) which is a great Argument againſt granting it; not that an Act of Parliament can be antiquated, but Non-uſer is a great Preſumption that the Law will not bear it; this is the Reaſoning of Littleton and Coke. Knight Service, p. 80, Sect. 108.(5) Moreover, when an Act of Parliament is not expreſs, but even doubtfull, and then has been neglected and not executed, in ſuch a Caſe the Preſumption is more violent.

Ch. Juſtice. (6) The Cuſtom Houſe Officers have frequently applied to the Governour for this Writ, and have had it granted them by him,(7) and therefore, though he had no Power to grant it, yet that removes the Argument of Non-uſer.

Mr. Thacher. If this Court have a Right to grant this Writ, it muſt be either *ex debita Juſtitia* or diſcretionary. If *ex debita Juſtitia*, it cannot in any Caſe be refuſed; which from the Act itſelf and its Conſequences, he argued, could not be intended. It can't be diſcretionary; for it can't be in the Power of any Judge at diſcretion to determine that I ſhall have my Houſe broken open or not. As ſays Juſt. Holt, "There can be no diſcretionary Power whether a Man ſhall be hanged or no." (8)

He moved further that ſuch a Writ is granted and muſt iſſue from the Exchequer Court, and no other

(4) *Paxton's caſe*, Auguſt term, 1755; *poſt*, 402–404, & notes.

(5) Co. Lit. 81 a, 81 b. S. P. 11 Met. 291.

(6) Hutchinſon, appointed November 13th, 1760. *Poſt*, 410, 411.

(7) S. P. 3 Hutchinſon's Hiſt. Maſs. 92. *Post*, 401.

(8) *Armſtrong* v. *Liſle*, (1697) Comb. 410. *S. C.* J. Kel. 95, 105; Skin.

other can grant it; 4 Inst. 103; and that no other Officers but such as constitute that Court can grant it.

1761.
PAXTON'S CASE.

Skin. 671; Holt, 63; 12 Mod. 109, 157; Carth. 395; 1 Salk. 63. The decision in that case was, that a conviction of manslaughter and allowance of benefit of clergy were a bar to an appeal of murder by the heir of the deceased; and that the defendant was entitled to be allowed his clergy at once, without waiting for the trial of the appeal, on which, if convicted, he might be hanged. S. P. 3 Inst. 130; *Smith* v. *Taylor*, (1771) 5 Bur. 2778.

Benefit of clergy in Massachusetts.

Benefit of clergy does not appear to have been allowed in the Colony of Massachusetts. 1 Hutchinson's Hist. Mass. (3d ed.) 388, note. At a later period, it was allowed in the Province in cases of manslaughter and burglary. *Trial of the British Soldiers*, (ed. 1770) 209. Washburn's Jud. Hist. Mass. 194. But it was not settled to what other crimes it extended. Resolution of General Court in February, 1768, 14 Mass. Archives, 507. 2 John Adams's Works, 534. Opinion of Trowbridge on "Benefit of Clergy respecting Rape," Keith MS. No. 11. (*Vid. post*, 478.) It was abolished here by St. 1784, c. 56.

Appeal of death in England.

The appeal of death was by Lord Holt "esteemed a noble remedy, and a badge of the rights and liberties of an Englishman." *Rex* v. *Toler*, 1 Ld. Raym. 557; 12 Mod. 375; Holt, 483. See Barrington on Sts. (5th ed.) 27. In the early part of the last century in England, persons who had been acquitted on indictments for murder, were often tried, convicted and executed on appeals. Kendall on Trial by Battel (3d ed.), 44-47. In 1770 its abolition was suggested in the House of Commons, but not pressed. 2 Cavendish Debates, 13. 20 Howell's State Trials, 716. An appeal of murder was brought in England as lately as 1817, but defeated by the appellant's declining to accept the wager of battel. *Ashford* v. *Thornton*, 1 B. & Ald. 403. Such appeals, as well as all trials by battel, were then abolished by St. 59 G. 3, c. 46.

Appeal of murder in the other Colonies.

The English Sts. of 9 H. 3, c. 34, & 6 Edw. 1, c. 9, concerning appeals of murder, were in force in the Provinces of Pennsylvania and Maryland. Report of Judges, 6 Binn. 599, 604. Kilty on Maryland Sts. 141, 143, 158. It is said that no such appeal was ever brought in Pennsylvania. Roberts on British Statutes in Pennsylvania, 59, 60. But in Maryland in 1765 a negro was convicted and executed upon such an appeal. *Soaper* v. *Tom*, 1 Har. & McHen. 227. The St. of 9 H. 3 was expressly adopted in South Carolina in 1712; and Mr. Cooper, the state editor of its statutes, doubts whether trial by battel and appeal of death were not both still in force there in 1837. 2 Sts. at Large of South Carolina, 401, 403, 715.

In Massachusetts Bay.

On the debate in the House of Commons in 1774 on the bill "for the better administration of Justice in Massachusetts Bay," a clause suspending

1761.

PAXTON'S CASE.

it. 2 Inſt. 551. That this Court is not ſuch a one, vid. Prov. Law. (9) This Court has in the moſt ſolemn Manner diſclaimed the Authority of the Exchequer; this they did in the Caſe of McNeal of Ireland & McNeal of Boſton. (10) This they cannot do in Part; if the Province Law gives them any, it gives them all the Power of the Exchequer Court; nor can they chuſe and refuſe to act at Pleaſure. But ſuppoſing this Court has the Power of the Exchequer, yet there are many Circumſtances which render that Court in this Caſe an improper Precedent; for there the Officers are ſworn in that Court, and are accountable to it, are obliged there to paſs their Accounts weekly; which is not the Caſe here. In that Court, there Caſes are tried, and there finally; which is another Diverſity. Beſides, the Officers of the Cuſtoms are their Officers, and under their Check, and that ſo much, that

---

ſuſpending the appeal of murder was vigorouſly aſſailed by Dunning, Burke, Fox, and others, and withdrawn. 17 Parl. Hiſt. 1291, 1292, 1296. And Mr. Kendall thinks, it exiſted in the Colonies. Kendall, 248, 249, 272. But Mr. Dane ſays, the appeal of felony did not exist here. 7 Dane Ab. 336. And ſee Conſtitution of Maſſachuſetts, c. 6, art. 6; Declaration of Rights, arts. 12, 15; U. S. Conſtitution, amendment 5.

Trial by battel.

In England, the last joinder of iſſue for trial by battel was on a writ of right in 1638; but the judges deferred the combat from time to time for error in the record until 1641, when the Houſe of Commons, upon the petition of the tenant, "ordered a bill to be brought in to take away trial by battel." *Claxton* v. *Lilburne*, 2 Ruſhw. Hiſt. Coll. 788, 790; 3 Ib. 356. Commons & Lords Journals 1620–1641, quoted in Kendall, 135, note. 3 Bl. Com. 337 *& ſeq.* But no ſuch bill was paſſed in England until 1820, *ut sup.* This mode of trial is not ſuppoſed to have been introduced in America, unleſs in South Carolina, *ut sup.* *Poſt*, 178. 3 Wilſon's Works, 142. 3 Dall. 350. 2 Sumner, 68.

(9) Prov. St. 11 W. 3, Anc. Chart. 330, 331.

(10) *McNeal* v. *Brideoak*, *post*, 470, note.

1761. PAXTON'S CASE.

that for Miſbehaviour they may puniſh with corporal Puniſhment. 3 & 4 Car. 2, § 8. (11) 7 & 8 W. & M. does not give the Authority. (12)

(*Mr. Otis* was of the ſame Side, but I was abſent, while he was speaking, moſt of the Time, and so have but few Notes.)

Mr. Otis. 12 Car. 2, 19. (13) 13 & 14 Car. 2, p. 56. Let a Warrant come from whence it will improperly, it is to be refuſed, and the higher the Power granting it, the more dangerous. The Exchequer itſelf was thought a Hardſhip in the firſt Conſtitution. Vid. Rapin, Vol. 1ſt, p. 178, 386, 403, 404. (14) Vol. 2, 285, (15) 375. (16)

It

---

(11) St. 13 & 14 Car. 2, c. 11, § 8.

(12) St. 7 & 8 W. 3, c. 22, § 6.

(13) St. 12 Car. 2, c. 19, *poſt*, 395, note.

(14) Rapin's Hiſt. of Eng. (2d ed.) London, 1732. The pages referred to in the firſt volume relate to the Court of Exchequer and proceedings therein.

(15) Where Rapin ſays, that in 1629 the privy council of Charles 1 gave orders, " impowering the officers of the cuſtoms to enter into any ſhip, veſſel, or houſe, and to ſearch in any trunk or cheſt, and break any bulk whatſoever, in default of the payment of cuſtoms. But beſides that this had never been practiſed before, another inconvenience aroſe. Theſe officers, under colour of ſearching, uſed many oppreſſions and roguerics, which cauſed the people ſtill the more to exclaim." See alſo 1 Ruſhworth's Hiſt. Coll. 665, 668, 669; 2 Ib. 8, 9.

Breaking of houſes, &c., by officers of cuſtoms in England in 1629:

Before writs of aſſiſtance were iſſued in Maſſachuſetts, the officers of the customs, " merely by the authority derived from their commiſſions, had forcibly entered warehouſes, and even dwelling-houſes, upon information that contraband goods were concealed in them." But " the people grew uneaſy under the exerciſe of this aſſumed authority," and reſiſted or ſued the officers. 3 Hutchinſon's Hiſt. Maſs. 92.

In Maſſachuſetts before 1755.

(16) The articles of impeachment againſt the Earl of Strafford in 1641, beginning with the ninth article, which charged him with iſſuing general warrants of arreſt. *S. C. & S. P.* in Ruſhw. Hiſt. Coll. 65, 236–240; 3 Howell's State Trial 1391, 1404, 1427.

Impeachment of Strafford.

1761. Paxton's Case.

It is worthy Conſideration whether this Writ was conſtitutional even in England; (17) and I think it plainly appears it was not; much leſs here, ſince it was not there invented till after our Conſtitution and Settlement. (18) Such a Writ is generally illegal. Hawkins, B. 2, ch. 1, Of Crim. Jur. (19) Viner, Tit. Commiſſion, A. (20) 1 Inſt. 464. (21) 29 M. (22)

Mr. Auchmuty. Bacon. (23) 4 Inſt. 100. From the Words of the Law, this Court may have the Power of the Exchequer. Now the Exchequer always had that Power; the Court cannot regard Conſequences, but muſt follow Law. As for the Argument of Non-uſer, that ends whenever the Law is once executed; and this Law has been executed in this Country, and this Writ granted, not only by the Governor, but alſo from this Court in Ch. Juſtice Sewall's Time. (24)

Mr. Gridley. This is properly a Writ of Aſſiſt- *ants,*

---

(17) An indication of the poſition, more diſtinctly ſtated in Otis's firſt argument in February, 1761: "An act of Parliament againſt the Conſtitution is void." *Vid. poſt*, 474, & Appendix I, J.

(18) *Qu.* Whether Otis here intended to deny that Acts of Parliament bound the Province. See Appendix I, J.

(19) 2 Hawk. c. 1, §§ 7, 8.

(20) "If commiſſion iſſues to take J. S. and his goods, without indictment, or ſuit of the party, or other proceſs, this is not good; for it is againſt the law."

(21) Probably 1 Inſt. 272 b, note to Lit. § 464: "The ſureſt conſtruction of a ſtatute is by the rule and reaſon of the common law."

(22) Probably c. 29 of Magna Charta: "*Nullus liber homo capiatur, vel impriſonetur,*" *&c.* 2 Inſt. 45 *& ſeq.* See Appendix I, E.

(23) Bac. Ab. Court of Exchequer.

(24) 1755–1759, *poſt*, 403–406.

1761. PAXTON'S CASE.

ants, not Aſſiſtance; not to give the Officers a greater Power, but as a Check upon them. For by this they cannot enter into any Houſe, without the Preſence of the Sheriff or civil Officer, who will be always ſuppoſed to have an Eye over and be a Check upon them. Quoting Hiſtory is not ſpeaking like a Lawyer. If it is Law in England, it is Law here; it is extended to this Country by Act of Parliament. 7 & 8 Wm. & M. ch. 18. (25) By Act of Parliament they are entitled to like Aſſiſtants; (26) now how can they have like Aſſiſtants, (26) if the Court cannot grant them it; and how can the Court grant them like Aſſiſtance, if they cannot grant this Writ. Pity it would be, they ſhould have like Right, and not like Remedy; the Law abhors Right without Remedy. But the General Court has given this Court Authority to grant it, and ſo has every other Plantation Court given their Superiour Court. (27)

The Juſtices were unanimouſly of Opinion that this Writ might be granted, and ſome Time after, out of Term, it was granted. (28)

---

(25) St. 7 & 8 W. 3, c. 22, § 6.

(26) Altered in the MS. from "Aſſiſtance" to "Aſſiſtants." The words of St. 7 & 8 W. 3, c. 22, § 6, are "like aſſiſtance."

(27) But it is ſaid that in other colonies the writs were refuſed. 7 John Adams's Works, 267. 4 Bancroft's Hist. U. S. 431, note.

(28) Judgment was given at the concluſion of the argument on the 18th of November, 1761. Boſton Gazette of November 23, 1761. And it appears by the court files that the writ was iſſued on the 2d of December, 1761. See App. I, C.

For a report of another caſe of public intereſt, decided ſoon after, to which Paxton was a party, ſee *Province of Maſſachuſetts Bay* v. *Paxton*, App. II.

February Term

III Geo. 3.

1763.

Ruddock v. Gordon.

Rec. 1763. Fol. 22.

A Collector of Taxes cannot maintain an Action to recover them where the Remedy given by Statute is by Diſtreſs.

The Want of Power to maintain ſuch Action is not Matter of Abatement.

Ruddock *verſ.* Gordon.

RUDDOCK was a Collector of Taxes in the Town of Boſton, and brought his Action, which was Treſpaſs upon the Caſe, for the Defendant's Tax, upon a general *Indebitatus Aſſumpſit.*

There were three Exceptions to the Writ, and Pleas in Abatement. Firſt, to the Looſeneſs of the Account, which was only in general for Tax for the Year 1761; and 'twas ſaid that the Account was Part of the Declaration, and that the Action would not be a Bar to another which might be brought hereafter for each Tax in particular. Secondly, that the Collector has no Right or Authority to bring ſuch Actions, the Law having pointed out another Way, viz., by Diſtreſs. Thirdly, that if any Action lay at all, it ſhould be Debt, and not Caſe. (1)

It

(1) The Rev. Sts. c. 8, § 15, provide that in certain caſes the collector "may maintain an action of debt or aſſumpſit." And by the St. of 1859, c. 171, the right of action is extended to all caſes of a neglect to pay for the ſpace of one year after the tax has been committed to the collector. Gen. Sts. c. 12, § 19.

It was anſwered to the firſt, that in the Town of Boſton all the Taxes were made up together, and that Tax was a Noun collective, including all, and would be a Bar; that as for the Collector's Right of bringing this Action, that ought to be conſidered upon the Merits and not in Abatement; and as for its being Debt, it is merely a Matter *in Pais*.

The Court ruled unanimouſly, that the Objection to the Collector's Power is not Matter of Abatement, but to be try'd upon the Merits. (2) But the Opinion of *the Court* being aſked by both Parties upon that Point, *the Court* were of Opinion that they had no ſuch Power, and that this Action can't be ſupported. (3)

Gardiner *verſ.* Purrington.

Gardiner v. Purrington.

Rec. 1763. Fol. 22.

In Trover for Trees, the Plaintiffs' Title to Land in another County, on which they were cut, cannot be given in Evidence where the Action might have been brought in that County.

THIS is an Action of Trover brought to the Inferiour Court in *Suffolk* for a Quantity of Timber cut in the County of *Cumberland*.

The

---

(2) The general principle has ſometimes been ſtated to be, that a perpetual diſability in the plaintiff is to be pleaded in bar, but if only temporary, then in abatement. 5 Dane Ab. 693. But this rule has many exceptions; and it ſeems to be now ſettled that a perpetual diſability, which forever deſtroys the plaintiff's right of action, is pleadable either in abatement or bar, (*Langdon* v. *Potter*, 11 Maſs. 313,) the rule that a plea in abatement muſt give a better writ having ſo many exceptions that it can hardly be called a general rule of law. 6 Pick. 369.

(3) S. P. *Crapo* v. *Stetſon*, 8 Met. 393. "A collector of taxes cannot maintain an action to recover them in any caſe beſides thoſe in which an action is given to him by Rev. Sts. c. 8, § 15." See alſo 6 Maſs. 44.

1763.
GARDINER
v.
PURRINGTON.

The Queſtion was, whether the *Title* of Land can be given in Evidence in Trover in *another* County than where the Land lies.

1 Bacon, 35; 1 Salk. 290, *Brown* vs. *Hedges;* Mod. Caſes, 322, *Walrond* vs. *Van Moſes*, (1) were cited in Favour of the Action; and it was ſaid by the Council on this Side, that the giving Title under this Action did not bar or affect an Action of Ejectment brought in the County where the Land lies.

Gridley. There is no ſpecial Pleading in Trover, except a Releaſe, which admits the Converſion. The Title is often given in Treſpaſs where the Poſſeſſion is not clear, 'tis what the Law calls incidental; yet 'tis neceſſary in Treſpaſs; juſt ſo in Trover. The Man cuts down the Timber—I may bring Treſpaſs; ſo I may Trover. The Timber is mine after it is cut down; the Tort never ſhall give him Property. It is mine in the Timber as it is mine in the Tree, and I may bring my Action: Now how can I prove my Property, unleſs I can give my Title in Evidence? When the Poſſeſſion ſeems mutual, it can never be determined, and though my own, (the Thing may be,) if I may not be admitted, I may never recover my own. In the Admiralty, many Things that are not naturally within its Juriſdiction may be tried there. Difference between an Inconvenience and a Miſchief—whenever the Law has once conſidered of this, it vaniſhes;

(1) *Anon.*, cited in *Walrond* v. *Van Moſes*, 8 Mod. 322.

1763.
GARDINER v. PURRINGTON.

vanifhes; in determining what is an Inconvenience, the Law is fettled.

Juft. Ruffell. Whether this Cafe is not different from the Cafe of Mod. Cafes, (2) where it was admitted for the Inconvenience, and is it not the fame in Effect as if the Title was determined?

Ch. Juft. Whether it will not operate againft another Rule of Law about Titles of Land coming in Queftion in another County?

Auchmuty. The Title is not determined.

Ch. Juft. As my Brother Ruffell obferves, is it not the fame Thing? It is not whether Trover is a tranfitory Action, (3) but whether that which is of the Nature of a real one fhall be given in Evidence.

Mr. Gridley cites Styles, 331.

Mr.

(2) The cafe cited in *Walrond* v. *Van Mofes*, *ub. fup.*, is as follows: "*Nota.* At the trial of this caufe a cafe was cited that trover lay in England for timber taken away and converted in Ireland; and this was by the opinion of the late Chief Juftice Holt, though it was objected that it might bring the title of lands in Ireland in queftion, which could not be tried here; but he anfwered that as trover was a tranfitory action it might be brought here for a converfion in Ireland; nor fhall any incident queftion which may arife on the fame bar the plaintiff of fuch action; for if it fhould, then a perfon being in England can have no remedy here when the defendant is guilty of a trover in Ireland, and comes from thence into this kingdom."

(3) Trover for cutting down trees is a tranfitory action. Steph. Nifi Prius, 2695. *Brown* v. *Hedges*, *ub. fup.* So alfo an action of trefpafs *de bonis afportatis* for burning down a fmall houfe erected for a temporary purpofe, and without a cellar. 15 Pick. 156.

1763.
GARDINER *v.* PURRINGTON.

Mr. Kent. 1 Bacon, 32. Mod. Cafes, . A perfonal Action may grow into a real one as here. 1 Lilly, 20.

The Court were of Opinion that the Cafes cited in Favour of this Evidence refpected only Cafes of Neceffity, and where they could not be tried in the fame County, which not being the Cafe here, they determined that in this Cafe it could not be admitted. (4)

ROGERS *v.* KENWRICK.

Rec. 1763. Fol. 46.

Rogers *verf.* Kenwrick.

(From Barnftable.)

It is no Objection to an Award that it fettles the Boundary Line between adjacent Lands of the Parties without ordering Releafes. *Hutchinfon, C. J., & Oliver, J., diff.*

THIS Action was Debt upon an Arbitration Bond. No Award pleaded. Award was read as follows: "We do determine and fettle the northweft Corner Bound as fettled by us is an Heap of Stones," &c., "which appears to be the reputed known N. W. Bound for many Years, and nothing appears

(4) Actions, perfonal in form, which involve or bring in iffue the title to land, have been held to become thereby real, within the meaning of the ftatutes concerning cofts and the jurifdiction of juftices of the peace. 4 Pick. 169 10 Pick. 473. But the point here decided appears to be, not that the action becomes local, but that the title to real eftate in another county fhall not incidentally be given in evidence to fupport a tranfitory action which might have been brought in that county. This feems a difficult pofition to fupport, as the title to the land is only offered as a means of proving a right to poffeffion of the trees when converted, on which latter point alone is the judgment conclusive.

1763. ROGERS v. KENWRICK.

appears but was always ſo," &c., "and that the ſaid Kenwrick pay," &c. (1) Now 'twas anſwered by

Mr. Paine. That the Arbitrators had taken upon them to determine a Title of Freehold, and therefore the Arbitration void and no Award. Where the Right of Freehold is in Debate, the Property cannot be transferred by an Award; the Arbitrators only are in Stead of the Parties, and can do no more than can be done by them. Now the Parties themſelves cannot paſs corporeal Inheritances without ſolemn Livery. 1 Roll. Abr. 242. 14 H. 4, 19, 24. 9 H. 6, 6. 3 H. 4, 6. 11 H. 4, 12. Keilw. 99. 1 Leon. 228. 1 Roll. Abr. 244. 1 Bacon, 132. But if Condition of the Obligation is to ſtand to Award of Arbitrators, who award the Land to one, and that the other ſhall releaſe, who does not, the Penalty of the Obligation is forfeited, but if no Act to be done by the Party, as releaſing, is awarded, it is not forfeited though the other do not convey to him a good Title. (2)

Mr. Otis, contra. I grant the Award to be void if

---

(1) The replication further alleged that the defendant had not kept up to the tenor of the award, but had broken over the line by cutting wood on the land of the plaintiffs. And among the papers on file appeared the depoſition of Jonathan Kenwrick, ſealed up and directed, "For the Clerk of y[e] Superiour Court of Judicature" &c. This being opened by the preſent Clerk of the Supreme Judicial Court, it appeared that the deponent teſtified to ſeeing the defendant "cutting wood about ſix rods to y[e] weſtward of y[e] range that was ſettled by y[e] arbitrators."

(2) Among the papers on file appears one which would ſeem to have been part of Mr. Paine's brief, ſince it contains the above argument and liſt of authorities almoſt *verbatim;* the whole being taken from Bac. Ab. Arbitrament, A.

1763. ROGERS v. KENWRICK.

if the Arbitrators have determined the Freehold; but here they have not, they have only determined the Line; the real Boundary is but a mathematical Line without Breadth or Thickneſs, the ſettling that does not affect the Freehold. 1 Bacon, Tit. Arbitra. I think then a Bond conditioned to abide by ſuch Award is good, and the Award good, and if not complied with, the Obligation ſhould be forfeited.

Paine. When they ſettle the Line, they ſay to whom the Land on each Side belongs. They have awarded Nothing to be done; they ſhould have ordered Releaſes.

Judgment for the Plaintiff. (3) *Ruſſell*, *Cuſhing*, *Lynde*, againſt *Oliver* & *Ch. Juſtice.*

Ch. Juſt. very warmly againſt the Determination.*

* *Quære*, if this Caſe is not agreeable to Law? Vid. Vol. 1, (4) p. 18, and the Authorities there cited.

---

(3) S. P. *Jones* v. *Boſton Mill Corp.* 6 Pick. 148. *Goodridge* v. *Duſtin*, 5 Met. 363. In this caſe the previous deciſion in *Whitney* v. *Holmes*, 15 Maſs. 152, was partially overruled, and the rule ſtated by Mr. Juſtice Hubbard to be, that an award which ſettles a boundary, "although it will not have the direct effect of conveying lands, will yet conclude the parties from diſputing the title or boundary which is diſtinctly ſettled by the award, and that it ſhall operate by way of eſtoppel." See alſo *Searle* v. *Abbe*, 13 Gray, 409.

(4) This volume is miſſing. Many other references to miſſing volumes are omitted. See Preface.

1763.

GRIDLEY v. BALSTON.

Gridley *verf.* Balfton & al.

Rec. 1763. Fol. 15.

The Eftate of a Teftator is not liable for the Negligence of Executors in carrying out and executing a Confignment made to the Teftator in his Lifetime.

BALSTON and others were Executors of Palmer of London, who was Agent for the Plaintiff in his Lifetime. A Ship was configned to Palmer by the Plaintiff, but Palmer died before her Arrival or Knowledge of it. The Executors undertook the Bufinefs and tranfacted it, and are now fued as Executors to Mr. Palmer for Breach of Truft. (1)

The Queftion was, as Confignment was made in Mr. Palmer's Life, and the Executors profecuted it, whether they fhould anfwer as Executors, and Palmer's Eftate be liable in their Hands. 2 Bacon, 144. (2)

It was faid, if the Breach of Truft was in Mr. Palmer — being a Tort, it dies with him; if not, he can't be chargeable.

On the other Hand that it was but a Continuance of the fame Affair, and they acted in his Stead. Viner, Tit. Executor, P. 4, Plea 39, 43. 1 Lill. 778, Let. H. Dyer, 324.

The

---

(1) The declaration alleged that the teftator, being factor of the plaintiffs, procured infurance on the freight of the plaintiff's galley from Jamaica to London; that when fhe arrived the teftator died; and that the executors undertook to fettle and manage the faid truft, but managed it ill, and "perfunctorily acted with great negligence" in fettling a leakage of fugars.

(2) Bac. Ab. Executor, P. 2. "The taking up of an executorfhip doth not embark executor in the perfonal trufts of the deceafed."

1763.
GRIDLEY v. BALSTON.

The Court unanimous that theſe Authorities are not in Point, and the Action will not lie.

BROWN v. CULNON.

Rec. 1763. Fol. 10.

A Town may recover of an Individual Money advanced by the Overſeers of the Poor for the neceſſary Support of his Wife and Children.

Brown *verſ.* Culnon.

(From Middleſex.)

UPON a ſpecial Verdict, which was: "The "Jury find that the Overſeers of the Poor in "the Abſence of the Defendant and without his "Requeſt advanced for the neceſſary Support of the "Defendant's Wife and Children a certain Sum, and "if by Law the Plaintiff as Treaſurer of the Town "ought to recover the ſame back from the Defend-"ant, they find for the Plaintiff — otherwiſe, for the "Defendant."

Judgment that the Defendant is liable. (1)

---

(1) S. P. *Hanover* v. *Turner*, 14 Maſs. 227. *New Bedford* v. *Chace*, 5 Gray, 28. But the town cannot recover for ſupplies ſuitable to the wife's condition in life, beyond her neceſſary ſupport as a pauper. *Monſon* v. *Williams*, 6 Gray, 416.

Dunten *verſ.* Richards.

(From Cambridge.)

Rec. 1763.
Fol. 12.

A Guardian who has executed his Ward's Indentures of Apprenticeſhip has no Power to releaſe the Maſter from his Covenant of Payment to the Ward, in Settlement of a Claim againſt himſelf for Deceit, grounded on the Ward's alledged Incapacity of performing his Covenants of Service.

PLAINTIFF was an Apprentice bound by his Guardian to the Defendant, who covenanted among other Things to pay the Plaintiff £80 (1) at the Expiration of the Time of his Service. This Action was Covenant broken. Oyer of the Indenture, upon which Defendant pleads that Plaintiff was not capable of ſerving him as he covenanted, and that in Conſideration thereof the Guardian had releaſed the Payment of the £80. The Queſtion was, whether the Guardian had Authority to make ſuch Releaſe.

It

(1) The declaration alleged that the plaintiff bound himſelf with the conſent of the guardian, and that the defendant covenanted to diſmiſs him at the end of the term "with two ſuits of apparell, one for the Sabbath and one for every day, and to give him eighty pounds in bills of public credit of the old tenor, or the value thereof in ſuch money as ſhall then be current," which value was alleged to have been £10 13*s.* 4*d.* The plea ſet forth that the defendant was deceived and impoſed upon by the guardian in binding the minor, whom he found deficient in underſtanding, and not capable of learning or ſerving him, wherefore he inſiſted that the apprentice ſhould be taken back, and, after much diſpute and controverſy, it was finally agreed that the maſter ſhould releaſe all demands on account of the impoſition, and that the guardian ſhould releaſe the £80 as aforeſaid, which was accordingly done. To this plea there was a "replication in writing, as on file, concluding to the country," and a rejoinder, after which the caſe was ſent to a jury, who found for the plaintiff "three pounds money damage and coſts." The caſe was continued for argument on the ſpecial plea, and judgment was finally entered for the full amount of £10 13*s.* 4*d.* It would ſeem that this argument muſt have been on a motion for judgment *non obſtante veredicto*, but as all the Middleſex files of court for 1763 are miſſing, no information can be obtained except from the record.

1763. DUNTEN *v.* RICHARDS.

It was ſaid by the Plaintiff that Guardians have no Right to releaſe or give Diſcharge but for Sums received. Moore, 852, *White* vs. *Hall.*

On the other Hand, the Guardian was a Party by their own ſhewing, and releaſed no other Contract than he made himſelf.

Court were unanimouſly of Opinion that the Guardian had no Right to Releaſe. (2)

---

(2) From the pleadings in this caſe it would ſeem that there was no attempt to affect the guardian with any liability on the covenants of the indenture, but that the maſter's claim was on the ground of deception and impoſition in inducing him to enter into it. See *Blunt* v. *Melcher*, 2 Maſs. 228. In that caſe it was held, that where a ward binds himſelf with the aſſent of his guardian, the words deſcribing his duties are not the covenants of the guardian, though he ſigns and ſeals the indenture. But in an indenture between father, ſon, and maſter, under 5 Eliz. c. 4, the father is anſwerable in covenant for what is to be performed by the ſon. Com. Dig. Covenant, A 2. Doug. 518. 8 Mod. 190. 3 Dane Ab. 588. Whether a father or guardian liable on a broken covenant for ſervice would have any power to releaſe the maſter from a covenant beneficial to the minor, is not here decided. It is a general rule that contracts beneficial to the ward cannot be avoided by the guardian. See 13 Maſs. 240.

Auguſt Term

III Georgii Ter. in Sup. Cur.

Preſent:

The Honourable

Thomas Hutchinſon, Eſqr., Chief Juſtice.
Benja: Lynde,
John Cuſhing,
Chambers Ruſſell,
Peter Oliver,
} Eſqrs., Juſtices.

1763.

BAKER *v.* MATTOCKS.

Rec. 1763. Fol. 118.

Baker *verſ.* Mattocks. (1)

The Prov. St. of 4 W. & M. by which Lands deſcend to all the Children, and which empowers the Anceſtor to convey or deviſe them at his Pleaſure, does not extend to Eſtates Tail, but leaves

THE Queſtion in this Caſe was, whether Eſtates in Tail are partable in this Province, by the Province Law.

Mr.

(1) *Formedon in the deſcender.* The declaration alleged a gift in tail to Samuel and Conſtance Mattocks, and a deſcent according to the form of the gift to Samuel, the ſon of the donees, and to the ſaid Samuel's eldeſt ſon, who died leaving the plaintiff and another daughter, who died leaving a ſon, who died without iſſue, "after whoſe death the whole right to the demanded premiſes came to the plaintiff according to the form of the gift." The ſpecial verdict found that Samuel, the grandfather of the plaintiff, made a deed of the premiſes to the defendant, one of his younger ſons, and that there were many other deſcendants

1763.

BAKER *v.* MATTOCKS.

them as at the Common Law. *Cuſhing, J.,* & *Hutchinſon, C. J., diſſ.*

Mr. Fitch in Favour of the Partability. The Deſign of the Province Law (2) was to alter the Common Law Deſcent. All Eſtates Tail at Common Law were Fee Simple conditional. Co. Lit. 20 a. 'Tis the Statute of Weſtminſter that forms Eſtates Tail. This Statute does not alter the Courſe of the Common Law Deſcents, it only limits them. Co. Lit. 19 a. Co. Lit. 110 b. This is the Caſe of Gavelkind Lands. Vin. Tit. Gavelkind, B.

Juſtice Ruſſell. The Common Law never took Place with Regard to Gavelkind Lands, but the Common Law takes Place here unleſs in Caſe of particular Eſtates.

Mr. Gridley. The Tail is only cut out of Fee Simple,

---

ants of the original donees beſides the parties to this caſe; "and if it ſhall appear to the Court upon the whole that the ſaid Samuel and Conſtance, the donees, took an eſtate in tail, and that the ſaid eſtate tail is not made partible by the law of this Province, then the jury find for the appellant poſſeſſion of the premiſes ſued for and coſts; otherwiſe they find for the appellee coſts."

(2) Prov. St. 4 W. & M. This was the law by which the right of primogeniture was firſt aboliſhed in the Province, for the reaſons ſet forth in the preamble as follows:

"Whereas eſtates in theſe plantations do conſiſt chiefly of lands which have been ſubdued and brought to improvement by the induſtry and labour of the proprietors, with the aſſiſtance of their children, the younger children generally having been longeſt and moſt ſerviceable unto their parents in that behalf, who have not perſonal eſtate to give out unto them in portions, or otherwiſe to recompenſe their labour.

"Sect. 1. Be it therefore enacted," &c., "that every perſon lawfully ſeiſed of any lands, tenements, or hereditaments within this province, in his own proper right in fee ſimple, ſhall have power to give, diſpoſe, and deviſe as well by his laſt will and teſtament in writing as otherwiſe by any act executed in his life, all ſuch lands, tenements, and hereditaments to or among his children or others as he ſhall think fit at his pleaſure, and if no ſuch diſpoſition, gift, or deviſe be made," then preſcribing the rules of deſcent to all the children. Anc. Chart. 230.

Simple, it is only excluding others to whom it would otherwiſe deſcend.

1763.
Baker v. Mattocks.

Mr. Thacher. But for the Province Law, neither Fee Simple or Tail would be partable. The Queſtion then is, whether this Law is extended to Eſtates Tail; by this Law, every Perſon ſhall have Right of Diſpoſition, and if no ſuch be made, then follow the Rules of Deſcent. 'Tis certain the Legiſlature had Fee Simple only in Contemplation; both would have gone according to the Common Law of England, but our Fee Simple is by this Act taken out of that Courſe, while the Fee Tail is not. The Statute of Weſtminſter left Gavelkind as it found it. Lilly, 648. 'Tis otherwiſe with Regard to our Province Law, which ſhall alter no further than its Deſign to alter.

Mr. Otis. The Manner of Succeſſion, if traced to its Original, is merely arbitrary; the Law of Nature is a Stranger to it; by that, no Man has a Right to more than his Life. States have an undoubted Right to ſettle it as they pleaſe: I ſay this in Anſwer to the Argument of the Natural Right of Deſcent to all the Children alike. When once any State has ſettled the Courſe of Deſcents among them, 'tis of great Importance that the Principles ſhould be kept to. The Method of Deſcent in England to the eldeſt Son is 700 Years—nay, as old as the Common Law itſelf. I conclude that before the Conqueſt the Right of Primogeniture did not take Place; ſomewhere between William 1 and Henry 1 it aroſe, but that does not affect the Caſe; it is now, and long has been ſo ſettled. Now as the Province

1763.
BAKER
v.
MATTOCKS.

Province Law has altered this Rule of Deſcent with Regard to the Fee, the Queſtion is, whether of Conſequence it has alter'd the Courſe of Tails. No Statute can alter the Courſe of the Law further than the expreſs Words of the Statute. Viner, Tit. Tail. It has been doubted whether any Alteration at all by our Province Law is good; it has been determin'd to be good at Home in the Caſe of Fee Simple, and for the Reaſon given in our Law, which does not hold with Regard to Tails.

Mr. Gridley. The Queſtion is, whether as Fee Simple is partable by Cuſtom or by Law of the Land, Tail is not alſo partable; that is the Caſe in the Cuſtom of Gavelkind. Fee Simple contains in it Fee Tail, which is a Part of it; as it was in the Fee Simple, ſo muſt be the Courſe of Deſcent in the Fee Tail. Heirs in Fee Simple are Heirs in Fee Tail; only certain Heirs are excluded, cut out, and 'tis an univerſal Interpretation of theſe limited Eſtates, that they ſhould follow the Rule of Fee Simple. Now ſhall we take the Courſe of our Eſtates Tail from our own Fee Simple, out of which they are created, and interpret the Rule of their Deſcent by it, or to interpret our Tails ſhall we have Recourſe to the Fee Simple of England to judge of our Tail?

Juſtice Oliver. Till the Statute *De Donis*, Tails were Fee Simple Conditional; by that, Eſtates Tail were created. We brought over both the Common Law and Statute with us. (3) This Law of ours relates

(3) S. P. 1 Maſs. 60, 61. 2 Maſs. 534. 8 Pick. 316. 13 Met. 68.

relates particularly to Fee Simple, and I think does not affect Eftates Tail, but leaves them as in England. I am againft the Partability.

1763.
BAKER
v.
MATTOCKS.

Juftice Ruffell. The very Intent of Tails was to fecure Eftates in Familys, and keep them together. The Intent ought to be obferved, but would be deftroyed by fuch a Conftruction of the Law. I am therefore againft the Partability.

Juftice Cufhing. This Point is of great Confequence to the Province, and it would be attended with great Difficulty at this Day to determine, that Eftates Tail were partable, the general Tenor having been otherwife, yet if the Law is plain, as I hold it is, I don't fee how it can be help'd. If there was no other than Fee Simple intended by the Prov. Law; yet as it was there fettled, who were Heirs, that fettled Eftates of Inheritance, all being made out of Fee Simple, and being a Limitation, not an Alteration. This is the Manner of Conftruction of the Law at Home: Where Fee Simple is partable, fo are Eftates Tail; and where Fee Simple defcends to the eldeft Son, fo does Tail.

Juftice Lynde. Had there been no particular Law of our Province, I fhould have thought Fee Simple and Tail would have gone alike, but now I think by our Law, Fee Tails are exempted and left at Common Law. Fee Eftates only are directed to defcend to all the Children, and with Reafon. It feems directly againft the Reafon and Intent of Eftates Tail that they fhould be partable, and that they

1763. BAKER v. MATTOCKS.

they are not made partable by this Law, is my Opinion.

Ch. Juſtice. It ſeems evident to me that it is the Spirit of the Engliſh Law, that all Inheritances ſhould follow the Method of Fee Simple: If it was now a thing intirely upon the Law I ſhould not have the leaſt Difficulty of thinking Fee Tail, as well as Fee Simple, was partable; but it has been ſo long thought otherwiſe here, and this has been the uninterrupted contemporaneous Expoſition of the Law, and many Judgments of Court founded on it, that it creates a great Difficulty, and I am glad that the Point is determined without me, for how ſuch a Cuſtom can prevail againſt plain Law, I doubt. (4)

SCOLLAY v. DUNN.

Scollay *verſ.* Dunn.

Rec. 1763. Fol. 107.

An Hoſtage ſent by the Maſter for the Ranſom of a Ship taken by the Enemy cannot maintain Admiralty Proceſs *in Perſonam* againſt the Owners for refuſing to pay the Money for his Liberation. *Oliver, J., diſſentiente.*

DUNN brought a Libel in the Admiralty againſt Scollay, for that he was a Mate on board a Veſſell of Scollay's, which was taken, and ranſomed by the Maſter, and Dunn went as an Hoſtage. He was

(4) Judge Trowbridge, in an opinion given upon the will of Shute Shrimpton Yeomans, who died in 1769, (for an opportunity of examining which we are indebted to Edmund Trowbridge Dana, Eſq.,) took the ſame view of the law as the Chief Juſtice and Juſtice Cuſhing in this caſe. But the law in this State has ſince been ſettled in accordance with the deciſion of the majority of the Court. *Corbin* v. *Healy*, 20 Pick. 516. *Wight* v. *Thayer*, 1 Gray, 284, 286. It was not until after the Revolution that the proviſions for barring entails by common deed of warranty were enacted. St. 1791, c. 60. And even at the preſent day this cannot be done by will. Gen. Sts. c. 92, § 1. 6 Gray, 24.

was long Priſoner, and at laſt releaſed by the Money raiſed by ſome of his Friends, and now returned to Boſton. Libels againſt Scollay and others, Owners of the Veſſell. A Prohibition was granted, and the preſent Queſtion was, whether the Prohibition ſtand or a Conſultation ordered; The Point was, whether the Proceſs in the Admiralty againſt the Owners' Perſons was good. (1)

1763.

SCOLLAY *v.* DUNN.

No Appeal lies to the King in Council from a Deciſion of this Court granting a Prohibition to the Admiralty in a Cauſe wherein the Matter in Controverſy is leſs than £300.

Mr.

---

(1) The writ of prohibition is addreſſed "to Chambers Ruſſell Eſq., Judge of our Court of Vice-Admiralty, Charles Paxton Eſq., Marſhal, Andrew Belcher Eſq., Regiſter, and all the officers of ſaid Court." The libel is alleged to have ſet forth as follows: "That the libellant was mate of the brigantine Peggy belonging to John Scollay and Thomas Fletcher, and Iſaac Freeman was maſter of her, and that ſhe was taken on the high ſeas as prize by a private French ſhip of war called the *Entreprenante*, belonging to Monſieur Boutellier at Nantes, and that the ſaid Iſaac ranſomed her and her cargo for 5000 livres, to be paid in ſix months, and that the ſaid John, at the ſaid Iſaac's requeſt and direction, became hoſtage for ſecuring the payment, and was by Peter Thibaut, the French captain of ſaid ſhip, carried to Nantes," &c., "and that the libellant was finally obliged to pay the ſum of £213 10*s*. of his own money to obtain his liberty." The petition further alleged that "the brigantine was not then here, and that the ſaid Court of Admiralty could not award any proceſs againſt her, and that the libellant did not allege that ſhe ever came to the petitioners' poſſeſſion, or that they ever agreed to the ſaid contract of ranſom, but that the deſign of the libellant was to make the petitioners' perſons and eſtates liable for the default of the maſter, whereof they were wholly unknowing." After reciting the petition at length, the writ concludes as follows:

"We therefore willing to maintain the Laws and Rights of our Judicatories and Courts of Record, and being unwilling our liege people "with delays to hurt, Command and firmly Enjoin you that you meddle "not further in the ſaid Plea or Cauſe, nor moleſt or cauſe to be moleſted "the ſaid John Scollay and Thomas Fletcher or either of them in the "Cauſe aforeſaid in the ſaid Court of Vice Admiralty neither attempt or "preſume to attempt anything more therein: Untill our ſaid Juſtices have "adviſed and conſulted therein at our Superiour Court of Judicature "Court of Aſſize, and general Goal Delivery to be holden at Boſton, "within and for our County of Suffolk on the third Tueſday of February inſtant, when and where you the ſaid Chambers Ruſſell and the "ſaid John Dunn or any other perſons may be preſent, if you or they "pleaſe

1763.
Scollay v. Dunn.

Mr. Auchmuty for the Juriſdiction. The firſt being taken upon the High Seas, Facts ariſing afterwards in Conſequence in the Body are within the Juriſdiction of the Court of Admiralty. Maſters may make Contracts that bind the Owners. Molloy, B. 2, C. 1, § 10; Ch. 2, §§ 14 & 16. Ib. B. 2, Ch. 2, § 2. Hardres, 183, *Sparks* vs. *Stafford.* In Salkeld the Caſe is not ſo well reported as the ſame in Mod. Rep. 'Tis unneceſſary to ſet forth Order to redeem; as the Maſter may juſtify throwing over Goods in Caſe of a Storm to ſave a greater Loſs, ſo may he redeem, as otherwiſe the Whole would be loſt. 2 Ld. Raym. 931, *Tranter* vs. *Watſon.* As for the Caſe of *Johnſon* vs. *Shippin* in Salkeld, that the Maſter by his Contracts cannot make the Owners liable, 6 Mod. 79 is the ſame Caſe, and not ſo reported, beſides there the Contract appeared to have been made at Land; as for the Veſſell's being loſt, 'tis of no Avail — the Owners muſt be bound inſtantly or not at all; if the Maſter has a Right to bind the Owners by his Contract, they are bound, and the Contract cannot be reſcinded but by the Parties, and not depend upon ſuch a Contingency as the Arrival of the Veſſell.

Mr. Gridley. If the Admiralty has Juriſdiction of the Principal, it has of the Incidents; if of the Thing, it has of the Perſon; as in the Caſe of Damage

---

"pleaſe to ſhow forth and maintain if you or they can, that the aforeſaid "Plea or Cauſe is cognizable in the ſaid Court of Vice Admiralty.

"Witneſs, Thomas Hutchinſon Eſq. at Boſton this twelfth day of "February in the third Year of our Reign *Annoque Domini* 1763.

"Nath'l Hatch, Cler."

age done by one Ship againſt another. Molloy, B. 2, C. 2, p. 2.

1763.
Scollay v. Dunn.

Thacher. Whether the Owners muſt anſwer in their Perſons for the Act of the Maſter at Sea, of which they were utterly unknowing, is the Queſtion; I take it not the Owners perſonally, for the Thing itſelf is bound. Every Ranſom is a new Purchaſe, and if the Owners are liable in this Caſe, they would be liable if the Maſter had contracted with the Captors for another Ship, and ſent an Hoſtage as a Pawn.

Ch. Juſtice. It differs from a new Purchaſe, for a new Purchaſe from an Enemy is void; 'tis a Redemption, a Saving it from being the Enemy's Property.

Thacher. If the Veſſell be liable for the Ranſom, and the Maſter may retain her for the Ranſom Money, then ſhe can't remain ſo abſolutely the Owner's Property as ſhe was before the Capture. 2 Ld. Raym. 932, *Tranter* vs. *Watſon.*

Ch. Juſtice. The Queſtion ſeems to me to be, whether the Contract of the Maſter upon the *High Sea* is the Contract of the Owner; and whether, if it is, there is any Inſtance of Suit in the Admiralty againſt the Perſons of the Owners.

Otis. The very Idea of Hypothecation is that the Maſter may bind the Owners, ſo far as that Intereſt of theirs goes, with what he is intereſted. Molloy, 15, 2, Ch. 11, § 11.

It

1763. SCOLLAY *v.* DUNN.

It is now ſettled that Owners ſhall not be liable for the Barratry of the Maſter further than the Ship and Freight. 7 G. 2.

The Power of the Maſter is confined to the Ship and Cargo. Holt's Rep'ts, 48. Viner, Tit. Court of Admiralty. The Caſe of Hardres is conſiſtent with the above Rule.

Gridley. There are ſome Things though tranſacted upon the High Sea are not of a Maritime Nature, are not within the Juriſdiction of the Court of Admiralty. Things of a Maritime Nature tranſacted at Sea are undoubtedly within its Juriſdiction. So there are ſome Things of a Maritime Nature, though not tranſacted upon the High Seas, that are within the Juriſdiction of the Admiralty; ſuch are Wages of Seamen. There is Nothing that Owners are not liable for, which is neceſſary for the Support of the Voyage; it is no Argument that becauſe the Veſſell is liable, the Owners are not alſo; Veſſell, Maſter, and Owners are all liable for Wages. Viner, Tit. Hypoth. 329, bot.

Otis. This is Nothing but Hypoth. Viner, Tit. Mariner, 236; Tit. Maſter of a Ship, 348.

Mr. Juſtice Oliver delivered his Opinion in Favour of the Juriſdiction of the Admiralty.

Juſtice Lynde. I take the Affair of Ranſom to be a Matter upon Sea, and therefore if the Libel was on the Ship or Cargo, I ſhould hold it good; but

but as it is not, I cannot but be for the Prohibition ſtanding. 1763.

SCOLLAY v. DUNN.

Chief Juſtice. Ranſom as far as it reſpects Maſter and Hoſtage maritime, ſo far as Owner and Maſter does not appear to be a Contract upon the High Seas. None of the Authorities maintain the Juriſdiction in this Caſe; and where it is doubtfull, I think 'tis a Rule that common Juriſdiction ought to be maintained, and that the Admiralty Juriſdiction ought to be made plain and clear, which I think is not the Caſe now.

Prohibition ſtands. (2)

Mr.

(2) There cannot be much doubt that the contract between the owner and the hoſtage who pawns himſelf for the ranſom, is maritime, and within admiralty juriſdiction. See the caſes cited above; alſo 3 Doug. 166; 1 Ld. Raym. 22. The concluſion arrived at by Mr. Juſtice Lynde is, that although the contract be maritime, yet that only the remedy *in rem* can be ſought in the admiralty. The oppoſite doctrine may now be conſidered as eſtabliſhed in this country, "if indeed," as ſays Mr. Juſtice Sprague, (21 Law Rep. 605,) "anything as to admiralty juriſdiction can now be deemed ſettled." See *Andrews* v. *Wall*, 3 How. 573, *Story*, *J.*—"Over maritime contracts the admiralty poſſeſſes a clear and eſtabliſhed juriſdiction capable of being enforced *in perſonam* as well as *in rem.*" *New Jerſey Steam Navigation Co.* v. *Merchant's Bank*, 6 How. 392, *Nelſon*, *J.*—"If the cauſe is a maritime cauſe, ſubject to admiralty cognizance, juriſdiction is complete over the perſon as well as over the ſhip; it cannot be confined to one of the remedies on the contract, when the contract itſelf is within its cognizance." Alſo *De Lovio* v. *Boit*, 2 Gallis. 462; Clerke's Praxis, Tit. 1. But that it was once ſo confined to one remedy in ſome caſes by the Engliſh law, ſee the diſſenting opinion of Mr. Juſtice Johnſon in *Allegre* v. *Ramſay*, 12 Wheat. 614. The reſolutions of 1632 gave the admiralty juriſdiction *in rem*, but not *in perſonam*, over contracts for "building or mending, ſaving or neceſſary victualling of a ship." And Mr. Juſtice Johnſon, *ub. ſup.*, contends that the only inſtance of admiralty juriſdiction *in perſonam* upon contracts was for ſeamen's wages, which was allowed on the principle of *communis*

error

1763.
Scollay v. Dunn.

Mr. Gridley then claimed an Appeal to the King and Council: Reaſon of Government requires that they ſhould have Power of final Judgment in Caſes of Importance; at Home, in Caſe of *Ejectione Firmæ* on a Leaſe, Appeal lies.

Auchmuty. This is a Matter that deſerves Appeal. Vaughan Rep. 290, 402. That Writs of Error lie in all inferiour Dominions, Ib. 418. Admiralty Juriſdiction is expreſſly excepted from our Charter; (3) and if no Appeal lies in this Caſe, it ſeems to me that Exception is of no Value. 1 Peere Wms. 330, *Chriſtian* vs. *Corren.*

Mr. Thacher. The laſt Clauſe of the Charter relative to this Matter of Appeals ſeems evidently explanatory

---

error facit jus. But ſee 3 Burr. 1740, where Dunning, *arguendo*, "admitted that actions had been brought in the admiralty by the hoſtage againſt the owners who refuſed to ranſom him." Alſo 5 Rob. 104, where it is ſtated that in ſuits for ranſom on the part of the enemy, "proceedings were always carried on againſt the owner in the name of the hoſtage ſuing for his liberty." Whether the claim of the hoſtage againſt the owners is in the nature of ſalvage, and therefore dependent on the ſafe arrival of the veſſel, or whether, as argued here, the owners are bound inſtantly by the act of redeeming her from her preſent peril — *quære.* A recapture of a ſhip from the enemy or from pirates is ſalvage. *The Trelawney*, 4 Rob. 227. And where the poſſeſſion has been parted with for the benefit of the owner, proceedings *in perſonam* may be ſuſtained. *The Hope*, 3 Rob. 216.

(3) "Provided always, and it is hereby declared, that nothing herein ſhall extend or be taken to erect or grant or allow the exerciſe of any admiral court, juriſdiction, power or authority, but that the ſame ſhall be, and is hereby reſerved to us and our ſucceſſors, and ſhall from time to time be erected, granted and exerciſed, by virtue of commiſſions to be iſſued under the Great Seal of England, or under the ſeal of the high admiral, or the commiſſioners for executing the office of high admiral of England." *Province Charter*, Anc. Chart. 36.

explanatory of the firft, (4) the Matter in Difference only is what is to be confidered in giving Jurifdiction, and not the Suggeftion of Damages.

Otis. It appears to me that by the plain Conftruction of the Words of the Charter, the Matter in Difference muft neceffarily be £300. Courts have conftantly denied Appeals where there has has been no Judgment for more than that Sum; this has been the contemporaneous Expofition of it.

Gridley. The Charter fhould be liberally conftrued in Favour of Appeals. I hold, this Court, by the Claufes in our Charter relative to this Matter, is to judge of the Limitations of Appeals. "In all Matters deferving the fame," are the Words upon which my Opinion is founded. It feems to be fettled that the Subject has a Right in all Caufes to appeal; therefore even the King cannot abridge it. "All Matters deferving the fame" ought to have a liberal Conftruction in Favour of the Subject. "We think it neceffary that our Subjects fhould have Liberty of Appeal to us in all Cafes that may deferve the fame." The Conftruction, the Gentlemen on the other Side would give, feems to be providing Appeals only for the Defendant; upon their Principles,

(4) "And whereas we judge it neceffary that all our fubjects fhould have liberty to appeal to us, our heirs and fucceffors, in cafes that may deferve the fame, we do by thefe prefents ordain, that in cafe either party fhall not reft fatisfied with the judgment or fentence of any judicatories or courts within our faid province or territory, in any perfonal action, wherein the matter in difference doth exceed the value of three hundred pounds fterling, that then he or they may appeal to us, our heirs and fucceffors, in our or their privy council." *Province Charter*, Anc. Chart. 32.

1763. SCOLLAY *v.* DUNN.

Principles, a Demurrer being to the Declaration, and Judgment againſt the Plaintiff, how can he ever appeal?

Juſtice Oliver. I take the firſt Clauſe in the Charter relating to Appeals to be only introductory to the ſecond, and that there can be no Appeal where the Matter in Difference is leſs than £300; and upon that ſecond Clauſe I am againſt granting an Appeal in this Caſe.

Juſtice Cuſhing. I take, the ſecond Clauſe is explanatory, and ſo I am againſt it.

Juſtice Lynde. With Regard to the firſt Clauſe, it appears to me to be only introductory, and therefore on that I am of the ſame Opinion; as to the ſecond I am doubtfull, but as I am in general againſt Appeals, I am againſt it in this Caſe.

Chief Juſtice. Firſt, whether the Subject Matter comes within the Clauſe of the Charter relative to Appeals, as it is an Affair begun in the Admiralty and brought here only by Prohibition; and for this we muſt look into the Charter, which entirely reſerves and excepts it, and 'tis by a ſubſequent Act we have any Right to iſſue Prohibitions to it; (5) and

(5) The Province Law of 11 W. 3, which gave the Superior Court general juriſdiction "as fully and amply to all intents and purpoſes whatſoever as the Courts of King's Bench, Common Pleas and Exchequer within his Majeſty's Kingdom of England, have or ought to have." Anc. Chart. 331. "The rights of the courts of common law within the Province of the Maſſachuſetts to reſtrain the exceſſes of the Admiralty Juriſdiction, are not derived from their charter, but from ſubſequent

1763.
SCOLLAY
v.
DUNN.

and if we have any Right to judge, I think it is the same as if the Matter came originally before this Court. Under the old Colony Charter, there was no Mention of Appeals; this was Objection against that Charter. One while in the Quo Warranto, that Clause in the new Charter was looked upon as a great Priviledge; (6) had it stood without any Clause, all Causes would have been appealable: I take it therefore to be a Priviledge in our Charter; "all Causes which deserve it," is explained to be above £300, but should it be admitted to be within the Discretion of the Court to grant Appeals, whether less or more, I should be against it, in Favour of Priviledge. As for this Case, whether it exceeds £300 or no, there is the Difficulty. I am considering the Allegations, &c., in Favour of Appeal. (7)

---

subsequent laws of the Province, confirmed afterwards by the Crown." Dummer's Defence of the New England Charters, (Boston ed. 1745,) 26.

(6) Under the Colony Charter no appeals to England were allowed. See the remonstrance of the legislature to the Long Parliament — "We have not admitted appeals to your authority, being assured they cannot stand with the liberty and power granted us by our charter." 1 Bancroft's Hist. U. S. 441. Afterwards in the reign of Charles 2, the colony "joined issue with the King by denying the right of appeal." 2 Ib. 74. And this was one of the principal causes of the subsequent issuing of the Quo Warranto, by which the charter fell.

(7) The appeal was not granted.

On a subsequent page in the MS. is the following memorandum: "*Dunn* v. *Scollay*, Case of Hostage & Ransom: Authorities in Favour of the Plaintiff were Molloy, (Old Edit.) 205 § 10, 212 § 14, 213 § 14. Molloy, (New Edit. 1744,) 358, 237, 8; 244, 5. 2 L'd Raymond, 931; Lord Holt's Opinion relied on; Sea Laws, 128. In Favour of the Defendant were 2 Chancery Cases, 239; 1 Salk. 35; 3 Bacon, 592, 595.

1763.

ANGIER
v.
JACKSON.

Rec. 1763.
Fol. 93.

It seems, that a new Trial may be granted where the Verdict is against Law and Evidence, but not where there is Evidence on both Sides.

Angier *vers.* Jackson.

MOTION was made for a new Trial. This Cause was from Middlesex. It seems the Jury gave a Verdict for Damages in Favour of Jackson, original Plaintiff, contrary to the Mind of the Court.

Trowbridge. When the Jury give a Verdict against Evidence, the Court may grant a new Trial. That Jury are not absolute Judges of Evidence and Damages, see Holt's Rep. 701, 702, *Ash* vs. *Lady Ash.* Jurys are to try Causes with the Assistance of Judges. Lucas's Cases of L. & Eq. 202. (1) Mistake of Judge or Jury good Cause for new Trial. Strange, 1105. Ibid. 584. Evidence doubtfull no new Trial should be granted, but here 'twas against direct Evidence. New Trial granted after Trial at Bar, is conceded. This Case is not like Ejectment — he may have a new Ejectment; not so here.

Auchmuty. If ever any Case was excepted from new Trials, this is. Trial at Bar is more favoured than Trial otherwise, because of its Solemnity. I confess I wish for a Power in the Court to set aside Verdicts, but not for an unlimited one. This Case was not against Evidence. I allow there was Evidence against Evidence; and two Verdicts, though no Rule of Controul, is yet of some Weight. (2) Strange,

(1) 10 Mod. 202, *The Queen* v. *Helston.*

(2) S. P. 7 Mass. 301. 9 Mass. 450. 18 Pick. 15. 8 Gray, 46.

1763.
ANGIER v. JACKSON.

Strange, 1105. Evidence doubtfull. Ibid. 1142. Salk. 648, *Sparks* vs. *Spicer*. The Court is not to be Judge of the Law and Fact too abſolutely; if it ſhould be, it takes away all Verdicts but ſuch as are agreeable to the Mind of the Court. It would be opening a Door to great Inconveniences to the Subject, even if Attaints did not lie; but here Attaint lies. (3)

Ch. Juſtice. Are you not agreed, that, were it evidently againſt Law and Evidence, there the Court may grant a new Trial, but not where there is Evidence on both Sides. (4)

Trowbridge. It can never be ſuppoſed that a Verdict will be given againſt direct Evidence, without Shadow of Evidence to ſupport it. This differs from the Caſe of *Fuller & Clark* at Cambridge — there was plainly Evidence againſt Evidence. I hold, this Court always have Right to grant new Trials when they think Injuſtice like to be done.

Juſtices Oliver, *Cuſhing*, *Ruſſell & Lynde* againſt a new Trial, becauſe the Court were not clear in the former Trial.

---

(3) It ſeems however that attaints had long been obſolete. See 3 Bl. Com. 390 — " The attaint is now as obſolete as the trial by battel which it ſucceeded, and we ſhall probably ſee the revival of one as ſoon as the revival of the other." But in *Aſhford* v. *Thornton*, 1 B. & Ald. 460, wager of battel was ſuſtained by the Court in 1818.

(4) See 20 Pick. 289, *Shaw, C. J.* — " For a long time it was conſidered that a new trial could only regularly be granted, where the verdict was without evidence or againſt the whole evidence. It has however been extended to caſes, where the verdict is clearly againſt the weight of evidence, although evidence was given on both ſides."

1763.
POOR
v.
DOBLE.

Poor *verſ.* Doble.

Rec. 1763. Fol. 113.

An Action on the Caſe for a Reſcue cannot be brought in a County where the Conſpiracy to reſcue, but not the Reſcue itſelf, took Place. *One Judge diſſenting.*

POOR brought an Action againſt one Jutſham, and, it being ſuggeſted to the Admiralty that Jutſham was on board a Veſſell in the Harbour, the Writ was committed to a Water Bailiff, who entered the Veſſell and took him. Doble interpoſed, went up to Boſton, and upon his Return forced the Defendant Jutſham from the Officer and carried him off; upon this the preſent Action was grounded. There were ſeveral Exceptions in Abatement of the Writ taken. The firſt was, "Not within the Juriſdiction of the Court;" it was ſaid they conſpired at Boſton, but the Act was done below. (1) *Mr.*

(1) The declaration ſet forth the original cauſe of action, the purchaſe of the writ, and the ſubſequent iſſue of a warrant from the Court of Admiralty, by virtue of which the deputy marſhal "went on board the ſloop Pompey, being then within the juriſdiction of the ſaid Court of Admiralty, and there found the ſaid Samuel Jutſham and him detained as a priſoner till he ſhould convene him to juſtice or deliver him to the ſheriff of this county or his deputy, that the ſaid writ of attachment might be duly ſerved on him." And it was further alleged that the defendants having conſpired and agreed to reſcue the priſoner, "in purſuance of the ſaid unlawful conſpiracy and agreement," "procured a boat at Boſton and went down to the ſaid ſloop Pompey, then lying at anchor in Nantaſket Bay, ſo called, about a quarter of a mile from the ſhore," that they reſcued the priſoner, forced the officer to return to Boſton without him, and the ſloop Pompey to put to ſea and carry him off, "whereby the plaintiff hath wholly loſt the benefit of the writ of attachment and his debt aforeſaid."

The defendants pleaded in abatement "that the ſaid Patrick hath not in ſaid declaration ſhown forth that the cauſe of the ſaid action aroſe within the county of Suffolk;" and the writ was abated "upon the firſt exception."

1763.
Poor
v.
Doble.

Mr. Thacher, in ſupport of the Writ ſaid, that the former Writ was ſaid to be purchaſed in Boſton, Complaint made there, Warrant procured there and Contrivance there.

Ch. Juſt. If Conſpiracy be in one County and Reſcous in another, could the Courts in both have Juriſdiction ?

Mr. Gridley. Juriſdiction of inferiour Courts muſt be ſhewn. This is a Court of a limited Juriſdiction; they have ſhewn the Conſpiracy to be within, but 'tis the Reſcue, and not Conſpiracy, which is the Cauſe of Action.

Writ abated, 3 *vs.* 1. (2)

---

(2) It appears to have been aſſumed that a civil action for a reſcue was local, and could only be brought in the county where the cauſe of action or ſome part thereof aroſe, and the deciſion was ſimply to the point that a conſpiracy alone within a county was not ſufficient to authorize the action to be brought there. No queſtion of admiralty juriſdiction could have ariſen, becauſe even if a ſhip " in Nantaſket Bay a quarter of a mile from ſhore " was not *infra corpus comitatus*, (12 Met. 387,) yet of torts upon the high ſea the common law had concurrent juriſdiction. 2 Gallis. 422.

For a ſomewhat analogous deciſion in a caſe in which the locality of the tort was the limit of juriſdiction, ſee *Adams* v. *Haſſard*, 20 Pick. 127, where it was held, that an impriſonment on ſhore, in purſuance of orders given on the high ſea, did not conſtitute a cauſe of action within admiralty juriſdiction.

But whether an action on the caſe againſt reſcuers is local at common law, *quære*. An action of eſcape againſt the officer is tranſitory. Bac. Ab. Eſcape, F. 2 Chit. Pl. (6th Am. Ed.) 736, 737, & note (d).

1763.

Lovell v. Doble.

Lovell *verſ.* Doble.

Rec. 1765. Fol. 129.

Exceptions to the Declaration ſhould be taken by Special Demurrer, and not by Plea in Abatement.

A Plea in Abatement to the Declaration, which does not point out a better Declaration, cannot be ſupported as in the Nature of a Special Demurrer.

THIS was for the ſame Cauſe, and the Declaration was the ſame.

Firſt Exception was, that it was not alledged in the Declaration that they ſet forth to the Admiralty that Jutſham had abſconded and concealed himſelf on board ſome Veſſell from the Service of the Writ.

Second Exception. They have not alledged that the Admiralty had Juriſdiction of the Matter of ſaid Complaint. *Given up.*

Auchmuty. Theſe Pleas are all negative; they find Fault with this, but do not point out a better. Pleas muſt be certain—not ſupported by Argument or Implication. 3 Doct. Plac. 54.

Gridley. They are defective in a material Point in their Declaration, your Honours will not ſupport it; our firſt Plea being over, and having been argued upon in Subſtance, they are too late to take Exceptions to this.

Auchmuty. The firſt Plea had no Exception to Form, but Subſtance; they are all ſeparate and diſtinct. All they verify is, that we have not done ſo and ſo—they do not verify it to be neceſſary. As for conſidering theſe Pleas as Special Demurrers, I think it cannot be intended here. He muſt conform to Rules of Abatement, and cannot avail himſelf

ſelf of what he might upon Special Demurrer; in Demurrer it might have been final againſt them, but in Abatement they plead over.

1763.
Lovell v. Doble.

Fitch. Abatement is regularly to the Writ; Exceptions to Form of Declaration is by Special Demurrer. Here they are generally taken in Abatement, not at Home, therefore we ought not to be taken up for conforming: However there are Inſtances of the like Pleas in Abatement; Lilly Ent. p. 9, Tit. Abatement; and many other Inſtances in Special Demurrer where the Plea is negative without pointing out a better. Lilly, Tit. Demurrer, 106, 186. (1)

Gridley. Theſe Pleas are in the Nature of Special Demurrer, but according to Cuſtom we have concluded in Abatement. When we have ſaid that there is an Omiſſion, do they ſay Anything new? Will your Honours go on with a Writ materially faulty, becauſe we have not pointed out?

Otis. They might have demurred, but have choſen Abatement, and ſo have entitled themſelves to all the Disfavour of Abatement.

Ch. Juſt. Plea in Abatement muſt be to the Writ, not Declaration. (2)

Otis.

---

(1) See 6 Pick. 369, *Wilde, J.*—"The exceptions to this rule [that the plea muſt give a better writ] are ſo numerous that it can hardly be called a general rule of law."

(2) A plea in abatement which concluded to the writ and declaration has been ſuſtained, on the ground that ſo much of the declaration as

12 would

1763.

Lovell v. Doble.

Otis. They may plead Matter of Fact in Abatement.

Exception not well taken.

Another Plea in Abatement was that they had not alledged the Admiralty to have had Juriſdiction of the Matter of the Complaint. Salk. 404, Tit. Juriſdiction.

Fitch. They have not alledged they had any Cauſe of Complaint to the Admiralty. Hobart, 129.

Auchmuty. We have ſet forth that he was concealed within their Juriſdiction. (3)

Rex v. Doaks.

Dom. Rex *verſ.* Doaks.

Rec. 1763. Fol. 110.

In Support of an Indictment for keeping a Bawdy Houſe, Evidence of Acts of Laſciviouſneſs by the Defendant while a Lodger, and before ſhe was Miſtreſs of the Houſe, is inadmiſſible.

On Trial of an Indict-

DOAKS was indicted before the Seſſions for keeping a Bawdy Houſe, found guilty there and fined; from thence ſhe appealed, and it appeared that Part of the Time ſhe was indicted for, ſhe was only a Lodger, and not Miſtreſs of the Houſe.

The King's Attorney offered to give Evidence of ſome Acts of Laſciviouſneſs before the Time in which

---

would be neceſſary to make a perfect writ, is a part of the writ, and may be excepted to in abatement. *Ilſley* v. *Stubbs*, 5 Maſs. 285.

(3) The ſecond exception was given up, and the caſe entered "Neither Party."

1763.

REX v. DOAKS.

which ſhe was proved to have been Miſtreſs of the Houſe. He ſaid it was by Way of Inducement, but *the Court ruled*, that no Evidence before ought to be admitted.

ment for keeping a Bawdy Houſe, Evidence of the Defendant's general Character is inadmiſſible for the Government, until the Defendant has attempted to ſupport it.

He likewiſe offered to prove her of general ill Character, but *the Court*, on that Point too, *ruled*, that he could not enter into that, before the other Side attempted to ſupport it. (1)

The Jury, by Direction of the Court, brought in their Verdict "*Not Guilty.*"

Dom. Rex *verſ.* Gay.

REX v. GAY.

Rec. 1763. Fol. 132.

A Juſtice has no Power to iſſue a Capias to bring before him a Perſon charged with Neglect in mending Highways.

A Warrant irregular on its Face is no Juſtification of the Officer.

GAY was indicted for aſſaulting and beating the Sheriff in the due Execution of his Office. The Caſe appeared to be this: Gay by Virtue of the Province Law relative to Highways, 5 W. & M. c. 8, & 11 G. 1, c. 3, (2) was warned to mend the Highways, and upon Complaint to a Juſtice that he had neglected his Duty therein, the Juſtice made out a Warrant to bring Gay before him to anſwer for

(1) S. P. *Commonwealth* v. *Hardy*, 2 Maſs. 318, *Parſons*, *C. J.*—"It is not competent for the proſecutor to go into this inquiry until the defendant has voluntarily put his character in iſſue."

(2) The proviſions of theſe ſtatutes are that in caſe of neglect "upon complaint and proof thereof before the next juſtice of the peace, without reaſonable excuſe made, and allowed by ſuch juſtice, he ſhall cauſe to be levied of every ſuch offender's goods the ſum or penalty of two ſhillings and ſixpence," &c. Anc. Chart. 268, 440.

1763. REX v. GAY.

for the Neglect. Dean, the Sheriff, having the Warrant, took Gay, who rescued himself and beat the Sheriff. The Question was, whether that Warrant should be given as Evidence of Dean's Right to take Gay, the Assault being confessed and justified.

Otis. The Justice had no Right to issue a Capias in this Case, and if so, Dean made the first Assault. A Warrant from an inferiour Court is less respected than from a superiour, yet even a Warrant issuing from this Court, illegally, would be a Trespass in the Person granting, and also in the Person executing it. It falls within that Rule, that the Officer executes at his Peril. This Court will not issue previous Process against the Body, when Execution can only go against the Goods; this is the Reason why original Summons issues against Executors and Administrators and Trustees of absconding Debtors. Difference between this Case and that of Assessors who have Authority of the Person. (3) Every Officer is bound to know what is within the Jurisdiction of the Court. Hawkins's Plea, 81. (4)

Thacher. The Justice has a Right to convene, and this Capias issued for that Purpose, &c.

Warrant not admitted, (5) 3 Judges against it, 2 doubtful. In Consequence of this,

Defendant acquitted.

N. B.

---

(3) Prov. Law, 4 G. 2, Anc. Chart. 477. Gen. Sts. c. 12, § 13. 8 Met. 102.

(4) 1 Hawk. c. 10, § 4.

(5) An illegal warrant is a justification only when regular on its face, and

1763.

Rex v. Gay.

N. B. Mr. Thacher ſays that in a Caſe at Barnſtable (*Mayhew & Wadſworth*,) the *Ch. Juſt. held*, an irregular Warrant might be admitted in Juſtification of the Officer, and that the Court were wrong in the Caſe of Gay on the other Side. (6)

---

and apparently within the juriſdiction of the court or magiſtrate iſſuing it. *Fiſher* v. *McGirr*, 1 Gray, 45. *Clark* v. *May*, 2 Gray, 410, 413.

Bassett v. Mayhew.

Rec. 1763. Fol. 47.

(6) The caſe referred to is *Cornelius Baſſett* v. *Wadſworth Mayhew & al.* May Term 1763, which was an action of treſpaſs for ſhooting the plaintiff, a deputy ſheriff, in the leg, while he was endeavoring to arreſt the defendant by virtue of the following warrant:

"Dukes County ſs: To the Sherriff of ſaid County, his Under Sher-"riff or Deputy, Greeting. Whereas Robert Allen of Chill-[SEAL.] "mark in ſaid County, Gent^n^. Has this Day appeared before "the Juſtices of our Lord the King at His Majeſty's Court of "General Seſſ:^s^ of The Peace, and made Complaint That he being in "the Execution of his office as Corroner, at the Houſe of Zacheus "Mayhew Eſq in Chillmark in the County aforeſaid: Lawfully au "thorized by a Mittimus to carry one Jeruſha Mayhew to his Majeſty's "Goal in Edgartown in ſaid County, he was there oppoſed in his ſaid "Office by one Wadſworth Mayhew of ſaid Chillmark by violently "ſeizing the body of the ſaid Jeruſha & holding her, and Prevented his "Carrying ſaid Jeruſha to his Majeſty's Goal: Which Doings of ſaid "Wadſworth is Contrary to Law, &c. Theſe are therefore in His "Majeſty's Name, To Require You or Either of You forthwith to "take the Body of the ſaid Wadſworth (if he may be found in your "Precinct), Againſt all Oppoſition to enter any Houſe where you ſhall "ſuſpect him ſaid Wadſworth to be, & to bring him forthwith before "the Juſtices of Our Lord the King at his Majeſty's Court of Gen^ral^ "Seſſ:^s^ of the Peace now Sitting in Seſſ:^s^ at Tiſbury: So that he may "be Dealt with According to Law in the Premiſes. Hereof fail not "& make Return of this Writ with your Doings therein into ſ'd Court.

"Dated at Tiſbury The 26th Day of Octo^r^. Anno Dom: 1762 & In "the Third Year of his Majeſty's Reign.

"Per Order of Court

"James Athearn *Cler.*"

Auguſt Term

IV Georgii Ter. in Sup. Cur.

Preſent:

The Honourable

Thomas Hutchinſon, Eſqr., Chief Juſtice.
John Cuſhing, Peter Oliver, } Eſqrs., Juſtices.

1764.

ALLISON *v.* COCKRAN.

Rec. 1764. Fol. 103.

Adminiſtrators are incompetent Witneſſes in Matters affecting the Eſtate of their Inteſtate, except where ſuch Eſtate is inſolvent.

The Report of the Commiſſioners is the only legal Evidence of ſuch Inſolvency

Alliſon *verſ.* Cockran.

TROVER* for a Negro. (1) The Adminiſtratrix of one Cockran, (Father-in-Law to the Defendant,)

* *Qu.* if this Action is well brought, for Trover lies not for a Negro. 2 Salk. 666. Ld. Raym. 1274, 146. Caſes in the Time of Holt, 495.

(1) In 1677, the Court of King's Bench, conſiſting of *Rainsford, C. J., Twiſden, Wild & Jones, JJ.*, expreſſed an opinion that trover would lie for negroes, who had been found, by ſpecial verdict, to be "infidels," and "uſually bought and ſold in America," [or, as other reporters have it, "in India,"] "as merchandiſe, by the cuſtom of merchants." *Butts* v. *Penny*, 2 Lev. 201; 3 Keb. 785; Freem. 452. But the record ſhows that the negroes in that caſe were "in India;" 20 Howell's State Trials, 52; and the deciſion, as reported by Freeman, was put upon

1764.

ALLISON v. COCKRAN.

Defendant,) deceased, was offered as an Evidence to prove the Sale from Allison to the Father.

Ruled

which can establish the Competency of the Administrator.

Whether Trover lies for a Negro — *quære.*

---

upon that ground only — " Held *per Curiam*, that although by the law with us a man cannot have an absolute property in the body of another, yet the custom of India concerning buying and selling of slaves being found, a trover and conversion would lie well enough." Freem. 452. This does not appear to have been known to the successors of those judges, (Freeman's Reports not being yet published,) when they " denied the opinion in the case of *Butts & Penny*." 2 Ld. Raym. 1275.

In the same court in 1680, *Dolben, J.*, said that trover, brought by one tenant in common " for half a negro," " has been allowed." 2 Show. 177. But it does not appear where that negro was. The decision referred to may have been in *Butts* v. *Penny, ub. sup.*, which is reported by Keble as " trover of 10 negroes and a half ; " 3 Keb. 785 ; (although the record of that case only mentions ten ; 20 Howell's State Trials, 51, note ;) or, more probably, the case thus quoted in the Court of Chancery in 1687 : " *Mr. Sergeant Maynard's case* was cited, who recovered a debt contracted here against the executor of an owner of a plantation in Barbadoes, and by his advice an action of trover was brought, and judgment obtained for the fourth part of a negro." 1 Vern. 453.

In 1689, Lord *Holt, & Rokeby & Turton, JJ.*, (three of the four judges who afterwards decided *Chamberlain* v. *Harvey, infra*,) joined in an opinion, given to the King and Council, that negroes were merchandise in the colonies. 1 Burge Col. & For. Laws, 736, note.

It is said to have been afterwards adjudged in the Common Bench that trover will lie for negroes. *Gelly* v. *Cleve*, (1693,) 1 Ld. Raym. 147, *ex rel.* Place. 3 Lev. 337. But it must be presumed that those negroes too were in the colonies ; for if they were in England, the decision is inconsistent with a series of cases in the King's Bench, (cited in Quincy's note, *supra*, 94,) by which it was very soon afterwards established as the law of England, that " as soon as a negro comes into England, he becomes free ; one may be a villein in England, but not a slave." 2 Salk. 666 ; Cas. temp. Holt, 495.

In those cases, it was held, that trespass would not lie for taking a negro in England, without declaring (as in the case of the taking away of any other servant) *per quod servitium amisit ; Chamberlain* v. *Harvey*, (1696,) 1 Ld. Raym. 146 ; 3 Ib. 129 ; 5 Mod. 182, 186 ; Carth. 397 : Nor *indebitatus assumpsit* for the price of a negro, without averring that at the time of the sale he was in a country by the laws of which he might be sold as a chattel ; *Smith* v. *Brown*, 2 Salk. 666 ; Cas. temp. Holt, 495 : Nor trover. *Smith* v. *Gould*, (1706,) 2 Ld.

1764. *Ruled by the Court,* (after hearing the Arguments of *Meſſrs. Gridley, Otis & Auchmuty, pro & con,*) that Adminiſtrators

ALLISON *v.* COCKRAN.

Ld. Raym. 1274; 2 Salk. 666. That the converſion alleged in the laſt caſe was in England is manifeſt from the grounds given for the deciſion by Lord *Holt* — "The common law takes no notice of negroes being different from other men. By the common law no man can have a property in another, but in ſpecial caſes, as in a villein," &c. "There is no ſuch thing as a ſlave by the law of England." 2 Ld. Raym. 1274, 1275. The ſtatement at the end of Salkeld's report of this caſe — "the Court ſeemed to think that in treſpaſs *quare captivum ſuum cepit* the plaintiff might give evidence that the party was his negro and he bought him" — appears to be an unwarranted inference of the reporter, inconſiſtent with Lord Raymond's report, and with the caſe of *Chamberlain* v. *Harvey*, *ub. ſup.*

There is no Engliſh adjudication ſince, which conflicts with theſe deciſions of Lord *Holt.* In *Pearne* v. *Liſle*, (1749,) Ambl. 75, Lord *Hardwicke* refuſed a writ of *ne exeat* againſt one who owed the plaintiff for the hire of certain negroes, upon the ground that it was a legal demand on which the defendant might be arreſted at law, ſaying: "As to the nature of the demand, it is for the uſe of negroes; a man may hire the ſervant of another, whether he be a ſlave or not, and will be bound to ſatisfy the maſter for the uſe of him." This paſſage accords with the ſuggeſtion in *Chamberlain* v. *Harvey*, *ub. ſup.*, that treſpaſs *per quod ſervitium amiſit* might be maintained in England for enticing away a ſlave; and concluſively ſhows that, even if the writ of *ne exeat* had been granted, the caſe would have involved no deciſion of the queſtion of what property one might have in a negro. The additional remark of the Lord Chancellor — "I have no doubt that trover will lie for a negro ſlave; it is as much property as any other thing" — is therefore wholly extrajudicial; and is moreover accompanied by a miſrepreſentation of the grounds of Lord *Holt's* deciſion, and by a manifeſt deſire to confirm the opinion given by Lord *Talbot* and himſelf in 1729 as attorney and ſolicitor general, in favor of holding ſlaves in England, of which Lord *Mansfield* ſaid that it "was upon a petition in Lincoln's Inn Hall, after dinner; probably, therefore, might not be taken with much accuracy." Lofft, 8; 20 Howell's State Trials, 70.

Lord *Hardwicke's* opinion on this ſubject has never been recognized as law by any court in England. In 1762, a bill in equity, filed by an adminiſtrator to recover back money given by his inteſtate to a negro who had been brought to England as a ſlave, (which was apparently founded on the ſuppoſition that the negro was ſtill a ſlave, and therefore incapable

Adminiftrators could not be Witneffes, except when the Eftate is infolvent. 1764.

ALLISON v. COCKRAN.

Meffrs.

---

incapable of receiving a gift,) was difmiffed by Lord *Northington*, who faid: "As foon as a man fets foot on Englifh ground, he is free; a negro may maintain an action againft his mafter for ill ufage, and may have a *habeas corpus* if reftrained of his liberty." *Shanley* v. *Harvey*, 2 Eden, 127.

It appears by *Granville Sharp's* MS. that Lord C. J. *Wilmot*, in 1768, held, that a female negro slave, married in England to a negro man who had alfo been brought from the Weft Indies as a flave, could not be carried back without the confent of the hufband; and that Lord C. J. *De Grey*, about the fame time, more than once expreffed the opinion, that there could be no property in the perfon of a flave by the law of England. Sharp's Memoirs, (2d ed.) 72, 110. The fame book contains a full account of Lord *Mansfield's* evafions of a decifion of the general queftion in the cafe of *Rex* v. *Stapylton*, in 1771. Ib. 82, 89-92.

It is clear from thefe authorities, (without relying on the cafe of the *Ruffian Slave* in 1569, mentioned in 2 Rufhw. Hift. Coll. 468,) that Lord *Mansfield's* reluctant difcharge of the *Negro Sommerfett* in 1772, (Lofft, 17-19; 20 Howell's State Trials, 79-82,) was but a re-affirmance of the law of England, as previoufly determined by Lord *Holt* and other eminent judges — notwithftanding the fubfequent ftatement of Lord *Mansfield*, in *The King* v. *Thames Ditton*, (1785,) 4 Doug. 301, that "the cafe of *Sommerfett* is the only one on this fubject;" and the affertion of Lord *Stowell*, in the cafe of the *Slave Grace*, (1827,) 2 Hagg. Adm. R. 106, 114, that Lord *Mansfield*, in *Sommerfett's cafe*, "made a change in the law." For an examination of fome of the *obiter dicta* of Lord *Stowell*, fee 20 Law Rep. 99, 105-107. That learned civilian does not manifeft any knowledge that one of his predeceffors, Sir *George Hay*, almoft as foon as *Sommerfett's cafe* was decided, twice held, upon full argument, that, before as well as fince that decifion, negroes could not lawfully be held or fold as flaves in England. *Cay* v. *Crichton*, (1773,) in the Prerogative Court; *Rogers* v. *Jones*, (1776,) in the High Court of Admiralty; both reported in Granville Sharp's "Juft Limitation of Slavery," (London, 1776,) App. 10 & 11, pp. 77-86.

Sir *William Blackftone's* ofcillations in this matter are too characteriftic to be paffed by, notwithftanding the length to which this note has already extended. In the firft edition of his Commentaries, publifhed in 1765, founding himfelf upon Lord *Holt*, ("Salk. 666,") he wrote: "This fpirit of liberty is fo deeply implanted in our Conftitution and rooted in our very foil, that a flave or a negro, the moment he lands in England, falls under the protection of the laws, and, with regard to

1764.

Allison v. Cockran.

Messrs. Otis & Gridley, Council for Defendant, said it was universally known that the Estate of Cockran, the Father, was insolvent, and appealed to the Chief Justice (who was likewise Judge of Probate) (2) for the Truth of their Suggestion.

The

all natural rights, becomes *eo instanti* a freeman." In his third edition, published in 1768, after the question had begun to be re-agitated in England, he altered the last clause of his statement to this: "and so far becomes a free man; though the master's right to his service may probably still continue." Against which Quincy has written, in the margin of his copy, "Curious!" In the fourth edition, published two years later, "*possibly*" was substituted for "probably." 1 Bl. Com. 127. After the passage had assumed this shape, Hargrave truly said of it, "There appears to be somewhat of very subtle distinction, if not rather of contradiction." 20 Howell's State Trials, 30, note.

Trespass will lie in England for taking slaves on the high seas, or in a country where slavery is not prohibited by law, from one who is not prohibited by the laws of his own country from trading in slaves. *Madrazo* v. *Willes*, (1820,) 3 B. & Ald. 353. *Buron* v. *Denman*, (1848,) 2 Exch. 167. But the commander of a British vessel is not liable to an action for refusing to deliver up to their master slaves who have escaped from a foreign country where slavery is recognized by law, and got on board his vessel, and are unwilling to return. *Forbes* v. *Cochrane*, (1824,) 2 B. & C. 448; 3 D. & R. 679.

By the English authorities, therefore, the right to maintain trover for a negro would seem to depend upon the question whether he may be held and sold as a chattel by the law of the country where his master's possession of him is interfered with. The fact suggested by Hargrave, *arguendo*, in 20 Howell's State Trials, 53, that "the master's power over the slave doth not extend to his life, and consequently the master's property in the slave is in some degree qualified and limited," would seem to be no valid objection to the maintenance of the action; for trover lies by one who has any special property in a chattel, with the right to immediate possession. 2 Saund. 47, & note.

At the time of the trial of the case here reported by Quincy, negro slaves were held and sold as property in Massachusetts. *Ante*, 29, note (2) to *Oliver* v. *Sale*, and authorities there cited. And in 1763 trover had been maintained in this court for a negro. *Goodspeed* v. *Gay*, in Barnstable, Rec. 1763, fol. 47. But it has been said, that in Connecticut, while slavery existed there, trover would not lie for a slave. Reeve Dom. Rel. 340.

(2) By the Province Charter the jurisdiction in matters of probate was

1764.

ALLISON *v.* COCKRAN.

The *Ch. Juſt.* ſaid that from the Accounts given him of the Eſtate, and from his own Knowledge, he had no Manner of Doubt but that the Eſtate was inſolvent; yet as the Commiſſioners had not made Report, there was no legal Evidence of the Inſolvency. And *the Court ruled*, that the Adminiſtratrix of Cockran the Defendant's Father ſhould not be ſworn. (3)

HANLON *v.* THAYER.

Hanlon *verſ.* Thayer.

Rec. 1764. Fol. 109.

Articles of Apparell and Ornament of a Wife, owned by her before her Marriage, (except neceſſary wearing Apparell,) are liable to Attachment for the Debts of the Huſband.

THE Plaintiff (Hanlon's Wife) (1) brings Trover againſt Thayer (a Sheriff) for attaching her Apparell. (2) There were two Queſtions in this

---

was veſted in the Governor and Council as a civil law court, who appointed judges of probate in each county as their delegates or ſubſtitutes. Anc. Chart. 32. Governor Pownall's Meſſage to the Council in February, 1760, App. III. 3 Hutchinſon's Hiſt. Maſs. 451, note. 2 Maſs. 154. 8 Cuſh. 541. 21 Law Rep. 78, 79.

(3) It is not eaſy to ſee why an adminiſtrator, not a party to the ſuit, and without any beneficial intereſt in the truſt fund, ſhould not be a competent witneſs for the eſtate, without regard to its ſolvency or inſolvency. 2 Stark. Evid. (2d Amer. ed.) 775. 3 Dane Ab. 420. 12 Maſs. 358. But it is probable that, in practice, adminiſtrators were paid by a commiſſion on the amount collected, as was afterwards expreſſly provided by the Rev. Sts. c. 67, § 8 — which might require a releaſe to make them competent witneſſes. 11 S. & R. 208. 15 Ib. 235. 7 Ib. 116. See alſo 16 Maſs. 118.

(1) Mark Hanlon was the plaintiff. The writ, however, was indorſed by Mary Hanlon, his attorney, who may have conducted the caſe, and thus occaſioned the miſtake.

(2) The common law proceeding by attachment was merely to compel the defendant's appearance where he failed to answer the ſummons. The Colony Law of 1644 gave plaintiffs the power to take out either ſummons or attachment in the firſt inſtance. Anc. Chart. 49. But the attachment

1764. HANLON *v.* THAYER.

this Caſe; one, whether, as the Apparell attached was the Property of Hanlon's Wife before the Intermarriage, it did not make a Difference in the Law from Caſes where Apparell after the Marriage came to the Wife; the other, whether the ſeveral Articles in the Schedule annexed were *all neceſſary* wearing Apparell.

Mr. Auchmuty, taking no Notice of the firſt Queſtion, endeavoured to prove the Apparell mentioned was neceſſary, by obſerving, what was neceſſary for one Station in Life was not ſo for another, and ſaid the Law never meant the Word "Neceſſary" in its ſtricteſt Senſe.

Mr. Chardon for Defendant. The Argument *ab Inconvenienti* is of very great Weight in the Law, and by admitting all theſe Things (in the Schedule) as *neceſſary* wearing Apparell, would be putting it in the Power of almoſt every Debtor to defraud his Creditor. (3) To explain and ſhow the Senſe in which

---

attachment being diſcharged by an appearance, as at common law, or at moſt by a judgment, twelve hours before execution, it was afterwards provided in 1650 that goods ſo attached ſhould "ſtand engaged" until the judgment ſhould be ſatisfied. Ib. 51. By the Prov. St. of 13 W. 3, the duration of the liability was limited to thirty days after judgment. Ib. 367. Gen. Sts. c. 123, § 42. The chattels liable to attachment have always been held to be ſuch only as may legally be taken on execution, and where this latter right is left at the common law, "ſo muſt the right to attach depend upon the common law." 6 Maſs. 244. By the Colony Law of 1647, officers were prohibited from levying execution on "any man's neceſſary bedding, apparell, tools or arms, neither implements of houſehold which are for the neceſſary upholding of his life." Anc. Chart. 155.

(3) The ſchedule compriſes earrings, necklaces, laces, ribbons, fans, &c.,

1764.

HANLON *v.* THAYER.

which the Law uses the Word *Necessary*, I cite 4 G. 2, c. 1. (4)

Mr. Gridley. Nothing is *necessary* in the *Law* but what is necessary to defend from the Inclemency of the Weather, (5) or necessary to the Degree: But before they can talk highly of Degree they must pay their Debts. If any besides what is barely necessary is allowed for Comfort, it is not the Law, but Humanity. The Law here wisely uses the Word *Necessary*, for the Boundary of Necessity is determinate, but Conveniency not, — Conveniency! What is convenient? &c. (a little Rhetorick and concludes.) *Mr. Gridley* also said: If a Judge of Probate grant to the Wife of an Intestate whose Estate is insolvent, two Beds, where *one only* was necessary, the other immediately became liable to be attached, and he cited *Hardistey & Barney*, (Comber. 356,) where *Holt* says if the Party have two Gowns, Sheriff may take one.*

Mr. Otis relied chiefly on the Evidence that proved Hanlon never bought or paid for a single Rag

* *Qu.* if 1 Inst. 351 b, top, would not have been a good Authority?

&c. There appears also a list of necessary articles which the defendant tendered back to Mrs. Hanlon before the date of the writ.

(4) Anc. Chart. 481.

(5) "1 Pr Gloshoes" (goloshes) and "1 Green Embrillo" appear upon the schedule, but were not among the articles tendered back as necessary. About this time, "Umbrillos" were first advertised in the papers, and were doubtless then considered articles of luxury. See Drake's History of Boston, p. 660.

1764. HANLON *v.* THAYER.

Rag of his Wife's Cloaths, but that ſhe brought all with her at the Marriage, and ſaid it had been the Cuſtom univerſally, never to take Cloaths ſo brought, for the Debts of the Huſband.

Juſtices Oliver & Cuſhing both ſaid the Caſe was very hard upon the Wife, who brought all theſe Cloaths at Marriage, yet "as they are perſonal Property, they become the Huſband's on Marriage, and therefore liable."

Ch. Juſt. I ſhould have been extremely glad if this Caſe had been argued a little more largely by the Gentlemen of the Bar, and more Authorities cited, in Matter of ſo great Conſequence. I always took it to have been the Cuſtom in ſuch Caſes as this, for the Wife to have her Cloaths; in Caſes that have come before me as Judge of Probate I never knew it denied to the Wife where the Eſtate was inſolvent. (6) In the Caſe cited (by Mr. G.) I ſuppoſe the Woman was a Party, and the Debt contracted

(6) The Prov. St. of 9 Anne reſerved only "the neceſſary bedding, utenſils and implements of houſehold," where the eſtate was inſolvent. Anc. Chart. 390. At common law, however, there ſeems to have been a queſtion to what extent the widow's "paraphernalia," beyond neceſſary wearing apparel, was liable to creditors of the huſband's eſtate. Bac. Ab. Baron & Feme, C. 3. 1 Dane Ab. 364. And the practice of allowing the widow her apparel in all caſes was afterwards confirmed by Sts. 1783, c. 36; 1802, c. 93; 1816, c. 95. The Reviſed Statutes, c. 65, § 5, excepted from the inventory of the eſtate "all the articles of apparel or ornament of the widow, according to the degree and eſtate of her huſband," "although his eſtate ſhould be inſolvent." The St. of 1838, c. 145, omits the limitation as to the huſband's degree, and provides that the articles aforeſaid ſhall be conſidered as excluſively belonging to the widow. Gen. Sts. c. 96, § 4.

1764.
HANLON
v.
THAYER.

contracted by her; this alters the Caſe much, but yet I apprehend (here *Ch. Juſt.* makes an Apology for what follows) that this may be one of thoſe Caſes where the Juſtice ſays a Thing *obiter*, or ſuddenly; for one Gown can never be ſuppoſed ſufficient — muſt ſhe go naked when that is waſhing? Upon the Whole I think it would be very hard upon the Wife, ſhould ſuch a Precedent as this take Place, that her *Cloaths* which ſhe *brought* in *Marriage* muſt go to diſcharge the Huſband's Debts. I ſhould think it ſafer to verge towards Conveniency than to ſtrain the Word *Neceſſary*. (7)

The *Ch. Juſt.* in the Courſe of this Caſe aſked if it would not have been better to have brought Detinue.

N. B. The Jury found for the Defendant Coſts.

Adjourned to September 11th — and then met
Chief Juſtice.
Lynde, } Juſtices.
Ruſſell, }

---

(7) Somewhat ſimilar opinions have been ſubſequently expreſſed. See 4 Cuſh. 361, *Shaw, C. J.* — "This word is not uſed in its moſt rigid ſenſe, as ſomething abſolutely indiſpenſable, and without which a debtor cannot live." And the exemption of "neceſſary wearing apparel" has been held to extend to cloth in the hands of a tailor. *Richardſon* v. *Buſwell*, 10 Met. 506.

Rex v. Pourksdorff.

Rec. 1764. Fol. 125.

A Conviction of Petit Larceny and Judgment thereon do not destroy the Competency of a Witness.

Dom. Rex *vers.* Pourksdorff.

INDICTMENT vs. Pourksdorff for Stealing. A Woman offered as Evidence who at the same Term had pleaded guilty to an Indictment of the same Nature. (1)

The Attorney General objected to her, that she pleaded guilty to an infamous Crime, and therefore no Witness, and cited Hawkins's Pleas of the Crown, B. 2, ch. 33, § 129; ch. 37, §§ 48 to 53.

Mr. Kent for the Prisoner. Law of Evid. 145. Judge Raymond, 32. 2 Sid. 51. (2)

The Attorney General then moved for Judgment; and

Granted.

The Question then arose, whether, when there is a Judgment, and not an infamous Judgment,* it bars the Person on whom Judgment is passed, from being a Witness.

Attorney General & Mr. Kent cited as above.

Ch.

* It is the Crime and not the Punishment that makes a Man infamous. Theory of Evid. 107, *q. v.*

---

(1) *Rex* v. *Pourksdorff & al.*, Rec. 1764, fol. 123.

(2) Where it is decided that a conviction without judgment thereon is not sufficient to disqualify a witness.

1764.
Rex
v.
Pourksdorff.

Ch. Juſt. When the Crime is ſo great and of ſuch a *Nature* (for Inſtance the *Crimen Falſi* in Law) as it is to be ſuppoſed that the Perſon guilty has loſt all Senſe of Truth, and would not heſitate at violating his Oath, in ſuch Caſe no Doubt not to be admitted, but even where the Judgment is infamous, (as that a Perſon ſhall ſit in the Pillory for writing a Libel,) yet if the Crime is not of ſuch a Nature as the leaſt to invalidate the Credit of the Witneſs's *Oath*, (as in the Caſe I mentioned, and that of the Witneſs now offered,) no Doubt they may be admitted.

Attorney General. Theft is infamous.

Kent. Petit Larceny is not.

Attorney General. There is no Difference between grand and petit Larceny.

Ch. Juſt. Do you ſuppoſe, Mr. Attorney, every Perſon convicted of petit Larceny at the Old Baily is ever after barred from being a Witneſs?

Attorney General. I don't know.

The Court unanimouſly *held*, No; (3) and ordered the

(3) It ſeems to have been aſſumed that the conviction in this caſe was for petit larceny. But the only indictment againſt a woman for larceny, on the record of this term, is againſt Margaret Knodle, joined with Pourkſdorff on a former indictment for grand larceny, to which ſhe pleaded guilty. In either caſe, however, the deciſion appears unaccountable, in view of the well-known rules of the common law on this ſubject, at that time unaltered by ſtatute. A conviction of felony de-

 ſtroyed

1764. REX v. POURKSDORFF.

the Witneſs to be ſworn, directing the Jury to give what Weight they pleaſed to her Evidence.

This Evidence alone cleared Pourkſdorff, by ſwearing ſhe ſtole the Goods herſelf.

Preſent:

Ch. Juſtice, Judge Lynde, Cuſhing & Oliver.

BALLARD v. MCLEAN.

Rec. 1764. Fol. 111.

Miſtake in the Addition of Place will abate a Writ of Review.

Ballard *verſ.* McLean.

THIS was a Writ of Review. McLean was called, of Milton, but it was fully proved that he did not belong to Milton. The Queſtion was, whether, this being a Writ of *Review*, which iſſues out of the *Clerk's Office*, it ſhould abate.

Mr.

ſtroyed the competency of a witneſs. Co. Lit. 6 b. And petit larceny was felony, although it did not produce a forfeiture of land. See 1 Hawk. (ed. of 1795) c. 36, § 6. But the puniſhment for grand larceny (burning in the hand) reſtored the competency of the witneſs (Com. Dig. Teſtmoigne — Witneſs A 3), while that for petit larceny had no ſuch effect, for which reaſon it was ſubſequently provided in England by 31 Geo. 3, c. 35, "That no perſon ſhall be an incompetent witneſs by reaſon of a conviction of petit larceny."

Whether the diſtinction between grand and petit larceny was ever adopted or recognized in Maſſachuſetts — *quære*. In *Commonwealth* v. *Keith*, 8 Met. 531, it was held that a conviction of larceny to the value of forty cents, before a juſtice of the peace, was ſufficient to exclude the witneſs. And there can be no doubt that any conviction of larceny had this effect until all incompetency from crime was finally aboliſhed by Sts. 1851, c. 233, § 97, & 1852, c. 312, § 60. *Commonwealth* v. *Green*, 17 Maſs. 515, 537. *Commonwealth* v. *Keith*, *ub. ſup.*

1764.
Ballard v. McLean.

Mr. Dana, in Support of the Writ, urged that the three Years (the Time limited by Law for bringing a Writ of Review) would expire before they could bring another Writ; and ſaid further that the Defendant was *late* of Milton, and was called in the original Writ, of Milton, which cauſed the Miſtake; and ſaid it would be a great Hardſhip upon the Plaintiff, when it was no Fault of his, for the Writ iſſued out of the Clerk's Office, that he ſhould be precluded from bringing his Review. Cited 2 Strange, 924, *Cortiſos* vs. *Munoz*.

Mr. Thacher, contra. Had he been named *nuper*, it might have done, but the Plaintiff has declared with Certainty. As to Writs of Review, they always have been and are ſubject to the ſame Rules with other Writs; and the Cuſtom has ever been in this Court to ſhow Writs of Review no more Favour than to other Writs.

Juſtices Lynde, Cuſhing & Oliver for abating it. (1)

Ch. Juſtice. Abſtracted from the Cuſtom, I ſee no Reaſon why it ſhould abate.

---

(1) Where a writ of review was improvidently iſſued, without notice to the oppoſite party, the Court ordered a hearing, but refuſed to quaſh the writ, becauſe, the three years having elapſed, the plaintiff would thereby loſe his right to bring another petition. *Clap* v. *Joſlyn*, 1 Maſs. 133. And in *Brewer* v. *Sibley*, 13 Met. 177, it is intimated that in caſe of review "it would be reaſonable to reſtrict the defence to the merits."

1764.

Preſent:

Ch. Juſtice, Juſtice Cuſhing & Juſtice Oliver.

BROMFIELD *v.* LITTLE.

Rec. 1764. Fol. 98.

It ſeems, that there is no Cuſtom of Merchants in this Country, of charging Intereſt after a Year on the Price of Goods ſold, which will raiſe an implied Contract to pay the ſame.

Bromfield *verſ.* Little.

IN this Action was a general *Indebitatus Aſſumpſit* on Account annexed. One Article was a Charge of Intereſt.

The Council for the Plaintiff urged, that it was a Cuſtom of Merchants here to charge Intereſt after a Year: (Several Merchants were ſworn on this Head, but they did not agree about the Time, neither whether they did or did not firſt inform the Debtor.) The Juſtneſs of the Charge was argued from the Charge of Intereſt after a Year, *at Home.*

In Behalf of Defendant, 'twas ſaid, there was no ſuch Cuſtom here at all; yet if it could be ſaid there was a Cuſtom here to charge after Notice either at or after Sale, certainly not before Notice.

Juſt. Oliver. Whether this is a reaſonable Cuſtom muſt firſt be conſidered. I think it is. I think, too, it appears to be a Cuſtom.

Juſt. Cuſhing. This Caſe is very different from what it is at Home; 'tis there the univerſal Uſage, which makes it the Suppoſition of every Party at firſt; and, as a Perſon purchaſing Goods without any ſpecial Promiſe is ſuppoſed to promiſe the Payment

1764. Bromfield v. Little.

ment of the Cuſtomary Price, ſo he is ſuppoſed to engage to pay the cuſtomary Allowance for Forbearance; but here, however reaſonable it may be, it is yet otherwiſe, nor is it implied in the Contract.

Ch. Juſtice. This Caſe is of much Importance to the Community. 'Tis agreeable to natural Equity that Intereſt ſhould be allowed; and I am glad it is growing into a Cuſtom; but the Rule is that both Parties ought at the Time of contracting to underſtand it ſo, and I doubt whether it is ſo general as that it can be ſuppoſed in this Caſe.

The Jury did not allow Intereſt.

N. B. The Superiour Court now altered, and the Sitting, inſtead of being the third Tueſday of February and third Tueſday of Auguſt, is the ſecond Tueſday in March and laſt Tueſday in Auguſt. March 12, A. D. 1765. (1)

---

(1) Prov. St. 5 G. 3, c. 6, Maſs. Perpet. Laws, 481.

March Term

V Geo. Ter. in Sup. Cur. &c.

Prefent:

The Honourable Ch. Juft., Lynde, & Cufhing.

1765.

CHARGE TO THE GRAND JURY.

The Charge to the Grand Jury by Ch. Juftice.

TO relieve the Oppreffed, to guard the Innocent, to preferve the Order of Society, and the Dignity of Government is a noble Principle of the Mind. This is the Duty of every Individual of the Community, but is more particularly incumbent, Gentlemen, upon you, as the Grand Inqueft for this County.

Our Bufinefs, Gentlemen, at this Time, is to diftribute Juftice, and to punifh all Crimes and Offences. It is this latter Part of our Duty that you, Gentlemen, are to affift us in; to point out and bring forward all Crimes and Offences againft the Tranquillity and Order of Society which fhall by any Means come to your Knowledge.

But before I enter upon the particular Branch of your Duty, I fhall obferve, that it is a very common

1765.
CHARGE TO THE GRAND JURY.

mon Thing in England to preſent Offences, when there is no Offender known, for wherever there is the one, there is always the other. Whenever there are any notorious Offences, as I obſerved before, in England, they always preſent them. I remember in particular (if it may be called an Offence) that at Middleſex, the Jury preſented, that there was unneceſſary Multiplication of licenſed Houſes, which tended greatly to the Deſtruction of the Health and Morals of the People. I do not mention this as the Caſe here, but only by Way of Example, to ſhow, that wherever you find any notable Things done that are detrimental, or any Things neglected which ought eſpecially to be done that are beneficial to Society, you have, Gentlemen, a diſcretionary Power to preſent them.

I would have you, Gentlemen, to enquire into the State of our Goal, for it has been repreſented, and I believe it but too true, that it is a moſt ſhocking, loathſome Place. For my own Part, when I have been obliged by the Nature of my Office to commit any of my Fellow Creatures, I could not help feeling for them, when I thought where I was ſending them — a dark, damp, and peſtilential Room — to ſuch a Place to ſend our Fellow Creatures muſt cauſe the moſt tender and exquiſite Senſations to Men of the leaſt Senſibility or Humanity. I do not think there is ſuch a Place for the Reception of Priſoners anywhere in the King's Dominions. I do not ſay this by Way of Reflection on the Gentlemen who have the proper Care of our Goal, nor upon the Sheriff* of this County, the Keeper

* Mr. Greenleaf.

1765. CHARGE TO THE GRAND JURY.

Keeper of our Prifon, who I know to be a Man of great Tendernefs: But from whatever Caufe, Gentlemen, it arifes, whether from Neglect or a Mifunderftanding among the Gentlemen whofe Province it is to look after it, or any Caufe whatever, 'tis your Duty to give your particular Attention to it. I remember, Gentlemen, a Cafe in fome late Reports, of a Sheriff committing a Man to a new plaiftered, wet and unwholefome Room, by which he was put into violent Fever and died; the Sheriff on this was committed, tried and hanged. (1) Our Goal is not intended as a Punifhment, it is only to keep Offenders for Trial, or after Trial till Sentence is fulfilled. Every Man in the Eye of the Law is prefumed innocent till proved guilty. How prepofterous then, Gentlemen, is it to commit a Man to a Place, who whether innocent or not muft run the Hazard of his Life—a Place which will bring a Man of the beft Conftitution in Danger of his Life; how long then will a Perfon of a weakly Conftitution furvive? I muft, Gentlemen, repeat it again, this demands your peculiar Attention, and the Attorney General will give any Directions you may want.

A Government always thinks itfelf happy when the Grand Jury can find no Offenders to prefent. This

---

(1) *Quære*, whether the Chief Juftice had not in his mind the cafe *Rex* v. *Huggins*, 2 Stra. 882; Ld. Raym. 1574, where the warden of the Fleet Prifon was indicted for the murder of a prifoner by confining him in a "new-built room, the walls being damp and unwholefome." The offence was held to be murder, but the prifoner was acquitted on the ground that it was the act of a deputy. A feries of fimilar cafes is reported in 9 Howell's State Trials, 146–234, but neither of them refulted in a conviction.

1765. CHARGE TO THE GRAND JURY.

This is not our Cafe. There has been a moft fcandalous and notorious Riot, not only againft Common Law, Natural Law, that is, the Law which every Man has implanted in him, but directly againft a Law of this Province;(2) nay the Offenders had Notice of the very Law, and warned againft a Violation of it; and I queftion whether there is any Law of this Province more univerfally known than this. For your Direction, Gentlemen—Riots, Routs, and unlawful Affemblies are where there are any Number not lefs than three, where they come with an Intent to commit fome unlawful Act—if they take not one Step they ought to be punifhed for this Intent; if they move forward, it is a Rout; if they commit any one Act, it is a Riot; every Man ought to ufe his utmoft Endeavour for the Suppreffion of fuch fcandalous Breaches of the Public Peace; and I am informed that the Magiftrates and others of this Town did their utmoft to prevent that Infult upon Government in this notorious Riot, but it feems all proved ineffectual—You cannot be infenfible that I have Reference to that lawlefs Mob who affembled on the 5th of laft November, (3) moft atrocioufly broke the Peace, put every

(2) Anc. Chart. 595. This ftatute was for the fuppreffion of diforders caufed by "tumultuous companies carrying about with them pageants and other fhews through the ftreets and lanes of the town of Bofton." See note (3) infra.

(3) The anniverfary of the Gunpowder Plot, known as "Pope Day," had been for many years the occafion of an annual riot between the "north-enders" and "fouth-enders" in the town of Bofton. Each of thefe rival factions celebrated the day by a proceffion carrying the effigies of the Pope, the Devil and the Pretender upon a platform, under which fmall boys, by means of rods connected with the figures, caufed them to rife up and look into chamber windows as they paffed. The

1765.
CHARGE TO THE GRAND JURY.

every Member of this Town in Confufion, and many in the utmoft Hazard of their Lives; and I would mention for the Benefit of all prefent, as they are a pretty large Concourfe of People, that Perfons in general do not know what a Danger they run, in mixing in fuch a Mob; if there had been any Perfon killed, every Man there would have been liable to be tried for his Life, and by a rigorous Conftruction of the Law, might have loft it: It would have lain upon every Perfon to have proved how he came there and what was his Bufinefs; and every Perfon who could have been proved to have been aiding before the Fact, encouraging and affifting after it was begun, and actually doing, or protecting and fcreening after it was committed, muft have come to his Trial, and for aught I fee muft have been convicted; for there are no Acceffories in Murder; all are Principals.

There is another Offence — you have feen it in the public Prints — of Robbery on the Highway — Money

---

The houfeholders were called upon for contributions for the celebration under the penalty of broken windows; and the two proceffions, after parading the town, met in Union Street, where they fought for the figures, which were afterwards burnt, either on Copps' Hill or the Common, according as victory remained with the north or fouth end. See Drake's Hiftory of Bofton, p. 661.

Before the next anniverfary in 1765, the general indignation occafioned by the Stamp Act had caufed a reconciliation to be effected, and both parties joined in the efcort of a "Union Pope," together with feveral additional figures reprefenting Tyranny, Oppreffion, Slavery, &c. Mafs. Gazette, Nov. 7, 1765; Bofton Evening Poft, Nov. 11, 1765. The defcription of this celebration which appeared in both the above papers, concludes as follows: — "This Union and one other more extenfive may be looked upon as the (perhaps the only) happy effects arifing from the S——p A——t."

1765.
CHARGE TO THE GRAND JURY

Money demanded and actually taken; an Offence very heinous in its Nature, and very rare in this Country, and I hope it will be univerſally diſcouraged; and I queſtion whether it is univerſally known, that by a late Law of this Province, it is Death to commit a Robbery on the Highway.

Another Offence — I take Notice of it with Pleaſure — that was formerly very common, but has not of late been heard of among us — I mean the Forgery and Counterfeiting our Public Bills of Credit: The Rigour of the Law, the Severity with which this Court has adjudged in ſeveral ſignal Inſtances, their full Determination to perſevere with the ſame Rigour in all ſimilar Caſes has happily been the Cauſe of its Suppreſſion.

Yet there is another Kind of Forgery, very pernicious to the Commonwealth, which will come before you; the Forgery of Notes of Hand: You perceive, Gentlemen, what Confuſion ſuch a Practice muſt introduce, how wicked a Crime this is in its Nature, and how deſtructive its Conſequences; on this Head I need ſay no more.

I will take up no more of your Time, Gentlemen. I will ſpare you, the Court and the Audience; only obſerving further that all Offences, from Murder, the higheſt of all Felonies, down to ſimple Felony, are ſubject to your Inquiry; yet though you ſhould be ſatisfied that there have been a Number of theſe leſſer Offences committed, as theſe come more immediately under the Cognizance of the lower Courts, you may omit taking Notice of ſuch Miſdemeanors,

1765. CHARGE TO THE GRAND JURY.

Misdemeanors, unless you should think there has been any gross Neglect in the Courts of Inferiour Jurisdiction.

But before I leave you, Gentlemen, I would observe one Word more relative to your Duty. In the Petty Jury, Gentlemen, you are sensible that all must agree in the Verdict; but to every Indictment the Agreement of twelve only is sufficient. One other Point there remains, Gentlemen, for you to observe, and that is, you are to keep your own and the King's Council; this, Juries in general, disregarding their Oaths, do not, strictly enough, observe — nay, I myself have often heard that the Jury had found a Bill, long before it was published in Court. But, Gentlemen, even after that, you are not liberated from your Oaths — you are to keep the Names of the Informers, and Everything else that comes before you in your present Capacity, secret; and unless this is done how will Offenders ever be brought to Justice? An Informer comes, purely for the public Good, to reveal some gross Abuse of the Laws, and hoping he may do some Good, yet unwilling that he should be known to be the Person. Soon after it is blazed abroad that he was the *Informer*, and every Circumstance aggravated to make him odious; will he ever again hazard his Reputation — nay, even his Property? will not this deter many good Men from doing eminent Services to the Public? In Consequence of which many heinous Crimes will go unpunished, many wholesome Laws will be broken with Impunity. (4)

And

(4) See John Adams's Diary, under the date of the following December.

1765.

CHARGE TO THE GRAND JURY.

And finally, Gentlemen, I would obſerve, that though it may give you great Uneaſineſs to bring Offenders to Puniſhment, yet this, Gentlemen, ſhould not prevent the Performance of what is incumbent on you as the Grand Inqueſt. 'Tis the Good of the Whole demands it; and that Self-Approbation which always attends a Conſciouſneſs of having diſcharged our Duty will ever be an ample Recompenſe.

I ſhall add no more; but only pray that Infinite Wiſdom may direct you, and that the Supreme Fountain of all Goodneſs may aſſiſt you in the Proſecution.

Present:

A full Court.

WHITNEY *v.* WHITNEY.

Whitney *verſ.* Whitney.

Rec. 1765. Fol. 136.

In a Declaration on a Note by the Payee, the Omiſſion of "Order" is an immaterial Variance. *Aliter*, in a Declaration by an Indorſee.

ASSUMPSIT on a Note. Note offered in Evidence to the Jury.

Mr. Adams (*objected.*) The Word *Order* is omitted; we take it to be an eſſential Variance. There is not a greater Difference between a Bond and

---

cember. — "Who has made it his conſtant endeavour to diſcountenance the odium in which informers are held? Who has taken occaſion in fine-ſpun, ſpick and ſpan, ſpruce, nice, pretty, eaſy, warbling declamations to Grand Inqueſts, to render the characters of informers honourable and reſpectable?" 2 John Adams's Works, 169.

1765.
WHITNEY v. WHITNEY.

and a Note, than between a Note negotiable, and not. Such kind of Variances are fatal. Vid. Fitzgib. 131, *Baynham's Caſe;* Law of Evid. 191.

Mr. Auchmuty. The Note is, to pay Plaintiff *Order:* The *or* is left out. Where a Note is nonſenſical we are not obliged to follow it. There can be no Doubt but whether this is Evidence to a Jury or not. In Favour of Juſtice doubtleſs it is. As to the Authorities the Gentleman cites — "a Note of a different Date," is a much ſtronger Caſe, for that is a totally different Note. Cites Trials per Pais. 399.

The Court ruled, that the Note ſhould go in as Evidence, on another Point.* That, as the Note *had not been indorſed,* the Omiſſion of *Order* was immaterial — *otherwiſe* had it been indorſed. (1)

Ch. Juſt. did not give his Opinion.

* Vid. the Caſe, *Ruſſell & Oakes.* (2)

---

(1) S. P. *Fay* v. *Goulding,* 10 Pick. 122 — "*Per Curiam.* As the action is brought by the payee this is not a material variance. If the plaintiff were an indorſee it would have been neceſſary to allege that the note was payable to the payee or his order."

(2) *Ante,* p. 50, where it is ſaid by *Ruſſell J.* that there is no difference between notes negotiable and not, until the indorſement.

1765.

Banifter *verf.* Henderfon.

BANISTER v. HENDERSON.

Rec. 1766. Fol. 80.

Meffrs. Dana & Gridley, for Banifter.
Meffrs. Auchmuty & Otis, (1) *for Henderfon.*

Special Verdict.

Cohabitation and univerfal Report are fufficient Evidence of a Marriage to eftablish the Legitimacy of the Demandant in a Real Action.

Devife as follows: "I give all my Houfes, Warehoufes, Lands, Mortgages, Money, Merchandife," &c. &c. "and all that of Right any Ways belongs and appertains to me," "to my three Sons, T., S., and J., to be equally divided among them in three equal Shares or Proportions, after my Debts, Legacies, and Funeral Expenfes are paid; and if either of my three Sons die without Heirs lawfully begotten

THOMAS BANISTER, Grandfather of the prefent Demandant, made his Will the 25 January, Anno 1708-9, and after divers Legacies follows:

"*Item*, after my juft Debts and Funeral Charges "are paid, I give all my Houfes, Warehoufes, "Lands, Mortgages, Bills, Bonds, Money, Plate, "Debts, Wares, Merchandizes, both at Sea and "Land, as alfo all Books, Bedding, Houfehold "Stuff, Horfes, Cattle, and all that of Right any "Ways belongs and appertains to me, whether "named or not named, to my three Sons, Thomas, "Samuel and John, to be equally divided among "them in three equal Shares or Proportions, after "my

(1) James Otis's will, made many years after, during the unfortunate condition of mental derangement in which his life ended, commences as follows: "In the name of God, Amen.—I, James Otis, being in no manner of fear of Death, though called by fome the King of Terrors, and by old Bannifter in his will, a fergeant—" Tudor's Life of Otis, p. 483. And in the will of Thomas Banifter, the teftator in this cafe, of which a copy is on file, appears the following:—"When Thou Jehovah fhall fend Thy inexorable ferjeant Death to arreft this body, and carry it to that dark prifon of the grave," &c.

——"Had I but time, (as this fell fergeant, Death
Is ftrict in his arreft,)"

HAMLET, Act V., Sc. 2.

1765.
BANISTER
v.
HENDERSON.

"my Debts, Legacies and Funeral Charges are paid, "*and if either of my three Sons die without Heirs* "*lawfully begotten in Wedlock, I will their Share or* "*Proportion to the surviving Sons or Son and their* "*Heirs forever.* And the Reaſon why I make my "eldeſt Son Thomas but *equal* with his Brothers "Samuel and John, is for theſe Reaſons; firſt, he "hath had a conſiderable Share already, Secondly, "I have given his Son £500 if the Lord ſpare his "Life — I need add no more Reaſons, but this — "they are all equally dear to me."

in Wedlock, I will their Share or Proportion to the ſurviving Sons or Son and their Heirs forever." Alſo a Legacy of £500 previouſly given to a Daughter was in a certain Event "to be paid to my three Sons or their Heirs, to be equally divided among them as I have willed the reſt of my Eſtate to be divided among them or the Survivors of them." *Held*, that the Brothers took an equal Tenancy in Common in Fee in the Real Eſtate, determinable on either's dying without Iſſue in the Life of ſome other Son, and an executory Deviſe over of ſuch Deceaſed's Share to the Survivor or

Afterwards: "I will to my beloved Wife Sarah "Baniſter, said Pew for her Life, to order who ſhall "ſit with her in it, and untill my Grandſon Thomas "Baniſter is of Age of twenty-one Years, if he liv-"eth to have *Male Heirs*, I give it to him and *to* "*his Male Heirs lawfully begotten in Wedlock forever*, "both Proprietorſhip and Pew, but if he dieth "without *Male Heirs*, I give it *to the next Male* "*Heirs, and to deſcend to the next Male Heirs, with-*"*out any Alienation forever.*" (2)

In

(2) The ſpecial verdict further found that the three brothers entered under the proviſions of the will aforeſaid, that Samuel and John (who ſoon after died without iſſue) made a letter of attorney to Thomas, who conveyed the premiſes to Giles Dyer, who reconveyed to Thomas, who conveyed again to Dyer one moiety of the premiſes. Thomas died, leaving the demandant his ſon and other children. Dyer then made a deed of the whole of the premiſes to Samuel, who afterwards, together with Frances, the widow of Thomas and mother of demandant, conveyed the premiſes to Peter Luce, who conveyed to John Henderſon, father of the tenant, after which Samuel died without iſſue. If the demandant was entitled to recover, the jury found for him poſſeſſion of the whole, or one moiety, or any leſſer part to which the Court decided that he was entitled. "But if he be intitled to no part thereof," then for

1765.

BANISTER v. HENDERSON.

Survivors. *Hutchinson*, C. J., & *Oliver*, J., *diss.*

If an Eftate Tail with Crofs Remainders, whether Conveyances by the Brothers with Collateral Warranty would not bind the Iffue, *quære?*

Under the Province Charter no Appeal lies to the King in Council, in a Real Action.

In fettling the special Verdict, there were three Points the Parties could not agree on. One was, whether the prefent Demandant was legitimate; or, in other Words, whether Thomas and Frances Banifter, Father and Mother of the Demandant, were legally married.

Thomas and Frances Banifter came over from England, and lived as Man and Wife, both in Old and New England.

Mr. Auchmuty, again the Legitimacy of the Demandant. Had it been perfonal Eftate, no Doubt common Report might have done to prove the Marriage, but here is a great Real Eftate to be determined—fhall common Fame be relied on in this Cafe? (3) No Certificate of the Marriage, the higheft, the only legal Evidence. Had it been in a new Country where Records are not kept, there might have been fome faint Colour for not producing a Certificate, but in England thefe Records are moft ftrictly kept; for they know it is the only Evidence that will ferve; the only Proof of the Legality of Marriage.

Mr.

---

for the tenant cofts. That part of the cafe between the ftatement of the devife and Mr. Dana's argument is reported in the MS. as of the previous term, after the cafe, *Rex* v. *Pourkfdorff.* For convenience the cafe is printed as a whole.

(3) See *Means* v. *Welles*, 12 Met. 361, *Hubbard*, J.—"It was argued that mere cohabitation was not a fpecies of evidence fufficient to fuftain a writ of right. But we are aware of no diftinction as to the amount of proof neceffary to eftablifh a marriage in any one cafe more than another, where marriage is a fact to be proved in order to fuftain an action."

1765.
BANISTER v. HENDERSON.

Mr. Gridley. In Strictneſs of Law they ought to produce a Copy, and not a Certificate, though generally allowed. It has been ſaid that a Certificate is the higheſt Evidence; but I ſay the Perſons preſent at the Marriage is Evidence higher in its Nature—for how will that ever prove the Identity of the Perſons? Cohabitation and univerſal Report have always been deemed ſufficient Evidence, and I never in the Courſe of my Practice heard it denied before.

Ch. Juſt. Have you no Authorities, Gentlemen?

Mr. Gridley. There is no Authority that the Sun ſhines.

Auchmuty. But there is Evidence.

Ch. Juſt. How do Quakers ever prove Marriage except by Report?

Mr. Auchmuty answered, Favour was ſhown them.

Mr. Gridley. There ſhall be no baſtardizing Iſſue after Death, is a Maxim of the Law.

Auchmuty. A Baſtard can't be Heir till Death, and after Death Baſtardy can't be proved.*

Juſt. Ruſſell only inſtanced in Quakers.

Juſt. Lynde. I can't think a Certificate alone is Evidence, or the beſt—that is greater which Mr. Gridley

* *Qu.* if Cases in Time of Holt, 287, would not have been pertinent.

Gridley mentioned. Perſons preſent at the Marriage can only prove the identical Perſons. (4) Univerſal Report is, in my Opinion, ſufficient Evidence, corroborated with other Circumſtances, of the Marriage.

Ch. Juſt. From Thomas and Frances Baniſter living in Old and New England as Man and Wife, I think it may well be inferred they were ſo. (5) I am ſorry for Want of Authorities, and that this Point was not left to the Court as well as the Reſt; for it is not properly a Matter of Fact.

The ſecond Point (Matter of a Perſon's Death) was proved to Satisfaction.

The third, whether there was an actual Entry into the demanded Premiſes was given (in Effect) up; for a Deviſe veſts the Eſtate immediately in the Donee; it does not mean an actual Seizin in Law, but Right to Seizin.

The Jury found the two Points in Favour of the Demandant.

N. B. The next morning *Ch. Juſt.* produced the following Authority from Burn's Eccleſiaſt. Law, vol. 2d, p. 36. (6) Tit. Marriage: "The Proof "of

---

(4) S. P. *Commonwealth* v. *Norcroſs*, 9 Maſs. 492. *Ellis* v. *Ellis*, 11 Maſs. 92.

(5) S. P. *Newburyport* v. *Boothbay*, 9 Maſs. 414. *Means* v. *Welles*, 12 Met. 361. *Aliter* in criminal proceedings before St. 1841, c. 20. *Commonwealth* v. *Littlejohn*, 15 Maſs. 163.

(6) Burn's Eccl. Law, Marriage, X. 5.

1765. BANISTER *v.* HENDERSON.

"of Marriage may be by Witnesses who were present at the Solemnization; by Cohabitation of the "Parties; by publick Fame and Report; by Confession of the married Persons themselves, although "their Acknowledgment might be only to avoid the "Punishment of Fornication, and by divers other "Circumstances which, if they amount to a half "Proof, ought to be extended in Favour of Marriage, rather than contrary to it. Wood, Civ. Law, "122."

Mr. Dana. The Demandant Banister demands by Force of the Will before me; his Pedigree is set forth in the special Verdict. I need not observe that the Intent of Testator is to be the sole Director for Construction of the Words, unless a new Estate is created contrary to Law. Now from the whole Tenor of the Will the Testator's sole Aim appears to be the keeping his Estate in his Family; and this Intention of his is the general Key to the Understanding the Will, and, if attended to, will show in the clearest Manner he designed an Estate Tail. He gives his Estate "*to his three Sons Thomas, Samuel and John, and if either of my three Sons &c., to the surviving* SONS OR SON;" Samuel, (I can't imagine how he came to take it in his Head) supposing he had a Fee, conveys away this Estate; but if this is an Estate Tail, it wipes away all Conveyances whatsoever; for Estates Tail are inalienable, except by Fine and Recovery, and that reduces it to Fee Simple.

I am sensible when a Man gives all his Estate without any otherwise expressing his Intent, a Fee passes.

paſſes.* 1 Salk. 239, *Hopewell* vs. *Ackland.* If the Teſtator had ſaid no more than "I give all my Houſes," &c., they would have had a Fee; but his Intent through the whole Will being not only to take Care of his Sons, but their Poſterity — and though he gives all "*to his three Sons Thomas, Samuel and John, to be equally divided among them, in three equal Shares or Proportions,*" yet he afterwards explains himſelf — "*If either die without Heirs,*" and he then explains *what Heirs*, "*Heirs lawfully begotten in Wedlock,*" then goes on — "*I will their Share or Proportion to the ſurviving Sons or* Son;" and though the Words following, "*their Heirs forever,*" are not aptly expreſſed, yet they ſhall not vitiate, for his Meaning is evident from all the Words taken together, and his Intent ſhall take Effect.† Cites 1 Salk. 226, 227, *Bliſſet* vs. *Cranwell,* and 2 Vent. 285.

As to his willing "all to his three Sons to be equally divided among them," there are numberleſs Authorities where the firſt Words give a Fee, by giving Lands to a Man and his Heirs forever, yet the after Words, explaining what Heirs he meant, make it a Tail. *Nottingham* vs. *Jennings*, 1 Salk. 233, as in our Caſe. *Soulle* vs. *Gerrard*, 1 Cro. 525. The after Expreſſions ſhew he meant Heirs lawfully begotten in Wedlock, and created a Tail: So in the Caſe laſt cited, the firſt Words ſhall be ſet aſide, becauſe contrary to his Intent. But full to

* Vide 3 Mod. 45, *Reeves* v. *Winnington.*

† *Qu.* whether 8 Rep. 95 b, would not have been a good Authority to this Point.

to our Point is the Cafe of *Chadock* vs. *Cowley*, 2 Cro. 695. Here —

Mr. Otis. Are you not fenfible, Sir, Lord Holt denies that Cafe to be Law? *

Mr. Dana. No: But if he does, he is not infallible: But the Authorities mentioned are fufficient. Cites 3 Lev. 70, *Parker* vs. *Thacker*, and 2 Cro. 415, *Webb* vs. *Hearing* — a Cafe in Point. It appears by all thefe Authorities, *una voce*, that Devifors' Intent fhall govern, the Intent fhall be collected from all the Words together; and though the fame Words give a Fee, yet if other Words explain what Heirs he means, viz[t] "Heirs of the Body," or "*Heirs lawfully begotten in Wedlock*," it fhall make a Tail; and in our Cafe it is a Tail with a Limitation over to "*either of the Sons or* SON," which the Law calls Crofs Remainders. The Intent of our Grandfather was fo fixed to keep his Eftate in his Family, and to make a Tail, that he extends it even to Perfonal Eftate, in which he is "againft the Rules of Law," therefore we don't demand it; † but his Intent in this is ftrongly marked. "*To the furviving Sons or* SON." The Iffue take, as much as if their Father had furvived.

Authorities to fupport the Crofs Remainders. T. Jones,

* *Qu.* if Mr. Otis was not miftaken, and that he blended it with the Cafe of *Hearn* v. *Allen*, 3 Croke, 57, which Ld. Holt feems to doubt of in the Cafe of *Nottingham* v. *Jennings*, 1 Ld. Raym. 570? and *qu.* if that Doubt of Lord Holt does not make againft Mr. Otis?

† *Qu.* if the Cafe *Nottingham* vs. *Jennings*, 1 Ld. Raym. 570, would not be in Favour of the Demandant.

1765.
BANISTER
v.
HENDERSON.

T. Jones, 172, *Holmes* vs. *Meynel.* Thomas Raymond, 452. This laſt Caſe is full in Point. "As for Authorities, you cannot expect many in a Will; every Will ſtands upon its own Legs." Pollexfen, 425. (This Caſe enlarged upon, therefore look into it more eſpecially.) Croſs Remainders may be by Implication. Dyer, 303, Tit. Deviſe. T. Jones, 172.

Ch. Juſt. But it muſt be expreſs Implication. Is this ſo?

Dana. Yes. Vid. Dyer, 303. (This Authority much relied on.)

Gridley. Dyer, Saunders, &c.; four of them of the ſame Opinion, that Croſs Remainders may be between three. 1 Vent. 224, *Cole* vs. *Levingſton.* By the whole Current of the Authorities, Croſs Remainders may be between three; our Caſe is much clearer than is common in theſe Caſes "*To the ſurviving Sons or* SON."

Ch. Juſt. "*And their Heirs forever.*"

Dana. I take it ſo: And he has ſhown what Heirs he meant; "*Heirs lawfully begotten in Wedlock.* The Expreſſion "*If either die,*" is an Anſwer to your Honour.

Ch. Juſt. Did the Teſtator intend a Tail to all of his Sons?

Gridley.

1765.

BANISTER v. HENDERSON.

Gridley. They took Tails with Crofs Remainders over.

Dana. On the Whole, the Teftator's fole Intent plainly appears to intail his Eftate; his Words aptly enough exprefs his Intent; and, as it is confiftent with the Rules of Law, it is the Bufinefs of the Law to fulfill that Intent.

Mr. Auchmuty. This is a Cafe of great Expectation and great Importance. We differ very much and very materially. In order to elucidate any Point in a Will, the other Parts connected with and referred to it muft all be confidered. Mr. Dana fays the Conveyances will not hurt, but will all be "wiped away" if this is an Eftate Tail: I fay not.

Ch. Juft. What do you fuppofe can bar an Eftate Tail?

Auchmuty. Conveyances with collateral Warranty.

Gridley. Abolifhed long ago by Act of Parliament.

Auchmuty. But firft to the Tail. He has expreflly given Money to go over as the other Eftate: "*My Will is that faid Legacy of £500 be equally* "*divided among my three Sons, Thomas, Samuel and* "*John, with the Reft of my Eftate as hereafter is men-* "*tioned.*" And afterwards, if certain Things happen, "*then I will the laft mentioned Sum of £500* "*fhall*

1765.

BANISTER v. HENDERSON.

"*ſhall at her Death be paid back again to my 3 Sons* "*or their Heirs, to be equally divided among them, as I* "*have willed the Reſt of my Eſtate to be divided among* "*them or the Survivors of them.*" Can his Intent* be ſuppoſed a Tail, when he deviſes Monies to go as his other Eſtate? He very expreſſly intails his Pew, very trifling in its Nature, in the ſtrongeſt Terms, which ſhews he was not ignorant of apt Words to make a Tail.

But to the Doctrine of Implication which the Gentlemen inſiſt on. The Expreſſions to make a Tail muſt be ſtrong and coercive. 2 Bac. 66. "No "Words ſhall be conſtrued to make a Tail without "*plain* Implication." The Courts will never extend Implications, againſt Eſtates Fee, the nobleſt Eſtates, to Fee Tail, Eſtates of a much baſer Nature. *Wild's Caſe*, 6 Coke, 16 b. To make Eſtates Tail "the "Intent ought to be manifeſt and certain, not ob-"ſcure and doubtfull." In the ſame Caſe: "The In-"tent, and not the Words only of the Deviſor, ought "to make it an Eſtate Tail, then this Intent ought "to be manifeſt and certain, and ſo expreſſed in the "Will;" and in our Caſe, as in *Wild's*, no ſuch Intent appears. They have cited no Authorities, but where the Implication has been ſo ſtrong that there was no avoiding the Conſtruction. Cro. Car. 368, *Spirt* vs. *Bence*. In this Caſe, where the Intent is not very clear, the Court will not conſtrue againſt the Common Law. I remember in Croke, Walmſley ſaid, Implication muſt be very ſtrong to diſinherit other

* *Qu.* Might not this be Evidence of his ſtrong Intent, as Mr. Dana hinted?

1765. BANISTER *v.* HENDERSON.

other Children, and to carry the Intent againſt the Rules of Deſcent. It is ſaid alſo in 3d Mod., the Court will not puzzle themſelves about the Intent of a Man who was perhaps ſick and confuſed in his Senſes at the Time of making the Will, but let it deſcend according to Law. 3 Mod. 104, *Hanchet* vs. *Thelwal.*—"No Reaſon can be given why this Court "ſhould not conſtrue Wills according to the Rules "of the Common Law, where an Eſtate by Implica-"tion is ſo uncertain; for when Men are ſick, yet "have a diſpoſing Power left, they uſually write "Nonſenſe, and the Judges muſt rack their Brains "to find out what is intended."

You are ſenſible when there are pecuniary Legacies to pay, *prima facie* a Fee. What an Eſtate ſoever they took, they had it charged with "*Funeral Charges, Debts and Legacies,*" &c., many of which were very large. Theſe and many other Things to be paid, no Perſonal Eſtate appears to be left wherewith to diſcharge them—none found in the Verdict; thus by Reaſon of theſe Charges, it converts the Eſtate into a Fee. 1 Lilly, 451, 2. To the ſame Point is 3 Rep. 21, *Boraſton's Caſe.*

Ch. Juſtice. The Books vary in that Point.

Auchmuty. Where there is a Sum in Groſs, that creates a Fee, but where a Sum is to be paid out of the Annual Profits, that do'n't alter; that I take to be the Rule.* Your Honours remember the Caſe

* *Qu.* if any Eſtate but an *Eſtate for Life* can be enlarged by *any Charge.* For it is Law that "no Eſtate ſhall paſs by Implication of Law

1765.

BANISTER v. HENDERSON.

Cafe *Elwell & Pierfon*, (7) and the Cafe of *Dudley* vs. *Dudley*. (8) This Point (of Charge) had great Weight, and juftly, in thofe Cafes.

The Words on which the Crofs Remainders are founded are Fee Simple; for it is, in Cafe of Death and no Iffue, to the Survivor and "their Heirs forever." Had Banifter the Grandfather intended a Tail, would he have ufed thefe Words,—efpecially when he fo well knew the Words of Tail, as in the Cafe of the Pew?

Ch. Juft. "Heirs lawfully begotten in Wedlock"— is that Tail or Fee?

Auchmuty. A Fee; for if a Man will depart from the Rules of Law, his Eftate fhall go according to the Rules of Defcent. But if there is any Doubt in this Cafe, it is at End: It is clearly then with us, both by the Principles of Law and Equity. 1 Lilly, 454. No Intent fhall go againft the exprefs Words of the Devifor; at this Rate from a Paffage or two inadvertently written, fhall go againft the general Tenor and plain Words of a Will. 2 Bac. 68. To conftrue the Intent againft the Words is directly againft all the Books. The Courts have always detefted Crofs Remainders among more than two; I

Law againft the *exprefs Limitation* of the Party, altho' the Limitation is void." 2 Rep. 55 b, and fo adjudged in the Cafe of *Hog* vs. *Croffe*, Cro. Eliz. 254. *Ideo* —

Qu. whether the Cafe of *Elwell* (cited above) was not adjudged againft Law.

(7) *Ante*, p. 42. (8) *Ante*, p. 12.

1765.
BANISTER
v.
HENDERSON.

I would obſerve upon Raym'd that the Caſes are different. In order to induce the Court to theſe Croſs Remainders, Mr. Dana has obſerved that the Deviſor's whole Intention was to keep his Eſtate in the Family. This is Implication upon Implication which no Lawyer ever heard of. This Intent is got by Implication, and Croſs Remainders are built on that Implication: But the moſt natural Implication is, that he never intended a Tail at all. According to theſe Gentlemen's Way, you may add Implication on Implication *in Infinitum*, and we ſhall have no ſettled Rules of Law to go by. In all their Authorities, the Deviſe was only to two, with Croſs Remainders over, but the Caſe they would extend it to, is among three; and the Reaſon is given—it is to avoid Confuſion by ſplitting Eſtates into a thouſand Parts, and to keep Peace among Men, from diſputing about ſo many confuſed Croſs Remainders: Beſides, the Remainders cited in the Books are not founded upon Implication, but upon Certainty. Mr. Dana has ſaid, there may be Words which import a Fee, changed into a Tail by after Words. Agreed; but no ſuch Words here—nay, the after Words are, "their Heirs forever," a plain Fee. They can't produce a ſingle Authority where the firſt Words controul the laſt; here the laſt Words are Fee. If any Parts claſh, I can't help that; if a Teſtator will deviſe in ſuch a Manner that there is no telling what Eſtate paſſes, it muſt paſs according to Law. "Where *a certain Intent* may be collected, it ſhall be "conſtrued according to that Intent, but where it is "uncertain, it is void. The Intent of the Deviſor "muſt be collected upon *plain* Words, and not "upon Words which engender Confuſion." And Walmſley

Walmſley ſaid, "It is a good Way when the Words "in a Will are ambiguous, ſo as the Intent may not "be collected, to expound the Will according to "the Law." Cro. Eliz. 742, *Taylor & Ux.* vs. *Sayer.* Is not the Intent here, at beſt, uncertain? Are the Deviſor's Words plain? Don't his Words engender Confuſion? Therefore by the laſt and the other Authorities, the Intent void, and the Rules of Deſcent muſt be obſerved.

The laſt Thing I ſhall mention, having already ſaid enough, is the ſeveral Deeds from Samuel, John and Frances, the Warrantys of which are collateral, and therefore bind the Iſſue. Lit. §§ 709, 716, 717, with Coke's Commentary read at large. 1 Inſt. 373 a, 375 b. 376 a. It is true there is a Statute about Warranties, but unleſs they produce, I ſhall not anſwer it.

Upon the Whole, Eſtates Tail are never implied except when the Intent is obvious — never have been, at Home or here. The Courts are very cautious how they give the Conſtruction of Tail to Words in a Will, eſpecially ſuch Words as theſe; and I believe never known to extend them to create Croſs Remainders among three. I ſhall not recapitulate my Arguments, but only obſerve that it will cauſe the utmoſt Confuſion thus to eject People out of Lands they have for ſo many years quietly enjoyed; and now to turn them out upon ſo ſtrained a Conſtruction of Words inadvertently dropped in a Man's laſt Illneſs, would be as much againſt Juſtice and Equity, as Law and Common Senſe.

Mr.

1765.
BANISTER v. HENDERSON.

Mr. Otis. The present Question arises on this Clause of Mr. Banister's Will: "*After my just Debts,*" &c. In the Course of my Argument I shall examine what Estate the Brothers took, whether Tail or Fee. 2dly. If a Tail, whether with Cross Remainders over. 3dly. If Remainders over, whether the Remainders were in Tail or in Fee. 4thly. If a Tail with Cross Remainders in Tail, whether the Collateral Warranty will not bind the Issue.

The Terms Fee Simple, Tail, general and special, Cross Remainders, Executory Devise are well known, but yet as this Case depends pretty much on having clear and precise Ideas of them, your Honours will pardon me, if to refresh our Memories, I just run over the several Definitions.

(Mr. O. then gave the several Definitions of the above Terms, chiefly from Black. Anal. q[d] vid.)

Cross Remainders, as commonly spoken of, mean implied Remainders. I will for the present allow a Tail, their Whole depending on their shewing implied Cross Remainders rationally and legally implied. Hobart, 29, 34, *Counden* vs. *Clerke.* Though the Intent of y[e] Devisor is justly called the Pole-Star of the Will, yet this is not the only Director; for this I cite the last Case. There are a Variety of Opinions on this Point, and that too among the most eminent Judges; some paying an unlimited Obedience to the Testator's Intention, and others as much slighting it. The true Medium, I take it, is laid down in this Case; "the "Devise

1765. BANISTER *v.* HENDERSON.

"Deviſe muſt be taken according to the Intent of "the Party Deviſor," yet "ſuch Intent muſt be ſo "expreſſ'd in the Will, that it may be *certain* to "the *Court*, and *not againſt Law.*" Hobart, 32. All the Vagaries of a diſeaſed Mind are not to be attended to; yet the rational and legal Intent of a Teſtator ſhould be obſerv'd.

(Relative to the Croſs Remainders, Mr. O. cited the following Authorities:) Viner, Tit. Remainder; the whole of this Chap. Here "Croſs Re-"mainders ſhall not riſe between 3, unleſs the "Words do very plainly expreſs the Intent of "the Deviſor to be ſo;" "between 3 the Law "will not endure Croſs Remainders, by Reaſon of "the Confuſion which will enſue." "Two Croſs "Remainders may well ſtand together, but *three* "*cannot well ſtand together*; for that would make "ſuch Confuſion as the Law abhors, and that was "the Reaſon of the Judgment in the Caſe of *Gilbert* "vs. *Witty*,* which *Pemberton*, *Ch. Juſt.* ſaid he took "to be ſound Law. 2 Show. 139, *Holmes* vs. *Meynill.*" And per *Holt*, *Ch. J.*—"a Croſs Remainder is an "awkward Sort of a Thing; the Caſe of *Holmes* vs. "*Meynill* † has prevail'd, and is not fit to be ſtirr'd "now;" "and *Powell*, *J.* ſaid that the Caſe never "went down with him, though affirmed on a Writ "of Error, and he has heard learned People ſpeak "againſt it"—(And goes on, and finiſhes the Chapter, and reads the whole of the Caſes cited above by Viner and others.) Viner, Tit. Rem. M. p. 1, 2. Ibid. Tit. Deviſe L. p. 1–6. 10 Rep. *Seymour's Caſe*, 1 Inſt. 1 b, (Fee Sim.)

From

* 2 Croke, 655. † 2 Show. 136.

1765.
BANISTER v. HENDERSON.

From all these Authorities there may be ſuch a Conſtruction as is conſiſtent with the Rules of Law, if it be conſtrued a Deviſe in Fee with an Executory Deviſe over. Theſe Authorities are againſt them directly: "3 Croſs Remainders cannot well ſtand together." "Between 3 the Law will not endure Croſs Remainders," and why? "'Twould make ſuch Confuſion as the Law abhors:" they are never favour'd in Law — Holt much againſt them; they are never raiſ'd by Implication; "Croſs Remainders will not ariſe to more than 2 by Implication." Viner, Tit. Rem. X. p. 4, Notes, cites 8 Mod.* 260, *Shaw* vs. *Weigh*; T. Raym'd, 455, *Holmes* vs. *Meynill.* Beſides from the plain Words, the whole Contexture and Tenor of this Will, 'tis plain he intended an Executory Deviſe over of the Deceaſed's Share to y[e] Survivors or Survivor; certain he never intended a Tail with Croſs Remainders over, — yet if there is the leaſt Doubt, the Caſe is with us. But which is likelieſt to get into the Head of a mere Layman — thoſe Croſs Remainders, which theſe Gentlemen contend for, which, after they have got beyond two, have puzzled the wiſeſt Heads in Europe, or that of an Executory Deviſe over, on a Fee determinable on either of his 3 Sons dying without Iſſue?

Mr. Gridley. Do you think the Teſtator had a clearer Idea of an Executory Deviſe than Croſs Remainders?

Mr. Otis. Though there may be ſome Niceties in the Difference between Executory Deviſes and other

* *Alias*, Caſes in Law and Equity.

1765. BANISTER *v.* HENDERSON.

other Devises, yet the general Idea is much more likely to enter into a Layman's Head, than that of Crofs Remainders.

'Tis manifeft from the Words of the Will he intended Equality among his Children. "*The Rea-*"*fon why I make my Eldeft Son but* EQUAL *with his* "*other Brothers*,"—"*They are all* EQUALLY *dear to me*:" Would what thefe Gentlemen contend for be confiftent with this intended Equality? Would not ours? An equal Tenancy in Common being, as we fay, devifed in Fee, determinable on either dying without Iffue in the Life of fome other Son, and then an Executory Devife over of fuch deceafed's Share to the Survivor or Survivors.

The Words in the Will do not make an Eftate Tail. *Hanchet* vs. *Thelwal*, 3 Mod. 105, 6.

In Order to make this Will agree with their Scheme, they are obliged to have Recourfe to double Implications; firft an Eftate Tail is to be implied and then Crofs Remainders. "An Eftate "by Implication was never thought of in a Deed, "nor in a Will, but in Cafes of Neceffity." Cafes in the Time of L'd Talbot, 3, *Glenorcky* v. *Bofville*. One would think this Rule would be fufficient to put an End to their Claim. But if they will have Implication, what fo ftrong for a Fee, as Charges of "Debts and Legacies," &c. This Implication of a Fee is confiftent both with Law and Equity—theirs directly againft both. "A. devifes his Brother, "Lands &c., and *all his Perfonal Eftate*, defiring him "to pay his *Debts and Legacies*,—*a Fee paffes*." 2 Vernon,

1765.
BANISTER v. HENDERSON.

non, 687, *Ackland* vs. *Ackland*. 3 Cro. 58. 2 Strange, 1175, *Barker* vs. *Suretees*. Thus there was not even an implied Tail in the three Brothers; next there were no Crofs Remainders: The Gentlemen can't find I believe, if they examine all the Books from William the Conqueror down to this Time, where there are Crofs Remainders by Implication, without an exprefs Tail. There are no Crofs Remainders between 3 Brothers to be found in any of the Books, not even that of Dyer, 303. That was nothing but *Talk*. (Mr. O. here expatiates on the aforecited Paffages of Viner.) But taking this Cafe of Dyer to have been adjudged (which is far from being certain), "It *feem'd* to the Court," &c.

Mr. Gridley. *Videbatur* was always ufed by the Roman Judges, and is often in the Books.

Mr. Otis. Let it be fo: It is well known there are *obiter* Opinions, which are properly enough expreffed by "*It feems*," yet are not to be relied on as Law. An *obiter* Opinion, I take it, is about a Medium between what the firft Council in England fay *arguendo*, and the folemn Judgments of the Court, after a full Hearing the Council. The Cafe of Dyer, 303, on which they bottom themfelves is totally different from the Cafe at Bar; excepting this Cafe of Dyer it is fettled that Crofs Remainders fhall not be among more than 2, and this Cafe being among 3, it falls to the Ground. 3 Leon. 115, *Brian* vs. *Cawsen*, as cited by Viner, Tit. Rem. X. p. 5. 1 Leon. 166. *Gilbert* vs. *Witty*, Cro. James, 655. Roll. Abr. 835. Viner, Tit. Devife, Let. K. 4 Mod. 282. Cro. Jam. 590, *Pells* vs. *Brown*. (Thefe

Authorities

Authorities cited by Mr. O. to ſhew the Brothers took by Executory Deviſe.)

I ſhall now ſhow, if all the foregoing Points were againſt us, yet the Collateral Warranty binds the Iſſue, and therefore the preſent Demandant muſt fail; but before I enter on this, the Deeds muſt be looked into, and your Honours will there ſee how the ſeveral Warranties deſcend. It is incumbent upon me to ſhew that Collateral Warranty is a Bar, without Aſſetts, notwithſtanding the Statute of Ann. 10 Rep. 95 b, *Edward Seymour's Caſe.* Lineal Warranty bars with Aſſetts, Collateral Warranty without; it may appear hard, but if the Reaſon is attended to, it will be cleared; it is for the Safety of Men's Eſtates, and that People ſhould not be defrauded of what they *bonâ fide* bought, many Years after Purchaſe. And there are other Artificial Reaſons, as no Man is preſumed to diſinherit his own Blood without leaving him greater Advancement, &c. 1 Inſt. 373 a, b, 375 b, 376 a, &c. Viner, Tit. Voucher, U. b. 2, to U. b. 6. *Holt, Ch. J.*, ſaid, "That the true Reaſon of Collateral "Warranty was the Security of Purchaſers, and for "their Encouragement; as alſo for the eſtabliſhing "and ſettling of ſuch as were in by Title or Deſcent "caſt, and this was the only Security ſuch Perſons "could have at Common Law; and becauſe the "Eſtates of ſuch Perſons as are in by Title, are "much favoured in Law, theſe Covenants that were "for ſtrengthening them were favoured likewiſe." Same Tit. U. b. 5. 12 Mod. 512. The Collateral Warranties which are made void againſt the Heir are thoſe made by any Anceſtor who has *no*

Eſtate

1765.
BANISTER
v.
HENDERSON.

Eſtate of Inheritance in Poſſeſſion of the Lands. 4 & 5 Ann, ch. 16. Now, according to their own Suppoſition and the Special Verdict, the Anceſtor making this Collateral Warranty had an Eſtate of Inheritance in Poſſeſſion, and therefore does not come within this Statute; but I deny the Statute of Ann to extend here.

The Common Law and Policy of England have been, this 4 or 500 Years, tired of theſe intailed Eſtates; and therefore every legal Method has been proſecuted for their Suppreſſion. Many have been the ill Effects felt both by State and Individuals, in Conveyance of theſe Eſtates; therefore ſo far from being favoured they have ever been diſcountenanced; and ſurely never was ſuch an Eſtate as is here contended for, favoured — big with the greateſt Confuſion and Injuſtice — inconſiſtent both with Law and Common Senſe. I therefore ſubmit it to your Honours' Judgment, not doubting that Judgment will be rendered according to Law.

Mr. Gridley. "*After my juſt Debts, &c., I give all,*" *&c.* "*If either,*" &c., "*to the ſurviving Sons or Son.*" The Queſtion is, whether there was a Tenancy in Common in Fee, with an Executory Deviſe over, or a Tail with Croſs Remainders: On the other Side they ſay, the firſt Words are Fee, and the after Clauſe, "*If either die without Iſſue,*" makes an Executory Deviſe over: We ſay, if there were no more Words, a Fee, but the after Words make a Tail, and the laſt, Croſs Remainders. When we read a Will, we aim at the Deviſor's Intent; we aim at the general governing Idea of the Teſtator's Mind. If we enter

1765.
Banister v. Henderson.

enter into the Will, you will find, that the grand and ſole Object of the Deviſor was the Emolument of his Poſterity, and the Perpetuity of his Eſtate in his Family. Let us ſee, if we can't make ſuch a System of Eſtate as will be conſiſtent with the Law, and enforce the Teſtator's Intent; if it is poſſible it ſhall be done: But theſe Croſs Remainders between 3 frighten the Gentlemen; no ſuch Thing in the Books; no ſuch Croſs Remainders by Implication: We will ſee. The firſt Words, "*All, &c.*" a Fee, the Words laſt, a Tail—as for "*Heirs,*" the other Words ſhew what he means. "*Heirs lawfully begotten in Wedlock.*" The Gentlemen talk of Implication upon Implication, and Implication upon that again; the Words by which the Tail is made are implied, but a neceſſary Implication. Heirs in general make a Fee, but he ſhews what Heirs he intended; "*If either die, then to the ſurviving Sons or Son,*" this makes the Croſs Remainders. The Sons Thomas, Samuel and John took Tails with Croſs Remainders over, each upon the other: Upon John's Death, Thomas and Samuel were jointly ſeized of John's Part; upon Thomas' dying, Samuel and Thomas' Iſſue were ſeized together; and upon Samuel's Death, the Whole remained to the Father of the preſent Demandant. This was the Intent of the Teſtator, that the Brothers took Tails with Remainders, one upon the other. It is the Buſineſs of the Law to explain the Pregnancy of Expreſſion, and when this Pregnancy is drawn out, this is the mighty Confuſion, this is the terrible Bugbear. The Lawyers who talk of the Abhorrence of the Law, the Confuſion, the Awkwardneſs, and I don't know what all, of Croſs Remainders, were

1765.
Banister v. Henderson.

were aſleep, I believe, and had their Heads muffled up in Napkins.

Mr. Auchmuty. I don't underſtand ſuch Reflections.

Mr. Gridley. I meant no Reflection on you, Sir.

Mr. Otis. Mr. Auchmuty, I did not take Mr. Gridley intended to reflect upon us, but on all the Judges of England.

Mr. Gridley. What mighty Difficulty to former People I can't tell; 'tis very plain now. Croſs Remainders may be among 2; why not 3? If John dies, then to Thomas and Samuel; if Thomas dies, then to Samuel; each have a Tail with a Remainder expectant upon the Death of the others dying without Iſſue. A Fee can't be limited upon a Fee — they ſtrived hard for it in the Caſe of Deviſes, but then it was only for Years. "All the Candles burning at once," as one of the Judges * expreſſed it. *Chadock* vs. *Cowley*, Cro. Jam. 695. Dyer, 303. Here is one Acre to A. and the Heirs Male of his Body, another to B. and another to C. in like Manner. "And if they all die without Iſſue of their or "any of their Bodies or either of them," Remainder over; here are Croſs Remainders among all the 3 Sons. Dyer, 303. The Darkneſs is here diſſipated from Croſs Remainders, the Words, dying "without

* *Twiſden.*

1765. BANISTER *v.* HENDERSON.

without Iſſue " are directly againſt Executory Deviſes.*

Mr. Auchmuty has endeavour'd from ſeveral Charges to prove it a Fee. The Manner of Conſtruction in Law is, *reddendo Singula Singulis;* every Thing muſt be rendered according to its Nature. An ample perſonal Eſtate was left — real ſhall never be taken in ſuch Caſe. The Charge was perſonal, and not upon the Land: Beſides, it does not appear that there was no perſonal Eſtate left; the Special Verdict ought to have ſet forth, there was no perſonal Eſtate left; this is not done, ſo that's at an End.†

It has been ſaid, Deviſor deſigned Equality — he did do Equality — all had Tails; the Event as to the Remainders was left to Chance.

I won't produce 20 Authorities where 1 is neceſſary; here have been numerous Authorities cited, to what Purpoſe I know not, unleſs *Show.*

Mr. Otis. You muſt allow Children a little Oſtentation.

Mr. Gridley. I won't ſay the Caſe of *Gilbert & Witty* is not Law, but I will produce Jones to ſhow wherein

* It is ſaid (in Carth. 310) that " It is a certain Rule that a Will ſhall never operate by Way of Executory Deviſe, if it may take Effect by Way of Remainder." *Qu.* if this Authority would have been impertinent.

† *Qu.* if perſonal Eſtate is not found in the Verdict, whether it is to be preſumed. Vid. 3 Mod. 45, 46.

1765.
Banister
v.
Henderson.

wherein it is wrong; Dodridge was certainly wrong, when he ſaid, no Croſs Remainders among 3. 7 Edward 6 (Year Book). Dodridge ought to have read this before he pronounced. It appears by this Book* that Dodridge was wrong, on whom the Gentlemen ſo much rely: 'Tis true I have not produced the Year Book, but I have produced Hobart, whom I can truſt, for he was an Oracle of the Law. 2 Jones, 172, *Holmes* vs. *Meynill.* Pemberton too is with us, one of the Miracles of Mankind; he was not afraid of the Reveries of Sick Men; was not afraid of plaguing his Mind in finding out the Meaning of diſeaſed Minds: He uſed the Aſſiduity becoming a Judge to get the Deviſor's Intent, and when he had found it, he had it fulfilled. 'Tis not the Part of Judges to ſtifle, but to enforce the Deviſor's Intent; you had Croſs Remainders among 3 at the Common Law, and Dyer, 303, has carried them as far as 4. Mr. Otis ſays there was no Judgment in this Caſe. Dyer ſeldom uſes more than "*it ſeems;*" this Mr. Otis knew: It is very ſtrange Dodridge ſhould ſay, no Croſs Remainders between 3, when here is 4, and I have ſhewn the Year Book; Dyer full with us, the greateſt Judge that ever ſat in the King's Bench, — as great in Law as Sir Iſaac Newton in Mathematicks and Philoſophy. Pollexfen, 413. So, taking theſe Authorities, we have 5 Judges againſt 3, Dodridge and other obſcure Names.† Skinner Rep. 17. Ld. Raym'd, *Meynill's Caſe.* I have looked over all their Authorities,

* Hob. Rep. 34. "A Deviſe to 3 Brothers in Tail, and that one shall be Heir to the other, this makes Croſs Remainders." Hob. 34.

† Holt and Powell.

ities, and theſe few I have ſelected as to the Point, and have obſerved on them what is neceſſary.

1765. Banister v. Henderson.

The Intent of the Teſtator is the *only* Rule, the *only* Director, whether that Intent is got by Implication or otherwiſe: His Intent can't be fulfilled without Croſs Remainders, and if Croſs Remainders are good among 2, certainly among 3; they have been carried to 3, and even to 4 according to the Authorities cited; therefore as his Intent is with us, and the Law is with us, your Honours will give Judgment accordingly.

N. B. Mr. Gridley made an Excuſe for not ſpeaking to the Collateral Warranty, as it was a Point he did not think would be ſtarted, and therefore begged time to look into the Books. This Requeſt was granted.

Afterwards Mr. Gridley ſpoke to this Point, of Collateral Warranty, and, as I heard, ſo concluſively that the Council for the Tenants waived the Matter.*

The Court deſiring that a brief State of the Caſe, *Baniſter* vs. *Henderſon* might be given in by the Council on both Sides, the following States were delivered to the Court.

The

* *Sed quære*, and ſee Dr. Sullivan's Lect. on the Laws of England, 182, 3, and *qu.* if ye Act of Parliament extends, or is binding here.

Qu. If 2 Strange, 969, 996, might not with Propriety have been produced in Favour of the Tenants. Vid. *Stephen* v. *Stephen*, Chan. Caſes, 168, 169, &c.; 1 Ld. Raym'd, 208. Vid. 2 Wilſon's Rep. 88 b. *Driver* v. *Standring*.

1765.
BANISTER
v.
HENDERSON.

The State of the Cafe by the Council for the Tenant.

Banifter's Cafe.

Whatever Eftate the Devifees took, was by Implication — not by exprefs Devife.

Implication muft be neceffary, and not barely poffible. 2 Bac. 66 (G). 6 Co. 17. Cro. Car. 368.

Intent to be collected from the whole Will — therefore the Devifes to the Grandfon and the Daughter, as well as joining real and perfonal Eftate muft be confidered. Alfo the Words in Remainder in the Claufe now in Difpute.

From all which it appears, the Teftator never meant to Entail; the Diftinction between the Devife of the Pew and the Reft of the Eftate proves the fame Point.

The Remainder being an Exprefs Eftate in Fee, argues that the firft Eftate was alfo intended in Fee.

The Teftator meant to convey an equal Tenancy in Common, in Fee, determinable on either's dying without Iffue in the Life of fome other Son, and an Executory Devife over, of fuch Deceafed's Share to the Survivor or Survivors.

The Eftate being fubjected to the Payment of Debts and Legacies, is equal to being fubject to Payment

Payment of certain Sums; and the Eſtate being implied makes a Fee Simple. 2 Vern. 687. 1 Lill. 451, 452. 3 Co. 19, *Boraſton's Caſe.* 1 Cas. Abr. Equ. 176, 9, 10, 12.

But if doubtfull, then Judgment muſt be for us, in Law and Equity; Law, that the Demandant clearly prove his Writ, and Cro. Eliz. 743 — what Walmſley ſaid; Equity — fairly purchaſed, long poſſeſſed, the Purchaſe Money uſed to ſupport the Family.

To prove it no Tail, 3 Mod. 104; 3 Cro. 57; 2 Strange, 1172.

Granting for Argument Sake, that the firſt Words create an Eſtate Tail by Implication, yet the Remainders not croſs. Hob. 34. Vin. Tit. Deviſe, X. pl. 1, and Notes. Vin. Remainder, *per tot;* 2 Cro. 655. 2 Show. 139. 8 Mod. 260.

When John died, Tom. and Sam., expreſſly by the Deviſe over, became Jointenants in Fee of his Part; and on Tom.'s Death, all his Part of John's Third that was undiſpoſed went to Sam., by Survivorſhip, and never can go back as a Remainder to the Heirs of Tom.

If Jointenants in Fee, there cannot be Croſs Remainders of that joint Eſtate, for that would be limiting a Fee on a Fee at Large.

The Collateral Warranty binds. 1 Inſt. §§ 709, 716. 1 Co. 63. 10 Co. 97. Vin. Tit. Voucher,

U.

1765.
BANISTER v. HENDERSON.

U. b. pl. 5, U. b. 6, pl. 1 & 2, & Notes. W. b. pl. 5. W. b. 4. Notes on pl. 2. U. b. 3, pl. 25, & Notes. Voucher, X. a. 2, pl. 5, U. b. 3, pl. 3. C. b. pl. 3, & Notes.

What is the Diſtinction between a Collateral and Lineal Warranty is proved by 1 Inſt. §§ 704, 705, & 717.

By the Council for the Demandant.

Caſe of Baniſter vs. *Henderſon.*

Mr. Thomas Baniſter by his laſt Will deviſed (among other Things) £500 to his Daughter Mary Baniſter; but if ſhe did not live to have Iſſue, then to be paid to his three Sons to be equally divided amongſt them, as he had willed the Reſt of his Eſtate to be divided among them, or the Survivors of them.

Item. He gave all his Houſes, Lands, Mortgages, Bills, Bonds, Money, Plate, Debts, Merchandizes, both at Sea and Land; as alſo all Books, Bedding, Houſehold Stuff, Horſes, Cattle, *and all that of Right any ways belonged or appertained to him whether named or not named* to his three Sons Thomas, Samuel, and John; to be equally divided amongſt them; and if either of his three Sons die without Heirs lawfully begotten in Wedlock, he willed their Share to the ſurviving Sons or Son, and their Heirs forever.

By this Deviſe the three Sons took an Eſtate in Common

Common in Tail general in the Lands &c. deviſed, with Croſs Remainders in Tail among them of each other's Shares.

1765.
BANISTER
v.
HENDERSON.

Firſt. By the Deviſe of all his Houſes and Lands &c., and all that of Right anyways belonged to him, whether named or not named, a Fee would have paſſed to his three Sons by Force of the Words taken by themſelves. Vid. 1 Salk. 239, *Hopewell* vs. *Ackland*, where Alleyn, 28, *Wheeler's Caſe*, and 2 Vent. 285, *Willow's Caſe*, are rely'd on; for the Words are as ſtrong and comprehenſive as thoſe made Uſe of in thoſe Caſes, and muſt comprehend all his Eſtate, which alone would paſs a Fee; and as by Deviſe of all his Lands an Eſtate for Life paſſed, the following Words, unleſs they comprehend his Eſtate in thoſe Lands, muſt be uſeleſs.

Secondly. The following Words, "equally to be divided among them," make them Tenants in Common of the Whole. Vid. 1 Salk. 226, *Bliſſet* vs. *Cranwell.*

Thirdly. By the ſubſequent Words — if either of his three Sons die without Heirs lawfully begotten in Wedlock, he wills their Share to the ſurviving Sons or Son, and to their Heirs forever — an Eſtate Tail general is created of their ſeveral Shares; for this ſhews the Intent of the Teſtator to be Heirs of their Bodies, by neceſſary Implication; ſo that Heirs here ſignifies the ſame as Iſſue; for they could not die without Heirs, living their Brother. Vid. Cro. James, 415, 416, *Webb* vs. *Hearing.*

1765.
BANISTER v. HENDERSON.

Hearing. Same, 448, *King* vs. *Rumball*.* 3 Lev. 70, *Parker* vs. *Thacker*. 1 Salk. 233, *Nottingham* vs. *Jennings*. Cro. James, 695, *Chadock* vs. *Cowley*.

Fourthly. By theſe Words — if either of his three Sons die without Heirs lawfully begotten in Wedlock, he willed their Share to ſurviving Sons or Son, and their Heirs forever — Croſs Remainders in Tail are created among them of their ſeveral Shares; for the Words "if either of them," &c. make Croſs Remainders, expreſs, and differs the Caſe from that of *Gilbert & Witty*. In 1 Vent. 224, *Cole* vs. *Levingſton*, *per Hale*, *C. J.* Vid. alſo Dyer, 303. Croſs Remainders expreſs among four, exactly agreeing with the preſent Caſe. 2 Jones, 172, *Holmes* vs. *Meynill*, a Croſs Remainder by Implication— whereas this expreſs, and conſequently a much ſtronger Caſe.

In both the ſaid Caſes the Croſs Remainders veſted in Tail, as well as the firſt Eſtate of each in their ſeveral Shares; and by the ſame Reaſon and Law, they ſhall veſt in Tail in the preſent Caſe; ſo that the Eſtate ſhall not revert till all the Sons are dead without Iſſue, and the whole Eſtate Tail entirely ſpent. And this is corroborated by the Limitation to the ſurviving *Son* as well as Sons, which plainly ſhows the Intent of the Teſtator was, that all theſe Remainders to each of the Sons, of the other's Shares, ſhould veſt in Tail immediately by the Deviſe; and this is perfectly agreeable to the Reſolution in

* By the firſt and laſt Caſes in Cro. James, it appears it was not a Contingent Eſtate, but took Place immediately by the Deviſe.

in the above Cafes, particularly that in Dyer, which correfponds exactly to it, and is full in Point; and this Conftruction renders the whole Devife in every Part of it perfectly confiftent and agreeable to the evident Defign and Intention of the Teftator.

Upon the Whole, the Devife then as was obferved at firft will ftand thus: To Thomas, Samuel and John, in Common in Tail general, with Crofs Remainders in Tail to each of the others' Shares; fo that when John died firft without Iffue, his Eftate was entirely fpent, and the Remainder of his Share came equally to Thomas and Samuel in Tail; when Thomas died leaving Iffue, his Moiety defcended to the Heirs of his Body in Tail, and alfo the Remainder in Tail of John's Moiety, which was vefted in Thomas, defcended upon the Death of Thomas to the Heirs of his Body in Tail; fo that when Samuel died without Iffue, his Moiety alfo came to the Iffue of Thomas in Tail; and no Part of the faid Eftate so devifed can revert to the Heirs of the Devifor till all the Iffue of the Body of Thomas is entirely fpent.

(*Another State of Banifter's Cafe which I received from Chief Juftice Hutchinfon, together with the foregoing State of that Cafe, by the Demandant's Council.*)

Cafe of Banifter vs. *Henderfon.*

The Teftator devifes all his Houfes, Lands, &c., *and all that of Right anyways belonged or appertained to him, whether named or not named*, to his three Sons Thomas,

1765.
BANISTER v. HENDERSON.

Thomas, Samuel and John, to be equally divided among them; and if either of his three Sons die without Heirs lawfully begotten in Wedlock, he willed their Share to the ſurviving Sons *or Son*, and their Heirs forever.

It was argued for the Defendant, that this was an Executory Deviſe, &c.

In Anſwer to which, it was urged for the Plaintiff, that it is a ſettled and certain Rule of Law, that a Will ſhall never operate by Way of Executory Deviſe, if it might take Effect by Way of Remainder, viz., if there is a particular Eſtate ſufficient to ſupport it. Vid. Carthew, 310, in the Caſe of *Reeve* vs. *Long*; 2 Saund. 380, *Purefoy* vs. *Rogers*, at the latter End of the Caſe; 2 Bacon, 72, where theſe and ſeveral other Caſes are cited.

By this Deviſe (as we ſhall ſhew clearly) an Eſtate Tail was created in the three Sons, of their ſeveral Shares; which is a particular Eſtate ſufficient to ſupport a Remainder; and therefore by the Rule, the Limitation ſhall take Effect by Way of Remainder, and cannot be conſtrued an Executory Deviſe.

It is inſiſted for the Plaintiff, that, by this Deviſe, the three Sons took an Eſtate in Common in Tail general in the Lands deviſed, with Croſs Remainders in Tail among them of each other's Shares.

To ſhew this, they obſerve —

Firſt. By Deviſe of all his Land, and all that of Right

1765.
BANISTER
v.
HENDERSON.

Right anyways belonged to him, &c., a Fee would have paſſed to the three Sons, by Force of theſe Words taken by themſelves; for this they rely on the Caſe of *Hopewell* vs. *Ackland*, 1 Salk. 239, where Alleyn, 28, *Wheeler's Caſe*, and 2 Vent. 235, *Willow's Caſe*, are rely'd on; for theſe Words are as full and ſtrong as thoſe made Uſe of in theſe Caſes, and muſt comprehend all his Eſtate.

Secondly. The following Words, "equally to be divided among them," make them Tenants in Common; for which Vid. 1 Salk. 226, *Bliſſet* vs. *Cranwell.*

Thirdly. By the ſubſequent Words — if either of his three Sons die without Heirs lawfully begotten in Wedlock, he wills their Share to the ſurviving Sons *or Son*, and their Heirs for ever. By the firſt Part of them, an Eſtate in Tail general is created of their ſeveral Shares: For this ſhows the Intent of the Teſtator to be, Heirs of their Bodies; ſo that Heirs here ſignifies the ſame as Iſſue, for neither could die without Heirs in the general Senſe of the Word, living his Brothers. For this they rely on Cro. James, 415, 416, *Webb* vs. *Hearing*; Same, 448, *King* vs. *Rumball*; Same, 695, *Chaddock* vs. *Cowley*; 3 Lev. 70, *Parker* vs. *Thacker*; 1 Salk. 233, *Nottingham's Caſe.*

N. B. By the above Caſes of *Webb & Hearing*, and *Chaddock & Cowley*, and their Analogy to the preſent, it appears that this was not a contingent Eſtate, but took Place and veſted immediately by the Deviſe.

 Fourthly.

1765.
BANISTER
v.
HENDERSON.

Fourthly. By the ſame Words, alſo (the latter Part of them), Croſs Remainders are created among the three Sons, of their ſeveral Shares. Theſe Words, "if either of them," &c., make Croſs Remainders expreſs, (1 Vent. 224, *Cole* vs. *Livingſton*) and is not by Implication, but as determinate as if Croſs Remainders had been drawn out at Length. And this differs the Caſe from that of *Gilbert & Witty*, produced on the other Side. Vid. also, Dyer 303, Croſs Remainders in Tail among 4, a Caſe in Point. Alſo 2 Jones, 172, *Holmes & Meynill*, where the Caſe of *Gilbert & Witty* is queſtioned. Vid. Hobart, 34, which Caſe, and that in Dyer, muſt have been overlooked by Juſtice Dodridge. He ſaid, in *Gilbert & Witty*, that it would not be found in any Book that Croſs Remainders could be between three.

It appears, alſo, by the Limitation being to the ſurviving *Son* as well as Sons, that it was the Intent of the Teſtator that the laſt ſurviving Son, the other two dying without Iſſue, ſhould take the Whole. This could not take Effect by any Conſtruction, but the above of Croſs Remainders in Tail executed; but upon this Conſtruction, no Part of the Eſtate could revert to the right Heirs of the Deviſor, until all the Sons were dead without Iſſue, and the whole Eſtate Tail in each ſpent, according to the above Caſe in Dyer.

Upon the Whole, therefore, the Deviſe ſtands thus: To Thomas, Samuel and John in Common, in Tail general; and if Thomas die without Iſſue, the Remainder of his Share to Samuel and John in Tail; and if Samuel dies without Iſſue, the Remainder

mainder of his Share to Thomas and John in Tail; and if John dies without Iſſue, the Remainder of his Share to Thomas and Samuel in Tail.

So that when John died without Iſſue, his Share came to Thomas and Samuel in equal Moieties in Tail, with Croſs Remainders in Tail between them of each other's Shares; and when Thomas died leaving Iſſue, his Share, and his Moiety of John's Share, came to his Iſſue in Tail; and when Samuel died without Iſſue, his Share, and his Moiety of John's Share, came to the Iſſue of Thomas in Tail.

The laſt Words, "*then to the ſurviving Sons or Son, and their Heirs for ever*," could not poſſibly make a Jointenancy in Fee, in Caſe of Death without Iſſue. The Survivor was to have the Whole, which might have been prevented by ſevering the Jointenancy; ſo that, to anſwer the Teſtator's Intent, a Remainder in Tail veſted in Thomas upon Samuel's Eſtate in Tail in this Moiety; and so *vice versa*, and upon Samuel's Death, this Remainder came veſted in Poſſeſſion.

Judgment was afterwards rendered at Worceſter Court for the Tenants: By the Opinion of *Lynde*, *Cuſhing* & *Ruſſell*: *Chief Juſtice* & *Oliver* full in Favour of the Demandant.* (9)

* *Qu.* if 2 Black. Comment. ch. 20, pp. 302, 303, and ch. 23, pp. 381, 382, would have been impertinent in this Caſe.

---

(9) It is to be regretted that we have no means of aſcertaining concluſively on what grounds this deciſion was given. The three points raiſed are briefly as follows: 1. Whether the words of the will created an

1765.
BANISTER v. HENDERSON.

an eſtate tail, or a fee with executory deviſes; 2. If an eſtate tail, whether croſs remainders can be created by implication among more than two; 3. Whether collateral warranty will not bind the iſſue. Quincy ſtates that the laſt point was given up by the tenant's counſel; and although it was inſerted in his "ſtate of the caſe," yet its not being mentioned in the others, would ſeem to ſhow that it was, in effect, abandoned. As to the ſecond point, it is true that moſt of the authorities at that day leaned ſtrongly againſt the eſtabliſhment of croſs remainders among more than two. See 3 Bl. Com. 381, 2, cited by Quincy *ſupra*. But upon this ground alone, it is difficult to ſee why the demandant ſhould not have had judgment for one third of the premiſes. And it was ſoon after eſtabliſhed that croſs remainders might ariſe among any number. Cowp. 780. 2 East, 36. *Hall* v. *Prieſt*, 6 Gray, 18, in which laſt caſe they were eſtabliſhed among eight. From theſe conſiderations, it ſeems to us more probable that the deciſion was given upon the firſt point; and we have, accordingly, ſo ſtated it in the marginal note.

But whether the point of collateral warranty was not well taken, *quære*. That the reporter ſo conſidered it, appears from his note, *ante*, 145, and his citation, *ſupra*, of 3 Bl. Com. 303, where it is laid down that collateral warranty is ſtill a bar, "notwithſtanding the ſtatute of Queen Anne, if made by tenant in tail in poſſeſſion."

Among the law papers of John Adams, for acceſs to which we are indebted to the kindneſs of Hon. Charles Francis Adams, we find a copy of an opinion given in 1745, by the diſtinguiſhed lawyer, John Read, upon a caſe which had ariſen upon the ſame clauſe in the will, and in which ſome of the ſame queſtions were involved. That opinion is printed below. The caſe reſulted in favor of the tenants; but it will be ſeen that Mr. Read's opinion coincided with that of the minority of the Court in *Baniſter* v. *Henderſon*, viz., that the deviſe created an eſtate tail with croſs remainders. It appears, alſo, that the point was raiſed which was afterwards decided in *Baker* v. *Mattocks* (*ante*, p. 69), viz., the partibility of eſtates tail; and that the opinion of Mr. Read, and alſo, it would ſeem, of Mr. Pratt (afterwards Chief Juſtice of New York), was in favor of the partibility, coinciding with that of the minority of the Court in *Baker* v. *Mattocks*, and with that of Judge Trowbridge. See *ante*, p. 74, note.

"*Mr. Baniſter's Caſe* v. *Nat. Cunningham.*

BANISTER v. CUNNINGHAM.
Rec. 1754. Fol. 148.

1692. The Province Law, p. 3, enacteth that any Man Seized in Fee Simple of Land in this Province may diſpoſe of it at Pleaſure by Deed or Will; or it ſhall be Subject to a Diviſion with his Perſonal Eſtate, viz[t], a double Portion to his eldeſt Son, and equal Shares to the Reſt of his Children.

1708. Mr. Thomas Baniſter deviſed, among other Things, £500 to his Daughter, Mary Baniſter, but if ſhe did not live to have Iſſue, then

1765.

BANISTER v. CUNNINGHAM.

then to be paid to his 3 Sons, to be equally divided among them, as he had willed the Reſt of his Eſtate to be divided among them or the Survivor of them."

Item. He gave all his Houſes, Ware-houſes, Lands, Mortgages, Bills, Bonds, Money, Plate, Debts, Wares, Merchandizes, both at Sea and Land, as alſo all Books, Bedding, Houſehold Stuff, Horſes, Cattle, *and all that of Right any ways belonged or appertained to him, whether named or not named, to his Three Sons, Thomas, Samuel and John, to be equally divided among them; and if Either of his Three Sons dye without Heirs lawfully begotten in Wedlock, he willed their Share to the Surviving Sons or Son, and their Heirs for ever.*

The Teſtator died; then his Son John died without Iſſue; then Thomas leaving Iſſue, whereof the Eldeſt Son is ſince deceaſed without Iſſue; but there are now living John, Samuel Anneſley, and Frances Wife of Wm. Bowen. The Teſtator's Son Samuel, ſurviving his two Brothers, mortgaged 7 Acres of Paſture in Boston, Part of the Eſtate deviſed them, to Nathaniel Cunningham, and his Heirs, by Force whereof he entered and held it, and then the Mortgagor died without Iſſue.

Q. Is Nath'l Cunningham's Eſtate in this Paſture good, or not?

A. His Eſtate is void, for the Mortgagor had but one Half, and that in Tail, by the Deviſe above.—

For the Deviſe above, giving all that of Right any ways belonged to the Teſtator, gave every Parcell of his Eſtate, and all the Right he had therein, and is as large as the Expreſſion in the Caſe of *Hopewell* vs. *Ackland*, 1 Salk. 239, viz[t]., "and whatſoever elſe I have not before diſpoſed of;" and therefore would by itſelf pass a Fee Simple to the Three Sons.

And theſe Words added, "to be equally divided among them," would make them Tenants in Common of the Whole. 1 Salk. 226, *Bliſſet* vs. *Cranwell.* But by farther deviſing the Remainder to the Survivor, if either of his Three Sons dye without Heirs lawfully begotten in Wedlock, the Teſtator createth an Entail of their ſeveral Shares. 1 Salk. 233, *Nottingham* vs. *Jennings.* Deviſe to his ſecond Son to hold to him and his Heirs for ever, and for Want of ſuch Heirs, then to his own Right Heirs—adjudged an Eſtate Tail; and the Word Heirs can import nothing more than Iſſue, for he could not die without Heirs, living Heirs of the Father.

Laſtly, by deviſing the Share of ſuch as dye without Heirs lawfully begotten in Wedlock, to the ſurviving Sons or Son, and their Heirs for ever, makes Croſs Remainders among them. So that when John died firſt without Iſſue, the Remainder of his Share came equally to Thomas and Samuel in Tail; when Thomas died leaving Iſſue, his Moiety deſcended to the Heirs of his Body in Tail; and when Samuel died without

1765.
Banister v. Cunningham.

without Iſſue, his Moiety came to the Heirs of the Body of Thomas in Tail. 2 Jones, 172, Holmes vs. Meynell, on Croſs Remainders by Implication, where Croke, James, 655, *Gilbert & Witty*, is queſtioned. See Dyer, 303, Deviſe. Croſs Remainders expreſs among 3, as this Caſe is. And Mr. Samuel Baniſter's ſurviving both his Brethren doth not change his Eſtate, which was an Entail immediate by the Will, Remainder to Thomas and John, and the Heirs of their Bodies. Cro. James, 695, *Chadock* vs. *Cowley*. Therefore by Samuel's Death without Iſſue, his Eſtate is determined; by the Death of John without Iſſue, and of Thomas leaving Iſſue, the Right to this Remainder, by Force of the Gift veſteth in Thomas's Iſſue in Tail, the Reverſion to the Right Heirs of the Donor.

Wherefore the Heirs of ye Body of Thomas ſhall demand and recover the Paſture of Mr. Cunningham by Force ofthe Deviſe aforeſaid.

Q. 2. To whom doth this Paſture fall, — to John the eldeſt Son ſurviving, or to the four Children of Thomas equally?

A. This Paſture deſcends to all his Children equally as Coparceners by the Prov. Law, and they muſt join in Suit.

The Teſtator was Seized of this Paſture as of an Inheritance deſcendible to all his Children as Coparceners as above, and therefore by giving it in Tail to his Sons and the Heirs of their Bodies, he could not alter ye Deſcent, and make that deſcendible to the Eldeſt Son only, which was by Law deſcendible to all ye Children; for —

1. The fulleſt Words of Limitation to make an Intail, as in a Gift to A. and his Heirs of his Body begotten, have no Tendency to alter the Courſe of Deſcent, but only to limit whoſe Iſſue ſhall inherit, and ſo how long the Inheritance ſhall endure; and when that Iſſue is ſpent, the Eſtate reverts to the Donor. Lit. Ten. § 18, 19.

2. The Stat. of Weſt. 2, c. 1, makes no Intail but of ſuch Eſtates as were Fee Simple Conditional at Common Law, and confirms them according to the Will of the Donor, but makes no Alteration of the Courſe of Deſcent. Co. Lit. 18, 19. Therefore Lands of Inheritance, whether intailed or not, always deſcended to the ſame Heirs. So Lands in Burrough Engliſh to the youngeſt Son. Co. Lit. 110, b. Lands in Gavelkind to all the Sons. Co. Lit. 175, &c.

3. If the Donor, intending by expreſs Words to alter the Courſe of Deſcents, gives Lands to a Man and his eldeſt Heirs females of his Body, or Lands holden in Gavelkind, to a Man and his eldeſt Heirs, he cannot thereby alter the Law; the Word Eldeſt ſhall be rejected, and all the Parceners ſhall inherit. Co. Lit. 27, § 31.

By y^e^ ſame Reaſon and Law, this Paſture, deſcendible to all his Children as Parceners in Fee Simple by the Prov. Law, now intailed deſcends to all the Children, and they muſt bring the Action.

Boſton, December 19, 1745. *John Read.*

Or

Or say, —

1. The Nature of an Intail confifts in limiting what Iffue fhall inherit, and how long the Inheritance shall endure, before the Donor or his Heirs may enter as in their Reverfion. Lit. Ten. § 18.

2. The Stat. of *Donis conditionalibus* creates no Eftate Tail but of fuch an Eftate as was Fee Simple at the Common Law, and is defcendible in fuch Form as it was at the Common Law. Co. Lit. 19, *Devant le dit Statute*, &c. — the penultimate Sentence of the fecond Paragraph. Therefore Lands of Inheritance, whether intailed or not, always defcend to y[e] Same Heirs in Either Cafe, Lands in Burrough Englifh to the youngeft Son. Co. Lit. § 165. *Toutes les Terres ou Tenements.* Lands in Gavelkind to all the Sons. Co. Lit. § 265.

N. B. This laft was, I think, in Mr. Pratt's Handwriting.

Rochefter Proprietors *verf.* Hammond.

ROCHESTER PROPRIETORS v. HAMMOND.

(*From Plymouth.*)

Pleas in Abatement.

Rec. 1764. Fol. 238.

In Ejectment, a Defcription of the Land as "120 Acres of Common Land that lieth in a Tract containing 210 Acres," and giving the Bounds of the whole Tract, is bad for Uncertainty.

THE Writ: Attach Nathan Hammond to anfwer the Proprietors of the common and undivided Land belonging to the Old Townfhip of Rochefter, in our County of Plymouth, in a Plea of Ejectment, wherein they demand againft the faid Nathan Hammond Poffeffion of 120 Acres of Common Land that lieth in a Tract of Land containing 210 Acres in Rochefter aforefaid; the whole Tract being bounded as follows, &c.; and fay that on the 20th of December, 1739, in a Time of Peace, in the Reign of our late royal Grandfather, George the 2d, that they, among other Common Lands in the faid Old Townfhip of Rochefter, were seized of faid 120 Acres of Land in their Demesne as of Fee,

1765.
Rochester Proprietors v. Hammond.

Fee, taking the Profits thereof to the Amount of £5 by the Year; and they ought to hold the same quietly; yet nevertheless the said Nathan Hammond has, within 20 Years last past, entered into the said Tract of Land, and now unjustly holds the Plaintiffs out of said 120 Acres of Common as aforesaid; and, tho' requested, refuses to deliver up the Possession thereof; to the Damage of the said Proprietors, &c.

Pleas: And the said Nathan Hammond comes and defends, &c., and saith the Plaintiffs' Writ and Declaration aforesaid is bad and ought to abate, for that the Proprietors therein demand against the said Defendant Possession of 120 Acres of Land, but have not therein set forth the Bounds of said Land, nor described the same with sufficient Certainty, as by Law they ought to have done; 2d, for that the Plaintiffs have not therein set forth that the Defendant ever ejected them from said Land, as they ought to have done; 3rd, for that the Plaintiffs have not set forth that they were seised of Land at the Time when the Defendant in said Declaration is said to enter into the same, as they ought to have done; and these Pleas the Defendant is ready to verify, and thereof prays Judgment.

R. T. Paine.

And the said Nathan comes and saith that he holds 98 Acres of Land within the Bounds set forth in the Plaintiffs' Declaration, by Virtue of a Deed of Bargain and Sale from his Father, N. Hammond, dated the 26th of March, 1734, who is since deceased, which Deed includeth a Covenant of

1765.
Rochester Proprietors v. Hammond.

of Warranty againſt all Perſons, and that his ſaid Father held the ſame by Deed of Bargain and Sale, dated January 30, 1699, of John Hammond, who is ſince deceaſed, and which laſt Deed contains a Covenant of Warranty general; and the ſaid Nathan alſo ſaith, that he holds twenty-two Acres of Land within the ſaid Bounds, of Joſeph Jenkins of Edgartown, in the County of Dukes County, by a Deed of Bargain and Sale from him, with a Covenant of Warranty general, dated March 3rd, 1763, and therefore prays Proceſs of this Honourable Court may iſſue to vouch in the Heirs of the ſaid John Hammond and the ſaid Joſeph, to defend his Title to ſaid Land.

R. T. Paine.

Mr. Paine. Your Honours will obſerve that there is not the leaſt Certainty in their Declaration. No Bounds are ſet to the Land demanded, but only the Bounds are given of a certain Tract from whence they are demanded. Now in England you muſt ſet forth not only the Bounds, but alſo the particular Sort of Land, whether Paſture, Meadow Land or not. As in *Savel's Caſe*, 11 Rep. 55. In this Caſe they have gone infinitely wide of the Mark. They have not told us whereabouts the Land they would eject us from lies; their Writ muſt of Conſequence fail.

Mr. Otis. Your Honours will preſume in Favour of the Writ, if not expreſs. The Lot from whence we demand this Land is clearly deſcribed; and we have ſet forth that we demand the ſoutherly Part of a 210-Acre Lot. The Sheriff, when he

21

gives

1765. ROCHESTER PROPRIETORS v. HAMMOND.

gives us Poffeffion, may affign to us the fouthernmoft Part of the Lot, and *Id Certum eft*, *quod*, &c. But let the Sheriff give us Poffeffion of the Whole, 'twill certainly be good for our Part recovered.

Mr. Gridley. They have failed in a material Point. No legal Judgment can ever be grounded on this Procefs. No Execution, which is the Fruit of Judgment, can ever be levied, fhould they recover; for a Sheriff fhall not make that certain which his Precept has not made fo.

Juft. Ruffell. If the Sheriff fhould lay out wrong, would not Hammond remain poffeft of the Whole?

Ch. Juftice. 'Tis impoffible for the Sheriff to lay out at all.

Unanimously abated. (1)

Dom. Rex *verf.* Mangent.

Life & Death.

DOM. REX v. MANGENT. Rec. 1765. Fol. 151.

A Certificate from a Minifter in another Province is admiffible in Proof of a Marriage,

THIS Caufe held from 10 in the Morning to 8 at Night, during which Time neither Judges or

---

(1) See *Atwood* v. *Atwood*, 22 Pick. 287, *Wilde*, J.—"When lands are demanded, the defcription of them muft be fo certain that feifin may be delivered by the fheriff without reference to any defcription dehors the writ."

1765.
DOM. REX
v.
MANGENT.

or Jury departed. It turned chiefly on Matters of Fact; and the Arguments too prolix to give even a Summary. The Indictment was for MURTHER of a bastard Child. (1)

without any Authentication from a Magistrate.

The Authorities on Behalf of the Prisoner were as follows: 2 H. P. C. p. 438, ch. 46, § 43, Tit. Evid. 1 & 2 Wm. & Mary, 2 H. P. C. 15 ch. p. 104, 105, § 61, p. 118. H. P. C. 428, Evid. § 5, 431. 1 Inst. 373. 1 Salk. 123. 1 Bac. 310, Bastardy. Kelyng, 32, an Authority much enlarged and insisted on.

No Authorities produced on behalf of the King.

N. B. It was ruled in this Cause, that a Certificate from a Minister in another Government, of the Marriage of two Persons, might be admitted to prove the Marriage, though the Certificate was without any Authentication from any Magistrate. The Reason for this Admission was, that this Court had no Power to compell any one in another Province to give Evidence in a Cause pending before this Court. In England it is otherwise, for a Latitat issues in similar Cases from the King's Bench. However, the Ch. Justice *seemed* to doubt.

Vid. Voltaire's Com. on ye Essays on Crimes, &c. p. 1st.

---

(1) It appears by the record that the prisoner was acquitted, the attorney general having agreed that she might give marriage in evidence, "tho' she answers to an indictment wherein she has the addition of spinster given her."

1765.

Draper (1) *verſ.* Bicknell.

(From Taunton.)

Special Verdict.

DRAPER *v.* BICKNELL.

Rec. 1765. Fol. 304.

A Perſon returned as a Soldier upon the Alarm-Liſt of a Military Company, and who receives a Notice from a Sergeant to appear at Muſter, is thereby rendered liable to the Penalty of the Law for Non-Attendance.

THE Queſtion in this Caſe was, whether a Man, having been only on the Alarm-Liſt for a Number of Years paſt, could be from thence ſo transferred by a general Warning from a Sergeant, or Notification, as to make him liable to the Penalty of the Law for Non-Attendance. (2)

Mr. Otis. Every man is preſumed, *prima Facie*, to be on the Train-Band-Liſt. 'Tis for him to ſhow himſelf exempted; the ſpecial Verdict does not find any ſuch Exemption. The Caſe is too plain to bear Argument.

Mr.

---

(1) In the MS. this caſe is entitled "*Clark* v. *Bicknall.*" Draper was "Clerk" of the company.

(2) The ſpecial verdict found as follows: —

"That in the year 1754, Japheth Bicknell, the plaintiff in review, was "returned to the Governour as a ſoldier upon the Alarm-Liſt of the Third "Military Company in the town of Attleborough. That afterwards, in "the year 1757, the ſaid Japheth was duly warned to appear as a trained "band ſoldier at what was called a little training, which preceded the "General Muſter of said Company, and alſo to appear at ſaid General "Muſter; and that his name was called among the trained band ſoldiers at both training and General Muſter, and that he did not appear "at either. They further find, that ſome time before ſaid little training, "the Captain of ſaid Company declared that the ſaid Japheth ſhould be "upon the trained band liſt; but whether ſuch declaration was made "before ſaid warning or not, doth not appear. And if, upon the "whole," &c.

The

1765. DRAPER v. BICKNELL.

Mr. Trowbridge. 'Tis found in the Verdiſt that Bicknell had been on the Alarm-Liſt. Now, will ſuch general Warning at once bring him into the Train-Band-Liſt? This, I take it, would be extending the Power of Officers beyond all Bounds. In ſuch Caſe no Man is ſafe; for when a Man is on the Alarm-Liſt, he is preſumed exempted from Training. Now, after this, how unjuſt is it, by ſuch a general Warning, to clap him on the Train-Liſt and make him liable to ſo heavy a Fine! It is putting it in the Power of every Officer to diſtreſs his Neighbours, who from long legal Exemption have thought themſelves not liable to be transferred without *ſpecial Notice;* and never was it till now pretended ſuch Transfer could be made by ſuch general

---

The notification to appear, of which a copy is on file, is as follows: —

" Mr. Japheth Bicknell, —

" You, being a Training Soldier in the Company of Militia, under "the Command of Capt. John Stearns, are hereby required in his " Majeſty's Name to appear at your Colours upon Tueſday the 22d of " March next, at the Meeting Houſe in the firſt Precinćt, at nine " o'clock in the Morning, on the ſecond Beat of the Drum, with Arms " compleat, according to law; Whereof you are not to fail; it being " according to an Aćt of the Great and General Court or Aſſembly of " this Province requiring the ſame upon a penalty of paying the Sum " of twenty Pounds for Non-Appearance.

" Attleborough, February 1757. JAMES PULLEN."

The aćt referred to was that of 1757 by which the Province provided for raiſing 1800 men to ſerve under Lord Loudoun againſt the French; and the muſter, for non-attendance upon which ſo heavy a fine was impoſed, was held for the purpoſe of raiſing the above force, " either by inliſtment or impreſs." It appears by the papers on file, that the abſent Bicknell was drawn for the expedition, but was afterwards excuſed on account of being " blind with the right eye."

1765. DRAPER *v.* BICKNELL.

general Warning. Your Honours will therefore be cautious how ſuch an arbitrary and unjuſt Precedent is made.

Mr. Gridley. 'Tis by Martial Law that every Perſon is obliged by ſuch Warning to attend, unleſs exempted. Some Exemptions are only temporary, and they have not shewn whether theirs is of this Kind or not. If they abſent themſelves without being legally exempted, they muſt bear the Conſequences.

Judgment for the Plaintiff. (3)

---

(3) The action here reported appears by the record to have been "a plea of review of a plea of review of a plea of debt," — the ſecond review "being authorized by an order of the Great and General Court." The case seems to have been obſtinately conteſted through ſeveral years. On the firſt trial in the Inferior Court, the plaintiff had judgment. The defendant appealed and ſucceeded in obtaining a reverſal. The plaintiff then brought his review, and obtained a ſecond judgment. The ſubſequent hiſtory of the caſe is recited as follows, in the defendant's petition for the order abovementioned:

——"Your petitioner manifeſtly made appear to this Honourable "Court, by former petitions, the hardſhip of that judgment; and it "appeared a ſubject worthy the juſtice of this Court to give him a new "trial.

"Accordingly, in the year 1761, the Honourable General Court "gave order for a new trial, and enabled your petitioner to bring a Writ "of Review for that purpoſe.

"This writ being bro't to the Superiour Court in Taunton, A. D. "1761, the defendant Draper pleaded in abatement thereto, that the "pet'r did not name his action, a plea of review of a plea of review, &c. — "for this exception the writ abated and the petitioner had new coſt to "pay to the adverſe party.

"On repreſentation of this matter to this Honourable Court, the "petitioner obtained an order for another Writ of Review, and that "the merits of the cauſe ſhould be conſidered and determined. In this "writ the petitioner took care to amend the fault found with his laſt Writ,

1765.
DRAPER
v.
BICKNELL.

" Writ, and named his plea, a plea of review of a plea of review of a plea " of debt; and, Alas! even ſo he could not be right; for it was objected " by motion that this Honourable Court's order authorized a writ of " review of the action of debt, but not a plea of review of a plea of re- " view, &c. So, on this motion the Court diſmiſſed the writ and " ordered the petitioner to pay coſt.

" Wherefore, the petitioner humbly prays an order may paſs this " Court to enable him to bring forward a new writ of review," " and " that the merits of his cauſe may be at laſt determined."

The prayer of the petition was granted, and an order paſſed, by virtue of which was iſſued the preſent writ, to which the defendant again pleaded in abatement, " that if any order of the Great and General Court of this Province authorizes the plaintiff to bring this writ, a profert of ye copy of ſuch order in Court is not ſufficient, as in this writ, but ſuch order and y[e] ſeſſion wherein it paſſed ought to have been particularly ſet forth above, and that such order appears by record of y[e] ſame Court." This plea, however, was overruled, and the caſe at laſt went to trial, and reſulted in the ſpecial verdict and deciſion above reported.

Auguſt 27th, A.D. 1765.

1765. DESTRUCTION OF THE HOUSE OF THE CHIEF JUSTICE.

THERE cannot, perhaps, be found in the Records of Time, a more flagrant Inſtance, to what a Pitch of Infatuation an incenſed Populace may ariſe, than the laſt Night afforded. The Deſtructions, Demolitions and Ruins cauſed by the Rage of the Colonies, in general perhaps too juſtly inflamed, at that ſingular and ever memorable Statute called the *Stamp Act*, will make the preſent Year one of the moſt remarkable Æras in the Annals of North America. And that particular Inflammation which fired the Breaſts of the People of New England in particular, will always diſtinguiſh them as the warmeſt Lovers of Liberty; though undoubtedly, in the Fury of Revenge againſt thoſe who they thought had diſclaimed the Name of Sons for that of Inſlavers, and oppreſſive Taxmaſters of their *native* Country, they committed Acts totally unjuſtifiable.

The Populace of Boſton, about a Week ſince, had given a very notable Inſtance of their Deteſtation of the above unconſtitutional Act; and had sufficiently

1765.

Destruction of the House of the Chief Justice.

ſufficiently ſhown in what Light they viewed the Man who would undertake to be the Stamp Distributor.* But, not content with this, the laſt Night they again aſſembled in King's Street, where, after having kindled a Fire, they proceeded, in two ſeparate Bodies, to attack the Houſes of two Gentlemen of Diſtinction,† who, it had been ſuggeſted, were Acceſſaries to the preſent Burthens, and did great Damage, in deſtroying their Houſes, Furniture, &c.; and irreparable Damage in deſtroying their Papers.‡ Both Parties, who before had acted ſeparately, then unitedly proceeded to the Chief Juſtice's § Houſe, who, not expecting them, was unattended by his Friends, who might have aſſiſted, or proved his Innocence. In this Situation, all his Family, it is ſaid, abandoned the Houſe, but himſelf and his eldeſt Daughter, whom he repeatedly begged to depart; but, as he found all ineffectual, and her Reſolution fixed to ſtay and ſhare his Fate, with a Tumult of Paſſions only to be imagined, he took her in his Arms and carried her to a Place of Safety, juſt before the incenſed Mob arrived. This filial Affection ſaved, 'tis more than probable, his Life. — Thus unexpected, and Nothing removed from the Houſe, an ample Field offered to ſatiate, if poſſible, this Rage-intoxicated Rabble.

* Andrew Oliver, Eſqr., Secretary of the Province, whoſe Loſs was eſtimated by the Committee of the Council at £129, 3, 0 Sterling.

† Benja: Hallowell, Eſqr., Comptroller, and Wm. Story, Eſqr., Deputy Regiſtrar of the Admiralty.

‡ The Loſs of Mr. Hallowell was eſtimated by the aforeſaid Committee at £412, 19, 1 Sterling, and Mr. Story's at £102, 1, 6 Sterling.

§ Thomas Hutchinſon, Eſqr., Lieutenant Governour of the Province.

1765.

DESTRUCTION OF THE HOUSE OF THE CHIEF JUSTICE.

ble. They beſet the Houſe on all Sides, and ſoon deſtroyed every Thing of Value.*

Furor Arma miniſtrat.
VIRG.

The Deſtruction was really amazing; for it was equal to the Fury of the Onſet; but what above all is to be lamented, is the Loſs of ſome of the most valuable Records of the Country, and other antient Papers; for, as his Honour was continuing his Hiſtory, the oldeſt and moſt important Writings and Records of the Province, which he had ſelected with great Care, Pains and Expenſe, were in his Poſſeſſion. This is a Loſs greatly to be deplored, as it is abſolutely irretrievable.

The Diſtreſs a Man muſt feel on ſuch an Occaſion can only be conceived by thoſe, who, the next Day,‡ ſaw his Honour the Chief Juſtice come into Court, with a Look big with the greateſt Anxiety, cloathed in a Manner which would have excited Compaſſion from the hardeſt Heart, though his Dreſs had not been ſtrikingly contraſted by the other Judges and Bar, who appeared in their Robes. — Such a Man, in ſuch a Station, thus habited, with Tears ſtarting from his Eyes, and a Countenance which ſtrongly told the inward Anguiſh of his Soul, — what muſt an Audience have felt, whoſe Compaſſion

* The Loſs ſuſtained by the Chief Juſtice ſuppoſed to be upwards £3000 Sterling.†

† Afterwards eſtimated by the Council Committee at £2376, 13, 4 Sterling.

‡ Firſt Day of the Superiour Court's Sitting.

Compaſſion had before been moved by what they knew he had ſuffered, when they heard him pronounce the following Words, in a Manner which the Agitations of his Mind dictated! — 1765.

DESTRUCTION OF THE HOUSE OF THE CHIEF JUSTICE.

Auguſt Term

V. Geo. 3 in Sup. Cur.

Preſent:

The Honourable

Thomas Hutchinſon, Eſqr., Chief Juſtice.

John Cuſhing, Peter Oliver, } Eſqrs., Juſtices.

THE Chief Juſtice, addreſſing the whole Court, ſaid, —

Gentlemen:

ADDRESS OF THE CHIEF JUSTICE.

There not being a Quorum of the Court without me, I am obliged to appear. Some Apology is neceſſary for my Dreſs — indeed I had no other. Deſtitute of Everything—no other Shirt—no other Garment, but what I have on. — And not one in my

1765. Address of the Chief Justice.

my whole Family in a better Situation than myſelf. The Diſtreſs of a whole Family around me, young and tender Infants hanging about me, are infinitely more inſupportable than what I feel for myſelf; though I am obliged to borrow Part of *this* Cloathing.

Senſible that I am innocent, that all the Charges againſt me are falſe, I cannot help feeling: — And, though I am not obliged to give an Anſwer to all the Queſtions that may be put me by every lawleſs Perſon—yet I call GOD to witneſs,—and I would not for a thouſand Worlds call my *Maker* to witneſs to a Falſehood,—I ſay, I call my *Maker* to witneſs, that I never, in New England or Old, in Great Britain or America, neither directly nor indirectly, was aiding, aſſiſting or ſupporting, or in the leaſt promoting or incouraging what is commonly called the Stamp Act; but, on the contrary, did all in my Power, and ſtrove as much as in me lay, to prevent it. — This is not declared through Timidity, for I have Nothing to fear. — They can only take away my Life, which is of but little Value when deprived of all its Comforts, all that is dear to me, and nothing ſurrounding me, but the moſt piercing Diſtreſs.

I hope the Eyes of the People will be opened, that they will ſee how eaſy it is for ſome deſigning wicked Man to ſpread falſe Reports, raiſe Suſpicions and Jealouſies in the Minds of the Populace, and inrage them againſt the Innocent — but, if guilty, this is not the Way to proceed — the Laws of our Country are open to puniſh thoſe who have offended.

1765.

ADDRESS OF THE CHIEF JUSTICE.

offended. — This deſtroying all Peace and Order of the Community — *all will feel its Effects.* — And I hope all will ſee how eaſily the People may be deluded, inflamed, and carried away with Madneſs againſt an innocent Man —

I pray GOD give us better Hearts!

The Court was then adjourned on Account of the riotous Diſorders of the preceding Night and univerſal Confuſion of the Town, to the 15th of October following.

Learn WISDOM from the preſent Times! Oh, ye Sons of *Ambition!* beware leſt a Thirſt of *Power* prompt you to inſlave your Country. Oh ye Sons of *Avarice!* beware leſt the Thirſt of GOLD excite you to inſlave your *native* Country. Oh ye Sons of *Popularity!* beware leſt a Thirſt of *Applauſe* move you groundleſſly to inflame the Minds of the People. — For the End of Slavery is Miſery to the World, your Country, Fellow-Citizens and Children, — the End of popular Rage, Deſtruction, Deſolation and Ruin.

Who, that ſees the *Fury and Inſtability* of the Populace, but would ſeek Protection under the ARM OF POWER? Who that beholds the *Tyranny and Oppreſſion* of arbitrary POWER, but would loſe his Life in Defence of his LIBERTY? Who, that marks the riotous Tumult, Confuſion and Uproar of a democratic — the Slavery and Diſtreſs of a deſpotic State, the infinite Miſeries attendant on both, but would

1765.

ADDRESS OF THE CHIEF JUSTICE.

would fly for Refuge from the mad Rage of the one, and oppressive Power of the other, to that best Asylum, that Glorious Medium, the BRITISH CONSTITUTION! Happy People! who enjoy this blessed *Constitution.* Happy! thrice happy People! if ye preserve it inviolate. May ye never lose it through a licentious Abuse of your invaluable Rights and Blood-purchased LIBERTIES! May ye never forfeit it by a tame and infamous Submission to the Yoke of Slavery and lawless DESPOTISM.

"Remember, O, my Friends, the LAWS, the RIGHTS,
"The generous Plan of Power, delivered down
"From Age to Age by your renown'd Forefathers;
"So dearly bought, the Price of so much Blood:
"O, let it never perish in your Hands,
"But piously transmit it to your Children.
"Do thou, great LIBERTY, inspire our Souls,
"And make our *Lives in thy Possession happy*,
"Or *our Death* GLORIOUS in thy just Defence." (1)

---

(1) Addison—*Cato*, Act IV. Sc. 5.

1765.

CHARGE TO THE GRAND JURY.

The Charge by the Chief Juſtice given on the Adjournment. (1)

GENTLEMEN of the Grand Jury: We, as the Superiour Court of the Province, are to carry the Laws into Execution, but in this we have Need of your Aſſiſtance. Your Buſineſs, Gentlemen, more immediately reſpects the Crown Law. It is my Duty to inform you what Steps you muſt take, and what Methods purſue. I have often, on theſe Occaſions, gone into a diſtinct Detail of the ſeveral Branches of our Duty that more particularly fall under your Cognizance, and given ſpecial Definitions of thoſe Crimes, Offences and Miſdemeanours, concerning which the Grand Jury are to enquire: But now our Time is too far ſpent to allow of this; and indeed there is the leſs Need, as our preſent Crimes ariſe not ſo much from Ignorance, as other Sources. I ſhall therefore only juſt touch on ſuch Definitions as I judge more eſpecially neceſſary.

In general, Gentlemen, then, you are to enquire into all heinous Offences: — And theſe in general are thoſe Crimes which hurt the Peace of the Community, and diſturb the Order of Society. One of the moſt renowned Men and greateſt Sages of the Law

---

(1) The adjourned ſitting.

1765. CHARGE TO THE GRAND JURY.

Law called himſelf the *Cuſtos Morum*, as well as *Cuſtos Legum*; and ſuch, Gentlemen, are you; you are to ſee that the Laws are kept inviolate, and the Manners of the People unpolluted.

You are to enquire into all Treaſons; and you are not to think there can be no Treaſons at this Diſtance from the Throne. Treaſons may be committed here, as well as nearer the royal Perſon; and if, from our Diſtance, we are exempted from thoſe more overt Acts of aſſaulting the Perſon of the King, yet Treaſon may be committed among us, by writing or ſpeaking againſt our Sovereign's Right to the Throne, conſpiring with others to levy War, and actually levying War againſt the King,* or the like.

You are to inſpect all Felonies, Burglaries, Thefts, high-handed Aſſaults, Riots and other Diſturbances: All Offences that more immediately reſpect the Morals of the People you are to enquire of; ſuch as the denying the Exiſtence of a God, Blaſphemy, or attributing to God what is inconſiſtent with God, or denying what belongs, and is due to him, a Denial of the eſtabliſhed Religion, all Profaneneſs, Lewdneſſes, and thoſe Crimes which a chaſte Ear cannot bear the Recital of, — indeed, there is no Offence whatever but may come under your Cognizance.

I

* *Qu.* Whether the Chief Juſtice had not in Contemplation the following, or ſome other ſimilar Authorities: — If the Intention of riotous Aſſemblies is to redreſs Grievances of a publick Nature, and ſuch Intention is executed, *it is a levying War againſt the King, and Treaſon.* Dalt. 322. 3 Inſt. 9. Kel. 70, 76. H. P. C. ch. 17, § 25. H. P. C. ch. 65, § 6.

1765.

CHARGE TO THE GRAND JURY.

I would eſpecially mention one or two Crimes which demand your immediate Attention. Burglary, Gentlemen, by the Rules of the Common Law, is a forceable Entry into the Houſe of another in the Night-Time, with an Intent to commit ſome Felony, whether ſuch Intent be executed or not; and I would obſerve, that there is no Need it ſhould be done ſecretly; it may be as well done when a great Number are preſent, as when there are but few. Riots is another very high Offence; this indeed does not ſtrike the Mind with ſo much Abhorrence, as ſome other Offences do, yet on the Diſcouragement and Suppreſſion of theſe, all Peace of Society depends. To prevent theſe, we muſt all lend our whole Aſſiſtance; for it is againſt the natural Light of Reaſon that ſuch Offences ſhould proceed with Impunity, and it greatly concerns every Individual to put a Stop to them. Such an Abhorrence has the Law, of Riots, that, if three or more aſſemble peaceably, and after, do ſome riotous Act, this is a riotous Aſſembly, notwithſtanding they did not at firſt aſſemble in a riotous Manner. The Law is thus ſevere, becauſe ſuch Aſſemblies, when not reſtrained, generally reſiſt all Oppoſition, and tend to the Subverſion of all Government: There is no knowing where they'll end. I ſhall not enlarge — indeed I may well be excuſed, being ſo much intereſted myſelf.

A ſacred Regard, Gentlemen, is to be had to your Oaths. You are to preſent no one through Malice, and leave no Man unpreſented, through Fear, Favour or Affection. Such a Situation are we in, at preſent, that 'tis very difficult to diveſt

1765. CHARGE TO THE GRAND JURY.

one's ſelf of all Connexions, and to preſerve that Firmneſs of Mind, on which depends the Well-being of us all.

The Truſt committed to you is very great and important. All Offences come under your Cognizance, and are to be preſented by you before they can be puniſhed. Sometimes Informations are filed by the Attorney General, and in certain Caſes admitted, though we are very tender how theſe are indulged, as 'tis a Hardſhip on the Subject; and I think there is no Caſe, in which a Man ſhall be tried for Life on an Information.* The Life of a Man ſhall not be endangered, unleſs twelve Men of the Grand Jury ſhall ſay, he ſhall be put on Trial, and twelve more of his Peers ſhall all agree that he is guilty, before he ſhall loſe his Life. This is a Priviledge of which the Court is as tender as any of the Subjects, and therefore do not allow Informations, only in particular Caſes, and thoſe very ſeldom. — It is of great Moment that you be very diligent in your Enquiry.

One Thing more I would mention: You are obliged, each of you, not only to take Notice of ſuch Offences as have been obſerved to you by the Court, or that ſhall be brought before you by the Attorney General, or others, but alſo of all thoſe Crimes which come within your own Knowledge, or where you have ſufficient Inducement to think Perſons have been guilty of Crimes, which have not been brought

* *Qu.* One may be convicted of Felony on Indictment or *Information* by 5 Geo. 1, ch. 4. Wood's Inſt. 654.

brought forward by any one. In such Cases, you ought to take Cognizance.

1765.
CHARGE TO THE GRAND JURY.

Further, Gentlemen, you will mind that Secresy you are obliged by your Oaths to observe. This is not observed commonly so much as it ought, but 'tis absolutely necessary now. You may discourse among yourselves, send for particular Persons, and examine them; and, whether what they testify is sufficient to find a Bill, or not, you are to keep all in Secresy. The Danger of revealing what may come before you at this Time is very obvious; 'twill not only prevent future Informations, but have a Tendency to countenance and increase Crimes which it nearly concerns all of us to suppress.

I shall only add, that you must use the strictest Impartiality through your whole Enquiry, and I pray God to direct you in it.

Pateshall *vers.* Apthorp & Wheelwright.

PATESHALL *v.* APTHORP.

Rec. 1765. Fol. 260.

In an Action of *Insimul Computassent* on an Account acknowledged by one Part-

ACTION upon an *Insimul Computassent.* It appeared that Wheelwright had made the Settlement, as joint Partner with Apthorp, and, on the Account so stated, the Company were indebted to the Plaintiff in a certain Sum, and that Wheelwright had given his single Note to balance the Company's

1765.
PATESHALL
v.
APTHORP.

Company's Debt. The main Queftion was, whether this difcharged the Company.*

An incidental Queftion was debated, whether Apthorp fhould be admitted to give Evidence, that, *in this particular Tranfaction*, there was no Privity between him and Wheelwright.

ner againft the Company, it is competent for the other to fhow that the Tranfaction was not in Partnerfhip. The Acceptance of the Note of one Partner for a Company Debt, and balancing the Company Account therewith, is no Difcharge of the Company. *Lynde*, J., *diffentiente.*

Mr. Auchmuty. One Partner can never be admitted to prove his Ignorance of his Partner's Tranfactions; for this would be to render all Tranfactions in Trade with Partners precarious and uncertain, and is directly againft all the Rules of Law.

Mr. Fitch. The *Infimul Computaffent* is figned only by Wheelwright, and not by Apthorp, and the fole Queftion is, if we may not prove Apthorp had Nothing to do with it.

Ch. Juft. Is there not a previous Queftion, whether it is in the Power of one Partner, thus to charge another?

Mr. Fitch. We have an Authority to that Point. 1 Salk. 126, *Pinkney* vs. *Hall.* It is not in every Cafe that one Partner fhall be bound down by the other's Act, fo as not to fhew he had no Concern in a certain Affair.

Mr.

* *Qu.* If thefe Authorities would not have been pertinent: 12 Mod. 537, 86, 406. Cunningham on Bills of Exch. 95, 96, 150, 151, 152. Vid. Noy, 140, *Oldfield's Cafe;* 5 Mod. 314; 1 Lutw. 466; 5 Co. 117; 4 Mod. 88; 2 Bac. Abr. 24; Str. 426; Burrow's Rep. 1 v. p. 9.

1765. PATESHALL v. APTHORP.

Mr. Gridley. The Exception is this — that it is to no Purpoſe to ſhew we had Nothing to do in this Matter, becauſe Wheelwright has ſaid, we had. Can it be imagined, that one Perſon has a Power by his Notes, his Bills, his Bonds, at his Caprice to charge his Partner? If this is Law, an End of Partnerſhips. The Authority we have produced is in Point. You ſhall not charge *ad Libitum*, but you may charge in the Affairs of the Partnerſhip, and no further. Leap this Boundary — no End — no ſeeing to the End of the infinite Miſchiefs which will flow in upon us. Shall one Partner's barely ordering certain Affairs into the Books, charge the other, and eſtop him from Proof of his having no Concern? It can never be.

Mr. Auchmuty. Their Authority is not in Point, for it is founded upon the Cuſtom of England.

Mr. Gridley. No: the Common Law.

Mr. Auchmuty. I take it to be only a particular Cuſtom; but if on the Common Law, let us ſee if the Inconveniences which will flow from their Doctrine, will not exceed any which may happen on admitting our Suppoſition. If it is once known that a Man may thus ſlip his Neck out of the Collar, who will have Anything to do with Partners? But there is an Authority right under theirs', clearly with us.

Mr. Gridley. There the Tranſaction was in Partnerſhip.

Mr.

1765.
PATESHALL
v.
APTHORP.

Mr. Auchmuty. To extend their Authority as far as is contended, would be inconvenient with a Witneſs. Who, if there muſt be an Inconvenience, is to ſuffer? — One who relies on the Faith and Credit of the Copartners, or the Partners themſelves who are thus ſolemnly united? Shall Apthorp be allowed to prove himſelf clear, when his Partner has declared, under his Hand, that he is jointly concerned?

Ch. Juſt. Suppoſe my Partner had charged me, by his Note of Hand — ſhall not I be admitted to prove that I had Nothing to do in that particular Tranſaction?

The Evidence was unanimouſly admitted, and the Chief Juſtice ſaid, that Want of Clearneſs, or Ambiguity, ought not to be an Objection to Evidence, but the Jury ſhould be left to judge.

On the main Queſtion, it was inſiſted by Mr. Auchmuty, that the Note given by Wheelwright was no Payment, and conſequently no Diſcharge of the Company. Words and Paper alone can never diſcharge a Debt without any Payment. Hob. 68, *Lovelace & ux.* vs. *Cocket.* Mod. Caſes in Law and Equity, (1) 290, *Springet* vs. *Chadwick.* 1 Salk. 124, *Clark* vs. *Mundal.* A Contract remains in full Force till diſcharged, and blank Paper will not diſcharge it; they have given us no more. Nothing but a Satisfaction can diſcharge; not even a Bond, by different Parties (ſays Lord Hobart), ſhall diſcharge

(1) 8 Mod.

1765.
PATESHALL
v.
APTHORP.

charge without Payment. And ſhall this Note diſcharge without Payment? Never! and why? "It is no Satisfaction *actual and preſent, as it ought to be.*" Hob. *ub. ſupra.**

Mr. Gridley & Mr. Fitch offered ſome Evidence to induce the Jury to think this was not a Partnerſhip Affair, and therefore Wheelwright could not make Apthorp chargeable. Upon the main Point, Mr. Gridley ſaid:

Mr. Gridley. The grand Queſtion is, whether Apthorp ſtands indebted to Pateſhall, according to the Settlement here produced. This is an *Inſimul Computaſſent*, a particular Mode of Action. You muſt prove as you declare, or you muſt fail, as in the Caſe of a Bond.

This is an Agreement of the Parties, in which Pateſhall has balanced the Account. The Agreement of the Parties muſt be taken altogether. — No dividing — No, ſays the Law — no Partition of what a Man ſays. What does Wheelwright here ſay? Why, that he and Apthorp owed. — Yes: but in the ſame Breath he ſays that he has paid Pateſhall. There it ends. A Settlement is one undivided, indiſſoluble Thing; and the Law ſays, if you ground yourſelf upon it, you ſhall take it altogether, or diſcard it altogether. — But let us ſee the Law.

Their firſt Authority is of a Bond; nothing to the Purpoſe. But one Note may diſcharge another; as

* *Qu.* If 2 L'd Raym'd, 928, &c., would not have been pertinent.

1765.
Pateshall
v.
Apthorp.

as where the Note is of later Date. The Cuſtom of the Place muſt always be regarded; and it has ever been here held, however it may have been in England, that one Note would diſcharge another. It is every Day's conſtant Practice, to ſettle Accounts and give Notes in Diſcharge. And I appeal to you, Gentlemen of the Country, what Confuſion would overwhelm us, if all Settlements ſhould be thus wiped away, and made of no Value. What is Law? What is the whole Common Law? It is the General Uſage. No Common Law found written, but handed down; and there is a Cuſtomary Law; and you, Gentlemen, know what has been the uninterrupted, unvarying Cuſtom of this Country.

The Settlement is what it is; and you cannot vary from it; if you do, you make it what it is not. The Conceſſion on one Side is, that Apthorp and Wheelwright are indebted; but the Conceſſion on the other Side is, that it is paid by Wheelwright's Note. One Note may balance another, and ſurely then it may balance an Account. 6 Mod. 36.

The Sum of what is ſaid is, that 'tis a Settlement. You muſt ſettle it as it is ſettled, or 'tis your Settlement — not ours. 'Tis like a Law, or a Will — you cannot alter or change it. You muſt take it as you find it. 'Tis as much a Conceſſion in the Plaintiff, that the Note balanced the Account, as it was in Wheelwright, that the Balance was owing from the Company. Wheelwright ſaid, there was a Debt due. Pateſhall ſaid, Wheelwright had paid it.

Oliver,

1765.
PATESHALL v. APTHORP.

Oliver, Juſtice. There are two Points. As to the firſt, it is pretty plain from the Evidence that Wheelwright and Apthorp were in Partnerſhip. The only Queſtion then is, if this Note was a Payment of the Company's Debt. I can't but think, as the Law ſtands, the Note was no Diſcharge of the Company.

Juſtice Cuſhing. I agree with my Brother Oliver in the firſt Point, but as to the chief Point, the Authorities produced don't ſeem to come up to the preſent Queſtion. Equity ſeems in Favour of the Plaintiff; and I don't know that the Law is againſt him.

Juſtice Lynde. There is Evidence under Wheelwright's own Hand, that this Matter was in Company; but there is a greater Difficulty on the other Point. The Plaintiff acknowledges, by relying on this Settlement, that he received the Note, in full Satisfaction. A new Agreement is entered into; for he diſcharges the Company and takes Wheelwright for his Security.

One can't very well account for the Caſe in Hobart. It is quite extraordinary, that a Man ſhould give a new Bond, and not take up the old. When Securities are changed, it ſeems to me that the old muſt be diſcharged.

Ch. Juſtice. The firſt Queſtion I take to be, Partnerſhip, or not. If one Partner receives Money, and carries it to the Company Account, clear Evidence that the Money was received in Partnerſhip.

 The

1765. PATESHALL *v.* APTHORP.

The ſecond Queſtion is, whether the Note given by Wheelwright diſcharged the Company. Had the Note been from Wheelwright and Apthorp, I ſhould have had more Doubt. The Plaintiff here gives Credit for Note of Wheelwright's. Now, whether the Contract with the Company can be ſuppoſed to continue, after Wheelwright had taken the Company's Debt upon himſelf, and Pateſhall had received the Note as a Balance of the Company Account, I doubt.*

The Jury found for the Plaintiff.

APTHORP *v.* PATESHALL. Rec. 1766. Fol. 9.

Afterwards, a Writ of Review being brought, the Cauſe was again argued, before the Chief Juſtice, Juſtice Lynde and Juſtice Ruſſell.

Juſtice Ruſſell was full with the original Plaintiff.

Lynde, Juſtice continued ſtrongly of his former Opinion; and was ſtrenuouſly in Favour of the Plaintiff in Review.

The Doubts of *the Chief Juſtice* were, on this Tryal, removed, and he ſaid that, from the Authorities, it was very clear, that the Note was no Diſcharge of the Company.† (2)

The

* Vid. Cun. L. Dict'y Tit. *Acceptance.*

† *Qu.* if theſe Authorities would not have been pertinent to the Point in Queſtion: 3 Cro. 85, 86. 2 Cro. 650. 1 Mod. Rep. 221, 225. 3 Lev. 55. 1 Brown. 47.

(2) The oppoſite doctrine has long been eſtabliſhed, both in this country and England. See Story on Partn. § 155 and note. *Arnold* v, *Camp*, 12 Johns. 409. *French* v. *Price*, 24 Pick. 23.

The Jury was of the ſame Opinion with the Jury upon the laſt Tryal.

Judgment being entered, Mr. Gridley moved for an Appeal Home, which, not being oppoſed, was granted.

Dunn *verſ.* Scollay. (1)

Caſe of Hoſtage & Ranſom.

DUNN v. SCOLLAY.
Rec. 1766. Fol. 10.

AUTHORITIES in Favour of the Plaintiff were, Molloy (old Edit.) 205, § 10, 212, § 14, 213, § 14; Molloy (new Edit. 1744) 358, 237–8,

(1) This action was firſt brought in the Court of Vice Admiralty, to which Court a prohibition was iſſued and confirmed, on argument, by the Superior Court. See *ante*, p. 74. The plaintiff then brought his action in the Court of Common Pleas, and recovered judgment for £700; from which judgment the defendants appealed to this Court. From the various papers on file, it appears that the caſe was as follows:

The Brigantine Peggy, belonging to John Scollay of Boſton, conſigned to Wm. Sitwell, London, was, on the 26th October, 1756, taken at ſea by the French privateer Entreprenante, then returning from trading in negroes on the coaſt of Guinea. The captain of the Peggy drew a ranſom bill on the conſignee, and ſent Dunn, the firſt mate, with the French captain as a hoſtage. The Peggy proceeded on her voyage, but again fell into the hands of the enemy, and was taken into Bourdeaux, where the captain died in priſon. Dunn in the meanwhile had been committed to the priſon of Bouffay at Nantz, where he remained in a ſick and deſtitute condition. Sitwell claimed that the underwriters ſhould pay the ranſom money for his diſcharge, but, as they refuſed, he wrote

1765. Dunn v. Scollay.

237–8, 244–5; 2 Ld. Raymond, 931; Ld. Holt's Opinion relied on; Sea Laws, 128.

In Favour of the Defendant were, 2 Chancery Caſes, 239; 1 Salk. 35; 3 Bacon, 592, 595. (2)

---

wrote to Dunn, that there was "no Way to compell them without Law, and that would be attended with great Uncertainty, as this, they ſay, is a Caſe has not been try'd" — and alſo that he was inſtructed by Scollay to ſettle without regard to the ranſom bill. He did, however, allow Dunn 1s. per day for his ſupport in priſon. In a letter from Scollay to Sitwell, after the former had heard of the firſt capture and ranſom, he claimed that, as he had given the captain no orders to ranſom the veſſel, if taken, the money muſt be paid either by the inſurers or the captain; but, as the latter might not be able to do ſo, if the ſhip were loſt, he directed Sitwell to inſure for Dunn's benefit the amount of the ranſom money on the veſſel and cargo, offering to be reſponſible himſelf for the premium. Before this letter was received, it is probable that news arrived of the ſecond capture. Dunn remained in priſon ſix years, and his final liberation is thus deſcribed in a letter from Sitwell:

"Jno. Dunn, y[t] was Freeman's Mate, has at length obtained his "Diſcharge. His Friends compounded y[e] Affair for about £200, and "have ſent about a Subſcription to raiſe y[e] Money. — I thought the "Affair would have ended here, but his Friends are of Opinion "y[t] y[e] Owners are liable to make good all Damages, & have adviſed "him to go over & endeavour to recover it. They have taken y[e] Opin-"ion of ſome of y[e] beſt Counſel here, w[ch] are in his Favour. — How "your Courts may determine this Affair, if it ſhould come to Tryal, I "know not."

From the authorities cited, it would ſeem probable that the caſe turned upon the queſtion of the maſter's power to bind the owner by a contract of ranſom, without ſpecial orders to that effect; and, that the ruling of the Court was againſt the plaintiff, ſeems probable from the verdict, which was for the appellant, reverſion of the former judgment and coſts.

(2) This liſt of authorities was at firſt ſuppoſed to refer to the former caſe, and was accordingly printed in a note to page 83.

1765.

NORWOOD v. FAIRSERVICE.

Norwood *verſ.* Fairſervice.

Rec. 1765. Fol. 238.

Whether an alleged Alteration in a Deed was made before or after its Execution, is a Queſtion of Fact for the Jury.

In Debt for Rent upon an Indenture, the Defendant may, under the Plea of *Non dimiſit*, give in Evidence the Counterpart of the Indenture which reſerves a different Rent.

NORWOOD brought his Action againſt Fairſervice on an Indenture, for that Fairſervice covenanted to pay £13., 6., 8. *per Quarter* for Rent of a Sand-Bank, and had not paid, &c. Defendant pleads, *Non dimiſit.* The Plaintiff produces in Evidence, to ſupport his Demand, one Part of the Indenture ſigned by the Defendant, wherein the Demiſe is acknowledged, and Payment of the above Sum per Quarter is covenanted.

Mr. Auchmuty, for the Defendant, offered to give in Evidence to defeat the Demand, the other Part of the Indenture, ſigned by Norwood, wherein he demiſes as aforeſaid, for the ſame Sum per Year.

Mr. Fitch, for Plaintiff, then ſuggeſted a Fraud in the Defendant, from whence this Difference aroſe, and prayed Judgment, whether this Indenture produced by Defendant ſhould go in Evidence to the Jury.

Mr. Auchmuty. I take it, the Gentleman is too early in his Objection; for Fraud or no Fraud ſhall be try'd by the Jury, and not by the Court. It is a plain Matter of Fact, of which the Jury are the ſole Judges. Beſides, of what Advantage will it be for the Court to determine this Matter? The Jury, after all, will determine whether this Variance was made before, or ſince the Execution of this Deed; and will give what Credit they pleaſe to it; ſo

1765. NORWOOD *v.* FAIRSERVICE.

ſo that for this Court to paſs their Judgment will avail Nothing. Neither do I think the Court have any Right to determine this Matter; for 'twill be abridging the Priviledges of the Subject, to settle a Point which wholly lies with the Jury to determine.

In Anſwer to which, it was urged by *Meſſrs. Gridley & Fitch*, that it had always been the Cuſtom of this Court to determine in ſuch Caſes. To which the Court agreed; and *Juſtice Lynde* said that he knew a ſimilar Caſe of one *Lanſon's*, in Middleſex: But the Chief Juſtice anſwered, that he had always doubted in thoſe Caſes, but whenever they aroſe, the Court always affirmed the conſtant Practice, and ſo he was ſilent.

'Twas then further urged by the Plaintiff's Council, that this Practice was well founded, and the Reaſon of it was this, that Nothing ſhould go to a Jury which would only tend to deceive and inveigle them; and that therefore when a Piece of Evidence was offered, on the Face of which Fraud appeared, the Court rejected the Evidence, as 'twould only tend to miſlead. And, as to what Mr. Auchmuty had ſaid, that the Court's Opinion would be of no Effect, 'twas anſwered, that, if the Court, upon Inſpection, were of Opinion that the Indenture had been fraudulently altered, it was then not Norwood's Deed — therefore no Evidence. For Courts will never admit that to go in as Evidence, which, *prima Facie*, they judge a Fraud; and the Jury can't judge of that which is not admitted to go to them.

Juſt.

1765.
NORWOOD *v.* FAIRSERVICE.

Juſt. Oliver. This properly belongs to the Jury. I am for admitting it to go in.

Juſt. Cuſhing. The Jury is ſole Judge of this; they muſt give what Credit they pleaſe.

Juſtice Lynde. As the Practice of this Court has always been otherwiſe, I am for viewing it.

Ch. Juſtice. I know the Cuſtom has been otherwiſe, but, for my Part, I think 'tis Time it was altered — am for admitting it. (1)

Another Objection was then made on Behalf of the Plaintiff, againſt this Counterpart of the Indenture being Evidence: For that the Indenture declared on was the Defendant's Deed — had been produced, and, by being admitted, the Defendant was eſtopped to ſay the contrary; that, if the Counterpart produced by the Defendant ſhould be admitted, it would prove Nothing againſt his own Deed.

Mr. Auchmuty. It has been ſaid, we have admitted the Indenture produced was our Deed. So far from admitting Anything, we have denied their whole Declaration; for we have pleaded, *Non dimiſit.* We could not poſſibly have been farther from admitting this Deed than by pleading as we have done.* Beſides, our Part and theirs make but one Inſtrument;

* *Sed vid.* 4 Bac. Abr. 84.

(1) See *Ely* v. *Ely*, 6 Gray, 442; 1 Smith's Lead. Cas. (Hare & Wallace's notes) 961, 2.

1765. NORWOOD v. FAIRSERVICE.

Inftrument; for in all the Books 'tis, *Hæc Indentura*. They have declared on a certain Indenture, made between the Plaintiff and Defendant, which is not complete without our Part, for they have produced only one Part, and the other lays with us to produce.

Mr. Gridley. We have declared, that, by one Part thereof, figned by the Defendant, he, in Confideration that we had demifed, &c., he covenanted, &c. He has pleaded, *Non dimifit*. To prove our Allegation, we have produced his Deed; and he is eftopped to fay the contrary, and offer in Evidence an Inftrument that he fays was figned by us. — What can it prove? That we did not demife? That is the Iffue. And here is his Deed in which he acknowledges that we did demife, and that he covenanted as we have declared. 'Tis abfurd to offer this Paper to defeat his own Deed. It can't be done.

Oliver, Juft. I think it can't be admitted.

Cufhing, Juft. He is eftopped, I think.

Lynde, Juft. I am very far from being fo clear in it.

N. B. No Authorities were produced, and the Council on each Side acknowledged the Points were unexpectedly ftarted.

The Chief Juftice, who had been abfent the whole Argument of this laft Objection, came into Court foon ſoon after this laſt Determination; upon which *Mr. Auchmuty* moved for his Opinion: But *Mr. Gridley* objected, his Honour not having heard the Argument, and the *Ch. Juſtice* ſaid, he the rather declined giving his Opinion, as there was but 4 Judges preſent; and two being againſt admitting it, his Opinion would avail Nothing. But, on the State of the Caſe by his Brethren, he ſeemed inclined to admit the Counterpart of the Indenture to go in as Evidence.

1765. NORWOOD *v.* FAIRSERVICE.

Mr. Auchmuty then ordered a Review to be minuted, and ſaid, if he was wrong now, he never was right in his Life.

At the next Trial, which I did not hear, *the Court* admitted the Counterpart of the Indenture to go in, as Mr. Auchmuty informed me. (2)

FAIRSERVICE *v.* NORWOOD. Rec. 1766. Fol. 7.

Pond *verſ.* Medway. (1)

(*About an Highway.*)

POND *v.* MEDWAY. Rec. 1765. Fol. 232.

On the Return of a Certiorari no Evidence is admiſſible dehors the Record.

RULED, on Argument, unanimouſly by all the 5 Judges, — That, on a Certiorari, no Evidence ſhould be admitted, but what came up in the

(2) The firſt judgment was reverſed on the review.

(1) In the MS. this caſe is entitled *Wrentham & Medway*. The petitioners were "John Pond of Wrentham and others."

1765.

POND v. MEDWAY.

the Case: (2) And the Council was not admitted to mention any Facts, but what appeared from the Record.

The Reason assigned by the Court was, that it would be Injustice to the Sessions to judge on Matters which from the Record returned, did not appear to have been before them.

Watts *vers.* Hasey.

WATTS v. HASEY.

Rec. 1765. Fol. 244.

In an appealed Action upon a Mortgage, Judgment for the Mortgagee is conditional, reserving two Months, according to Prov. St. 10 W. 3, although the Case was defaulted in the Inferiour Court, and two Months have elapsed since the Judgment appealed from.

WATTS sued Hasey upon a Mortgage, and Hasey was defaulted at the lower Court, but appealed. Judgment was entered up in the Inferiour Court, agreeable to the Province Law, 10 Wm. 3, (1) reserving two Months.

Mr. Kent now brought a Complaint, praying that, as the two Months had already been allowed, Execution might issue in twenty-four Hours after Judgment. He urged, that in the Province Law the Words were, "in all Cases *brought for Tryal* in the Superiour Court," &c. Now, he said, this Action was not brought for Tryal; for it was defaulted in the Court below, and therefore could not be try'd now. Besides, if Execution did not issue till

---

(2) S. P. *Rutland* v. *Worcester*, 20 Pick. 78. *Per Curiam*, "When the record is before the Court upon the return of the writ, the Court will look only at the record." See 10 Met. 219.

(1) Anc. Chart. 324.

1765.

WATTS *v.* HASEY.

till the Expiration of two Months, the Stamp-Act would take Place, and then Execution could not be had at all. Moreover, as the Equity of the Law had been satisfy'd, he prayed that Custom might not bar him, which had prevailed, because never before asked to be altered, and never before a like Reason for granting such a Request.

The Justices, Oliver, Russell, Cushing & Lynde said, the Usage had been uninterrupted, and the Construction of the Law thereby established; therefore they would make no Innovation.

Ch. Justice. All Cases brought to this Court are certainly brought for Tryal, let them come up how they will. *Nolumus mutare Leges Angliæ.*

Tyler *vers.* Richards, Administrator.

TYLER *v.* RICHARDS.

Rec. 1765. Fol. 243.

Indebitatus Assumpsit for Boarding and Schooling Defendant's Son, is not supported by Proof of a

INDEBITATUS ASSUMPSIT, for Boarding and Schooling Intestate's Son. Proof that the Intestate promised *to pay honourably.*

Mr. Auchmuty. This Action will not lye; they ought to have brought a *Quantum Meruit.* Law of Evid. 190.

Messrs. S. Quincy & Adams. It has always been the

1765.
TYLER
v.
RICHARDS.

Promiſe "to pay honourably."

the Cuſtom of this Court, to allow an *Indebitatus Aſſumpſit* to lye, if the Services alledged were proved to have been done. As every Man is ſuppoſed to aſſume to pay the cuſtomary Price. Aſſumpſit is always brought for Work done by Tradeſmen, and is always allowed. The Price for Boarding and Schooling is as much ſettled in the Country, as it is in the Town for a Yard of Cloth, or a Day's Work by a Carpenter.

Mr. Auchmuty. It is high Time ſome Rule was ſettled by this Court in Relation to theſe Actions; For if a *Quantum Meruit* is not neceſſary here, 'tis neceſſary in no Caſe. The Practice has always been varying, the Court ſometimes denying, and ſometimes allowing ſuch Proof, to ſupport theſe Actions. But had *Indebitatus Aſſumpſit* been brought for a Yard of Cloth, and the Evidence had been a Promiſe to pay *honourably*, I'm ſure 'twould have defeated the Action. My Lord Gilbert ſays, "Courts muſt go according to the *Allegata et Probata.*" Now, what is alledged here? That my Client promiſed to pay abſolutely ſo much. What is the Proof? That he promiſed to pay *honourably*. If this Proof is admitted, there will be an End of any Diſtinction between *Indebitatus Aſſumpſit* and a *Quantum meruit.*

The whole Court, abſente Ruſſell, were unanimous that this Evidence would not ſupport the Declaration; on which the Plaintiffs diſcontinued, paying Coſts.*

* *Sed vid.* the cauſe of *Pyncheon* vs. *Brewſter*, poſt.

At the Cloſe of this Term, the Chief Juſtice thus addreſſed himſelf to the Bar.

GENTLEMEN of the Bar: I cannot but with Pleaſure obſerve to you the Harmony which has ſubſiſted between all of you in our preſent Seſſion, and that Unanimity and Order which has prevailed univerſally amongſt us through this whole Term. I the rather obſerve this, becauſe, in moſt Parts of the Province there has been great Diſturbances. I thought this Notice juſtly due, and cannot but hope 'twill ſerve as a future Precedent to us all, and a good Example to the Community.

ADDRESS BY THE CHIEF JUSTICE.

N. B. Through this Term James Otis, Jr., Esq., was abſent at the CONGRESS, held in New York, relative to the Stamp-Act, which was to take Place the firſt of November next.

1765.

THE SUPERIOUR COURTS, in their feveral Circuits, having, for the Want of Stamp-Papers, done no Bufinefs, except barely opening the Court, and continuing all Matters over to the next Term, ever fince the Stamp-Act was to have taken Place in the Colonies; —

The Town of Bofton, at a Meeting on December the 18th, 1765, voted, that the following Memorial be prefented to his Excellency the Governour, *in Council*. And that Jeremy Gridley, James Otis, Jr., and John Adams, Efqrs., be applied to as Council to appear in Behalf of the Town in Support of the faid Memorial.

MEMORIAL OF THE TOWN OF BOSTON.

Town Rec. 1765. Fol. 669.

PROVINCE OF THE MASSACHUSETTS BAY.

To his Excellency the Governour *in Council*.
The Memorial of the Town of Bofton.

Humbly fhews, —

THAT your Memorialifts, having a juft Senfe of the Value of the Britifh Conftitution of Government, under which they have enjoyed all the

1765.
MEMORIAL OF BOSTON.

the Bleſſings of civil Life, cannot but be deeply affected, when the Channels through which theſe Bleſſings are derived to us are obſtructed; which, at Preſent, is our unhappy Caſe. The Courts of Law within the Province, in which alone Juſtice can be diſtributed among the People, ſo far as reſpects Civil Matters, are to all Intents and Purpoſes ſhut up; for which your Memorialiſts apprehend no juſt and legal Reaſon can be aſſigned.

We have always underſtood, that the Law is the great Rule of Right, the Security of our Lives and Property, and the Beſt Birthright of Engliſhmen.

Under theſe Apprehenſions, we make our humble Application to your Excellency in Council, with whom the Executive Power within the Province is conſtitutionally lodged, that you would be pleaſed to give ſuch Directions, to the ſeveral Courts and their Officers, as that, under no Pretence whatever, we may be any longer deprived of this invaluable Bleſſing. And your Memorialiſts pray that they may be heard upon this moſt important Subject by their Council learned in Law.

And, as in Duty bound, they ever pray, &c.

Atteſt, W. C., Town Clerk.

1765.
Memorial of Boston.

Council Chamber.

Prefent:

His Excellency
Francis Bernard, Efqr., Governour, &c.,
in Council.

MR. ADAMS. Innumerable are the Calamities which flow from an Interruption of Juftice. Neceffity requires that the Doors of Juftice fhould ever be open to hear the Complaints of the Injured and Oppreffed.

The Stamp-Act, I take it, is utterly void, and of no binding Force upon us; for it is againft our Rights as Men, and our Priviledges as Englifhmen. An Act made in Defiance of the firft Principles of Juftice; an Act which rips up the Foundation of the Britifh Conftitution, and makes void Maxims of 1800 Years ftanding.

Parliaments may err; they are not infallible; they have been refufed to be fubmitted to. An Act making the King's Proclamation to be Law, the Executive Power adjudged abfolutely void.

The

The Stamp-Act was made where we are in no Senfe reprefented, therefore no more binding upon us, than an Act which fhould oblige us to deftroy One Half of our Species. 1765. MEMORIAL OF BOSTON.

There are certain Principles fixed unalterably in Nature. Convention and Compact are the Requifites to make any Law obligatory. That the Subject is not bound by Acts, when he is not reprefented, is a found Maxim of the Law, and not peculiar to the Britifh Conftitution, but a Maxim of the antient Roman Law: "What concerns All fhall be judged of by All."

The only Reafon of the Power of the Parliament in England is, becaufe they are elected by the People, who, if their Liberties are infringed, have a Check at the next Election. Have Americans any fuch Check? Have they any Voice in Deputation? A Parliament of Great Britain can have no more Right to tax the Colonies than a Parliament of Paris.

This Act has never been received from Authority, therefore in a legal Senfe we know Nothing of it.

The Neceffities of Bufinefs, the Cries of the People, call aloud for Juftice. It has become impoffible to execute this Act, therefore, if it were binding, we are excufed by every Law, human or divine, from a Compliance with it. Wood's Inft. The King's Writs are *ex debitâ Juftitiâ*, and cannot be denied the Subject. And in *Magna*

 Charta,

1765. MEMORIAL OF BOSTON.

Charta, it is ſaid, we deny no Man Juſtice, we delay no Man Juſtice. 2 Inſt. ch. 29, p. 56. (1)

Mr. Otis (opened with Tears). It is with great Grief that I appear before your Excellency and Honours on this Occaſion. A wicked and unfeeling Miniſter has cauſed a People, the moſt loyal and affectionate that ever King was bleſſed with, to groan under the moſt inſupportable Oppreſſion. But I think, Sir, that he now ſtands upon the Brink of inevitable Deſtruction; and truſt that ſoon— very ſoon, he will feel the full Weight of his injured Sovereign's righteous Indignation. I have no doubt, Sir, but that the loyal and dutiful Repreſentations* of nine Provinces, the Cries and Supplications of a diſtreſſed People, the united Voice of all of His Majeſty's moſt loyal and affectionate Britiſh-American Subjects, will obtain all that ample Redreſs they have a Right to expect; and that e'er long, they will ſee their cruel and inſidious Enemies, both at Home and abroad, put to Shame and Confuſion.

My

* Alluding to the Tranſactions at the late Congreſs.

(1) See John Adams's Diary, December 20, 1765. "I grounded my argument on the invalidity of the Stamp-Act, it not being in any ſenſe our act, having never conſented to it. But leſt that foundation ſhould not be ſufficient, on the preſent neceſſity to prevent a failure of juſtice, and the preſent impoſſibility of carrying that act into execution.

Mr. Otis reaſoned with great learning and zeal on the judges oaths, &c.

Mr. Gridley, on the great inconveniences that would enſue the interruption of juſtice." 2 John Adams's Works, 158, 9.

1765.

MEMORIAL OF BOSTON.

My Brother Adams has entered ſo largely into the Validity of the Act, that I ſhall not enlarge on that Head. Indeed, what has been obſerved is ſufficient to convince the moſt illiterate Savage that the Parliament of England had no Regard to the very firſt Principles of their own Liberties.

Only the Preamble of that oppreſſive Act is enough to rouſe the Blood of every generous Briton. — "We your Majeſty's Subjects, the Commons of Great Britain, &c., do Give and Grant" — What? Their own Property? No! The Treaſure, the Heart's Blood of all your Majeſty's dutiful and affectionate Britiſh-American Subjects.

But the Time is far ſpent — I will not tire your Patience. It was once a fundamental Maxim, that every Subject had the ſame Right to his Life, Liberty, Property and the *Law*, that the King had to his Crown; and 'tis yet, I venture to ſay, as much as a Crown is worth, to deny the Subject his *Law*, which is his Birth-right. 'Tis a firſt Principle, "that Majeſty ſhould not only ſhine in Arms, but be armed with the Laws." The *Adminiſtration* of Juſtice is neceſſary to the very Exiſtence of Governments. Nothing can warrant the ſtopping the Courſe of Juſtice, but the impoſſibility of holding Courts, by Reaſon of War, Invaſion, Rebellion or Inſurrections.* 1 Inſt. 249, a & b. This was Law at a Time when the whole Iſland of Great Britain was divided into an infinite Number of petty Baronies and Principalities; as Germany is, at this Day. Inſurrections

* Vid. Molloy *de Jure Mar.* p. 6, § 9.

1765.
MEMORIAL OF BOSTON.

Inſurrections then, and even Invaſions, put the whole Nation into ſuch Confuſion, that Juſtice could not have her equal Courſe; eſpecially as the Kings in antient Times frequently ſat as Judges. But War has now become ſo much of a Science, and gives ſo little Diſturbance to a Nation engaged, that no War, foreign or domeſtic, is a ſufficient Reaſon for ſhutting up the Courts. But, if it were, we are not in ſuch a State, but far otherwiſe; the whole People being willing and demanding the full Adminiſtration of Government. Vid. Bracton, 240.

The ſhutting up of the Courts is an Abdication, a total Diſſolution of Government. Pollexfen's Argument at the Revolution Conference, Rapin's Hiſtory, 790. Jones, 773, 774. Whoever takes from the King his executive Power, takes from the King his Kingſhip. Vid. the Speeches of Holt, Somers, Nottingham and other Lords. Rapin, 790. Vid. Bracton, 107.

"The Laws which forbid a Man to purſue his Right one Way, ought to be underſtood with this equitable Reſtriction, *that one finds Judges to whom he may apply*. When there are no Courts of Law to appeal to, it is then we muſt have Recourſe to the Law of Nature," &c.* Hugo Grotius, *de Jure B. & P.* Lib. 1, C. 3, § 2. Lib. 2, C. 4, § 9. C. 7, § 2, n. 2. C. 20, § 2, p. 4 & 5, with Mr. Barbeyrac's Notes. Code, Lib. 1, Tit. 9, *De Jud. & Cœl.*

I

* Vid. Molloy *De Jure Mar.* ch. 2, § 5.

1765. MEMORIAL OF BOSTON.

I can't but obſerve that cruel and unheard of Neglect of that Enemy to his King and Country, the Author of this Act, that, when all Buſineſs, the very Life and Being of a commercial State, was to be carried on by the Uſe of Stamps, that wicked and execrable Miniſter never paid the leaſt Regard to the Miſeries of this extenſive Continent, but suffered the Time for the taking Place of the Act to elapſe, Months before a ſingle Stamp was received. Though this was a high Piece of Infidelity to the Intereſt of his royal Maſter, yet it makes it evident that it could never be intended, that if Stamps were not to be had, it ſhould put a Stop to all Juſtice; which is *ipſo Facto* a Diſſolution of Society.

It is a ſtrange Kind of Law, which we hear advanced now-a-days, that, becauſe one unpopular Act can't be carried into Execution, that therefore there ſhall be an End of all Law. We are not the firſt People who have riſen to prevent the Execution of a Law; the very People of England themſelves roſe in Oppoſition to the famous Jew-Bill, and got that immediately repealed. And Lawyers know that there are Limits, beyond which if Parliaments go, their Acts bind not. 4 Inſt. 122.

The King is always preſumed to be preſent in his Courts, holding out the Law to his Subjects; and when he ſhuts his Courts, he unkings himſelf in the moſt eſſential Point. 18 E. 3, ch. 1. 1 H. 4. 20 E. 3, ch. 2. 4 H. 4, ch. 1. Vattel, p. 20. And Magna Charta, and the other Statutes are full, "That they will not defer, delay or deny to any Man Juſtice or Right." "That it ſhall not be commanded

1765. MEMORIAL OF BOSTON.

commanded by the Great Seal, or *in any other Way* to diſturb or delay Common Right." The Judges of England are "not to counſel, or aſſent to any Thing which may turn to the Damage or Diſheriſon of the Crown." They are ſworn not to deny to any Man Common Right, by the King's Letters, nor none other Man's, *nor for none other Cauſe.* Is not the Diſſolution of Society a Disheriſon of the Crown? The "Juſtices are commanded, that they ſhall do even Law and Execution of Right to all our Subjects, rich and poor, without having Regard to any Perſon, without letting to do Right for any Letters or Commandment which may come to them from Us, or from any other, or by any other Cauſe." 4 Inſt. 70. (2)

His Excellency the Governour. The Arguments made Uſe of, both by Mr. Adams and you, would be very pertinent to induce the Judges of the Superiour Court to think the Act of no Validity, and that therefore they ſhould pay no Regard to it; but the Queſtion with me is, whether that very Thing don't argue the Impropriety of our Intermeddling in a Matter which ſolely belongs to them to judge of in their Judicial Department. And can it be proper for us to command them to act in any particular Way, relative to a Matter which is to come before them in their Judicial Capacity? eſpecially, as from ſome of the very Authorities you have cited, it appears, that the Judges are to obey no Mandate, come it from whomſoever it will.

Mr.

(2) See Boſton Gazette, December 30, 1765, January 6, 1766. 2 John Adams's Works, 174.

1765. MEMORIAL OF BOSTON.

Mr. Otis. Thoſe Mandates ſpoken of in the Authorities, are ſuch as are made to *delay Juſtice*, and command the Judges *not to proceed.* That very Thing, I take it, ſhews that Juſtice is never to be ſtopped, but that the Law ſhall always have its own Courſe. And ſurely your Excellency muſt ſee a great Difference between a Command in Delay of Juſtice, and one made in its Furtherance. There is certainly a very wide Diſtinction to be made, between ſaying, Juſtice ſhall ſtop, and a Command or Recommendation to the Judges, to proceed in the ſeveral Courts of Judicature, according to the Laws and Cuſtoms of the Country.*

Mr. Gridley. The Queſtion now before your Excellency and Honours, is of great Conſequence, of very great Weight. The Safety of the whole People, the Preſervation of all Government is in Iſſue. All Laws are divided into public and private, criminal and civil. The Criminal Law is as free as ever; for the Act excepts Criminal Matters.

The Benignity of the Law ſays, if the Intention of the Party cannot operate one Way, it ſhall another. 'Tis ſo in all private Tranſactions:— How much more ſo in Things of a publick Nature! Though the criminal Law is free, yet there is ſuch an intimate Connection between this and private Law, that the one cannot ſubſiſt without the other. Deprive me of the one, and 'tis worſe

* *Qu.* if Foſter's Crown Law, 269, might not have been argued upon by way of Analogy.

1765. MEMORIAL OF BOSTON.

worſe than if you deprived me of both. My Property is invaded, but the Invader is no Criminal. Where then is my Remedy? He, who deprives me of my Remedy, deprives me of my Right. What ſhall be done? To ſhut up the Courts is a Renuntiation of Government. What! ſhall I live in a Society, and yet have no Redreſs of my Wrongs? Shall I have no Remedy againſt him who has broken his moſt ſolemn Contracts and Engagements? Shall I bear the Inſults of Inſolence, and have no Recompence for my Damage and Sufferings as a private Individual? I have an Eſtate, but I have no Security. — Purſue the Thought, and it is dreadfull. Hunger will break through a Stone Wall. Diſputes, Animoſities, Wrangles, Diſaffections, Hatreds, Heart-burnings, Tumults, Confuſions, — 'tis eaſy for the Imagination to trace the infinite Miſeries which ruſh in upon us like an Inundation; — no Need to purſue it further.

What was the Law inſtituted for? For the Protection of my Perſon and Eſtate. Government is ſubverted if the Law is not open. 'Tis abſurd to ſuppoſe that Society can take away from me my Right of Self-preſervation as a Man, and not protect my Property as a Citizen. The People muſt return to a State of Nature. And I had much rather be a Barbarian of the Woods, than live in a State once under Government, but now reduced to Anarchy and Confuſion. The Knowledge obtained in Society has only fitted them to execute their Perpetrations with more Dexterity, and rendered their Plots the more terrible.

But

1765. MEMORIAL OF BOSTON.

But let me put the Caſe, that all the Stamp-Papers had been deſtroyed by Tempeſt, or ſome other Caſualty: The Courts in ſuch a Caſe muſt have proceeded. There is now as much an Impoſſibility to uſe thoſe Papers, as though they were all in the Bottom of the Ocean.

There is not a Syllable in the Act which has the leaſt Aſpect, that Courts ſhould ſtop, if Stamps were not to be obtained. A Mulct is the Puniſhment for Non-uſer, — which ſhows that if a Perſon will ſubmit to that, the End of the Act is complied with: But Impoſſibility in ſuch Caſe would aſſuredly excuſe: That the Law never requires Impoſſibilities is a Maxim of the Law.

Neceſſity demands Juſtice ſhould have its Courſe. It is no Laches, no Default of ours, that the Act cannot be put in Force. The Innocent ſhall never be involved in the ſame Fate with the Guilty if it can be avoided. It is not in the Power of any one to obtain a Stamp-Paper. A Thing that is impoſſible is as though it were not. He who is a Citizen ſhall never be denied his Law.* (3)

* *Qu.* If Locke on Government, ch. 19, § 219, would not have been pertinent to the Queſtion.

Qu. If the Authority from the Year-Book, 19 H. 6, p. 63, would not have been pertinent in the preceding Debate. — "The Law is the greateſt Inheritance the King has, for by the Law *He Himſelf*, and all his Subjects are governed; and if there was *no Law*, there would be *no King*, nor Inheritance.

---

(3) The reſult of theſe arguments and the action taken by the Council in the premiſes will appear from the following record of a Town Meeting held on the 21ſt of December, 1765. Town Records, 1765, Fol. 670:

" 3 o'clock P. M. Met according to Adjournment.

 " Mr.

1765.

MEMORIAL OF BOSTON.

" Mr. Adams again Reported — That the Honourable the Council " had come into ſome Reſolves relative to the Memorial of the Town " to His Excellency in Council, a Copy of which had been handed him " by the Deputy Secretary, which Reſolves being read, it was Voted " that the ſame be entreed upon the Town Records — and they are as " follows — vizt —

" ' At a Council held at the Council
" ' Chamber in Boſton upon Sattur-
" ' day the 21st Day of Decem^r.
" ' 1765,

" ' The Board proceeded to the Conſideration of the Memorial of the " ' Town of Boſton, and came to the following Reſolves, vizt. —

" ' That a Queſtion in Law neceſſarily ariſes from ſaid Memorial, " ' namely, Whether the Officers of the Courts of Law can be juſtified in " ' proceeding in their reſpective Offices with unſtamp'd Papers, and it is " ' thereupon — Reſolved that it is the Buſineſs of the Courts of Law to " ' determine Points of Law, nor can the Board with any Propriety direct " ' or adviſe the ſaid Courts in ſuch Judgements or determinations, and " ' in this particular point of Law under the preſent ſtate of the Province " ' the Board are deſirous that the ſaid Courts ſhould be free in their " ' Judgments, without any apprehenſion of cenſure from the Board. It " ' is therefore further —

" ' Reſolved, that the Subject-Matter of this Memorial is not proper " ' for the determination of this Board, nor is it in the power of the Board " ' to afford relief in the way and manner pray'd for, but the Board rec- " ' ommend it to the Juſtices of the Inferior Court of Common Pleas for " ' the County of Suffolk to determine the aforeſaid Point of Law as ſoon " ' as may be, and to the other Courts within the Province to determine it " ' at or before their reſpective Terms.

" ' A true Copy. Att. JN^O. COTTON, D Sec^ry.'

" Upon a Motion made and ſeconded — the Queſtion was put. " Viz^t. — Whether the Town apprehend the above Reſolves *of Council* " in conſequence of their Memorial to *His Excellency* in Council to be " ſatisfactory — Paſſed in the Negative unanimouſly."

" Adjourned to Thurſday next 10 o'clock A.M.

" Thurſday December 26th, 1765. Met according to Adjourn^t.

" The Town being acquainted by ſeveral Gentlemen preſent, that " the Courts of Probate within this Province would be opened; that the " Sheriff of the County of Suffolk had ſerved, and was ready to ſerve all " Writts brought to him, and that the Court of Common Pleas for ſaid " County next in courſe to ſit, would meet & proceed to Buſineſs; and " that Mr. Sheriff Greenleaff, and Mr. William Mollineux could give " the Town further ſatisfaction relative to theſe particulars —

" It was therefore Voted, that Mr. Sheriff and Mr. Mollineux be " deſired to inform the Town reſpecting theſe Matters — Mr. Sheriff accordingly

"accordingly declared that he had duly ſerved all the Writts which had "been given him for Service to this Day — and Mr. Mollineux that "having diſcourſed the Judges of the Inferior Court, he had no reaſon "to doubt but that the aforeſaid Court would at their next Term pro-"ceed to Buſineſs as uſual.

"Upon a Motion made and ſeconded — Voted that when this Meet-"ing be adjourned, it ſhall be to Thurſday the 16th Day of January "next.

"Thurſday the 16th of January 1766. Met according to Adjourn-"ment.

"Whereas the Inferior Court of Common Pleas for the County, "together with the Court of Probate, is now open, and Buſineſs going "on as uſual — Voted unanimouſly that the Repreſentatives of the Town "be and hereby are Inſtructed to uſe their utmoſt endeavours with the "General Aſſembly at the preſent Seſſion, that Meaſures may be taken "that Juſtice be alſo duly Adminiſtred in all the Countys throughout "the Province, and that enquiry may be made into the Reaſons why "the Courts of Juſtice in the Province has been in any Meaſure "obſtructed.

"It is further Voted unanimouſly that the Repreſentatives be alſo "Inſtructed to uſe their Influence in the General Aſſembly that proper "enquiry may be made into the behavior of any Perſon, or Perſons, "who by their miſconduct have either contributed toward the Difficul-"tys we labour under reſpecting the Stamp Act, or have baſely neglected "to uſe their upright and beſt endeavors to relieve us from those Diffi-"cultys.

"Voted that the Thanks of the Town be, and hereby are given to "the Honourable James Otis, Eſq., the Moderator of this Meeting, for "diſpatching the Buſineſs thereof.

"Then the Meeting was diſſolved."

Governor Bernard thus deſcribes theſe occurrences in a letter to the Lords of Trade, dated January 18, 1766, for a copy of which with others we are indebted to the kindneſs of Hon. George Bancroft:

Gov. Bernard to Lords of Trade, Jan'y 18, 1766.

——"They next began with the Courts of Juſtice, & for that pur-"poſe preſented a Memorial to the Governor and Council. This "Memorial was conſidered in a full Council of 15; & the prayer of it, "that the Governor & Council would give orders that the Courts "ſhould be opened, was unanimouſly rejected. This reſolution of the "Council was reported at a Town Meeting the ſame day & unani-"mouſly voted unſatisfactory. Neverthelesſ means were found that the "Courts of this County ſhould be opened; the Judges as I ſuppoſe, ſub-mitting

1766. MEMORIAL OF BOSTON.

"mitting to the despotism of the people. It was then hoped that all "things would be quiet; but no such thing: it was then insisted in this "Town they should not be satisfied with their own Courts being opened, "unless all the Courts of the Province, who tho' very much dissatisfied "with the Stamp Act, would not proceed in open defiance of an Act of "the Parliament, & a great part of the people were quite satisfied with "waiting until the success of the last application to Parliament could be "known. But Boston must govern the whole Province, & the Delin-"quency must be rendered universal."

It will be remembered that Chief Justice Hutchinson had been also Judge of Probate for the County of Suffolk. *Ante*, p. 98. Having refused to open the Court or to allow any business to proceed without stamps, he considered himself compelled either to resign or quit the country, and chose the former alternative. 3 Hutch. Hist. Mass. 142.

On the 18th, the House of Representatives in reply to the Governor's address at the close of the last session, presented a message to his Excellency which was published in the Massachusetts Gazette of the 23rd, and which contains the following language:

"The Courts of Justice must be open — open immediately; and the "Law, the great Rule of Right in every County in the Province exe-"cuted — The stopping the Course of Justice is a Grievance which this "House must enquire into — Justice must be fully administred through "the Province, by which the shocking Effects which your Excellency "apprehended from the People's non-compliance with the Stamp Act "will be prevented."

And on the 24th, the House, probably in consequence of the votes of the Town, passed the following resolve:

"Resolved that the shutting up of the Courts of Justice in general "in this Province, particularly the Superiour Court, has a manifest "Tendency to dissolve the Bonds of civil Society, is unjustifiable upon "the Principles of Law and Reason, dangerous to his Majesty's Crown "and Dignity, and a very great Grievance to the Subject that re-"quires immediate Redress; and that therefore the Judges and Justices, "and all other publick Officers in this Province ought to proceed in the "Discharge of their several Functions as usual."

This resolve was sent up for concurrence to the Council, where the proceedings are thus described by Governor Bernard.

Gov. Bernard to Lords of Trade, March 10, 1766.

—— "The Council after a short Debate ordered it to lye on the Ta-"ble; the House sent up a Message to desire they would pass on it. The Council

1766. MEMORIAL OF BOSTON.

" Council resumed the consideration of it, and it having been said that " it did not appear that the Judges would not proceed in Business at the " usuall Time, it was ordered that the Judges be desired to meet together, " and after consideration to signify to the Council whether they intended " to proceed in Business at the usual Time. The Judges accordingly " met, and signified to the Council by Letter that it was impossible for " them to determine absolutely what they should do at so distant a Time " (5 Weeks); but they were of Opinion that if the Circumstances of the " Province were the same at the Time of opening the Court as they " were now, and the Lawyers should urge their proceeding, they should " find themselves obliged to proceed. The Council voted this to be " satisfactory and passed upon the Resolve by non-concurring it. The " House sent down for the Judges Letters, and voted that the Informa- " tion was unsatisfactory, and so the Matter ended. — In the first Debate " upon the Resolve, the Lieutenant Governour bore a principal Part. " In the next Boston Gazette came out a Letter signed Freeborn Arm- " strong, containing virulent Abuse of the Lieutenant Governour, mis- " representing what he said in the Council, and arraigning him upon the " very Falsities of the Misrepresentation. This was a Breach of Privi- " ledge tending to overturn all Government by destroying a main Pillar " of it — Freedom of Debate in Councils of State. Upon this Princi- " ple the Council were earnestly urged by myself and some of the most " reputable of their own Body, to resent this in a Parliamentary Way. " But it could not be obtained, — it was said that, if they committed the " Printers, they would be rescued by the Mob, — that if the Author was " discovered in Form, as he was known to be a Member of the House " (Mr. Otis) they should be involved in a Quarrel with the House; that " this was not a Time to resent Indignities. So they contented them- " selves with vindicating the Lieutenant Governour's Character by a " Publication of their own. Boston Gazette, Jan'y 27 & Feb. 3."

This reply was also published in the Massachusetts Gazette of January 30th, as follows:

" Province of
" *Massachusetts Bay.* }

IN COUNCIL Tuesday the 28th Day of January 1766.

" Sixteen Gentlemen of the Board being then present, who had been " likewise present on Friday the 24th Instant:

" A Paragraph in the Boston Gazette of the 27th Inst. was read at " the Board, containing a Resolve of the Honourable House of Repre- " sentatives of the 24th Instant, respecting the shutting up the Courts of " Justice in this Province and asserting That ' The Resolves was the same " ' Day sent up to the Hon. Board for their Concurrence when the " ' Hon. Thomas Hutchinson, Esq; Lieutenant Governor, and Chief Justice

1766.

MEMORIAL OF BOSTON.

"'Juſtice of the Superiour Court, who, on this Occaſion alſo ſits as "'Preſident of the Council, a Place he has uſurped, after engroſſing all "'the Places of Honor and Profit in the Province moved to give it the "'go-by, ſaying it was Impertinent, and beneath the Notice of the Hon. "'Board, or to that Effect.'

"Whereupon a Debate was had at the Board upon the ſaid Para-"graph; and the following Queſtions were thereupon put,

"Q. 1. Whether any Gentlemen preſent at the Board on Friday "laſt heard the Lieutenant Governor expreſs himſelf in the Manner "mentioned in the Boſton Gazette of Yeſterday, viz. That the Reſolve "of the Houſe was impertinent, and beneath the Notice of the Hon. "Board, or Words to that Effect?

"*It paſſed unanimouſly in the Negative.*

"2. Whether the Words the Lieutenant Governor uttered in that "Debate carried any Reflection on the Honorable Houſe of Repre-"ſentatives?

"*It paſſed unanimouſly in the Negative.*

"3. Whether his Honor the Lieutenant-Governor hath uſurped the "Place of Preſident of the Board?

"*Reſolved*, That when his Honor firſt took the Place of Preſident "of the Board, it was determined by the Reſolution of the Board at that "Time, after ſearching the Books for Precedents in the like Caſes: "And it was declared by ſome Gentlemen who were then preſent, that "the Motion was made, and the Queſtion determined by the Board, the "Lieutenant-Governor himſelf being altogether ſilent on the Occaſion.

"*THE foregoing is a true Copy, and publiſhed by Order of the Board.*

"*Atteſt.* A. OLIVER, Secr'y."

1766.

March Term

VI. Geo. 3.

THE Chief Juſtice, who was Lieutenant Governour of the Province, was not preſent through the whole of this ſhort Term.

OPENING OF THE COURT.

The Charge was given the Grand Jury by Juſtice Lynde, who touched upon Nothing but what related to Matters which were to come before them, as the Grand Inqueſt for the County.

But *what* and *how* the Buſineſs of this Term was tranſacted; together with the political Fineſſe of the Game that was played, muſt be left to be reported by another Hand, at a future Day. (1)

---

(1) See John Adams's account of this ſeſſion given in his "Diary," under the date of March 11, 1766, 2 John Adams's Works, 189:

"11. Tueſday. Went to Boſton. The Chief Juſtice not there; a "piece of political fineſſe to make the people believe he was under the "neceſſity of going a journey this week, but would be here by the next "was put about, while care was taken to ſecure an agreement to an ad-"journment for three or four weeks; ſo that Hutchinſon is to trim and "ſhift, and luff up, and bear away, and elude the blame of the miniſtry "and the people. Cuſhing ſpoke out boldly and ſaid he was ready to go on;

1766. OPENING OF THE COURT.

"on; he had no difficulty about going on. Lynde ſaid, we are here. "Oliver ſaid, here am I in dureſs, and, if I muſt go on, I muſt. Thus "popular compulſion, fear of violence of the Sons of Liberty, &c., was "ſuggeſted to be the only motive with him to go on."

We give alſo Governor Bernard's account of the proceedings, contained in a poſtſcript to his letter of March 10th, from which an extract was printed on p. 212.

Gov. Bernard to Lords of Trade, March 10, 1766.

"P. S. Mar. 12. I have an opportunity to add an account of what "has been done at the opening of the Superior Court, at the uſual time, "which was yeſterday. It is uſual for the Lawyers in a body to wait on "the Judges on the firſt day of the Term before they go into the Court. "At this meeting, the Chief Juſtice not attending, one of the Judges, "Mr. Peter Oliver, ſaid that he attended the Court according to his "duty; that he underſtood that it would be expected, that he & his "Brethren ſhould proceed in buſineſs in defiance of the late Act of Parliament; that ſuch proceeding was contrary to his judgment & opinion; & that if he ſubmitted to it, it would be only for ſelf preſervation, "as he knew he was in the hands of the populace, & therefore he previouſly proteſted that all ſuch acts of his, if they ſhould happen, would "be acts done under dureſs. To which the other Judges aſſenting, it "was propoſed to each of the Lawyers ſingly, whether he deſired that "the buſineſs ſhould proceed, contrary to the Act of Parliament: when "every one of them anſwered in the Negative; even Mr. Otis himſelf "who has for 4 months paſt been labouring indefatigably to bring about "this particular miſchief. But they ſaid it would be proper to try a "cauſe or two to quiet the people; accordingly one cauſe, which had "been at iſſue before the Stamp Act took place, was tryed and all other "civil buſineſs was poſtponed to the middle of April, by which time "they expect to know the determination of the parliament. So evident "is it that this ſcheme, for obliging the Judges of the Superior Court to "proceed in defiance of the Stamp Act, which has agitated the Governor & the General Court at different times for 5 months paſt, was not "calculated for the eaſe or convenience of the people who wanted no "ſuch expedient, but was contrived to oblige the Government to join in "an inſult upon the Parliament, or elſe to remain expoſed to the reſentment of the people for not ſo doing.

F. B.

"(Indorſed)
"Recd. May 19th } 1766.
"Read May 29th }

The

1766.

OPENING OF THE COURT.

The adjournment was to the 29th of April, on which day the Court again met and again adjourned without proceeding to businefs. Adams's defcription of this meeting is as follows:

"29. Tuefday. At Bofton. To this day the Superior Court was "adjourned. Hutchinfon, Lynde and Cufhing were prefent. Two of "the bar agreed to continue an action. Hutchinfon leans over, and or- "ders Winthrop to minute an agreement to continue. We will confider "of it, fays he. Another of the bar moved for a continuance, and no "oppofition. Hutchinfon orders the clerk to enter it, motion for a con- "tinuance, &c. Then the Court went to playing off a farce, and try- "ing to get a caufe for the jury, but none was then ready. Then "Hutchinfon propofed, — 'What if we fhould adjourn to the firft Tuef- "day in June?' . . . . Thus the Chief Juftice is now muftering up "fortitude enough to make public, to manifeft his defire to comply with "the Stamp Act and to affift in carrying it into execution, in order to "lay claim to the protection of the Houfe of Commons, and to claim a "compenfation for his damages. . . . . I faid not one word for or againft "the adjournment; I faw the Court were determined before I came in, "and they had no right to expect that I would fall in with that determi- "nation; and I had no difpofition to foment an oppofition to it, becaufe "an oppofition made with any warmth might have ended in the demoli- "tion of the earthly houfe of his Honor's tabernacle." 2 John Adams's Works, 193, 4.

On the fixteenth of May, a copy of the repeal of the Stamp Act arrived in Bofton.

Auguſt Term

VI. Geo. 3.

Charge to the Grand Jury by the Chief Juſtice.

1766.

CHARGE TO THE GRAND JURY.

GENTLEMEN of the Grand Jury: When we opened the Court in this Place, this Time Twelvemonth, the Diſorders through the Continent, in general, were very great. Here, it was ſo great, that a Stop was put to the Courts of Juſtice, and this Court was adjourned to a diſtant Day, becauſe it was not *ſafe* * to proceed. But, through the Favour of Divine Providence, we are now in a better State, and it may perhaps be prudent to ſay Nothing

* *Qu. de hoc*, & vid. the Votes of the Town of Boſton, on the Day, to which the Chief Juſtice referred. (1)

---

(1) The following is a copy of the votes referred to, from the town records for 1765, fol. 647:

" At a legal Meeting of the Freeholders and other Inhabitants of " the Town of Boſton at Faneuil Hall, Auguſt 27th, *Anno Domini* " 1765,—

" The Hon'ble James Otis Eſq. was choſen Moderator.

The

Nothing of what is paſt. Diſorders, ariſing from what was eſteemed a Violation of our Right, had better be gone over in Silence; for it is difficult to draw the Line, where Duty ceaſes, and Oppoſition may begin. Yet, for Perſons under Pretence of Rectifying publick Wrongs, to invade private Rights is highly criminal.

1766. CHARGE TO THE GRAND JURY.

This Town is the firſt in the Province, and indeed generally takes the Lead through the Continent: I ſhould therefore be culpable, did I not ſay Something reſpecting our future Conduct. Our Grievances being removed, it will be beſt for us to return to our uſual Order. A Time, perhaps, will never arrive in the Life of the longeſt Liver of us, nor

---

" The Town having an utter deteſtation of the extraordinary & vio-
" lent proceedings of a number of Perſons unknown againſt ſome of the
" Inhabitants of the ſame the laſt Night — Vote unanimouſly that the
" Selectmen and Magiſtrates of the Town be deſired to uſe their utmoſt
" endeavors agreeable to Law to ſuppreſs the like diſorders for the future,
" and that the Freeholders and other Inhabitants will do everything in
" their power to aſſiſt them therein.

" VOTED, That the Inhabitants of this Town will be ready on all
" occaſions to aſſiſt the Selectmen and Magiſtrates in the ſuppreſſion of
" all Diſorders of a like nature that may happen, when called upon for
" that purpoſe.

" VOTED, That the Thanks of the Town be, and hereby are given
" to the Hon[ble] James Otis Eſq. the Moderator of this Meeting, for diſ-
" patching the Buſineſs thereof.

" Then the Meeting was diſſolved."

The only mention of any further diſturbance is by Hutchinſon himſelf, who ſays that on the next evening an attempt was made " to collect " the people together in order to further rapine; but a military watch hav- " ing been ordered, and the Governor's Company of Cadets appearing in " arms, and ſhewing great ſpirit, the mob was diſperſed." 3 Hutch. Hiſt. Maſs. 127.

1766.

CHARGE TO THE GRAND JURY.

nor of our Children's Children, when ſuch an Attempt will again be made: And if not, why ſhould we ſtill continue thoſe Broils and Animoſities, which diſturb our internal Peace and Tranquillity. Is it not better to go on, as formerly, with the Exerciſe of Government, than unneceſſarily to provoke the Parliament of Great Britain to Acts, which otherwiſe might never be thought on?

As the Behaviour of this Town has great Influence through the whole Province, and, as I obſerved before, has its Weight through the whole Continent, this is the Reaſon, Gentlemen, why I mention Things of ſo general a Nature, and which do not ſo immediately relate to you; but you, Gentlemen, being returned from the Body of the County, may, in Reſpect to the Reſtoration of Harmony and Order among us, be extenſively uſefull.

I do not know how it happens, but Diſorders are ſeldom confined to one Point. People who begin with one View, ſeldom end there.

Every one muſt have obſerved, the Court I am ſure have, through the Province, a general Diſpoſition to Diſorder, Confuſion and Riot, Breaches of the Peace, and what is commonly called Mobs. Laws have been thought rigorous, hardly to be borne, which heretofore were never thought ſevere. The Minds of the People are diſturbed, their Sentiments divided, but it is abſolutely neceſſary for us to unite; and as our Intereſt is the ſame, ſo our Wills ſhould be in Concert with Great Britain.

It

1766.

CHARGE TO THE GRAND JURY.

It is an old Maxim of the Law, Gentlemen, that the Laws may ſometimes ſleep, but they never die. It lays a great Deal with you, Gentlemen, to revive thoſe, which are abſolutely neceſſary for the Safety of the Community and good Order of Government; and I hope that you will ſet an Example to the Reſt of the Province.

The Buſineſs that immediately concerns you, Gentlemen, reſpects the Crown Law; And you are ſenſible, Gentlemen, that there is a ſtanding Grand Jury, which meet four Times a Year, and preſent all leſſer Offences cognizable at the Seſſions. Capital Offences, being extremely dangerous to Society, will demand your higheſt Attention. High Treaſon is another Crime which may be committed here, but in few Inſtances. I will mention ſome which I recollect. Levying War againſt the King is High Treaſon; as where People ſet about redreſſing public Wrongs; this, Gentlemen, the Law calls levying War againſt the King; becauſe it is going in direct Oppoſition to the King's Authority, who is the Redreſſer of all Wrongs.

Counterfeiting the King's Coin is High Treaſon at Home, but we have not ſettled that Point here. We have a particular Province-Law, which makes it a leſſer Offence; how far this will operate upon the Law of England, we have never determined; tho' there is no Negative Clauſe in our Act. (2) Another

(2) Anc. Chart. 745.

1766. Another Inſtance of High Treaſon here, may be committed by counterfeiting the King's Seal; but this has never yet happened. Theſe are all the Inſtances of High Treaſon here, which now occur to me.

CHARGE TO THE GRAND JURY.

Homicide, Gentlemen, is another Offence which you are to take Notice of, and this, Gentlemen, may be done, either by ſhooting, ſtriking, poiſoning, or any other Way, however ſecret, by which the Life of a Man is deſtroyed. Homicide is either voluntary or caſual: The former is Murder, the latter may be Manſlaughter, Chancemedley, or otherwiſe, as the particular Caſe may happen.

Burglary is another Offence which will come under your Examination, and is, in the Law, defined, breaking open in the Night-time, and entering into any Dwelling-houſe with a felonious Intention, whether ſuch Intention be executed or not. There has been a Difficulty in the Minds of Some, as to the felonious Intention; As where a Man enters without a felonious Intention, and afterwards commits a Felony, whether ſuch an Offence come under the Denomination of Burglary. Now I would obſerve, that the only Rule of Law is, to judge of the Intention by the Act; and, this Rule adhered to, there can be no Difficulty.

Blaſphemy, Gentlemen, is another Offence, and in the Law is a very high Crime, being of the moſt dangerous Nature; for it tends to the Diſſolution of all the Ties of Government, and ſaps the very Foundation of Society.

I

1766.

CHARGE TO THE GRAND JURY.

I am deſired to mention another Offence, which does not immediately relate to your Conduct. There has been of late, a great Number of Thefts and Robberies committed in the Day-time in many of the neighbouring Towns; particularly, I am informed, in Roxbury, Dorcheſter, Brookline and Milton: And an Offence which is of very dangerous Tendency, has been frequent, that in Law is called Theft-bote; where the Perſon robbed has taken back the Goods ſtolen, and received a Satiſfaction in Order to a Concealment. Indeed I ſhould give you this particularly in Charge, had I not great Reaſon to think the Inſtance I have a more immediate Reference to, was committed through pure Simplicity and Ignorance; but I hope this publick mentioning of it, will have the ſame Effect, and prevent the like Evil for the Future.

In a word, all high Crimes and Offences, all high-handed Riots, which any of you know, you are obliged by your Oaths to communicate to your Brethren, that they may judge of, and preſent them.

You muſt act, through the whole, with Impartiality, without Prejudice in Favour of, or againſt any One. You are bound by your Oaths to Secreſy, which Jurors do not always obſerve, not conſidering their Oath, and the Hurt they do the Community; and eſpecially to Individuals, who, by their revealing Matters, which came before them, are rendered obnoxious to thoſe whoſe paſt Offences have made them Criminals.

Gentlemen:

1766.

Charge to the Grand Jury.

Gentlemen: You, and we are all of us accountable to the Supreme Governour of the Univerſe, for our Conduct in our ſeveral Departments.

Pynchon v. Brewster.

Rec. 1766. Fol. 83.

Indebitatus Aſſumpſit lies for Phyſicians' Attendance, Travel and Drugs.

In *Indebitatus Aſſumpſit* the Plaintiff may recover a leſs Sum than that laid in the Declaration.

Pynchon, Executor, *verſ.* Brewſter.

INDEBITATUS *Aſſumpſit* upon a long Doctor's Bill for Medicines, Travel into the Country and Attendance.

In this Caſe it was ſtrongly urged by *Mr. Adams* for the Defendant, that this Action lay not, but that a *Quantum Meruit* ſhould have been brought; and he relyed much on the Caſe of *Richards & Tyler*, tried laſt Auguſt Term, *q. v.* p. 195.

But the *Chief Juſtice* ſaid, that Boarding and Schooling were uncertain as to Price, and a *Quantum Meruit* muſt be brought; but that Travel for Phyſicians, their Drugs and Attendance, had as fixed a Price as Goods ſold by a Shopkeeper, and that it would be a great Hardſhip upon Phyſicians to oblige them to lay a *Quantum Meruit.* And the *Chief Juſtice*, who alone ſummed up this Caſe to the Jury, ſaid that the Cuſtom here had always been in ſuch Caſes to lay an *Indebitatus Aſſumpſit*,* though in

* *Qu.* and vid. 2 Vol. p. 113, *Dr. Holden* vs. *Day.* *Qu.* Where is the true Boundary Line between an *Indebitatus Aſſumpſit*, and a *Quantum Meruit*, on this Side the Water?

in England it would not do; and *that the Jury might, upon an Indebitatus Aſſumpſit, if they thought it reaſonable, leſſen the Charges in the Account.* This was ſolemnly affirmed by all the five Judges, in the Courſe of this Debate, to be Law here; though it was not, in Great Britain.*

1766. PYNCHON *v.* BREWSTER.

The Jury did, according as the Law was laid down to them, and ſtruck off about £7 from the Account, lowering the Charges, probably, to what they thought "*reaſonable.*"

* The Reſolution in this Caſe was denied to be Law by the whole Court, *Ch. Juſt. abſente*, in the Caſe of *Leteſtu & Glover*, Auguſt Term, 1770. (1)

---

(1) We find a report of the caſe of *Glover* v. *Le Teſtue* among John Adams's papers, as follows:

GLOVER *v.* LE TESTUE. Rec. 1771. Fol. 11.

"*Glover* vs. *Le Teſtue*, Aug. 1770.

"*Indebitatus Aſſumpſit* for Viſits and Medicines. The Queſtion "whether *Indebitatus* will lie, or *Quantum meruit?* — Ans. *Indebitatus* "will not, becauſe no Contract for a certain Price for the Viſits or "Druggs. 2 *Inſtructor Cler.* 162, 'if one ſue upon a Promiſe to ſatisfye "him for Work done, he muſt ſhew in his Declaration how much he de- 'ſerved for his Work.' So if one ſue for a Thing ſold, where no Price "was agreed upon, he muſt aver, and ſhew it to be worth ſo much.

"2 *Inſtructor Cler.* 151. Aſſumpſit for Wines ſold and delivered — "Note in the Margin. 'On this Count (*Ind. Aſs.*,) the Plaintiff muſt "prove the expreſs Price agreed on.' — Page 152. Note in the Margin. "'But on this Count (*Quant. Mer.*) the Delivery only is ſufficient.'

"1 Salk 23, *Hard's Caſe*. *Indebitatus Aſſumpſit* will lie in no Caſe, "but where Debt lies, &c. But ſee 1 Burrows, 374, *Harris* vs. *Hunt-* "*bach*. 2 Burrows, 1006, *Moſes* vs. *Macfarlan*, page 1008 — Ld. Manſ- "field. 'The firſt Objection is, y^t an Action of Debt would not lie here; "and no aſſumpſit will lie where an Action of Debt may not be brought. "Some ſayings at *Niſi Prius* reported by Note-Takers, who did not un- "derſtand the Force of what was ſaid, are quoted in Support of that "Propoſition. But there is no Foundation for it,' &c., An Action of "Aſſumpſit will lie in many Caſes where Debt lies, and in many where "it does not lie.' *Slade's Caſe*, 4 Co. 92.

"1 Fitzherb.

1766.
Glover
v.
Le Testue.

"1 Fitzherb. 119. 'A Writ of Debt properly lieth where a Man "oweth another *a certain Sum of Money* by Obligation or by Bargain for "a Thing sold, or by Contract, or upon a Loan made by ye Creditor to "ye Debtor,' &c.

"1 Mod. Ent. 299. There are two Sorts of Promises, express or "implied,—an express Promise is where a Person promises, yt he will "pay a Sum of Money, &c.

"At the Bottom, 5,—'An implied Promise is such as is raised by Im-"plication of Law upon the Nature of the Case, as where a Man sells, and "delivers Goods to another, tho' he cannot prove an express Promise to "pay for them; and where the Price is not of ascertained Value between "the Parties, ye Law implies that the Defendant promised to pay for "such Goods, so much as they were worth; So if a Man sets another to "Work, and no Price is agreed, nor any express Promise to pay, the "Law implies that the Person who set the Man to work contracted with "him and promised to pay him so much as he deserved.'

"*The Court unanimously adjudged*, that *Indebitatus Assumpsit* would "not lie upon the Account in this Case, neither for Visits, Bleeding nor "Medicines, but allowed Plaintiff to file a new Declaration on *Quantum* "*Meruit* on Payment of Costs.

"A Tender may be pleaded to a *Quantum Meruit.* 5 Bac. Abr. 27. "1 Str. 576, *Johnson* vs. *Lancaster.*"

A declaration on an implied promise "is said to be in *general assumpsit:* which is either *indebitatus assumpsit*, wherein the plaintiff generally states that the defendant being indebted in a certain specific sum promised to pay that sum, or upon a *quantum meruit* or *quantum valebant.*" Lawes on Pleading in Assumpsit, 2. And it was formerly held that under the former count, only the exact sum laid could be recovered, because otherwise "the same assumpsit was not found that the plaintiff did declare upon." *Bagnal* v. *Sacheverell*, Cro. Eliz. 292. But in *Thompson* v. *Spencer*, 8 Geo. 3, it was held that the plaintiff might in such case recover what was justly due. Id. (5th ed.) *in notis.* It would appear therefore that the decision in *Pynchon* v. *Brewster* was in accordance with the law of England, when overruled, in 1770, though not when made in 1765.

1766.

Box v. Welch.

Rec. 1767. Fol. 190.

Entries in a Plaintiff's Book of Account, charging two Defendants jointly, but not as Copartners, are admiſſible, together with his Oath, without previous Evidence of the joint Contract. *Hutchinſon, C. J., diſſentiente.*

Box & al *verſ.* Welch & al.

INDEBITATUS ASSUMPSIT on Account annexed. The Plaintiff's Book and Oath were offered as Evidence to the Jury, to which an Objection was made by Mr. Auchmuty — the Charge ſtanding "Dr. J. W. & J. W. Jr.," and not "J. W. & Co."

Mr. Auchmuty. We never yet have extended the Rule of the Plaintiff's Oath to his Book ſo far as this Caſe would carry it. The Oath of the Party is allowed in any Caſe only from Neceſſity. You muſt bring Proof of the joint Contract and Sale to both the Defendants, and then your Oath and Book will be good Evidence of this Charge. We admit the Plaintiff to his Oath, when the Action is brought againſt one, becauſe he may come in and defend himſelf. He can never prove a Negative, viz[t], that he did not contract. In the Caſe of known Partnerſhips, poſſibly, we may have gone ſo far as to admit the Plaintiff to his Oath, becauſe here each uſually contracts for the other, and the Contract of one for both ſhall bind both; but at this Rate it will be in the Power of any one to bind who he pleaſes.

Mr. Otis. 'Tis agreed, if the Charge was againſt one, the Plaintiff might be admitted to his Oath: Why not, when it is againſt two? Either of them may defend himſelf as well now, as when charged ſingle. Any Evidence that would diſcharge in one Caſe, will in the other; and it has ever been the Cuſtom,

1766.
Box
v.
Welch.

Cuſtom, as I conceive, in ſuch Caſes to admit the Plaintiff to his Oath.

Ch. Juſtice. Suppoſe, Mr. Otis, that you and I were charged together, — muſt not ſome Evidence be given of the Contract with both, before the Plaintiff can be admitted to his Oath?

Mr. Auchmuty. And if your Honour and Mr. Otis can be bound in this Manner, why not me and twenty more? If this Rule is eſtabliſhed, ſome of your ſharp Folks, who ſtick at Nothing, will never loſe their Debts, — 'tis only clapping in one or two ſubſtantial Men, and your Debt's ſecure. Beſides, if you admit his Oath, we can never prove a Negative.

Mr. Otis. Prove a Negative! He may prove Anything in Diſcharge, now, as well as when one is charged, and he pleads, he never promiſed. As to the charging one, two or three, — you may charge three Million, and the Plaintiff's Oath and Book ſhall go in, as Evidence to the Jury, who will judge of that and all Circumſtances. The moſt we have contended for in theſe Caſes, has been, when the Charge was againſt A. B. & Co., we, I believe, may have gone ſo far as to make the Plaintiff ſhow the Company, before we admitted his Oath.* But this is not our Caſe; we don't pretend a Company. The Charge in our Books ſtands againſt J. W. & J. W., Jr. We ſay they jointly bought theſe Goods, and that we delivered the Goods upon their joint Credit; and we offer our Oath and Book to ſupport

* *Quære.*

ſupport our Charge, the only Evidence that ever has been, or can be expected.

Four Judges againſt the Chief Juſtice, that the Plaintiff's Oath and Book ſhould go as Evidence to the Jury, who would judge of all the Evidence with all the Circumſtances.

The Plaintiff was ſworn accordingly.

Apthorp & al *verſ.* Eyres.

Apthorp v. Eyres.

Rec. 1766. Fol. 100.

A Depoſition *in perpetuam Rei Memoriam* is admiſſible to ſatisfy the Court of the Death of a Party to a Suit, on a Motion to minute the ſame on Record, though the Witneſs is alive and might eaſily be produced. *Oliver & Ruſſell, J J diſs.*

WHEELWRIGHT, one of the Plaintiffs in this Action, having died ſince the Commencement of it, a Motion was made, that a Minute ſhould be made of Wheelwright's Death, becauſe, ſhould ſuch a Minute be omitted, it would be Error. (1)

Mr. Fitch. I have a Depoſition in my Hand, taken *in perpetuam Rei Memoriam*, which I offer to the Court as Evidence of Mr. Wheelwright's Death. This is Evidence to ſatisfy the Court, and not a Jury. If your Honours are ſatisfyed of the Fact, whether by Attendance on his Funeral, or ſeeing his Corpſe, or otherwiſe, you will order the Minute to be made by your Clerk.

Mr. Gridley. When we produce Depoſitions as Evidence to a Jury, we muſt proceed in a certain Manner

---

(1) Tidd Prac. 1056, 1107.

1766. APTHORP *v.* EYRES.

Manner in the Caption, according to the Province Law. All the great Courts at Home conſtantly produce Affidavits to ſuch Points. Lilly, 44. Your Honours are as well ſatisfy'd as if the Depoſition was taken according to the ſtricteſt Rules of the Province Law.

Mr. Auchmuty. Affidavits are received at Home when properly taken, but the Courts never receive them, when improperly taken. Will your Honours receive a Depoſition *in perpetuam*, &c., which were never received at Home, or anywhere elſe, while the Perſon was living, and might be produced to give his Teſtimony *vivâ Voce.* What if your Honours were ſatisfy'd of the Fact?—will your Honours make Minutes in your Records from your own Knowledge? Your Honours would then be Witneſſes, and not Judges.

Juſt. Oliver. They might have produced the Witneſs; I am therefore for not making the Minute, as there is no Evidence to the Court.

Juſt. Ruſſell. If they could not *eaſily* have produced the Witneſs, I ſhould have been for receiving this Evidence, but as they can *eaſily* produce him, I think they ought.

Juſt. Cuſhing. I think this is good Evidence to ſatisfy a Court, and better than ever I knew in a like Caſe.

Juſt. Lynde. I am for admitting this Evidence, for I am ſatisfy'd of the Fact.

Ch.

1766.
APTHORP v. EYRES.

Ch. Juſtice. Certainly Courts are not tied up to ſuch ſtrict Rule in Admiſſion of Evidence, as when it is to go to Juries. I am very full, that the Court have ſufficient Evidence from this Depoſition to ſatisfy them of Mr. Wheelwright's Death, and am for the Minute's being made.

*Which was done accordingly.** (2)

* Vid. L'd Raym[d] 174, *Faux* vs. *Barnes*.

---

(2) But see *Coffin* v. *Abbot*, 7 Maſs. 225, where it was held, that on the hearing of a petition for review, depoſitions are inadmiſſible, unleſs taken with the ſame forms as if to be uſed in the trial of a cauſe.

March Term

VII Geo. 3.

Charge to the Grand Jury by the Chief Juſtice.

1767.

CHARGE TO THE GRAND JURY.

BEFORE I ſay Anything to the Grand Jury, it is highly proper that I ſhould take Notice of the Death of One of the Judges of this Court. I have no Talent for it, and am an Enemy to traducing and vilifying the Characters of Men, when alive, and flattering them when dead. Yet Juſtice to Judge Ruſſell obliges me to ſay Something of his Death. Every one who knew him in private Life, muſt acknowledge him a moſt amiable Man. I ſcarce ever knew his Equal. He might be truly characterized as a Lover of Mankind, and no higher Character can, I think, be given of any One. Nothing more need be ſaid to recommend him, *eſpecially at this Time.*

The ſeveral Poſts of Honour which he bore, he ſuſtained

1767. Charge to the Grand Jury.

fuftained with Dignity. As a Legiflator, I had an Opportunity to obferve his Conduct, both as a Member of the Council and Houfe of Reprefentatives: And I know that he ever engaged on that Side which had Truth and Juftice for its Support. As a Judge of the Admiralty, his Conduct was moft unexceptionable: And I believe none of his Decrees, but met with univerfal Approbation, except at Times, when Party-fpirit and Animofities ran high, and made it a Thing impoffible, for any Judge, in any Department, to give Satisfaction. His Conduct in this Court — I appeal to the Gentlemen of the Bar — was fuch as pronounced him the Judge, and a Man of ftrict Integrity. Although we all have fome Byafs, — 'tis impoffible for human Nature to be without, — yet if he had any Byafs, it was ever in Favour of Virtue.

Juftice has been done this worthy Character, already, in publick, in an unexceptionable and elegant Manner. (1) The beft Ufe that we can make, is to follow his Path and imitate his Virtues; efpecially, as we all muft fhortly follow him to give our Account to the Judge of us all. — Now,

Gentlemen of the Grand Jury:

You are fent here from your feveral Towns, upon Bufinefs of great Importance to your Country. I will not go fo largely and particularly into the Duty of Grand Juries in general, as many of you have been on Juries before, and moft of you have been converfant with the Duty of your Office.

There

(1) Maffachufetts Gazette, January 15th, 1767.

1767. Charge to the Grand Jury.

There is one general Obſervation I would make; that the End of Government is the Happineſs of every Individual, ſo far as is conſiſtent with the Good of *the Whole.* To attain this End is impoſſible without Laws, and their due Execution. 'Tis neceſſary that Laws ſhould be eſtabliſhed, elſe Judges and Juries muſt go according to their Reaſon, that is, their Will; and this is in the ſtricteſt Senſe arbitrary. On this Reaſon, I take to be grounded that well-known Maxim, that *the Judge* ſhould never be *the Legislator:* Becauſe, then, the Will of the Judge would be the Law; and this tends directly to a State of Slavery. The Rules and Orders of a State muſt be known, and muſt be certain, that People may know how to act; or elſe they are equally uncertain, as if the Law depended upon the arbitrary Opinion of Another.

Let the Body of Laws be ever ſo good,—if they are not executed, 'tis worſe than a State of Nature, becauſe we guard ourſelves in a State of Nature, and therefore are more ſecure than in a Society, where we depend on the Laws for our Protection, which are not put in Force.

There has been a Failure of Law amongſt us, which has been very detrimental. Doubts and Differences in Opinion have been, which has cauſed a great Deal of Confuſion. 'Tis to be hoped we are returning again to good Order. I wiſh the Laws to be put in due Execution for the publick Good, and am as much for the Liberties of the People, as any Man, *ſo far as is conſiſtent with the Welfare of the Community.*

In

1767.

CHARGE TO THE GRAND JURY.

In this Country we have always been happy in a good Set of Laws. The principal Crown-Law of this Province is grounded on our provincial Laws; where theſe fail, the Common Law of England is the Rule. The Principle of the Crown-Law is, eſtabliſhing Puniſhment, not according to the Degree of moral Evil in the Offence, but according as the Crime affects the Peace of the Community.

There is a Difference between Peace, as uſed in the Common Acceptation of the Word, and Peace as it is uſed in a Law-ſenſe. Offences which are much greater in their Nature, are puniſhed in a much milder Manner, than Offences leſs heinous, which affect the publick Peace more.

I ſuppoſe there is no one whom Blaſphemy does not ſtrike with greater Horrour, than the Crime of Treaſon againſt the Prince; yet the *latter* is juſtly puniſhed with Death, when the *former* is not, becauſe it does not tend ſo immediately to deſtroy the Happineſs of the State. Many other Things I might inſtance in, but this is ſufficient. The Principle that the Law goes upon, is, that the Supreme Being will avenge his own Wrongs. I don't know a Nation in the World, that makes that Diſtinction between Murther and Manſlaughter, which the Engliſh do. It was not made in this Country before the Charter; for our Forefathers founded their Laws upon the Law of Moſes, which makes no ſuch Diſtinction. This may properly be called the Benignity of the Engliſh Law.

(The Chief Juſtice then proceeded to charge the Grand

1767. CHARGE TO THE GRAND JURY.

Grand Jury relative to thoſe particular Crimes, which it was probable would come before them, and then continued as follows:)

I would now only add, Gentlemen, that you carefully obſerve the Oath of God which is upon you: It contains many good Rules for your Conduct, and lays you under the greateſt Obligations to diſcharge your Duty with Fidelity.

All Crimes you have Cognizance of, from the higheſt to the loweſt, though leſſer Offences are commonly left to the Inſpection of Juſtices of the Peace, and the Seſſions. But, if they are negligent, it is your Duty to preſent all Offenders againſt the publick Peace, in the Common Acceptation of that Word.

I know that it is impoſſible for Men in any Society to be all of the ſame Mind. Doubts and Diſagreements in Sentiment will ariſe; it is not only neceſſary, but uſeful; for by this Means, the Good of the Community is often attained, the moſt ſalutary Plans of Government adapted, and the whole Buſineſs of the publick Weal better executed.

But, becauſe we do not think alike, becauſe we diſagree in our ſeveral Opinions, let us not ſlander and traduce one another's Characters. We might as well quarrell, and deſtroy Men for their different Looks, or Complexions. But to reproach and vilify each other in publick Print, is a Crime of a much higher Nature, and it is more miſchievous ſtill, when it is pointed againſt all in Authority.—

Shall

1767. CHARGE TO THE GRAND JURY.

Shall no one's Character be ſafe, becauſe he does not think as we would chooſe? — For my Part, I know no more dangerous Symptom in any State, than when its Rulers are ſlandered, and the Authority of thoſe who govern, is deſpiſed and trampled upon.

I am ſure I never promoted any ſuch Spirit among us; and heartily do I wiſh, that I could help to reſtore the Peace of this Community. But I doubt whether there is any Room to hope, *at this Time*, any Good from my Recommendation.

I have known the Time, when a Man could not more recommend himſelf than by promoting Peace, Harmony and good Order; And there have been Times, when a Man might obtain greater Applauſe in promoting the Contrary, and ſtirring up Contentions, Diviſions, Animoſities and Factions.

But I know that it has been ſaid by our Great Lord and Saviour, that "Bleſſed are the Peacemakers," and if I might obtain His Approbation, I am not anxious for any other Events.

Bromfield *verſ.* Lovejoy.

BROMFIELD *v.* LOVEJOY.

Rec. 1767. Fol. 190.

PLEA in Abatement by *Mr. Auchmuty*, that the Defendant bore a Captain's Commiſſion, and ſo a *Gentleman* by Office, and therefore, Yeoman, was not

1767. BROMFIELD *v.* LOVEJOY.

not his due Addition. Cited 2 Inſt. 666, 668; 1 Inſt. 66 a.

A Captain of Militia, commiſſioned by the Governour, is a Gentleman by Office, and if ſued by the Addition of Yeoman may abate the Writ.

Mr. Otis. Lovejoy is certainly no Gentleman by Office; for no Commiſſion from any Governour whatever, can make a Man Gentleman by Office. Lovejoy is then a Gentleman, if any Way, by Curteſy, or Reputation, and, Gentleman, would be a good Addition, "but if he be named Yeoman, he cannot abate the Writ." Viner, Tit. Additions, C. pl. 29, p. 85. "Yeoman or Gentleman are Additions *ad Placitum*, and *ad Libitum*, are no Part of the Name, but Additions *ad Libitum*, as People pleaſe to call them." Viner, Ibid. pl. 33, 34.

The Court took a Diſtinction between Gentleman by Curteſy, and Reputation, and *ſeemed* to be of Opinion, that, if a Man was Gentleman by Curteſy, Yeoman was not his due Addition; *aliter* if Gentleman by Reputation only. In the preſent Caſe they were of Opinion, that Lovejoy was a Gentleman, both by his Commiſſion and by Curteſy. Therefore they *ruled, that the Writ abate*, though they ſaid it was a very great Hardſhip upon the Bar.*

* Vid. 3 Bac. Abr. 618, where Brook, 44, is cited. Vid. 2 Ld. Raym'd, 849.

1767.

CARPENTER *v.* FAIRSERVICE.

Rec. 1767. Fol. 196.

Whether a Promiſſory Note in which the Words "in one Month" appear to have been eraſed is admiſſible in Support of a Declaration on a Note payable on Demand, in Connexion with Evidence that the Alteration was made after Execution — *quære.*

Carpenter *verſ.* Fairſervice.

Preſent:

All the 4 Judges.

ASSUMPSIT upon a Note of Hand, payable upon Demand. Theſe Words "~~in one Month~~" were thus daſhed out.

Mr. Auchmuty objected, that the Note thus eraſed did not ſupport the Declaration; therefore not Evidence to ſupport it; and prayed Judgment whether it ſhould go in.

A Witneſs was ſworn, who declared, he wrote the Note, and gave a Reaſon why thoſe Words were inſerted, and ſaid they had, ſince the ſigning of Fairſervice, been eraſed.

Mr. S. Quincy, to what Mr. Auchmuty had objected, reply'd, that the Jury were Judges of this Matter, and would determine whether the Razure was before, or after ſigning.

The Point was not much laboured on either Side: And *Juſtices Oliver & Lynde* were of Opinion, that, as the Note did not ſupport the Declaration, it ſhould not go in as Evidence.

The Chief Juſtice & Juſtice Cuſhing were full for the Caſe, with all its Circumſtances to be left to the Jury.

1767.
CARPENTER v. FAIRSERVICE.

Jury. And the *Chief Juſtice* ſaid, that ſurely the Court could not determine the Weight of the Evidence of the Witneſs; but that the Jury are the ſole Judges of the Credibility of this Witneſs, upon whoſe Teſtimony alone it reſts, whether this Razure was before or after ſigning.* (1)

The Court being divided, the Plaintiff diſcontinued, paying Coſts.

* Vid. *Norwood* vs. *Fairſervice*, ante, p. 189.

---

(1) The queſtion as to the time when an alteration of a written inſtrument was made, is for the jury. 6 Gray, 442. 20 Vermont, 205. 11 New Hampſhire, 395.

Auguſt Term

VII Geo. 3.

Thomas Hutchinſon, Eſqr., Chief Juſtice.
Benjamin Lynde,
John Cuſhing,
Peter Oliver,
Edmund Trowbridge,* } Eſqrs., Juſtices.
Jonathan Sewall, Eſqr., Solicitor General.†

Preſent:
The whole Court.

The Charge of the Chief Juſtice to the Grand Jury.

1767. CHARGE TO THE GRAND JURY.

GENTLEMEN of the Grand Jury: When I had Occaſion laſt to ſpeak from this Place to the Grand Jury, I made ſome general Reflections

* The late Attorney General. This was the firſt Time of his ſitting as a Judge in the County of Suffolk. He was ſucceeded in the Office of Attorney General by Jeremy Gridley, Eſqr.

† N. B. Mr. Sewall was the firſt Officer of the Kind ever known in the Province. He was, prior to this Appointment, made *Special* Attorney

1767.

CHARGE TO THE GRAND JURY.

Reflections upon the Nature and End of Civil Government. I then remarked, that it was eſſential to a Free People, that they ſhould be governed by known and certain Laws.* From thence I took Occaſion to obſerve upon a well known Maxim of Government, that the Perſon of *the Judge* and *the Legiſlator* ſhould never be united in the ſame Perſon. — I don't know how it happened, but this Obſervation of mine was ſoon after remarked upon in the Papers,† and a Suggeſtion thrown out, that I had been, for a Number of Years paſt, acting in direct Oppoſition to this Principle of mine; and, in Violation of my own Conſcience, had continued a Practice diametrically repugnant to my own Sentiments and Opinion. — This was a pretty Home Reflection. I ſhould not have mentioned this Matter now, but from a firm and hearty Regard to my Country, — to ſhow People the great Impropriety of ſuch Reflections, and to let them know the Dangers

ney *General*, but this being diſagreeable to Mr. Gridley, and carrying Something of an Abſurdity in the very Term, he was tranſlated to his preſent novel Office of Solicitor.

* Vid. *ante*, p 234.

† Boſton Gazette, April 27, 1767. (1)

---

(1) This paper contains a long political article on the then approaching election of Repreſentatives, ſigned " Freeborn American." The paſſage alluded to is as follows:

" It is a doctrine lately advanced by an executive J—ge in a public
" aſſembly, and is manifeſtly agreeable to liberty and law, *that a legiſlator*
" *and judge in the ſame perſon are incompatible with that freedom & in-*
" *dependence neceſſary to an impartial adminiſtration of government;*
" and yet this very J—ge for a long time was elected a legiſlator, and
" ſerved as ſuch."

gers they are expoſed to from countenancing ſuch Reflections, and the Puniſhment thoſe are obnoxious to, who publiſh Things of this Nature. 1767.

CHARGE TO THE GRAND JURY.

To ſuffer the Tranſactions and Opinions of the Executive Court to be illiberally animadverted upon is of the moſt dangerous Tendency to the Community: — For, if the Authority of the Executive Courts is brought into Contempt, what Miſchiefs will not infeſt Society!

It is really amazing to me, how I could be miſunderſtood, unleſs through Willfullneſs, in a Matter, in which, if I had been attended to, it was evident I leaned quite the other Way. — For, at that very Time, I mentioned, as the Reaſon why the Judge and Legiſlator ſhould not be the ſame Perſon, was becauſe the Will of the Judge would then be Law, and that in ſuch a Caſe, the Law would be uncertain, depending upon the arbitrary Will of another.

This I ſaid, to elucidate the main Object I had in View, that the Laws of every State ought always to be fixed, certain and known; and that ſuch Laws ſhould ever be put in due Execution. — For, when the arbitrary Will of the Judge is the Law, the Laws will be perpetually fluctuating and uncertain, ſo that the Subject can never know what Laws to obey, nor the Executive Officer what Laws to execute. — The whole Tenor, Scope and Connexion of what I ſaid, very plainly ſhowed my Meaning. — But, becauſe I advanced, that the Direction, Opinion and Will of the Judge ſhould never be the Law

1767.
Charge to the Grand Jury.

Law — could it be reaſonably inferred that the Judge ſhould never participate in the Legiſlative at all? — could it juſtly be concluded that I meant, that a Judge ſhould never ſhare at all in making the Laws? It was very obvious my Meaning was directly the reverſe.

It is very extraordinary to find the ſame Perſons contending for an unlimited Freedom of Thought and Action, which they would confine wholly to themſelves? We find one Side hardly allowed to contradict what the other advances, and not permitted even to reaſon, without being treated in the moſt abuſive Manner, and vilifyed beyond all Bounds. — Nothing can be more unjuſt than this.

Pretty high Notions of the Liberty of the Preſs, I am ſenſible, have prevailed of late among us; but it is very dangerous to meddle with, and ſtrike at this Court.

The Liberty of the Preſs is doubtleſs a very great Bleſſing; but this Liberty means no more than a Freedom for every Thing to paſs from the Preſs without a Licence. — That is, you ſhall not be obliged to obtain a Licence from any Authority before the Emiſſion of Things from the Preſs. Unlicenced Printing was never thought to mean a Liberty of reviling and calumniating all Ranks and Degrees of Men with Impunity, all Authority with Ignominy. — To carry this abſurd Notion of the Liberty of the Preſs to the Length ſome would have it — to print every Thing that is Libellous and Slanderous

Slanderous — is truly aſtoniſhing, and of the moſt dangerous Tendency.

1767.
CHARGE TO THE GRAND JURY.

To publiſh that a Man was a Bankrupt, a Villain or the like, would aſſuredly be liable to a civil Action, if not an Indictment. — To ſtrike a Man in the King's Court will ſubject the Offender to the Loſs of his Hand and Impriſonment for Life. — And yet, ſhall that ſame Court tolerate the groſſeſt Abuſe in the publick Prints, and let all Inſults paſs with Impunity? — Shall a Man be allowed to publiſh openly of an Executive Court, in Print, what he dares not charge a private Man with, in Converſation?

I don't give the Abuſe in this Matter in Charge to you, Gentlemen, becauſe I conceive that this Court have full Power to proceed in a much more Summary Way to execute Juſtice on the Offenders.

We often hear of very ſevere Strictures made upon the Conduct of Miniſters of State in Great Britain; but we never hear of ſimilar Reflections upon the Judges of Weſtminſter Hall. — They would iſſue a Proceſs for Contempt of the Court, and commit the Printer inſtantly, if he did not expoſe the Authors — and, if he did, very like, both Author and Publiſher.

'Tis on the Dignity and Support of the Executive Courts that your own Liberty depends. Let the Reſpect due to theſe Courts be loſt, let their Dignity not be kept up, by a Support of Authority, and

1767.
Charge to the Grand Jury.

and all Order and Government will ſoon be at End. For what Order can there be in a Society where the Courts which are to carry the Laws into Execution are treated with a contemptuous Diſreſpect? — If ſuch an unlimited Liberty is indulged and carried on, we ſhall ſoon approach near to that Licentiouſneſs which is worſe than Tyranny.

I would mention, in Order to ſhow People the Hazard they run, in treating this Court abuſively, and to caution all againſt a like Conduct for the Future, that we are not obliged to have the Matter preſented in the firſt Place by the Grand Jury, then to have it left to a Petit Jury to be decided, before the Offence can be puniſhed; but this Court may proceed in a far more ſummary Manner, to bring the Offender to Juſtice. — This Court will ever take proper Care to ſecure their Honour by keeping up their Authority.

I have ſaid thus much, that a general Abhorrence of ſuch groſs Abuſe may take Place for the Future, and every Thing of the like Kind hereafter be univerſally diſcountenanced among us.

(Here I was called out of Court: — The Chief Juſtice then, as I was informed, went on to hint, as ſome thought, at what Major Hawley had publiſhed in the Papers relative to the Berkſhire Affair. (2) When I returned, the Chief Juſtice was paſſing very high Encomiums upon the Judges of England,

(2) See note at the end of the charge.

1767.

Charge to the Grand Jury.

land, and ſpeaking upon thoſe Judges who were guilty of Unfaithfullneſs, Bribery and Corruption. He ſaid, —)

They muſt certainly be the moſt abandonedly wicked of all Men. — They deſerve the worſt Puniſhment, and I pray God they may always meet with it. — But I believe, whenever ſuch Characters have appeared, of which, to the Glory of the Engliſh Nation, there have been very few Inſtances, they have never been attacked in the publick Prints.

(The Judge here charged the Jury about the criminal Affairs, which in this Court were numerous, and then concluded with ſaying, —)

We frequently hear Talk of Tumults and Diſorders — but few know the Danger they run, in engaging in ſuch Diſorders. For, if a Man is attacked, upon any Pretence whatever, in his own Houſe, whether it be to treat him contemptuouſly for the Diverſion and Sport of thoſe who aſſault him, or for whatever other Cauſe, if the Man who is thus beſet kills any one or all of thoſe who thus abuſe him, he is only guilty of Manſlaughter, for which he ſhall have his Clergy; whereas, if any one of the others ſhould unfortunately happen to kill a Man, all thoſe, who anyways aſſiſted or abetted the Offenders, are every one of them guilty of Murder, and muſt ſuffer the Pains of Death.

Gentlemen of the Grand Jury: —

You muſt carefully attend to all the Obligations which

1767.

CHARGE TO THE GRAND JURY.

which you brought into Court with you, and, more eſpecially, to that additional Obligation you are now under, by the Oath of God which is upon you. You are to inquire into and preſent all heinous and dangerous Offences. You are not to ſuffer yourſelves to be guided or in the leaſt governed by Hatred, Envy or Malice, or Favour or Affection.

Be careful to obſerve your Oath, and keep the Fear of God before your Eyes — I cannot end with a better Caution.

NOTE.

The "Berkſhire Affair" alluded to on p. 246 was the trial of Seth Warren, indicted with others for a riot and reſcue of one Franklin, arreſted on civil proceſs, while the Courts were cloſed by the Stamp Act. Major Hawley was counſel for the priſoner; and from his account of the affair, publiſhed in the "Boſton Evening Poſt," July 6th and 23rd, 1767, we compile the following brief statement:

One Morse, a deputy ſheriff of Berkſhire, having arreſted a priſoner on a juſtice's execution, he was reſcued by the defendant and others, "the "ſaid Warren and others declaring to the ſaid Morſe that it would be in "vain for him to attempt to take any perſon from Laneſborough to "priſon for debt, ſo long as priſoners when committed could not be al- "lowed to have the liberty of the priſon yard upon any terms, but muſt "be kept in as close cuſtody as felons, and until the Court ſhould be "open, and people ſhould be admitted, by ſome courſe or proceſs of "law, to recover their dues as formerly. And, to be explicit, it ap- "peared in evidence that the plain ſenſe of what thoſe perſons at that "time declared to Morſe was, that they deſired he would not attempt any "more to take any perſon from Laneſborough to goal on writs purchaſed "or ſued out before the firſt of November for debt, ſo long as they could "not have their lawful right, viz., the benefit and priviledges of the "King's writs for the recovery of their juſt dues of thoſe who were in- "debted to them; and that if he ſhould attempt it, and ſhould actually "take, and arreſt any perſon in Laneſborough for that purpoſe, he might "depend on it, that they would be reſcued — A noble reſolution, worthy of

1767.

" of every Engliſhman, and all who have the principles of a free government interwoven in the conſtitution of their minds." — " This reſolution of the ſaid Warren and others then together was, ſoon after the ſaid ſixth of November, communicated to ſeveral others of the inhabitants of Laneſborough, who, on conſideration of the ſtate of the province & country, judged the reſolution reaſonable & proper, joined therein, and agreed to abide by it." Afterwards, " at a raiſing in the ſaid Laneſborough, when the greateſt part of the men of that town were aſſembled, it was propoſed to a conſiderable number of them, that all the inhabitants ſhould join together, and ſtand by each other in preventing the officers from arreſting and impriſoning any one of the town for debt, ſo long as the then preſent ſtate of things, as to proceedings in law, ſhould continue — ſeveral of the company to whom the propoſition was then made expreſſed their approbation thereof — none of them objected to it. — In the evening, the company went to the tavern," where the ſame officer, aided by a poſſe, endeavored to execute a writ againſt one Franklin, then preſent, — a ſcuffle enſued, and the officer and poſſe were driven off. " The evidence that there was at the trial, of this previous confederacy, and that Warren with the other perſons charged acted purſuant to ſuch confederacy in the reſcue of Franklin, was what the attorney-general ſpecially relied on in arguing the caſe, to ſhow it was a riot, and to confute my hypotheſis of its being but a ſudden treſpaſs and affray; and two of the Juſtices, viz., Judge Cuſhing and Judge Oliver, in delivering the caſe to the jury, ſpecially obſerved and inſiſted upon it, that it was plain from the evidence that the aſſault," &c., " was committed in conſequence and purſuance of the previous agreement and confederacy above mentioned." " The Chief Juſtice did not give his opinion upon the circumſtances in the evidence which ſhewed it to be in execution of a previous confederacy, but, for reaſons beſt known to himſelf, choſe to make a different ſtate of the caſe, which indeed was ingenious enough, but not altogether ſo pertinent and proper, becauſe it was (as I humbly conceive) ſhort of the evidence. — It is to be obſerved that the preſentment charged the defendants with a riot, and the Court ſuppoſed the only doubt of the jury would be, whether the aforeſaid facts, as they appeared in evidence, conſtituted a riot; and therein the Court ſuppoſed it was proper the jury ſhould be determined by their opinion, and therefore particularly informed the Jury it was clearly the opinion of the Court that the facts proved conſtituted a riot, and that therefore the jury, in their opinion, could have no difficulty in finding Warren guilty according to the preſentment." The jury were charged with the caſe at night. The next morning, " either before they delivered their verdict, or before ſentence," the priſoner's counſel " did ſuggeſt to the Chief Juſtice that it was clear from Hawkins' Pleas of the Crown, 1st Book, Chapter 65, Sect. 6, which ſection I turned to and he read, that, ac-

1767. "cording to the evidence, the crime which the defendant had been guilty "of, (if of any), was High Treaſon; to which the Chief Juſtice replied, "he was well apprized of what Hawkins ſaid, and that he knew, if an "aſſembly of men, combined for the purpoſe, ſhould by force oppoſe the "execution of one ſingle ſtatute, they would be guilty of High Treaſon, "which moſt certainly is in general true, ſound doctrine and clear law. "3 Inſt. 9–10 — 5 Bacon's Abr. 117 — Hawk. P. C. *ubi ſupra* — The "ſame in Burn's Juſtice."

Nevertheleſs, the priſoner was convicted of a riot, and fined three pounds. In the article from which we quote, Major Hawley argues with great force that the priſoner was either guilty of High Treaſon, or, owing to the ſtate of nature to which the cloſing the courts had reduced ſociety, of no crime at all, — judged merely by the light of reaſon. — "But" (he ſays) "I think that the puniſhing him for *a riot* cannot be juſti-"fied upon any principle or hypotheſis; for it plainly appears, that his "conduct was either innocent and juſtifiable, or that he was guilty of "the higheſt crime, viz., *High Treaſon:* And if it appeared to the court "and the King's counſel, that his crime was High Treaſon, which, I "think, muſt have been the caſe *on their principles*, would it not have "been more becoming the character of the firm and intrepid judge, to "have adviſed that he ſhould have been diſmiſſed from the preſentment "of a riot, and charged anew, and brought to trial for his true offence, "than without any intimation of his Majeſty's pleaſure, to have pro-"ceeded to convict him of a riot, and fine him *in the ſum of three* "*pounds.*"

This article by Major Hawley was in reply to what he conceived to have been a miſſtatement of the facts, by a writer ſigning himſelf "Philanthrop," who habitually wrote in ſupport of the government. See 3 Hutch. Hiſt. Maſs. 164, 175.

1767.

Malcolm *verf.* Gleafon.

MAICOLM *v.* GLEASON.

Rec. 1767. Fol. 101.

The Acceptor of a negotiable Order is liable to a fubfequent Indorfee, without Notice of the Indorfement.

A. drew a negotiable Order upon B. B. accepted the Order, and after Acceptance the Order was indorfed over. The Queftion was, if the *Indorfee* could fupport an Action againft B. (upon his Acceptance aforefaid upon the Prefentment of the Order by the Payee) before perfonal Notice given B., of Indorfement.

Ruled, unanimoufly, by all the five Judges, on Argument, that the Action was well brought, and that Notice to B. of Indorfement was not neceffary; for B. was liable to *Indorfee* in the fame Manner that he was to *Payee*, on the Acceptance.

Gibbs *verf.* Gibbs.

GIBBS *v.* GIBBS.

Rec. 1767. Fol. 113.

Queftions of Law on the Conftruction of a Will muft be raifed by fpecial Verdict, and not by an Objection to the Admiffion of the Will in Evidence, on the Ground that it does not fupport the Declaration.

Prefent:
The whole Court.

THE Demandant counts as Heir in Tail under a Will.

Mr. Auchmuty objected to the Will going in as Evidence to the Jury, becaufe the Will did not fupport the Declaration, as it gave only an Eftate for Life to the Anceftor of the Demandant.

The

1767.
GIBBS
v.
GIBBS.

The Court, after a short Argument, were unanimously of Opinion that the Exception was the first of the Kind ever made; that, if allowed, would destroy all Wills from being Evidence, as it would bring the real Point in (as they expressed it) upon a Side Motion, and would be subversive of the hitherto uninterrupted Course of Practice. The Exception being overruled, *the Court* said, the Will should go in, as Evidence to the Jury, who, upon finding the special Matter, would bring the Point of Law properly before the Court.

HALL
v.
MILLER.

Rec. 1767.
Fol. 118.

Evidence of a Sale upon a Credit will support a Declaration upon a Promise to pay on Demand, where the Time of the Promise is laid after the Expiration of the Credit.

Hall *vers.* Miller.

THE Plaintiff brought Assumpsit *to pay on Demand*, upon Account annexed, (1) and gave in Evidence his Book, in which was a Memorandum of an Agreement made at the Day of Sale, that Months Credit was given the Defendant. The Time alledged in the Declaration, of the Defendant's being indebted, *was, after a Lapse of the Months Credit.* Now, the Question was, whether this Evidence supported the Declaration.

Mr.

(1) The sufficiency of the common form of declaration in assumpsit, upon account annexed, was questioned in the case of *Rider* v. *Robbins*, 13 Mass. 284, and it was there held to rest on immemorial practice. See 2 Mass. 398; also Dummer's Defence of the New England Charters, (ed. 1745,) 20, where a description is given of the early practice in the courts of law.—"If it be Matter of Account, the Account is annexed to the Writ, and Copies of both left with the Defendant."

1767.
HALL
v.
MILLER.

Mr. Auchmuty urged, that this Evidence proved a different Contract from that alledged by the Plaintiff; for he declares upon a Promiſe *to pay upon Demand*, and brings in Evidence that the Contract was not to pay on Demand, but that a long Credit was given: And, though the Promiſe is not alledged to be upon Demand, *till after the Time of Credit was elapſed*, yet, that can never alter the Nature of the original Agreement. There never was a Promiſe *to pay upon Demand*, if we believe the Plaintiff's own Book; and the Proof varying from the Allegation, the Plaintiff muſt, in this Action, fail.

But it was anſwered, and *Reſolved by the whole Court*, (unanimouſly) that the *Promiſe* to pay *on Demand* being laid *after the Time of Credit was elapſed*, was well ſupported by this Evidence; for, the Defendant having neglected Payment at the Time limited, *after that Time paſt*, the Law raiſes a Promiſe to pay on Demand, and the Plaintiff may *then* well declare ſo. And *the Court* relied on Gilbert's Law of Evid. 191, where "one brought "Aſſumpſit for £20, and gave in Evidence a Prom- "iſe that if two would ſurrender their Right, he "would pay them £20 apiece, and that they did "ſurrender their Right, this is good Evidence to "ſupport the Declaration; for the Promiſe is laid "abſolutely in the Declaration, and the Promiſe in "Proof is upon Condition, yet, when that Condi- "tion is performed, the Duty becomes abſolute, and "ſo is good Proof upon this Declaration."

1767.
Noble v. Smith.

Rec. 1767. Fol. 121.

A partial Confideration of a Promiffory Note cannot be fhewn, in Reduction of Damages, in an Action by the Promifee.

Noble *verf.* Smith.

S. Quincy & *J. Adams*	*for Pl'ff.*	*J. Otis* & *R. Auchmuty*	*for De't.*

THIS Cafe was very largely debated by the Council on both Sides; and the Queftion was, if Evidence might be given to the Jury, of a partial Confideration of a Note of Hand, upon which the Plaintiff, Promifee in the Note, had brought his Action.

The Books produced by the Bar were, Trials *per Pais*, 408; Cunningh. Bills of Exch. 122, 141; 1 Salk. 25, *Meredith & Short;* 2 Ld. Raym'd. 1430, 1431; 1 Stran. 674; 2 Bac. 4; Gilbt. Rep. 154.

Juft. Trowbridge was for admitting the Evidence to go in, in Mitigation of Damages.

Oliver, Juft. was againft the Admiffion.

Cufhing, Juft. of the fame Opinion.

Lynde, Juft. was of Judge Trowbridge's Opinion, for Admiffion.

The Chief Juftice acknowledged the Point was of confiderable Importance, and not without its Difficulties on either Side. Many Mifchiefs and Inconveniences

1767. NOBLE v. SMITH.

veniences, he ſaid, might ariſe, upon the Refuſal or Admiſſion of ſuch Evidence. On the one Hand, a Note to a conſiderable Amount may be obtained upon a very trifling Conſideration: It ſeems hard that an Inquiring into the Conſideration ſhould be denied, and that Evidence ſhould be refuſed in Diminution of Damages. On the other Hand, People, upon a Settlement of Accounts, or Matters in Diſpute, think themſelves quite ſafe in taking a Note for the Sum due, and reaſonably ſuppoſe all Neceſſity of keeping the Evidence of the Conſideration at an End; it would be big with Miſchief to oblige People to ſtand always prepared to conteſt Evidence that might be offered to the Sufficiency of the Conſideration. This would be doubly ſtrong in Favour of an Indorſee. Upon the whole, as many more, and, I think, greater Inconveniences would naturally ariſe, if ſuch Examinations into the Conſideration of Notes were admitted. I am therefore againſt it in this Caſe. (1)

The Council for the Defendant, upon this Reſolution of the Court, given *ſeriatim*, confeſſed Judgment for the Sum ſued for.*

* *Vid.* Styles, 58, *Bruer & Sowthwell*, and 1 Vin. 332, bot., 332 top. Actions (of Aſſum.) (Y).

---

(1) The oppoſite doctrine has long been eſtabliſhed. *Pariſh* v. *Stone*, 14 Pick. 210, *Shaw, C. J.* — "It ſeems very clear that want of conſideration either total or partial may always be ſhown by way of defence; and that it will bar the action or reduce the damages, as it is found to be total or partial reſpectively."

1767.
CURTIS v. NIGHTINGALE.

Rec. 1767. Fol. 117.

Aſſumpſit for Money had and received will not lie to recover the Conſideration Money paid for land originally conveyed to the Plaintiff, and ſubſequently to a third Party, on the Plaintiff's Deed being deſtroyed before recording.

Curtis *verſ.* Nightingale.

INDEBITATUS ASSUMPSIT for Money had and received to the Plaintiff's Uſe. The Caſe was,— Nightingale, for a good Conſideration, ſold a Tract of Land to the Plaintiff, by Deed; and afterwards, the Plaintiff's Deed being burnt before recording, the ſaid Nightingale conveyed the ſame Land to another Perſon. The Plaintiff now brought this Action to recover back the Conſideration Money.

Mr. Dana objected, that this Action would not lie, but that a ſpecial Action of the Caſe, upon the Fraud, ſhould have been brought. 1 Salk. 22. Comb. 341. 2 Stran. 916. 1 Bac. 167.

A Majority of the Court was of Opinion that this Action for Money had and received would not lie, and ſo directed the Jury, who found accordingly.* (1)

N. B.

* Vid. 2 Ld. Raym'd. 1216, 1217.

(1) It was formerly the rule, that what was a tort in its inception could not be made the ſubject of an implied aſſumpſit. But many exceptions to this rule have been eſtabliſhed. Where goods tortiouſly obtained or held have been ſold by the wrong doer, the owner may waive the tort, confirm the ſale and maintain aſſumpſit for the price received. 2 Ld. Raym. 1216 (cited by the reporter *ſupra*). *Jones* v. *Hoar*, 5 Pick. 285. Whether in a caſe like the one above reported the plaintiff would not have an election, either to conſider the ſale as reſcinded, and recover his original conſideration, or to treat the defendant as his agent in

1767.

CURTIS v. NIGHTINGALE.

Rec. 1768. Fol. 139.

A Deed caſually deſtroyed by Fire may be proved by Witneſſes.

N. B. A ſpecial Action on the Caſe was afterward brought, and, on Demurrer to the Declaration, the Superiour Court (March Term, Suffolk, 1768) gave Judgment in Favour of the Plaintiff, on the Authority of 10 Rep. 92, b.* (2)

* Viner, Evid. (T. b. 22) pl. 1, 3, & ye Note, & ye Authorities there cited. Ib. (T. b. 65) pl. 3.

---

in the ſecond conveyance, and recover the laſt received purchaſe-money — *quære*. On a ſubſequent page of the MS., this caſe is again reported, and the action is there ſtated to have been brought "to recover back the Conſideration Money, either of the 1ſt or 2d Deed." By the record, however, it appears that the action was brought for the original price paid by the plaintiff.

(2) *Doctor Leyfield's Caſe*, where it is laid down that a deed caſually deſtroyed by fire may be "proved in evidence to the jury by witneſſes, that affliction be not added to affliction." The demurrer was evidently on the ground that the deed was not pleaded with a *profert*. Formerly, in caſe of a loſt deed, relief could only be had in equity. Id. (ed. of 1826) *in notis*.

March Term

VIII Geo. 3.

1768.

CHARGE TO THE GRAND JURY.

The Charge given to the Grand Jury by the Chief Juſtice was as follows.

GENTLEMEN of the Grand Jury: At the Opening of the Court you are ſenſible that the Path of your Duty ſhould be pointed out to you; and, in Order that you may have an Apprehenſion of what is incumbent on you, I ſhall endeavour to give you ſome Idea of thoſe Principles, on which the Law is founded.

Our Anceſtors, Gentlemen, when they came over to this Country, brought with them the Common Law of our Mother Country, (which is with great Propriety ſo called,) and, although their firſt Charter bound them down to make no Laws contrary to the Law of England, yet, from the Situation they were then in, and from their peculiar Circumſtances, they

1768.

CHARGE TO THE GRAND JURY.

they then apprehended they had a Right to adopt the Judicial Laws of Mofes which were given to the Ifraelites of Old. They, at that Time, confidered, not how Crimes affected the Peace and Harmony of Society, but, almoft always adapted their Punifhment to the real Guilt of the Criminal. Thus, they punifhed Adultery, with Death (1); Blafphemy, with Death (2); nay, they carried it fo far, that a refractory, difobedient Child, if he continued obftinate and incorrigible after Admonition and Reproof, was punifhed by whipping very feverely; and, if that Punifhment did not reclaim or work fome Reformation, he was put to Death. (3) I can't but regret that we have departed fo far from the Spirit of our Fathers, under the old Charter, as that a refractory, difobedient Child has become fo common * among us as fcarce to be noticed. I could mention many other Crimes and Punifhments under the old Charter, all of which went on this fame Principle I before obferved.

Upon a Judgment given againft the old Charter, the People could never obtain fo great a Boon, as they thought their old Charter: Since, you are fenfible,

* *Qu.* of the Juftice of this Remark.

(1) Anc. Chart. 59.

(2) This act was paffed in 1646, and by its terms was expreffly extended to "pagan indians"—"albeit we compel them not to the "Chriftian faith — neverthelefs, the blafpheming of the true God cannot "be excufed by any ignorance or infirmity of human nature, the Eter-"nal Power and Godhead being known by the light of nature, and the "creation of the world." Anc. Chart. 61.

(3) Anc. Chart. 60.

1768.

CHARGE TO THE GRAND JURY.

ſible, they appointed all their Officers, made all their Laws, without any Controul from Home. At this Day, our Governour, Lieutenant Governour and Secretary are appointed from Great Britain, and our provincial Acts are all ſubject to a Negative from thence. We ſtand, therefore, upon quite a different Footing from our Forefathers, and the Principle of our Laws is very variant from that which governed them under the old Charter. There were ſeveral Attempts made, ſince our preſent Charter, to enact Laws upon Old-Charter Principles; but they all failed, and the Laws were diſallowed in Great Britain.

The Principle of Law which now governs us, is to puniſh Crimes, only as they affect Society. From hence it is, we ſee, many Offences in England are puniſhed, often in no Ways proportioned to the real Heinouſneſs of the Crime: — Thus, to counterfeit a Shilling is a higher Crime than to kill one's Father. One is High Treaſon — the other is only Felony.

High Treaſon, Gentlemen, is the higheſt Offence our Law knows of, and is a Crime againſt the very End of Government, and tends to deſtroy its very Being. Moſt of the Offences which amount to High Treaſon, we, here, by Reaſon of our Diſtance from the Perſon of our Sovereign, cannot commit; ſome we may, which, before I cloſe, I may have Occaſion to mention.

(Here the Chief Juſtice was conciſe upon the Articles, Felony, Burglary, Forgery, Arſon, Sodomy and

1768.

CHARGE TO THE GRAND JURY.

and Theft; upon which laſt, he obſerved, that our provincial Law had reduced the Penalty ſo low, he wiſhed the Government would, ſince the great Increaſe of that pernicious Crime, make ſome further Proviſion againſt it.)

Perjury, Gentlemen, is not, by the Law of England, or our Provincial Law, made capital, which has often excited my Wonder. There is no Crime I now think of, more pernicious to Society. Perjury, in a legal Senſe, is a falſe Swearing in a Court of Record, in a Point material to the Iſſue. But that Man muſt be abandoned to all Senſe of Religion, who can call his God to witneſs a Falſehood, even where, in a Law-Senſe, it might not amount to Perjury. The lighteſt Puniſhment ſuch a Man muſt expect to feel, is to be perpetually goaded with the Stings of his own Conſcience. Surely, the Time or Place can be no Ways material in the Divine Mind, where a Man willfully ſwears a Falſehood. He, who can deliberately call his Maker to witneſs to a Lie, muſt live in Horror all his Days. I am ſorry we have ſo much Reaſon to think this Crime is ſo frequently committed in our Cuſtom-Houſe Oaths.

There are a Multitude of other Crimes of the moſt dangerous Tendency, which ſtrike the Mind of the Generality, when we hear Rumours of them, with no great Horror—yet are plainly introductive of the utmoſt Confuſion into Society, deſtroy its Harmony, produce Bloodſhed and Murder—in ſhort, if allowed to increaſe, they muſt ſap the Foundation of all Government. Such are Riots, Routs

1768.

CHARGE TO THE GRAND JURY.

Routs and unlawful Affemblies. Yet, who would live in a State where he was frequently alarmed with Reports of the Kind? You, Gentlemen, who live in the Country, feldom hear of these Things, but we, who live in Town, fee, feel and hear of them often — that there is a going to be a Rumpus, as it is called — a cant Word for a Riot. This excites no great Horror in our Mind; but if we were told, that fuch a Man's Houfe was to be deftroyed — fuch a Man to be killed — it would fill us with great Dread of the Confequences. — Yet the plain natural Tendency of thefe Things is to this very End.

An Infult, only, may, at firft, be defigned to a private Perfon; but, when once an Affembly is gathered, any one of that Company who has a private Pique againft any Individual, and has a Hand in the Lead, may eafily draw fuch a Multitude to commit Crimes which, at firft, they had not the leaft Intention to do; nay, would have fhuddered at, if mentioned.

(Here the Chief Juftice went into the well-known Law of Aggreffors and Defenders in Riots and Affaults, and recommended to the Inhabitants of Bofton a watchful Eye over their Servants.)

One other Offence, which tends much to difturb the Peace and deftroy the Order of the Community, is that of Libelling.*

This

* If the Severity of the Law, touching Libels, as it hath fometimes been laid down, be duly weighed, it muft ftrike both Houfes of Parliament with Terror and Difmay. The Lords' Proteft, in November, 1763. p. 9.

1768.

CHARGE TO THE GRAND JURY.

This Offence has increaſed very much, of late, and threatens the Subverſion of all Rule among us. There are People who make it their Buſineſs to furniſh the Preſs with the moſt ſcandalous and defamatory Pieces.

No Government,—in Europe, I am ſure,—not one that is counted the moſt free, would have tolerated thoſe libellous Pieces which we have ſeen in the publick Prints, within this Twelve-month paſt. Theſe Publications have often brought to my Mind a Story I have heard of one Wilkes, of whom you all have heard—and whom, I am ſorry to ſay it, ſome among us ſhow too great a Deſire to imitate. That Perſon was once aſked, while he was writing, how far a Man in an Engliſh Government might go, in his Publications, and not come within the Laws of High Treaſon. To which he anſwered, he was juſt then trying how far he could go. Theſe Authors among us ſeem to be trying the ſame dangerous Experiment. I will not pronounce thoſe Authors guilty of High Treaſon; but I will venture to ſay, they come as near it as poſſible, and not come within it.

For theſe ſeven or eight Years, I have made it my conſtant Practice to read every Book upon the Crown-Law I could meet with; and I never yet read or heard, till of late, the Doctrine that ſome particular Perſon muſt be ſtruck at—that Names of particular Perſons were neceſſary—that the initial or final Letters muſt be inſerted, in Order to make a Libel.

This

1768.
CHARGE TO THE GRAND JURY.

This Notion which has lately prevailed ſeems to ariſe from a Miſtake of ſome of our Books, where ſome defamatory Pieces have been adjudged Libels, becauſe the Authors had put down the initial or final Letters of the Names of certain Perſons. But, ſurely, it never follows from hence, that this is the only Way of making a Libel.

The Rule of Law is, that the Perſon libelled muſt be ſufficiently marked out; for, if the Perſon is ſo fully delineated, that he is well known without putting his Name, it rather adds to the Heinouſneſs of the Offence, as it ſhows the deliberate Malice of the Author, and his wicked Endeavours to elude the Law.

Neither is it neceſſary to a Libel, that any Perſon at all be mentioned: As in a Libel againſt the Government, wrote in Queen Ann's Time, which contained a Defence of Hereditary Right, and a Denial of the Right of Parliament to fix the Crown where it then was. (1) So there may be a Libel upon Religion, — as I remember, when I was quite young, to have heard of one Woolſton who wrote ſeveral Treatiſes againſt the Miracles of Our Saviour. (2) Thus, in publiſhing of a very obſcene Book, as the Earl of Rocheſter's Works. And one Curl, I think, was condemned to the Pillory for a Libel of the ſame Sort. (3) The Duke of Wharton too, who wrote a Book called Ezeriph and Sophron, in which a Parallel was run between thoſe two Characters,

---

(1) *Dr. Sacheverell's Caſe*, 15 Howell's State Trials, 1.

(2) See 26 Howell's State Trials, 676.

(3) 10 Howell's State Trials, 153.

1768.

CHARGE TO THE GRAND JURY.

acters, making Sophron, by whom was meant the Pretender, a very wise Prince, and Ezeriph, by whom was intended the King then on the Throne, a very weak and wicked Man. (4) In all these Writings and many more I might name, no Names were mentioned nor ever supposed necessary to make them Libels; but the Authors or Publishers were committed, and punished in the severest Manner.

And one Franklin, who wrote against Ministers, was imprisoned and punished; though it was objected, that there were Ministers of Religion, as well as State. (5) Nothing can be clearer, than that a Libel may as well be without a Name, as with one, and without any initial or final Letters. As painting a Sign, drawing a Man's Picture with a Gallows near it, or any other Way sufficiently descriptive of the Person intended.

I remember that Lord Talbot, one of the greatest Judges that ever sat on the English Bench, lays it down as the Rule of Libels, that, if, upon the Connexion and Comparing of the several Parts, and then taking the Whole together, the Person was plainly pointed out and easily known to every Reader, it was sufficient to constitute it a Libel.— It is enough if the Thing is obvious to a common Understanding.

I expect some will cry out, our Liberties are endangered — the Liberty of the Press is struck at — but

(4) 17 Howell's State Trials, 666, & note.

(5) 17 Howell's State Trials, 626.

1768.
CHARGE TO THE GRAND JURY.

but let ſuch People conſider, that, if we may write, why not ſpeak as freely of Men? Shall a Man print that, of the firſt Ruler of a State, which he will not ſpeak of any one Man in the Community? Shall our first Magiſtrate be thus ſlandered with impunity in an *infamous* Paper?* — I believe I may ſay thus much, without incurring the Imputation of prejudging.

Formerly, no Man could print his Thoughts, ever ſo modeſtly and calmly, or with ever ſo much Candour and Ingenuouſneſs, upon any Subject whatever, without a Licence. When this Reſtraint was taken off, then was the true Liberty of the Preſs. Every Man who prints, prints at his Peril; as every Man who ſpeaks, ſpeaks at his Peril. It was in this Manner I treated this Subject at the laſt Term, yet the Liberty of the Preſs, and the Danger of an *Imprimatur* was canted about, as if the Preſs was going under ſome new and illegal Reſtraint. No Gentleman of the Bar, I am ſure, could have ſo miſunderſtood me. This Reſtraint of the Preſs, in the Prevention of Libels, is the only Thing which will preſerve your Liberty. To ſuffer the licentious Abuſe of Government is the moſt likely Way to deſtroy its Freedom. — But ſhall a Printer be puniſhed? — why, it is ſaid, it is his Living. — Shall a Highwayman be puniſhed? To rob is his Living. Shall a Thief? — to ſteal is his Living.† Whence

* *Vide* the Supplement to the BOSTON GAZETTE, February 29, 1768, Boſton Gazette, March 7, 1768, March 14, 1768. (6)
† *Vid.* Kelyng, 23.

(6) See note at the end of this charge.

Whence is it, that this Difference is made between him who robs me of my Reputation, and who takes away my Property? The former is the worſt of the two.

1768. CHARGE TO THE GRAND JURY.

You, Gentlemen, may be at ſome Loſs, what is Evidence of publiſhing a Libel. I will briefly mention what is undoubted Law in this Caſe. A Bookſeller having a libellous Book in his Shop to ſell is full Evidence enough to you, Gentlemen, of the Publiſher. To ſend a Libel about by one's Servant to ſell is Evidence alſo. Gentlemen, the general Rule of Law here takes Place, that who ever does a Thing by another, does it himſelf.

A Libel may be as well againſt a private Perſon, Gentlemen, as againſt one in a publick Station; and the Diſturbances Things of this Sort are likely to breed, is very obvious to every Man; but the Conſequences are infinitely more miſchievous when the Chief Ruler is openly attacked. — There is no End to theſe Things.

But, it is ſaid, if we have a bad Ruler, there is no other Means of Redreſs. This is a Miſtake. To be ſure the *Chief Ruler* of the Province *is not to be brought into this Court to anſwer for any Miſdemeanour:* but we muſt ſeek Relief from Great Britain. (7) *Qu.*
If our Governour acts in an illegal Manner, we have a good King, and can *eaſily* have him removed. *Qu.*
Upon

(7) For an article by Quincy on the liability of all officers to impeachment, and the cauſes therefor, publiſhed in the "Boſton Gazette" of Jan. 4, 1768, ſee App. IV.

1768.

CHARGE TO THE GRAND JURY.

Upon a juſt Complaint we may have a Governour ordered to Weſtminſter and there tryed and puniſhed. We have ſeen Inſtances of this. But, I am ſure, I do not believe our preſent Governour is deſerving of ſuch Treatment: I am myſelf fully convinced of his Uprightneſs and Integrity.

Judge Foſter, who is one of the cleareſt and moſt accurate Writers I ever met with, upon the Crown-Law, lays it down, that no Subject, in Society, has a Right to avenge his own Wrongs, but muſt ſeek his Redreſs in the Method the Laws of his Country allow. And if it ſhould unfortunately happen, that any one Individual ſhould be injured, or greatly wronged, by thoſe appointed to rule over him, and the Laws of the Land afford him no Remedy, he ought patiently to bear his unhappy Lot; and it is incumbent on him to have Recourſe to that Maxim, that Vengeance belongeth only to the *Moſt High.**

Gentlemen of the Grand Jury: You are to remember the Oath of God which is upon you. You are ſworn truly to preſent all ſuch Matters and Things

* *Qu.* if his Honour (the Chief Juſtice) don't refer to Foſter's Crown Law, 296, *q. v.* And

Qu. if Judge Foſter's Words will bear the Conſtruction (as here given) in its full Extent. (8)

---

(8) The paſſage referred to is as follows:

" No man under the protection of the law is to be the avenger of his " own wrongs. If they are of ſuch a nature for which the laws of ſociety " will give him an adequate remedy, thither he ought to reſort: but be " they of what nature ſoever, he ought to bear his lot with patience and " remember, *That Vengeance belongeth only to the Moſt High.*"

1768.

CHARGE TO THE GRAND JURY.

Things as ſhall be given you in Charge.* — Go now and ſee how you can get over your Oath: — Go now and ſee if you can avoid making a Preſentment of thoſe heinous Offences with which you have now been charged. — In doing your Duty and in the Obſervance of your Oath, you may cauſe a Clamour againſt you; Reproach may be thrown on you; you may be vilified and ſlandered; — but remember your own Conſciences. In the faithful Diſcharge of your Duty, you will find, at leaſt, the Approbation of a good Conſcience. You ought not, by any Means, to regard the Cenſure you may meet with, from the Performance of your Duty as Grand Jurymen. Remember that you and I are to give an Account to our God at his awfull Tribunal, how we have diſcharged our reſpective Duties, and of our Obſervance of the ſeveral Oaths of God, with which each of us is laid under the greateſt Obligations. — I hope, Gentlemen,

* *Qu.* if the Words of the Oath will bear any ſuch Conſtruction; and ſee the precedent Words of the Oath in the Law-Book. (9)

---

(9) Prov. St. 4 W. & M. (ed. 1759) 26, where the oath of the foreman and other grand jurors is thus:

"YOU as Foreman of this Inqueſt for the Body of this County of S. You ſhall diligently enquire and a true Preſentment make "of all ſuch Matters and Things as ſhall be given you in Charge; the "King and Queen's Majeſties Counſel, your Fellows and your own, you "ſhall keep ſecret; you ſhall preſent no Man for Envy, Hatred or "Malice; neither ſhall you leave any Man unpreſented for Love, Fear, "Favour or Affection, or Hope of Reward: But you ſhall preſent "Things truly as they come to your Knowledge according to the beſt of "your Underſtanding. *So help you GOD.*"

"THE ſame Oath which your Foreman hath taken on his Part, you and every of you on your Behalf ſhall well and truly "obſerve and keep. *So help you GOD.*"

1768. tlemen, you will bear in Mind what I have now ſaid, and pray that we may all finally be acquitted at the Bar of God.

N. B. The Grand Jury found no Bill for Libelling.

At the Superiour Court held ſhortly after, at Charleſtown, the Chief Juſtice, (as I was well informed,) in his Charge to the Grand Jury, gave a gentle Touch upon the Conduct of this (Suffolk) Grand Jury, in not finding a Bill, after ſuch a Home-Charge.

Qu. of ſome Points of Law laid down in the preceeding Charge:— And *vide* Bollan on the Freedom of Speech and Writing upon Publick Affairs, p. 45, 46, 47, and onward.

Vide 2 Lord Raymond, 879.

NOTE.

The circumſtances which gave riſe to the alleged libel referred to by the Chief Juſtice were as follows: Hutchinſon had been a member of the Council for ſome years before he became Lieutenant Governor. After receiving this appointment, though no longer elected to the Council, he continued to occupy a ſeat in that body, on the ground that the Lieutenant Governor poſſeſſed ſuch a privilege *ex officio*. This claim was the occaſion of a warm controverſy between the Houſe of Repreſentatives and the Governor, the former aſſerting that it afforded "a new and additional inſtance of ambition and a luſt of power" on the part of the Lieutenant Governor, which charge Hutchinſon declares to have been the work of Major Hawley, in revenge for imagined ill-treatment in Court. 3 Hutch. Hiſt. Maſs. 175 (*ante*, p. 249, 50). The Governor repreſented the affair to Lord Shelburne, then Secretary of State, and received a reply, approving of his conduct, cenſuring the Houſe in general, and ſeveral members in in particular. This excited much indignation in the Houſe, who thereupon charged the Governor with miſrepreſenting the character of their members, and alſo prepared a letter to the Secretary of State, praying for an opportunity of vindicating themſelves and their conſtituents. 1768.

It was at this time that the article in queſtion appeared in the ſupplement to the "Boſton Gazette" of February 29, 1768, referred to by the reporter, together with the two following papers, containing the proceedings of the Council and Houſe, and other communications relating to the affair. The file of Boſton newſpapers for that year, from which we copy, is in the poſſeſſion of the Maſſachuſetts Hiſtorical Society, and contains many pen and ink notes, references, &c., by the original owner and compiler, Harbottle Dorr, a Boſton merchant of the period. Theſe we have encloſed in brackets where they occur.

From the ſupplement to the "Boſton Gazette," Feb'y 29, 1768:

[*By Doctor Warren.*]

"Meſſieurs EDES & GILL,

"*Pleaſe to inſert the following.*

"MAY it pleaſe your ———, We have for a long time known your Enmity to this Province. We have had full Proof of your "Cruelty to a loyal People. No Age has perhaps furniſhed a more glar-"ing Inſtance of obſtinate Perſeverance in the Path of Malice, than is "now exhibited in your ———. Could you have reaped any Ad-"vantage from injuring this People, there would have been ſome Excuſe "for the manifold Abuſes with which you have loaded them. But when "a diabolical Thirſt for Miſchief is the alone Motive of your Conduct, "you muſt not wonder if you are treated with open Diſlike; for it is "impoſſible, how much ſoever we endeavour it, to *feel* any Eſteem for "a Man like you ——— Bad as the World may be, there is yet in every "Breaſt ſomething which points out the good Man as an Object worthy "of Reſpect, and marks the guileful treacherous Man-hater for Diſguſt "and Infamy. ———

"Nothing has ever been more intollerable than your Inſolence upon a "late Occaſion, when you had by your jeſuitical Inſinuations, induced a "worthy Miniſter of State, to form a moſt unfavorable Opinion of the "Province in general, and ſome of the moſt reſpectable Inhabitants in "particular. You had the Effrontery to produce a Letter from his Lord-"ſhip, as a Proof of your Succeſs in calumniating us.—— Surely you muſt "ſuppoſe we have loſt all Feeling, or you would not dare thus tauntingly to "diſplay the Trophies of your Slanders, and, upbraidingly, to make us "ſenſible of the inexpreſſible Misfortunes which you have brought upon "us.—— But I refrain, leſt a full Repreſentation of the Hardſhips ſuffered "by this too long inſulted People, ſhould lead them to an unwarranta-"ble Revenge. We never can treat good and patriotic Rulers with too "great

1768. "great Reverence —— But it is certain that Men totally abandoned to "Wickedneſs, can never merit our Regard, be their Stations ever ſo high.

"'*If ſuch Men are by God appointed,*
"'*The Devil may be the Lord's anointed.*'"

[*By Dr. Warren.*] A TRUE PATRIOT."

[*This was ſuppoſed to be a great Libel on the Governor: he recommended it to the Houſe and Council to conſider it. The Grand Jury were inſtructed to find a Bill, but they did not.*]

Bancroft attributes the above article to Otis as "bearing the marks of his excited mind." VI. Bancroft's Hiſt. U. S. 131.

From the "Boſton Gazette," March 7, 1768:

"BOSTON, March 3, 1768.

"Tueſday laſt his Excellency the Governor was pleaſed to ſend the "following Meſſage to the Honorable His Majeſty's Council:

"*Gentlemen of the Council,*

"I HAVE been uſed to treat the Publications in the *Boſton-Gazette* with the Contempt they deſerve, but when they are carried to a "length, which if unnoticed, muſt endanger the very Being of Govern-"ment, I cannot conſiſtently with the Regard to this Province which I "profeſs and really have, excuſe myſelf from taking Notice of a Publica-"tion in the *Boſton-Gazette* of Yeſterday, beginning at the top of the ſec-"ond Column of the ſecond Page of the Supplement. I therefore con-"ſulted you in Council thereupon, and have received your unanimous "Advice that I ſhould lay the ſaid libellous Paper before your Board in "your legiſlative Capacity, and likewiſe before the Houſe of Repreſent-"atives.

"In purſuance of which Advice, I have ordered the Secretary to com-"municate to you the ſaid libellous Paper, that you may take the ſame "together with all the Circumſtances attending it, into your ſerious Con-"ſideration, and do therein as the Majeſty of the King, the Dignity of his "Government, the Honor of this General Court, and the true Intereſt "of this Province, ſhall require.

"FRA. BERNARD.

"Council Chamber, March 1, 1768."

"*In Anſwer to which, there being the full Number of the Council preſent "excepting three Gentlemen, the Board unanimouſly Voted the following "Addreſs to His Excellency.*

"To His Excellency FRANCIS BERNARD, Eſq; Captain General and "Governor in Chief, in and over his Majeſty's Province of the *Maſſa-"chuſetts-Bay* in *New-England*, and Vice-Admiral of the ſame.

"The

" The ADDRESS of His Majesty's Council of the Province aforesaid.

" *May it please your Excellency,*

"THE Board have taken into serious Consideration your Excellency's Message of the first Instant, with the *Boston-Gazette* " communicated therewith.

" The Article in said *Gazette*, refer'd to by your Excellency, gave the " Board a real Concern, not only as it is mischievous in its Tendency, but " as it is a false, scandalous and impudent Libel upon your Excellency.

" Altho' the Author of it may endeavour to screen himself by the " Omission of a Name, yet as it refers particularly to a Transaction so " lately had in the General Court, there is the highest Presumption the " Intention of it could be no otherwise than to place your Excellency in " the most odious Light.

" Such an insolent and licentious Attack on the Chief Magistrate (the " King's Representative in the Province) involves in it an Attack on " Government itself; as it is subversive of all Order and Decorum; and " manifestly tends to destroy the Subordination, that is absolutely necessary " to good Government, and the Well-being of Society. It would have " been flagitious at any Time, but being perpetrated while the General " Court is sitting, and a Transaction in the Court the alledged Occasion of " it, it becomes from these and other Circumstances, in the highest degree " flagitious; and may justly be deemed, not only an Insult on the General " Court; not only an Insult on the King's Authority, and the Dignity of " his Government, but as it concludes with the most unwarrantable Pro- " faneness, an Insult upon the King of Kings.

" The Board therefore cannot but look upon the said Libel with the " utmost Abhorrence and Detestation: and they are firmly persuaded " the Province in general view it in the same light: The Threats there- " fore implied in the said Libel cannot be the Threats of the Province, " but of the Libeller.

" The Board take this Opportunity, with one Voice to assure your Ex- " cellency that, to the utmost of their Power, they will always defend and " support the Honor and Dignity of the King's Governor; and will be " ever ready to do, in this Affair, as in every other, whatever the Majesty " of the King, the Honor of the General Court, and the true Interest of " this Province, shall require.

" In COUNCIL, 3rd March, 1768.

" ORDERED UNANIMOUSLY, That the foregoing Address be presented " to His Excellency the Governor, and that *Samuel Danforth, Benja-* " *min Lincoln, William Brattle, Thomas Hubbard, and Harrison Gray,* " Esqrs., be a Committee to wait on His Excellency therewith.

" A. OLIVER, Secr'y.

35

1768.

" *His Excellency was pleased to return the following Answer:*

" Gentlemen,

"I Thank you most heartily for this Address, in which you express so full and unanimous a Sense of your Duty to the King, and your " Resolution to support his Government in this Province. For myself, I " am so fortified in a Consciousness of my own Integrity, which has hith- " erto defied the utmost Malice to impeach it publickly, that I am not to " be moved by the impotent Attacks of an anonymous Libeller. I should " not have taken Notice of the Libel in question, if I had not apprehended " it pregnant with Danger to the Government. As you are of the same " Opinion, I have only to assure you that I will at all Times most readily " join with you in all proper Measures to maintain the Authority of the " King, and promote the Welfare of the People, within the Province, " committed by His Majesty to my Charge.

" Fra. Bernard.

" Council Chamber,
" March 3, 1768.

" *His Excellency sent the like Message to the House of Representatives* " *as the preceding to the Council,* mutatis mutandis; *to which the House* " *made the following Answer,*

" *In the House of Representatives, March* 3, 1778.

"ORDERED, That Mr. *Hancock*, Mr. *Otis*, Col. *Ward*, Mr. *Spooner*, and Capt. *Bradford*, be a Committee to wait on his " Excellency the Governor, with the following Answer to his Message " of the 1st Instant.

" T. Cushing, Spk'r.

" *May it please your Excellency,*

"IN Duty and great Respect to his Majesty's Representative and Governor of the Province, this House have given all due Atten- " tion to your Message of the first Instant. You are pleased to recom- " mend to their serious Consideration, a publication in the *Boston Gazette* " of Monday last as ' being carried to a length, which if unnoticed, must " endanger the very Being of Government.' In this View, your Excel- " lency, in the Notice you have taken of it, without doubt, acted ' con- " sistently with the Regard to this Province, which you profess.'

" We are very sorry that any Publication in the News Paper, or any " other Cause, should give your Excellency an Apprehension of Danger " to the Being or Dignity of His Majesty's Government here. But this " House, after Examination into the Nature and Importance of the Pa- " per referred to, cannot see Reason to admit of such Conclusion as your " Excellency has formed. No particular Person publick or private is

" named

" named in it: And as it doth not appear to the House, that any thing " contained in it can affect 'the Majesty of the King, the Dignity of the " Government, the Honour of the General Court or the true Interest of " the Province,' they think they may be fully justified in their Determi- " nation to take no further Notice of it.* 1768.

" The Liberty of the Press is a great Bulwark of the Liberty of the " People: It is therefore the incumbent Duty of those who are consti- " tuted the Guardians of the People's Rights to defend and maintain it. " This House, however, as one Branch of the Legislature, in which Ca- " pacity alone they have any Authority, are ready to discountenance an " Abuse of this Privilege, whenever there shall be Occasion for it: Should " the proper Bounds of it be at any Time transgressed, to the Prejudice " of Individuals or the Publick; it is their Opinion at present, that Pro- " vision is already made for the Punishment of Offenders in the common " Course of the Law. This Provision the House apprehend, in the pres- " ent State of Tranquility in the Province, is sufficient, without the " Interposition of the General Assembly; which however, it is hoped, " will, at all Times, be both ready and willing, to support the executive " Power, in the due Administration of Justice, whenever any extraor- " dinary Aid shall become needful."

*" *The Division upon this Question was* 56 *to* 18. *The Division in the House upon this Message was* 39 *to* 30."

From the same paper:

" *Messieurs* Edes & Gill,

" *Please to insert the following:*

"MY *first performance*, has by a strange kind of compliment, been by some applied to his Excellency Governor Bernard. " It is not for me to account for the construction put upon it. Every " man has a right to make his own remarks, and if he satisfies himself, " he will not displease me. I will however inform the Public, that I " have the most sacred regard to the characters of all good men, and " would sooner cut my hand from my body, than strike at the reputation " of an honest member of the community: But there are circumstances, " in which not justice alone, but humanity itself, obliges us to hold up *the* " *villain to view*, and expose his guilt, to prevent his destroying the " innocent. — Whoever he is whose *conscience* tells him he is not the " monster I have portraited, may rest assured I did not aim at him; but " the person who *knows* the black picture exhibited, to be his own, is " welcome to take it to himself. — The Imputation of disaffection to the " King and the Government, brought against me by his Majesty's coun- " cil, I shall answer only by a quotation from the paper which they have " been pleased to censure, where I say, 'We can never treat good and " patriotic rulers with too great reverence.' In which sentence I hope " the

1768. " the honorable Board will not ſay I have omitted to declare my ſentiments of the duty which every good ſubject owes to his preſent Majeſty, " and all worthy ſubordinate magiſtrates. And I flatter myſelf, that the " ſentiments of the Board coincide with mine; if they do not, I muſt " diſſent from them. — Their charge of profaneſs, I humbly apprehend, " was occaſioned by their *forcing* a ſenſe upon the two laſt lines, totally " different from what I intended they ſhould convey — My deſign was to " compare wicked men, and eſpecially wicked magiſtrates, to thoſe enemies to mankind the devils, and to intimate that the devils themſelves " might boaſt of divine authority to ſeduce and ruin mankind, with as " much reaſon and juſtice, as wicked rulers can pretend to derive from " God, or from his word, a right to oppreſs, harraſs and enſlave their " fellow-creatures. The beneficent Lord of the univerſe delights in " viewing the happineſs of all men: And ſo far as civil government is " of divine inſtitution, it was calculated for the greateſt good of the " whole community: And whenever it ceaſes to be of general advantage, it ceaſes to be of divine appointment; and the magiſtrates in ſuch " a community have no claim to that honor which the divine Legiſlator " has aſſigned to magiſtrates of his election. I hope the honorable Board " will not condemn a man for expreſſing his contempt for the odious doctrines of divine hereditary right in princes, and of paſſive obedience, " which he thinks diſhonorary to almighty God, the common and impartial Father of the ſpecies, and ruinous both to Kings and Subjects; " and which if adhered to, would dethrone his preſent Majeſty, and deſtroy the Britiſh nation. The honorable Board is humbly requeſted " to examine whether the above is not the moſt natural and obvious " ſenſe of the quoted lines: Certainly when I read them, I thought it " the only ſenſe; and I ſhall think myſelf very *unhappy* in my readers, " ſhould they generally put that conſtruction upon them which the honorable Board have been pleaſed to adopt.

" I ſhall at all times write my ſentiments with freedom, and with decency too; the rules of which I am not altogether unacquainted with. " — While the Preſs is open, I ſhall publiſh whatever I think conducive " to general emolument; when it is ſuppreſſed, I ſhall look upon my " country as loſt, and with a ſteady fortitude expect to feel the general " ſhock!

" A TRUE PATRIOT."

" PRINTERS!

" *Insert the following!*

" A *libel* on a *Lobſter.*

" I Hope none will be offended; but I really prefer a *Crab* to a *Lobſter.**

" *Libellus Famoſus.*

" * *See* 5 *Report.* 125.

"*A Libel on Crabs.*

"I Care not a Farthing who is offended; I would not give one Lobſter for Ten Crabs.*

"*Famoſus Libellus.*

"* *See* Weſtminſter *Journal.*"

From the "Boſton Gazette," March 14, 1768.

"*Meſſieurs* Edes & Gill, [*Dr. Warren.*]

"*Pleaſe to inſert the following:*

"WITH Pleaſure I hear the general Voice of this People in favor of freedom; and it gives me ſolid ſatisfaction to find "all orders of unplaced independent men, firmly determined, as far as in "them lies, to ſupport their own RIGHTS, and the Liberty of the "PRESS. The hon. houſe of Repreſentatives have ſhewed themſelves "reſolute in the cauſe of juſtice — The Grand Jurors have convinced us, "that no influence is able to overcome their attachment to their country, "and our free conſtitution — they deſerve honor — But this is one of "thoſe caſes, in which by doing as they have done, they really merit "praiſe; yet the path was ſo plain, that to have done otherwiſe, would "have rendered them ——— indeed!

"While this People know their true intereſt, they will be able to diſtin-"guiſh their friends from their enemies; and with uniform courage, will "defend from tyrannic violence, all thoſe who generouſly offer themſelves "volunteers in the cauſe of truth and humanity. But if ever a miſtaken "complaiſance leads them to ſacrifice their privileges, or the well-mean-"ing aſſertors of them, they will *deſerve* bondage, and ſoon will find "*themſelves in chains.*

"Every ſociety of men have a clear right to refute any unjuſt aſper-"ſions upon their characters; eſpecially when they feel the ill effects of "ſuch aſperſions: And though they may not purſue the ſlanderer from "motives of revenge, yet are obliged to endeavour to detect him, that ſo "he may be prevented from injuring them again. — This province has "been moſt barbarouſly traduced; and now groans under the weight of "thoſe misfortunes which have been thereby brought upon it; we have "detected ſome of the authors; we will zealouſly endeavour to deprive "them of the power of injuring us hereafter. —— We will ſtrip the ſer-"pents of their ſtings, & conſign to diſgrace, all thoſe guileful betrayers "of their country. —— There is but one way for men to avoid being ſet "up as objects of general hate, which is, NOT TO DESERVE IT.

"A true Patriot."

1768.

"*To the PRINTERS.*

[*S. Adams.*]

"THERE is nothing so *fretting* and *vexatious*, nothing so justly TERRIBLE to tyrants, and their tools and abettors, as a FREE "PRESS. The reason is obvious; namely, Because it is, as it has been "very justly observed, in a *spirited* answer to a *spirited* speech, '*the* "*bulwark of the People's Liberties.*' For this reason it is ever watched "by those who are forming plans for the destruction of the People's "Liberties, with an *envious* and *malignant* eye. If a villain is por-"traited and held up to the public, rather than fail in the attempt to cast "an odium upon the press, they will even *own the character*, and pro-"nounce it a libel; for it is their absurd doctrine, *the more true*, *the* "*more libellous.* It is not at all surprizing, that *your* press is hated, and "*your* paper branded with the name of '*infamous*,' by *some* men: "These are the men who formed and pushed to the utmost of their "power, the late *detested Stamp-Act*: These are the men who have been "forging chains and manacles; and when they could not, after the most "impudent attempt, *force* them upon the people, have with intollerable "insolence endeavored to perswade them that they had better *put them on* "*themselves*: But *your Press* has sounded the alarm; or to use the words "of a *minion*, 'rung the alarm bell:' *Your Press* has spoken to us the "words of truth: It has pointed to this people, their danger and their "remedy: It has set before them Liberty and Slavery; and with the "most perswasive and pungent language, conjured them, in the name of "GOD, and the King, and for the sake of all posterity, to chuse Liberty "and refuse Chains: Go on, for you have been already prosper'd. "The People have listned with attention: They have pursued *such* "measures as in spite of the slanderous tongues of their malicious enemies "*must* and *will* be succesful: While these measures have been taking, "*your* Press has been incessantly calling upon all to be quiet; and pa-"tiently to wait for their political salvation — NO MOBBS — NO CON-"FUSIONS — NO TUMULTS — This has been the language of YOUR — "'*infamous*' Paper — Let this be the language of ALL ——— *We* know "WHO have abused us — We owe them *Contempt*, and we will treat them "with it in full measure: But let not the hair of their scalps be touched: "The time is coming, when they shall lick the dust and melt away.

"POPULUS."

The next week's "Gazette," published March 21st, contains an account of the celebration of the anniversary of the repeal of the Stamp Act, (March 18th,) and among the toasts drank at a dinner of fifty gentlemen at the British Coffee House, appear the following:

"5. *The Boston-Gazette and the worthy members of the House who* "*vindicated the freedom of the PRESS.*

"6. *The worthy and independent Grand Jurors.*"

1768.

RICHMOND
v.
DAVIS.

Rec. 1768.
Fol. 134.

An Officer receiving an Execution without any ſpecial Directions from the Creditor, is holden by Law to levy the ſame on ſuch Goods or Eſtate as may have been attached on the Writ. *Trowbridge, J. diſſentiente.*

Silveſter Richmond, Eſqr., Appellant, *verſ.* Benja: & Edward Davis, Appellees. (1)

THE Jury find ſpecially: 1. That the Goods and Eſtate of Ebenezer Stetſon were legally attached, on the third Day of May, by the Appellant, to anſwer the Demand of the Appellees againſt ſaid Stetſon.

2. That ſaid Stetſon doth not appear to us to be an abſconding Debtor, till the ſixth Day of ſaid May.

3. That the Execution in the Caſe was delivered to the Appellant, before thirty Days after Judgment were expired.

4. That the ſaid Appellees gave the Appellant no Orders, or Directions, concerning the attached Effects.

5. That, if the Appellant was held by Law to levy his Execution on ſaid Effects, without any ſpecial Directions from the Creditors, the Jury find for the Appellees the Sum of £762. 7. 10, Money, Damage and Coſts, otherwiſe they find for the Appellant. This

(1) This was an action originally brought againſt the appellant as ſheriff, to recover damages for the default of his deputy in not levying an execution upon certain property of the judgment debtor, which had been attached on the writ.

1768. RICHMOND *v.* DAVIS.

This Caſe was largely handled at the Bar, by the Council on both Sides. But, as the Arguments were all taken up by the Bench, we proceed to the Learned Argument of the puiſne Judge.

The Writ of Execution, and the Officer's Duty thereon, conſidered by Judge Trowbridge, in the Caſe of Davis & Richmond.

A common Judgment Creditor, *in England*, has his Election to ſue out a *Levari Facias*, a *Fieri Facias*, *Elegit*, or *Capias ad Satisfaciendum*, but can execute but one of them at the ſame Time.

The *Levari Facias* commands the Sheriff, that, of the Lands, Goods and Chattels of the Debtor, he cauſe *to be Levied*, the Sum recovered, ſo that he have it in Court, &c., to be delivered to the Creditors.

The *Fieri Facias* commands the Sheriff, that he cauſe *to be made*, of the Goods and Chattels of the Debtor, the Sum recovered, and to have the *Money* in Court, &c., to render the Creditor his Debt, &c.

The *Elegit* commands the Sheriff to *deliver* the Debtor's Goods and Chattels (except his Cattle of the Plough,) and half of his Land, *at a reaſonable Price and Extent*, to hold untill the Debt is *Levied.*

The *Capias ad Satisfaciendum* commands the Sheriff to take the Debtor's Body, and bring him into

into Court, at the Return-Day, that he may pay the Debt, &c.

1768.
RICHMOND *v.* DAVIS.

All theſe Writs are directed to the Sheriff only, and he only is to make Return thereof. Upon the *Levari Facias*, the *Money* is to be *levied by Sale* of the Goods and Chattels. Upon the *Fieri Facias*, the Sheriff is to *make the Money*, by Sale of the Goods and Chattels. Upon the *Elegit*, the Sheriff cannot *ſell*, but muſt *deliver* the Goods and Chattels, and half the Lands to the Creditor, at the Value put on them by a Jury of twelve Men under Oath, and if there be Goods and Chattels enough to anſwer the Debt, &c., the Land is not to be extended.* If the Debtor pays the Money, the Sheriff ought not to ſell the Goods on the *Levari Facias*, or *Fieri Facias*, or deliver them, or extend the Land on the *Elegit.* Though, by the *Capias ad Satisfaciendum*, the Sheriff is commanded to bring the Body into Court, yet, if he receive the Money of the Debtor, and bring it into Court, or pay it to the Creditor, the Court will excuſe him.

A Common Judgment-Creditor *here* can have but one Execution, and that is directed to the Sheriff, his Underſheriff, or Deputy; reciting the Judgment, and commanding them, that, of the Goods, Chattels, or Lands of the Debtor, they cauſe to be paid and ſatisfied to the Creditor, *at the Value thereof in Money*, the aforeſaid Sums, and thereof alſo to ſatisfy themſelves for their own Fees, and, for Want of Goods, Chattels, or Lands of the Debtor, ſhewn,

* 2 Inſt. 396.

1768.
Richmond v. Davis.

ſhewn, or found, to *the Acceptance of the Creditor*, they are commanded to take the Debtor and commit him to Goal, and there detain him untill he pays *the full Sums aforeſaid*, with their Fees, or that he be diſcharged by the Creditor, &c., and to make Return of Doings, &c. The Officer is not commanded to Levy ſuch Sum *of Money*, of the Goods, &c., and to bring it into Court, (as by the *Levari Facias*,) or to pay it to the Creditor, or to make of the Goods and Chattels of the Debtor, the Sums recovered, and bring *the Money* into Court, (as by the *Fieri Facias*,) or to pay the Money to the Creditor, — but is, of the Debtor's Goods, Chattels, or Lands, to cauſe to be paid and ſatisfied to the Creditor, *at the Value thereof in Money*, the Sums recovered, &c.; that is, to cauſe the Creditor to be paid and ſatisfied his Debt *in* the Goods, Chattels, or Lands of the Debtor, at a reaſonable Price and Extent, as in the *Elegit;* and the Officer being alſo commanded for Want of Goods, &c., *to the Acceptance of the Creditor*, to take the Debtor and impriſon him, ſhews that the Creditor has his Election to take his Satisfaction *in* the Goods, Chattels, or Lands of the Debtor, or to have his Body impriſoned untill he pays the *Money;* and that he has no other Choice. He cannot oblige the Officer to take the Debtor's Goods, Chattels or Lands, and ſell them, and thereby raiſe Money to pay the Debt; nor can he do it, without the Conſent of the Debtor.

The Sheriff has no Right to take a Debtor's Eſtate and ſell it, unleſs he is impowered by Law to do it; and neither the Common Law, nor any Statute or Law of the Province impowers him to do do it here, unleſs it be the Execution eſtabliſhed by Law; and that neither expreſſly impowers him to do it, nor requires him to do any Thing, that he cannot do without having ſuch a Power, as doth the *Levari Facias* and *Fieri Facias*; and therefore, he has no ſuch Power.

1768. RICHMOND *v.* DAVIS.

Of what Conſequence will it be to the Creditor, whether Goods or Eſtate, tendered or found, was *to his Acceptance*, or not, if the Creditor was not to receive *the Same* in Satisfaction of his Debt, but the Officer was obliged to raiſe the Money by the Sale thereof? It ſhould, in that Caſe, rather have been, to the Acceptance of the Officer, than the Creditor; but the Writ expreſſly makes the Debtor's being impriſoned or not depend on the Goods or Eſtate, tendered or found, being to the Acceptance of the Creditor, or not; or, in other Words, on his being content to receive the Same at the appraiſed Value, in Satisfaction of the Judgment.

There is neither Price nor Value mentioned in the *Fieri Facias*, nor the *Levari Facias*; nor was it proper for either to be inſerted in either of thoſe Writs, as the Eſtate was to be ſold for the moſt it would fetch, be it more or leſs: Becauſe, if either the Words, "at a reaſonable Price," as in the *Elegit*, or "at the Value thereof in Money," as in our Writ, had been in the *Levari Facias* or the *Fieri Facias*, the Sheriff muſt have cauſed the Eſtate to be appraiſed, before he ſold it for the moſt it would fetch, and made return thereof accordingly;* and that

* 2 Inſt. 396.

1768.
RICHMOND v. DAVIS.

that would have been attended with confiderable Expenfe to no good Purpofe, and for that Reafon was not inferted in either of thofe Writs, upon which the Money was to be raifed by the Sale of the Eftate; but with great Propriety was inferted in our Writ, whereby the Creditor was to receive his Satisfaction *in* the Eftate, if he pleafed, and was not, by the Proceeds of the Sale of it.

The Words "*to the Acceptance of the Creditor*" were not in the Writ when it was firft eftablifhed, as it appears by the 4th and 5th of Wm. & Mary, c. 21, but were inferted by Force of that Act, on Purpofe to give the Creditor the Election aforefaid, and to oblige the Officer to govern himfelf accordingly. The Claufe of the Act to this Purpofe is not in either of the laft Impreffions of our Laws, but is in the Province Law-Book printed in 1726, p. 35. The Words are thefe, viz[t]., "And whereas, by the "Precedent or Form of an Execution, the Officer "is commanded for Want of Goods, Chattels or "Lands of the Debtor, to be by him fhewn or "found, within the Precinct, to take the Body of "fuch Debtor and commit him to Prifon: — It is "hereby *explained*, enacted and *declared* by the Au-"thority aforefaid, that where Judgment is granted "for Money, or any particular Specie, the Creditor "*fhall not be compelled* to take any other Specie, but "in every fuch Cafe, for Want thereof, the Officer "fhall take the Body of the Debtor in Execution "and imprifon him, unlefs fuch Creditor fhall be "content to receive his Satisfaction *in* fuch other "Eftate as may be tendered or found. And the "Words 'to the Acceptance of the faid A. B.' fhall "be "be ſupplied and inſerted in the Writ of Execution, "to follow next the Word 'Precinct.'"

1768.
RICHMOND
v.
DAVIS.

Here is not the leaſt Intimation given, that the Officer was to raiſe the Money by the Sale of the Debtor's Eſtate; but, on the contrary, it plainly appears, that the Makers of this Act thought that, upon the old Writ, the Creditor was *obliged* to take his Satisfaction *in* ſuch Eſtate of the Debtor as was tendered or found, or go without Satisfaction; which could not be the Caſe, if the Officer was obliged to raiſe the Money by the Sale of the Eſtate; and therefore, they enact, that, where Judgment is for Money, he ſhall not be compelled to take any other Specie, but, for Want of it, the Officer *ſhall* impriſon the Debtor, unleſs the Creditor is content to receive his Satisfaction *in* ſuch other Eſtate as may be tendered or found; but don't add, "or unleſs the Officer can raiſe the Money by Sale of the Eſtate," or Words to that Effect — as they doubtleſs would have done, had they ſuppoſed he was obliged to do it, if the Creditor choſe he ſhould, rather than receive the Eſtate, or have the Body impriſoned. It is plain alſo, that the Makers of this Act thought, that the inſerting thoſe Words, "to the Acceptance of the Creditor," in the Execution, would give the Creditor, for Want of the Money being paid by the Debtor, his Election to receive his Satisfaction *in* other Eſtate, or to have the Debtor impriſoned untill he paid the Money; and they intended it ſhould have that Effect, and, therefore, the preſent Writ ought to be ſo underſtood and conſtrued. Eſpecially, as this is the Senſe put upon it by an explanatory

1768. RICHMOND *v.* DAVIS.

explanatory Act. Carth. 396. 4 Bac. Abr. 650. 10 Co. 101. 11 Co. 73.

In England, the Creditor has this Election, and makes it by suing out the *Elegit* or *Capias ad Satisfaciendum*, and here, the same Election is given him, though both those Writs are included in one. As, on the *Elegit*, the Sheriff could not extend the Lands, if there were Goods or Chattels enough to answer the Debt, &c., so the Act of 8 W. 3, c. 3, subjects the Land to be taken in Execution, unless the Debtor or his Attorney tenders the Officer personal Estate sufficient to pay the Debt, &c.; But this don't take from the Creditor his Election of receiving his Satisfaction in the Estate tendered or found, or having the Body imprisoned; nor doth it impower the Officer to sell the Estate tendered, unless the tendering it to him be considered as an Evidence of the Debtor's Consent that he should sell it, which ought not to be. For the Debtor may well be presumed to choose to pay his Creditor in Personal Estate, at the appraised Value, rather than his Real — especially, as then (*a*) he could not redeem either — and to choose to take the Chance of his being taken and imprisoned, untill he raised the Money, by pawning, mortgaging or selling his Estate to the best Advantage; rather than to put it in the Power of an Officer, to sell it for the most it would fetch — perhaps, for half its Value.

Again, if the Legislature had designed, the Sheriff should

(*a*) The Act for redeeming real Estate taken in Execution was not made, till the 12th of Ann.

ſhould ſell a *living* Debtor's Eſtate, and thereby raiſe Money to pay the Debt, &c., they would not have made the Precept in the Form they did; but would either have expreſſly required him to ſell it, or to have done that which could not be done without ſelling the Eſtate; as is done in the *Levari Facias* or the *Fieri Facias;* or would by ſome expreſs Law have empowered the Sheriff to ſell the Debtor's Eſtate, as they by the 2 An. c. 5, impowered him to ſell a *deceaſed* Debtor's Eſtate, where the Creditor had Judgment and Execution for Money, and was not content to receive Satisfaction *in* the Goods or Eſtate of the Deceaſed, at an appraiſed Value. Here, the Creditor has his Election to take his Satisfaction *in* the Eſtate, or the Proceeds of the Sale of it. But, in the former Caſe, to have the Debtor's Eſtate, or his Body impriſoned, which would oblige him to raiſe the Money and to pay the Debt: And becauſe the Body of the Executor or Adminiſtrator could not be impriſoned for the Deceaſed's Debt, and thereby be compelled to pay the Money, the Legiſlature, agreeable to the Spirit of the explanatory Act aforeſaid, in Order to prevent the Creditor's being obliged to take his Satiſfaction in the Deceaſed's Eſtate, at an appraiſed Value, enabled the Sheriff to ſell it, and thereby to raiſe the Money and pay the Debt. There is a good Reaſon for the Sheriff's being impowered to ſell a deceaſed Debtor's Eſtate, which doth not hold good in the other Caſe. — What Reaſon can be aſſigned for the Sheriff's being ſo expreſſly impowered by this Act to ſell in this Caſe, if he was before, by the Writ of Execution or any prior Law impowered to do it? Surely, no good Reaſon can

1768. RICHMOND v. DAVIS.

can be aſſigned for it. The Words of the Execution, ſo far as reſpects the Eſtate, are the ſame in both Caſes.

The Legiſlature hath, in many Caſes, impowered Officers, as well as others, to ſell Eſtates; but, then, it hath always been done by expreſs Words, plainly and clearly giving them Power to do ſo. From thence may be deduced an additional Argument to prove that they did not intend, by our Writ of Execution, to impower the Sheriff to ſell any Debtor's Eſtate.

By our Writ of Attachment, or Capias, the Sheriff, his Underſheriff or Deputy are commanded to attach the Goods or Eſtate of a ſuppoſed Wrongdoer, to a certain Value, &c., and for Want thereof, to take his Body, ſo that they have him at Court, to anſwer the Plaintiff, and to make Return of their Doings. And by 13 W. 3, c. 15, the Eſtate ſo attached is not to be diſcharged, untill thirty Days after Judgment for the Plaintiff; to the Intent, he may take the ſame by Execution, for ſatisfying the Judgment, ſo far as the Value thereof can extend, if he think fit, unleſs the Judgment be ſooner, or otherwiſe ſatisfied. And the ſame Act provides, that, if the Body be taken and impriſoned on that Writ, it ſhall be held the ſame Time after Judgment for the Plaintiff, that it may be taken in Execution; if the Plaintiff don't order the Sheriff to diſcharge him before. The Difference in the Mode of Expreſſion in the ſame Act is obſervable; the Body is to be held, that *it may be taken in Execution* — the Eſtate is to be held, that *the Plaintiff may take*

1768.
RICHMOND
v.
DAVIS.

take the ſame in Execution to ſatisfy the Judgment, *ſo far as the Value thereof can extend*, if he think fit: — that is, if he chooſes to receive the ſame at the apprized Value. This Act ſtrongly implies that the Judgment may be ſatisfied within the 30 days, otherwiſe than by the Eſtate attached, or the Body's being taken in Execution; and the 6 Geo. ch. 2, expreſſly impowers the Creditor to cauſe the Judgment to be otherwiſe ſatisfied; for it is thereby enacted, that, when any Perſon recovers Judgment for Money, or any other Specie, and the Debtor is either unwilling or unable to ſatisfy the Judgment by Money or other Specie, and the Creditor, finding no other perſonal Eſtate to his Acceptance, doth therefore think fit to levy upon the Real Eſtate of the Debtor, rather than on the Perſon of the Debtor, the Officer ſhall cauſe it to be apprized and ſet out by three Perſons ſworn and appointed as the Act directs, and deliver the Creditor Poſſeſſion thereof, and make return thereof accordingly. And, if the Real Eſtate cannot be divided and ſet out by Meets and Bounds, then he ſhall extend the Rents, &c.

This Act extends to all Caſes where the Debtor is unwilling or unable to pay the Money or other particular Specie the Judgment is for; and his not paying it, eſpecially if demanded, will be an Evidence of his being either unwilling or unable to do it; — and, therefore, it muſt extend to the Caſes, where the Body or Eſtate is taken upon the Capias, or Attachment, and the 30 days not expired: Becauſe the Debtor's being in Priſon don't ſhow him to be able or willing to pay the Money; — nor

 doth

1768. RICHMOND v. DAVIS.

doth the Officer's attaching Eſtate, though by Direction of the Plaintiff, ſhew, that, when the Plaintiff has recovered Judgment, he is content to receive his Satisfaction in the Eſtate ſo attached, rather than in other Eſtate of the Debtor, or rather than the Debtor's Body ſhould be impriſoned untill he pays the Money, which this Act intends, by levying on the Perſon of the Debtor. And this Act alters the Condition upon which Real Eſtate might be taken in Execution by the 8 W. 3, from a Tender, to an Acceptance; and giving the Creditor his Election to take his Satisfaction in any Part of the Debtor's Eſtate, Real, or Perſonal, or to have his Body impriſoned untill he pays the Money.

As the Creditor has this Right of Election, ſo the Debtor, in Conſequence thereof, has a Right to his Liberty, if Goods, Chattels or Lands are ſhewn or found, to the Acceptance of the Creditor, to ſatisfy the Judgment, &c. And it is at the Peril of the Officer, that he infringes the Right of the one or the other. As the Officer's Duty, as well as the Debtor's Right, depends upon the Creditor's Election, the Officer cannot poſſibly know what he ought to do, and therefore, neither in Reaſon or Law is obliged to act, untill that Election is expreſſly made, or, by ſome Act of the Creditor, is reaſonably ſuppoſed to be made. If the Creditor, inſtead of Money, is willing to accept the Debtor's Goods, Chattels or Lands, in Satisfaction of his Debt, it is the Officer's Duty to cauſe him therewith to be ſatisfied; but, if he is not willing, it is the Officer's Duty, for Want of Money, to take ye Debtor, and impriſon him. As ſoon as the Officer has the Writ of Execution, he

1768. RICHMOND *v.* DAVIS.

he ought to know what he is to do by Force of it; or at leaſt the firſt Step he is to take; and, if that depends upon the Will of the Creditor, he only can, and therefore ought to make it known to the Officer, as ſoon as he delivers to him the Writ.

The Debtor is allowed 24 hours, after Judgment, to pay the Money, and thereby prevent the Execution's iſſuing againſt him; and, if he does not pay it in that time, it is ſuppoſed he cannot or will not do it; — and thereupon the Execution iſſues in the Form preſcribed; and wherein no Mention is made of the Money's being paid, or to be paid by the Debtor, or of its being demanded of him, and, therefore, the Officer is not obliged to demand the Money of the Debtor, or even let him know he has an Execution againſt him, before he arreſts him or takes his Eſtate. The firſt Step, therefore, the Officer is to take, is to find and take the Debtor's Body or Eſtate. If the Officer, by Force of the Writ, has a Right to take the Debtor's Goods and Chattels, and doth take of them to the Value of the Debt, &c., the Debtor may be thereby diſcharged of the Debt, and the Creditor obliged to look to the Officer. For if (2 Bac. 355)* the Officer is not obliged to ſeek for any Eſtate, which, when found, it is not lawfull for him to take, and he has no Right to take the Eſtate, unleſs the Creditor is content to receive it inſtead of the Money, and is a Treſpaſſer if he doth it

* Ld. Raymond, 1075. If the Sheriff ſeizes Goods, on a *Fi. Fac.*, and they are reſcued out of his Hands, he is anſwerable for them, and for the ſame Reaſon muſt be ſo, if he takes them from the Debtor, on the *Elegit.*

1768.
RICHMOND *v.* DAVIS.

it againſt the Will of the Debtor, it cannot be thought reaſonable that the Officer ſhould be obliged to find and take the Debtor's Goods and Chattels from him, and carry them to the Creditor, or keep them untill he will come to ſee if he is content to receive them at the Value they may be apprized at, inſtead of the Money; and, if he will not, that the Officer ſhould be obliged to return them back to the Debtor, or to his Houſe, and then look out for the Debtor, and impriſon him. The Creditor may as well ſay, that he will not make his Election, untill the Eſtate, Real and Perſonal, be apprized; whereas, by 6 Geo., it is plain the Election muſt be before the Apprizement; becauſe it is on the Creditor's *thinking fit to levy* on the Real Eſtate, that the Officer is to cauſe it to be apprized, ſet out, and delivered to the Creditor. Indeed, if he thinks an unreaſonable Value is ſet upon the Eſtate, he may apply to the Court whence the Execution iſſued, to prevent the Officer's Return being filed and recorded; and, upon juſt Cauſe ſhewn, they will not allow it to be done; and then the Creditor may have an Alias-Execution. But, if the Officer returns, that he has cauſed the Eſtate to be apprized, &c., and has delivered poſſeſſion thereof to the Creditor, and the Return be filed and recorded, the Creditor is bound thereby, but may have an Action of Ejectment, to recover the Land, if Poſſeſſion thereof was not actually given him; and that Return will enable him to do it, if the Land was the Debtor's in Fee, when extended. Ld. Raymond, 346. Cro. Jam. 246. Holt, 348. L. R. 77.

Upon

1768. RICHMOND v. DAVIS.

Upon the Whole, ye Creditor ought to make his Election as ſoon as ye Officer has ye Writ of Execution; and, if he delivers, or ſends ye Execution to him without declaring his being content to receive his Satisfaction in ye Debtor's Eſtate, or giving the Officer any Direction concerning it, it is to be preſumed he is not content to receive his Satisfaction in any other Eſtate of the Debtor's, than Money; for, his Willingneſs not appearing, when it ought to appear, if he is willing — he, in Judgment of Law, is not willing, according to the Rule, that, that which doth not appear, is not; eſpecially, as ye Officer muſt, for Want of the Money, take the Debtor and impriſon him, if to be found, which is eſteemed, in Reaſon and in Law, the higheſt and beſt Execution, and moſt forceable. Hob. 61.

And, that, if Goods, Chattels or Lands were taken, ye Creditor muſt appoint one of the three Apprizers. The Officer, upon an Execution here, cannot determine the Value of Goods, Chattels or Lands, any more than the Sheriff, in England, can, ye Price and Extent on the *Elegit;* and therefore, he muſt find the Value by ye Verdict of a Jury, that being the Rule at Common Law; unleſs that Rule be altered by ſome Statute or Law of the Province. Now, although there is no Act of Parliament, or of this Province, touching this Matter, that expreſſly mentions Goods or Chattels, yet, as the 6 Geo. directs, that ye Value of Real Eſtate taken in Execution ſhall be determined by three Freeholders, under Oath, one of whom to be appointed by ye Creditor, it may be reaſonably ſuppoſed,

1768. RICHMOND *v.* DAVIS.

posed, that ye Makers of that Act intended the Officer should observe the same Rule in Regard to Goods and Chattels; and, therefore, that Act is, by an equitable Construction, extended to Goods and Chattels. So that, if the Creditor is content to receive his Satisfaction in Goods, Chattels or Lands, he must appoint one of the Persons who are to apprize the same. And he must also, by himself or by somebody else, receive the Goods and Chattels after they are apprized; for the Officer is not obliged to carry them to the Creditor, whatever they are, or wherever he be. And, therefore, if the Creditor points out no particular Estate, nor nominates or appoints any Person to apprize the Estate that may be found, or receive it for him, or give any particular Directions concerning it, it is reasonable to suppose he has no Thought of taking Anything but the Money or Body, although Goods, Chattels or Lands were attached, even by the Plaintiff's Orders, on the original Writ; for, after Judgment, he is not obliged to take them, as appears above. And a Creditor may, and often doth think himself in Danger of losing the Debt, and therefore directs the Officer to attach Estate that he would be very unwilling to take, at the apprized Value, instead of the Money, if he had any Prospect of getting the Money any other Way: — And, sometimes, directs Estate to be attached, which he only suspects to be the Debtor's, and that, before Judgment, he finds the Debtor has no Right in. And, therefore, as ye Creditor is not obliged to take the Estate in Execution that was attached by his Order, on ye original Writ; so neither is any Attachment of Estate

1768. RICHMOND *v.* DAVIS.

Eſtate of yᵉ Debtor, any Evidence of the Creditor being after Judgment content to receive it, in Satisfaction of his Debt, as will juſtifie yᵉ Officer's taking it by yᵉ Execution — much leſs oblige him to do it.

It has been ſaid, the Sheriff, his Underſheriff and Deputies are but one, and all Acts done by the Underſheriff and Deputies, are, in Law, conſidered as done by the Sheriff himſelf. If this be Law, in this Province, it affords a very ſtrong Argument, that the Plaintiff's directing an Officer to attach Eſtate on the original Writ, is not, without further Directions, ſuch Evidence as will make it the Officer's Duty to take it by the Execution; becauſe the Rules muſt be the ſame, whether the Execution be delivered yᵉ Perſon who made yᵉ Attachment, or to another. Suppoſe, then, the Sheriff of Middleſex attaches Eſtate by Force of a Writ returnable to Worceſter Inferiour Court, and returns it, and Judgment is obtained, and Execution iſſues thereon, and is ſent to a Deputy Sheriff, at Malborough, within yᵉ 30 days, without any ſpecial Direction, or Notice given that any Eſtate was taken, and yᵉ Deputy knows not that any was attached, and doth not take it, but looks out for the Debtor — is he guilty of any Fault; or ſubject to an Action, when he is guilty of none; (2) or is yᵉ Sheriff in Fault for not taking the Eſtate, by the Execution, when he had it not; or ſubject to an Action for not doing that,

(2) See 12 Met. 537, where it is intimated that want of knowledge of an attachment returned in another county will excuſe the officer.

1768.
RICHMOND
v.
DAVIS.

that, which, without any Fault of his, he never had it in his Power to do; — or for the Default of his Deputy, who had not been guilty of any? — Surely Natural Juftice forbids it; and therefore, he, who affirms, muft fhew fome clear, exprefs, pofitive Law, fubjecting the Sheriff to an Action in fuch Cafe as this, before he can be believed. And it may, and frequently doth happen, that Attachments are made by one Perfon, and the Execution delivered to another: But, then, if the Creditor would have the Eftate that was attached taken in Execution, he tells the Officer to whom he gives ye Execution, of it, and directs him to take it in Execution. And furely, it is much more reafonable that a Creditor fhould let ye Officer know, when he gives him the Execution, that he is content to take his Satisfaction in ye Debtor's Eftate, than that the Sheriff fhould be obliged to give Notice to his Underfheriff and Deputies of what he doth on every Writ of Attachment, and that they fhould do the like to him, and to each other; which muft be done to fave the Sheriff from being fubject to an Action, in fuch a Cafe as is before mentioned, if the Law be as is fuggefted. In England, where ye Writ is directed to the Sheriff, and returned by him only,* it may reafonably be fuppofed he knows what is done by himfelf, or his Underfheriff, or Deputies, who make Return of their Doings to him, for him to make his Return by; but here, where ye Writs are directed and delivered to ye Deputies, as well as ye Principal, and executed and

* See Dalton Sher. 96, 181 — to whom original Writs are to be directed and by whom to be returned.

1768. Richmond v. Davis.

and returned by them to ye Court, according to ye Command therein, it cannot reaſonably be ſuppoſed he ſhould know what they have done; or they, what he and each other have done; and, therefore, the Creditor muſt make his Election after Judgment, although Eſtate be attached by his Order, on the original Writ. (3)

But the four other Judges were of a different Opinion. They did not give their Opinions at large, as Judge Trowbridge had done, but ſeemed to ground themſelves upon the contemporaneous Expoſition of our Laws (which they conceived to have been againſt Judge Trowbridge's Opinion) and the uninterrupted Practice of the Sheriffs in this Province. (4)

Judgment was thereupon rendered for the Appellees, for the Sum of —— and Coſts. From which

---

(3) This opinion of Judge Trowbridge is alſo publiſhed in the ſupplement to 14 Maſs. 473, from a copy taken by Hon. Increaſe Sumner, formerly Juſtice of the Supreme Judicial Court. We have not, however, on that account, thought beſt to omit Quincy's report from the term where it properly belongs.

(4) This "practice of the ſheriffs" appears to have been that of ſelling perſonal property on execution; for, a few years later, an act was paſſed, reciting that doubts had ariſen as to their right to do ſo, and formally eſtabliſhing the ſame. Anc. Chart. 675.

At the preſent day although the creditor may make his election, and if he would levy on real eſtate or the body, muſt do ſo; yet in the abſence of any inſtructions it would ſeem that the officer's neglect to take and ſell perſonal property, known to be attached, would be againſt the creditor's "manifeſt intereſt," and "would not bind him to loſe a ſecurity which he had previouſly and lawfully obtained." See 11 Maſs. 321. Alſo 12 Met. 532, by Shaw, C. J., in deſcribing the duties of an attaching officer. — "If, within thirty days after judgment, the execution is delivered to him for ſervice, he muſt take the property on the execution."

1768.
RICHMOND
v.
DAVIS.

which Judgment, the Appellant claimed his Appeal to y[e] King in Council.

Qu. whether there is any Reliance to be made on a contemporaneous Expofition of Laws, unlefs fuch Expofition has been made, *feriatim*, by the King's *Judges.* — Now fuch Expofition was never pretended: — And if the Laws will not warrant certain Proceedings, can any Practice whatever eftablifh them againft Law?

——— "*Marcellus* ———
"*Ingreditur — Viros fupereminet omnes.*"

APTHORP
v.
SHEPARD.

Rec. 1768.
Fol. 351.

Indebitatus Affumpfit will not lie upon an Account which has been adjufted by the Parties, and where a Note has been given for the Balance.

Apthorp *verf.* Shepard.

Special Verdict.

INDEBITATUS ASSUMPSIT for Merchandife. The Cafe was: Goods were delivered in A. D. 17—. Afterwards an Abatement was made, the *Account adjufted*, and a Note given for the Balance; but this Action was brought upon the open Account. (1)

It

(1) This action was brought by Apthorp, as furviving partner of the firm of Apthorp & Wheelwright, againft the defendant and one Miller (not ferved). The fpecial verdict found that Shepard & Miller had paid part of the account, " befides a deduction allowed for damaged goods and overcharge," " that the parties fettled and adjufted their accounts as above, and the appellee Shepard gave his promiffory note negotiable and endorfed, and which is in the cafe for faid ballance, payable on demand," and that Apthorp & Wheelwright gave credit to Shepard & Miller therefor.

1768. Apthorp v. Shepard.

It was urged for the Defendant that, where there had been an Adjuſtment, no Action would lie upon the *open* Account; but *Inſimul Computaſſent* was the only Action. To ſupport which, 2 Mod. 43, 44, *Millwood & Ingraham*, was cited by Mr. Auchmuty.

But it was anſwered, that y[e] ſame Caſe is in 1ſt Mod. 205, 206 — where there is but *one Debt*, an Adjuſtment will not deſtroy y[e] original Contract, and the ſame Remedy remains as before ſuch Adjuſtment. And, in 12 Mod. 537, 538, *May* v. *King*, the Caſe of *Millwood & Ingraham* is denied by Holt to be Law. Alſo Fitzgib. 44; 1 Salk. 124; Caſes in Law & Eq. (or 8 Mod.) 290; Str. 426; 1 Burrow, 9, *Rhoads* vs. *Barnes*; Ibid. 375; & Hob. 68 were cited.

The Court took Time to adviſe. Afterwards the *Chief Juſtice* delivered the Opinion of the *Court* (which he ſaid was unanimous,) that this Action after Adjuſtment would not lie. He alſo informed the Bar that the Court, in forming their Opinion, had Regard to the following Caſes offered by *Judge Trowbridge*, which were not produced by the Council on Argument: Far. (2) 139; 1 Show. 155, 156; Mod. Caſes, 36; 2 Salk. 442; 12 Mod. 86; Ld. Raym'd. 680 — and alſo 1 Mod. 261 — ſtated Accounts may be pleaded in Bar of an Action of Covenant, &c. (3)

Memorandum.

---

(2) 7 Mod.

(3) The objection taken by Mr. Auchmuty was, that the action ſhould have been *inſimul computaſſent* on the adjuſted account. But from the authorities cited by Judge Trowbridge, it would ſeem that he at leaſt

1768.

MEMORANDUM.

Memorandum.

Jonathan Sewall, Efq'r., being now fixed Attorney General, we hear Nothing more at Prefent, of a *Special* Attorney *General*, or of the novel Office of Solicitor General. (1) *Vide ante*, p. 241.

---

leaft inclined to place the decifion on the broader ground that the note given by Shepard was a payment, and extinguifhed the original claim againft the firm. This would be in accordance with law as now eftablifhed, and in oppofition to the cafe of *Patefhall* v. *Apthorp*, ante 179, decided before Judge Trowbridge took his place on the bench.

(1) The next incumbent of this newly created office was Samuel Quincy, elder brother of the reporter. See *poft*, April Term, Middlefex, 1772.

Auguſt Term

VIII Geo. 3.

Chief Juſtice's Charge to the Grand Jury.

1768.

CHARGE TO THE GRAND JURY.

GENTLEMEN of the Grand Jury: I have frequently in this Place *freely* given my Sentiments upon ſuch Subjects as I thought of the higheſt Importance to Society. The Nature of Government in general, and the particular Form of it, in this Province, I have pointed out to Grand Juries, in the Courſe of my Charges to them, at the Opening of the Courts. This, I am ſenſible, has been done in an imperfect Manner: — but it was in the beſt Manner I was capable of.

I obſerve, Gentlemen, many among you, who are well acquainted with the Nature of your Duty, and what belongs to y[e] Buſineſs of a Grand Jury: — I ſhall therefore content myſelf with one or two Obſervations on the Conſtitution of this Court.

The

1768. Charge to the Grand Jury.

The Conſtitution of this Court is ſet forth in your Charter; (1) and by this Charter we are diſtinguiſhed from moſt of the Provinces on the Continent. And, beyond Diſpute, we are favoured more, in this Reſpect, than any People on the Continent.

The King is, in our Laws, called the Fountain of all Juſtice: — and, at Home, the Judges are appointed directly by the King, and hold their Commiſſions during their good Behaviour. The Commiſſions of the Judges of this Court are, it is true, during Pleaſure (2); — but when we conſider by whom our Judicatories are appointed, we ſhall find that we approach very near the Priviledge enjoyed by our Brethren, in England: At leaſt, we are in a Middle between them, and ſome of our Brethren in America, whoſe Judicatories are erected at Home, their Judges appointed from thence, and are removeable at Pleaſure.

Our Judicatories are erected by the General Court; — thus the Crown and Province are, finally, the Fountain of Juſtice. The Houſe of Repreſentatives,

(1) Anc. Chart. 31, 2.

(2) In 1772 ſalaries were granted by the Crown to the Juſtices of the Superior Court, and they were forbidden to receive their uſual compenſation from the Legiſlature of the Province. This excited the greateſt alarm and indignation among the people, as an act which completed the dependence of the Judiciary on the Crown. Brigadier-General Brattle, ſenior member of the Council, in behalf of the government party, publiſhed an article in the "Maſſachuſetts Gazette," Jan. 4, 1773, in which he attempted to prove that the Judges' commiſſions were not, (as Hutchinſon here acknowledges,) during pleaſure, but for life. He was moſt concluſively anſwered by John Adams. 2 John Adams's Works, 316. 3 Ib. 511.

1768.

CHARGE TO THE GRAND JURY.

ſentatives, in the Erection of a Court, are under no Controul; and we muſt preſume they will ever conſtitute ſuch a Court as is agreeable to the old Form of Government and the Tempers of the People. — This is certainly no ſmall Priviledge. The Judges of this Court derive all their Power from the Government; they are appointed by the King's Governour, with the Advice and Conſent of yᵉ Council, and are only removeable by the Governour and *Council* at Pleaſure. — This, I think, amounts to near the Priviledge of yᵉ People in England: — *There*, the Judges hold *quamdiu*, *&c.*; and *here*, they are diſplaced by the Governour, *with the Conſent of Council*. Now, unleſs you can ſuppoſe a Houſe of Repreſentatives who would join in erecting Judicatories unknown to the Conſtitution, and inveſting them with Powers inconſiſtent with the Priviledges of the People — the Governour and Council appointing Judges unworthy their Station, and removing them for their Integrity — this People are as ſecure, and as firmly eſtabliſhed in their *Liberties*, as they are in Great Britain. I know of no Difference. Certainly, if they are not up to Great Britain, they are the neareſt that can be; — nearer than any other Government on the Continent. Senſible of this, in a Converſation, ſome Time ago, with one of the Judges from New York, he expreſſed his Surpriſe at our happy Circumſtances, relative to the Conſtitution of our Courts and the Appointment and Removal of our Judges. There, they are appointed from Home, and removed by the Governour at Pleaſure, and no one to call to Account. Certainly, Gentlemen, we cannot too highly value theſe Priviledges. It has, therefore, much excited my Wonder

Qu.

Qu.

1768.

CHARGE TO THE GRAND JURY.

der and Aſtoniſhment, when I have heard Men talk ſlightly of our Charter, as if it was not worth Anything at all. Such Perſons muſt ſurely be very ignorant or very bad Men. Our Anceſtors thought it, in their Day, a great Bleſſing; and what is there to alter its Nature ſince their Time? What I have only now mentioned is enough to make it an Object of our higheſt Regard.

This leads me to mention a Report which has lately prevailed, very much to my Surpriſe and Concern: — it has been given out, with a great Deal of Confidence, and believed, as I learn, by many People, that I have received from Great Britain a Commiſſion to be Chief Juſtice of this Court. The firſt Time I ever ſaw or heard of any ſuch Thing, was ſeeing it ſuggeſted in our publick Prints. — For a Judge of this Court to endeavour to obtain a Commiſſion of this Sort, ſo directly againſt our Charter, would be unpardonable: He would, in my Opinion, be guilty, not only of Infidelity to ye People, but of a plain Violation of his Oaths, by attempting an Innovation unknown to the Laws of the Land, and in Breach of ye Charter of Government. I have been employed now, I think it is upwards of thirty Years, in publick Affairs, and I can ſay, with ye utmoſt Sincerity, that I never attempted or countenanced, directly or indirectly, any Invaſion of any one Priviledge the People are intituled to by the Royal Charter.

For the Reaſon I mentioned in the Opening of this Charge, I ſhall not, Gentlemen, be particular upon the Crown Matters.

You

1768.

CHARGE TO THE GRAND JURY.

You will, Gentlemen, diligently inquire of all Riots, unlawful Aſſemblies, flagrant Breaches of the Peace, Theft, Robberies, Burglaries, Murders, Treaſons and Felonies of every Kind, — all inflammatory, ſeditious Libels upon Government or the Rulers in Government, which tend to deſtroy all civil Peace, and ſtrike at the Root of all Order and Government; In ſhort, Gentlemen, every Crime and Offence of every Denomination comes with Propriety before you. If, when you come together, you find no Offences preſented, and none come within your own Obſervation and Knowledge, — in ſuch Caſe, you will find no Bills. — But if, when you come together, you have Offences brought before you, or others which moſt certainly fall within your own Knowledge and Obſervation, — in ſuch Caſes, you muſt find Bills: But, Gentlemen, if you neglect your Duty, from any Cauſe or Motive whatever, you are not only criminal in the Sight of God, by a direct Violation of your Oaths, but, inſtead of being the Aiders and Supporters of Peace, Order and good Government, and rendering that Service to the Country which is your indiſpenſable Duty, you do it the greateſt Diſſervice in your Power, by introducing the worſt of civil Evils.

My Abſence from the Court, and other Engagements, during this Term, prevented my taking any Minutes of Arguments at the Bar.

March Term

IX Geo. 3.

N. B. This was the firſt Court held in the New Court Houſe in the County of Suffolk.

1769.
CHARGE TO THE GRAND JURY.

Charge of the Chief Juſtice.

GENTLEMEN of the Grand Jury: We are met here together in Order to maintain the juſt Rights of the People of the County. The bare Mention of the Word *Rights* always ſtrikes an Engliſhman in a peculiar Manner. — But, in Order to ſupport and defend the Rights, of which we are ſo fond, we ought to have a juſt Apprehenſion of what they are, and whereon they ſtand. I do not intend to go very largely into the Matter, but only touch upon a few Fundamental Principles on which thoſe Rights all ſtand.

As Men, in our natural Capacity, we have a Right

1769. CHARGE TO THE GRAND JURY.

Right to do as we pleaſe, without any Controul whatever; but, as Members of Society, we are abridged of this our natural Liberty, and are obliged to ſubmit to the Laws of the State. Now, as the End of Society is to preſerve to us that Security in our Perſons and Property which we could not have in a State of Nature, we are under a Neceſſity of giving up ſome of our original Rights, in Order to a full Enjoyment of the Remainder. And the beſt Conſtitution of Government muſt certainly be that, in which we part with the feweſt of our natural Rights; — that is, where we part with no more than is abſolutely neceſſary to attain the very Ends of Society and Government. — All this is obvious on the firſt Mention. The Conſtitution of Government, under which we have the Happineſs to live, is, therefore, the moſt happy, becauſe we have never yielded up more of the private Rights of Individuals than was needful to inveſt the Government with Power ſufficient to protect us as Citizens. — It is, therefore, the Duty of every good Citizen, who is bound to preſerve the Laws of the State under which he lives, to apply to the Legiſlative Body for a Redreſs of all Grievances which ariſe from the Laws. To aim at a Redreſs in any other Way is to bring Everything into Confuſion.

We, Gentlemen, who are to execute the Law, are not to enquire into the Reaſon and Policy of it, or whether it is conſtitutional or not; — whether one Part of the Community are oppreſſed, and whether another Part oppreſs: We, and you, Gentlemen, as the Executive Body, are to enquire what is Law, and ſee that the Laws are inforced.

If

1769.

CHARGE TO THE GRAND JURY.

If we ſtep over this Line, and judge of the Propriety or Impropriety, the Juſtice or Injuſtice of the Laws, we introduce the worſt Sort of Tyranny: — the moſt abſolute Deſpotiſm being formed by a Union of the Legiſlative and Executive Power. I mention this, Gentlemen, becauſe, from my own Obſervation, both in this and ſome other Counties, I have found Juries taking upon them to judge of the Wholeſomeneſs of the Laws, and thereby ſubverting the very End of their Inſtitution.

Gentlemen of the Grand Jury: You are to enquire into all Things given you in Charge. Every Crime is cognizable in this Court; but it has generally been our Rule to leave the leſſer Offences againſt y[e] Laws, to inferiour Jurisdictions. And although, Gentlemen, few of you can be ſuppoſed to be Lawyers, yet you are all Men of Reaſon, and will be able to diſtinguiſh between thoſe groſſer Offences and high Immoralities which deſerve the moſt immediate and full Exertion of the Laws in this Court, and thoſe leſſer Matters which will receive an adequate Puniſhment in the lower Courts.

I need not inform you, Gentlemen, that High Treaſon is the higheſt Offence our Law knows of; as unhinging all Society, and demands the moſt entire Suppreſſion.

(Murder — Arſon — Burglary — Forgery — Thefts — the common Learning on theſe Topicks here laid down to the Grand Jury, by the Chief Juſtice.)

Not

April Term

Middlesex ss.

XII Geo. 3, 1772.

Honourable Peter Oliver, Esquire, Chief Justice.
Honourable Edmund Trowbridge, Foster Hutchinson, Nathaniel Ropes, William Cushing, } Esqrs., Justices.

Jonathan Sewall, Esq., Attorney General.
Samuel Quincy, Esq., Solicitor General. (1)

Reed's Case.

Standing Grand Jurors of a County for a Year are exempt from serving on petty Juries.

A *Venire facias* issued to Littleton for a Juryman, and Mr. Reed was returned, who was a Standing Grand Juror of the County for the Year, which

(1) This office is said to have been created especially for the purpose of winning over Sewall to the government party. See 10 John Adams's Works, 179; *Ante*, 241. After Sewall was raised to the office of Attorney General, that of Solicitor General remained vacant until March,

1772. REED'S CASE.

which was known, but, being in Doubt if that exempted him, he was returned.

The Court, on hearing the Facts, told him he was not obliged to ſerve, and, if he declined, they would order a new *Venire* to iſſue.

Flagg *verſ.* Hobart.

FLAGG *v.* HOBART.

Rec. 1772. Fol. 40.

Where, in an Action for Words, Juſtification is pleaded to Part, and to the Reſidue, not guilty, the two Iſſues will be tried ſeparately; and, on the firſt, the Defendant is entitled to open. Damages will be aſſeſſed ſeparately upon each Iſſue.

ACTION for Words, and Special Damages alledged. Defendant juſtified ſpeaking the firſt Words, and plead not guilty to the Reſt.

Dana, for the Plaintiff, going on to open the Cauſe —

Quincy, for the Defendant, moved that he (Quincy) might open it.

Sewall, alſo for the Plaintiff, ſaid, if the Defendant inſiſts

---

March, 1771, when the place was given to Samuel Quincy; he alſo having embraced the cauſe of the government.

It is intimated by John Adams that Samuel Quincy's adherence to this party was cauſed by jealouſy of the greater profeſſional ſucceſs and reputation of his younger brother, who had openly and with great fervor eſpouſed the patriotic cauſe. 10 John Adams's Works, 195. It may well be that the government leaders were induced to attempt his converſion on the ſuppoſition that he might be ſo influenced; but that their ſucceſs was in fact attributable to this unworthy motive, we do not believe. The correſpondence between the brothers, eſpecially on the ſide of the elder, evinces the tendereſt fraternal affection, even at a time when party animoſity was at its height. See Quincy's Life of Quincy, 160.

infifts on trying the Iffues feparately, they have a Right to open; but, if they will try them together, we muft open; for Part of our Declaration is denied; we ought, therefore, to proceed and prove what we have firft alledged. (1)

Trowbridge, *Juftice*, afked, if the Action had been Trefpafs, Affault and Battery, and Plea, as to the Force and Arms, not guilty; and Juftification as to the Refidue, who fhall open there? — the Law is, if the Juftification be found, Nothing more is to be done, as to the Force and Arms.

Sewall anfwered, he could not think that a parallel Cafe — he thought *Claufum fregit*, and Juftification as to Part, and, as to the Refidue, not guilty, rather in Point; there, he faid, the Plaintiff might open.

But *the Court* directed the Iffues to be tried feparately. (2)

It became a Queftion, at the Trial, on the firft Iffue, whether Damages fhould be affeffed feparately on that Iffue, or whether they fhould be paffed over till the other Iffue was alfo tried, and then affeffed *in toto*: And *per Curiam* — The Damages muft be affeffed

(1) Acc. *Davis* v. *Mafon*, 4 Pick. 156; *Ayer* v. *Auftin*, 6 Pick. 225. But by the prefent rules of practice in this ftate, the plaintiff has the right to open and clofe in all cafes, even when the only iffue is on the defendant's declaration in fet-off. 8 Cufh. 603, *note*. 2 Gray, 260.

(2) S. P. *Morfe* v. *Jewett*, Mafs. S. J. C., June Term, 1781, where, in affault and battery, "the defendants juftified moderate correction," "there were feveral iffues joined," and "as to the moderate correction, the defendant opened and clofed." 5 Dane Ab. 564.

1772. FLAGG v. HOBART.

affeffed on each Iffue; for, perhaps, the other Iffue will be found againft the Plaintiff; then Damages will be paffed over; or, perhaps, if Damages are affeffed jointly, there may be a Motion in Arreft of Judgment, that the Words in the laft Iffue are not Actionable, and then it may be faid that Judgment muft be ftayed for the Whole; and other Reafons may be given alfo. (3)

Whitney *verf.* Haven.

WHITNEY v. HAVEN. Rec. 1772. Fol. 41.

Where a Warrant from a Juftice is pleaded in Juftification of an Arreft, an attefted copy of the fame is admiffible, notwithftanding Evidence is offered tending to invalidate its correctnefs. *Cufhing, J. diffentiente.* Evidence is admiffible to fhow a Difference between the Warrant on which the Arreft was made, and that fet forth in the Juftification. It is not effential that

TRESPASS. To the Force and Arms, not guilty. Juftification for the Refidue under a Warrant from Juftice Jones, directed to an Officer, who took the Defendant for Aid, and, as fuch, arrefted the Plaintiff. And, to fupport his Juftification,

(3) This action was for words fpoken againft the plaintiff in his trade and bufinefs of a millwright, — accufing him of ruining defendant's mills, and afferting that "it would have been better to have given any "Wages to a Workman than to have had my Mills fo fpoiled by fuch a "Blunderbufs." Thefe words and others were juftified, as fpoken "with Defign only to prevent the faid Eleazer from hurting others by his bad Work." The plea of not guilty as to the refidue, applied to the charge of calling the plaintiff "a Logerhead," "a Deceiver," and a "fractious Fellow," and of afferting that "there was fo much Liquor "ftirring that Flagg hardly knew what he was about." The plaintiff joined iffue on the fecond plea, and replied, *de injuriâ, &c.*, to the firft; on which replication, iffue was alfo joined. In the Inferiour Court, the jury found generally for the plaintiff, and affeffed damages at £30. On the appeal, the verdict conformed to the iffues, viz.: "the Jury find "upon the firft Iffue that the Appellant fpoke the Words in his Plea of "Juftification mentioned, of his own Wrong, without fuch Caufe as he "has pleaded, and affefs Damages for the Appellee Thirty Pounds; and "upon the fecond Iffue they find the Appellant guilty, and affefs Dam-"ages for the Appellee upon that Iffue, Five Pounds."

1772.

WHITNEY *v.* HAVEN.

tion, Defendant produced an attefted Copy from the faid Juftice's Records. Plaintiff objected to its being received, for he had Evidence to fhew that the Warrant on which he was arrefted had no Seal — whereas this Copy came with a *Loco Sigilli.**

the Juftice fhould aver himfelf to be fuch in the Body of the Warrant.

Trowbridge, Juftice. If there be Anything in the Objection, it is to invalidate the Copies. But *the Court* accepted them, contrary to the Opinion of *Cufhing, Juftice.*

Afterwards, the Plaintiff was admitted to give Evidence that the pretended Warrant whereby he was arrefted was different from that fet forth in the Defendant's Juftification. The Proof was not fufficient.

Judgment for Defendant.

Tuttle *verf.* Willington.

TUTTLE *v.* WILLINGTON.

Rec. 1772. Fol. 44.

PLAINTIFF declared on a promiffory Note made by the Defendant to one Winfhip, and by him indorfed to the Plaintiff. There was a Payment to Winfhip before Affignment. When this

Payment by the Maker to the Promifee of a Note on Demand is a good Defence to a fubfequent Indorfee for Value without Notice.

* The Plaintiff alfo objected, that the Juftice had not averred himfelf a Juftice in his Warrant, but the Objection had no great Weight with the Court. The Warrant in the Juftification was introduced thus, viz: "the Tenor of which faid Warrant is as follows," — the Warrant fet out *verbatim.*

N. B. The Foreman on the other Jury, withdrawn to agree on ye Verdict, was fent for to teftify in this Caufe.

1772.
TUTTLE v. WILLINGTON.

this appeared, the Court told the Plaintiff that this Point was ſettled againſt him on a Special Verdict, found at Cambridge, Auguſt Term, 1763, in the Cauſe of *Ruſſell & Oaks* (1); and ſo ſolemnly determined on full Argument in the Court-Houſe in Boſton.

Judgment for Defendant.

FOWLE v. WYMAN.

Rec. 1773. Fol. 162.

The Levy of an Execution on Land is good Evidence of Poſſeſſion in an Action of Treſpaſs *qu. cl.*, notwithſtanding the Omiſſion by the Officer to certify that the Appraiſers were "indifferent and diſcreet Men."

It ſeems that a Declaration deſcribing the Cloſe as abutting "weſterly on a Way" is ſufficiently ſupported by Proof of an Abutment weſterly on a Way and Land of J. S.

Fowle *verſ.* Wyman.

TRESPASS. Lands were attached by Fowle. The Defendant then conveys to Wyman. (1) Execution levied in due Time and regular Return, &c., except the Officer did not certify, the Appraiſors were *indifferent and diſcreet Men.* Plaintiff offered this Evidence of his Poſſeſſion; to which the Defendant objected, but *admitted.* (2)

Then

---

(1) *Ante*, p. 48.

(1) The date of the attachment appears by the return to have been November 1, 1770. The conveyance to Wyman was merely a leaſe "for and during the Term of Sowing and Ingathering one Crop of Winter Rye." The date of this leaſe is prior to that of the attachment; but there is on file the depoſition of Elizabeth Richardſon, to the effect that the delivery of the premiſes to the leſſee did not take place until ſome time near the middle of November; when the deponent, "being called as an Evidence, ſaw the ſaid David cut up out of the ſaid "Land, Turffe and Twigg, and deliver the Same unto the ſaid Benja. "Richardſon and Joſhua Wyman reſpectively, and therewith the Poſ-"ſeſſion of the ſame Lands."

(2) A regular and complete levy under an execution has been held ſufficient proof of poſſeſſion to ſuſtain this action. 3 Maſs. 215, 523. But the omiſſion to certify that the appraiſers were indifferent and diſcreet men has been held a fatal defect. *Williams* v. *Amory*, 14 Maſs. 20. *Bradley* v. *Baſſett*, 2 Cuſh. 417.

1772. FOWLE v. WYMAN.

Then 'twas ſaid by Defendant that the Plaintiff had produced no Evidence of Treſpaſs on the Lands ſet forth in the Declaration, which he there bounds, 'Weſterly on a Way;' the Land whereon the ſuppoſed Treſpaſs was done, was bounded, Weſterly on a Way and Lands of J. S. — therefore the Declaration is not ſupported; *and ſo ruled* unanimouſly by *the Court.* (3)

Note. The Defendant cited an Authority out of Salkeld, and one out of Hobart, of which inquire. (4) *Sewall for the Plaintiff,* inſiſted that where there was only an Omiſſion of ſome of the Abuttments, it was not fatall, for then what Abuttments were ſet out were only Surpluſſage, that where there were falſe and contradictory Abuttments ſet out, they were bad. (5)

---

(3) Although the firſt impreſſion of the Court may have been in favor of the defendant, yet that the point muſt have been reſerved for adviſement and the objection finally overruled appears probable from the fact that the caſe reſulted in a verdict, judgment, and execution for the plaintiff.

(4) 2 Salk. 453. Hob. 16, 176.

(5) Although before the St. of 1839, c. 151, § 3, in this commonwealth, and the Reg. Gen. Hil. T. 4 W. IV., in England, it was not neceſſary to name or deſcribe the plaintiff's cloſe in the declaration, yet if this were done by abuttals, they muſt be proved as laid. 2 Rol. Ab. 678. Bul. N. P. 89. 3 Stark. Evid. (ed. of 1832) 1435. But a general accuracy of deſcription has been held ſufficient. See *Webber* v. *Richards*, 1 Q. B. 443, where the rule is ſtated to be "that the party is not to be turned round on account of ſome minute variance in one out of ſeveral particulars, but that there muſt be a general accurate correſpondence faithfully deſcribing the cloſe in ſubſtance, and conveying full information to the defendant of the place in which he is alleged to have committed the treſpaſs. Alſo *Wheeler* v. *Rowell*, 6 N. H. 215, — a caſe in point, in which it was held that a deſcription of a cloſe as "abutting ſoutherly on W.'s land" "did not imply that it was abutting all the way ſoutherly on W.'s land," and that the omiſſion of a rod or two of abutment was immaterial.

1772.

THWING v. DENNIE.

Thwing *verſ.* Dennie.

Rec. 1772. Fol. 43.

An Attempt to ſnatch Papers from the Hand of the oppoſite Party in Court is a Contempt.

DENNIE was opening his Papers and Evidences; Thwing in a moſt ſavage Manner attempted to ſnatch ſome of them out of Dennie's Hand; and thereby tore ſome Papers very eſſential in the Cauſe.

The Court, ſeeing Thwing's Behaviour, ordered the Sheriff to take him immediately into Cuſtody, which he did, and committed him to Priſon.

LITTLE v. HOLDIN.

Little *verſ.* Holdin.

Rec. 1772. Fol. 44.

It ſeems, that under the Prov. Sts. 11 W. 3, c. 3, and 13 W. 3, c. 5, on Failure of the Appellant to appear and proſecute his Appeal in the Superiour Court, the Appellee cannot have Judgment for Damages without filing a Complaint.

LITTLE had Judgment on a Verdict below, and Holdin appeals, and entered his Appeal, and the Cauſe was continued one Term, &c.

Now, the Action called, Holdin failed to appear and proſecute. And thereupon Little files his Complaint, agreeable to the Prov. Stat. 13 W. 3, c. 5, and had Judgment as the ſaid Statute directs.

Note. The Prov. Stat. 11 W. 3, c. 3, (1) gives this Court Cognizance of all Actions brought by Appeal, &c., which gives ſome Colour to ſuppoſe

(1) Anc. Chart. 330.

1772.

LITTLE v. HOLDIN.

poſe that the Appeal being entered, the Appellee (having the Copies) might on Motion prove his Demand and have Judgment for his Damage and Coſt, or as the Caſe may require, he ſtill continuing Plaintiff, *quoad* the Trial; but the Law ſeems to conſider the Appellant as Plaintiff or *Actor*, *quoad* the Support of the Suit; then he, being called, does not appear,— the Suit which he ſupported falls of Courſe, and is diſcontinued, or the Appellant is become nonſuit; and though perhaps the Appellee might thereupon have his Coſts at that Court, yet Judgment for his Damages could not be ſupported; wherefore came ye 13 W. 3, c. 5, (2) which ſeems the only Way for the Appellee to proceed in ſuch Caſes againſt the Appellant.

DEWING v. TRAIN.

Dewing *verſ.* Train.

Rec. 1777. Fol. 81.

No Action lies for Money recovered of the Plaintiff by Suit on a Note given by him to ſecure the Defendant againſt a contingent Liability on an Execution which the Plaintiff has ſubſequently paid.

ASSUMPSIT for Money had and received to he Plaintiff's Uſe. The Caſe was, that one Ball, a Deputy Sheriff, had an Execution againſt the Plaintiff iſſuing on a former Suit brought by J. S., and Train paſſed his Word for Dewing's Appearance at a Day then to come; and Dewing gave Train a promiſſory Note for the Contents of the Execution; notwithſtanding which, Train ſued Dewing on the Note, on which Suit Dewing never

(2) Anc. Chart. 356.

1772. DEWING *v.* TRAIN.

never appeared, and Train had Judgment againſt him, — and, in the Courſe of the Affair, Dewing was committed by Ball on the Execution in Favour of J. S., and cleared it, and alſo cleared Train's Judgment on the Note; and then brings this Action to recover back the Money which Train had taken by his Suit on the Note.

Sewall, for the Plaintiff, in opening, diſcovered the Opinion of *the Court*, that the Action was not maintainable on theſe Facts, (1) adviſed his Client, (who before had refuſed,) to refer the Cauſe, which was accordingly done.

NOTE.

This action was continued under reference from term to term until October, 1774. At this date, there appears on the docket the uſual heading for the term, with the exception of a blank in the place of the names of the juſtices by whom it ſhould have been holden; and after the liſt of continued actions appears the following entry:

" N. B. The ſuperior Court did not ſit in the County of Middleſex " in October, 1774, by reaſon of the difficulty of the times, & there was " no term of the ſaid Court in that County until October, 1776. And " the continued actions are carried forward by a ſpecial order of the gen- " eral Court."

The circumſtances which prevented this ſeſſion of the Court were as follows: Articles of impeachment had been drawn up by the Houſe of Repreſentatives againſt the Chief Juſtice, and, although the Council would take no action in the matter, yet, the articles being publiſhed, the effect

---

(1) On the general principle that money paid under legal proceſs cannot be recovered back. The plaintiff's remedy ſhould have been ſought by review. 16 Maſs. 308. 17 Maſs. 394. 1 Pick. 440. 4 Gray, 148. 13 Gray, 70.

effect, as described by John Adams, was that "when the Superior Court "came to sit in Boston, the grand jurors and petit jurors, as their names "were called over, refused to take the oaths," on the ground that "the "Chief Justice of that Court stood impeached of high crimes and mis-"demeanours before his Majesty's Council, and they would not sit as "jurors while that accusation was depending. At the Charlestown "Court the jurors unanimously refused in the same manner." 2 John Adams's Works, 332. On the 19th of July, 1775, the General Court holden at Watertown, while the American army was at Cambridge, and the British in Boston, passed the act removing all officers appointed by the Governor, whether civil or military, from their respective offices, from and after the 19th of September then next. On the 11th of the following October, a majority of the Council reorganized the Superior Court by appointing John Adams Chief Justice, and William Cushing, William Read, Robert Treat Paine, and Nathaniel Peaslee Sargent, Esqrs., Associate Justices thereof. Adams accepted the appointment, but resigned in 1777, never having taken his seat on the bench. 3 Ib. 23, 24. Read, Paine, and Sargent at first declined the office, and their places were filled by James Sullivan, Jedediah Foster, and James Warren. The latter also declined the appointment, but the two former accepted it, and were commissioned March 20, 1776. Foster had occupied a seat in the Council, which he at once resigned, as incompatible with the office of judge. In his letter of resignation he says: "It has for sundry Years past been a prevailing Opinion that a "Seat at the Hon'ble Council, and on the Superiour Court Bench ought "not to be held by the same Person at one and the same Time: an "Opinion I think founded in the highest Reason, and should be supported "in a free Constitution." 195 Mass. Archives, 14. See *ante*, p. 242.

In May, 1776, was passed the act changing the style of commissions, writs, processes, and proceedings in law, from the name and style of the King of Great Britain, France, and Ireland, Defender of the Faith, &c., to the name and style of the Government and People of the Massachusetts Bay in New England. Anc. Chart. 798. The first Court held under the new organization appears to have been in Ipswich, for the County of Essex, on the 3rd Tuesday in June, 1776. The records of this term are entitled "Colony of Massachusetts Bay," and the Court was held by "Wm. Cushing, Jedediah Foster, and James Sullivan, Esqrs., Justices," "They having first produced Commissions under the Government Seal, severally appointing them Justices of the said Court." Rec. 1776, Fol. 2.

In February, 1776, was passed an act altering the place of holding Courts in Suffolk, from Boston to Dedham and Braintree, the former being made the shire town of Suffolk, — the preamble reciting that "Boston, *the Place appointed by Law for holding the Superiour Court*," &c., "*is now made a Garrison by the Ministerial Army, and become a*

"*common*

1772. "*common Receptacle* (1) *for the Enemies of* America." In accordance with this act, the first term of Court for Suffolk was holden at Braintree, in September, 1776. Rec. 1776, Fol. 29. In the following November, the act was repealed, and the first term holden in Boston appears to have been in February, 1777. Rec. 1777, Fol. 67.

The first term for Middlesex was, as before stated, in October, 1776, when the Court met and adjourned to the following February. The adjourned session was held by Cushing, Foster, Sullivan and Sargent, the latter having been reappointed on the 19th of the preceding September, and this time accepting the office. At this term there appear the first instances of appeals claimed to the "General Congress of the United States of America." Rec. 1776, Fol. 51. "Middlesex Minute Book, October, 1776." The case of *Dewing* v. *Train* was continued to the following April Term, which was the first holden at Concord under the act passed in February, 1776, changing the places of holding Court in Middlesex, "*as* Charlestown *is destroyed by the Enemy*." At this term the referees made their report in favor of the plaintiff for £18, 8, 6, for which sum judgment was entered, and execution issued November 3, 1777.

---

(1) "Old receptacles, common sewers" ——
Pericles, Act IV. Sc. 6.

April Term

XII Geo. 3.

Worcester ss.

Hooton *verſ.* Grout. (1)

1772.

HOOTON *v.* GROUT.

Rec. 1772. Fol. 54.

QUESTION: Whether Lands and Tenements mortgaged may be taken in Execution for ſatisfying the Mortgagee's juſt Debts.

Lands and Tenements mortgaged may be taken in Execution for ſatisfying the Mortgagee's juſt Debts.

Anſwer: The Province Law, 8 W. 3, c. 3, provides that all Lands and Tenements belonging to any

A Deed was received in Boſton by the Regiſter of Deeds for Worceſter, for Record. Five Days after, the Land was attached, and ſubſequently on the ſame

---

(1)The following opinion is by Judge Trowbridge. See note at the end of the caſe. The queſtions of law were raiſed as uſual by a ſpecial verdict, as follows:

——" That David Page, who was vouched in and admitted to defend " this Action on the 30th day of June, A. D. 1761, was ſeized of the " demanded premiſes in fee & on the ſame day gave his bond conditioned " for the payment of One Thouſand Pounds Lawful Money to Nathan- " iel Wheelwright, ſince dece'd, in one year, which is in the Caſe; and " alſo at the ſame time gave his deed of Mortgage to the ſ'd Wheel- " wright of the ſaid premiſes and other Lands as a Collateral Security " for the payment of the money due on ſaid Bond, which deed is alſo " in the Caſe, that the ſaid Nath'l, on the 10th day of January, A. D. " 1765,

1772.

HOOTON
v.
GROUT.

Day the Deed was filed and recorded in the Regiſtry at Worceſter. *Held* that the Record was good againſt the Attachment.

any Perſon in his own proper Right in Fee ſhall ſtand charged with the Payment of his juſt Debts, as well as his Perſonal Eſtate, and be liable to be taken in Execution for ſatisfying the ſame. (2)

The Act of 6 Geo. 1, c. 2, ſubjects the Debtor's Real Eſtate to be taken in Execution to ſatisfy any Judgment recovered againſt him, if he doth not ſatisfy it by Money or other Specie; and directs how the Value ſhall be aſcertained. (3)

The Act of 8 and 9 G. 2, c. 5, ſubjects the Right ye Mortgagor hath in Equity to redeem the Land, &c., to be attached and taken in Execution for ſatisfying his Debts: (4) ſo that the Whole of the Debtor's Real Eſtate, and the Right he has to redeem any Real Eſtate mortgaged, is, by the Laws of

" 1765, (the money due on ſaid Bond being then unpaid,) by his Deed of " Aſſignment duly Executed which is in the Caſe Conveyed and Aſ- " ſigned the ſaid Bond and the money due thereon & the ſaid Mortgaged " premiſes to Charles Ward Apthorp Eſqr., that the ſaid Deed of " Aſſignment was, on the 16th day of ſaid January Rec'd at Boſton by " Timothy Paine Eſq. as Regiſter of Deeds for the County of Worceſ- " ter, in which ſaid premiſes lay, for Record. That on the twenty-firſt " day of ſaid Month the ſaid John, by Virtue of a Writ duly purchaſed " by him againſt the ſaid Nathaniel, Cauſed the ſaid Demanded premiſes " to be attach'd as the Eſtate of the ſaid Nathaniel for a Debt due from " him, and afterwards on the ſame day the ſaid Deed of Aſſignment was " filed in the Office for the Regiſtry of Deeds for ſaid County of Worceſ- " ter to be recorded, & was accordingly afterwards on the ſame day there " Recorded at length." The verdict further ſet forth that judgment was recovered and execution regularly levied by the plaintiff on the demanded premiſes then in the poſſeſſion of the mortgagor, who afterwards paid the bond to Apthorp, and alſo conveyed to him the premiſes which were held by Grout as his tenant. On this verdict, judgment was entered for the tenant. See note at the end of the caſe.

(2) Anc. Chart. 292. (3) Ib. 423. (4) Ib. 501.

1772.
Hooton
v.
Grout.

of this Province, made liable to be taken in Execution for satisfying his Debt.

A Mortgage is where one borrows Money of another and pledges his Land or Tenements, &c., to the Lender, to secure to him y[e] Repayment, at a future Day, of the Money lent. 1 Inst. 205 a. Treat. in Eq. 86, 7, 91. Abr. Cas. Eq. 311, 327. 3 Bac. Abr. 632, 641. 2 Black. Com. 157, 8.

This is done by the Borrower's conveying his Land, &c., to y[e] Lender to hold to him, for a certain Number of Years or in Fee, upon Condition that if the Money, &c. be repaid by the Day, that then the Mortgagor may re-enter, &c. 3 Bac. Abr. 632. 2 Black. Com. 157, 8.

The former is called a Term, and is a Chattel Real, which doth not descend to the Heir, unless it be attendant on the Inheritance, but goes to y[e] Executor, is Legal Assets after his Entry or Recovery, and may be sold by him, without the Aid of the Court of Chancery, in England. 3 Bac. Abr. 632. 1 P. Will. 730, 1. Or the Superiour Court here.

A Term, not attendant on the Inheritance, may, in England, on a *Fi. Fa.*, be taken and sold by a Sheriff; and, on an *Elegit*, he may deliver it to the Creditors at the appraised Value as Personal Estate, or extend it as Real. *Comyn* vs. *Brandlyn*, Moor, 873. 2 Inst. 395 b. 4 Rep. 74. 8 Rep. 96, 171. It may be sold as well as other Goods without Appraisement. Wood's Inst. 632.

 When

1772.
Hooton
v.
Grout.

When Lands or Tenements are mortgaged in Fee, the Land, &c., and the Mortgagor's whole Eſtate therein paſſes preſently to the Mortgagee; ſo that ſuch a Mortgagor, in England, has by Law Nothing left but the bare Condition. 1 Inſt. 205 a. 210. Str. 689. Ca. Temp. Talb. 66, 68. 2 Cha. Ca. 97. 2 P. Will. 416.

The Mortgagor has a Right in Equity to redeem the Land, &c., at any Time within 20 Years after Forfeiture for Condition broken, if the Right be not forecloſed or releaſed before; but it is only a naked Right and not liable to be taken in Execution, in England. 2 Atk. 292. Nor is it Legal Aſſets there. 2 Vern. 62. Though here, by Force of the Province Law, 8 & 9 G. 2, c. 5, it may be attached and taken by Execution for ſatisfying the Mortgagor's Debt.

Though the Eſtate of a Mortgagee in Fee is only a Fee Simple conditional at firſt, and while it is uncertain whether y[e] Condition will be performed or not, — yet the Mortgagee has as ample and great an Eſtate in the Land as if it was an abſolute Fee Simple, though it may not be ſo durable. 1 Inſt. 18 a.

If the Condition be not performed, the Mortgagee's Eſtate in y[e] Land, be it an Eſtate for Years or of Inheritance, becomes abſolute; and, at Law, in England, is the ſame as though it had not been Conditional; and the Mortgagor could have no Relief in the Common Law Courts, untill the Stat. of 7 G. 2, c. 20, was made, which provided that

1772. HOOTON v. GROUT.

that on Ejectment brought by the Mortgagee, &c., if the Mortgagor, &c., pay the Principal, Intereſt, &c., the Mortgagee ſhall reconvey the Eſtate to the Mortgagor, &c.; which ſhews plainly the Senſe of the Parliament, that the Legal Eſtate is in the Mortgagee; or they would not have obliged him to reconvey it to a Mortgagor in Actual Poſſeſſion of the Land; as he muſt be ſuppoſed to be, when Ejectment is brought againſt him. 2 Black. Com. 158, 9, & Stat. 7 G. 2, c. 20.

Though the Court of Chancery, upon Conſideration that the Land was at firſt intended by the Parties only as a Pledge and Security for the Repayment of the Money lent, &c., allow the Mortgagor, his Heirs, Executors, Adminiſtrators or Aſſigns, upon Payment of the Money lent, &c., to redeem the Land, though forfeited, and in the Poſſeſſion of the Mortgagee, his Heirs or Aſſigns; yet that Court alſo conſiders the Legal Eſtate in the Land mortgaged to be in the Mortgagee; and, if it be a Mortgage in Fee, that the Mortgagor has no Eſtate at all left in the Land. 1 Vern. 412. 2 Cha. Ca. 97, 187. 2 Vent. 337.

This laſt Point came directly in Queſtion before Sir Joſeph Jekyll, Maſter of the Rolls, in the Caſe of *Haſkett* vs. *Strong*, 12 G., which was thus:— Mr. How mortgages certain Lands to Neal for 500 Years; and afterward mortgages them to Haſkett in Fee. Neal aſſigns his Term to Strong, who advanced more Money to How, and took of him a Deed of ye Inheritance. Haſkett contended that the Term was merged in the Inheritance; but his

1772. Hooton v. Grout.

his Honour decreed that it was not; becaufe How, after he had mortgaged to Hafkett in Fee, had no Eftate in him to grant, and then the Term could not be merged in a void Grant of the Inheritance. Stra. 689. Lord Chancellor Talbot in 1734 made a like Decree in the Cafe of *Collet* vs. *De Gols & Ward*, — that Ward, the Mortgagee, had the legal Eftate in the Land, and that Tyffen, the Mortgagor, had no Eftate in it to convey. Ca. Temp. Talb. 66, 68.

Upon this fame Principle it is, that a third Mortgagee, without Notice, by buying in the firft Mortgage, fecures himfelf againft the fecond Mortgagee; for, being equally intituled in Equity to a Repayment of the Money lent on the third Mortgage, as the fecond Mortgagee is on his, and having by the Purchafe of the firft Mortgage obtained the legal Eftate in the Land, a Court of Equity will not take that from him, in Favour of one who has no more Equity on his Side than the third Mortgagee hath. 2 Vent. 338. 1 Vern. 187. 2 Vern. 29, 157, 159. Abr. Ca. Eq. 322. 1 Cha. Ca. 162, 201. Hard. 173, 318. Fra. Max. 64.

It alfo is upon this fame Principle, that the Mortgagee, after having received the Money due to him, is, by the Court of Equity, confidered as a Truftee to the Mortgagor, and holding the Eftate in Truft for him, untill he reconveys it to him. 3 P. Will. 252, Note. That the Heir of the Mortgagee has the Ufe and Benefit of the Land, untill it is redeemed. It defcends to him, and he holds it as a Truftee

Truſtee for ye Executor. Abr. Ca. Eq. 327.— That, upon the Mortgagee's dying inteſtate, the Land mortgaged in Fee deſcends to his Heirs, he holds it in Truſt for the Adminiſtrator untill the Money is paid. Pre. Chan. 265. Abr. Ca. Eq. 327. 3 Bac. Abr. 641. Treat. Eq. 86, 88.— That the Mortgagee may deviſe the Land as Part of his Real Eſtate, and it ſhall paſs accordingly. 2 Vern. 583. Ca. Eq. 3. 3 Bac. Abr. 642. 2 Burr. 978.—That, although a ſecond Mortgage in Fee is conſidered as ſuch, between the Parties, yet Nothing paſſes by it but the Mortgagor's Right of Redemption; and, on a third Mortgage, only the Right of redeeming the firſt and ſecond Mortgages. Abr. Ca. Eq. 312.

Objection 1ſt. But it is objected, that Ld. Ch. Juſt. Mansfield, in the Caſe of *Martyn & Mawlin*, B. R. 1760, ſaid that "a Mortgage is a Charge upon "the Land, and whatever would give the Money "will carry the Eſtate in the Land along with it to "every Purpoſe." "The Eſtate in the Land is the "ſame Thing as the Money due upon it. It will "be liable to Debts; it will go to Executors; it "will paſs by a Will not executed with the Solemni-"ties required by the Statute of Frauds. The Aſ-"ſignment of the Debt, or forgiving it, will draw "the Land after it, as a Conſequence. Nay, it "would do it, though the Debt were forgiven by "Parol; for the Right to the Land will follow, "notwithſtanding the Statute of Frauds."—And that Lord Hardwick says, "the principal Right of "the Mortgagee is to the Money, and the Land is "but an Accident."

In

1772.
Hooton v. Grout.

In the Cafe of *Martyn & Mawlin*, there were but two Points confidered or determined by the Court, viz[t]: Firft. If the Father did, by his Will, give his Son and Daughter an Eftate Tail in a certain Clofe, mortgaged to the Father in Fee, and into which he had entered for the Condition broken, and the Mortgage had run 8 or 9 Years. Secondly. If the Son and Daughter took fuch an Eftate in the Clofe, whether it was well barred by the Surrender. And the Court determined, that the Teftator did not give his Son and Daughter an Eftate Tail in the Land, and that, if he had, the Eftate would have been well barred by the Surrender; — but it was not becaufe the Court thought the Teftator could not give his Son and Daughter the Clofe to hold as an Eftate Tail, but becaufe it appeared to the Court, upon Confideration of the whole Will, that the Teftator did not intend to give them the Land, but only the Money due upon it. For Lord Mansfield, in the Cafe, expreffly fays, if the Reporter is not miftaken, that — "if it appeared that "the Teftator really meant and intended to devife "the Clofe, as Land, it would be a Devife of the "Land, the Mortgage being forfeited by Law, and "the Eftate in the Land become abfolute." And Lord Keeper Cowper fays, — "If a Man, feifed of "Lands in Fee which were only mortgaged to "him, devifes them to his Son and his Heirs, and "fays, they fhall go as an Inheritance, furely the "Heir, if the Mortgage be paid off, fhall receive "the Money, and not the Executor; for the Father, who had the governing Power over the "Eftate, may difpofe of it as an Inheritance so long "as it continues fo, and y[e] Money, when paid off, "fhall "ſhall go as he intended the Land ſhould." Gilb. Ca. Eq. 3. That is, to y[e] Heir, and not to y[e] Executor.

So, a Deviſe to the Heir, of the Land mortgaged, will intitle the Heir to the Money, if the Land be redeemed. And, on the other Hand, if the Mortgagee give the Money due on the Land to his Daughter, and the Mortgagor pays it to her, the Court of Chancery will oblige the Heir, to whom the Land *deſcended*, to *reconvey* it to the Mortgagor; but, if he refuſes to pay the Money and redeem the Land, the Court will order the Land to be ſold to raiſe the Money for the Daughter, or conveyed to her *by the Heir*, unleſs he will forecloſe the Mortgage, pay the Money and keep the Land, as he may. 2 Vern. 67.

In this Senſe, and in this Manner, a Gift of the Money may eventually carry the Eſtate in the Land, and indeed, the Land itſelf along with it. But, if Lord Mansfield ſaid, "that y[e] Eſtate in the Land is the ſame Thing as the Money due upon the Land," it is not very eaſy to underſtand what he meant or intended thereby; for, if that be literally true, it neceſſarily follows, that the Money due upon the Land is the Eſtate in it; which is not only abſurd, but at once deſtroys the Diſtinction between a Mortgage of Land for a Term only, and a Mortgage in Fee, — if it be for the ſame Sum, — as the Mortgagee's Eſtate, in that Caſe, muſt be the ſame in both; which his Lordſhip could not poſſibly mean. If his Lordſhip meant that the Mortgagee's Eſtate in the Land was worth no more than the Money

1772. HOOTON v. GROUT.

Money due upon the Land, that may be true. But, that the Mortgagee's Eſtate in the Land will be liable to Debts, go to Executors, and paſs by a Will not executed by the Solemnities required by the Statute of Frauds is not true with Regard to Mortgages in Fee or for a Term attendant on the Inheritance. Sir Joſeph Jekyll, Maſter of the Rolls, decreed, that a Term attendant on the Inheritance would not paſs by ſuch a Will; and, upon an Appeal, his Decree was affirmed by the Lords Gilbert and Raymond, as Commiſſioners of the Great Seal, in the 8 G. 1 Gilb. Ca. Eq. 168. And, ſurely, if a Term attendant on the Inheritance will not paſs by ſuch a Will, the Inheritance itſelf will not. Nor do Lands mortgaged in Fee go to Executors, but deſcend to the Heir; and the Executor cannot obtain the ſame without the Aid of the Court of Chancery. And then they are not Legal Aſſets in the Hands of the Executor, but Equitable Aſſets only. Theſe Propoſitions, therefore, could not be intended by his Lordſhip as extending to all Mortgages, though they may be true as to Mortgages for Terms not attendant on the Inheritance. — "That the Aſſignment of the Debt, or the Forgiving of it, upon Parole, will draw the Land after it as a Conſequence," without the Aid of the Court of Chancery, is not true, unleſs Lord Hardwick was greatly miſtaken, when he ſaid, in the Caſe of *Harriſon* v. *Owen*, 1 Atk. 520, "That, if a Mortgagee "cancells a Mortgage, and it is found in his Poſſeſ-"ſion, it is as much a Releaſe (of the Debt, he muſt "mean) as cancelling a Bond; but it doth not con-"vey or reveſt the Eſtate in y[e] Mortgagor; for that "muſt be done by ſome Deed." If aſſigning the Debt

Debt or forgiving it, would reveſt the Eſtate in the Mortgagor, ſurely his paying the Money would do it; and yet the Mortgagee, after he has received the Money, is a Truſtee to the Mortgagor, untill he hath reconveyed the Eſtate. 3 P. Will. 252, Note.

1772. HOOTON v. GROUT.

To what End are all the Applications to Chancery to compel the Mortgagee, his Heirs or Aſſigns to reconvey the Eſtate, if paying the Money or tendering it would reveſt the Eſtate in the Mortgagor? As none of theſe Points came directly in Queſtion in the Caſe of *Martyn & Mawlin*, and it doth not appear that either of the other Judges concurred with Lord Mansfield in thoſe Propoſitions (if they ever fell from him), they cannot ſtand in Competition with contrary Decrees and Determinations, regularly made upon the Points when directly in Queſtion before the Court. But we have no Aſſurance theſe dark Sayings were ever uttered by Lord Mansfield. For the Reporter, Burrow, in his Preface, p. 8, ſays, "I do not take my Notes in "Short Hand,—I watch the Senſe, rather than the "Words, and, therefore, very often uſe ſome of my "own. I do not always take down the Reſtrictions "with which the Speaker may qualify a Propoſi-"tion, to guard againſt its being underſtood univer-"ſally or in too large a Senſe. And, therefore, I "caution the Reader always to *imply* the Exceptions "which ought to be made, when I report ſuch "Propoſitions as falling from the Judges." So that it is not certain that any of the Propoſitions are laid down in Lord Mansfield's own Words, nor that they were laid down without Reſtrictions and

 Limitations;

1772. HOOTON v. GROUT.

Limitations; and, as they are inconſiſtent,—one plainly diſtinguiſhing between the Eſtate in the Land, and the Money due upon it, and the next aſſerting that they are the ſame Thing—and almoſt all of them being inconſiſtent with the Decrees and Determinations of ſome of the great Men in the Nation and the conſtant Courſe of the Court of Chancery, they can be of no Authority, ought not to be palmed upon Lord Mansfield, but attributed to the inaccuracy of ye Reporter. Lord Mansfield certainly knew the Difference between Money and an Eſtate in Land,—between a Term and an Eſtate of Inheritance,—and between Legal and Equitable Aſſets;—which the Propoſitions, as they ſtand, abſolutely confound, and, therefore, are not to be regarded.

Objection 2nd. But Lord Chancellor Hardwick ſays,—"The principal Right of the Mortgagee is to the Money, and the Land is but an Accident." This is, doubtleſs, true; and no Ways inconſiſtent with what his Lordſhip and others have ſaid reſpecting Mortgages. Lord Hardwick alſo ſays, "That a Mortgage is a Debt by Specialty, and the Land is regarded, in this Court, (Chancery) only as a Pledge and Security for the Payment of the Money." 2 Atk. 435, 445. In Fra. Treat. Eq. 91, it is ſaid, "the Principal Right of the Mortgagee is to the Mortgage-Money, and his Right to ye Land is only as a collateral Security for the Payment of it,"—and, in England, it always is ſo, becauſe the Court of Chancery look upon a Mortgage as a general Debt, and the Land only as a Security. 2 Atk. 437. That Court conſiders the borrowing the Money

Money as creating a Debt, which, in good Conſcience, is due and ought to be paid: And, therefore, that Court will, ſometimes at leaſt, enforce the Payment of ſo much as the Proceeds of the Land, when ſold, fall ſhort of anſwering the Debt, though there was neither Bond nor Covenant in the Deed to oblige the Mortgagor to repay the Money. Salk. 449. 3 P. Will. 360, 1. So that the Debt is conſidered, in Chancery, as ſubſiſting independent of the Land. And the Mortgage as not eſſential to the Debt, but only additional and collateral Security for the Payment of it. Fra. Treat. Eq. 91.

An Accident is a Non-eſſential; and therefore Lord Hardwick with ſtrict Propriety ſaid, "The Land is but an Accident," it being not eſſential to the Debt. But, if the Mortgagee has no Eſtate in the Land, how can it be any Security to him for the Repayment of the Money lent, or how can it be ſaid to be pledged for the Security of the Repayment of the Money, if the Mortgagee has not the Land nor any Eſtate in it, according to the legal Senſe of the Word? Surely it cannot. Where then is the Eſtate? It is not in the Mortgagor; he, though in actual Poſſeſſion of the Land, is but Tenant at Will to the Mortgagee. *Newport's Caſe*, Skin. 424. Fra. Treat. Eq. 91. Carth. 414. Comb. 249, 250. Salk. 245, 6.

A Mortgagor in Fee, in England, has no Eſtate left in the Land that can be taken from him by Execution, though all Perſonal Eſtate and a Moiety of the Real may be ſo taken. 2 Atk. 292.

Though

1772. Hooton v. Grout.

Though a ſecond or third Mortgage in Fee be conſidered as a Conveyance of the Land between the reſpective Parties, becauſe the Deed eſtops the Mortgagor and his Heirs from ſaying he had not the Land, or ſuch an Eſtate in the Land as he hath taken upon him to grant, yet, in Fact, Nothing paſſes by the ſecond Deed, but y[e] Right of redeeming the Mortgage, or by the third than the Right of redeeming both the former. Fra. Treat. Eq. 90.

This Right of Redemption is not Legal Aſſets, in England. 2 Vern. 61. Nor are Mortgages in Fee Legal Aſſets in the Hands of the Executor or Adminiſtrator, unleſs the Money be paid them: Nor has the Ordinary Anything to do with them, unleſs the Money be paid. If it is not paid, the Heir may foreclоſe the Mortgagor; and then the Court of Chancery will not oblige the Heir to reconvey the Land to y[e] Executor, if he will pay him the Money due upon it. 2 Vern. 61, 67. Fra. Treat. Eq. 91, 92.

Objection 3rd. Mortgages are looked upon as Parts of the Perſonal Eſtate; the Money lent coming out of the Perſonal Eſtate, it ought to return there.

It is ſo conſidered in the Court of Chancery, unleſs the Mortgagee in his Lifetime or by his laſt Will, doth otherwiſe declare, or diſpoſe of the Mortgage. Fra. Treat. Eq. 91, 2. But where the Mortgagee enters for a Forfeiture, and abſolutely ſells the Land to J. S. and his Heirs, it ſhall not be looked

looked upon in his Hands as a Mortgage ſo as to make it Perſonal Eſtate. 1 Vern. 271, *Cotton* v. *Iles*, 1684. So, if Mortgagee in Fee, after Forfeiture and Entry, deviſes the Land to his two Daughters and their Heirs, and his other Mortgages to them and their Executors, the Daughters take the Land mortgaged in Fee as Real Eſtate, diſcendible to their Heirs untill it is redeemed. 2 Vern. 582. If Land mortgaged in Fee be deviſed as Real Eſtate, and afterwards redeemed, the Money ſhall go to him to whom the Land would have gone, and not to the Executors, as Part of the Perſonal Eſtate. 1 Vern. 4. 3 Bac. Abr. 642. Gilb. Ca. Eq. 3.

Charles Cox, poſſeſſed of a Term, mortgaged it, and died poſſeſſed of the Equity of Redemption of the Mortgage: — and, upon the Queſtion, if this mere Equity of Redemption was Legal, or Equitable Aſſets only, Sir Joſeph Jekyll, Maſter of the Rolls, after taking Time to conſider it, delivered his Opinion, with Solemnity, that this Equity of Redemption was Equitable Aſſets only; the Mortgage being forfeited at Law, and *the whole Eſtate thereby veſted in the Mortgagee.* 3 P. Will. 342.

Aſſets are of two Sorts, — one, by Deſcent — the other, in Hand. By Deſcent is where the Teſtator binds himſelf and his Heirs and dies ſeiſed of Lands in Fee Simple which deſcend to his Heirs; ſuch Lands are Aſſets by Deſcent. But where one is indebted and makes an Executor and dies, leaving ſufficient Eſtate that by the Courſe of the Law comes into the Hands of the Executor, or Profits come

1772. come into the Hands of the Executor in Right of his Teftator, this is called Affets in Hand. Terms of Law. 2 Burn, Eccl. Law, 668.

Hooton v. Grout.

Affets are also divided into Legal and Equitable. Legal Affets are fuch as are liable to Debts and Legacies by the Courfe of the Law; Equitable Affets are fuch as are only liable by the Help of a Court of Equity. Ib. 669.

It has before been obferved that the Mortgage of Land for a Term of Years is but a Chattel Real; and, unlefs attendant on the Inheritance, goes to the Executors without the Aid of a Court of Equity, and, confequently, is Legal Affets as foon as the Executor enters or recovers it; as it may be fold by him, without the Aid of any other. 1 P. Will. 730, 1. 3 Bac. Abr. 632. But Mortgages in Fee are not Chattels, but Eftates of Inheritance that may, by the Mortgagee, be granted or devifed as Real Eftate; and, if they are not, will defcend to his Heir; and the Executor cannot avail himfelf thereof, without the Aid of the Court of Chancery, if the Mortgagor is not willing to redeem and there is neither Bond nor Covenant to oblige him to do it. And, therefore, a Mortgage in Fee, as fuch, in England, is not liable to Debts in general or Legacies, by the Courfe of the Law, as Goods and Chattels are, though fuch Mortgages may be Affets by Defcent, and make the Heir anfwerable for the Value of it, if it is not redeemed. The mortgaged Premifes are confidered, in Chancery, after Forfeiture, as being the Eftate of the Mortgagee, vefted in him, and become abfolute by the

1772.

Hooton v. Grout.

he Forfeiture; That he, who comes into Chancery o redeem the Eſtate, ſhall pay the Coſts in Chancery, which are very great. 3 P. Will. 342.

The Mortgagee of a Term, though he, after Forfeiture, has the abſolute Eſtate for the Term, yet cannot make it Real Eſtate by deviſing it as ſuch; and, therefore, though it be deviſed in Tail, he Executor ſhall have it. 1 Roll. Abr. 915. 2 Burn's Eccl. L. 646. And yet, a Mortgagee in Fee may conſider y[e] Eſtate as Real or Perſonal, and diſpoſe of it accordingly; becauſe, the Land being Real Eſtate, the Mortgagee in Fee, having the Land and the whole Eſtate in the Land veſted in him, may grant or deviſe it as Real Eſtate; and it ſhall paſs accordingly; and being alſo intituled to y[e] Money lent and due on the Land, either by Bond, or Covenant in the Deed (as is moſt commonly the Caſe,) and alſo in good Conſcience, the Mortgagee may give y[e] Money; and, if it be paid the Legatee, he ſhall have it; or, if it can be recovered by the Bond or Covenant, he may get it in the Courſe of Law; or he may obtain it by the Aid of the Court of Chancery, in ordering y[e] Land to be ſold to raiſe the Money, or conveyed by the Heir to the Legatee, &c.; and, in that Senſe, the Gift of y[e] Money may be ſaid to draw y[e] Land after it.

This evidently ſhows that the Legal Eſtate in the Land is in the Mortgagee, as well as a Right to y[e] Money which the Land is pledged as a collateral Security for the Payment of; or elſe it could not paſs by his Gift or Deviſe of it, as an Inheritance. Not only the Act of Parliament, but alſo the Prov. Law,

1772.

Hooton v. Grout.

Law, 10 W. 3, c. 14, (5) ſhews that the Makers of thoſe Acts ſuppoſed that a Mortgagee in Fee had an Eſtate of Inheritance which he might aliene; and, if he did not do it, that it did deſcend to his Heirs. The Prov. Law provides that the Mortgagee, his Heirs, or the Tenant in Poſſeſſion, being the Purchaſer, and holding in his own Right, upon the Mortgagor, or Vendor, or his Heirs, tendering Payment of the original Debt, &c., ſhall accept the ſame and reſtore Poſſeſſion of the Land to the Mortgagor, &c., and *releaſe their Right therein.* There is no Mention made of the Money being paid to y[e] Executor or Adminiſtrator of y[e] Mortgagee, or their releaſing their Right to y[e] mortgaged Premiſes. The Legiſlature well knew, that, after Forfeiture and Entry for the Condition broken, the Eſtate was abſolutely in the Mortgagee, his Heirs or Aſſigns, and would remain ſo forever here, unleſs they provided for the Relief of y[e] Mortgagor, &c.; which they did by that Act. It is the only Relief he has here, and it is a Relief given by Law. So that it is not in the Diſcretion of y[e] Juſtices of the Inferiour or Superiour Courts, whether the Mortgagor, &c., ſhall, by paying the Mortgage Money, &c., redeem the Land within the Term appointed by the Act, nor whether he ſhall do it after the Expiration of y[e] Term, as it is in the Court of Chancery. Therefore, after the Time allowed by Law for Redemption is paſt, the Eſtate is irredeemable, and the Mortgagee has the ſame Right, Eſtate and Intereſt in and to the Land as if it had been granted to him at firſt abſolutely and without any Condition at all. And he then may,

(5) Anc. Chart. 324.

may, in every Senſe, be as properly ſaid to be ſeiſed in his Demeſne, as of Fee, of the Land, if it was mortgaged in Fee, as any Tenant in Fee Simple can be; and the Land may be by him ſold and deviſed as an Eſtate in Fee Simple, and, if it is not, it will deſcend to his Heirs in Fee, ſubject only to his Widow's Dower, and to be ſettled by the Court of Probate on one or more of the Children, as it will accommodate beſt; and the Widow has not the leaſt Colour nor Pretence for taking a Third of it as Perſonal Eſtate, becauſe it was a Mortgage, and holding that Third as an Eſtate of Inheritance, in Fee. Becauſe it is a Real Eſtate, and, if she don't hold it ſo, it cannot deſcend to her Heirs, nor can ſhe convey the Inheritance.

In England, the Common Law Courts hold, that the Eſtate paſſes preſently upon executing the Deed and Livery of Seiſin. The Court of Chancery holds, that the Mortgagee's Eſtate in the Land becomes abſolute upon the Condition not being performed. Our Law provides, that, upon the executing the Deed, acknowledging and regiſtering it, the Land ſhall paſs, without any other Act or Ceremony whatever; ſo that the Land paſſes, here, as much as if there was Livery of Seiſin given, and the Mortgagor's Eſtate in the Land mortgaged paſſes with it, here, as much as in England. Can there, then, a Queſtion ariſe in a Common Law Court here, whether any Eſtate in the Land mortgaged paſſes to the Mortgagee preſently upon the Regiſtry of the Deed, when the Court of Chancery allows, that, by the Forfeiture, the whole Eſtate is in the Mortgagee; and that it is abſolute; and that the Mortgagor

1772. HOOTON v. GROUT.

gagor has no Eſtate left in him. Shall the Common Law Courts here ſay, the Mortgagee has no Eſtate in the Land? No, ſurely, unleſs they take it upon them to be wiſer than the Law.

A Tenant in Fee Simple of Land has the largeſt Eſtate in it that a Subject can have. He can convey it abſolutely or conditionally, for a limited Time or forever. If he mortgages the Land for a Time only, the Fee remains in him, and the Mortgagee has the Land during the Time, if it is not redeemed, and no longer; but, if it is mortgaged in Fee, the Land and all the Mortgagor's Eſtate therein paſſes preſently to the Mortgagee. A Mortgagor in England has Nothing by Law left but the bare Condition, though here he has not only the Condition, but alſo a legal Right, by 10 W. 3, c. 14, to redeem the Land after Forfeiture, at any Time within three Years after Entry for the Condition broken.

The Mortgagor, continuing in Poſſeſſion, doth not hold the Land in his own proper Right here, any more than he doth in England, but is Tenant at Will of the Mortgagee here, as much as there; the Land therefore cannot be attached and taken in Execution as Land belonging to the Mortgagor in his own proper Right in Fee, by Force of 6 G. 1, c. 2, becauſe the Land is not his, nor has he any Eſtate in it. The Right the 10 W. 3, c. 14 gives him to redeem the Land doth not give him any Eſtate in it before it is redeemed and reconveyed, any more than the Right in Equity to redeem doth, in England; that is but a naked Right, and cannot

1772.
HOOTON v. GROUT.

cannot be taken by Execution there; Here, indeed, the legal Right the Mortgagor hath to redeem may be taken in Execution for ſatisfying his Debts: But the Creditor cannot avail himſelf of any more than what the Land is worth, above what it is mortgaged for: If the Mortgagor's Creditor by Execution does not pay the Money due on the Land to the Mortgagee, he cannot have the Land; nor has he any Eſtate in or Right to it, but upon Condition of paying the Mortgage Money, &c., to the Mortgagee.

Where the Land is mortgaged for the full Value of it or more, the Right of Redemption is not only a naked Right, but it is of no Value to the Mortgagor, cannot be attached or taken in Execution by his Creditors with any Advantage to themſelves, and, therefore, will not. In ſuch Caſes, then, if the Land cannot be taken in Execution as the Mortgagee's Eſtate, it will not be taken at all, but muſt be exempt ſo long as it is redeemable; which may be an hundred Years after the Forfeiture for the Condition broken. That, ſurely, will be of no Advantage to Trade or the Community.

But why may not the Land be taken as the Mortgagee's Eſtate for ſatisfying his Debts, as well as the Mortgagor's Right of Redemption may, for ſatisfying his? If it belongs to the Mortgagee in his own proper Right in Fee, it doubtleſs may, by Force of ye Province Law, 8 W. 3, c. 3. Where doth or can the Eſtate in Fee in the Land veſt, if it doth not in the Mortgagee in Fee? It muſt be in him or the Mortgagor or in Abeyance.

It

1772.

Hooton v. Grout.

It is plain it cannot be in the Mortgagor, nor can a Feoffment or Grant of Land in Fee annihilate the Eſtate in the Land, any more than it doth the Land itſelf. It ſerves only to paſs yᵉ Land and the Mortgagor's Eſtate in it to the Mortgagee; therefore the Eſtate in Fee cannot be in Abeyance. Then it muſt be in the Mortgagee in Fee; and that as ſoon as the Grant is made. It is not granted *in Futuro*, but *in Preſenti*. Upon the executing, acknowledging and recording the Deed, all the Mortgagor's Eſtate in the Land paſſes with it to the Mortgagee, and all the Eſtate then veſts in him, that can veſt. There is no future Act to be done by the Mortgagor or Mortgagee to make yᵉ Eſtate veſt in the Mortgagee, or to deveſt the Mortgagor of it. By the Mortgagor's performing the Condition upon which the Eſtate in the Land is granted, and the Mortgagee's acknowledging it in the Margin of the Record, the Land and the Mortgagor's former Eſtate in it, upon his Entry, will return to him, and he will be in as of his former Eſtate. That is, yᵉ Eſtate in Fee will be reveſted in yᵉ Mortgagor ſo as to avoid all meſne Incumbrances. But, if the Condition be not performed, nor the Land redeemed within the Time limited by Law, the firſt Grant remains in Force, and the Eſtate at firſt granted to yᵉ Mortgagee remains and continues in him without any Increaſe of Eſtate at all. Though the Land be irredeemable, the Mortgagee's Eſtate in the Land is not enlarged, though it may be more certain and durable, as Lord Coke ſays. 1 Inſt. 18. And it is evident that yᵉ Makers of yᵉ Stat. 4 and 5 W. 3, c. 16, ſo underſtood it, when they provided that a ſecond Mortgagee, without Notice of the

1772.
Hooton v. Grout.

the firſt, ſhould hold the Land for ſuch Eſtate and Term therein, as was granted to him againſt the Mortgagor, &c., freed from ye Equity of Redemption as fully as if ye Land had been purchaſed abſolutely and without Liberty of Redemption. See ye Stat. or 3 Bac. Abr. 648.

No poſſible Inconvenience can attend the attaching and taking in Execution the Lands mortgaged for ſatisfying ye Mortgagee's Debts, as to ye Mortgagee, beyond what would attend ye taking his other Real Eſtate in Execution. Nor will any other Inconvenience attend the Mortgagor than doth every Purchaſer of Real Eſtate: He may redeem it as well after it is taken in Execution as before. If the Whole is taken in Execution and the Year is elapſed, the Land is become irredeemable by ye Mortgagee; and then, if ye Mortgagor pays ye Money to ye Creditor by Execution, who, in Fact, holds the ſame as a Purchaſer, his Reconveyance of ye Eſtate to ye Mortgagor is ſufficient. If but Part of ye Land is taken, and the Mortgagor would redeem, the Mortgagee and his Creditor may together, on Payment of ye Money, reconvey ye Eſtate. If they will not do it, ye Mortgagor may file his Bill againſt them, and upon lodging ye Money in Court, they muſt reconvey ye Land to ye Mortgagor, or he will have Judgment and Execution for Poſſeſſion of it.

It is true, the Mortgagor may pay ye Money to ye Mortgagee, after his Creditor has attached the Land for his Debt, without ye Mortgagor's knowing it is attached, and thereby loſe his Money: And ſo

1772. HOOTON v. GROUT.

ſo a Purchaſer may purchaſe Land after it is attached, and thereby loſe his Money; but that has never been thought ſufficient to prevent a Debtor's Land being attached and taken in Execution for ſatisfying his Debts.

It might be of Advantage to make ſuch Attachments more public, by certifying them to the County-Regiſter, or otherwiſe. If Lands mortgaged could not be taken for ye Mortgagee's Debts, not only the Land will be exempt, but ye Money alſo. For, as our Mortgages in general are without any Bond, or Covenant in the Deed, the Money cannot, upon the Mortgagee's abſconding, be attached in Hands of the Mortgagor; for here ſuch a Mortgage is only a Conditional Sale, and none of the Executive Courts can compel the Mortgagor to repay the Money. 3 Bac. Abr. 638, 9. Cro. Jac. 281. Yelv. 206. 2 D'Anv. Abr. 53.

Though it may be a Debt in Conſcience, neither the Juſtices of the Inferiour Court or Superiour Court have, by Force of the Prov. Law 10 W. 3, c. 14, the Power of the Court of Chancery in ſuch Caſes. Their Power is limited. All the Power they have for determining Caſes in Equity is given them by that Act, and the obliging a Mortgagor to redeem the Land comes neither within the Words nor Meaning of the Act. So that, if the Land cannot be taken as Mortgagee's Eſtate to ſatisfy his Debts, he may have Ten or a Hundred Thouſand Pounds ſecured to him by the Mortgage, which his Creditors, by no Poſſibility, can come at; he may ſhut himſelf up and bid Defiance to them all. Surely

1772.
Hooton v. Grout.

Surely this is not to be endured, if it can poſſibly be avoided: Much leſs ſhould firſt Principles of Common Law, Judgments and Determinations of the Common Law Courts and Courts of Chancery alſo, be ſet at Nought and diſregarded in Order to ſubject Creditors to ſo great an Evil.

It has been objected, that, if the whole Eſtate in the Land is in the Mortgagee in Fee, all after Deeds of Conveyance of the Land, made by the Mortgagor, muſt be void and ineffectual to paſs the Land to the Purchaſer or give him any Eſtate in it, and all ſuch Purchaſers muſt loſe the Land they have paid their Money for, and ſuppoſed they held in Fee Simple.

This was ſaid without due Conſideration, — for, although Nothing doth, in Fact, paſs by ſuch after Deed, but ye Mortgagor's Right of Redemption, yet, as between the Grantor and Grantee, it is a good Grant of the Inheritance. It enables the Purchaſer to redeem the Land, obtain Poſſeſſion thereof and a Releaſe of the Mortgagee's Right and Intereſt in and unto the ſame. By the Mortgagee's releaſing to the Purchaſer in actual Poſſeſſion of the Land, the Eſtate which the Mortgagee had in the Land paſſes to the Purchaſer, and he thereby becomes ſeiſed in Fee of the Land.

If the ſecond Deed be made before the Time appointed in the Mortgage Deed for the Payment of the Money, and the Money is paid at the Day, and the Mortgagee acknowledges the Payment thereof on ye Record, that, by the Prov. Law 9 W.

3,

1772. HOOTON *v.* GROUT.

3, c. 8, difcharges the Mortgage and bars all Action thereon, (6) fo that neither the Mortgagee, his Heirs or Affigns can demand or recover the Land; and the Eftate in Fee which he had in the Land paffes to the Purchafer with the Land, or revefts in the Mortgagor: If it paffes to the Purchafer, he has it directly:—If it reveft in the Mortgagor, his second Deed eftops him and his Heirs from demanding the fame; for, as between the Parties to that Deed, it is a Conveyance of the Inheritance, and the Grantor and his Heirs, at leaft, are eftopped to fay the Contrary; and the Purchafer being in Poffeffion of the Land, and the fecond Deed being acknowledged and regiftered, the original Mortgagor cannot grant or convey the Land to another; and fo the Purchafer will thereby be quieted in the Poffeffion of the Land, and it will defcend from him to his Heirs, as an Inheritance.

Such Purchafers, therefore, are in no Danger of lofing their Eftates by the Court's determining, that a Mortgagee in Fee has an Eftate in Fee in the Land mortgaged, as not only the Common Law Courts, but alfo the Courts of Equity have before done.

NOTE.

The foregoing opinion is by Judge Trowbridge, the original MS. in his handwriting, though without title, having been found among his law papers, to which the editor was allowed accefs by the kindnefs of E. T. Dana, Efq. The fame point was decided in *Symes* v. *Hill*, *ante*, 318, and, among John Adams's papers, we find minutes of this

(6) Anc. Chart. 304.

1772.
HOOTON
v.
GROUT.

this opinion, and of the arguments of counſel, under the joint title "*Symes* vs. *Hill* & *Hooton* vs. *Grout*,"—ſuggeſting the probability that both caſes were argued together, ſo far as they were ſuppoſed to depend on this queſtion of the liability of mortgaged eſtates to attachment. But it would ſeem that the latter caſe muſt have been in fact decided on the firſt point raiſed by the ſpecial verdict, — viz., the effect of the leaving the aſſignment for record, — as the only other ground for judgment for the defendant would have been that the eſtate of a mortgagee was *not* attachable. Such we might have thought the deciſion in the caſe, overruling *Symes* v. *Hill*, and that this opinion of Trowbridge was a diſſenting one, but for the facts above mentioned tending to ſhow that the caſes were argued together and that this opinion was the reſult, although the point was neceſſarily decided in the caſe of *Symes* v. *Hill* alone.

The law in this commonwealth has long been ſettled in oppoſition to the doctrine here laid down. 13 Maſs. 207. 16 Maſs. 345. 3 Pick. 484. Another opinion upon the ſame point by Judge Trowbridge, of which the original alſo remains among his papers, is publiſhed in the ſupplement to 8 Maſs. 551.

1770.

ANONYMOUS.

While a Grantee of Land is in open Possession thereof under his Deed, Nothing passes by a subsequent Deed by the Grantor to a third Person, although recorded before the first.

Land, of which the Grantee is in open Possession under an unrecorded Deed, is not liable to Attachment by the Creditors of the Grantor.

Anonymous. (1)

A. SEISED in Fee of Land in Cambridge, by his Deed, in Consideration of £50, bargains and sells it to B., who enters and improves the Land as his own for several Years; and, while he is so possessed thereof, A., for £50 more, paid by C., by another Deed, bargains and sells ye Land to him, acknowledges the Deed, and it is recorded before the first; after which the first Deed is recorded, — whereupon these Questions arise:

1. If, by ye 2d Deed, ye Land, or any Estate in it passed to C.

2. If the Land, at ye Time of ye making ye 2d Deed, might have been lawfully taken in Execution by a Creditor of A. for Satisfaction of his Debt.

In

---

(1) The following opinion is without title, and occurs in the MS. between the memoranda at August Term 1769, *ante*, p. 316, and some unfinished notes of a case in Middlesex at October Term, 1771. In the case of *Fowle* v. *Richardson*, October Term 1770, in which the reporter was counsel for the defendant, this point was raised and decided as above. See Judge Trowbridge's reading on the provincial registry act, in the supplement to 3 Mass. 579. We should have supposed it probable that the opinion here copied into Quincy's book was that of Judge Trowbridge in the case referred to, but that the facts do not correspond: the land in *Fowle* v. *Richardson* being situated in Woburn, and the consideration in the deeds being also different. Whether these discrepancies can be accounted for on the supposition that the opinion was written out some time after the argument, and without the papers or record for reference, we leave the reader to judge.

1770.
ANONYMOUS.

In Order to determine these Questions aright, it will be necessary to consider not only ye Prov. Law 9 W. 3, 8, but how ye Law stood when that Act was made.

The Statute of 27 H. 8, 10, commonly called ye Statute of Uses, after reciting in ye Preamble, that "by ye common Laws of ye Realm, Lands, "Tenements and Hereditaments, be not devisable "by Testament, nor ought to be transferred from "one to another, but by solemn Livery of Seisin, "Matter of Record, Writing sufficient made *bona* "*Fide* without Covin or Fraud," enacts "that when "any Person shall be seised of Land," &c. "to the "Use, Confidence or Trust of any other Person or "Body Politic, the Person, or Corporations intitled "to the Use in Fee Simple, Fee Tail, for Life or "Years, or otherwise, shall from thenceforth stand "and be seised or possessed of ye Land, &c. of and "in ye like Estates as they have in the Use, Trust, "or Confidence; and that the Estate of ye Person "so seised to Uses shall be deemed to be in him or "them that have ye Use, in such Quality, Manner, "Form and Condition, as they had before in y^{e} "Use."

At common Law, a Bargain and Sale was a real Contract, whereby ye Bargainor, for a pecuniary Consideration, bargained and sold, or rather contracted to bargain the Land to ye Bargainee, and became, by such Bargain, a Trustee for, or seised to the Use of ye Bargainee, and the above Statute of Uses compleated ye Purchase; thus, as ye Bargain vested ye Use, ye Statute vested ye Possession in him

y^{t}

1770. ANONYMOUS. y[t] had y[e] Ufe, fo foon as it arofe, and thereby y[e] *Ceftuy que Ufe* became compleat Owner of y[e] Land, in Law as in Equity. 2 Bla. 338.

But, to prevent clandeftine Conveyances of Freeholds, y[e] Statute of 27 H. 8, 16, commonly called y[e] Statute of Inrollment, was made, whereby it is enacted, that no Land, &c. fhall pafs from one to another, whereby any Eftate of Inheritance or Freehold fhall be made or take Effect, or any Ufe thereof be made, by Reafon only of any Bargain and Sale, except it be made by Writing indented, fealed, and inrolled in one of y[e] Courts of Weftminfter or in y[e] County or Counties where y[e] Land lies, before the *Cuftos Rotulorum*, &c., within fix Months after the Date of y[e] Indenture.

All Conveyances made by a Bankrupt of his Land, &c. are, by the Statute of Eliz. & James, made void, and y[e] Commiffioners are expreffly empowered to fell and convey y[e] fame by Deed indented and inrolled in one of y[e] Courts of Record, although they may have been conveyed by y[e] Bankrupt to another; and fuch Conveyances by y[e] Commiffioners are made good and effectual in Law. But no Time is limited for the inrolling y[e] Deed.

In 1641, the Maffachufetts Colony made an Act, that no Mortgage, Bargain, Sale or Grant made of any Houfes or Lands, Rents or other Hereditaments, where y[e] Grantor remained in Poffeffion of y[e] Lands, fhould be of any Force againft any other Perfon, except y[e] Grantor or his Heirs, unlefs y[e] fame be acknowledged before fome Magiftrate and

and recorded by ye Clerk of ye County Court where ye Land lies. Old Colony Law Book, 33. (2) And in 1652 they made another Law, that no Sale or Alienation of Houſes and Land ſhould be held good, except it was done by Deed, and Poſſeſſion delivered upon Part in ye Name of ye Whole, unleſs ye Deed be acknowledged and recorded according to Law. *Idem*, 32. (3) No Time is limited by either of ye Acts, for recording the Deed.

By ye Province Law 9 W. 3, 8, (4) it is enacted, that all Deeds or Conveyances of any Houſes or Lands, ſigned and ſealed by ye Party granting y^e^ ſame having good and lawfull Right and Authority thereto, and acknowledged by ye Grantor, before a Juſtice of ye Peace, and recorded at Length in ye County where ye Lands lie, ſhall be valid to paſs y^e^ ſame, without any other Act or Ceremony in the Law whatſoever. And, that, after three Months, no Bargain, Sale, Mortgage or other Conveyance of Houſes or Lands, made and executed in the Province, ſhall be good and effectual in Law to hold ſuch Houſes or Lands againſt any other Perſon but ye Grantor and his Heirs only, unleſs ye Deed thereof be ſo acknowledged and recorded; and ye Act requires ye Regiſter to note ye Time when ye Deed is received by him into ye Office, and y^t^ ye Record ſhall bear ye Date; but no Time is limited for recording ye Deed. This Act and the Old Colony Law alſo empowers ye Grantee to compell ye Grantor to acknowledge ye Deed; and this Act provides that ye Vendee, by filing a Copy of ye Deed proved in

(2) Anc. Chart. 86. (3) Anc. Chart. 85. (4) Anc. Chart. 303.

1770. Anonymous. in yᵉ Regiſter's Office, ſhall thereby ſecure his Title in yᵉ mean Time, and that it ſhall be accounted ſufficient Caution againſt purchaſing yᵉ Eſtate in yᵉ Deed granted, and there is a Clauſe in yᵉ Old Colony Law of the like Import.

Upon yᵉ Whole, it is obſervable, that there is a material Difference between yᵉ Statute of Inrollment and yᵉ Statute of Bankrupts, as to Time of inrolling yᵉ Deed; yᵉ latter limiting no Time, but yᵉ former making it abſolutely neceſſary to be done within ſix Months from yᵉ Date of yᵉ Deed; elſe no Eſtate paſſes or Uſe ariſes by yᵉ Deed. If yᵉ Indenture of Bargain and Sale be ſuch as would have raiſed a Uſe at common Law,* and is inrolled within yᵉ ſix Months, yᵉ Inrollment has ſuch a Relation to yᵉ Deed, as that yᵉ Land paſſes from yᵉ Execution of yᵉ Deed, not by Force of yᵉ Statute of Inrollment, but by Force of yᵉ Deed, that raiſes yᵉ Uſe to yᵉ Bargainee, ſo ſoon as it is made, and the Statute of Uſes, that veſts yᵉ Poſſeſſion ſo ſoon as yᵉ Uſe ariſes. Hob. 136. Cro. Ja. 408, *Dimmock's Caſe.* 2 Jones, 196, *Perry* v. *Bowers.*

Upon a Queſtion, whether yᵉ Vendee of yᵉ Commiſſioners on yᵉ Statutes of Bankrupts, of Lands, by Deed indented, could maintain, by his Leſſee, an Ejectment before Inrollment of yᵉ Deed, though it was inrolled after Action brought, it was *held* by yᵉ King's Bench, that he could not, becauſe yᵉ Conveyance muſt be by Deed indented and inrolled, and that it would be very inconvenient and dangerous to admit of Relation, no Time being prefixed for

* 2 Inſt. 673.

for yᵉ Inrollment, which might be 7 or 20 Years or more after yᵉ Execution of yᵉ Deed. 2 Jones, 196, and 1 Vent. 360, *Perry* v. *Bowers*.

Whether yᵉ Makers of yᵉ Old Colony Law or yᵉ Province Law knew of theſe Determinations is not certain, but it is highly probable ſome of them did, and, to avoid yᵉ Inconveniences that might attend a Relation, they thought it beſt to prefix no Time for recording yᵉ Deed, and, for that Reaſon, among others, did not do it: But, inſtead of it, the Province Law requires the Regiſter to note yᵉ Time when yᵉ Deed is received by him into yᵉ Office, and that yᵉ Record ſhall have that Date; which, to be ſure, is altogether vain, if the Recording is to have yᵉ like Relation to yᵉ Execution of yᵉ Deed, as yᵉ Inrollment within ſix Months has; but is neceſſary, where yᵉ Eſtate is not to paſs, to every Purpoſe, untill yᵉ Deed was recorded: and, was it not for yᵉ Exception in yᵉ reſtrictive Clauſe of yᵉ Province Law, as well as yᵉ Old Colony Law, of "yᵉ Grantor and his Heirs," there would be yᵉ ſame* Reaſon for yᵉ Eſtate's not being adjudged to paſs here in any Caſe or to any Purpoſe, untill yᵉ Deed is recorded, as there is for its not doing ſo on Sales made by yᵉ Commiſſioners of yᵉ Bankrupt Eſtates.

But, although yᵉ Eſtate doth not paſs, here, ſo as to avoid all meſne Conveyances, untill yᵉ Deed is recorded, it doth not thence follow, that it doth not paſs before to ſome particular Purpoſes, and yet not to others, — as, in all fraudulent Conveyances, yᵉ Eſtate

* *Qu*. If yᵉ Eſtate is not in them; and alſo, if yᵉ Matter of yᵉ Exception would not have been implyed. See 3 Co. 82 b.

1770. ANONYMOUS. Eſtate paſſes from yᵉ Grantor to yᵉ Grantee, although yᵉ Deed be void as to Creditors: So, here, if yᵉ Deed be ſuch as would have raiſed a Uſe at Common Law, it veſts yᵉ Uſe in yᵉ Vendee upon yᵉ Execution of yᵉ Deed, and yᵉ Statute of Uſe veſts yᵉ Poſſeſſion in him that has yᵉ Uſe, ſo ſoon as it ariſes, whereby yᵉ Purchaſe is compleat as between yᵉ Parties, though not with Regard to others. This is what is meant and intended by yᵉ Deed's not being good and effectual to hold yᵉ Eſtate againſt any other Perſon, except yᵉ Grantor and his Heirs, unleſs it be recorded.

The Vendee cannot, with any Propriety, be ſaid to hold yᵉ Eſtate, until he has it; the Eſtate don't remain in yᵉ Vendor untill yᵉ Deed is recorded: The Grantor, between the Execution and recording yᵉ Deed, has no Right of Entry into yᵉ Land, nor can he recover it by Action, nor will it deſcend to his Heirs, yᵉ Deed being effectual in Law, without recording, to hold yᵉ Land againſt yᵉ Grantor or his Heirs. But, on the other Hand, if, upon yᵉ Delivery of yᵉ Deed, yᵉ Grantee enters into yᵉ Land, as he has a Right to do, he may convey it, and, if he doth not, but dies ſeiſed of yᵉ Land, it will deſcend to his Heirs, although yᵉ Deed be not recorded; which would not be the Caſe if yᵉ Eſtate never veſted in him; for he could not convey that which he had not; and very great Part of yᵉ People of yᵉ Province hold their Eſtates by ſuch Titles.

If, upon yᵉ Delivery of yᵉ Deed, yᵉ Grantee enters, holds and improves yᵉ Land as his own, while he is ſo poſſeſſed thereof yᵉ Grantor cannot, by a ſecond

1770.
ANONYMOUS.

ſecond Deed, convey ye Land to another; for, although y^e^ ſecond Deed ſhould be recorded before ye firſt, yet neither ye Land nor any Eſtate in it will paſs to y^e^ ſecond Bargainee, becauſe no Uſe would at Common Law have ariſen by ſuch Deed. Lord Coke, in his 2 Inſt. 673, ſays, ye Statute of Inrollment is to be intended of lawfull and effectual Bargains and Sales, ſuch as would have raiſed an Uſe at Common Law; and doth reſtrain ye Execution of them only that would be of Effect, if inrolled in ſix Months.

That Rule holds good here. The ſecond Bargain and Sale cannot be better than it would have been, had there not been a firſt. And "that no Man can, by Deed, convey Land to another, which a third Perſon is in Poſſeſſion of, claiming it as his own"* is a Maxim of ye Common Law which is by no Means altered by ye Province Law. That rather confirms and eſtabliſhes ye Rule: For it enables no other Perſons to convey Land by Deed acknowledged and recorded, but ſuch as "have good and lawfull Right and Authority ſo to do." And, though this Clauſe, when taken together with ye reſtrictive Clauſes in ye Act, muſt be conſtrued to extend to ſuch Perſons as have an apparent Right and Authority to convey, yet that don't deſtroy, but eſtabliſhes ye Rule of ye Common Law; ſince no Man has even an apparent Right to convey Land to another, that a third Perſon is in Poſſeſſion of, claiming it as his own.

Blackſtone

* 9 Inſt. 266.

1770.
ANONYMOUS.

Blackstone says, a Lease for Years gives ye Lessee a Right to enter, and when he enters, he is then, and not before, compleat Tenant for Years. — That such Entry serves ye Purpose of Notoriety, as well as Livery of Seisin from ye Grantor would have done. 2 Bla. 314. If so, surely ye Entry of ye Bargainee, having a Deed which not only gives him a Right of Entry into ye Land, but vests ye Fee in him, to certain Purposes at least, must alike serve ye Purpose of Notoriety. The Lease is not inrolled, any more than ye Deed is recorded, the former may be as secret as ye latter; and ye Entry and Occupancy, which is alike in both, equally serve ye Purpose of Notoriety. The Occupant, in both Cases, is *prima Facie* supposed to be the Owner of ye Land, and, upon Inquiry, will be found so. No fair Purchaser, in such Cases, is in Danger of being defrauded, if he uses ye Caution he ought to do. The Design of ye Province Law, as well as ye Statute of Inrollment, is to prevent fair Purchasers being defrauded and injured.

The restrictive Clause in ye Old Colony Law is expressly confined to Deeds made by a Grantor remaining in Possession after ye Grant, and ye Deed not recorded. A second Conveyance, in such Case, ought to take Place, because ye Grantor then was ye apparent Owner of ye Land, and an honest, fair Purchaser ought reasonably suppose him to be so.

The first Deed may be deemed fraudulent upon ye same Principles yt a Bill of Sale of Goods is, where they remain in Possession of ye Vendor; but when ye Deed is recorded or ye Grantee enters into Possession

Posseffion of ye Land, and improves it as his own, every one, thereby, is sufficiently cautioned against purchasing ye Land of ye former Posseffor, and is in no Danger of being injured or defrauded, unless it be by an Attempt to defraud a fair *bona Fide* Purchaser.

The restrictive Clause in ye Province, though not in ye very Words of ye Colony Law, is of ye like Import, and establishes ye same Rule; it is designed to prevent clandestine Conveyances, operating to ye Prejudice of *bona Fide* Purchasers; and it will have ye desired Effect, if it be so construed, as that a Deed of Conveyance, not accompanied with Posseffion, nor recorded, may not prevent Houses and Lands or any Estate therein passing by such an after Conveyance as would have been effectual for that Purpose, had ye first Deed never been made. The Words of ye Act will well bear such Construction, ye Act, so expounded, will stand with ye Reason of ye Common Law, and, therefore, ought to be so expounded: — If it is, it is plain, that Land will not pass by a second Bargain and Sale thereof, made while ye first Bargainee is in Posseffion of ye Land, claiming it as his own; and, consequently, that the second Bargainee cannot recover or hold ye Land.

Nor can ye Land, in such Case, be taken in Execution by a Creditor of ye Bargainor for Satisfaction of his Debts; because it is not, in Fact, his Land, nor is it apparently so. He has no Estate, Right or Interest, in or to ye Land, nor Posseffion of it, by himself or his Tenant. The Bargainee is not a Tenant at Will to ye Bargainor, nor doth he hold y^e

1770. ANONYMOUS. yᵉ Land in Right of yᵉ Bargainor, but in his own Right; nor is he a Diſſeiſor; the Deed gives him a Right to enter into yᵉ Land, and hold it againſt yᵉ Bargainor, and, conſequently, he is not a Tenant at Will or a Diſſeiſor. He is a Tenant in Fee Simple; he may convey yᵉ Land to another in Fee, or deviſe it; if he does neither, but dies ſo ſeiſed thereof, it will deſcend to his Heirs, and neither yᵉ Land nor any Right or Eſtate in it will deſcend to yᵉ Heirs of yᵉ Bargainor.

Nor is yᵉ Conveyance fraudulent in Fact, but is a *bona Fide* Purchaſe, and yᵉ Land is liable to be taken in Execution for ſatisfying yᵉ Bargainee's Debts. — Surely, it is not yᵉ Eſtate of both, and liable to be taken in Execution for yᵉ Debts of both, at the ſame Time.

If it be objected, "that yᵉ Conveyance will be effectual againſt other Perſons beſides yᵉ Grantor and his Heirs, if yᵉ Land may not be attached by his Creditors, againſt yᵉ Intent as well as expreſs Words of yᵉ Act," — in Anſwer thereto, it may be ſaid: — 1ſt, That yᵉ Objection is of equal Force, upon the Suppoſition that yᵉ Land may be attached as the Bargainee's Eſtate, by his Creditors; for yᵉ Deed, though not recorded, ſecures yᵉ Land againſt yᵉ Bargainor and his Heirs, ſo that yᵉ Bargainee cannot be removed by them; and, if his not recording yᵉ Deed will alſo ſecure it againſt yᵉ Bargainee's Creditors, then yᵉ Conveyance will not only be effectual againſt other Perſons beſides the Grantor and his Heirs, but be a ſtrong Inducement to many Purchaſers not to record their Deeds, leſt their

their Land ſhould be taken from them by their Creditors.

2. It is not by Force of y[e] Deed of Conveyance only, that y[e] firſt Grantee is enabled to hold y[e] Land againſt y[e] Creditors and Vendee of y[e] Bargainor; but by that accompanied with an Entry and continued Poſſeſſion, which Blackſtone ſays is of equal Notoriety with Livery of Seiſin; and that was y[e] common Evidence of y[e] Alteration of Property at Common Law. (5)

---

(5) Under the early regiſtration acts, it was conſtantly held that open and notorious poſſeſſion conſtituted ſuch implied notice of a conveyance as to preclude a ſubſequent vendee or creditor of the grantor from taking advantage of a neglect to record the ſame. 2 Maſs. 506. 4 Maſs. 637. 6 Maſs. 487. 10 Maſs. 60. 1 Pick. 164. 3 Pick. 149. But ſince the Rev. Sts. c. 59, § 28, actual notice only will have this effect, which poſſeſſion alone, however notorious, will not prove. *Pomroy* v. *Stevens*, 11 Met. 244. As to what degree of knowledge will amount to actual notice of a prior deed, ſee *Curtis* v. *Mundy*, 3 Met. 405.

May 20th, A.D. 1771.

Court of General Seffions of the Peace.

1771.

PETITION OF JURORS.

Under the Prov. St. 4 W. & M. c. 12, the Jufti-ces of the Seffions have no Power to raife Money from the County for an ex-traordinary Allowance to Jurors or Of-ficers of Court for Services on a criminal Trial.

The Petition of the Jurors in the Trials of Captain Prefton and the Britifh Soldiers. (1)

AT laft Auguft Term the Honourable Juftices of the Superiour Court paffed the following Order:

"Ordered, that it be recommended to the Court "of General Seffions of the Peace to make the Ju-"rors that were impannelled and fworn for the Trial "of Thomas Prefton, Efq., and the Soldiers, as alfo "the Officers who kept them, a reafonable Allow-"ance for faid Services: faid Prefton's Trial hold-"ing

(1) The following report of this decifion, and the remarks thereon, were publifhed by Quincy in the "Bofton Gazette," May 20, 1771, as appears by the memorandum endorfed upon the MS. In the celebrated trials of Capt. Prefton and the foldiers indicted for the murder of Crifpus Attucks and others in the "Bofton Maffacre," Adams and Quincy were counfel for the prifoners. A report of Prefton's trial was taken in fhort hand, and fent to England, but has never been publifhed. 2 John Adams's Works, 236. 10 Ib. 201. A report of the trial of the foldiers was taken by the fame hand, three editions of which have been publifhed in Bofton; the firft in 1770, the fecond in 1807, and the laft in 1824.

"ing six Days, and said Soldiers' nine Days; said "Jurys being kept together every Night by two or "more Officers." (2) 1771. PETITION OF JURORS.

In

---

(2) These trials would seem to have been the first in the province which lasted more than a day. Among Judge Trowbridge's papers is a list of "*Tryals by Jury cont'd for several Days*," which may have been drawn up for this case, and which comprises the trials of *John Lilburne*, 2 Hargr. St. Tr. 19, & 7 Ib. 354; *Peter Cook*, 4 Ib. 738; *Capt. Kidd*, 5 Ib. 287, and quotes from the trial of *Elizabeth Canning*, as follows:

"Emlyn in his Opinion says y[e] Law will not allow a Jury to go at "Large in a Criminal Case while ye Tryal is depending but y[t] they "may take Refreshm'ts & retire to rest in a place provided for them if "Guarded by a sworn Officer," &c., and that "Perhaps y[e] suffering y[e] "Jury to go at Large in y[e] midst of y[e] Tryal may be Cause for arresting "Judgm't. 10 Vol. State Tryal, 407."

In the margin of the record of Preston's case appears the following memorandum:

"N. B. The Court being unable to go through this Trial in one Day, "the King's Attorney and the Prisoner consent that the Court shall "adjourn over Night during the Trial; the Jury being kept together by "two Keepers, one chosen by the King's Attorney, the other by the "Prisoner or his Council; besides the Officer appointed by the Court." Rec. 1770, fol. 52.

A like memorandum appears on the record of the trial of the soldiers, except that, in this case, the prisoners did not enjoy the privilege of appointing a keeper, "the Jury being kept together by proper Officers appointed & sworn by the Court." Rec. 1770, fol. 52.

In 25 Mass. Archives, 414, appears the following letter, written by Oliver to Hutchinson during the trial of Preston; Hutchinson having ceased to act as Chief Justice, shortly after assuming the administration in consequence of the departure of Governor Bernard. See *ante*, p. 316.

"Dear Brother, "Saturday Night.

"After having had the Pleasure of seeing you to Day, I now give "myself the Pleasure of writing to you. I know you think you would "have finished the Cause in half the Time, & I know it would not have "taken half a Day at the Old Bailey; but we must conform to the "Times. We have not finished yet. Mr. Paine has now to close for "the

1771. PETITION OF JURORS.

In Consequence of this Order, the Jurors above named petitioned the Court of Sessions for the above Allowance, and the Court, having a Doubt of their Power touching the Grant of the Prayer thereof, ordered the Petition to stand over for Argument at the Sessions in April; and, on last Wednesday, THE POWER OF THE COURT to grant the Prayer of the Petitioners was argued by four Gentlemen of the Bar (*pro & con*) by Desire of the Honourable Justices of the Sessions.

It seemed agreed by Bench and Bar that the only Power of the Sessions to *grant Monies* must be derived from *provincial Law;* that such a Power could be derived from no where else. — And the Question was, whether the Act of 4 of W. & M. c. 12,

---

"the Crown, & he was so unfit, that to avoid as much as possible all "popular Censure we indulged him till Monday morn; for Mr. Auch-"muty did not finish till ½ past 4 o'clock. We shall finish I believe by "one or two o'clock on Monday. Hard upon the Jury, you say, it is "so, but we have allowed them the Liberty of the Court House to-mor-"row with their Keepers. It is best on the whole.

"I have a Quarto Volume of Evidence which I have pretty minutely "taken. I have reviewed it, & it turns out to the Dishonour of the In-"habitants, & appears quite plain to me that he must be acquitted; that "the Person who gave Orders to *fire* was not the Capt., & indeed if it "had been he, it at present appears justifiable. What the Verdict will "be, Monday I suppose will declare.

"I shall be glad to be released from this Prison, but it will be only an "Exchange to others.

"Farewell, Dear Brother.

"Yours affectionately,

"PETER OLIVER."

"To

"His Honour

"Mr. Hutchinson,

"Milton."

c. 12, (3) gave the Court a Power to grant Monies for the Allowance before mentioned. 1771.

PETITION OF JURORS.

The Act is intituled "An Act for the Settlement "of the Bounds and defraying the PUBLICK and "NECESSARY CHARGES *arising within each respective* "*County* in this Province." "And for the due and "equal *raising of Monies* for *defraying of the Charges* "*arising within each respective County*, for the necessa-"ry Repairs and Amendments of Bridges, Prisons, "the Maintenance of poor Prisoners, and ALL OTHER "PROPER COUNTY CHARGES, It is enacted, that, when "and so often as there shall be NEED OF RAISING "MONEY FOR THE ENDS AFORESAID in any County, "the Justices in Quarter Sessions for such County "receiving Information thereof from the County "Treasurer, shall agree and determine the whole "Sum to be raised, &c., and issue their Order," &c., "to assess the same upon the Inhabitants," &c.

The Debates at the Bar took up the Day. And the Justices after this solemn Hearing (only *Mr. Justice Dunbar doubting*) were unanimously of Opinion that the Prayer of the Petition of the Jurors should not be granted; and the Petition was accordingly dismissed.

It gives a most sensible Pleasure *in these Times* to find a Court of Justice deciding a *Point of Law* against an Extension of *their Power: especially* as that

(3) Anc. Chart. 245.

1771.
Petition of Jurors.

that Power would affect *the Purfe of the Subject.* — This Decifion is of no fmall Moment; its Importance will appear more confpicuous upon a clofe Examen and Reflection. However, it is yet a Matter of deep Concern with fome that the Superiour Court feem to entertain a different Opinion on the Point in Queftion. *They ordered a Recommendation of the Allowance to be made.* They are prefumed to know the Law, and we are willing to fuppofe they would not *influence*, and *much lefs recommend* to a fubordinate Court the Exertion of an illegal Power; a Power derogatory to the natural and primary Right of the Subject over his Property; and of the higheft Confequence to the Community, confidered in a feparate or collective View.

The Exiftence and Exertion of fuch a Power in the Seffions are of very extenfive Concernment; we therefore imagine all due Confideration was had at paffing the above *Order of Recommendation:* and, if fo, does not a becoming Deference to the Supreme Court lead us to conjecture that they were of Opinion that the Court of Seffions was by Law vefted *with Power to take Money out of the Pocketts of the People* to make that Allowance which it was thought expedient thus formally to recommend?

Printed in Bofton Gazette (Edes & Gill)
Monday, May 20, 1771.

Motto:
Intelligentibus.

December, A.D. 1763.

Curia Admiral.

Coram Honor. Chambers Ruſſell, Armigero.

Biſhop *verſ.* Brig Freemaſon.* (1)

1763.
THE FREEMASON.

Landing is not eſſential to conſtitute an Importation of Goods contrary to the Act of 15 Car. 2, c. 7, § 6.

A bringing into Port of prohibited Goods, under Circumſtances ſhowing a fraudulent Intent, though without Landing or breaking Bulk, is ſufficient, under that Act, to work a Forfeiture of Ship and Cargo.

MR. AUCHMUTY. I ſhall conſider firſt the Act of 15 Car. 2. (2) The Words are confined to *Importation*. Importation is to be a Forfeit; this

* Vid. Wilſon's Reps. 257, *Smyth* v. *Reynolds*.

(1) This was a libel by Captain Biſhop as a Cuſtom Houſe Officer, againſt the Freemaſon, as forfeited for importing European goods not ſhipped in Great Britain, in violation of the Act of 15 Car. 2, ch. 7, § 6. See note at the end of the caſe. *Auchmuty* was Advocate General — *Gridley* & *Thacher* for the claimants. No copies of the proceedings can be found, for moſt of the Admiralty records and files of Court prior to 1765 were deſtroyed in the ſtamp act riot of the 26th of Auguſt, in that year, (2 Minot's Hiſt. Maſs. 215. *Ante*, 169,) and what remained are ſuppoſed to have been carried away, either to Halifax or England. 10 John Adams's Works, 205, 354.

(2) The act of 15 Car. 2, c. 7, § 6, provides that " no Commodity of " the Growth, Production or Manufacture of *Europe* ſhall be imported " into any Land, Iſland, Plantation, Colony, Territory, or Place to His " Majeſty belonging " " in *Aſia*, *Africa*, or *America*, (*Tangier* only excepted)

1763. THE FREEMASON.

this four Times mentioned in the ſame Act; from this I reaſon that 'tis not a Landing that is required, but that a bare Importation will be a Forfeit. 15 Car. 2, ch. 7, § 6, p. 16. Acts of Parliament are to be conſtrued as we find them; Courts have no Power to controul them. Foſter's Crown Law, 20, 21, *Alexander Kinlock & Chas. Kinlock*, two Perſons indicted for Treaſon; ſpecial Plea, that, by Cuſtom, they were to be tried in Scotland: — This, only to ſhow how Acts are to be conſtrued. — The Offence is allowed to be within the Letter, but not within the uſual Conſtruction. That the Veſſel has imported theſe Goods is very certain. She was ſome Time below, was above the Caſtle (3) ſome Time. (He then obſerves upon the Evidence to ſhew there was a Deſign of fraudulent Importation.)

2. Whether ſhe is within the Meaning of this Act, which is for the Encouragement of Trade: What the Trade is that is to be encouraged, Sec. 5 ſhews: It is to render Great Britain the Staple. The only ſenſible Meaning of Importation is *Bringing in*, excluſive of Landing. 13 & 14 Car. 2, ch. 13, ſhews this ought to be the Conſtruction. In the ſame Senſe 'tis taken in 13 & 14 Car. 2, ch. 19, and in 13 & 14 Car. 2, ch. 11, §§ 22, 23, and in 22 & 23 Car. 2, ch. 26. From theſe Acts, I think it was evident that *Bringing in* is all they meant by Importation,

"cepted) but what all be *bona fide* and without Fraud laden and "ſhipped in *England*, *Wales* or the Town of *Berwick* upon *Tweed*, and "in *Engliſh* built Shipping."

(3) Caſtle Iſland, on which Fort Independence now ſtands, is within the mouth of the harbor, and about two and a half miles from the city.

1763. The Freemason.

tion, as all theſe Acts uſe the Words. The Statute 6 Geo. 2, ch. 13, §§ 2 & 3, makes a Diſtinction between Landing and Importing: They deſigned to make a Diſtinction between Goods that are cuſtomable, and not forfeited till Landing, and thoſe which, being prohibited, are forfeited by bare Importation. If theſe Laws ſhould be otherwiſe conſtrued, they would be compleatly evaded. — For, if they have not a fair Opportunity of *Running*, they will *Report.* The Conſequences of this Act to any particular Plantation cannot now be conſidered. There is a great Difference between Goods that may be imported and pay a Duty, and thoſe which are abſolutely prohibited.

Mr. Thacher. I aſk no Favour againſt Law. There is a Preliminary to be ſettled before the Merits. I queſtion the Power the preſent Libellant had to ſeize — and, if ſo, the Seizure is abſolutely void. (Upon this, Capt. Biſhop's Commiſſion was read, which was from three of five Commiſſioners of the Cuſtoms — and a Power to ſeize ſuch and ſuch contraband Goods wherever he ſhould find them.) By the 13 & 14 of Car. 2, ch. 11, § 15, none but an Officer can ſeize. 2 Strange, 952, *Horne* v. *Booſey.* If ſeized and condemned, the Owner ſhall afterwards recover in Trover, if the Perſon who ſeized was not a proper Officer. Now, every Officer is to be over ſome Port, Harbour, Town, &c.; Captain Biſhop's Commiſſion is general. No Plantations are mentioned, but it extends through the Globe. Have the Commiſſioners alone a Power to grant ſuch Commiſſions? I can't find their Appointment, therefore ſuppoſe that it is by the King's Prerogative,

Prerogative, and that he might farm the Cuſtoms or appoint Commiſſioners. This, with Regard to the Realm, not the Plantations, as their Planting is within Memory. There were no Officers for a long Time known as Officers of the Cuſtoms, but they were ordered to the Governour, or Officers by him appointed. And 'tis by expreſs Acts of Parliament that their Appointment here is. 25 Car. 2, ch. 7, § 4. I find by the Records in the Council-Chamber, that the Commiſſioners ground themſelves upon this Act, which reſpects only Collection of Cuſtoms. 'Tis 7 & 8 W. 3, ch. 22, § 11, this Warrant is grounded, if upon any. By this Act, Power is given to the Lord Treaſurer or Commiſſioners of the Treaſury (theſe are ſynonymous) and the Commiſſioners of the Cuſtoms, jointly. This Warrant is only from the Commiſſioners of the Cuſtoms, whereas no excluſive Power is given to either. Further, Officers who ſhall be thus appointed ſhall be particularly limited, they are ſtill to appoint in ſome particular Place, and over ſome particular Department. By the 13 & 14 Car. 2, ch. 11, § 14, it ſeems that the Officers, even in England, are limited; and it ſeems to be divided into Diſtricts Officers are obliged to reſide in; ſo that, had there been no Claim, the Party might have brought his Action. This late Act gives no new Power, but only to appoint Ships. There is an Act in 10 of Wm. 3, which impowers Ships to ſeize, which is only on the Coaſts, and this is only to extend that coaſting Power to the Plantations.

Let us conſider whether it comes within the Letter of this Act. If any Veſſell approaches or comes into

1763. THE FREEMASON.

into a Port, without any Intent to unload, ſhall her Cargo be ſaid to be imported? Can a Thing be ſaid to be imported, becauſe the Veſſell that holds it comes into Port? What Miſchief do they mean to ſuppreſs? 'Tis lawfull for us to be Carriers from one French Port to another. Shall then an Engliſh Veſſell, Carrier for other Nations, leaking and wanting Proviſions, with Liberty from the Owner to touch at an Engliſh Port for a few Days to procure Stores, not be permitted to touch at ſuch Engliſh Port? I challenge an Inſtance of a Seizure on this Act, till Landing or Bulk broken. Can it be ſaid that this Stopping is the Miſchief? 'Tis ſupplying the Colonies that is intended to be prevented. This will be ſtill plainer from ſeveral Acts the Advocate has cited. 13 & 14 Car. 2, ch. 13, § 2. What they mean by Importation is bringing in as Merchandize, ch. 19, § 2. The Meaning muſt ſtill be the ſame.

Mr. Gridley. The Expreſſion in this Libel, that they are imported into the Port, is different from the Language of the Act, which generally runs, "imported into any Lands, Territories," &c. The importing into a Port, is quite a different Thing from importing into a Land or Territory. In the 15 Car. 2, upon which this is grounded, it is, 'imported into any Iſland,' &c. and to ſay any Thing is imported into any Land without Landing, ſeems to be downright Soleciſm. The Wiſdom of the Nation has ſeen fit to gain a Profit from Merchandize, but ſtill that the greateſt may ſtill remain with the Merchant. Shall ſuch a Catch as this be the Deſign of the Wiſdom of the Nation?

1763. THE FREEMASON.

tion? 28 Edw. 3, ch. 13. 20th R. 3, ch. 4. These were before the feudal Tenures were taken away, and, upon their ceasing, Customs were introduced. Carkesse, Book of Rates, 767, 772. In the Act of Tonnage and Poundage, instead of importing, it is said, brought into England, 12 Car. 2, ch. 4. 15 Car. 2, ch. 7, § 8, shews there is *importing by Land*, so that the Word can't have a necessary Regard to Port. 7 & 8 of Wm. 3, ch. 22, §§ 6, 14, it is, to put on Shore. 9 & 10th of Wm. 3, ch. 43, § 1, is an Importation into a Port. 10 & 11 W. 3, ch. 10, § 19, Export is by Land, — so is 11 & 12 W. 3, ch. 10, § 3. Never was an Instance of importing into a Port being an Importation. (4)

---

(4) The report of this case in the MS. here breaks off. A full statement of the facts, the questions raised, and the decree of the Court, appears in the following letter from Governor Bernard to the Earl of Halifax, for a copy of which the editor is indebted to the kindness of Hon. Jared Sparks.

" My Lord, BOSTON, Decr. 2-th, 1763.

" Pursuant to the order received from Lord Egremont to send to his " office exact accounts of what shall happen in the execution of the " Laws of trade, I proceed to give an account of the prosecution of the " Brigantine & cargo, of the seizure of which I gave a short information " in my letter dated Octr. 25.

" The Brigantine Free Mason laden with french goods, chiefly wines, " at Bourdeaux took her departure for Boston at which place she ar- " rived (having first touched at Liverpool in Nova Scotia,) on fryday " the 21st of Octr. & came to anchor within the harbour about 6 miles " distance from the Town. There she lay at anchor all the rest of that " & the next day untill the Evening when it was dark, when she went " up to town. Being hailed in passing the Castle, they answered, from " Newcastle; & being boarded by the Man of War's barge They an- " swered from Newcastle laden with Coals. But it appearing that she " had a Cargo of Wine, Capt. Bishop commander of the sloop of War " Fortune, who had qualified himself in this Province as a Custom house " Officer, seized her. Soon after she was seized they owned that the Brig- antine

1763. THE FREEMASON.

" antine was loaded with french Wines &c. & came from Bourdeaux being " bound to St. Eustatia. And on the monday following, being the first " time the Custom houſe was open after the ſeizure, the Master made a " report of his Cargo, (which in the courſe of the tryal was falſified) & " his destination & praied that he might be permitted to proceed to St. " Eustatia. But the Captain, as a Custom houſe officer, by the advice of " the Advocate General, libelled the Veſſell & Cargo in the Court of " Vice Admiralty as forfeited for importing European goods not shipt " in Great Britain, contrary to the Act of the 15th of Cha. 2. Upon " which the Veſſell was claimed by owners living in this Province, & as " for the Cargo, a claim was entered on the behalf of Mr. " a french Merchant at Bourdeaux & Mr. a Dutch Mer- " chant at St. Eustatia; and it was alledged that theſe goods were " freighted by one to the other, and that leave was given for this Veſſell " to take Boston in her way to St. Eustatia: and that they had a Right " to come into this Port ſo long as they reported & did not break bulk.

" This produced a Question very interesting to the Crown, that is, " whether a Veſſell laden with prohibited goods & pretended to be bound " from a foreign European port to a foreign American port, might come, " ever ſo much out of their way, into a British American port & there " lie at anchor upon the credit of reporting her Cargo & pretended deſ- " tination. The affirmative of this Question had been pronounced to be " law in ſome popular declamations in the cauſes which were carried on " here against the Custom houſe officers about 3 years ago: but there " never was a cauſe, that I know, in which this point was adjudged. I " therefore determined, whenever a Caſe should happen in which this " Doctrine should come into Question to oppoſe it with all my power; " ſince it is obvious, that if this was determined to be law, it would be " neceſſary to apply to Parliament for an amendment of the 15th of " Char. 2, ſince it would be impoſſible to prevent foreign European goods " coming into America, if Veſſels laden with ſuch goods had a right to " come to British American ports only by reporting the Cargo & a pre- " tended destination to a foreign Port.

" Upon this account I took upon me the overlooking the conduct of " this proſecution in a manner more earnest & public than I have uſed in " other cauſes of this kind. The advocate general conducted it with a " ſpirit & Judgment not to be enough commended. The most mate- " rial Question was whether there could be an importation (ſo as to for- " feit) without landing. The judge having heard Council for two whole " days, gave his opinion that landing was not neceſſary to make an im- " portation contrary to that Act, & having shown how effectually the " Act would be defeated if a liberty for Veſſells laden with prohibited " goods, to come into British Ports at their own diſcretion was allowed, " & having mark't out ſeveral particular Circumstances which showed a " fraudulent intention in the preſent caſe, decreed the Veſſel & Cargo to " be forfeited.

1763.

THE FREEMASON.

" From this Decree the Claimers have appealed to the High Court of " Admiralty. Upon this occaſion I must, *in purſuance of the orders I " have received to impart to your Lordſhip, ſuch hints as may occur to me " for the better execution of the laws of trade*, earnestly recommend to " your Lordship, that the defence of this Decree against the appeal may " be ſupported at the expence of his Majesty. As one third part of this " forfeiture is decreed to his Majesty, his interest in it requires the ſupport " of his Officers *pro tanto*. But that is not all: if theſe extraordinary " Custom houſe officers, whoſe ſervice, as it's new, is the more invidious, " do not appear to have the public ſupport of the Crown in what they " do according to the best advice they can procure, I am convinced that " a Combination will ſoon be made to distreſs & embarraſs them by ap- " peals & actions at common law for doing their duty in the most plain " & poſitive caſes. This I have ſeen experienced in the confederacy " which was formed against the ordinary custom houſe officers of this port " about 3 years ago, which was effectually diſcouraged by one instance " only of a defence being carried on at the expence of the Crown.

" Copies of the proceedings are making out, which, together with an " abstracted state of the caſe & of the arguments uſed for the forfeiture, " will be ſent by the first opportunity. Captn. Bishop has alſo ſeized a " ship for loading with Rice without giving bond. I adviſed & assisted " him in this proſecution, & the ship was condemned together with the " Rice without any defence.

" I am with great regard

" My Lord your Lordships

" most, &c. &c. &c.

" FRA: BERNARD.

" The Rt. Hon'ble

" The Earl of Halifax."

APPENDIX I.

A. What are Writs of Aſſiſtance?

THIS term has been applied in the books of the law to many different proceſſes, which may conveniently be claſſed under three heads.

Different kinds of Writs of Aſſiſtance.

1. Writs of aſſiſtance, more uſually called "writs of aid," iſſuing from the Court of Exchequer, addreſſed to the ſheriff, and commanding him to be in aid — "*quod ſit in auxilium*" — of the King's tenants by knight ſervice, or the King's collectors, debtors, or accountants, to enforce payment of their own dues, in order to enable them to pay their dues to the King. Theſe writs are very ancient. (1) A like

1. Writs of Aid in the Exchequer.

(1) 1 Madox Hiſt. Exch. (2d ed.) 675, 677, 678, & notes. 2 Ib. 192. Reg. Brev. 87 a. 1 Rapin Hiſt. Eng. (2d ed.) 404, which was cited by *Otis*, *ante*, 55. 2 Bell Com. (4th ed.) 53. Manning's Exch. Pract. in Revenue, (2d ed.) 74, 75, 323; 332, 333, where the forms of one of theſe writs and of the affidavit and fiat therefor are given.

One of the writs of aid in the Regiſter (from what court iſſued is not ſtated) might almoſt be uſed for a precept to a marſhal of the United States to aſſiſt the maſter of a fugitive from ſervice under the Act of Congreſs of 1850, viz:

"*REX vicecomiti ſalutem. Præcepimus tibi quod ſis in auxilium A. de B. ubi ipſe non ſufficit ad diſtringendum villanos ſuos de N. ad* "*faciendum ei conſuetudines & ſervitia debita & conſueta. T. &c.*"

"*De auxilio habendo ad diſtringendum villanos.*" Reg. Brev. 87 b.

It is a curious coincidence that the word *conſuetudines*, uſed therein, is like writ, iſſued in 20 James I., to levy debts due to the Prince of Wales, is entitled on the record "*breve de aſſiſtendo.*" (2)

Under this head may conveniently be mentioned the writs iſſued by King Edward I. to the Barons of the Exchequer, commanding them to aid a particular creditor to obtain a preference over other creditors of the ſame debtor, out of a ſurplus of his goods remaining in the Exchequer, after paying a debt due to the King, or to ſome other creditor who had ſued there. (3)

2. Writs of Aſſiſtance in Chancery.

2. Writs to the ſheriff, to aſſiſt a receiver, ſequeſtrator, or other party to a ſuit in chancery, to get poſſeſſion, under a decree of the Court, of lands withheld from him by another party to the ſuit. Theſe writs, which iſſue from the equity ſide of the Court of Exchequer, or from any other Court of Chancery, are at leaſt as old as the reign of James I., and are ſtill in common uſe in England, Ireland, and ſome of the United States. (4) But, whether from the odium attached to the name here, or from the practice in this Commonwealth to conform proceſſes in equity to thoſe at law, no inſtance is known of ſuch a writ having been iſſued in Maſſachuſetts.

3. Writs

---

is the ſame word uſed in the old law books to denote cuſtoms on imports. Magna Carta of H. 3, c. 30. 2 Inſt. 58, 59. Lord Hale concerning the Cuſtoms, Hargrave's Law Tracts, 131 & *ſeq.*

(2) Manning's Exch. Pract. in Revenue, 388, note.

(3) *Memoranda in Scaccario*, 6, 13, 14. Manning's Exch. Pract. in Revenue, 75. 2 Madox Hiſt. Exch. 85, 86, & notes.

(4) Lord *Hardwicke* in *Penn* v. Lord *Baltimore*, 1 Ves. Sen. 454. 1 Sanders, Orders in Ch. 110, 237, 746, 879. "*Brev. de Aſſiſten.*" in Reg. Brev. app. 46, 47 — mentioned by *Thacher*, *arguendo*, 2 John Adams's Works, 522; *poſt*, D. 2 Fowler's Exch. Pract. in Eq. 186. 1 Ib. 161, where a form is given. *Greenſlade* v. *Baker*, 2 Ib. 182, & Bunb. 168. 3 P. W. 379, note. *Bird* v. *Littlehales*, 3 Swanſt. 299, note. *Bower* v. *Cooper*, 2 Hare, 412. *White* v. *Phibbs*, Sauſſe & Scully, 88, & note. 1 Smith's Ch. Pract. 447–449. 1 Grant's Ch. Pract. (5th ed.) 132; 606, (the form). 2 Dan. Ch. Pract. (Amer. ed.) 1267, & notes, & caſes cited. *Kerſhaw* v. *Thompſon*, 4 Johns. Ch. 615, 618. *Ludlow* v. *Lanſing*, Hopk. 232. *Valentine* v. *Teller*, Ib. 422. Blake's Ch. Pract. 97.

3. Writs of aſſiſtance to ſeize uncuſtomed goods were introduced by a ſtatute of Charles II., (5) and were perhaps copied

3. Writs of Aſſiſtance to ſeize uncuſtomed goods.

English Statutes on Writs of Aſſiſtance.

(5) By St. 12 Car. 2, c. 19, (confirmed by Sts. 13 Car. 2, St. 1, c. 7; 1 Anne, St. 1, c. 13, § 2; 9 Anne, c. 6, § 2; and 3 G. 1, c. 7, § 2,) if uncuſtomed goods are "landed or conveyed away without due entry thereof firſt made, and the cuſtomer or collector, or his deputy, agreed with, then and in ſuch caſe, upon oath thereof made before the Lord Treaſurer, or any of the Barons of the Exchequer, or chief magiſtrate of the port or place where the offence ſhall be committed, or the place next adjoining thereunto, it ſhall be lawful to and for" either of thoſe officers "to iſſue out a warrant to any perſon or perſons, thereby enabling him or them, with the aſſiſtance of a ſheriff, juſtice of peace, or conſtable, to enter into any houſe in the day time, where ſuch goods are ſuſpected to be concealed, and in caſe of reſiſtance to break open ſuch houſes, and to ſeize and ſecure the ſame goods ſo concealed; and all officers and miniſters of juſtice are hereby required to be aiding and aſſiſting thereunto." § 1.

"Provided always, That no houſe ſhall be entered by virtue of this act, unleſs it be within the ſpace of one month after the offence ſuppoſed to be committed." § 2.

"Provided alſo, That if the information whereupon any houſe ſhall come to be ſearched ſhall prove to be falſe, then and in ſuch caſe the party injured ſhall recover his full damages and coſts againſt the informer, by action of treſpaſs to be therefor brought againſt ſuch informer." § 4.

By St. 13 & 14 Car. 2, c. 11, § 5, "it ſhall be lawful to or for any perſon or perſons, authorized by writ of aſſiſtance under the ſeal of his Majeſty's Court of Exchequer, to take a conſtable, headborough, or other public officer, inhabiting near unto the place, and in the day time to enter and go into any houſe, ſhop, cellar, warehouſe, or room, or other place, and in caſe of reſiſtance to break open doors, cheſts, trunks, and other packages, there to ſeize, and from thence to bring, any kind of goods or merchandize whatſoever, prohibited and uncuſtomed, and to put and ſecure the ſame in his Majeſty's ſtorehouſe, in the port next to the place where ſuch ſeizure ſhall be made."

Both theſe acts were repealed by St. 6 G. 4, c. 105, §§ 17, 19. But the ſubſtance of the proviſion of St. 13 & 14 Car. 2 as to writs of aſſiſtance has been repeatedly reënacted. Sts. 6 G. 4, c. 108, § 40; 16 & 17 Vict. c. 107, § 221. Hamel's Laws of the Cuſtoms, 215, & app. cx.

Writs of aſſiſtance continue in force until the demiſe of the Crown, and for ſix months afterwards. Sts. 1 Anne, St. 1, c. 8, § 5; 6 G. 4, c. 108, § 41; 16 & 17 Vict. c. 107, § 221. And they are not affected by the death, reſignation, or removal of any of the commiſſioners named therein. St. 54 G. 3, c. 46.

copied from the ſheriff's patent of aſſiſtance. (6) The book of precedents, (7) quoted at the firſt argument here in 1761, (8) is ſo rare, and the form therein given is ſo curious a juſtification of Otis's ſuggeſtion that it was framed "by ſome ignorant clerk of the Exchequer," (9) that it is exactly reprinted in the margin. (10) The ſame form, with very little

---

(6) By Sir *Thomas Plumer*, *arguendo*, and Lord *Mansfield*, C. J., in *Cooper* v. *Boot*, 4 Doug. 347. In Dalton's Sheriff is the following form:

"The Patent of Aſſiſtance." Dalton's Sheriff, 8.

"*CAROLUS Dei Grat' Angliæ, Scotiæ, Franciæ, & Hiberniæ, Rex, fidei defenſor, &c. Archiepiſcopis, Epiſcopis, Ducibus, Comiti-*
"*bus, Baronibus, Militibus, liberis Hominibus, & omnibus alijs de com.*
"*Cantabr. ſalutem. Cum conceſſerimus dilecto nobis A. B. Militi officium*
"*vicecom. noſtri præd. cum pertinent', habend. quamdiu nobis placuerit,*
"*prout in literis noſtris patentibus ei inde confectis plenius continetur,*
"*vobis mandamus quod eidem A. B. tanquam vicecom. noſtro com.*
"*prædict' in omnibus quæ ad officium illud pertinent. intendentes ſitis*
"*auxiliantes & reſpondentes. In cujus rei teſtimon. has literas noſtras*
"*fieri fecimus patentes. Teſte meipſo apud Weſtm. die*
"*Anno regni noſtri, &c.*"

(7) "Compendium of the Several Branches of Practice in the Court of Exchequer at Weſtminſter," by W. Brown. London, 1688. The copy once owned by Judge *Lynde* is in the library of the American Antiquarian Society at Worceſter. The remnant of the firſt edition was publiſhed in 1699 as a ſecond edition, and entitled "The Practice of his Majeſties Court of Exchequer at Weſtminſter."

(8) 2 John Adams's Works, 523; *poſt*, D. (9) Ib.

"*Breve Aſſiſten' pro Officiar' Cuſtum'.*" *Temp. Jac.* 2. Brown's Exch. Pract. 358.

(10) "REX, &c. Omnibus & ſingulis Officiar' & Miniſtr' qui nunc habent aut impoſterum ſunthabitur' aliquod Offici-
"um poteſtatem vel auctoritatem ab vel ſuper Juriſdiction' Dom̄ Magni
"Admiralli ſeu Admiralitat' regni noſtri Angliæ Omnibus & ſingulis
"Vice-admirallis Juſticiar' noſtris ad pacem Major' Vic' Conſtabular'
"Ballivis les Headboroughs ac omnibus aliis Officiar' Miniſtris & Subdit'
"noſtris de & infra quemlibet Civitatem Burgum Villam & locum hujus
"regni Angliæ dominii Walliæ & vill' Berwici ſuper Twed' & veſtrum
"cuilibet ſalutem Cum nos per literas noſtras Paten' ſub magno ſigillo
"noſtro Angliæ geren' dat' tertio die Decembris anno regni noſtri
"viceſimo ſeptimo Aſſignaverimus dilectos nobis T. V. & R. B. Ar'
"Collector' Cuſtum̄ nrar̄ infra Port' Dover & in omnibus locis &
"crecis eidem Portui &c. (**take the granting word in the Patent**)
"prout per eaſdem literas Paten' inter alia plenius liquet & apparet
"Vobis

little change, is ſtill followed in England, as appears by comparing the old writ with one iſſued in the firſt year of the preſent reign, for a copy of which the writer is indebted to Henry T. Parker, Eſq., of London. (11)

"Vobis igitur & cuilibet veſtrum præcipimus & firmiter iujungengo "mandamus quod omni excuſatione ceſſante permittatis & quilibet veſ-"trum permittat præfat' T. V. & R. B. & eorum alterum deputat' "& ſervien' eorum & eorum quemlibet de tempore in tempus ad eo-"rum & cujuſlibet eorū volunt' & placitum tam nocti quam die intrare "& ire Anglice **to goe on board** aliquam navem cimbam vel aliud "vas fluctuan' Anglice **riding** jacen' vel exiſten' infra vel venien' ad "Portum præd' aut in aliquas Portus loca ſeu crecas eidem Portui adja-"cen' talem navem cimbam vel vas tunc & ibidem invent' videre ſcru-"tare & ſupervidere ac perſon' in eiſdem ſtricte examinare tangen' vel "concernen' Cuſtum̄ & Subſid' nobis debit' Ac etiam in tempore di-"urno unacum Conſtabular' Præpoſito Anglice **Headborough** aut alio "publico officiario prope inhabitan' intrare & ire in aliquas Cellas Ang-"lice **Vaults** Cellur' Repoſitor' Anglice **Warehouses** Shopas vel alia "loca ſcrutare & videre utrum aliqua bon' res vel merchandizas in "eiſdem navibus cimbis vel vaſis cellis cellur' repoſitor' ſhopis vel aliis "locis ſint vel erint ibi abſcondit' vel concelat' exiſten' fact' vel induct' "vel eſkippat' vel onerat' ad tranſportand' ab vel extra Port' D. p̄d' aut "aliquos Portus vel crecas eidem Portui adjacen' Ac aperire aliquos "riſcos Angiice **Truncks** ciſtas pixid' fardell' Packs fatt' vel de le Bulke "quecunque in quibus aliqua bona res vel merchandiz' erint ſuſpect' fore "paccat' vel concelat' Ac ulterius ad faciend' et exequend' omnia ea "que de jure & ſecundum legem & ſtatut' hujus regni Angliæ in hac "parte fuerit faciend' Ac vobis & cuilibet veſtrum præcipimus & fir-"miter injungend' mandamus quod eiſdem T. V. & R. B. deputat' & "ſervien' eorum & eorum cuilibet in executione præmiſſorum de tempore "in tempus auxiliantes aſſiſten' & adjuvan' ſitis & quilibet veſtrum auxil-"ians aſſiſtens & adjuvans ſit prout decet Et hoc nullattenus omittatis "& quilibet veſtrum omittat periculo incumbente Teſte, &c."

Writ of Aſſiſtance to Commiſſioners of the Cuſtoms in England in the reign of Victoria.

(11) "VICTORIA," &c. "To all and every the Officers and Miniſters who now have or hereafter ſhall have any "office power or authority derived from or under the Commiſſioners of "our Admiralty or our High Admiral of our United Kingdom for the "time being and to all and every our Vice Admirals Juſtices of the "Peace Mayors Sheriffs Conſtables Bailiffs Headboroughs and all other "our Officers Miniſters and Subjects within every City Borough Town "and County of England the Dominion of Wales and Town of Ber-"wick upon Tweed and to every of you Greeting Know ye that "Whereas We by our Commiſſion or Letters Patent under the Great "Seal

" Seal of our United Kingdom of Great Britain and Ireland bearing date " at Westminster the Twenty-fourth day of November in the first year " of our reign have constituted appointed and assigned our trusty and well " beloved Richard Betenſon Dean " and others " to be our Commiſſion- " ers for and during our pleaſure for the collection and for the manage- " ment of our Customs in and throughout the whole of our ſaid United " Kingdom of Great Britain and Ireland " &c. &c. " as by our ſaid " Commiſſion or Letters Patent inrolled amongst the Remembrances of " our Court of Exchequer at Westminster (amongst other things) is " more fully contained We therefore command you and every one of you " that all excuſes apart you and every one of you permit and ſuffer the " ſaid Richard Betenſon Dean " and others " and the Deputies Miniſ- " ters Servants and other Officers of them the ſaid Commiſſioners and " each of them from time to time as they shall think proper as well by " night as by day to enter and go on board any Ship Boat or other " Veſſel riding lying or being within and coming into any Port Creek " or Haven of England Dominion of Wales and Town of Berwick " upon Tweed and ſuch Ship Boat or Veſſel then and there found to " ſearch and ſurvey and the perſons therein being strictly to examine " touching and concerning the premiſes aforeſaid according to the form " effect and true intent of our ſaid Commiſſion or Letters Patent and " the Laws and Statutes of England or the United Kingdom of Great " Britain and Ireland in that behalf made and provided And in the " day time to enter and go into the Houſes Shops Cellars Warehouſes " Rooms and other places where any Goods Wares or Merchandizes lye " concealed or are ſuſpected to be concealed which are prohibited or " for which the Duties of Customs and other the rates and ſums of " Money aforeſaid are not or shall not be duly paid and truly ſatisfied " anſwered and paid unto our Collectors or Deputy Collectors Miniſ- " ters Servants and other Officers reſpectively or otherwiſe agreed for " according to the true intent of the Laws in force or hereafter to be made " and ſuch Houſes Shops Cellars Warehouſes Rooms and other pla- " ces to ſearch and ſurvey for the ſaid Goods Wares and Merchandizes " And further to do and execute all things which of right and according " to the Laws and Statutes of England and of the United Kingdom of " Great Britain and Ireland in this behalf shall be to be done according " to the effect and true meaning of our ſaid Commiſſion or Letters " Patent and the Laws and Statutes of England and of the ſaid United " Kingdom And we further strictly enjoin and command you and every " one of you that to the ſaid Richard Betenſon Dean " and others " our " ſaid Commiſſioners and to their Deputies Ministers Servants and " other Officers and each of them you and every one of you from time to " time be aiding assisting and helping in the execution of the premiſes as " is meet and this you or any of you are in no wiſe to omit at your perils " In Witneſs whereof we have cauſed theſe our Letters to be made pa- " tent Witneſs James Lord Abinger " &c.

B. Writs of Aſſiſtance granted in Maſſachuſetts Bay in the Reign of George II.

1755. Hutchinſon's ſtatement.

HUTCHINSON ſays, that under the adminiſtration of Governor *Shirley*, (which ended in 1756,) "he, as the civil magiſtrate, gave out his warrants to the officers of the cuſtoms to enter;" (1) and "theſe warrants were in uſe ſome years," until a diſpute of their legality cauſed the Governor "to direct the officers to apply for warrants from the Superior Court; and, from that time, writs iſſued, not exactly in

---

(1) In 65 Maſs. Archives, 77, is the following draft of a warrant, in Secretary *Willard's* handwriting, indorſed, "Warrt. to Coll. Greenleaf Febry. 28, 1755," and alſo (in Governor *Shirley's* hand) "Let it wrote fair and brought to-night to me to ſign"—which affords a curious example of confounding judicial and miniſterial duties.

Warrant from Governor Shirley to ſtop illegal trade.

"WILLIAM SHIRLEY Eſqr. To John Greenleaf Eſqr. Greeting:

"WHEREAS I have recd. Information that one Follingworth who ſails "from Newbury has made a Voyage already from thence to Cape Bre- "ton, or other Settlemts. near thereto, with a Load of Beef for their Sup- "ply, & is now fitting out with Proviſions for the ſame Purpoſe in "Contempt of the Authority of this Governmt. and to the great Preju- "dice of his Majeſtys Interests;

"THESE are therefore to deſire & direct you forthwith to make strict "Inquiry into this Affair & take Evidence upon Oath thereon; & "with the Advice of other Juſtices of the Peace to uſe all the Methods "you can by Law effectually to prevent this pernicious Trade in your "Place, & for the Proſecution of ſuch Perſons as have violated or ſhall "violate the Laws & Orders of this Governmt. for ſtopping all Veſſels "from going to Sea at this time without my ſpecial Leave, as alſo for not "carrying Proviſions & Ammunition off without Giving Bond at the "Impoſt Offices; eſpecially that the ſaid Follingworth be ſtop'd from "Proceeding on his Voyage: And all his Majeſtys Officers and other "his Majeſtys Subjects are hereby required to aſſiſt you herein.

"GIVEN under my hand & ſeal."

1755. in the form, but of the nature of writs of affiftance iffued from the Court of Exchequer in England." (2) The accuracy of this laft ftatement is fully corroborated by the contemporaneous records. The foremoft to apply to the Court was *Charles Paxton.* (3)

1. Paxton's Petition in 1755.

" Province of the
" Maffachufetts Bay }

"TO the Honourable his Majeftys Juftices of his Superiour Court for faid Province
" to be held at York in and for
" the County of York on the
" third Tuefday of June 1755.

" HUMBLY SHEWS Charles Paxton Efq[r] That he is lawfully authorized to Execute the Office of Surveyor of all " Rates Duties and Impofitions arifing and growing due to " his Majefty at Bofton in this Province & cannot fully " Exercife faid Office in fuch Manner as his Majeftys Ser- " vice and the Laws in fuch Cafes Require Unlefs Your " Honours who are vefted with the Power of a Court of " Exchequer for this Province will pleafe to Grant him a " Writ of Affiftants, he therefore prays he & his Deputys " may be Aided in the Execution of faid office within his " Diftrict by a Writ of Affiftants under the Seal of this " Superiour Court in Legal form & according to Ufage in " his Majeftys Court of Exchequer & in Great Britain, & " your Petitioner &C[a]

" CHAS PAXTON " (4)

This

(2) 3 Hutchinfon's Hift. Mafs. 92, 93.

(3) Bofton Gazette of November 23, 1761. If, as there ftated, the application was firft made in 1754, the reafon for its poftponement may perhaps be found in this entry on the docket of Auguft term 1754:

" The Court appoint Jam[s] Otis jun[r] Gent[n] to act as Attorney for the " King at this Term in the abfence of the Attorney General."

(4) The original petition, in the handwriting of *Samuel Winthrop* (then one of the clerks of the Superior Court) and figned by *Paxton,* is in

This caſe firſt appears on the records of the Court at the enſuing Auguſt term in Suffolk, (which the docket ſhows to have been held by *Sewall*, C. J., *Lynde*, *Cuſhing & Ruſſell*, JJ., and which was finally adjourned on the 30th of Auguſt,) in this form: 1755.

" Order on Paxton Eſq[rs] Petition." Rec. 1755. Fol. 148.

" UPON READING the petition of Charles Paxton Eſquire " wherein he ſhewed that he is lawfully authorized to exe- " cute the office of Surveyor of all Rates Duties and Impo- " ſitions ariſing & growing due to his Majeſty at Boſton in " this Province, and could not fully exerciſe ſaid office in " ſuch manner as his Majeſtys Service and the Laws in ſuch " caſes require, unleſs ſaid Court who are veſted with the " power of a Court of Exchequer for this province would " grant him a writ of Aſſiſtants, he therefore prayed that " he and his Deputies might be aided in the Execution of " ſaid office with his Diſtrict by a writ of Aſſiſtants under " the Seal of ſaid Court in Legal form and according to " Uſuage in his Majeſtys Court of Exchequer & in Great " Britain. ALLOWED, AND 'TIS ORDERED BY SAID COURT " that a writ be iſſued as prayed for." (5)

The

---

in the Library of the Maſſachuſetts Hiſtorical Society, in a MS. Collection of " Letters and Papers, Boſton, 1631–1783," fol. 98.

The form of petition, preſerved by *John Adams* at the end of his notes of the argument in February, 1761, and mentioned in 2 John Adams's Works, 523, note, is preciſely ſimilar, from the words " that he is lawfully authorized " to the words " in Great Britain," having only theſe words prefixed: " Petition. To the honbl &c humbly ſhews " ; and at the end " C. P——."

(5) The York docket for 1755 has not been found. The only Suffolk docket on which the caſe appears is that of Auguſt term 1755, upon which it is entered, without any number, as follows:

" The petition of Charles Paxton Eſq[r] ſurveyor of the Rates Du- " ties & Impoſitions ariſing & growing due to his Maj[ty] in this Province, " that the Court wou'd grant him a Writ of Aſſiſtants; allow'd: & " order'd that a Writ be iſſued as pray'd for."

1755. The writ was afterwards issued (6) in the following form: (7)

First writ issued to Paxton.

"Province of the
"Massachusetts Bay.

"GEORGE the Second by the Grace of God of Great Brit-
"ain, France and Ireland King,
"Defender of the Faith &c —

"To all and singular Justices of the Peace, Sheriffs and "Constables, and to all other our officers and Subjects "within said Prov. & to each of you Greeting —

"WHEREAS the Commissioners of our Customs have by "their Deputation dated the 8th day of Jany 1752, assignd "Charles Paxton Esqr Surveyor of all Rates, Duties, and "Impositions arising and growing due within the Port of "Boston in said Province as by said Deputation at large ap-"pears, WE THEREFORE command you and each of you that "you permit ye said C. P. and his Deputies and Servants "from Time to time at his or their Will as well in the day "as in the Night to enter and go on board any Ship, Boat "or other Vessel riding lying or being within or coming to "the said Port or any Places or Creeks appertaining to said "Port, such Ship, Boat or Vessell then & there found to "View & Search & strictly to examine in the same, touch-"ing the Customs and Subsidies to us due, And also in the "day Time together with a Constable or other public officer "inhabiting near unto the Place to enter and go into any "Vaults, Cellars, Warehouses, Shops or other Places to "search and see whether any Goods, Wares or Merchan-"dises, in ye same Ships, Boats or Vessells, Vaults, Cellars, "Warehouses,

(6) "*Sub silentio.*" Boston Gazette of November 23, 1761. The writ is said in the Gazette, as well as by *Thacher*, *arguendo*, *ante*, 52, not to have been issued until 1756.

(7) This writ (which is a close translation of the earliest precedent, *ante*, 398, note 10,) is printed, by permission of Mr. *Charles Francis Adams*, from the form preserved by *John Adams*, and mentioned in 2 John Adams's Works, 523, note.

1755.

"Warehouſes, Shops or other Places are or ſhall be there "hid or concealed, having been imported, ſhip't or laden in "order to be exported from or out of the ſaid Port or any "Creeks or Places appertain'g to the ſame Port; and to "open any Trunks, Cheſts, Boxes, fardells or Packs made "up or in Bulk, whatever in wh any Goods, Wares, or "Merchandiſes are ſuſpected to be packed or concealed and "further to do all Things which of Rt and according to "Law and the Statutes in ſuch Caſes provided, is in this "Part to be done: And We ſtrictly command you and every "of you that you, from Time to Time be aiding and aſſiſt-"ing to the ſaid C. P. his Deputies and Servants and every "of them in the Execution of the Premiſes in all Things "as becometh: Fail not at your Peril: WITNESS Stephen "Sewall Eſqr &c —"

1758.

Upon the record of January term 1758, in Middleſex, held by the ſame Juſtices, is the following entry:

2. Richard "Lechmere's Petº Writ iſſued Feby: 1758." Rec. 1758. Fol. 256.

"THE PETITION of Richard Lechmere, Eſqr Collector "of the port of Salem &Ca for a Writ of Aſſiſtants as on "the file: ORDERED that a writ be iſſued as pray'd for."

---

3. Waldo's Petition. "Writ of Aſſiſtants iſſued April 1758." Rec. 1758. Fol. 297.

In Suffolk, February term 1758. Preſent: The ſame Juſtices and *Oliver*, J.

"THE PETITION of Francis Waldo Eſqr Collector and "Surveyor of the Port of Falmouth, (8) for a Writ of Aſ-"ſiſtants, GRANTED."

In Middleſex, January term 1759. Preſent: All the Judges but *Oliver*, J.

"THE

---

(8) In Caſco Bay, Maine—now Portland. St. 1786, c. 14.

1759.

4. "Nevin's Pet.° Granted." Rec. 1759. Fol. 519.

"The Petition of James Nevin Eſq.r Collector of the "port of Newbury &C.a for his Majeſty's Writ of Aſſiſt-"ants; Granted; the ſaid James having produced his "commiſſion."

---

5. Thomas "Lechmere's Pet.° Order thereon." Rec. 1759. Fol. 548.

6. "Order on Sheaf's Pet.°" Rec. 1759. Fol. 553.

In Suffolk, February term 1759, theſe two caſes:

"The Petition of Thomas Lechmere Eſq.r Surveyor "General of his Majeſty's Cuſtoms, for a Writ of Aſſiſt-"ants; Granted." (9)

"The Petition of William Sheaf Eſq.r Collector of the "Port of Boſton, for a Writ of Aſſiſtants, as on file, Al-"low'd."

1760.

7. "Cradock's Pet.° W.t iſſued 1.st Mar, 1760." Rec. 1760, Fol. 28.

8. "Walter's Pet.° Allow'd." Rec. 1760, Fol. 30.

And in Suffolk, February term 1760, two caſes, viz:

"The Petition of George Cradock Eſq.r Collector of "the Port of Boſton, for a Writ of Aſſiſtance, as on file "Allow'd."

"The Petition of William Walter Eſq.r Collector of "the Ports of Salem and Marblehead, for a Writ of Aſſiſt-"ance, as on file, Allow'd; W.t iſſued 1.st Mar, 1760."

At each of theſe laſt two terms, as appears by the records, the whole court was preſent, viz: *Sewall*, C. J., *Lynde*, *Cuſhing*, *Ruſſell & Oliver*, JJ. (10)

---

(9) Upon the margin of the docket oppoſite this caſe is this entry: "Hatch, Dr. Writ iſſued 8th March 1759. Dld Petitio.r" And there is a ſimilar entry in the margin of the docket oppoſite *Richard Lechmere's caſe*, *ſupra*, 405. It may be conjectured that the words "Hatch, Dr." were intended as a charge of the clerk's fees to *Nathaniel Hatch*, Comptroller of the Port of Boſton, who had perhaps preſented theſe petitions. *Vid. poſt*, 422.

(10) Theſe are all the applications for Writs of Aſſiſtance, which have been found in the time of Chief Juſtice *Sewall*, who is ſaid to have had doubts of the legality of ſuch writs. 3 Hutchinſon's Hiſt. Maſs. 89. 10 John Adams's Works, 183, 247. Each of the petitions in 1758 and

1760.

and 1759 is entered on the docket of the term at which the order was paſſed, and numbered with the civil actions. The Suffolk Docket for 1760 and the court files of all theſe terms are wanting.

Governor Bernard's Papers.

Much light is thrown upon the ſubject of the Writs of Aſſiſtance by the very valuable collection of Governor *Bernard's* letter-books and manuſcripts in the poſſeſſion of Mr. *Jared Sparks*, who has kindly and liberally given the writer every facility for examining and making copies of them.

The King's inſtructions of March 18, 1760, to Sir *Francis Bernard*, at the time of his appointment to the Government of Maſſachuſetts Bay, contained an order, in the moſt general terms, to "be aiding and aſſiſting to the collectors and other officers of our admiralty and cuſtoms, in putting in execution" the Acts of Trade. 13 Bernard Papers, 149, 196.

On the 18th of Auguſt 1760, Governor *Bernard*, in announcing to the Lords of Trade his arrival in Boſton, wrote: "There are no diſputable points of government remaining unſettled; and this people are better diſpoſed to obey their compact with the Crown, than any other on the continent, that I know. I may add that I enter on the government without any party being formed againſt me." 2 Ib. 37.

Some weeks before this letter reached England, *Pitt*, as Secretary of State, ſent the following inſtructions to the Governors of the American Colonies:

"Whitehall, 23d Auguſt 1760."

"Sir,

Pitt's inſtructions in 1760 to prevent trade with the Enemy.

"The Commanders of His Majeſty's Forces, & Fleets, in North "America, & the Weſt Indies, having tranſmitted repeated & certain "Intelligence of an illegal & moſt pernicious Trade, carried on by The "King's Subjects in North America, and the Weſt Indies, as well to "the French Iſlands, as to the French Settlements on the Continent of "America, and particularly to the Rivers Mobile, & Miſſiſſippi, by "which the Enemy is, to the greateſt Reproach & Detriment of Govern-"ment, ſupplied with Proviſions, and other Neceſſaries, whereby They "are principally, if not alone, enabled to ſuſtain, & protract this long & "expenſive War; And it further appearing, that large Sums in Bul-"lion are alſo ſent, by The King's Subjects, to the above Places, in "Return whereof, Commodities are taken, which interfere with the "Produce of the Britiſh Colonies Themſelves, in open Contempt of the "Authority of the Mother Country, as well as to the moſt manifeſt Pre-"judice of the Manufactures, & Trade of Great Britain; In order "therefore to put the moſt ſpeedy and effectual Stop to ſuch flagitious "Practices, ſo utterly ſubverſive of all Law, and ſo highly repugnant to "the Honor and Wellbeing of this Kingdom, It is his Majeſty's expreſs "Will & Pleaſure that you do forthwith make the ſtricteſt, & moſt dili-"gent Enquiry into the State of this dangerous & ignominious Trade,

"and

1760. "and that you do uſe every Means in your Power, to detect and diſcover "Perſons concerned, either as Principals, or Acceſſories, therein, & "that you do take every Step, authorized by Law, to bring all ſuch "heinous Offenders to the moſt exemplary, and condign Puniſhment; "And you will, as ſoon as may be, & from Time to Time, tranſmit to "me, for the King's Information, full & particular Accounts of the "Progreſs you ſhall have made in the Execution of theſe His Majeſty's "Commands, to which The King expects that you do pay the moſt "exact Obedience: And you are farther to uſe your utmoſt Endeavours, "to trace out and inveſtigate the various Artifices and Evaſions, by "which the Dealers in this iniquitous Intercourſe find Means to cover "their criminal Proceedings, & to elude the Law, in order that, from "ſuch Lights, due & timely Conſideration may be had, what farther "Proviſions ſhall be neceſſary to reſtrain an Evil of ſuch extenſive & "pernicious Conſequences.

"I am, Sir,

"your moſt obedient humble Servant,

"W. Pitt."

Theſe inſtructions are preſerved in 22 Maſs. Archives, 163–165; and there is a duplicate original in 9 Bernard Papers, 121–123. There is no evidence in this or any other public act of *Pitt* of an intention to put new reſtrictions on the trade of the Colonies, beyond cutting off ſupplies to the enemy in time of war. See 4 Bancroft's Hiſt. U. S. 375–377.

Governor Bernard's anſwer.

Governor ***Bernard*** anſwered, that on his arrival in Auguſt, 1760, he ſatisfied himſelf that no ſuch trade was carried on here; and incloſed the report of a committee, approved by the Council, to the ſame effect; and added: "If I apprehended that there was the leaſt danger that this trade would be carried on from this Province, I would immediately communicate your orders by circular letters to the ſeveral officers of the ports within my government: But I apprehend that, as things are, ſuch public notifications would anſwer no other purpoſe than to imply a charge againſt the Province of what I believe it is quite free from." Bernard to Pitt, November 8, 1760, 1 Bernard Papers, 284. Council Rec. 1760, fol. 280, 285.

In a letter to Secretary ***Pownall***, of June 15, 1761, the Governor particularly mentions theſe inſtructions and his anſwer. 1 Bernard Papers, 317. But no more ſpecific order in 1760 for the execution of the Acts of Trade has been found in the Bernard Papers or in the Maſſachuſetts Archives or Council Records.

It would ſeem therefore that the above inſtructions muſt be thoſe which *John Adams* mentions in his autobiography as "ſent to the cuſtom houſe officers, to carry the Acts of Trade and Navigation into ſtrict execution;" and which in his correſpondence he leſs accurately deſcribes as ſpecific orders to the officers of the cuſtoms to apply for Writs of Aſſiſtance.

ance. 2 John Adams's Works, 124, note. 5 Ib. 492. 7 Ib. 267. 10 Ib. 246, 274. It ſhould be remembered that even the autobiography was not written until twenty-five years afterwards. 2 Ib. Pref. vii.

Death of Chief Juſtice Sewall.

The records quoted in the text ſhow that the officers of Boſton and moſt of the other principal ports of the Province had been previouſly ſupplied with Writs of Aſſiſtance, which would continue in force until the death of the King and for ſix months afterwards. *Ante*, 397, note 5, *ad fin.* Chief Juſtice *Sewall* died on the 10th of September, 1760. *Mayhew's* Sermon on his Death. Boſton Gazette of September 15, 1760. And no application for a Writ of Aſſiſtance appears upon the record or docket of the autumn term in 1760 of the Superior Court in Eſſex, which began and ended in October. Rec. 1760, fol. 154–160. There could hardly be more conclusive proof of the inaccuracy of the ſtatement in *Adams's* autobiography (repeated in his correſpondence) that the firſt application for a Writ of Aſſiſtance was made by *Cockle*, Collector of Salem, to the Superior Court "at their seſſion in November, 1760, for the County of Eſſex," and that "Mr. *Stephen Sewall* was then Chief Juſtice." 2 John Adams's Works, 124, note. 10 Ib. 183, 246, 247, 274. By a ſimilar error of date, in his preface of 1819 to *Novanglus*, *Adams* puts Chief Juſtice *Sewall's* death "in December, 1760, or January, 1761." 4 Ib. 7. As a Writ had been iſſued to *Paxton* in Boſton ſome years before, (*ante*, 403,) and the Collectors of Boſton had obtained them there in this and the previous year, (*ante*, 406,) the application can hardly have been made in Salem becauſe "Mr. *Paxton* thought it not prudent to commence his operations in Boſton," as ſuggeſted by *Adams*. 10 Ib. 246. Indeed there is no ſufficient evidence that any application was made in Salem. The ſtatement in *Adams's* later correſpondence that *Otis* was retained by the merchants of Salem as well as of Boſton to oppoſe the iſſuing of the Writs (Ib. 247, 275,) receives no confirmation from the names ſubſcribed to the petition of the merchants; and is inconſiſtent with the counter memorial of the Surveyor General, and with *Otis's* own ſtatement in opening his argument. *Poſt*, 412, 413, 414. 2 John Adams's Works, 523. 2 Minot's Hiſt. Maſs. 91. *Poſt*, D, note. *Adams* ſeems to have made a miſtake of a year, at leaſt, and may have been miſled by ſome recollection of *Paxton's* application having been made in York, (*ante*, 402,) or of the ſubſequent doings of *Cockle*, whoſe unpopularity was ſecond to *Paxton's* only. *Vid. poſt*, 422, 423, & notes. The reaſons, derived from the court records, for believing that no application was made in writing at this time, are ſtated *poſt*, 418, note 3. And both *Bernard* and *Hutchinſon* imply that the application which was oppoſed was made after the appointment of the latter to be Chief Juſtice. See 3 Hutchinſon's Hiſt. Maſs. 95; Hutchinſon to Conway, and Bernard to Lords of Trade, and to Franklin, *poſt*, 415, 416, note. But it is poſſible that *Cockle*, who had been very recently appointed, (*poſt*, 423,) and to whom no Writ of Aſſiſtance had been iſſued, did orally apply for one before the end of the year.

Adams's account of Cockle's application in 1760.

1760.

Hutchinson's appointment to be Chief Justice.

Upon the death of Chief Justice *Sewall*, *Hutchinson's* friends at once began to move for his appointment to fill the vacancy. 3 Hutchinson's Hist. Mass. 86. Andrew Oliver to Israel Williams, September 30, 1760, 2 Williams Papers, 102, in Mass. Hist. Soc. Lib. *John Adams's* Diary of November 5, 1760, 2 John Adams's Works, 99, 100. *James Otis* in Boston Gazette of April 4, 1763. *Gordon* (who did not arrive in Massachusetts until ten years later—see his preface) asserts that "Mr. *Hutchinson* hurried to Mr. *Bernard*, procured a promise, which being once given the Governor would not retract, and got himself appointed Chief Justice." 1 Gordon's Hist. U. S. 141. See also Adams to Niles, February 13, 1818, 10 John Adams's Works, 285. But *Hutchinson's* own statement in his history that the appointment was unsought by him is well attested by the letter, above referred to, in which *Oliver*, his brother-in-law, wrote to *Israel Williams*, his intimate friend: "If his Excellency & the Lieutenant Governor were to confer together on the Subject the matter might be accommodated. The Lieutenant Governor is so diffident of his own fitness, that if he could be brought to accept of the place, yet I am persuaded he would never move in it." See also Williams to Hutchinson, December 3, 1760, 2 Williams Papers, 118. Even *Otis* in the Gazette (*ub. sup.*) does not show that *Hutchinson* did more than accept the office of Chief Justice, after promising to use his influence to have *Otis's* father appointed the youngest judge, according to a promise which Governor *Shirley* had made some years before. 3 Hutchinson's Hist. Mass. 86. 4 Bancroft's Hist. U. S. 379. And it is due to *Hutchinson* to add his explanation that "the Governor declared that, if the Lieutenant Governor should finally refuse the place, the other person would not be nominated." 3 Hutchinson's Hist. Mass. 87.

On the 17th of November, 1760, *Bernard* wrote to Lord *Halifax*: "No public business of consequence has been moved of late, except I may reckon the filling up the place of Chief Justice. This office became vacant on the 10th of September, and last Thursday I appointed the Lieutenant Governor to it. I propose to explain my motives to your Lordship for this proceeding; but I must wait for another opportunity, as this must go to the Post office." 1 Bernard Papers, 283. The Governor apparently never found time to explain his motives, and they are therefore merely matters of conjecture. But it would appear from the statements of *Bernard* and *Hutchinson* that the first controversy with the officers of the customs was the claim in behalf of the Province for moneys illegally received, which arose after this appointment. Bernard to Secretary Pownall, January 19, 1761, & February 13, 1762, 1 Bernard Papers, 296; 2 Ib. 30. Hutchinson to Williams, January 21, 1761, 2 Williams Papers, 155. 3 Hutchinson's Hist. Mass. 89, 92. *Post*, Appendix II. & notes. And, considering how many of the officers already held Writs of Assistance, there seems to be no good reason for adopting the suspicion expressed by *John Adams* in 1780, which thirty-five

five years later grew into an affertion, that *Hutchinfon* was appointed for the fpecial purpofe of fecuring a decifion in favor of thefe writs. 7 John Adams's Works, 267. 10 Ib. 183, 247, 280. 1760.

All the accounts fhow that Governor *Bernard* confidered it neceffary that candidates for judicial office fhould make perfonal applications to him. And the truth feems to be that *Otis* and *Hutchinfon* each had ftrong partizans; that the Governor was determined to appoint a Chief Juftice who would fuftain the Crown and its officers in any controverfy which might arife, while the *Otises* were indignant that he fhould difregard the promife of his predeceffor; and that each party put the worft interpretation poffible upon the action of the other. But the charge commonly made by the fupporters of prerogative againft *James Otis*, that his fubfequent public courfe was dictated folely by revenge for his father's difappointment, (3 Hutchinfon's Hift. Mafs. 88; Judge *Oliver*, quoted in *John Adams's* Diary of June 5, 1762, 2 John Adams's Works, 135; Bernard to Shelburne, December 22, 1766, 4 Bernard Papers, 275,) may be claffed with *D'Ifraeli's* infinuation that *John Hampden's* refufal to pay Ship Money was occafioned by an ancient grudge againft the fheriff who levied it. See 1 Nugent's Life of Hampden, 224.

George 2 died on the 25th of October, 1760. News of his death reached Bofton on the 27th of December, and *George* 3 was proclaimed on the 30th, without waiting for any official notice of his acceffion. *Hutchinfon*, who had been appointed on the 13th of November, was commiffioned as Chief Juftice on the 30th of December, and firft took his feat upon the Bench on the 27th of January, 1761, in Middlefex. But (probably from fome doubt of the regularity of his appointment) he was included in the renewal of the commiffions of the Judges after the demife of the Crown, on the 15th of April, 1761. Bernard to Secretary Pownall, January 11, 1761, 1 Bernard Papers, 285. 3 Hutchinfon's Hift. Mafs. 88, 95, 96. Rec. 1761, fol. 161, 188. Council Rec. 1760, fol. 288, 298; 1761, fol. 382; Book of Commiffions 1756–1767, fol. 191, 199, 201.

C. Writs of Aſſiſtance in Maſſachuſetts Bay in the Reign of George III.

1761.

Records and files of Court.

AMONG the few files of the Superior Court of Judicature in Suffolk of ſo early a date, now remaining in the cuſtody of the clerk of the Supreme Judicial Court of Maſſachuſetts, one bundle, labelled in the handwriting of *John Tucker*, who was clerk of this Court from 1784 to 1825, "Boſton Mixed Papers down to A. D. 1762," fortunately includes the papers relating to the Writs of Aſſiſtance granted by *Hutchinſon*, as well as the caſe of *the Province of Maſſachuſetts Bay* v. *Paxton.* (1) The papers on file in the matter of the Writs of Aſſiſtance are as follows:

The Petition of the Merchants. (Indorsed "Greene & al petition ab[t] Writ of Aſſiſt[s].")

Petition of Merchants of Boſton for a hearing upon the Writs of Aſſiſtance.

"TO the Honb[le] the Juſtices of the Superiour Court "of Judicature, Court of Aſſiſe & General Goal "Delivery to be holden att Boſton within & for "the County of Suffolk on the third Tueſday "of February ADom. 1761.

"THE PETITIONERS Inhabitants of the Province of the "Maſſachuſett's Bay Humbly Pray That they may be heard "by themſelves and Council upon the ſubject of Writs of "Aſſiſtance & your Petitioners ſhall (as in Duty bound) ever "pray.

"Samuel Auſtin	Sam[l] Grant	Thos: Greene
"Edw[d] Davis	Nat Wheelwright	Joſhua Winſlow
"Jon[a] Maſon	Tho[s] Tyler	Jos. Green
"Sam Ph Savage	Nath[el] Holmes	John Spooner

John

(1) *Poſt*, Appendix, II.

1761.

" John Scollay
" James Perkins
" Timo Newell
" John Waldo
" Wm Greenleaf
" Joseph Scott
" Thomas Gray
" Jont Amory
" Chris. Clarke
" Jonathan Sayward
" Jams Warden
" Peter Boyer
" Geoe Erving
" John Baker
" Thoms Greene Jr

John Gooch
W Molineux
Ezekl Goldthwait
Samuel Welles Jun
Benj Auftin
Arnold Welles
Sam. Dexter
Jona Williams
Sol. Davis
Henderfon Inches
John Boylfton
James Pitts

Jno Barrett
John Tudor
John Avery
John Dennie
John Rowe
Sam Wentworth
J Erving junr
Jas Boutineau
Fitch Pool
John Lowell
Melatiah Bourn
John Winniett
John Browne
Timo Fitch
Danl Malcom
Saml Gridley
Tho Boylfton
Saml Hughes
Jofeph Domett
Jams Thompfon
John Welch Junr:
Shrimpt Hutchinfon
John Greene
Wm Thompfon"

The Memorial of *Thomas Lechmere*, the Surveyor General. (Indorsed "Lechmere's petn")

Memorial of the Surveyor General in favor of the Writs.

" Province of the
" Maffachufetts Bay
" Suffolk fs.

TO the Honourable His Majefty's Juftices of the Superior Court of Judicature Court of Affife and General Goal Delivery held at Bofton within & for faid County on the third Tuefday of february, 1761.

"THE MEMORIAL of Thomas Lechmere Surveyor General of His Majefty's Cuftoms for the Northern Diftrict of America.

"WHEREAS a petition is enter'd in this Honble Court "fign'd

1761. "ſign'd by a great number of Merchants and Traders be- "longing to the Town of Boſton praying to be heard upon "the Subject of Writs of Aſſiſtance Your Memorialiſt "therefore prays that Council may be heard on his Majeſ- "ty's behalf upon the ſame Subject: And that Writs of Aſ- "ſiſtance may be granted to him and his Officers, as uſual. (2)

"THO[s] LECHMERE."

The

---

(2) In the previous reign *Lechmere* as Surveyor General, *Paxton* as Surveyor of the Port of Boſton, and the Collectors of the Ports of Boſton, Salem and Marblehead, Newburyport, and Falmouth, had been ſupplied with Writs of Aſſiſtance. *Ante*, 404–406. But thoſe writs were about to expire. *Ante*, 397, note 5, *ad fin.*

Arguments.

The queſtion whether new ones ſhould be iſſued was argued at this term, beginning on the 24th of February, 1761, by *Otis* and *Thacher* againſt the writ, and by *Gridley* alone in its favor. This is the argument reported by *John Adams*. *Vid. poſt*, D. Judgment was ſuſpended; and at the next term, on the 18th of November, 1761, the queſtion was argued again by *Otis* and *Thacher* againſt the writ, and by *Gridley* and *Auchmuty* in its favor. This is the argument reported by *Quincy*, *ante*, 51 & *ſeq.*, and mentioned in the Boſton Gazette of November 23, 1761, *poſt*, F.

Judgment, and iſſue of the Writ.

At the concluſion of this argument, "judgment was immediately given in favor of the petition." Boſton Gazette of November 23, 1761. So *Quincy* ſays: "The Juſtices were unanimouſly of opinion that this writ might be granted, and ſometime after, out of term, it was granted." *Ante*, 57. The court adjourned on the 19th of November, (*ante*, 51, note) and on the 2d of December, the writ was granted to *Paxton*, according to an elaborate form, prepared by *Hutchinſon*, and reciting all the ſtatutes relied upon. *Infra*, 418.

Hutchinſon's account of the judgment, in his hiſtory.

Hutchinſon, in his hiſtory, after ſtating that the writs were objected to becauſe they did not ſpecify the place to be ſearched, and were not ſupported by information upon oath, ſays: "The Court was convinced that a writ, or warrant, to be iſſued only in caſes where ſpecial information was given upon oath, would rarely, if ever, be applied for, as no informer would expoſe himſelf to the rage of the people. The ſtatute of the 14th of Charles II. authorized iſſuing writs of aſſiſtance from the Court of Exchequer in England. The ſtatutes of the 7th and 8th of William III. required all that aid to be given to the officers of the cuſtoms in the Plantations, which was required by law to be given in England. Some of the judges, notwithſtanding, from a doubt whether ſuch writs were ſtill in uſe in England, ſeemed to favour the exception, and, if judgment

The other papers and memoranda concerning Writs of Affiftance to various officers of the cuftoms may be conveniently arranged under diftinct numbers. 1761.

Firft.

---

judgment had been then given, it is uncertain on which fide it would have been. The chief juftice was therefore defired, by the firft opportunity in his power, to obtain information of the practice in England, and judgment was fufpended. At the next town [term], it appeared that fuch writs iffued from the Exchequer, of courfe, when applied for; and this was judged fufficient to warrant the like practice in the Province. A form was fettled, as agreeable to the form in England, as the circumftances of the Colony would admit, and the writs were ordered to be iffued to cuftom-houfe officers, by whom application fhould be made to the Chief Juftice by the Surveyor General of the cuftoms." 3 Hutchinfon's Hift. Mafs. 94.

In applying to the Englifh government, in 1765, for compenfation for his loffes by the Stamp Act Riot, (*ante*, 168,) *Hutchinfon* enlarges upon his own fervices in overruling the fcruples of the other judges, and upon the unworthy motives of thofe who oppofed the writ. In a letter of September 12, 1765, he fays: "Three or four years ago, after a long argument in the Superior Court, which has by its conftitution the power of the Court of Exchequer, as well as that of the Common Pleas and King's Bench, it was determined to grant writs of affiftance to the cuftom houfe officers, no other provifion being made by law for entering fufpected houfes or warehoufes. This was a great mortification to the illicit traders, who found no great difficulty in running goods and houfing them; the great difficulty is after they are landed." 26 Mafs. Archives, 153. "In the year 1761 application was made by the officers of the cuftoms to the Superior Court, of which I was then Chief Juftice, for writs of affiftance. Great oppofition was made by fome who profeffed themfelves friends to liberty, and by others who favoured illicit trade, and the court feemed inclined to refufe to grant them; but I prevailed with my brethren to continue the caufe until the next term, and in the mean time wrote to England, and procured a copy of the writ, and fufficient evidence of the practice of the Exchequer there, and the like writs have ever fince been granted here." Hutchinfon to Secretary Conway, October 1, 1765, 26 Mafs. Archives, 155. "About three years ago, upon application made to the Superior Court, of which I am Chief Juftice, writs of affiftance were granted in aid of the officers of the cuftoms, which were complained of as grievous by the illicit traders, and by them a notion was put into the heads of the common people in general that thefe writs were contrary to their liberties as Englifhmen." Hutchinfon to Earl of Kinnoull, October 27, 1765, Ib. 164. "With refpect to the writs

In his letters in 1765.

1761. *First.* The earliest in date of the remaining papers is the following certificate:

"Boston 2d decem^r, 1761.

1. Surveyor General's Certificate for Paxton.

"Sir

"Do me the favour to issue a Writ of assistance to "Charles Paxton Esquire Surveyor & Searcher of his "Majestys Customs in the Port of Boston,

"Sir, Your most Obedient
"and most humble Servt
"JOHN TEMPLE."

"To the Honble Thomas
"Hutchinson Esqr Chief
"Justice of the Superior Court
"of this Province."

This

---

writs of assistance, I was well satisfied after great deliberation that in issuing them I did what the law required me to do, and if I was mistaken, which I am not yet convinced of, it was an error in judgment only." Hutchinson to Lords of Trade, November 3, 1765, Ib. 160.

Governor Bernard's statement.

Governor *Bernard*, in a letter to the Lords of Trade, of November 30, 1765, describing the Stamp Act Riot, says: "Last of all the (Lieutenant Governor) Chief Justice's house destroyed with a savageness unknown in a civilized country. I mention him as Chief Justice, as it was in that Character he suffered; for this connecting him with the Admiralty & Custom house was occasioned by his granting writs of assistance to the Custom house officers, upon the Accession of his present Majesty; which was so strongly opposed by the Merchants that the Arguments in Court from the Bar and upon the Bench lasted three days. The Chief Justice took the lead in the Judgement for granting Writs, and now he has paid for it." 4 Bernard Papers, 176, 177. And on the 24th of March, 1768, (after the passage of the St. of 7 G. 3, c. 46, *infra*,) he wrote to Lieutenant Governor *Franklin* of New Jersey: "Writs of Assistance were first granted by Chief Justice *Sewall* many years ago. Upon Chief Justice *Hutchinson* coming to the Bench, there was a formal Opposition to the renewing them after the Demise of the late King, which was prosecuted with such earnestness, that the hearing lasted three days successively. The Court was unanimous for granting them as the Laws then stood." 5 Ib. 261.

Adams's account of the judgment,

John Adams, in two letters to *William Tudor*, half a century afterwards, says that the Chief Justice, some days after the argument in February,

This paper, which forms the wrapper of all the others filed 1761.

February, 1761, on ordering the caſe to be continued to the next term, ſaid that the court " could not at preſent ſee any foundation for the Writ of Aſſiſtance ;" and adds, that no judgment was ever given in public, nor anything more ſaid in court about the Writs of Aſſiſtance. 10 John Adams's Works, 233, 248. If this laſt ſtatement were not concluſively diſproved by the contemporaneous evidence, any truſt in its accuracy would be much ſhaken by the contradictions in thoſe letters, on the queſtion whether the writs were ever actually executed. On the 18th of December, 1816, he writes, " After ſix or nine months we heard enough of cuſtom-houſe officers breaking houſes," &c., " by virtue of writs of aſſiſtance ; " and, on the 29th of March, 1817, " It was generally reported and underſtood that the Court clandeſtinely granted them, and the cuſtom-houſe officers had them in their pockets, though I never knew that they dared to produce them or execute them in any one inſtance." It is an unpleaſant duty to point out inaccuracies in ſo ſpirited an account of this memorable cauſe. But ſimilar doubts have been expreſſed by more competent and experienced judges. 10 John Adams's Works, 362, note. 4 Bancroft's Hiſt. U. S. 417, note. And in the examination of this matter the writer has from the beginning (*ante*, 409) but ſtrictly followed *Adams's* own directions in a letter to *Benjamin Waterhouſe* a year later: " You need not take my word. Look into Judge *Minot's* Hiſtory of Maſſachuſetts Bay, *anno* 1761 ; ſearch the records of the Superior Court of Judicature, Court of Aſſize and General Gaol Delivery, at Salem term, 1760, and Boſton term, 1761 ; look up the newſpapers of 1761 ; aſcertain the time when Chief Juſtice *Stephen Sewall* died ; call for Dr. *Mayhew's* printed ſermon on his death ; ſearch the date of Chief Juſtice *Thomas Hutchinſon*'s commiſſion as Chief Juſtice." 10 John Adams's Works, 280.

and of the execution of the writs.

Tudor's ſon diſpoſes of the contradiction in *Adams's* letters to his father by ſuppreſſing the firſt letter, and aſſerting that the ſtatement in the other " is unqueſtionably correct." Tudor's Life of Otis, 87, note. This concluſion is reached by aſſuming that though " *Minot's* hiſtory ſays, ' the writ of aſſiſtance was granted,' and refers to the court records for authority, yet this was probably a mere form to ſave the pride of the adminiſtration ; " and that " nothing was afterwards heard of this odious inſtrument." Indeed, *Tudor's* whole account of the Writs of Aſſiſtance is a mere digeſt of *Adams's* letters, without attempting to verify their ſtatements by the records or files of the Court, (of which his father was then a clerk,) or even examining the newſpapers of the time. Upon him falls, with ſpecial weight, Lord *Coke's* reproof: " It appeareth that the reporter never ſaw the ſaid record, only took it by the care of that which was ſpoken in court, (a dangerous kind of reporting, and

Tudor's account worthleſs.

 ſubject

1761. filed in the case, bears these indorsements, in the handwriting of *Hatch*, one of the clerks of the court: (3)

"Certificate of the Surveyr General for a Writ of Assistts for Mr Paxton.

"1761. 2d Decr wt issued.

"With Thomas Green & als petition & T. Lechmere's memorial." To which is subsequently added in *Winthrop's* hand: "and others papers are filed herein." (4)

Writ issued to Paxton. There is also a much worn form of a Writ of Assistance, of which the following is an exact copy, the words in brackets being interlined, and those in italics erased — the whole in the handwriting of *Hutchinson*, except the words "Annoque Dom 1761" at the end, which are apparently in the handwriting of *Hatch*, and "Cler." in the handwriting of *Winthrop*:

"Prov. of
"Mass Bay }

GEORGE the third by the grace of God of Great Britain France & Ireland King Defender of the faith &ca

"To

---

subject to many mistakings, for seldome or never the right case is put,) as in this case it fell out." 4 Inst. 17.

(3) *Samuel Winthrop* and *Nathaniel Hatch* had been re-appointed clerks in August, 1761. Rec. 1761, fol. 220.

(4) Under these, in the handwriting of *William C. Aylwin*, clerk of the Supreme Judicial Court from 1825 to 1827, are references to *Nevin's case*, (*ante*, 406,) and to the record book of 1761. *Tudor's* mistakes had been published in 1823. *Supra*, 417, note.

Record entries. Rec. 1761, Fol. 225, 226. In the index to the volume of the records of the Superior Court 1760–1762 are the following references: "Greene & al Petn 225," "Lechmere, Survr Genl his petition. 226." On referring to the places indicated, which are in August term 1761, the latter part of fol. 225 is found to be blank, with this entry on the margin: "Green & others Petition. No papers are on file." And the first page of fol. 226 is entirely blank. A temporary absence of these papers from the files may have been the cause of their escape from the fate which has befallen most of the court papers of that time. The dockets of 1761 and 1762 in Suffolk are missing, and the subsequent dockets and records contain no entries of applications for Writs of Assistance. But the entry of the case on the record under no other names than those of the merchants and the Surveyor General shows that no written application for the writ had been previously filed in the case.

1761.

SEAL.

"To ALL & ſingular our Juſtices of the peace "Sheriffs Conſtables and to all other our Officers "and Subjects within our ſaid Province and to "each of you Greeting.

"KNOW YE that whereas in and by an Act of Parliament "made in the *thir*[four]teenth year of [the reign of] the late "King Charles the ſecond *it is declared to be* [the Officers of "our Cuſtoms & their Deputies are authorized and impow-"ered to go & enter aboard any Ship or Veſſel outward or "inward bound for the purpoſes in the ſaid Act mentioned "and it is *alſo* in & by the ſaid Act further enacted & de-"clared that it ſhall be] lawful [to or] for any perſon or "perſons authorized by Writ of aſſiſtants under the ſeal of "our Court of Exchequer to take a Conſtable Headborough "or other publick Officer inhabiting near unto the place "and in the day time to enter & go into any Houſe Shop "Cellar Warehouſe or Room or other place and in caſe of "reſiſtance to break open doors cheſts trunks & other pack-"age there to ſeize and from thence to bring any kind of "goods or merchandize whatſoever prohibited & uncuſ-"tomed and to put and ſecure the ſame in *his Majeſtys* "[our] Storehouſe in the port next to the place where ſuch "ſeizure ſhall be made.

St. 13 & 14 Car. 2, c. 14, § 5.

"AND WHEREAS in & by an Act of Parliament made in "the ſeventh & eighth year of [the reign of the late] "King William the third there is granted to the Officers "for collecting and managing our revenue and inſpecting "the plantation trade in any of our plantations [the ſame "powers & authority for viſiting & ſearching of Ships & "alſo] to enter houſes or warehouſes to ſearch for and ſeize "any prohibited or uncuſtomed goods as are provided for "the Officers of our Cuſtoms in England by the ſaid laſt "mentioned Act made in the fourteenth year of [the reign "of] King Charles the Second, and the like aſſiſtance is "required to be given to the ſaid Officers in the execution "of their office as by the ſaid laſt mentioned Act is pro-"vided for the Officers in England.

St. 7 & 8 W. 3, c. 22, § 6.

"AND

1761.

Prov. St. 11 W. 3.

"AND WHEREAS in and by an Aƈt of our ſaid Province "of Maſſachuſetts bay made in the eleventh year of [the "reign of] the late King William the third it is enaƈted & "declared that our Superior Court of Judicature Court of "Aſſize and General Goal delivery for our ſaid Province "ſhall have cognizance of all matters and things within "our ſaid Province as fully & amply to all intents & pur-"poſes as our Courts of King's Bench Common Pleas & "Exchequer within our Kingdom of England have or "ought to have.

Paxton's appointment.

"AND WHEREAS our Commiſſioners for managing and "cauſing to be levied & colleƈted our cuſtoms ſubſidies and "other duties have [by Commiſſion or Deputation under "their hands & ſeal dated at London the 22[d] day of May "in the firſt year of our Reign] deputed and impowered "Charles Paxton Eſq[r] to be Surveyor & Searcher of all the "rates and duties ariſing and growing due to us at Boſton in "our Province aforeſaid and [in & by ſaid Comiſſion or "Deputation] have given him power to enter into [any Ship "Bottom Boat or other Veſſel & alſo into] any Shop Houſe "Warehouſe Hoſtery or other place whatſoever to make "diligent ſearch into any trunk cheſt pack caſe truſs or "any other parcell or package whatſoever for any goods "wares or merchandize prohibited to be imported or ex-"ported or whereof the Cuſtoms or other Duties have not "been duly paid and the ſame to ſeize to our uſe In all "things proceeding as the Law direƈts.

Precept to officer.

"THEREFORE we ſtriƈtly Injoin & Command you & every "one of you that, all excuſes apart, you & every one of "you permit the ſaid Charles Paxton according to the true "intent & form of the ſaid comiſſion or deputation and the "laws & ſtatutes in that behalf made & provided, [as well "by night as by day from time to time to enter & go on "board any Ship Boat or other Veſſel riding lying or being "within or coming to the ſaid port of Boſton or any Places "or Creeks thereunto appertaining ſuch Ship Boat or Veſ-"ſel then & there found to ſearch & overſee and the per-"ſons therein being ſtriƈtly to examine touching the prem-

iſes

1761.

" iſes aforeſaid & alſo *according to the form effect and true* " *intent of the ſd comiſſion or deputation*] in the day time to " enter & go into the vaults cellars warehouſes ſhops & other " places where any prohibited goods wares or merchandizes " or any goods wares or merchandizes for which the cuſ- " toms or other duties ſhall not have been duly & truly " ſatisfied and paid lye concealed or are ſuſpected to be " concealed, according to the true intent of the law to " inſpect & overſee & ſearch for the ſaid goods wares & " merchandize, And further to do and execute all things " which of right and according to the laws & ſtatutes in " this behalf ſhall be to be done. And we further ſtrictly " INJOIN & COMMAND you and every one of you that to " the ſaid Charles Paxton Eſqr you & every one of you " from time to time be aiding aſſiſting & helping in the " execution of the premiſes as is meet. And this you or " any of [you] in no wiſe omit at your perils. WITNESS " Thomas Hutchinſon Eſq at Boſton the day of De- " cember in the Second year of our Reign Annoque Dom " 1761.

Precept for aſſiſtance.

Teſte.

" By order of Court

" N. H. Cler." (5)

Second.

Charles Paxton.

(5) *Paxton* made all the ſeizures at this time. Bernard to Pitt, May 5, 1761, 1 Bernard Papers, 311. Bernard to Egremont, May 17, 1764, 3 Ib. 216. Boſton Gazettes, quoted *poſt*, G. *Gray, treaſurer*, v. *Paxton, poſt*, Appendix II. & notes.

He was appointed on the 8th of January, 1752, by the Commiſſioners of the Cuſtoms in England, Surveyor and Searcher of the Port of Boſton, and as ſuch obtained the firſt Writ of Aſſiſtance ever iſſued in the Province. Book of Commiſſions &c. 1628–1763, in the office of the Secretary of the Commonwealth, fol. 79. *Ante*, 402–404. His renewed commiſſion after the demiſe of the Crown, recited in the new writ now iſſued to him, (*ſupra*, 420,) is not recorded in either of the books there preſerved; but doubtleſs correſponded with his firſt commiſſion in 1752, which, like all the other commiſſions from that time to 1765, referred to below, was preciſely ſimilar to that iſſued in 1764 to *Hallowell, infra*, 432, note.

Paxton was alſo Marſhal of the Courts of Vice Admiralty of Maſſachuſetts, New Hampſhire, and Rhode Iſland, at leaſt as early as 1756. *Poſt*,

1761.

2. Certificate for Cockle at Salem.

Second. A certificate of the Surveyor General, dated December 4, 1761, and otherwise precisely similar to that for *Paxton*, (*supra*, 416,) for a Writ of Assistance to "James Cockle Esqr Collector of his Majesty's Customs at the Port of Salem."

Writ issued to Cockle.

This certificate is indorsed, apparently by *Hatch*, "*Writ issd 8th Decr*" [erased, and these words added by *Winthrop* :] "Wt issued 5th Feby 1762 : dld Cockle." (6)

On

Post, Appendix II. Commission as Marshal of July 20, 1761, Book of Commissions &c. 1628–1763, fol. 214. In 1755, he resigned the office of Crier of the Superior Court of Judicature. Rec. 1755, fol. 148.

The mob that destroyed the houses of *William Story*, the Registrar of the Admiralty, Comptroller *Hallowell*, and Chief Justice *Hutchinson*, on the night of August 26, 1765, went first to the house occupied by *Paxton*, which was saved by a present of a barrel of punch from the owner of the house. Bernard to Halifax, August 31, 1765, 4 Bernard Papers, 150. 1 Gordon's Hist. U. S. 176. In the library of the American Antiquarian Society is an old portrait of *Paxton*, with a patch in the canvas, said to have been put in to repair a breach made by a brickbat thrown by the mob.

In October 1766, *Paxton* went to England, for the purpose of assisting in remodelling the American revenue system; and, upon the establishment of the new Board of Customs in Boston, procured his own appointment as one of the Commissioners. 6 Bancroft's Hist. U. S. 32, 41, 50, 102. As such, on the 20th of June 1768, he wrote one of the letters to England, asking for a military force, which were afterwards denounced by the House of Representatives. Representations in Letters of Hutchinson, Oliver, &c. (Boston, 1773) 37, 67. See also 2 John Adams's Works, 220, 318; 10 Ib. 298; Sabine's American Loyalists, 510.

James Cockle.

(6) In the Boston Gazette of May 10, 1762, under the custom house advertisements, is a notice, of which the first paragraph is a sufficient specimen, viz:

"Port of *C—k—le Borough.*

"Now riding at Anchor and ready for Sailing, the Idiot of full "Freight, with Ignorance, no Commission, few Guns; any necessitous "Person that wants daily Sustenance may meet with suitable Encour- "agement by applying to *J—s C—k-le* the Commander, at the King's "Arms in *S*———."

Cockle's predecessors, *Richard Lechmere*, and *William Walter* (who is mentioned as *Cockle's* deputy in the notice just cited), had been furnished

On a separate flip of paper is this memorandum, by which probably to draft the writ to *Cockle:* 1761.

" By Commiffion or deputation dated at London the fixth " day of May 1760 — appointed James Cockle Efq Col- " lector of all Rates &c at the port of Salem Marble- " head, &ca." (7)

Third.

---

nifhed with Writs of Affiftance in the previous reign. *Ante*, 405, 406. *Nevin*, who had alfo obtained a Writ of Affiftance then as Collector of " Newbury &c.," publifhes notices in the Bofton Gazette in January 1764 as " Collector of the port of Pifcataqua."

(7) His commiffion of this date from the Commiffioners of Cuftoms in England is recorded in the Book of Commiffions &c. 1628–1763, fol. 171. A renewal of it, dated London, July 24, 1762, is recorded in a book of Records of the Salem Cuftom Houfe, May 1761 — April 1775, in the poffeffion of the Effex Inftitute, which is particularly defcribed by *David Roberts*, Efq., in the fecond volume of their Hiftorical Collections, 169 *& feq.* But to guard against mifapprehenfion of that defcription, it fhould be added that that record contains no evidence of *Cockle's* application for a Writ of Affiftance in 1760 or 1761, (*ante*, 409,) nor of any reftoration of *Cockle* after his removal by the Surveyor General in 1764. Cockle's appointment.

In February 1764 the Commiffioners of Cuftoms in London publifhed in the Bofton Gazette offers of reward for the difcovery to *Temple*, the Surveyor General, or any other principal officer of the cuftoms in North America, of any perfon guilty of entering into or conniving at any compofition for duties. On the 28th of September, 1764, *Temple* vifited Salem; and removed *Cockle* from office, for compounding for duties, and concealing from him information received from Anguilla, " and above all for the Infult offered me by you in the Tender of a Bribe to pafs over fuch your proceedings without punifhment;" and appointed *William Brown* in his ftead. Salem Cuftom Houfe Record, 43, 44. Compare 3 Hutchinfon's Hift. Mafs. 162. Governor *Bernard*, who was accuftomed to confult with *Cockle*, was indignant at this, and pretended that the Surveyor General was poffeffed with " a moft extreme and haughty jealoufy " of the Governor and his office, and that the real caufe of *Cockle's* removal was his having advifed with him on one occafion; and earneftly defended *Cockle* — *Paxton* alfo " teftifying his good opinion of his integrity in his office." Bernard to Jackfon, October 5, and to Jackfon and other perfons in England, November 30, 1764, 3 Bernard Papers, 256, 265–270. But the Governor was obliged to admit that " in truth, if conniving at foreign fugar & molaffes, & Portugal wines & Fruit, is to be reckoned Corruption, there was never, I believe, His removal.

1761.

3. Certificate for Waldo at Falmouth.

Third. A ſimilar certificate of the Surveyor General, dated December 17, 1761, for a Writ of Aſſiſtance to "Francis Waldo Eſquire Coll^{r}. & Surveyor of his Majeſtys Cuſtoms at Falmouth."

Indorſed in *Hatch's* handwriting: "M^{r}. Waldoe's Commiſſ^{n}. dated 18 March 1761." (8)

1762.

4. Certificate for Sheafe, Collector at Boſton.

Fourth. A certificate of the Surveyor General, dated January 4, 1762, of his having "this day appointed William Sheafe

---

I believe, an uncorrupt Cuſtom houſe Officer in America, till within twelve months; and therefore Incorruption in the beſt of them muſt be conſidered, not as a poſitive, but comparative term;" and to doubt whether his own certificate of *Cockle's* good conduct "is not too free to be laid before a public Board, altho' it might ſafely and properly be communicated to every member of it." Ib. 267.

Governor Bernard's corruption.

The Surveyor General charged the Governor with ſharing *Cockle*'s illegal gains; and an affidavit of *Sampſon Toovey*, *Cockle's* clerk, made the day before his removal, ſupports this charge. Bernard to Temple, September 29, 1764, Ib. 43. Boſton Gazettes of June 12 & October 9, 1769; 5 Bancroft's Hiſt. U. S. 158, note. *Hutchinſon* in May 1765 wrote, with his uſual caution: "Mr. *Temple* it is evident has a very great perſonal prejudice againſt the Governor, which it is ſaid aroſe from an apprehenſion that he had not all that reſpect ſhown him which he ſuppoſed to be due." "Whether he [the Governor] ever took any improper ſteps will be determined in England. I do not know that he has done more than all his predeceſſors uſed to do." 26 Maſs. Archives, 138. And a writer in the Boſton Gazette of November 3, 1766, ſpeaks of the Governor of New York as "A G. that has not turned cuſtom-houſe officer, and *cockled* the ſimple merchant out of his intereſt to the prejudice of the King's revenue, at the ſame time repreſenting to the miniſtry his deſire to cruſh a trade upon which he placed his great dependence to inrich himſelf." Notwithſtanding Governor *Bernard's* efforts in his behalf, *Cockle* was never reſtored. 3 Hutchinſon's Hiſt. Maſs. 163. The Surveyor General afterwards appointed *Toovey* a waiter and preventive officer at Cape Ann. Salem Cuſtom Houſe Record, 53.

Waldo's commiſſion.

(8) His commiſſion of this date from the Commiſſioners of Cuſtoms in England is recorded in Book of Commiſſions &c. 1628–1763, fol. 216. A Writ of Aſſiſtance was iſſued to him. See account, *infra*, of a riot in Falmouth upon an attempt to ſeize goods under it in Auguſt 1766. He had received a ſimilar commiſſion, dated October 25, 1757, and a Writ of Aſſiſtance, in the preceding reign. Ib. 163. *Ante*, 405.

Sheafe Eſq.[r] Collector of his Majeſtys Cuſtoms at the port of Boſton," and requeſting a Writ of Aſſiſtance for him. (9) 1762.

Fifth.

---

(9) *Sheafe's* appointment of this date is announced in the Boſton Gazette of the ſame day, and recorded in Book of Commiſſions &c. 1628–1763, fol. 219. He was ſubſequently made deputy of *Roger Hale* and *Joſeph Harriſon*, his own ſucceſſors in the office of Collector. Book of Commiſſions 1764–1774, fol. 43, 68, 69. *Infra*, 428. It does not appear whether a Writ of Aſſiſtance was iſſued to him in this reign; but in 1766 he aſſiſted *Hallowell*, the Comptroller, who had ſuch a writ, in attempting to ſearch a cellar. *Infra*, note 22. Sheafe's appointment.

In the preceding reign *Sheafe* had been repeatedly appointed by *Henry Frankland*, then Collector, his deputy in his abſence. Book of Commiſſions &c. 1628–1763, fol. 110, 163. At laſt *Frankland* was ſuſpended by the Surveyor General "for being abſent from his duty," and *Sheafe* appointed in his ſtead on the 10th of March, 1759, and as ſuch ſupplied with a Writ of Aſſiſtance. Book of Commiſſions 1756–1767, fol. 80. *Ante*, 406. Frankland Collector.

He was ſucceeded by *Benjamin Barons*, who was appointed by the Commiſſioners of Cuſtoms in England on the 11th of May, 1759, and who took the oath of office on the 25th of September, 1759. Book of Commiſſions &c. 1628–1763, fol. 170, 171. *Barons* was ſuſpended by *Lechmere*, the Surveyor General, who appointed *George Cradock* temporary Collector in December 1759, and finally, upon charges filed by *Paxton*, removed *Barons* and appointed *Cradock* on the 24th of June, 1761. Governor *Pownall's* certificate of December 20, 1759, on file in *Erving* v. *Cradock*, *poſt*, Appendix II. Boſton News Letter, December 20, 1759. *Bernard's* Letters of February 21 & June 28, 1761, 1 Bernard Papers, 297, 320. Book of Commiſſions 1756–1767, fol. 203. *Barons* immediately commenced actions againſt *Lechmere* for ſuſpending him, againſt *Cradock* as an abetter of his ſuſpenſion, and againſt *Paxton* for having made to the Surveyor General the complaint upon which he was removed; but brought none of theſe actions to trial. Bernard to Lord Barrington, February 20, 1762, 2 Bernard Papers, 27. Bernard to Lords of Trade, Auguſt 6, 1762, Ib. 45. Barons Collector.

Paxton's articles of complaint againſt *Barons* alleged *inter alia* that "he procured a Meeting of Merchants, in which he was conſidered as principal, to act againſt the Court of Admiralty," who accordingly "preſented a petition to the Aſſembly," (*poſt*, Appendix II.) and that "he hath declared that the Superior Court's granting Writs of Aſſiſtance is againſt Law, and he hath encouraged a Repreſentation from the [ſame] Meeting of Merchants to the Superior Court againſt granting ſuch Writs." *James Otis*, under the name of *Hampden*, in Boſton Gazette of September 18, 1769. Paxton's charges againſt him.

Governor *Bernard* charged *Barons* and *Otis* with being the chief inſti-

 gators

1762.

5. Certificate for Hatch, Comptroller at Boston.

Fifth. A precisely similar certificate of the same date, for a Writ of Assistance to "Nathaniel Hatch, Esqr Comptroller of his Majestys Customs at the Port of Boston." (10)

And

---

gators of the controversy of the merchants with the custom house officers, and especially of the actions of *the Province* v. *Paxton*, and *Erving* v. *Cradock*, *post*, Appendix II. On the 19th of January, 1761, he wrote to Secretary Pownall: "Mr *Barrons* has plaid the Devil in this Town. He has put himself at the head of a combination of Merchants all raised by him with the Assistance of two or three others to demolish the Court of Admiralty & the other Custom House officers, especially one who has been active in making seizures." 1 Bernard Papers, 296. And on the 6th of July, 1761, he wrote: "The Assembly keeps in very good temper; all necessary business is properly done, notwithstanding an opposition is kept up (seldom raising the minority to one third) by Mr *Otis* Junr who has been Mr *Barrons* faithfull Councellour from the first beginning of these Commotions to the hour of this present writing." Ib. 323. To the like effect are his letters of July 12 & August 28, 1761, & January 12, 1762, 2 Ib. 7, 9, 25; December 22, 1766, & January 24, 1767, 4 Ib. 275, 299.

Bernard's opinion of Barons.

Cradock Collector.

Cradock was furnished with a Writ of Assistance in the preceding reign, (*ante*, 406,) but was succeeded by *Sheafe* on the 4th of January, 1762, as above stated, before any new writs were issued, except to *Paxton* and *Cockle*. Before and after this time he was Deputy Judge in Admiralty here. Decrees on file in *Gray, treasurer*, v. *Paxton*, *post*, Appendix, II. Washburn's Jud. Hist. Mass. 184.

Comptroller Hatch.

(10) This appointment is announced in the Boston Gazette of the same day, and recorded in Book of Commissions &c. 1628–1763, fol. 220. *Hatch* acted as Comptroller for a year at least. Boston Gazettes of January, 1764. He was also clerk of the Superior Court, and on the 10th of January, 1771, while continuing to hold that office, was made a Justice of the Inferior Court of Common Pleas. *Supra*, 418, note 3. Book of Commissions 1767–1775, fol. 181. Mein & Fleeming's Registers for 1772–75. 2 John Adams's Works, 194, 196, 251. Sabine's Amer. Loyalists, 351.

Plurality of offices —

The custom of combining incongruous offices in the same person was a prevailing abuse in the Province, and therefore very carefully guarded against in the State Constitution adopted in 1780. Declaration of Rights, art. 30. Constitution of Massachusetts, c. 6, § 2.

Hutchinson.

Hutchinson was Chief Justice, Lieutenant Governor, a Councillor, and Judge of Probate for the County of Suffolk. 2 Minot's Hist. Mass. 79 note. 2 John Adams's Works, 124 note, 151. "Instances may be found, where a man of abilities shall monopolize a power proportionate to all those of lord chief baron of the exchequer, lord chief justice of both branches, lord high treasurer, and lord high chancellor of

Great

And a Writ of Aſſiſtance, in *Winthrop's* hand, and under the ſeal of the court, to *Nathaniel Hatch*, (11) in the corrected form above printed (*ſupra*, 418,) except in reciting the appointment of *Hatch* on the 4th of January 1762 by "John Temple, Eſq[r], Surveyor General of our Cuſtoms for the Northern Diſtrict of America, to be Comptroller of all the rates and duties ariſing and growing due to us at Boſton in our province aforeſaid," and with this teſte: 1762. Writ made out to Hatch.

"WITNESS Thomas Hutchinſon Eſq: at Boſton the "third day of June, in the ſecond year of our Reign, An-"noq Domini 1762. (12)

"By order of Court.

"SAML WINTHROP Cler." (13)

Sixth.

Great Britain, united in one ſingle perſon." *James Otis*, in Boſton Gazette of January 11, 1762.

Chambers Ruſſell, (alſo "one of the original conſpirators againſt the public liberty" — 2 John Adams's Works, 333,) while Judge both of the Court of Admiralty and of the Superior Court of Judicature, was firſt a Councilior, and then a member of the Houſe of Repreſentatives. Bernard to Lord Barrington, October 15, 1766, 5 Bernard Papers, 164. The Judges were often members of either houſe. 3 Hutchinſon's Hiſt. Maſs. 148, 150. 2 John Adams's Works, 151, 195. 4 Ib. 72. Ruſſell.

It was very common for the ſame perſon to hold offices in the cuſtoms and in the courts of juſtice. *Paxton* was Surveyor of the Port of Boſton, Crier of the Superior Court of Judicature, and Marſhal of the Court of Admiralty. *Supra*, 421, note 5. *George Cradock* was Collector of the Cuſtoms, and Deputy Judge in Admiralty. *Supra*, 426, note 9, *ad fin.* *Edward Winſlow* was Collector of the Cuſtoms and Clerk of the Courts in Plymouth. *Infra*, note 25. Paxton. Cradock. Winſlow.

(11) The reaſon why this Writ of Aſſiſtance was never iſſued may have been either that *Hatch* neglected to pay the clerk's fee, or that he was ſuperſeded before he had occaſion to uſe the writ. *Vid. ante*, 406, note 9; *infra*, 432. However that may have been, we are indebted to his neglect for the preſervation of the only original Writ of Aſſiſtance, iſſued in the Province, that has come down to us.

(12) The years of each king's reign were computed from the day of his acceſſion. 2 Foſs's Judges of England, 1. *Ante*, 411, 420, 421.

(13) The General Court, on the 6th of March, 1762, paſſed a bill authorizing any Judge or Juſtice of the Peace, upon information on oath by any officer of the cuſtoms, to iſſue a ſpecial writ or warrant of aſſiſtance; and prohibiting all others. But the Governor, after adviſing with the Judges of the Superior Court, refuſed to ſign it. *Vid. poſt*, G. Action of the General Court.

The

1762.

6. Certificate for Hale, Collector at Boston.

Sixth. A requeſt of the Surveyor General, dated July 25, 1762, for a Writ of Aſſiſtance to "Roger Hale, Eſq[r] Collector of his Majeſtys Cuſtoms for the Port of Boſton. (14)

1763.

7. Certificate for Dowſe at Salem.

Seventh. A ſimilar requeſt, dated December 10, 1762, for a Writ of Aſſiſtance to "Joſeph Dowſe, Eſq[r]. Surveyor and Searcher of his Majeſtys Cuſtoms at Salem and Marblehead." (15)

8. Writ iſſued to Surveyor General.

Eighth. The form of writ printed above (*ſupra*, 418,) bears theſe indorſements in the handwriting of *Hatch:*

"Writ iſſ[d] to the Survey[r]. General 27th. May, 1763" (16)
"1st. Dec. 1760." (17)

Ninth.

Reduction of ſalaries of Judges.

The General Court, at the ſame ſeſſion, "not only reduced the allowance to this Court in general, but refuſed to make any allowance at all to me as chief juſtice." Hutchinſon to Bollan, March 6, 1762, 26 Maſs. Archives, 8. *Vid. infra*, 435, *per Marſhall, C. J.*

Hale's appointment.

(14) *Hale's* commiſſion from the Commiſſioners of Cuſtoms in England bears date of February 8, 1762. Book of Commiſſions &c. 1628–1763, fol. 227. For the form of his inſtructions, *vid. infra*, 433, note.

Dowſe's appointment.

(15) *Dowſe* was commiſſioned by the Surveyor General on the 31ſt of March, 1760, and by the Commiſſioners of Cuſtoms in England on the 5th of June, 1760, and again on the 22d of May, 1761. Book of Commiſſions &c. 1628–1763, fol. 172, 174, 217. But it would ſeem that he never obtained a Writ of Aſſiſtance; for the Commiſſioners of Cuſtoms appointed in 1767, in a letter dated "Caſtle William, Boſton Harbor, 17th Oct[r] 1768," directing him to ſearch certain ſtores at Squam River, ſay: "If Mr *Dowſe* is not furniſh'd with a Writ of Aſſiſtants it will be neceſſary that the Comptroller ſhould attend him in this Service." Salem Cuſtom Houſe Record, 253. *Maſcarene* was then Comptroller at Salem, and had a Writ of Aſſiſtance. *Infra*, note 24.

(16) No certificate or application in writing ſeems to have been made. Probably none was required of the Surveyor General.

Temple's appointment.

(17) Probably the date of *John Temple's* appointment by the Commiſſioners of Cuſtoms in England in place of *Thomas Lechmere.* He was certainly appointed before February 12, 1761. Inſtructions of that date from Commiſſioners of Cuſtoms to Governor of Connecticut, but not received by Governor *Fitch* (as appears by his indorſement) until November 12, 1761. 2 Trumbull Papers, 6, in Maſs. Hiſt. Soc. Lib. It would ſeem that *Temple*, who was born in Boſton, (R. C. Winthrop's Addreſſes, 112,) brought theſe credentials with him on his return. In

June

1763.

Ninth. A certificate from the Surveyor General, dated November 5, 1763, of "the Commiffioners of the Cuftoms having appointed Thomas Bifhop Efq$^{r.}$ to be an officer of his Majeftys Cuftoms for feizing prohibited & uncuftomed goods," and requefting a Writ of Affiftance for him.

9. Certificate for Captain Bifhop.

On which the Chief Juftice iffued the following order:

Order for Writ to Captain Bifhop.

"Bofton 4 Nov. 1763.

"Gent$^{n.}$

"Thomas Bifhop Efqr, Comander of His Majef-"ty's Ship Fortune having applied to me for a writ of affift-"ance as an Officer of His Majefty's cuftoms you are to "caufe fuch writ to be iffued a certificate being firft pro-"duced from the Surveyor general & lodged in the office "fignifying that the faid Thomas Bifhop Efqr is fuch an "Officer

"T HUTCHINSON"

"To Samuel Winthrop Efq
"or Nathanael Hatch Efq
"Clerks of the fuperior court."

At the foot of this are added thefe minutes in *Winthrop's* handwriting:

Writ iffued to Bifhop.

"twenty third day of June 1763." (18)
"W^{t} iffued Nov. 1763, was dld Cap. Bifhop."

Tenth.

June *Lechmere* was ftill acting as Surveyor General, and recognized by the Governor as entitled to do fo "till Mr. *Temple* arrives to take upon him the office." *Supra*, 425, note. Bernard to Lechmere, June 2, 1761, 2 Bernard Papers, 113. The firft notice of this arrival of *Temple* in the Province is the following in the Bofton Gazette of November 23, 1761.

"Laft Night came to Town, from New York, the Hon. *John Temple*, Efq; Lieut. Governor of the Province of New-Hampshire, and "Surveyor General of his Majefty's Cuftoms for the Northern Diftrict "of America."

In the fame paper is the report of the decifion in favor of the Writs of Affiftance, the enforcement of which was among *Temple's* earlieft official acts. *Vid. fupra*, 416, 422; *infra*, 437; *poft*, G.

(18) The date of the appointment by the Commiffioners of the Cuftoms

Bifhop's appointment.

1765.

10. Certificate for Folger at Nantucket.

Tenth. A certificate of the Surveyor General, dated February 25, 1765, ſtating the appointment of "Mr Timothy Folger to be a ſearcher and preventive officer in the Cuſtoms

---

toms in England of Captain Biſhop to be an officer of the cuſtoms. Book of Commiſſions &c. 1628–1763, fol. 247.

Commanders of ſhips made officers of the cuſtoms.

In this year the commanders of all ships ſtationed on the American coaſt were authorized and directed to act as officers of the cuſtoms. St. 6 G. 3, c. 22. Order in Council of July 8, 1763, Book of Commiſſions &c. 1628–1763, fol. 255. Lord Egremont's Inſtructions to Governor Bernard, July 9, 1763, 10 Bernard Papers, 120. Governor's Proclamation of November 16, 1763, in Boſton Gazette. Surveyor General's Inſtructions to Cuſtom Houſe Officers, December 26, 1763, Salem Cuſtom Houſe Record, 6. 5 Bancroft's Hiſt. U. S. 92, 161.

Hutchinſon's remarks.

This meaſure was a ſurpriſe to the Province. On the 17th of September, 1763, *Hutchinſon* wrote to *Richard Jackſon*, *Grenville's* Secretary: "The firſt intelligence was from the Act itſelf and the proclamation and inſtructions conſequent, which came to my hands two days ſince in the Governor's abſence from Lord Egremont. I fancy many of the Weſt India traders will be ſurpriſed. Such indulgence has been ſhown of late to that branch of illicit trade that nobody has conſidered it as ſuch; veſſels arriving and making their entries for ſome ſmall acknowledgments as openly as from our own Iſlands without paying the duties." "The real cauſe of the illicit trade in this province has been the indulgence of the officers of the cuſtoms, and we are told that the cauſe of their indulgence has been that they are quartered upon for more than their legal fees, and that without bribery and corruption they muſt ſtarve. If the venality of the preſent age will not admit of reform in this reſpect, perhaps the proviſion now made may be the next beſt expedient." 26 Maſs. Archives, 69.

Bernard's anſwer to the inſtructions.

On the 25th of October the Governor wrote to Lord *Egremont* in anſwer to the inſtructions, ſaying: "Ever ſince I have been in this Government, I have exerted the beſt of my powers to maintain a due obedience to the abovementioned Laws; and I can with pleaſure add, that I believe they are nowhere better ſupported than they are in this Province. When firſt I came to this Government, about three years ago, ſome of the Merchants of this Town, provoked with liberties allowed at Ports allmoſt under their eye, & really injured by them, did endeavour to enforce the allowance of the ſame liberties within this Port, by divers ~~irregular~~ ~~violent~~ means. But my Reſolution & the Steadineſs of the Judges of the Superior Court defeated this Scheme; & they became content to wait till meaſures ſhould be taken for putting all the Ports in America upon the ſame footing. Before this Commotion & ſince, the Merchants here in general have acted in ſuch a manner as to intitle themſelves to all proper favour.

toms to refide at Nantucket," and requefting a Writ of Affiftance for him. 1765.

Folger's

---

favour. I do not pretend that this Province is intirely free from the breach of thefe Laws, but only that fuch breach, if difcovered, is furely punifhed. There has been an Indulgence time out of mind allowed in a trifling but neceffary article, I mean the permitting Lifbon Lemons & wine in fmall quantities to pafs as Ships Stores. I have allways underftood that this was well known in England, and allowed, as being no object of trade, or, if it was, no way injurious to that of Great Britain." He then goes on to fpeak of Lemons as "in this Climate not only neceffary to the comfort of Life, but to health alfo;" fays: "The wine generally ufed in this Country heretofore has been Madeira, but of late that has grown fo extravagantly dear, that few People can afford it. The Wines of the Weftern Ifles are now in the general ufe of this Country. But fome Gentlemen prefer Portugal Wines. French Wines can never be an article of Trade here, as what comes to America is in general bad and very perishable; & when it is good, it comes as dear as Madeira, & is not near fo much efteemed;" and clofes by "befpeaking your Lordfhip's favor that this intimation may not be underftood to contain an admiffion that I myfelf have been knowingly concerned in or confenting to the aforefaid indulgence." 3 Bernard Papers, 99; Bernard's Select Letters, 1. The Governor's innocent ignorance of an indulgence which he "always underftood was well known in England, and allowed," was not univerfally believed. See 5 Bancroft's Hift. U. S. 158, & note; 4 Franklin's Works, 469; *fupra*, 424, note 7.

Wines in the Province.

On the 26th of November, 1763, the Governor wrote to *Jackfon* as follows, erafing the words in italics: "The Merchants here are greatly alarmed at the prefent proceedings to guard this coaft & efpecially the appointing the Captains of the Men of War to be Cuftomhoufe Officers. They are ftrange People; they are either for *taking the Government by ftorm &* enforcing fuch a remiffion of the laws of trade as they think fit; or elfe in a fit of Defpondency they give up themfelves & their trade to ruin. They never think of a middle way; to remonftrate, with decency, upon the real hardships they lay under, & to crave redrefs, which I cannot think would be hard to obtain." 3 Bernard Papers, 106.

Bernard's ftatement.

Compare *Burke's* account of the abufes and evils of this fyftem of employing officers of the navy as cuftom houfe officers. 8 Annual Regifter, 18–21. "If thefe gentlemen did not underftand all thofe cafes in which ships were liable to penalty, they as little underftood thofe in which ships were exempt even from detention; and, of courfe, hurt the interefts of trade in the fame proportion that they difappointed the expectations

Burke's account.

1765.

Order for Writ to Folger.

Folger's certificate is indorſed by the Chief Juſtice "The writ is allow'd to iſſue." (19)

11. Certificate for Hallowell, Comptroller at Boſton.

Eleventh. The following requeſt of the Surveyor General:

"Boſton, 14 March 1765.

"Sir,

"I Believe it is Neceſſary for the Service of the Rev-"enue that Mr Hallowell the Comptroller of the Cuſtoms "for the Port of Boſton ſhould have a Writ of Aſſiſtance. "If you think proper to grant him one you will much "oblige me. I am with Great Reſpect,

"Sir, Your moſt obedient
"and moſt humble Servant
"J. TEMPLE.

"To the Hon[l]. M[r] Hutchinſon."

On

---

pectations of the treaſury; ſo that, through the natural violence of their diſpoſition, and their unacquaintance with the revenue buſiness, the trade ſtill carried on between British ſubjects was very much injured." Ib. 18.

Biſhop's ſervices.

When Captain *Biſhop* was about to return to England, Governor *Bernard*, in a letter of July 5, 1766, to the Secretary of the Admiralty, commended him for his vigilance and aſſiſtance, and wrote that "upon his firſt arrival here he engaged in the particular buſineſs for which he was ſent here, with great diligence and alertneſs;" and by two ſeizures "ſo diſcouraged the practice of illicit trade, that I believe we are indebted to him for having leſs of it in this port than in other places." 4 Bernard Papers, 243. See *The Brig Freemaſon*, *ante*, 387; Bernard to Halifax, December 24, 1763, printed from 3 Bernard Papers, 111, *ante*, 392–394. On the arrival of the ſtamps Captain *Biſhop* had charge of their removal to the Caſtle; and he took them back to England when he returned. Bernard to Biſhop, and to Halifax, Auguſt 22, 1765, 4 Ib. 61, 145. Bernard to Biſhop, July 17, 1766, 5 Ib. 186. Bernard to Grey Cooper, July 18, 1766, Ib. 138.

Folger's appointment.

(19) It was iſſued on the 2d of February 1765, more than three weeks before the date of the certificate. *Infra*, 434. *Folger* was appointed by *Temple* on the 17th of Auguſt, 1764. Book of Commiſſions 1764–1774, fol. 39. Among *John Adams's* MS. notes of his caſes in court are memoranda of "*Folger* vs. *Hallowell*" and "*Butler* vs. *Brig Union*," by which it appears that the queſtion of the right of a preventive

On which this order is indorſed by the Chief Juſtice : 1765.

Order for Writ to Hallowell.

"Agreeable to the within Requeſt you are to cauſe a "Writ of Aſſiſtance to iſſue. (20)

"T HUTCHINSON.

"Mr. Winthrop or
"Mr. Hatch."

On

---

tive officer, deputed by the Surveyor General, or by the Board of Cuſtoms here, to make a ſeizure, was argued in the Court of Vice Admiralty by *Adams* in favor of the right, and by *Otis* and *Sewall* againſt it; but the deciſion is not ſtated. See *the Ship Columbus*, (High Court of Admiralty, 1789,) 1 Collect. Jurid. 105.

Hallowell's commiſſion.

(20) A writ was accordingly iſſued on the 22d of March 1765. *Infra*, 434. In the Library of the American Antiquarian Society is the original commiſſion from the Commiſſioners of the Cuſtoms in England to "Mr. Benjamin Hallowell the younger to be Comptroller of all the Rates Duties and Impoſitons ariſing and growing due to His Majeſty at Boſton in New England in America by Vertue of" the act of 25 Car. 2, c. 7, "WHEREBY he hath power to enter into any Ship, Bottom, Boat, or other Veſſel; As alſo into any Shop, Houſe, Warehouſe, Hoſtery or other place whatſoever to make Diligent Search into any Trunk, Cheſt, Pack, Caſe, Truſs or any other Parcel or Package whatſoever for any Goods Wares or Merchandize prohibited to be Imported or Exported, or whereof the Cuſtomes or other Duties have not been duly paid; And the ſame to Seize to His Majeſties Uſe; And alſo to put in Execution all other the lawful powers and Authorities for the better managing or Collecting the ſaid Duties, In all things proceeding as the Law Directs, HEREBY praying and requiring all and every His Majeſties Officers & Miniſters, and all others whom it may Concern, to be Aiding and Aſſiſting to Him in all things as becometh." This commiſſion, printed on parchment from an engraved plate, is dated March 9, 1764; bears a certificate of Governor *Bernard*, dated July 18, 1764, that *Hallowell* had taken the oaths of office; and is recorded in Book of Commiſſions 1764–1774, fol. 35. *Hallowell's* appointment was rumored two months earlier. Boſton Gazette of May 7, 1764.

Hallowell's inſtructions.

In the ſame library are the original printed inſtructions from the English Commiſſioners of Cuſtoms to *Hallowell* as Comptroller, dated July 13th 1764, conſiſting almoſt wholly of a copy of the printed inſtructions of the ſame date, to *Roger Hale*, Collector of Cuſtoms at Boſton, (in a form which muſt have been then recently eſtabliſhed, inaſmuch as it mentions the St. of 4 G. 3, c. 15,) which contains no mention of Writs of Aſſiſtance, otherwiſe than by directing the Collector to execute the

powers

1765. Writs iſſued to

On the back of the precedent above printed, (*ſupra*, 418,) under the memoranda of the iſſuing of a writ to the Surveyor General, (*ſupra*, 428,) are the following, in *Winthrop's* handwriting :

10. Folger. " to Tim° Folger Feby 2nd 1765 (21)
11. Hallowell. " to B. Hallowell Eſq : 22 Mar, 1765 (22)
12. Fiſher. " to Jn° Fiſher 1 April 1768 (23)
13. Maſcarene. " to Jn° Maſcarene 1 April 1768 (24)
14. Winſlow. " to Edwd Winſlow 8 Feby 1769 (25)
15. Capt Reid. " to Captn Wm Reid of ye Sloop Liberty 10th Feby 1769." (26)

---

powers and authorities given him by the act of 7 & 8 W. 3, c. 22, § 6, and other Acts of Parliament " for entering any Houſes or Warehouſes to ſearch for and ſeize any ſuch Goods, under the Regulations preſcribed by Law ;" and informing him that " the like Aſſiſtance is to be given to you, and the other Officers in the Execution of your and their Duties as by the 14th of Cha. II. is provided for Officers in Great Britain."

In a collection of folio pamphlets in the Boſton Athenæum, labelled " Tracts, A. 23," are copies of ſuch inſtructions ; and alſo of ſimilar inſtructions iſſued from the London Cuſtom Houſe to Collectors in America in 1707, which do not ſubſtantially vary in this reſpect, except in omitting the words " under the Regulations preſcribed by law."

Hallowell. *Hallowell* was one of the moſt active and unpopular of the officers of the cuſtoms. His houſe was ſacked on the 26th of Auguſt 1765, with thoſe of Chief Juſtice *Hutchinſon*, and *William Story*, the regiſtrar of the Vice Admiralty Court. *Ante*, 168. In 1766 he and *Sheafe*, the deputy collector, were ſucceſsfully oppoſed by *Malcolm* in the execution of a Writ of Aſſiſtance. *Infra*, 446. In June 1768 he was forward and violent in ſeizing *John Hancock's* Sloop *Liberty*, and was ſent to England to miſrepreſent the behavior of the people upon that occaſion. Franklin's True State of the Proceedings in Maſſachuſetts, 4 Franklin's Works, 481. 6 Bancroft's Hiſt. U. S. 156, 161, 164. He was afterwards " appointed one of the Commiſſioners of the Board of Cuſtoms in America, in the Room of the Hon. *John Temple*, Eſq." Boſton Evening Poſt, December 31, 1770.

(21) *Vid.* certificate and order, *ſupra*, 430–432, & note 19.

(22) *Vid. ſupra*, 432, 433, & note 20. Writs of Aſſiſtance had now been iſſued to officers of all the principal and ſome of the ſmaller ports of the Province, and there ſeems to have been no difficulty in executing them until after the paſſage of the Stamp Act.

Chief Juſtice *Marſhall*, ſpeaking of the condition of the American Colonies

1763.

Colonies in 1763, ſays: "At no period of time was the attachment of the coloniſts to the mother country more ſtrong, or more general, than at preſent." To which he adds this note: "After the expulſion of the French from Canada, a conſiderable degree of ill humour was manifeſted in Maſſachuſetts with reſpect to the manner in which the laws of trade were executed. A queſtion was agitated in the court in which the Colony took a very deep intereſt. A cuſtom-houſe officer applied for what was termed 'a writ of aſſiſtance,' which was an authority to ſearch any houſe whatever for dutiable articles ſuſpected to be concealed in it. The right to grant ſpecial warrants was never conteſted, but this grant of a general warrant was deemed contrary to the principles of liberty, and was thought an engine of oppreſſion equally uſeleſs and vexatious, which would enable every petty officer of the cuſtoms to gratify his reſentments by haraſſing the moſt reſpectable men in the province. The ill temper excited on this occaſion was ſhewn by a reduction of the ſalaries of the judges, but no diminution of attachment to the mother country appears to have been produced by it." Marſhall's American Colonies, 377. Such is the ſummary of the greateſt authority on American conſtitutional law, in a work of which a moſt competent critic has ſaid: "Every part of it is marked with the ſcrupulous veracity of a judicial expoſition." Binney's Eulogy on Marſhall, 59. And ſee Otis's Rights of the Britiſh Colonies, 48, 60; 3 Hutchinſon's Hiſt. Maſs. 102, 103.

Chief Juſtice Marſhall's account of the Writs of Aſſiſtance.

Hutchinſon, at this time, took the part of the Colony. "The Molaſſes Act as it now ſtands was undoubtedly intended to have the force of a prohibition. To reduce the duty to a penny per gallon I find would be generally agreeable to the people here, & the merchants would readily pay it; but do they ſee the conſequence? Will not they be introductory to taxes, duties & exciſes upon other articles, & would this conſiſt with the ſo much eſteemed privilege of Engliſh ſubjects — the being taxed by their own repreſentatives?" Hutchinſon to Jackſon, Auguſt 3, 1763, 26 Maſſ. Archives, 65, 66. So in July, 1764 (eraſing the words in Italics, and inſerting thoſe in brackets): "The coloniſts like all the reſt of *his Majeſty's ſubjects* [the human race] are of different ſpirits and diſpoſitions, ſome more calm & moderate, others more violent & extravagant; and if now & then ſome rude & indecent things are thrown out in print, in one place & another, I hope ſuch things will not be conſidered as coming from the Coloniſts in general, but from particular perſons warmed by the [intemperate] zeal, ſhall I ſay of Engliſhmen, in ſupport of what upon a ſudden appear to them to be their rights." Ib. 90. And on the 9th of November, 1764, he wrote to Mr. *Bollan*: "If the Parliament begin with internal taxes, I know not where any line can be drawn. If it be ſaid there is none but their diſcretion, we are in danger of unequal diſtreſſing burdens, which finally muſt affect the nation as much as the colonies themſelves." Ib. 117.

Hutchinſon in 1763–64.

Governor *Bernard* wrote to *John Pownall*, May 6, 1765: "I am ſorry that this Province ſuffers in the opinion of their Superiors for the miſdeeds

Bernard in May, 1765.

1765.

misdeeds of a few particulars. I can assure you that the people in general is extremely well disposed to Government; & it is owing only to the Wickedness & folly of a few politicians, chiefly of this Town, that it does not always appear so." 3 Bernard Papers, 289. Compare Franklin's Examination before the House of Commons, 4 Franklin's Works, 169.

Still the Acts of Trade were occasionally violated, and on grounds of right. The independent spirit of Rhode Island was a principal source of uneasiness to the Crown officers.

Illegal trade in Rhode Island.

In the Old French War the Governor of Rhode Island granted licenses to trade with the enemy, which were decided by the High Court of Admiralty in 1762 to be invalid. *The Chester*, MS. Index to Admiralty Cases 1758–1766, purchased in London at the sale of the Library of Doctors' Commons in 1860, and in the possession of the writer, pl. 145. See also Lieutenant Governor Delancey to Lords of Trade, June 3, 1757, 7 N. Y. Col. Doc. 225; Governor *Hopkins's* reply to *Pitt's* circular of August 23, 1760, and General *Amherst's* letter of May 7, 1762, to the Governor of Rhode Island, 6 Rhode Island Col. Rec. 263, 317. But that practice was not confined to Rhode Island; indeed it was said that "Governor *Bernard* in particular has also done business in the same way." Lieutenant Governor *Sharpe* of Maryland, quoted in 4 Bancroft's Hist. U. S. 377.

Governor Bernard's complaints.

However that may have been, Governor *Bernard* was constant in his complaints of smuggling in that Colony. On the 9th of May 1761 in a letter to *John Pownall*, describing a seizure of a vessel for being concerned in the Mississippi Trade, he wrote: "These practices will never be put an end to till Rhode Island is reduced to the subjection of the British Empire; of which at present it is no more a part, than the Bahama Islands were, when they were inhabited by the Buccaneers." 2 Bernard Papers, 312. On the 5th of October, 1761, he wrote a detailed account of "the notorious manner" of carrying on contraband trade in Rhode Island, in a letter addressed to *Pitt*, but which was never sent. 2 Bernard Papers, 14. 9 Ib. 229. And in another letter to *John Pownall*, on the 10th of February, 1764, after stating that the support which he had given Captain *Bishop* as a seizing officer had occasioned a confederacy among the unfair traders to get him displaced from his government, he added: "They are not so temperate in Rhode Island: they cant submit to the Laws of Great Britain as yet. When an Act of Parliament is quoted, they say they cant find it in their law book. The Surveyor general lately appointed a Comptroller of the port of Newport, an officer before known in that port. The Governor promised to swear him into his office; but before he could do it, the Assembly made an order that the Governor should not admit him into Office; & the Governor obeyed. Upon which the Surveyor went thither himself & swore him in. Soon after, A Vessel coming up to Providence passed by the Custom house without reporting & immediately proceeded to land her Cargo. Soon after she was seized by the officer stationed

1765.

tioned at Providence: but it ſignifyed nothing; for the ſame night a parcel of people with blacked faces entered her, fitted her for ſea & loaded her as well as they could, & put to ſea before morning: And yet this veſſel is known to belong to one of the Superior Court Judges." "It is not eaſily conceived, how much hurt this lawleſs independent Colony does to our orderly government." 3 Bernard Papers, 130. The Surveyor General's offer of reward for the diſcovery of theſe offenders is in the Boſton Gazette of February 6, 1764. In a later letter about the ſame tranſaction, Governor *Bernard* reports that the Governor of Rhode Iſland "ſaid publickly that the parliament of Great Britain had no more right to make laws for them than they had for the Mohawks." Bernard to Halifax, December 14, 1764, 3 Bernard Papers, 200. And ſee *Hutchinſon's* letters in 1766, *infra*, 442, 443.

Reſcue of Sloop Polly.

On the 12th of April 1765 the Surveyor General made a repreſentation to the Governor of a riotous reſcue of the Sloop *Polly* in Taunton River from *Robinſon*, the Collector of the Cuſtoms in Rhode Iſland, and Captain *Antrobus* of the *Maidſtone*, who had on the 3d of October 1764 been appointed by the Surveyor General, purſuant to the inſtructions of 1763, (*ſupra*, 429,) "an Officer of the Cuſtoms to ſeize prohibited and uncuſtomed goods." Book of Commiſſions 1764–1774, fol. 39. The Surveyor General eſpecially complained that the Governor had not ſupplied him with a Writ of Aſſiſtance. Bernard to Temple, April 12, 1765, 4 Bernard Papers, 40. Governor *Bernard's* Statement, 66 Maſs. Archives, 286. Surveyor *Dowſe's* Narrative, Ib. 291. Council Rec. 1765, fol. 368. The Council, after notice to the Surveyor General, and his refuſal to attend, on the 15th of April (preſent: Governor *Bernard*, Lieutenant Governor *Hutchinſon*, *Andrew Oliver*, *John Erving*, *James Bowdoin*, *Thomas Hubbard*, *Harriſon Gray*, *Thomas Flucker*, & *Edmund Trowbridge*) unanimouſly reſolved "That the Surveyor Generals expectation that the Governor ſhould have applied to the Chief Juſtice for a Writ of Aſſiſtance was improper, it being the practice for the Surveyor General to apply for ſuch Writ himſelf, and this Board are informed by the Chief Juſtice that he has done it in many Inſtances, and has never yet been refuſed in any one Inſtance. It further appears to the Council that the Governor during his Adminiſtration has given all Support and Encouragement to the Officers of the Cuſtoms, in carrying the Acts of Trade into Execution, and that nothing has greater tendency to weaken his hands, than ſuch undue Return as has been made on this Occaſion." 66 Maſs. Archives, 296, 297. Council Rec. 1765, fol. 369. The correſpondence of the Surveyor General with the Governor and Council, and other documents relating to this buſineſs, are in 56 Maſs. Archives, 442–448, and 66 Ib. 280–301.

Proceedings in Council.

Surveyor General.

The Surveyor General had no confidence in the Governor's integrity, and had indeed directly charged him with corruption in the adminiſtration of the revenue laws. *Supra*, 424, 430, 431, notes, and authorities there

1765.

there cited. The Governor professed a desire to have these charges investigated, and relied mainly on the testimony of the inferior custom house officers (his alleged accomplices) to clear himself. Bernard to R. Jackson and to J. Pownall, May — August, 1765, 4 Bernard Papers, 1–10. He also recriminated by charging the Surveyor General with remissness in executing the Acts of Trade; and vehemently complained that none of the officers of the Navy except Captain *Bishop* would consult with him about seizures. Bernard to Halifax, July 1, 1765, Ib. 130.

Charges against the Justices of Bristol.

On the 9th of May Collector *Robinson* and Captain *Antrobus* laid an information before the Governor, that after their seizure of said vessel and her cargo, and while *Nicholas Lechmere*, searcher and landwaiter of the customs in Rhode Island, and his servant, in whose custody the vessel had been left, "were refreshing themselves on shore within One hundred yards of the Vessel," the cargo was carried away, and the vessel unrigged and scuttled, by persons unknown. 44 Mass. Archives, 554. On the 11th of May, *Robinson*, by the Governor's request, at a special meeting of the Council summoned for the purpose, filed a complaint against divers Justices of the County of Bristol, for not yielding him proper assistance in the recovery of the goods. Ib. 556. Council Rec. 1765, fol. 373. Bernard to Robinson, May 8 & 9, 1765, 4 Bernard Papers, 44, 45. Bernard to Halifax, May 11, 1765, 3 Ib. 211. The Justices were summoned to appear, and made answers, to which *Robinson* replied, and depositions were taken. Proceedings in Council, June 5 & 13, 1765, Copy in Secretary's Office of Council Rec. 1765–1774, fol. 3, 9. 44 Mass. Archives, 559. 56 Ib. 450. 66 Ib. 312, 313, 320–328. One of the Justices was *Samuel White*, of Taunton, who was Speaker of the House of Representatives this year, and who, as tradition reports, was "famed for his accuracy in making writs." Holmes's Address to the Bristol Bar, 8. The others were *Timothy Fales*, *James Williams*, *Ezra Richmond*, and *Jerathmeel Bowers*.

Answer of the Justices.

The Justices answered that *Robinson*, when he applied to them, would not submit his commission to their inspection, but "Immediately demanded a Warrant to search the Stores of Job Smith and all other Suspected places, without prefering any Written Complaint or offering to make Oath to his Suspicion of the facts. Whereupon we severally told him it was a new matter, & that we Doubted of our Power to Grant such a Warrant as he Demanded and chose to Consider of the Matter, and under these Circumstances we Suspended the Matter for Consultation. May it please your Excellency we beg leave to observe that Mr Robinson doth not pretend that he had any Writ of Assistance or if he had that he shewed it to any of us; whereupn we Considered whether as Justices of the Peace we were obliged to Grant a General Warrant to break up all Suspected Houses or Even any particular House to Search for goods taken away as these were. Especially to a person who Shewed us no Power he had to demand one and who presented us no Regular Complaint

1765.

plaint Tho' Requefted We thought it not Incumbent on us by the Common Law if not Repugnant to it. And if there is any act of Parliament Injoy^ng it upon us it had not come to our knowledge, we thought it our Duty to attend to the obfervance of all Laws and not to take fuch Steps in the Execution of any Suppofed one as to Infringe on others that were known." And they add that *Robinfon* by their affiftance obtained entrance without a warrant into every houfe which he defired to fearch. The original anfwers, drawn by *Samuel White*, are in 44 Mafs. Archives, 560–564.

Committee appointed.

On the 24th of July 1765, the Chief Juftice and the Attorney General were appointed by the Governor and Council a Committee " to confider whether Juftices of the Peace in America are obliged or impowered by Law to grant Warrants to break open Stores or other Houfes to fearch for Cuftomable Goods; " and on the 31ft of July, at a Council at which the fame perfons, except *Hubbard*, were prefent as on the 15th of April, (*fupra*, 437,) and alfo *James Otis* (of Barnftable) & *Royall Tyler*, made this report, the original of which, with the order thereon, both in *Hutchinfon's* handwriting, are preferved in 66 Mafs. Archives, 329–332, and copied in Council Rec. 1765–1774, fol. 24 & *seq.*:

" To His Excellency Francis Bernard Efq^r Governor in chief &c.

Opinion of Hutchinfon and Trowbridge on the Power of Juftices of the Peace to grant Warrants to break Houfes.

" In obedience to the Order of Your Excellency in Council we " have confidered the Points referred to us, and find That by the Act " of Parliament of the 14th of Charles the fecond intitled An Act for " preventing frauds & regulating abufes in His Majeftys cuftoms it is " among other things enacted ' that it fhall be lawful to or for any per- " fon or perfons authorized by writ of affiftance under the feal of His " Majefty's court of exchequer to take a conftable, headborough or " other publick officer inhabiting near unto the place & in the day " time to enter & go into any houfe fhop cellar warehoufe or room or " other place and in cafe of refiftance to break open doors chefts trunks " and other package, there to feize & from thence to bring any kind " of goods or merchandize whatfoever prohibited and uncuftomed ' And " that by a fubfequent claufe in the fame Act it is further enacted ' that " all Officers belonging to the Admiralty Captains & Commanders of " Ships Forts Caftles & Blockhoufes, as alfo all Juftices of the Peace " Mayors Sheriffs Bailiffs & Headboroughs and all the King's Majefty's " Officers Minifters & Subjects whatfoever whom it may concern shall " be aiding and affifting to all and every perfon or perfons which are or " fhall be appointed by His Majefty to manage his cuftoms and their " refpective deputies in the due execution of all and every act and " thing in and by this prefent Act required and enjoined.' And that by " the Act of the feventh & eighth of William the third intitled ' An " Act for preventing frauds & regulating abufes in the Plantation " trade ' the fame Powers and authorities are given to the Officers of " the

1765.

"the customs in the Plantations for visiting & seizing ships & taking "their entries & for seizing securing & bringing on shore any prohibited "or uncustomed goods as are provided for the Officers of the customs "in England by the Act of the 14th of Charles the second and that "by the same Act of William the Third it is further provided 'that the "like assistance shall be given to the said Officers in the execution of "their office as by the said last mentioned Act is provided for the Offi- "cers in England.' But we do not find that Justices of the Peace by "any clause in the aforesaid Act of 14th of Charles the second or by "any clause in any other Act of Parliament which extends to the Plan- "tations or by the common law or by any law of this Province are "obliged or impowered to grant Warrants to break open stores or other "houses to search for customable goods, and we apprehend the only "provision for that purpose is by a writ of assistance from the Superior "Court of judicature &c. to which Court the Act of this Province "constituting the same gives the like Powers with those of the court of "exchequer in England. All which is humbly submitted to your Ex- "cellency's judgment.

"Boston, July 31, 1765.

"T Hutchinson
"Edm: Trowbridge."

Complaint against Bristol Justices dismissed.

"The foregoing Report was accepted, and the Opinion therein given was unanimously declared to be the Opinion of the Board;" and it was Resolved, that "Mr. Robinson not having then procured a Writ of Assistance (as he hath since done)" the Justices were justified in doing as they did, and the complaint was dismissed.

The fact that *James Bowdoin* and *Otis's* father concurred with the rest of the Council in this Opinion goes far to show that the legality of Writs of Assistance was then considered to be established beyond controversy. But such acquiescence did not last much longer.

Hutchinson's letters to Jackson in 1765.

The development of public sentiment in this year is well shown in the familiar letters of *Hutchinson* to *Jackson*, agent of the Province in England. On the 5th of May, 1765, he said: "I do not believe that the officers of the customs are better supported in the execution of their trust in any government upon the continent than they are in this. The charge against the governor seems to be that he is too active. The council are always ready to do what is proper on their part. Every officer for whom it has been desired has been furnished with a writ of assistants, which have been refused in most of the other governments." 26 Mass. Archives, 138. In a letter of June 4, 1765, but marked in his letter-book "not sent," he wrote: "I think the Acts of Trade are better observed than in any time past. All the officers of the customs in this Province have been furnished with writs of assistance. I have also issued them to the officers in Rhode Island for that part of their district which lyes in this Province." Ib. 139. In a similar letter of the next day: "The stamp act is received with us as decently as could be expected.

expected. The act will execute itſelf, & there is no room for evaſion ; and if there was, I am ſure the executive court would ſhow no countenance to it." Ib. 140. On the 6th of Auguſt : "I hope we ſhall be able to keep peace in the execution of the ſtamp act, notwithſtanding all the newspaper threats ; but pray do not be in great haſte with more of the ſame ſort. I do not mean to inſinuate that they would not be ſubmitted to, but they will cauſe an alienation of affection which muſt have an ill effect." Ib. 145. Ten days later, after the diſtributor of ſtamps had been burned in effigy, and ten days before the deſtruction of the Chief Juſtice's own houſe by the mob, he wrote : "I made a poor judgment when I wrote you before, & find I promiſed myſelf what I wiſhed rather than what I had reaſon to expect. I am now convinced that the people thro' the continent are impreſſed with an opinion that they are no longer conſidered by the people of England as their fellow ſubjects & entitled to engliſh liberties ; & they expect ſome tragical events in ſome or other of the colonies ; for we are not only in a deplorable ſituation at preſent, but have a diſmal proſpect before us as the commencement of the act approaches. If there be no execution of it all buſineſs muſt ceaſe ; and yet the general voice is, it cannot be carried into execution." Ib. 145, ſupplemental leaf. In a letter to the ſame of September 12, 1765, he wrote : "The late acts of Parliament for raiſing a revenue from Molaſſes & a duty on Stamps have cauſed great part of the people in the Colonies to run diſtracted. The poſts I ſuſtain have made me their object in this Province." [Then follows the ſtatement of the caſe of the Writs of Aſſiſtance, already quoted, *ſupra*, 415, note.] "The Stamp duty, although I always feared the conſequence of it would be bad, both to the nation & colonies, and privately & publickly declared my thoughts upon it, yet after the paſſing the act I could not avoid conſidering it as legally right, the Parliament being beyond diſpute the ſupreme legiſlature of the Britiſh dominions ; but our friends to liberty take advantage of a maxim they find in Lord *Coke* that an act of Parliament againſt Magna Charta or the peculiar rights of Engliſhmen is *ipſo facto* void. This, taken in the latitude the people are often enough diſpoſed to take it, muſt be fatal to all Government & it ſeems to have determined great part of the colonies to oppoſe the execution of the act with force & to show their reſentment againſt all in authority who will not join with them." He then gives an account of the deſtruction of his houſe and papers ; and adds : "I am ſtill of the mind I always have been that thoſe acts of Parliament have been unſeaſonably puſhed." Ib. 153, 154.

1765.

"The change of the currency, writs of aſſiſtance, & letters in favour of the ſtamp act are ſaid to be the reaſons of my being particularly obnoxious ; but the diſpoſition to tumult in general is undoubtedly occaſioned by an apprehenſion prevailing among the People that they are deprived of the liberties of Engliſhmen ; & every attempt to maintain in them a due ſenſe of their connexion with Great Britain is miſconſtrued into an

Hutchinſon to Conway, October, 1765.

1765. attempt to inſlave them, & the officers of the crown for doing what at any other time would be thought their duty are now charged with ſupporting the meaſures of the miniſtry & ſacrificing the rights of the People." Hutchinſon to Seymour Conway, October 1, 1765, Ib. 155. See other quotations from *Hutchinſon's* letters, *ſupra*, 415, note.

Bernard & Hutchinſon on Otis.

Bernard and *Hutchinſon* were very bitter againſt *Otis*. "Some of them talk as if this Town was to remain forever independent of the King's Government: One ſays, Let us ſee now, who will ſeize Merchants Goods, what Judge will condemn them, what Court will dare grant writs of aſſiſtance now; Other talk as familiarly of turning out the Governor, (for adhering to the King & Parliament) as they could do at Rhode Iſland or Connecticut." [The Governors of thoſe Colonies were elected, inſtead of being appointed by the King, as in Maſſachuſetts Bay.] "Mean while, *Otis* (who perhaps is as wicked a man as lives) publiſhes every week inflammatory invectives againſt the Governor & Government." Bernard to John Pownall, November 26, 1765, 5 Bernard Papers, 46. "I will hold out as long as poſſible. To die by inches will pleaſe my great adverſary the preſent champion for liberties. What will poſterity ſay of him when they reflect upon or feel the ruin he has brought upon his country." Hutchinſon's letter of December 24, 1765, "not ſent," 26 Maſs. Archives, 185. & *vid.* Ib. 187. In a ſubſequent letter to Governor *Pownall*, (quoted at ſome length *infra*, 444, 445,) *Hutchinſon* ſpoke of *Otis* as "a meteor which has appeared ſince you left the Province in the Maſſachuſetts." Ib. 215.

"The man is mad."

Two years later *Hutchinſon* wrote: "We have now and then flaſhes from our firebrand. I wish I could think them preſages of his extinction." Letter of February 17, 1768, Ib. 289. In January 1768 he reported that during the election of Councillors "*Otis* like an enraged Dæmon ran about the houſe." 25 Ib. 262. And the Governor ſaid that *Otis* at the ſame ſeſſion "behaved in the houſe like a madman." Letters of Bernard, Gage & Hood, (Boſton, 1769) 9. It is not quite clear whether the writers perceived (what was probably the fact) that the mind of *Otis* was already affected. See 2 John Adams's Works, 163, 214, 219, 220; Tudor's Life of Otis, 174, 356, 364; 1 Gordon's Hiſt. U. S. 204; 6 Bancroft's Hist. U. S. 120, 310; Maſs. Hiſt. Soc. Proceedings 1858, p. 53; Oliver to Bernard, December 3, 1769, *infra*, 462. Perhaps the more natural inference is that they only reëchoed the voice of the Houſe of Lords in February 1766—"the man is mad." Holliday's Life of Mansfield, 248. 16 Parl. Hiſt. 172.

The effect of the Stamp Act.

At the end of 1765 *John Adams* wrote in his diary: "The Stamp Act has raiſed and ſpread through the whole continent a ſpirit that will be recorded to our honor with all future generations. In every colony, from Georgia to New Hampshire incluſively, the ſtamp diſtributers and inſpectors have been compelled by the unconquerable rage of the people to renounce their offices." "The people, even to the loweſt ranks, have become more attentive to their liberties, more inquiſitive about

about them, and more determined to defend them, than they were ever before known or had occaſion to be." 2 John Adams's Works, 154. & *vid.* Ib. 169, 173; Trowbridge to Hutchinſon, December 2, 1765, 25 Maſs. Archives, 39; Otis's Argument on the 19th of December, 1765, for the Opening of the Courts, *ante*, 202; Franklin's Examination before the Houſe of Commons in February, 1766, 4 Franklin's Works, 167, 169, 176, 178, 196, 198, & 16 Parl. Hiſt. 140, 141, 145, 147, 159, 160; 5 Bancroft's Hiſt. U. S. cc. 19, 20.

Hutchinſon's change of tone.

At the ſame time *Hutchinſon's* tone changed — ſtretching the authority of Acts of Parliament beyond what had ever been aſſerted in England, (*Vid. poſt*, H) and more than inſinuating the neceſſity of forcible meaſures, and habitual interference with the internal affairs of the Colony. "I thought we had ſettled a tolerable ſyſtem of colony law in this province — that where the local laws did not provide, the law of England, not meerly as it ſtood when we came over here, but as it has been from time to time amended by ſubſequent ſtatutes, except ſuch ſtatutes as apparently were confined to the realm, was the only certain rule of law in judicial proceedings, and that upon other plans the law would be vague and uncertain, & I was in hopes to have lived to ſee no body doubt of the reaſonableneſs of it. But all of a ſudden from this fatal act we have it advanced that acts of parliament of England or Great Britain have no more relation to us than acts of parliament of Scotland had before the Union. The King of Great Britain indeed is our Sovereign, but we have no repreſentation in parliament, & ſtrictly ſpeaking, not meerly thoſe acts which lay taxes upon us, but no other acts any further than we adopt them, are binding upon us. In converſation with *Hopkins*, the late Governor of Rhode Iſland, a few weeks ago, who profeſſes to be of this principle, I aſked him what conſtruction he gave to the reſtraint in their charter from making laws repugnant to the laws of England. 'Oh! the common law as it ſtood when their charter was granted.'" "If laws immediately reſpecting us are not obligatory, ſurely thoſe of a more general nature are not ſo, & I know not by what law I am to judge or be governed." "In order to our future peace & happineſs, it ſeems abſolutely neceſſary that the relation between Great Britain and her colonies ſhould be made certain, & then that the authority in each colony ſhould be ſtrengthened ſo as to maintain and preſerve this relation. But this requires ſuperior wiſdom. All the ſervice I ever hoped to be capable of is to repreſent the true ſtate of our caſe." Letter of February 26, 1766, 26 Maſs. Archives, 197, 198. "As Chief juſtice I am ſworn to judge according to law. I look upon acts of parliament, not reſtrained to the realm, as binding the coloniſts where the local laws are ſilent, and controlling thoſe laws themſelves where they are made to reſpect them. The chief juſtice of Rhode Iſland ſuppoſes no act of parliament can controul a law of that colony. Should there be allowed ſuch diſſonance in a point of this importance? I wiſh to ſee known eſtabliſhed principles,

1766.

principles, one general rule of ſubjection, which once acknowledged, any attempts in oppoſition to them will be more eaſily reſiſted and cruſhed. When this is done, will it not be convenient to familiarize to acts of parliament made immediately to reſpect us? Should a ſeſſion paſs without one or more acts of this ſort; ſometimes general, ſometimes they may reſpect a particular colony. Proper ſubjects will always occur." Letter of April 21, 1766, Ib. 228.

Hutchinſon on abridging Engliſh Liberties.

But *Hutchinſon* was never very ſcrupulous about reſtraining the liberties of the people. As early as July 1764 he not only agreed that "it is poſſible for Parliament to paſs Acts which may abridge Britiſh Subjects of what are generally called natural rights," but was "willing to go farther, & ſuppoſe that in ſome caſes it is reaſonable & necessary, even though ſuch rights should have been ſtrengthened & confirmed by the moſt ſolemn ſanctions & engagements. The rights of parts & individuals muſt be given up when the ſafety of the whole shall depend upon it." 26 Maſs. Archives, 90. Compare his Charge to the Grand Jury in 1767, *ante*, 234; his well known ſaying in January 1769 — "There muſt be an abridgment of what are called English liberties —" Letters of Hutchinſon, &c. (Boſton, 1773) 16; and Edmund Quincy to John Hancock, March 25, 1776, Maſs. Hiſt. Soc. Proceedings 1858, p. 30.

Hutchinſon to Pownall on thoughts of Independence.

On the 8th of March 1766, *Hutchinſon* wrote a long letter to Governor *Pownall*, for the avowed purpoſe of acquainting him "with the riſe and progreſs of this taint of principles and the degree to which it prevails," an outline of which is shown by the following extracts: "I have often had occaſion to reflect upon your ſentiments of the People of America, more juſtly formed, from the experience of a few years, than my own, from living among them all my days. A thought of independence I could not think it poſſible should enter into the heart of any man, in his ſenſes, for ages to come. You have more than once hinted to me that I was miſtaken, and I am now convinced that I was ſo." "It is not more than two years since it was the general principle of the coloniſts, that in all matters of privilege or rights the determination of the Parliament of Great Britain muſt be deciſive." "Until the late act which lowered the duties upon molaſſes & ſugar, with a profeſſed deſign to raiſe a revenue from them, few people in the colonies had made it a queſtion how far the Parliament, of right, might impoſe taxes upon them. When this firſt became a topick for converſation, few or none were willing to admit the right, but the power, and from thence the obligation to ſubmit, none would deny. The Maſſachuſetts assembly was the firſt repreſentative body, which took this matter into conſideration." He then deſcribes the addreſſes from Maſſachuſetts and New York to the Houſe of Commons, (ſubſtantially as in the third volume of his Hiſtory, 113–115,) and adds: "It had not however been ſuggeſted that the ſtamp act would not be executed." But ſoon after, "the

1766.

" the reſolves of the Virginia aſſembly were ſent hither. A new ſpirit appeared at once. An act of Parliament againſt our natural rights was *ipſo facto* void, and the people were bound to unite againſt the execution of it." " If the act should be repealed, we shall ſtill be in a deplorable condition. In the capital towns of ſeveral of the colonies, & of this in particular, the authority is in the populace, no law can be carried into execution againſt their mind. I am not ſure that the Acts of Trade will not be conſidered as grievous as the ſtamp act. I doubt whether at preſent, any cuſtom houſe officer would venture to make a ſeizure." 26 Maſs. Archives, 207–210.

Reſcue of goods ſeized at Newbury.

In a poſtſcript of a few days later to the ſame letter, *Hutchinſon* mentions " a ſeizure of molaſſes & ſugar at Newbury; half a dozen boats, well manned, went after the officer, took the goods from him and the boat he was in, and left him all night upon the beach. A proclamation with promiſe of reward upon diſcovery is nothing more than the shew of authority, no man will venture a diſcovery, and I imagine a few more ſuch inſtances will make it ſettled law that no act but thoſe of our own legiſlatures can bind us." 26 Maſs. Archives, 214. The Governor's proclamation, which ſtates that this reſcue was on the 10th of March, is in the Boſton Gazette of March 17, 1766. On the ſame day the Governor wrote to Secretary *Conway* and to the Lords of Trade: " Upon this occaſion People do not wonder at the goods being reſcued, but at an Officer's being ſo hardy & fooliſh as to ſeize them & think he would be able to retain them. Under the preſent dominion of the People I have never expected that any goods, tho' ever ſo notoriouſly forfeited, would be ſeized, or ſecured or proſecuted; an attempt of that kind being judged impracticable in every ſtep by ſome of the moſt diligent & diſcrete Cuſtom houſe officers." 4 Bernard Papers, 218.

Hutchinſon on the Repeal of the Stamp Act.

Hutchinſon wrote again to Governor *Pownall* on the 11th of May, 1766, of the anticipated repeal of the Stamp Act: " Our advices are as late as the 8 of March, & though we do not know the act of repeal has paſſed through all branches, yet we are told it certainly would paſs." " We were in ſuch a ſtate that nothing short of an armed force in every colony could have carried the ſtamp act into execution, nor do I think the people ever will ſubmit to internal taxes. It is well if no oppoſition is made to other duties. I hear the great haranguer told the inhabitants of Boſton in town meeting laſt week the merchants were fools for ſubmitting to duties and reſtraints upon trade. P—— had information of a veſſel unloading dutch goods from Statia a few days ago, but he did not think it ſafe to go himſelf, nor could he find anybody elſe who would venture to ſeize her." 26 Maſs. Archives, 231.

Bernard's account of Otis's ſpeech thereon.

Governor *Bernard*, ſomewhat later, wrote: " M[r] *Otis* at a meeting at the town hall (which I think was to fix a time for rejoicings for the repeal) in a ſet Speech told the People that the diſtinction between inland taxes & port Duties was without foundation; for whoever had a right

1766. right to impofe one had a right to impofe the other: & therefore as the Parliament had given up the one, (for he faid the Act fecuring the dependency had no relation to Taxes) they had given up the other; & the Merchants were great fools, if they fubmitted any longer to the Laws reftraining their Trade, which ought to be free. This Speech made a great deal of Noife; & it was obferved by ferious Men, that *Otis* had thereby made himfelf anfwerable for all the difturbances which should thereafter happen in the execution of the Laws of Trade. But the natural Confequence, & what immediately followed was, that a common talk prevailed among the People that there should be no more Seizures in this Town. There have been but two Seizures made in the Province since; & they have been both refcued with an high hand. In that at Bofton, it is remarkable that the Man who oppofed the Officers fent for *Otis*, & he went thither as his Councellor. This is the manner, in which this Man & his Faction, after they had heard of the Repeal of the Stamp Act, prepared to make a return for it, on the part of the Province." Bernard to Shelburne, December 22, 1766, 4 Bernard Papers, 282.

Both thefe feizures were made under Writs of Affiftance. Neither of them feems to have been confidered by *Hutchinfon* important enough to be mentioned, either in his correfpondence or his Hiftory.

Falmouth Riot. The firft was on the 7th of Auguft, 1766, in the houfe of *Enoch Ilfley* in Falmouth, now Portland, and was forcibly and publicly refcued by a large number of Perfons. Copies of Council Rec. 1765–1774, fol. 145. Directions of Auguft 18, 1766, to Collector and Comptroller of Falmouth, in 5 Bernard Papers, 195. Governor Bernard's Proclamation of fame date in Bofton Gazette of August 25. In a letter of Auguft 18 to the Lords of Trade upon this affair, Governor *Bernard* fays: "As often as any Seizures are made in this Province, in its prefent ftate, fo often shall I have a proclamation of this kind to iffue, which is now become a meer farce of Government; since no one dares to difcover or profecute the Offenders, if they were fo difpofed; & indeed the Offenders are fome times, as in this Cafe, the greateft part of the Town. Formerly a refcue was an accidental or occasional Affair; now, it is the natural & certain Confequences of a feizure, & the Effect of a predetermined Refolution that the Laws of Trade fhall not be executed." "Thefe are the Confequences of the general Weaknefs of the Government, which is become a meer Shadow. I expect to have frequent occasion to repeat to your Lordships, that this Government is not like, by any internal powers of its own to recover itfelf from the great blow it has lately received. The popular Leaders have laboured fo fucceffully, that the very Principles of the Common People are changed; & they now form to themselves pretensions & Expectations, which had never entered into their Heads a year or two ago." 4 Bernard Papers, 245. See also Bernard to Shelburne, February 28, 1767, 6 Ib. 197.

Contraft

1766.

Contraft with these *Adams's* Diary, November 11, 1766, 2 John Adams's Works, 203; & Otis to Conway, June 9, 1766: "Should any persons attempt to persuade the adminiftration, that the colonifts are in the leaft difpofed to forget their duty and loyalty to the beft of Kings, they will foon find themfelves confuted." 2 Sparks's Amer. Biog. 2d feries, 145, 146.

The other affair, called by the Governor in his letter of February 28, 1767, "the Riot at Bofton," and in that of the previous December (*fupra*, 446,) a feizure "refcued with an high hand," was as follows:

Malcolm's oppofition to a Writ of Affiftance.

On the 24th of September, 1766, *Hallowell*, the Comptroller of the Cuftoms of the Port of Bofton, and *Sheafe*, the Deputy Collector, informed the Governor and Council that, upon going to the cellar of the houfe of *Daniel Malcolm* in the north part of Bofton with a Writ of Affiftance and a Deputy Sheriff to feize uncuftomed goods, they had been denied admittance, and oppofed by *Malcolm* with fword and piftols, and threats of death to any one who should attempt to open the door. The Council (Prefent: the Governor, *Danforth*, *Erving*, *Bowdoin*, *Hubbard*, *Gray*, *Ruffell*, *Flucker*, *Tyler & Pitts*) advifed the Governor to inform the officers "that this Board are willing to do what in them lies for the affiftance of the officers in the execution of his warrant, when their interpofition shall appear to be neceffary, but that it is their opinion that as the sheriff has it in his power to raife the *Poffe Comitatus*, any aid from his Excellency and the Board does not appear at prefent to be needful." The Collector and Comptroller accordingly went with the Sheriff to the houfe, but, as the Governor the next day informed the Council, "found the houfe shut up clofe and furrounded with a great number of people, fome of the moft credible of which informed the officers that if they offered to force the houfe they would be in danger of their lives, and they were thereby prevented entering the houfe." The officers and other witneffes were called in, and gave their affidavits before the Council. Copies of Council Rec. 1765–1774, fol. 157, 158. 88 Mafs. Archives, 191–198. Bernard to Lords of Trade, October 10, 1766, 4 Bernard Papers, 252.

Proceedings in Council.

Legal knowledge of the people.

The teftimony taken on this occafion fhows how well inftructed the people were in the principles of law applicable to the cafe, perhaps by *Otis*, who was counfel for *Malcolm*. Bernard to Shelburne, December 22, 1766, *fupra*, 446. But compare Gage to Hillfborough, October 31, 1768; "Copies of Letters from Governor Bernard, &c. to the Earl of Hillfborough," 25; *Burke's* Speech in 1775 on Conciliation with America, 2 Burke's Works, (Bofton ed. 1839) 36, 37; Attorney General *De Grey*, January 26, 1769, 1 Cavendish Debates, 196.

Sheriff's teftimony.

Stephen Greenleaf, the Sheriff, teftified, that he "left the Officers of ye Cuftoms & went singly up to a great Number of people who were collected

1766.

collected at the head of ye Street leading to Malcolm's houſe & expoſtulated with them ſome time; that he was Civilly treated by them, but was aſſured that no admiſſion into Capt Malcolms houſe would be ſuffer'd except the Cuſtom houſe Officers would go before a Juſtice & make Oath who their Informer was; the declarant then inform'd them, as he had before desired Capt Nicholls to inform Mr Malcolm, that the Collector & Comptroller had both made Oath before Mr Juſtice Hutchinſon that they had receiv'd ſuch information as the Warrant ſet forth, and that he did not apprehend that the Laws oblig'd them to tell who their Informer was; a reply was then made from ye Crowd but by whom the declarant does not know, that *they* knew better, and that ye Officers should Sware to their informer before they should go into the Houſe; the declarant then inform'd them that if the Cuſtom houſe Officers should think proper to force the houſe & should be oppoſ'd, they knew it was his Duty to command their Aſſiſtance, and he hop'd that no man there would refuſe it; to which ye general voice was that they hop'd that no body would hurt *him*, they knew he was obliged to do what he did, but they believ'd that he would have no Aſſiſtance except the Informer was diſcover'd or delivered up; the declarant remembers to have heard one voice from behind him ſay 'Aye *we'll* aſſiſt you,' but by the manner of pronunciation & tone of voice he took it to be Ironical & either by way of Ridicule or threatning. The declarant ſays that it appearing to him that the people were determin'd, & that any further expoſtulations would be fruitleſs, return'd to ye Officers (who were ſtanding at a little diſtance) and obſerv'd to them that it grew late & night would ſoon come on, that the ſtreets were continually filling with people, that *they* muſt be ſenſible of the difficulty of the affair they were upon & that the warrant would not Juſtify a forcible Entrance into any dwelling houſe after Sunſet;" and they then retired. 88 Maſs. Archives, 196, 197.

Town Meeting.

On the 13th of October the Inhabitants of Boſton in town meeting unanimouſly appointed *James Otis*, *Joſeph Jackſon*, *Samuel Sewall*, *John Hancock*, *William Phillips*, *Timothy Newell*, *John Rowe*, *Samuel Adams* and *Joſhua Henſhaw* "a Committee to wait on his Excellency the Governor in Behalf of the Town, and to desire he would be pleaſed to give the Secretary Orders to furnish the Town-Clerk with Copies of all the Depositions relating to the Informations given the Cuſtom-Houſe Officers, and the Proceedings thereon, that ſo the Town having Knowledge of their Accuſers, and of the Nature and Design of the Teſtimonies taken, may have it in their Power to rectify Miſtakes, and counterwork the Designs of any who would repreſent them in a diſadvantageous Light to his Majeſty's Miniſters." Boſton Gazette of October 13, 1766.

Letter of Boſton to town agent.

The Committee obtained the copies, and took other depoſitions, and reported a letter to *Dennis De Berdt*, the agent of the town in England, which

1766.

which was approved in town meeting on the 22d of October, and contained theſe paſſages: "Whatever repreſentation may have been made to our prejudice, which we think we have ſome good reaſon to ſuſpect, our most inveterate enemy dare not openly aſſert that the civil authority in this county & even thro' the province has not as good reason to be aſſured of the aſſiſtance of the people in the legal exerciſe of power as in any county in England." "M[r] *Malcomb* admitted them into every appartment ſaving one which being let he told them the key was not in his poſſeſſion. They threatened to enter by force, which Mr *Malcomb* told them they muſt do at their peril. However not having ſufficient authority as they apprehended, they then retired. Mr *Malcomb* ſuppoſing they would return, determined to faſten his houſe that if they entred it should be forceably, being aſſured from the declarations of the perſon who hired the aforeſaid cellar & his own knowledge of the other appartments, that no counterband goods were there. The officers returned in the afternoon & after ſome attempt tho' without violence to get an entry they again retired and came no more." Boſton Town Rec. 1766, fol. 721–726. See alſo Boſton Gazette of October 27, 1766, which ſtates "That there really were no goods in the Houſe liable to a Seizure; and that as for the good People, who were *curious ſpectators*, they behaved as orderly, to uſe the words of ſome of the Deponents, as if they were at Church." And the Gazette of November 24 declares that "the Metropolis has shared largely in theſe vile and falſe Repreſentations, from the Days of that worthy and conſciencious C——r Mr. *B——ns*, to the Affair of Capt. *M–lc—b's*, and they have, and are taking proper Measures to ward off the Evils they have been threatened with." See also Gazette of March 20, 1769; & *ſupra*, 425, note.

Remark of Otis.

In the following December, the Governor's proceedings were denounced by *Otis* in the Houſe of Repreſentatives, "when," if the Governor's account is to be truſted, "a Member obſerved that 'He knew the Time when the Houſe would have readily aſſiſted the Governor in executing the Laws of Trade, inſtead of being moved to oppoſe him in it.' To this *Otis* replied that 'the Times were altered; they now knew what their Rights were; then they did not.'" Bernard to Shelburne, December 24, 1766, 4 Bernard Papers, 289.

1767.

Acts of Parliament of 7 Geo. 3.

In 1767 Parliament paſſed new ſtatutes to promote the execution of the Acts of Trade. The St. of 7 G. 3, c. 41, authorized the appointment of Commiſſioners of the Cuſtoms to reside in America; and the St. of 7 G. 3, c. 46, § 10, declared the highest Court of Juſtice in each Province to be authorized to iſſue Writs of Aſſiſtance. See Opinion of Attorney General *De Grey*, *infra*, 452.

American Board of Cuſtoms.

The new Board of Commiſſioners conſiſted of *Henry Hulton*, *John Temple*, *William Burch*, *Charles Paxton*, and *John Robinſon*. *Hulton* and *Burch* were newcomers. *Hulton* had previouſly been ſecretary of the Commiſſioners of the Cuſtoms in England; and his name is ſigned

 at

1767. at the foot of the commiſſion of Harriſon to be Collector of Cuſtoms at Boſton, dated July 11, 1766, and recorded in Book of Commiſſions 1764–1774, fol. 68, and of ſimilar earlier commiſſions. *Temple* had previouſly been Surveyor General of the Northern Diſtrict of America; *Paxton*, Surveyor of the Port of Boſton; and *Robinſon*, Collector of Newport. *Vid. ſupra*, 421, 428, 437. Their commiſſion is dated September 8, 1767, recorded in Book of Commiſſions 1764–1774, fol. 83–92, publiſhed entire in the Boſton Evening Poſt of September 26, 1768, and quoted, in part, in the Report of the Committee of Boſton in November 1772, *infra*, 466. *Hulton*, *Burch*, and *Paxton* arrived in Boſton on the 5th of November 1767. *Temple* and *Robinſon* were here before. Boſton Evening Poſt, November 9, 1767. 3 Hutchinſon's Hiſt. Maſs. 183.

1768.

Their inſtructions and commiſſions to their ſubordinates.

In a "general letter," dated "Cuſtom Houſe, Boſton, 11 Jany 1768," and ſigned by all of them, they ſaid to their ſubordinate officers: "You are to mention if you have received the Act of the 7th of his preſent Majeſty ch. 46, the directions of which you are ſtrictly to obſerve, and particularly, if you are not already furniſh'd with Writs of Aſſiſtants, you are to apply by letter for ſuch writs to the Juſtice or Juſtices of the Superior Court of your Province or Colony, who are empowered by ſaid act to grant the ſame." Salem Cuſtom Houſe Record, 216. Their printed inſtructions and commiſſions to their inferiors varied from the forms of 1764, (*ſupra*, 433, note,) in expreſſly mentioning Writs of Aſſiſtants. The inſtructions were altered by ſtriking out the words "under the Regulations preſcribed by Law," and inſerting theſe: "Obſerving that you are not to enter any Houſe, Shop, Cellar, or Warehouſe, but in the Day time, and taking with you a Writ of Aſſiſtants, and a Conſtable, Headborough, or other Civil Officer next inhabiting." Printed inſtructions of February 28, 1769, to *John Mascarene*, Comptroller of Salem, in Maſs. Hiſt. Soc. Lib. In the ſame library is an impreſſion of the plate, engraved in London, for commiſſions to their ſubordinates, "By virtue whereof He hath power to enter into any Ship, Bottom, Boat or other Veſſel, & also in the day time with a Writ of Aſſiſtants granted by *his Majeſtys Superior or ſupreme Court of Juſtice*, and taking with him a Conſtable, Headborough or other publick Officer next inhabiting, to enter into any Houſe, Shop, Cellar, Warehouſe, or other place whatſoever, not only within the ſaid Port but within any other Port or place within our juriſdiction, there to make diligent Search, and in caſe of reſiſtence, to break open any Door, Trunk, Cheſt, Case, Pack, Truſs, or any other parcel, or package whatſoever," &c. This is also printed (though miſpunctuated) in the Society's Proceedings of 1859, p. 324. See also Salem Custom House Record, quoted in 2 Eſſex Inſtitute Hiſt. Coll. 173.

Removal of Folger.

One of the firſt acts of the Commiſſioners was to remove *Folger*, Collector at Nantucket, (*ſupra*, 430,) for voting in the House of Repreſentatives for the reſolves in favor of American manufactures. Boſton

Boſton Gazette of February 29, March 14, & April 11, 1768. Hutchinſon's Letter of December, 1769, 26 Maſs. Archives, 417.

Fiſher Collector at Salem.

(23) *Fiſher* was Collector at Salem and Marblehead, having been appointed by the Commiſſioners of Cuſtoms in London on the 10th of January, 1765. Book of Commiſſions 1764–1774, fol. 45. Bernard to Fiſher, April 20, 1765, in which the Governor cautions *Fiſher* againſt "employing in your ſervice one *Toovey* whom you find in the office: When you know his Story, as an honeſt Man, you will abhor him; as a prudent Man you will have no Communication with him." 4 Bernard Papers, 41. For the reaſon of the Governor's feeling, *vid. ſupra*, 424, note. *Fiſher* had previouſly been a naval officer, as appears by an earlier letter to him, in which the Governor alſo ſays: "I am fully ſatisfied of the right of the Naval Officers to ſeize & proſecute for all breaches of the laws of trade equally with the Cuſtom houſe Officers. I have therefore propoſed to the chief Juſtice, this morning, to grant you a ſtanding Writ of Aſſiſtance as he does to the Cuſtom houſe Officers who apply for the ſame. As this writ has never been, as yet, granted to Naval officers, he has deſired to conſider of it & conſult with his Brethren. They meet again in a fortnight's time & then I will move the Matter again; but will not take out the writ without you deſire." Ib. 38. *Fiſher* was ſuſpended by the Commiſſioners of Cuſtoms at Boſton on the 30th of September 1768; but reſtored on the 4th of Auguſt 1769, by direction of the Commiſſioners of Cuſtoms in London. Salem Cuſtom Houſe Record, 247, 251, 301. Boſton Gazette, November 7, 1768, & Auguſt 28, 1769.

Maſcarene Comptroller at Salem.

(24) *Maſcarene* had been appointed by the Commiſſioners of Cuſtoms in England Comptroller at Salem and Marblehead on the 15th of Auguſt 1764. Book of Commiſſions 1764–1774, fol. 40. For the form of his inſtructions *vid. ſupra*, 450.

Form of Writ of Aſſiſtance unchanged.

The writs to *Fiſher* and *Maſcarene* were probably in the ſame form as thoſe previously iſſued; for on the 24th of March 1768 Governor *Bernard*, in ſending to Lieutenant Governor *Franklin* of New Jerſey forms of Writs of Aſſiſtance, which he hoped would "remove the Difficulties your chief Juſtice lies under," ſaid: "It is not improbable but that, as there is now a Commiſſion of Cuſtoms in America, the Form of the Writ may be alterd ſo as to be made more conformable to that uſed in England. But no Steps have been taken towards this as yet." 5 Bernard Papers, 261.

Hutchinſon's repreſentations in 1768.

Hutchinſon, in a letter dated May 26, 1768, manifeſtly written with a view of ſetting the Commiſſioners in the moſt favorable light, at the expenſe of the Province, but marked in his letter-book "not ſent," wrote: "The Commiſſioners of the Cuſtoms will repreſent the breaches of the Acts of Trade notorious enough, & yet they are not able to prevent or puniſh them. Writs of Aſſiſtance are iſſued whenever they have been applied for, but the Civil Officers are not regarded. The laws have loſt their force, & upon the riſing of a Mob I should have

1768. have no dependance upon any civil or military officer to ſuppreſs it; the only chance would be from private perſons of ſpirit, who being alarmed with the fear of having their property deſtroyed might perhaps combine together & make reſiſtance; but this is very uncertain at any time, and when a mob is raiſed meerly to reſcue ſeized goods, ſuch a combination is not to be expected." 26 Maſs. Archives, 306, 307.

English views of the lawfulneſs of Writs of Aſſiſtance.

In the Boſton Gazette of September 5, 1768, under date of London, June 20, 1768, it is reported that "more than one very eminent Lawyer have publickly declared that a certain method of proceeding appears to them equally as unconſtitutional as general warrants." But on the 20th of Auguſt 1768 the Attorney General of England gave the following opinion, which is here reprinted from a copy remaining upon the files of March term 1769 of the Superior Court of Judicature of the Colony of Rhode Iſland.

"CASE.

Opinion of Attorney General De Grey upon Writs of Aſſiſtance.

"7th Geo. 3d, "Ch. 46. "BY this Act of Parliament, after reciting 'That by an Act of Parliament made in "the 14th Cha. 2d, intitled an Act for preventing Frauds and regu-"lating Abuſes in His Majeſty's Cuſtoms, and ſeveral other Acts now "in Force, it is lawful for any Officer of His Majeſty's Cuſtoms, au-"thorized by Writ of Aſſiſtants under the Seal of His Majeſty's Court "of Exchequer, to take a Conſtable, Headborough, or any other pub-"lic Officer inhabiting near unto the Place, and in the Day Time, to "enter and go into any Houſe, Shop, Cellar, Warehouſe or Room, or "other Place, and in Caſe of Reſiſtance to break open Doors, Cheſts, "Trunks and other Package, there to ſeize, and from thence to bring "any kinds of Goods or Merchandize whatſoever, prohibited or uncuſ-"tomed; and to put and ſecure the ſame in His Majeſty's Storehouſe, "next to the Place where the Seizure shall be made. And further re-"citing, That by an Act made in the 7th and 8th of William the 3d, "intitled an Act for preventing Frauds and regulating Abuſes in the "Plantation Trade, it was amongſt other Things enacted, That the "Officers for collecting and managing His Majeſty's Revenue, and in-"ſpecting the Plantation Trade in *America*, ſhould have the ſame Pow-"ers and Authorities to enter Houſes or Warehouſes, to ſearch for and "ſeize Goods prohibited to be imported or exported into, or out of, any "of the ſaid Plantations, or for which any Duties were payable, or "ought to have been paid, and that the like Aſſiſtance ſhould be given "to the ſaid Officers in the Execution of their Office, as by the ſaid re-"cited Act of the 14th Cha. 2d, is provided for the Officers in *England*, "but no Authority being expreſſly given by the ſaid Act of 7th and 8th "of William 3d, to any particular Court to grant ſuch Writs of Aſſiſt-"ants for the Officers of the Cuſtoms in the ſaid Plantations, it was "doubted

"doubted whether ſuch Officers could legally enter Houſes and other "Places on Land to ſearch for and ſeize Goods in the Manner directed "by the ſaid Acts; to obviate which Doubts for the future, and in order "to carry the intention of the ſaid Acts into effectual Execution. 1768.

"*It is enacted*, 'That after the 20th of *November*, 1767, ſuch Writs "'of Aſſiſtants to authorize and empower the Officers of His Majeſ-"'ty's Cuſtoms to enter and go into any Houſe, Warehouſe, Shop, "'Cellar or other Place, in the *Britiſh* Colonies or Plantations in "'*America*, to ſearch for and ſeize prohibited or uncuſtomed Goods in "'the Manner directed by the ſaid recited Acts, ſhall and may be "'granted by the Superior or Supreme Court of Juſtice having Juriſ-"'diction within ſuch Colony or Plantation reſpectively.'

"IN PURSUANCE of this Act of Parliament, the Officers of the "Cuſtoms in *America*, have applied to the Judges of the Superior "Courts of Judicature in the reſpective Provinces, for Writs of Aſſiſt-"ants, but moſt of them have refuſed to grant ſuch Writs, ſeemingly "for this Reaſon, that no informations had been made to them of any "ſpecial Occaſion for ſuch Writ, and that it will be unconſtitutional to "lodge ſuch Writ in the Hands of the Officer, as it will give him a "diſcretionary Power to act under it in ſuch Manner as he ſhall think "neceſſary.

"But it muſt be obſerved, that if ſuch a General Writ of Aſſiſtants "is not granted to the Officer, the true Intent of the Act may in almoſt "every Caſe be evaded, for if he is obliged, every Time he knows, or "has received information of prohibited or uncuſtomed Goods being "concealed, to apply to the Supreme Court of Judicature for a Writ of "Aſſiſtants, ſuch concealed Goods may be conveyed away before the "Writ can be obtained. Inquiry has been made into the Manner of "granting Writs of Aſſiſtants in *England*, and it appears that ſuch "Writs are iſſued out of the Court of Exchequer whenever the Com-"miſſioners of the Cuſtoms apply for them. Every Officer of the Cuſ-"toms here, is armed with ſuch a Writ, and whenever a new Officer is "appointed, the Commiſſioners direct their Sollicitor to procure a Writ "of Aſſiſtants, which is iſſued as a matter of Courſe by the Clerks of "the Exchequer without any Application to the Court. This Writ is "directed to all Officers and Miniſters who have any Office, Power or "Authority from or under the Juriſdiction of the Lord High Admiral "of *England*, to all and every Vice Admirals, Juſtices of the Peace, "Mayors, Sheriffs, Conſtables, Bailiffs, Headboroughs, and all other "the King's Officers, Miniſters and Subjects, commanding them to be "aiding, aſſiſting and helping the Commiſſioners of the Cuſtoms and "their Deputies, Miniſters, Servants, and other Officers in the Execu-"tion of their Duty.

"Queſt. *Whether the Superior Courts of Juſtice in the* Britiſh *Col-"onies or Plantations in* America, *ought not upon Application, to iſſue "Writs of Aſſiſtants in the ſame Manner as is practiſed in the Court of "Exchequer*

1768. "*Exchequer in* England, *and what steps should be taken by Government in Order to Enforce the Issuing of these Writs for the Protection of the Officers of the Customs abroad?*

"There can be no doubt, but that the Superior Courts of Justice in *America* are bound by the 7th GEO. 3d. to issue such Writs of Assistants, as the Court of Exchequer in *England* issues in similar Cases, to the Officers of the Customs.

"As this Process was probably new to many of the Judges there, and they seem to have had no Opportunity of informing themselves about it, it is perhaps in some measure excusable, that they wished to have time to consider of it, and to inquire into the Practice of the Court of Exchequer and of other Colonies; and I think it can only be because the Subject was entirely misunderstood, and the Practice in *England* unknown, that the Chief Justice of *Pennsylvania*, who is generally well spoken of, could imagine, that 'He was not Warranted by Law' to issue a Writ commanded by the Legislature; which Writ was founded upon the Common Law, enforced by Acts of Parliament and in daily use in *England*, and which from the general import of the 7th WILL. 3d. ought to have been set on foot from that time in *America*, and which Statute the late Act only meant to Explain. And it appears accordingly that in *Boston* where a very able Judge presides and some Experience had been had upon the Subject, no Difficulty was made in granting it.

"I think therefore it is advisable that the Form of the Writ issued by the Court of Exchequer in *England*, should be sent over to the several Colonies in *America*, together with the Manner of applying for it and of granting it, by which they will see, that the Power of the Custom House Officers is given by Act of Parliament and not by this Writ, which does nothing more than facilitate the Execution of his Power by making the Disobedience of the Writ a Contempt of the Court: The Writ only requiring all Subjects to permit the exercise of it and to Aid it. The Writ is a Notification of the Character of the Bearer to the Constable and others to whom he applies, and a Security to the Subject against others who might pretend to such Authority. No Body has it but a Custom House Officer armed with such a Writ. The Writ is not granted upon a previous Information, nor to any particular Person, nor on a special Occasion. The inconvenience of that was experienced upon the Act of 12th CHA. 2d, C. 19. and the present Method of proceeding adopted in lieu of what that Statute had prescribed.

"*Wm DeGrey.*

"20*th August*, 1768."

On the evening of August 31, 1768, during a visit of *John Robinson* to Newport, notice having been publicly posted that he had "boasted among his brother Commissioners that he could be well supported in the Execution

cution of his Office at *Rhode-Iſland*, and be fully protected from the leaſt inſult," a great mob collected about the tavern. "But after a very diligent Search, (not by Virtue of any Writ of Aſſiſtance, but by Candle Light,) of the Houſe, Out-Houſes, Bales, Barrels, Meal Tubs, Trunks, Boxes, Packs and Packages, packed and unpacked, and in ſhort of every Hole and Corner ſufficient to conceal a *Ram Cat*, or a Commiſſioner, they could find neither." Boſton Gazette of September 5, 1768.

1768.

Parody of Writ of Aſſiſtance.

On the 20th of December 1768 the Commiſſioners of the Cuſtoms in Boſton wrote to Chief Juſtice *Hutchinſon*: "Having directed our Sollicitor to prepare a form of a Writ of Aſſiſtants, copies of which are intended to be ſent to the different ports in America, to be applied for in the reſpective Courts by our Officers, as occaſions may require, We herewith encloſe the ſame, and a copy of the Opinion of the Attorney General in England for your Honor's peruſal, and ſhould be glad to receive your opinion, whether the Form is ſuch as you would chooſe to iſſue to our ſeveral Officers within the Province of Maſſachuſets Bay." The letter is ſigned by *Burch*, *Hulton*, and *Temple*. 44 Maſs. Archives, 670.

Change in form of Writ of Aſſiſtance.

That the changes propoſed were merely formal is evident from the following reply of *Hutchinſon*: "I have received from your Board the Copy of a Writ of Aſſiſtants framed by your Sollicitor upon which you deſire my opinion. I have compared it with the Writ iſſued from His Majeſty's Court of Exchequer in England, and I do not find that the two Writs vary from each other any farther than the different circumſtances of Place make neceſſary, only I obſerve in the direction you have omitted the word *Mayors*. We have no Mayors in this Province at preſent, no more have we Headboroughs. I think the Writ ſhould either be reſtrained to ſuch Officers only as are exiſting in the Colony where it iſſues, or elſe take in all that are named in the Writ which iſſues at home. If it ſhould be the latter that part which expreſſes ſuch Officers as have at that time no exiſtence would be conſidered as ſurpluſage. I am for keeping to the very words of the Exchequer Writ as far as different circumſtances of place will admit. I ſhould be willing immediately to iſſue Writs in the form propoſed only I think it convenient my brethren ſhould be firſt conſulted. Our next Term will begin the 2d Tueſday in March. I imagine no inconvenience can ariſe by deferring the matter until that time, your Officers being already furniſhed with Writs as agreeable to the form propoſed as the Circumſtances of the Colonies before your Board was conſtituted would admit, but if you think otherwiſe I will conſult my brethren as ſoon as may be." 44 Maſs. Archives, 671.

Hutchinſon's comments thereon.

(25) Edward Winſlow was Deputy Collector at Plymouth, appointed by the Surveyor General on the 27th of March, 1765, and reappointed by the Commiſſioners of Cuſtoms in 1768; and was alſo clerk of the courts and regiſter of probate in Plymouth County. Book of Commiſſions

Winſlow Collector at Plymouth.

1768.

miſſions 1764–1774, fol. 44. Boſton Evening Poſt of June 6, 1768. Mein & Fleeming's Regiſter for 1769, 58, 60.

Sloop Liberty ſeized at Boſton —

(26) The Sloop *Liberty*, *Barnard* Maſter, originally belonged to *John Hancock*, and was ſeized at Boſton by the Commiſſioners of the Cuſtoms near ſunſet on the 10th of June, 1768, for landing Madeira Wines without paying the duties; and, at Comptroller *Hallowell's* ſuggeſtion, was taken out from the wharf by armed boats from the *Romney* Man of War, and anchored under her guns; which occaſioned a riot. For thoſe proceedings, and the diſcuſſions about them, ſee Letters of Bernard, Gage & Hood, (Boſton, 1769) 20–28, 85–108; "A third extraordinary Budget" of Letters, &c. between Governor Bernard and the Miniſtry, 2–8; 6 Bernard Papers, 311–326; Bernard to Hillſborough, December 12, 1768, 7 Ib. 115; Letters of Hutchinſon, &c. (Boſton, 1773) 3–9; John Powell to Collector Harriſon, and Harriſon to Powell, June 13, 1768, 3 Chalmers MS. New England Papers, 2, in the poſſeſſion of Mr. *Jared Sparks*; W. Molineux to Harriſon, June 15, 1768, Ib. 1; Affidavit of Richard Silveſter, Ib. 12, 13; Joſhua Henſhaw to William Henſhaw, June 15, 1768, a copy of which is in Maſs. Hiſt. Soc. Lib.; Proceedings in Council, 50 Maſs. Archives, 287–300, Copies of Council Rec. 1765–1774, fol. 333–342, & Bradford's State Papers, 156–158; Boſton Gazette, June 20, Auguſt 8, & October 10, 1768; Vindication of Town of Boſton, 9–15; Franklin's True State of Proceedings in Maſſachuſetts Bay, Almon's Prior Documents, 262, 263; 1 Gordon's Hiſt. U. S. 230–237; 3 Hutchinſon's Hiſt. Maſs. 188–193, 488–491; 6 Bancroft's Hiſt. U. S. 155–162, 174; Richard Frothingham in 9 Atlantic Monthly, 708. The popular objection, that this ſeizure near ſunſet was unprecedented and unlawful, was founded, *Hutchinſon* ſays, on a miſapprehenſion that the direction in a Writ of Aſſiſtance, to enter houſes "in the day time only," applied to all ſeizures of veſſels or goods. 3 Hutchinſon's Hiſt. Maſs. 190, note.

Adjudged forfeit by Court of Admiralty —

The Commiſſioners, in ſeizing the *Liberty*, acted upon the written opinion of their Solicitor, *David Liſle*. Collector Harriſon to John Powell, June 13, 1768, 3 Chalmers New England Papers, 2. The ſloop was libelled in the Court of Vice Admiralty, and "adjudged forfeit for breach of the Acts of Trade," and an order of ſale paſſed on the 31ſt of Auguſt, and publiſhed on the 5th of September, under which ſhe was ſold by auction on the 6th of September, and was bought by the Collector of the Port of Boſton, to be uſed as a cruiſer for the protection of trade. Boſton Evening Poſt of September 5 & 12, 1768. See also "Journal of the Times" of November 3, 1768, in Boſton Evening Poſt of January 9, 1769. In the ſpring of 1769 ſhe cruiſed as a "*guarda-coſta*" on the ſhores of Connecticut and Rhode Iſland, and ſeized ſeveral veſſels. Boſton Gazette of January 9, May 1 & 15, and Evening Poſt of May 15, & June 19, 1769.

Used as a "guarda-coſta" —

Deſtroyed at Newport.

On the 19th of July 1769 a mob at Newport, provoked by her ſeizures of veſſels on unfounded ſuſpicions, and by the inſolence of her crew,

crew, fcuttled and burned her. Affidavit of Captain Reid, 2 Trumbull Papers, 219, in Mafs. Hift. Soc. Lib. Letters of Commiffioners of Cuftoms in Boston, and of Collector and Comptroller of New London, to Governor of Connecticut, Ib. 221, 223. Proclamations of Governor of Rhode Ifland and of Commiffioners of Cuftoms, and extracts from Rhode Ifland Newspapers, 6 Rhode Ifland Col. Rec. 593–596. Boston Gazette and Evening Post of July 24 & August 7, 1769. "Journal of the Times" in Boston Evening Post of December 11, 1769. Boston Gazette of December 18, 1769, and March 5, 1770. 1 Cavendish Debates, 495, 496. 2 Arnold's Hift. R. I. 297. The Rhode Ifland hiftorians, in the books juft cited, confider this the firft overt act of refiftance to the authority of Parliament. But in 1765 the execution of the Stamp Act had been rendered impoffible by compelling the refignation of all the stamp diftributors throughout the Continent. *Supra*, 442, 443. And if a fingle act of violence is to be deemed of fuch importance, a veffel had been refcued from the custom houfe officers in Newport in 1764. *Supra*, 436.

1768.

The identity of *John Hancock's* Sloop *Liberty* with the revenue veffel destroyed at Newport feems to have escaped the notice of historians. But the evidence of her forfeiture, fale, fubfequent ufe, and destruction, is perfectly conclusive, notwithstanding the vague statements of fome writers that *Hancock's* floop was restored after a long detention. See Almon's Prior Documents, 263, note; 1 Gordon's Hist. U. S. 240. The miftake probably arose from confounding the proceeding against the vessel with the information against her owner. It would seem that no defence to the libel *in rem* was attempted; for *John Adams's* "Admiralty Book" contains no note of it; although it does contain a full report of the proceeding *in perfonam*, which is fo like the account in the "Journal of the Times" in the Boston Evening Post of 1769 as to raife a fufpicion that fo much at least of that journal is by the fame hand.

Miftaken ftory that fhe was reftored.

This cafe affords fuch curious examples of the Admiralty proceedings and of the conftitutional arguments of that period, as to excufe the insertion here of a full report. *Adams's* notes begin with the information and order for process, as follows:

"Jonathan Sewal *vs.* John Hancock.

ADVOCATE GENERAL *v.* HANCOCK.

" Prov. &c. Before the Hon[l]. Robert Auchmuty Efq[r]

"BE it remembered, that on the 29 day of October in the Ninth "Year of the Reign of his Majefty George the Third, Jona- "than Sewall Efq[r] Advocate General for the faid Lord the King, in his "proper Perfon comes and as well on behalf of the faid Lord the King, "as of the Governor of this Province, gives the faid Court to underftand

Information.

 "and

1768. ADVOCATE GENERAL *v.* HANCOCK.

" and be informed, that on the ninth day of May laſt, a certain Sloop " called the Liberty, arrived at the Port of Boſton in said Province, from " the Iſlands of Madeira, having on Board, one hundred and twenty ſeven " Pipes of Wine of the Growth of the Madeira's; of which ſaid Sloop, " one Nathaniel Barnard was then Maſter, and that in the Night Time " of the ſame day the ſaid Nathaniel Barnard with Intent to defraud the " ſaid Lord the King of his lawfull Cuſtoms, did unlawfully and clan- " deſtinely unship and land on Shore in Boſton aforeſaid one hundred of " the aforeſaid Pipes of Wine of the Value of Thirty Pounds Sterling " Money of Great Britain, each Pipe, the Duties thereon not having " been firſt paid, or ſecured to be paid, agreeable to Law. And that " John Hancock of Boſton aforeſaid Eſq^{r} was then and there *willfully* " *and unlawfully aiding and aſſiſting in unſhiping & landing* the " ſame one hundred Pipes of Wine, he the ſaid John Hancock, at the " ſame time *well knowing, that the Duties thereon were not paid or* " *ſecured* and that the unshipping and landing the ſame, as aforeſaid, " was with Intent to defraud the ſaid Lord the King as aforeſaid, and " contrary to Law; againſt the Peace of the ſaid Lord the King and " the Form of the Statute in ſuch Caſe made and provided, whereby " and by Force of the ſame Statute, the ſaid John has forfeited Treble " the Value of the ſaid Goods, ſo unshipped and landed as aforeſaid, " amounting in the whole to the Sum of Nine Thouſand Pounds Ster- " ling Money of Great Britain, to be divided, paid and applied in man- " ner following, that is to ſay, after deducting the Charges of Proſe- " cution, one Third Part thereof to be paid into the Hands of the " Collector of his Majeſty's Cuſtoms for the ſaid Port of Boſton, for the " Uſe of his Majeſty, his Heirs and Successors, one Third Part to the " Governor of ſaid Province, and the other Third Part to him that in- " forms for the ſame.

" Whereupon as this is a matter properly within the Juriſdiction of " this Hon^{l} Court, the ſaid Advocate General prays the Adviſement of " the ſaid Court in the Premiſes, and that the ſaid John Hancock may " be attached and held to anſwer to this Information, and may by a " Decree of this honourable Court be adjudged to pay the aforeſaid ſum " of Nine Thouſand Pounds to be applied to the Uſes aforeſaid.

" JON SEWALL Adv^{o} for the King."

Warrant iſſued.

" Octr 29, 1768. Filed and allowed and ordered that the Regiſter " of this Court or his Deputy iſſue out a Warrant for the Marshall of " this Court or his Deputy to arreſt the Body of the ſaid John Hancock " and him keep in ſafe Cuſtody ſo that he have him at a Court of Vice " Admiralty to be holden at Boſton on the ſeventh day of November " next at Nine of Clock before noon and that he take Bail for Three " Thouſand Pounds Sterling Money of Great Britain.

" ROBERT AUCHMUTY Judge &c."

Hancock

1768.

ADVOCATE GENERAL v. HANCOCK.

Hancock was arreſted on the night of November 2d, and gave the required bail. "Journal of the Times" of November 3, 1768, in Boſton Evening Poſt of January 9, 1769. The Court adjourned from time to time until January 2d, when "a number of witneſſes were examined by the court in a moſt extraordinary and curious manner; Mr. *Hancock's* neareſt relations, and even his tradesmen, were ſummoned as evidences;" and the Court afterwards ſat repeatedly and examined other witneſſes. "Journal of the Times" of December 5 & 14, 1768, January 2, 5, 7, 23, 28, 30, February 11, 18, 21, 1769, in Boſton Evening Poſt of January 30, February 6, 20, 27, March 13, 20, 27, April 10, 17, 1769. Obſervations published by the Merchants of Boſton in 1769, 19, note. The grounds of defence, as ſtated in the notes of *John Adams*, were as follows:

Further proceedings.

Argument of John Adams.

1ſt. That even if Captain *Marſhall* had landed the wines before the duties were paid, (of which there was evidence,) Mr. *Hancock*, if he "neither conſented to this Frolick, nor knew of it," could not be held to be "aſſiſting or otherwiſe concerned in the unſhipping or landing inwards," within St. 4 G. 3, c. 15, § 87, which *Adams* compared with St. 8 Anne, c. 7, § 17.

1. Defendant did not aſſiſt.

2d. That the St. of 4 G. 3 was to be conſtrued with the utmoſt ſtrictneſs; becauſe it was "the moſt pœnal of almoſt any Law in the whole Britiſh Pandect," forfeiting the whole ſhip and cargo for witholding a ſmall amount of duties.

2. St. 4 G. 3 to be conſtrued ſtrictly —

"But among the Groupe of Hardships which attend this Statute, the firſt that ought always to be mentioned, and that ought never to be forgotten is

"That it was made without our Conſent. My Clyent Mr Hancock never conſented to it. He never voted for it himſelf, and he never voted for any Man to make ſuch a Law for him. In this Reſpect therefore the greateſt Conſolation of an Englishman, ſuffering under any Law, is torn from him, I mean the Reflection, that it is a Law of his own Making, a Law that he ſees the Neceſſity of for the Public. Indeed the Conſent of the ſubject to all Laws, is ſo clearly neceſſary that no Man has yet been found hardy enough to deny it. The Patrons of theſe Acts allow that Conſent is neceſſary, they only contend for a Conſent by Conſtruction, by Interpretation, a virtual Conſent. But this is only deluding Men with Shadows inſtead of Subſtances. Conſtruction, has made Treaſon where the law has made none. Conſtructions, in short and arbitrary Diſtinctions, made in short only, for ſo many by Words, ſo many Cries to deceive a Mob have always been the Inſtruments of arbitrary Power, the means of lulling and enſnaring Men into their own Servitude, for whenever we leave Principles and clear poſitive Laws, and wander after Conſtructions, one Conſtruction or Conſequence is piled up upon another untill we get at an immenſe diſtance from Fact and Truth and Nature, loſt in the wild Regions of Imagination and Poſſibility, where arbitrary Power ſitts upon her brazen Throne

Becauſe "made without our conſent."

1769.
ADVOCATE GENERAL v. HANCOCK.

Throne and governs with an iron Scepter. It is an Hardſhip therefore, ſcarcely to be endured that ſuch a penal Statute, ſhould be made to govern a Man and his Property, without his actual Conſent and only upon ſuch a wild Chimæra as a virtual and conſtructive Conſent.

Becauſe no trial by jury.

"But there are greater Proofs of the Severity of this Statute, yet behind. The Legiſlative Authority by which it was made is not only grievous, but the Executive Courts by which it is to be carried into Effect, is another. In the 41st § of this Act 4 G. 3, c. 15, we find that all the forfeitures and Penalties inflicted by this or any other Act of Parliament, relating to the Trade and Revenues of the ſaid British Colonies or Plantations in America, which ſhall be incurred there, ſhall and may be proſecuted, ſued for, and recovered, in any Court of Record, or *in any Court of Admiralty*," &c. "Thus, theſe extraordinary Penalties and Forfeitures are to be heard and try'd, — how? Not by a Jury, not by the Law of the Land, but by the civil Law and a Single Judge. Unlike the ancient Barons who *unâ Voce responderunt, Nolumus Leges Angliæ mutari* — The Barons of modern Times, have anſwered, that they are willing, that the Laws of England should be changed, at leaſt with Regard to all America, in the moſt tender Point, the moſt fundamental Principle. And this Hardſhip is the more ſevere as we ſee in the ſame Page of the Statute and the very preceeding Section, § 40, That all Penalties and Forfeitures, herein before mentioned, which shall be incurred in Great Britain, shall be proſecuted, ſued for and recovered in any of his Majeſty's Courts of Record in Weſtminſter or in the Court of Exchequer in Scotland reſpectively. Here is the Contraſt that ſtares us in the Face! The Parliament in one Clauſe guarding the People of the Realm, and ſecuring to them the benefit of a Tryal by the Law of the Land, and by the next Clauſe, depriving all Americans of that Priviledge. What shall we ſay to this Diſtinction? Is there not in this Clauſe, a Brand of Infamy, of Degradation, and Diſgrace, fixed upon every American? Is he not degraded below the Rank of an Englishman? Is it not directly, a Repeal of Magna Charta, as far as America is concerned. It is not att all ſurpriſing that the Tryals of Forfeitures & Penalties are confined to the Courts of Record at Weſtminſter, in England — The Wonder only is that they are not confined to Courts of common Law here." He then refers to the attachment of Englishmen to c. 29 of Magna Charta; and to Lord *Coke's* commentary thereon in 2 Inſt. 51, as "concluding with a Reflection, which if properly attended to might be ſufficient even to make a Parliament tremble." This paragraph of the argument, ſomewhat expanded, was inſerted by *John Adams* in the inſtructions of the town of Boſton to their repreſentatives in May 1769, 3 John Adams's Works, 508, 509; and abridged in the "Journal of the Times" in the Boſton Evening Poſt of July 10, 1769. See alſo Letter of Houſe of Repreſentatives to Franklin, November 6, 1770, Maſſachuſetts Papers published by the Seventy-Six Society, 174.

3d. Adams

1769.

ADVOCATE GENERAL *v.* HANCOCK.

3d. Adams alſo ſaid: "We are here to be tryed by a Court of civil not of common Law, we are therefore to be tryed by the Rules of Evidence that we find in the civil Law, not by thoſe that we find in the common Law.—We are to be tryed, both Fact and Law is to be tryed by a ſingle Judge, not by a Jury.—We therefore claim it as a Right that Witneſſes not Preſumptions nor Circumſtances are to be the Evidence." And he argued that by the rules of the civil law, in order to convict a perſon of any crime, there muſt be two witneſſes, free from all exception; that "if there were two or ten ſuch Witneſſes as *Mezle*, they would not amount to Proof ſufficient for condemnation;" that the reſpondents had "a right to examine the Witneſſes whole paſt life, and his Character at large;" and to prove by other witneſſes that (as it is ſtated in the "Journal of the Times") "he was a *fugative* from his native country to *avoid the puniſhment* due to a very *heinous crime;*" for which he cited the following authorities: "New Inſt. Civil Law, 315, 316. Dig. Lib. 22, Tit. 5, §§ 3, 12. Codicis, Lib. 4, Tit. 19, § 25; Tit. 20, s. 9, § 1, & note 32. Deut. 19, 15. Calv. Lex Teſtis. Forteſcue de Laudibus Legum, c. 21, p. 38. Wood Inſt. 310. Domat, V. 1, p. 13, Preliminary Book, Tit. 1, § 2, IV. 15."

3. Inſufficiency of the teſtimony.

"On the contrary," *Adams* argued, "if we are to be governed by the Rules of the common Law we ought to adopt it as a whole and ſummon a Jury and be tryed by Magna Charta — Every Examination of Witneſſes ought to be in open Court, in Preſence of the Parties, Face to Face — and there ought to be regular Adjournments from one Time to another. What other Hypotheſis shall we aſſume? Shall we ſay that we are to be governed by ſome Rules of the common Law and ſome Rules of the civil Law, that the Judge at his Diſcretion shall chooſe out of each Syſtem ſuch Rules as pleaſe him, and diſcard the reſt, if ſo, *Miſera ſervitus est.* Examinations of Witneſſes upon Interrogatories, are only by the Civil Law. Interrogatories are unknown at common Law, and Engliſhmen & common Lawyers have an averſion to them if not an abhorrence of them. Shall we ſuffer under the odious Rules of the civil Law, and receive no advantage from the beneficial Rules of it? This, inſtead of favouring the Accuſed, would be favouring the Accuſer, which is againſt the Maxims of both Laws."

This point, which is alſo reported in the "Journal of the Times," was argued on the 24th of February, and decided on the 1ſt of March. Boſton Evening Poſt of April 17 & 24, 1769. It is followed in *Adams's* MS. by this "Interlocutory Decree," entitled "Advocate General *vs.* John Hancock Eſq."

Interlocutory decree.

"The Subſtance of the Point before the Court, is, whether a Witneſs "shall be examined to charge another Witneſs in the Cauſe with a "particular infamous Crime.

"It is urged by the Advocates offering the firſt mentioned Witneſs, "firſt, that this is a civil Law Court, and Secondly, by that Law ſuch "Evidence is admiſſible. To the laſt Point ſeveral authorities were "cited, but the principal one from the Digeſt 22. 3. 2. 3.

"To

1769.
ADVOCATE GENERAL v. HANCOCK.

"To which it was anſwered by the Advocates on the other Side that "this is not a civil Law Court in ſuch Caſes as the preſent. And that "the Authorities produced were not to be underſtood in the Senſe con-"tended for by the Reſpondent's Advocates. In Support of the laſt, "the Notes under the aforeſaid 3 Law in the Digeſt were read and re-"lyed on. It was alſo urged, that admitting the civil Law to be as "contended for, the Argument would prove too much, becauſe it would "exclude relations in certain Degrees, intimate Friends, Perſons under "the age of Fourteen &c. from teſtifying.

"I take the Senſe of the Authority firſt mentioned, to be no more "than a general deſcription of what are good objections againſt perſons "being admitted to their Oaths as Witneſſes without deſcribing the "mode whereby ſuch diſqualifications are to be aſcertained. If ſaid Au-"thority is not ſo conſtrued, it certainly clashes with the notes, which "clearly relate not to the Admiſſion of Witneſs, but the Credit or Rep-"utation of their Evidence. The reaſon why proof by record ought to "be exhibited againſt a Witneſs, when charged with a Crime, appears "clear from the Queſtion put in the Note, under D. 22, Tit. 3. *Quis* "*enim si ſufficiat accuſaſſe, innocens fiet?* Such a reading reconciles the "Text and comment in the Dig: to each other, and the former to "Reaſon. I am therefore of Opinion the motion is not well ſupported, "even by the Rules of the civil Law. In addition to which, when I "conſider the proceſs now in queſtion, is founded on an Act of parlia-"ment, originally intended to be guided by the Rules of the common "Law, that the Practice of the Court has ever been to hear and deter-"mine ſimilar caſes, according to thoſe rules, the manifeſt and great "inconveniences which muſt accrue, by the admiſſion of ſuch evidence, "I am clearly of Opinion, the Queſtion put is improper, and therefore "Decree the ſame to be withdrawn.

"ROBT AUCHMUTY Judge &c."

Adams's comments thereon.

Upon this decree, *Adams* makes the following obſervations, with which his report ends:

"1. The Advocates for the Crown, did not argue that our Argument would exclude Relations, Friends, Perſons under 14, &c—But the Advocates for the Reſpondent, inſiſted that all thoſe Rules of the civil Law ought to be adopted, becauſe they were beneficial to the Subject the Reſpondent.—We had no difficulty at all in admitting the Conſequence as far as it is here mentioned. So far from it that we deſired it, becauſe Mr *Hancock's* Relations, Friends, and many Perſons under Age have been examined in this Caſe.—It is true Mr *Fitch* did argue that our Principle would juſtify the Introduction of Torture, and this he thought was proving too much, and this was well obſerved by Mr *Fitch* and was the beſt argument I have heard in the Caſe.

"2. The Judge has totally miſtaken the 'Senſe' of the Authority, for inſtead of being a Deſcription of Objections againſt Perſons being admitted

admitted to their Oaths it is wholly confined to thoſe who are already Sworn.—It is *Teſtium Fides examinanda eſt*, not *Perſonarum Fides*, and as a Witneſs in Engliſh implies the Competency of the Perſon, ſo *Teſtis* in Latin implies the Same and a Perſon cannot be *Teſtis*, untill he is admitted, to tell what he knows, *i. e.* to give Evidence."

1769.

This ſuit was dropped on the 26th of March. "Journal of the Times," in Boſton Evening Poſt of May 22, 1769. See alſo Obſervations published by the Merchants of Boſton in 1769, 19, note; Almon's Prior Documents, 263, note. The ſtatement in *Adams's* autobiography (2 John Adams's Works, 216) that "this odious cauſe was ſuſpended at laſt only by the battle of Lexington" is manifeſtly an exaggeration. It is not the only inſtance of a miſtake of date in his autobiography. *Vid. ante*, 409.

End of this ſuit.

About the ſame time the grand jury found an indictment for perjury at the trial of this caſe againſt "one *Joſeph Muzzele*" or "*Mayſel*," (evidently the ſame as *Mezle*, *ſupra*, 461,) which could not be immediately tried, "as this fellow, to whom a poſt has been given by the recommendation of the com—ſſi—ners, on board the Sloop Liberty, late Mr. *Hancock's*, now a Guarda-Coſta, is upon a cruiſe in ſaid Sloop." "Journal of the Times" of March 26 & 27, & April 22, in Boſton Evening Poſt of May 22 & June 19, 1769. As this indictment does not appear on the records of the court, it was probably withdrawn by the Crown officers.

Mezle indicted for perjury.

Governor *Bernard's* ſubſequent repreſentations and conduct afford a fair example of his policy. Much feeling having been excited by the manner of ſeizing the *Liberty*, (*ſupra*, 456,) the Governor had the next veſſel ſeized left in a place convenient for the reſcue of the cargo; and, when it was reſcued according to his expectation, and reſtored the next day, pretended that the reſtoration was only made "upon pain of the diſpleaſure of the town." Letters of Bernard, Gage & Hood, 38–41. Vindication of Boſton, 22. He wrote to Lord *Hillſborough* that "every ſeizure made or attempted to be made on Land in Boſton, for three Years paſt, before theſe two Inſtances, has been violently reſcued or prevented;" and immediately afterwards, in his "Obſervations upon the Anſwer of the Council," ſaid, "That there has been no reſcue lately is very True; & the reaſon is that there has been no Seizure;" and was obliged to fall back upon *Malcolm's* caſe of two years before, *ſupra*, 447. Letters of Bernard, Gage & Hood, 39. 12 Bernard Papers, 293. Contraſt with Governor *Bernard's* ſtatements the Reſolves of the Houſe of Repreſentatives of June 29, 1769, Bradford's State Papers, 179; 6 Bancroft's Hiſt. U. S. 272; Richard Frothingham in 9 Atlantic Monthly, 708. The friends of America in the Houſe of Commons ſaw and expreſſed the truth. Colonel *Barré* ſaid: "May not a little mob have been called a tumult, and a little inſurrection a rebellion? In being riotous, the Colonies have mimicked the mother country." 1 Cavendish Debates, 44. And Governor *Pownall* ſaid: "Rebellion

Governor Bernard's miſrepreſentations.

1769.

"Rebellion is not in their hearts; independence is not in their heads." Ib. 220. & *vid.* Ib. 205, 393. Compare this ſaying of Governor *Pownall* with *Hutchinſon's* reflections in 1766 on *Pownall's* hints of the poſſibility of a thought of independence, (*ſupra*, 444,) and *Camden's* prophecy to *Franklin* eight years earlier. Quincy's Life of Quincy, 270.

Rejoicings of crown officers over inſanity of Otis and deaths of Malcolm and others.

It would be hard to find more bitterneſs of party ſpirit than is shown in a letter of December 3, 1769, from *Andrew Oliver*, the Secretary of the Province, to Governor *Bernard* in London, written three months after Commiſſioner *Robinſon's* aſſault upon *James Otis*, and narrating as "curious anecdotes concerning Mr. *Otis*," the following: "Doct. *Gardner* has not ſcrupled declaring to one and another, that upon his applying to him to argue a cauſe, he told him he could not do it, for his Lungs were gone, nor could he ſufficiently collect himſelf, for he had ruined his Country; but that he had acted with a good intention, & ſtretching forth his hand, curſed the day on which he was born. To another perſon from whom I had it he ſaid, He wondered what our parſons meant by thanking God for their exiſtence; for his part he never did nor never would, or never could. He is become the Sport of the young Gentn of the Bar, and he was greatly mortified on looking over the Entries this preſent term of the Supr. Court, to find he had but 4 when the youngeſt *Quincy* had 9 & *John Adams* had 60. It is remarkable that there have been three untimely deaths among thoſe concerned in running the Sloop Libertys Cargo, viz Capn. *Marſhall* the next day, Capn. *Barnard* afterwards drownd at Sea, & Capn. *Malcolm* ſince, who I hear ſaid he catchd his death at that time. Should this other Perſon's Fate prove as is expected, we might be juſtified in looking to the hand of Providence in the diſpoſal of theſe Events." 12 Bernard Papers, 163, 164. In a letter of October 30, 1769, another of the ſame party (ſuppoſed by *Chalmers* to have been *Auchmuty*) expreſſed ſimilar ſentiments: "*Otis* by a kind providence of heaven is generally ſuppoſed to be delirious. It is beyond doubt he has given signal proofs of it in his late conduct." 3 Chalmers New England Papers, 48.

Daniel Malcolm.

Daniel Malcolm was one of the moſt active merchants on the popular ſide, and was proportionably hated and abuſed by the Crown officers. *Supra*, 413, 447–449. Letters of Bernard, Gage & Hood, 18, 50. *Hutchinſon* in 25 Maſs. Archives, 262. Hillſborough to Bernard, July 11, 1768, 11 Bernard Papers, 222. Bernard's Obſervations on the Anſwer of the Council, 12 Bernard Papers, 293, 294. *Ante*, 313. 1 Gordon's Hiſt. U. S. 219, 232, 234. 6 Bancroft's Hiſt. U. S. 139. His epitaph thus expreſſes his character: "A true Son of Liberty, A Friend to the Publick, An Enemy to Oppreſſion, And one of the foremoſt in Oppoſing the Revenue Acts on America." Boſton Evening Poſt, November 20, 1769.

"At the Superiour Court held at Charleſtown, application was made by the Cuſtom-Houſe Officers for a full ſupply of Writs of Aſſiſtance, which

1769.
New Writs of Aſſiſtance iſſued.

which were accordingly granted." "Journal of the Times," under date of April 28, 1769, in Boſton Evening Poſt of June 26, 1769. April term 1769 of the Superior Court of Judicature in Middleſex laſted from the 11th to the 14th of April. Rec. 1769, fol. 41–56. It may be conjectured that theſe writs were in the amended form. *Supra*, 455. But Writs of Aſſiſtance had now become ſo much a matter of courſe, that no notice appears on the record, dockets, or files of court, of this iſſue, except to Collector *Winſlow* and Captain *Reid*, (*ſupra*, 434,) who may have been the only perſons to whom they were now firſt granted. On the 20th of April 1769 the Commiſſioners of the Cuſtoms wrote from Boſton to the Officers of the Cuſtoms of other ports in the Province, ſaying: "Gentlemen, Writs of Aſſiſtants having been iſſued by the Superior Court of this Province for the Officers of your Port, we direct you forthwith to apply for them to the Clerk of that Court, ſo that you may be furniſhed with the ſame, to be uſed as occaſion may require." This letter was ſigned by the whole board. Salem Cuſtom Houſe Record, 279.

1770.
Hutchinſon's opinion on Duty of Sheriff in executing Writs of Aſſiſtance.

Hutchinſon's opinion of the part to be taken by the ſheriff in the execution of a Writ of Aſſiſtance, is shown in his anſwer, dated February 11, 1770, to an inquiry of *William Tyng*, Sheriff of Cumberland County, in which he ſays: "It always appeared to me to be the more immediate buſineſs of the Officers of the Cuſtoms to enter ships &c. and alſo to break open Cellars, Warehouſes & other places, to ſearch for contraband & uncuſtomed goods, but they are required in certain caſes to have a Writ of Assiſtants, which is directed to all Officers and all His Majeſty's ſubjects in general, who are requeſted to permit the Officers of the Cuſtoms to do their duty & to be aiding & assisting. I think every perſon may be juſtified who shall prevent the Officers of the Cuſtoms from being impeded in the diſcharge of their duty, & that it is the eſpecial buſineſs of the Civil Officers to whom the writ is directed to ſee that the Officers of the Cuſtoms are protected & aided & assiſted whenever they shall be obſtructed in the diſcharge of their duty, but in the particular caſe that you refer to I do not ſee that you was obliged to furnish hands to unrigg the Veſſel, but it is to be ſuppoſed there are inferior Officers or Servants of the Cuſtoms to be employed in ſuch Services. Had there been an attempt to reſcue I think you would have done well in requiring aid to prevent &c. Notwithſtanding the remarks you have ſeen in the newſpapers, this Writ of Assiſtants, after a long argument, by the unanimous voice of the Judges of the Superior Court has been determined to be legal and conſtitutional, & by a late Act of Parliament the Court is required to iſſue it, & undoubtedly all who oppoſe the due execution of it muſt be conſidered as offenders." 26 Maſs. Archives, 439. See alſo Comptroller Savage to Hutchinſon, February 20, 1770, 25 Ib. 355–360; 2 Willis's Hiſt. Portland, 132.

The Commiſſioners of the Cuſtoms, in a "general letter" of October 11, 1771, inſtructed their officers: "You are alſo to acquaint us

1771.

Inſtructions by Commiſſioners.

whether you have been furniſhed with Writs of Aſſiſtants by the Superior Court of this Province, agreeably to the form tranſmitted by our Solicitor, and if you have not, you are to aſſign the reaſons why you have not been able to obtain them." Salem Cuſtom Houſe Record, 342. This letter was ſigned by *Hulton*, *Burch*, and *Hallowell*, who was the ſucceſſor of *John Temple*.

Temple's previous conduct

Temple had never had any ſcruples about Writs of Aſſiſtance. *Supra*, 416 & *seq.*, 429, note, 437, 450, 464. But he did not agree with the Commiſſioners in other meaſures, and did not ſhare their unpopularity. Boſton Gazette, February 6, 1769. Letters of Bernard, Gage & Hood, 107. Bernard to Barrington, February 20, 1769, 7 Bernard Papers, 260. Hutchinſon in December, 1769, 26 Maſs. Archives, 417. Proceedings of Town Meeting of October 4, 1769, 3 Chalmers's New England Papers, 37. 1 Gordon's Hiſt. U. S. 236. 3 Hutchinſon's Hiſt. Maſs. 193, 194. 6 Bancroft's Hiſt. U. S. 249. *Adams* and *Hutchinson* both teſtify to *Temple's* intimacy with *Otis*. 7 John Adams's Works, 457. 3 Hutchinſon's Hiſt. Maſs. 293. It is therefore not improbable that Governor Bernard's diſtruſt of him was not wholly unfounded. *Vid. supra*, 423, 438; Bernard to Hillſborough, February 21, and to John Pownall, June 12, 1769, 7 Bernard Papers, 141, 297. He was appointed in 1771 Surveyor General of the Cuſtoms in England; was removed in 1774 for his attachment to the American cauſe; returned to America in 1781; and, after the Revolutionary War, was appointed Conſul General of Great Britain in the United States. *Supra*, 434, note 20. R. C. Winthrop's Addreſses, 112–115. John Adams to Preſident of Congreſs, Auguſt 16, 1781, 7 John Adams's Works, 457. Adams to Jay, April 13, 1785, 8 Ib. 234.

and ſubſequent hiſtory.

1772.

Committee of Boſton on Rights of Coloniſts.

At a meeting of the inhabitants of Boſton in Faneuil Hall on the 2d of November 1772, a committee of twenty-one was appointed "to ſtate the Rights of the Coloniſts, and of this Province in particular, as Men, as Chriſtians, and as Subjects; to Communicate and Publiſh the ſame to the ſeveral Towns in this Province, and to the World, as the Senſe of this Town, with the Infringements and Violations thereof that have been, or from Time to Time may be made." The three firſt named on this Committee were *James Otis*, *Samuel Adams*, and *Joſeph Warren*. *Joſiah Quincy* was alſo a member. The report of this committee, which was accepted on the 20th of November, is ſaid to have been written by *Adams* and *Warren*. Its formal preſentation was the laſt public act of *Otis*. 6 Bancroft's Hiſt. U. S. 431. One article in its "Liſt of Infringements and Violations of Rights" is ſo curiouſly like *Otis's* argument upon the Writs of Aſſiſtance in 1761, which had been the beginning of his public career, that with it this ſketch of the hiſtory of thoſe Writs in Maſſachuſetts Bay, already too much extended, may fitly cloſe.

Their Report.

"Theſe Officers are by their Commiſſions inveſted with Powers altogether unconſtitutional, and entirely deſtructive to that Security which we we have a right to enjoy; and to the laſt degree dangerous, not only to our property, but to our lives: For the Commiſſioners of his Majeſty's Customs in America, or any three of them, are by their Commiſſions impowered, 'by writing under their hands and ſeals to conſtitute and appoint inferior Officers in all and ſingular the Port within the Limits of their Commiſſions.' Each of theſe petty officers ſo made is intruſted with Power more abſolute and arbitrary than ought to be lodged in the hands of any Man or Body of Men whatſoever; for in the Commiſſion aforementioned, his Majeſty gives and grants unto his ſaid Commiſſioners, or any three of them, 'and to all and every the Collectors, Deputy Collectors, Miniſters, Servants, and all other Officers ſerving & attending in all and every the Ports & other Places within the Limits of their Commiſſion, full Power and Authority from time to time, at their or any of their Wills and Pleaſures, as well by Night as by Day, to enter and go on board any Ship, Boat, or other Veſſel, riding, lying, or being within, or coming into, any Port, Harbour, Creek or Haven, within the limits of their Commission; and alſo in the day-time to go into any Houſe, Shop, Cellar, or any other Place, where any Goods, Wares or Merchandises lie concealed, or are *ſuſpected* to lie concealed, whereof the cuſtoms and other duties, have not been, or shall not be, duly paid and truly ſatisfied, anſwered or paid unto the Collectors, Deputy-Collectors, Miniſters, Servants, and other officers reſpectively, or otherwiſe agreed for; and the ſaid Houſe, Shop, Warehouſe, Cellar, and other Place to ſearch and ſurvey, and all and every the Boxes, Trunks, Cheſts and Packs then and there found to break open.' 1772.

"Thus our Houſes, and even our Bed-Chambers, are expoſed to be ranſacked, our Boxes, Trunks and Cheſts broke open, ravaged and plundered, by Wretches, whom no prudent Man would venture to employ even as Menial Servants; whenever they are pleaſed to ſay they *ſuſpect* there are in the Houſe, Wares, &c. for which the Duties have not been paid. Flagrant inſtances of the wanton exerciſe of this Power, have frequently happened in this and other ſeaport Towns. By this we are cut off from that domeſtic ſecurity which renders the Lives of the moſt unhappy in ſome meaſure agreeable. Theſe Officers may under color of Law and the cloak of a general warrant, break through the ſacred Rights of the *Domicil*, ranſack Mens Houſes, destroy their Securities, carry off their Property, and with little Danger to themſelves commit the most horrid Murders." Report of the Committee, as published by Order of the Town, 15–17. Compare Junius Americanus in Boſton Gazette of December 24, 1770, & January 28, 1771.

1774. Boſton Port Bill.

Nothing later than this, tending to illuſtrate the matter of Writs of Aſſiſtance, has come to the notice of the writer. The port of Boſton was cloſed by the Boſton Port Bill on the 1st of June, 1774. St. 13 G. 3, *c*. 45. 34 Maſs. Hiſt. Coll. 1.

1775. Change of Government.

On the 28th of July 1775 the Council, elected according to the Province Charter, with the conſent of the Houſe of Repreſentatives aſſumed the

1775.

New Seal of the Colony —

the government, upon the ground that the Governor and Lieutenant Governor "have abſented themſelves, and have refuſed to govern the Province according to ſaid Charter." Journal H. R. 1775, p. 21.

On the ſame day a committee was appointed, of which *James Otis* (of Barnſtable) was chairman on the part of the Council, and *Joſeph Hawley* on the part of the Houſe, "to conſider what is neceſſary to be done relative to a Colony Seal;" and on the 5th of Auguſt was directed "to ſit forthwith," and reported that the Old Province Seal (which bore the Royal Arms) "be not taken up," but that "the eſtabliſhed form of a Seal for this Colony, for the future," ſhould be an Indian holding a Tomahawk and Cap of Liberty, with the motto *Petit ſub libertate quietem*. The idea of the Indian was doubtleſs derived from the ruder figure on the firſt Seals of the Colony, brought over by Endicott in 1629 and Winthrop in 1630. 1 Maſs. Col. Rec. tit. & pp. 24, 55, 59, 73, 392, 396. The Council accepted the report of the committee, ſubſtituting however for the Indian "an Engliſh American, holding a ſword in the Right Hand, and Magna Charta in the Left Hand, with the words '*Magna Charta*' imprinted on it." The Houſe of Repreſentatives concurred, with this ſignificant amendment, that "in the Device previous to the Word '*Petit*,' be inſerted the Word '*Enſe*,' and ſubſequent to it, the Word '*Placidam*.'" 137 Maſs. Archives, 14. 86 Ib. 340, 364. Journal H. R. 1775, pp. 20, 46, 47, 48. The ſame image and motto, and the words "Iſſued in Defence of American Liberty," were ſtamped on the bills of credit iſſued by the Colony until ſome time after the Declaration of Independence, when the letters "IND" took the place of "Magna Charta." Sts. of 1775, cc. 2, 9; 1776, cc. 11, 16, 26; Acts & Laws of the Colony of Maſſachuſetts Bay 1775–1776, pp. 2, 71, 72, 75, 84, 99. Journal H. R. September 1776, p. 109.

"Engliſh American" with Magna Charta — *Enſe* petit placidam ſub libertate quietem —

1776.

Independence.

1780.

Conſtitution. Image on ſeal changed, retaining ſuperſcription.

Maſſachuſetts, in 1780, after framing a Conſtitution of her own, (the Declaration of Rights prefixed to which repeated the chief articles of Magna Charta, and condemned general warrants,) replaced the image on the ſeal by her ancient emblem, in a more heraldic form, and eſtabliſhed the following as the Seal and Arms of the Commonwealth: "*Sapphire*, an Indian dreſſed in his Shirt, Moggoſins, belted, proper, in his right Hand a Bow *Topaz*, in his left an Arrow, its point towards the Baſe; of the ſecond, on the Dexter ſide of the Indian's head, a Star, *Pearl*, for one of the United States of America. Crest — On a Wreath a Dexter Arm cloathed & ruffled proper, graſping a Broad Sword, the Pummel & Hilt *Topaz*, with this Motto, *Enſe petit placidam ſub libertate quietem*." Council Rec. December 13, 1780, fol. 49. Theſe Arms, aſſumed in the midſt of the Revolutionary War, years before the adoption of the Federal Conſtitution, are ſtill unchanged. And the motto, eſtabliſhed by the firſt legiſlature of the Revolution, recognizing that the quiet of liberty is to be ſought, if need be, by the ſword, remains the device, and governs the action, of Maſſachuſetts to-day.

D. John Adams's Report of the Firſt Argument in February 1761. (1)

GRIDLEY. — The Conſtables diſtraining for Rates. more inconſiſtent with Eng. Rts. & liberties than Writts of affiſtance. And Neceſſity, authorizes both. Gridley.

Thatcher. I have ſearched, in all the ancient Repertories, of Precedents, in Fitzherberts Natura Brevium, and in the Regiſter (Q. w[t] y[e] Reg. is) and have found no ſuch Writt of affiſtance as this Petition prays. — I have found two Writts of aſs. in the Reg. but they are very difft, from y[e] Writt prayd for. — (2) Thacher.

In

(1) This report, which has been once published in 2 John Adams's Works, 521–523, is by the courteous permission of Mr. *Charles Francis Adams* here reprinted as exactly as possible, with the original paragraphs, ſpelling, and punctuation, from the MS. notes of *John Adams*, who was preſent at the argument, though he was not admitted as a barriſter until the 14th of November following. 2 John Adams's Works, 124 & note, 133. 10 Ib. 245. Rec. 1761, fol. 239. The only other contemporaneous report is an enlargement of this. *Vid. infra*, 477, note 39.

The elaborate narrative given more than half a century afterwards by *Adams* to *Tudor*, who printed an abſtract of it as the argument of *Otis* in this caſe, is rather a recollection of the ſentiments of the coloniſts between 1761 and 1766. 10 John Adams's Works, 232–362, & note. Tudor's Life of Otis, 68–86. 4 Bancroft's Hiſt. U. S. 417, note. *Ante*, 409, 417. It would ſeem to have been written by *Adams* without even referring to his own notes; for it ſubſtitutes Raſtall's Entries for Regiſtrum Brevium; and aſſerts that no precedent could be found of a writ of aſſiſtance to a cuſtom houſe officer — in direct oppoſition to all the counſel in the caſe, as reported by himſelf in the text. 10 John Adams's Works, 322, 342. He ſeems alſo to attribute to *Otis* his own argument ſeven years later in the caſe of *The Liberty*, *ante*, 460, 461. 10 John Adams's Works, 348, 349.

(2) Reg. Brev. app. 46, 47; *ante*, 396 & note 4.

1761. In a Book, intituled the Modern Practice of the Court of Exchequer there is indeed one ſuch Writt, and but one. (3)

By y[e] Act of Pal[t] any other private Perſon, may as well as a Cuſtom Houſe Officer, take an officer, a Sheriff, or Conſtable, &c and go into any Shop, Store &c & ſeize: any Perſon authorized by ſuch a Writt, under the Seal of the Court of Exchequer, may, not Cuſtom Houſe Officers only. — Strange. (4) — Only a temporary thing.

The moſt material Queſtion is, whether the Practice of the Exchequer, will warrant this Court in granting the ſame.

The Act impowers all the officers of y[e] Revenue to enter and ſeiſe in the Plantations, as well as in England. 7. & 8 W[m] 3, C. 22, § 6, gives the ſame as 13. & 14. of C. gives in England. (5) The Ground of M[r] Gridleys arg[t] is this, that this Court has the Power of the Court of Exchequer. — But This Court has renounced the Chancery Juriſdiction, w[h] the Exchequer has in Caſes where either Party, is y[e] Kings Debtor. (6) — Q. into y[t] Caſe. (7) In

---

(3) Copied in full *ante*, 398, note 10, *qu. vid.*

(4) Probably *Horne* v. *Boosey*, 2 Stra. 952, in which, notwithſtanding a condemnation of goods in the Exchequer, trover was maintained against "one not the proper officer" for ſeizing them, on the ground of his "being a tideſman, who could not enter a houſe without a writ of aſſiſtance and a peace officer, the words of his warrant being ſo reſtrained."

(5) *Vid.* Sts. 13 & 14 Car. 2, c. 11, § 5; 7 & 8 W. 3, *c.* 22, § 6; quoted in full by *Gridley arguendo*, *infra*, 480, 481.

(6) 3 Bl. Com. 45. That juriſdiction was transferred to the High Court of Chancery by St. 5 Vict. c. 5.

(7) That caſe was again cited by *Thacher* at the argument in November 1761, as "the Caſe of McNeal of Ireland & McNeal of Boſton," *ante*, 53. The only trace of it to be found in the clerk's office is the following entry on the records of February term, 1754, in Suffolk, which was held by *Sewall*, C. J., *Saltonstall*, *Lynde*, *Cushing* & *Oliver*, JJ.

"McNeal *v.* Brideoak." "Ann McNeal Widow and Mary McNeal Spinſter both of the "City of Dublin in the Kingdom of Ireland Debtors and Accountants "to his Majeſty Compl[ts] againſt Sarah Brideoak of Boſton in the "County

In Eng. all Informations of uncufted (8) or prohibited Importations, are in y[e] Exchequer. — So y[t] y[e] Cuftom Houfe officers are the officers of y[t] Court. — under the Eye, and Direction of the Barons. 1761.

The Writ of Affiftance is not returnable. — If fuch feifure were brot before your Honours, youd often find a wanton Exercife of their Power.

At home, y[e] officers, feife at their Peril, even with Probable Caufe. — (9)

Otis. This Writ is againft the fundamental Principles of Law. — The Priviledge of Houfe. A Man, who is quiet, is as fecure in his Houfe, as a Prince in his Caftle — notwithftanding all his Debts, & civil proceffes of any Kind. — But Otis.

For flagrant Crimes, and in Cafes of great public Neceffity, the Priviledge may be incrohd (10) on. — For Felonies an officer may break, upon Profcefs, and oath. — i. e. by a Special Warrant to fearch fuch an Houfe, ~~fufp~~ fworn to be fufpected, and good Grounds of fufpicion appearing.

Make oath cor[m] Ld. Trea[er], or Exchequer, in Eng[d] or a Magiftrate

---

" County of Suffolk in faid Province Spinfter commonly called Sarah " McNeal of faid Bofton Widow Defendant on a Bill in Equity filed " in Court Decem[r] the 20th 1752 (and on file). This Bill hath been " continued from the Term of this Court for this County held at faid " Boston in November A D 1752 by Adjourn[t] from the third Tuefday " of Auguft preceeding by Confent of both Partys unto this Court & " now both Partys appear'd & the faid Bill is Difmist and the faid " Sarah Brideoak is allowed her Cofts Taxed at £ . Rec. 1754. Fol. 150.

" The compl[ts] moved that they might be allowed an appeal to y[e] " King in Council : Allow'd."

(8) Uncuftomed. Compare enlarged report, *infra*, 482.

(9) S. P. *Shipley* v. *Redmain*, before Lord *Camden*, cited in 4 Doug. 347. *Per* Lord *Mansfield*, *Cooper* v. *Boot*, 4 Doug. 348, & 3 Esp. R. 145.

(10) This looks in the MS. like an indiftinct abridgment of " incroached."

1761. Magiſtrate here, and get a Special Warrant, for ye public good, to infringe the Priviledge of Houſe. (11)

Genl. Warrant to ſearch for Felonies. Hawk. Pleas Crown. (12) — every petty officer from the higheſt to ye loweſt, and if ſome of 'em are ~~com̄, others~~ uncom̄ others are uncomm̄. (13) Gouv^{t} Juſtices uſed to iſſue ſuch perpetual Edicts. (Q. with w^{t} particular Reference ?) (14)

But one Precedent, and y^{t} in ye Reign of C. 2 when Star Chamber Powers, and all Powers but lawful & uſeful Powers were puſhed to Extremity. — (15)

The authority of this Modern Practice of the Court of Exchequer. — it has an Imprimatur. (16) — But w^{t} may not

---

(11) *Vid.* St. 12 Car. 2, c. 19, quoted *ante*, 397, note 5.

(12) 2 Hawk. c. 13, § 10 — that such a warrant is illegal.

(13) The MS. is very obſcure here; but this ſeems to be the true reading, and to indicate that Adams, heſitating whether to put "commiſſioned" or "uncommiſſioned" firſt, accidentally repeated the latter. This interpretation makes the paſſage accord with the argument urged by *Thacher*, *supra*, 469, by *Otis*, *infra*, 475, and in the Boſton Gazette of February 4, 1762, *post*, F. — that by the words of St. 13 & 14 Car. 2, "any perſon" might execute the writ.

(14) Probably Dalton's Juſtice, 401, 402. See 3 Hutchinson's Hiſt. Maſs. 93; 2 Minot's Hiſt. Maſs. 94; 2 John Adams's Works, 524. *Otis* admitted that ſpecial Writs of Aſſiſtance, to ſearch ſpecified places, might be granted upon information on oath. Ib.

(15) The one precedent of iſſuing general warrants in the time of Charles 2 was by Chief Juſtice *Scroggs*, for which he was afterwards impeached by the Houſe of Commons. Vid. 8 Howell's State Trials, 192, 193, 200; 19 Ib. 1071, 1072. In the extended ſketch of *Otis's* argument, the positions taken in this and the following paragraph are confuſed thus: "Not more than one inſtance can be found of it in all our law-books; and that was in the zenith of arbitrary power, viz. in the reign of Charles 2, when Star-Chamber powers were pushed to extremity by ſome ignorant clerk of the Exchequer." 2 Minot's Hiſt. Maſs. 98. 2 John Adams's Works, 525. It is hard to underſtand how ſuch extraordinary powers could be wielded by a clerk of the Exchequer; and the book of that ignorant clerk was not published until the laſt year of the reign of James 2; yet it is poſſible that it was the precedent therein to which *Otis* referred. *Vid. ante*, 398, notes 7, 8.

(16) Vid. *infra*, 476, & note 35.

not have? — It may be owing to ſome ignorant Clerk of ye Exchequer. 1761.

But all Precedents and this am'g ye Reſt are under ye Control of ye Principles of Law. Ld. Talbot. better to obſerve the known Principles of Law y^n^ any one Precedent, tho in the Houſe of Lords. — (17)

As

---

(17) The caſe here referred to is evidently *Clare* v. *Clare*, where Lord *Talbot* diſregarded the decisions of Lord *Cowper* in *Higgins* v. *Dowler*, 2 Vern. 600, and Sir *Joſeph Jekyll* in *Stanley* v. *Leigh*, (ſince reported in 2 P. W. 686,) ſaying, "I think it much better to ſtick to the known general rules, than to follow any one particular precedent which may be founded on reaſons unknown to us;" and, after citing a deciſion of the Houſe of Lords in favor of his own concluſion, added, "Even had it not been in the Houſe of Lords, I ſhould have thought myſelf bound to go according to the general and known rules of law." Cas. temp. Talb. 26, 27. But the authority of the two caſes doubted by Lord *Talbot* has been ſince fully eſtabliſhed. Williams's note, Ib. 27. Cox's note to *Higgins* v. *Dowler*, 1 P. W. 98.

It is ſtill a vexed queſtion in England whether the Houſe of Lords can overrule or diſregard a previous deciſion of its own in another caſe; but it is well ſettled that a final deciſion of the Houſe of Lords is concluſive in the caſe in which it is made, and cannot be recalled or ſet aſide, even at the ſame term, except for fraud, or by a ſpecial Act of Parliament. *Bright* v. *Hutton*, 3 H. L. Cas. 388, 392. *Tommey* v. *White*, 3 Ib. 69–71, & 4 Ib. 334. *Wilſon* v. *Wilſon*, 5 Ib. 58, 63, 71. *Thelluſſon* v. *Rendleſham*, 7 Ib. 529, 530. *Attorney General* v. *Dean & Canons of Windſor*, 8 Ib. 381, 391–393, 459.

In the United States, the line between the legiſlative and judicial departments is better defined. The Supreme Court of the United States does not hold itſelf bound by its own erroneous deciſion in another caſe. *Geneſee Chief* v. *Fitzhugh*, 12 How. 456. *Louiſville, Cincinnati & Charleſton Railroad* v. *Letſon*, 2 Ib. 555. *Ohio & Miſſiſſippi Railroad* v. *Wheeler*, 1 Black, 296. And a rehearing may be granted at the ſame term at which judgment has been entered. *United States* v. *Knight*, Ib. 490. In ſome of the Colonies the legiſlature habitually exerciſed the power of granting reviews and new trials. St. 1642, Maſs. Col. Laws (ed. 1672) 152; Anc. Chart. 199. *Draper* v. *Bicknell*, *ante*, 166, note. Governor Hutchinſon's Speech to the General Court, April 8, 1772, Bradford's State Papers, 314. *Calder* v. *Bull*, 3 Dall. 392, 393, 395, 398. And this practice was continued in Maſſachuſetts and ſome of the other States even after the adoption of written Conſtitutions, eſtabliſhing diſtinct departments of government. But it is now well ſettled that the legiſlature cannot

ſet

1761. As to Aćts of Parliament. an Aćt againſt the Conſtitution is void: an Aćt againſt natural Equity is void: and if an Aćt of Parliament ſhould be made, in the very Words of this Petition, (18) it would be void. The Executive Courts (19) muſt paſs ſuch Aćts into diſuſe — 8. Rep. 118. from Viner. (20) — Reaſon of ye Com̄ Law to control an Aćt of Parliament. — Iron Manufaćture. noble Lord's Propoſal, y^t we ſhould ſend our Horſes to Eng. to be ſhod. — (21)

If an officer will juſtify under a Writ he muſt return it. 12th Mod. 396. — perpetual Writ. (22)

Stat.

ſet aſide a judgment or grant a new trial in a particular caſe. *Holden* v. *James*, 11 Maſs. 396. *Denny* v. *Mattoon*, 2 Allen, 379. *Lewis* v. *Webb*, 3 Greenl. 326. *Durham* v. *Lewiſton*, 4 Greenl. 140. *Merrill* v. *Sherburne*, 1 N. H. 199. *Taylor* v. *Place*, 4 R. I. 339. *People* v. *Superviſors of New York*, 16 N. Y. 432. *De Chaſtellux* v. *Fairchild*, 15 Penn. State R. 18.

(18) It would ſeem from this expreſſion, as well as from the enlarged report of *Gridley's* argument, *infra*, 478, that *Adams* ſuppoſed a written petition to have been filed in this caſe. But it is more probable that the counſel referred to the form of petition which had been previouſly uſed; for there does not appear to have been any application in writing for the writ at this time, except the memorial of the Surveyor General in behalf of himſelf and all his officers. *Ante*, 413, 418, & note.

(19) The term "executive courts" was commonly applied to Courts of Juſtice, as diſtinguiſhed from the Legiſlature or "General Court." *Ante*, 200, 245, 280, 307. Quincy's Life of Quincy, 68. 2 John Adams's Works, 135, 155, 194, 234, 235. 3 Ib. 481. 3 Hutchinſon's Hiſt. Maſs. 505. 1 Doug. Hist. N. A. 517, 520.

(20) *Bonham's caſe*, 8 Rep. 118. Vin. Ab. Statute, E. 6, pl. 15. *Vid. poſt*, I.

(21) Perhaps in the debate in 1750 on St. 23 G. 3, c. 29, which prohibited the erećtion or maintenance in the Colonies of any rolling or ſlitting mill, plating forge, or furnace for making ſteel. See 1 Minot's Hiſt. Maſs. 170. *John Adams*, in a letter to Tudor of Auguſt 21, 1818, makes *Otis*, in 1761, quote, with this, the ſimilar remark "that a hobnail ſhould not be manufaćtured in America" — which was in faćt a threat of *Chatham's* in 1766, in caſe the Americans should deny the power of Parliament over their trade. 10 John Adams's Works, 350. 4 Bancroft's Hiſt. U. S. 417, note. 5 Ib. 387.

(22) "He, that has not shewed to the Court that he hath done his duty in what the proceſs of the Court required him, shall not be juſtified

Stat. C. 2. We have all as good Rt to inform as Cuſtom Houſe officers (23) — & every Man may have a general, irreturnable ~~Writ~~ Commiſſion to break Houſes. — 1761.

By 12. of C. on oath before Ld Treaſurer, Barons of Exchequer, or Chief Magiſtrate to break with an officer. (24) — 14th C. to iſſue a Warrant requiring ſheriffs &c to aſſiſt the officers to ſearch for Goods not entrd, or prohibitd.(25); 7 & 8th W. & M. gives Officers in Plantations ſame Powers with officers in England. — (26)

Continuance of Writts and Proſceſſes, (27) proves no more nor ſo much as I grant a ſpecial Writ of aſſ. on ſpecial oath, for ſpecl Purpoſe. —

Pew indorſd Warrant to Ware. — (28) Juſtice Walley

---

fied by the proceſs." *Freeman* v. *Bluet*, 12 Mod. 396. In that caſe, the precept directed the officer to return it. *Otis* argued that the Writ of Aſſiſtance, not being returnable, was perpetual. 2 Minot's Hiſt. Maſs. 95. 2 John Adams's Works, 524.

(23) Compare *ſupra*, 469, 472, & note 13.

(24) St. 12 Car. 2, c. 19.

(25) St. 13 & 14 Car. 2, c. 11, § 5.

(26) St. 7 & 8 W. & M. c. 22, § 6.

(27) By St. 1 Anne, St. 1, c. 8, § 5, relied on by *Gridley*, *infra*, 481.

(28) In the fuller report of Otis's ſpeech this illuſtration is thus introduced: "This wanton exerciſe of this power is not a chimerical ſuggeſtion of a heated brain. I will mention ſome facts. Mr. Pew had one of theſe writs, and when Mr. Ware ſucceeded him, he endorſed the writ over to Mr. Ware: ſo that theſe Writs are negotiable from one officer to another; and ſo your Honours have no opportunity of judging the perſons to whom this vaſt power is delegated." 2 Minot's Hiſt. Maſs. 96, 97. 2 John Adams's Works, 524, 525.

In April 1860, the ſergeant-at-arms of the United States Senate indorſed over to another perſon a precept, addreſſed to himſelf by name, to arreſt a witneſs who had refuſed to appear before a committee of the Senate; and the witneſs was arreſted by the deputy, but diſcharged by Chief Juſtice *Shaw*, with the concurrence of the other judges of the Supreme Judicial Court of Maſſachuſetts, upon the ground that the deputation was invalid. *Sanborn* v. *Carlton*, 15 Gray. In June 1860, the Committee on the Judiciary of the Senate, through Mr. *Bayard* of Delaware, their Chairman, made a report on this ſubject, controverting this deciſion, and accompanied by a bill expreſſly conferring on the ſergeants-at-arms of the Senate and Houſe of Repreſentatives

1761. ley ſearc'd Houſe. (29) Law Prov. (30) Bill in Chancery. — this Court confined their Chancery Power to Revenue &c. (31)

Gridley. By the 7. & 8 of Wm. C. 22. § 6th. — This authority, of breaking and entering Ships, Warehouſes Cellars &c given to the Cuſtom Houſe officers in England by the Statutes of the 12th. and 14th of Charl. 2d, is extended to the Cuſtom Houſe officers in ye Plantations: (32) — and by the Statute of the 6th of Anne, (33) ~~this~~ Writts of Aſſiſtance are continued, in Company with all other legal Proſceſſes for 6 months after the Demiſe of the Crown. — Now what this Writ of aſſiſtance is, we can know only by Books of Precedents. — And we have produced, in a Book intituld the modern Practice of the Court of Exchequer, a form of ſuch a Writ of aſſiſtance to the officers of the Cuſtoms. (34) The Book has the Imprimatur of Wright C. J. of

---

atives the power to ſerve or execute by deputy the mandates, precepts, and warrants of their reſpective houſes. But Congreſs did not paſs the bill.

(29) "Another inſtance is this: Mr. Juſtice Walley had called this ſame Mr Ware before him by a conſtable to anſwer for a breach of Sabbath-day acts, or that of profane ſwearing. As ſoon as he had finished, Mr. Ware aſked him if he had done. He replied, Yes. Well then, ſaid Mr. Ware, I will shew you a little of my power. I command you to permit me to ſearch your houſe for uncuſtomed goods; and went on to ſearch his houſe from the garret to the cellar; and then ſerved the conſtable in the ſame manner." Otis's argument, as reported in 2 Minot's Hiſt. Maſs. 97, and 2 John Adams's Works, 525.

(30) Probably Prov. St. 11 W. 3, defining the juriſdiction of the Court, quoted by *Gridley*, *infra*, 479.

(31) *Vid ſupra*, 470, & notes 6 & 7.

(32) For theſe ſtatutes, *vid. ante*, 397, note 5; *infra*, 479, 480.

(33) St. 1 Anne, St. 1, c. 8, § 5, the context of which however is quite as conſiſtent with the ſuppoſition that only the ordinary writs of aſſiſtance, iſſuing out of chancery, were intended — "That no commiſſion of aſſociation, writ of admittance, or *ſi non omnes*, original writ, writ of *niſi prius*, writ of aſſiſtance, nor any commiſſion, proceſs, or proceedings whatſoever, in or iſſuing out of any Court of equity," &c. &c. should be determined by the demiſe of the King.

(34) Printed *ante*, 398, note 10.

of the K.'s B. (35) w[h] is as great a sanction as any Books of Precedents ever have. altho Books of Reports are usually approved by all the Judges (36) — and I take Brown the author of this Book to have been a very good Collector of Precedents. — I have two Volumes of Precedents of his Collection, (37) w[h] I look upon as good as any, except Coke & Rastal. 1761.

And the Power given in this Writ is no greater Infringement of our Liberty than the Method of collecting Taxes in this Province. — (38)

Every Body knows that the Subject has the Priviledge of House only against his fellow Subjects, not vs y[e] K. either in matters of Crime or fine. (39)

---

(35) The value of the Imprimatur of *Wright, C. J.* may be judged from these facts: "He was so poor a lawyer, that he could not give an opinion on a written case, but used to bring such cases, as came to him, to his friend Mr. *North*, and he wrote the opinion on a paper, and the lawyer copied it, and signed under the case as if it had been his own." 2 North's Lives, (ed. 1826) 94. At the instance of Chief Justice *Jeffreys*, he was appointed by *James* 2 a Baron of the Exchequer, notwithstanding the remonstrances of Lord Keeper *Guilford* that he was "the most unfit person in England to be made a judge," "a dunce, and no lawyer," and "of no truth nor honesty." Ib. 96, 97. By the same influence he was afterwards successively advanced to be a Judge of the King's Bench, Chief Justice of the Common Pleas, and Chief Justice of England; and signalized the last appointment by ordering a capital execution to take place, according to the King's will, in a different county from the conviction, which Chief Justice Herbert, who was removed to make way for him, and another Judge who "had his *quietus* the night before," had just decided could not be done. 3 Mod. 71, 124, 125. For Lord *Camden's* opinion of him, see 19 Howell's State Trials, 989, 990, 991, 993. Character of Chief Justice Wright.

(36) See Wallace's Reporters, (3d ed.) 34, & note.

(37) Probably W. Brown's "*Praxis Almœ Curiœ Cancellariœ*," 2 vols., London, 1704.

(38) Prov. Sts. 4 & 10 G. 2, Anc. Chart. 471, 512.

(39) These notes, the handwriting of which exhibits the haste with which they were made, are followed by more distinctly written "extracts from the Acts of Parl[t]" and "Prov. Law, Page 114" — being the same provisions which are incorporated into the extended sketch of *Gridley's*

1761.

Extended report from Keith MS.

Gridley's argument, *infra*, 479, 480; and by the forms of petition and writ printed *ante*, 402 & note, 404.

A more extended ſketch of this argument is contained in a manuſcript book entitled on the fly leaf "Iſrael Keith's Pleadings, Arguments, Extracts, &c.," in the poſſeſſion of *John G. Newell*, Eſqr., of Pittsford in the State of Vermont, who has kindly furniſhed the writer with the following information: "From what I can learn, *Iſrael Keith* was born in Boston; educated at Cambridge, Maſs.; was for a short time in the practice of the law in Boſton; and in 1798 or near that time he moved to this place, where he lived and. died. He was 67 years of age. He died 5th June 1819, as appears from the record upon his monument. Col. *Keith* was a gentleman of the old ſchool; while living, ſuſtained the reputation of ſtrict integrity and correct morals. It was ſaid of him, that becauſe he could not be at the head of his profeſſion, he gave up the practice of the law, and left for the wilderneſs of Vermont. At one time he was aid to General *Waſhington* during the American Revolution. I have underſtood that while he was ſtudying his profeſſion, he took the notes of Mr. *Otis's* ſpeech. It is in Col. *Keith's* handwriting, and the manuſcript has been in my poſſeſſion ſince 1825, and before that time it was in poſſeſſion of his widow, Mrs. *Caroline Keith*. She died 23d May 1834, and was buried in this town." It may be added that *Iſrael Keith* appears in the Harvard College Catalogue among the graduates of 1771, and was admitted to practice as an attorney of the Superior Court of Judicature at March term 1780 in Suffolk, (Rec. 1780, fol. 155,) and is mentioned as an attorney of the Supreme Judicial Court in the Boſton Regiſters from that time until 1791, but not afterwards.

The book itſelf contains ſufficient evidence that Mr. *Keith* was a careful ſtudent of law, and had acceſs to ſome of *John Adams's* materials. Besides other curious caſes, opinions and extracts, it contains Governor *Pownall's* meſſage on Courts of Probate (*poſt*, Appendix, III.); the caſe of *Glover* v. *Le Teſtue*, decided in 1770, (printed *ante*, 225, note, from *Adams's* original notes); "Lord C. J. *Hale's* advice for the ſtudy of the Common Law" (being one long paragraph out of his preface to Rolle's Abridgment, reprinted 1 Collect. Jurid. 276, 277); "Lord C. J. *Reeve's* Advice to his nephew on the ſtudy of the Law" (ſince published by Mr. Hargrave from a leſs perfect copy in 1 Collect. Jurid. 79); a letter from Dr. *Dickins*, Regius Profeſſor of Law at Cambridge, to Mr. *Gridley* on the books neceſſary to a knowledge of the Civil Law; and a letter from Mr. *Gridley* to Judge *Lightfoot* of the Admiralty Court in Rhode Iſland on the ſtudy of the Admiralty Law. The four laſt were recommended in 1758 by *Gridley* to *Adams*, when a ſtudent at law. 2 John Adams's Works, 46.

Mr. *Keith's* cannot be an original report of the argument upon the Writs of Aſſiſtance; for he was only nine years old at the time of that argument. And the miſtakes of "2 W. 3" for "11 W. 3," and "Chance

" Chance of Juriſdiction " for " Chancery Juriſdiction " (*infra*, 480, 481,) are not thoſe of one who had heard the argument, though eaſily made in copying.

But there are many reaſons for preſuming that it is a copy of a ſketch made by *John Adams*, from which the ſpeech of Otis, printed in 2 Minot's Hiſt. Maſs. 91–99, and, with ſome variations, in 2 John Adams's Works, 523–525, formed a part. *Otis's* argument is given, almoſt word for word, as in *Minot's* Hiſtory; and the arguments of *Gridley* and *Thacher* are evidently reported by the ſame hand, and correſpond with the abſtracts and quotations of parts of them by Minot, and in a remarkable degree with *Adams's* original notes. *Adams*, in his diary of the ſpring of 1761, quotes ſome one as praiſing the ſtyle of his "abſtract of the argument for and againſt the Writs of Aſſiſtance," and eſpecially of *Gridley's*, in a way that could hardly have been applied to his firſt rough notes, printed in the text. 2 John Adams's Works, 124, 125. And *Adams* himſelf many years after ſaid that the more extended notes printed by *Minot* were his own, except ſome paſſages which he pointed out. Ib. 525–527. A compariſon of his report with thoſe preſerved by *Minot* and *Keith* tends to the conviction that in repudiating thoſe paſſages he was guided by his taſte rather than his notes or his memory. The form of writ and petition preſerved by *Adams* correſpond with thoſe quoted by *Gridley*, according to this report. *Ante*, 403, note 4; *infra*, 480.

The antiquity and accuracy of the report copied by Mr. *Keith* are curiouſly corroborated by the following order, entered at the end of the Docket of Auguſt term 1759 of the Superior Court of Judicature in Suffolk:

Order of Court as to Special Matters.

" N. B. The Court determin'd that for the future the ſpecial pleadings shall come on the ſecond Tueſday in each term & continue from day to day till finish'd, & to allow the Bar the preceding Monday to prepare therefor."

In Mr. *Keith's* manuſcript the introductory ſtatements and the reports of the arguments of *Gridley* and *Thacher* (which have never been printed) are as follows:

" Boſton Superior Court February 1761.

" On the ſecond Tueſday of the Court's sitting, appointed by the rule of the Court for argument of ſpecial matters, came on the diſpute on the petition of Mr. Cockle & others on the one side, and the Inhabitants of Boſton on the other, concerning Writs of Aſſiſtance. Mr. *Gridley* appeared for the former, Mr. *Otis* for the latter. Mr. *Thacher* was joined with him at the desire of the Court.

Gridley's argument.

" Mr. *Gridley*. I appear on the behalf of Mr. Cockle & others, who pray 'that as they cannot fully exerciſe their Offices in ſuch a manner as his Majeſty's Service and their Laws in ſuch caſes require, unleſs your Honors who are veſted with the power of a Court of Exchequer for this

1761. this Province will pleaſe to grant them Writs of Aſſiſtance. They therefore pray that they & their Deputies may be aided in the Execution of their Offices by Writs of Aſſiſtance under the Seal of this Court and in legal form, & according to the Uſage of his Majeſty's Court of Exchequer in Great Britain.'

"May it pleaſe your Honors, it is certain it has been the practice of the Court of Exchequer in England, and of this Court in this Province, to grant Writs of Aſſiſtance to Cuſtom Houſe Officers. Such Writs are mentioned in ſeveral Acts of Parliament, in ſeveral Books of Reports; & in a Book called the Modern Practice of the Court of Exchequer, We have a Precedent, a form of a Writ, called a Writ of Aſſiſtance for Custom houſe Officers, of which the following a few years past to Mr Paxton under the Seal of this Court, & tested by the late Chief Justice Sewall is a literal Tranſlation." [Here follows the writ printed *ante*, 404.]

"The first Queſtion therefore for your Honors to determine is, whether this practice of the Court of Exchequer in England (which it is certain, has taken place heretofore, how long or short a time ſoever it continued) is legal or illegal. And the ſecond is, whether the practice of the Exchequer (admitting it to be legal) can warrant this Court in the ſame practice.

"In anſwer to the firſt, I cannot indeed find the Original of this Writ of Aſſistance. It may be of very antient, to which I am inclined, or it may be of modern date. This however is certain, that the Stat. of the 14th Char. 2nd has eſtabliſhed this Writ almoſt in the words of the Writ itſelf. 'And it shall be lawful to & for any perſon or perſons *authoriſed by Writ of Aſſiſtance under the ſeal of his Majeſty's Court of Exchequer* to take a Conſtable, Headborough, or other public Officer, inhabiting near unto the place, & in the day time to enter & go into any houſe, Shop, Cellar, Warehouſe, room, or any other place, and in caſe of Reſiſtance, to break open doors, Cheſts, Trunks & other Package, & there to ſeize any kind of Goods or Merchandize whatever prohibited, and to put the ſame into his Majeſty's Warehouſe in the Port where Seiſure is made.'

St. 13 & 14 Car. 2, c. 11, § 5.

"By this act & that of 12 Char. 2nd all the powers in the Writ of Aſſiſtance mentioned are given, & it is expreſſly ſaid, the perſons shall be authoriſed by Writs of Aſſistance under the ſeal of the Exchequer. Now the Books in which we should expect to find theſe Writs, & all that relates to them are Books of Precedents, & Reports in the Exchequer, which are extremely ſcarce in this Country; we have one, & but one that treats of Exchequer matters, and that is called the 'Modern practice of the Court of Exchequer,' & in this Book we find one Writ of Aſſiſtance, tranſlated above. Books of Reports have commonly the Sanction of all the Judges, but books of Precedents never have more than that of the Chief Juſtice. Now this Book has the Imprimatur of Wright, who was Chief Juſtice of the King's Bench, and

St. 12 Car. 2, c. 19, § 1.

and it was wrote by Brown, whom I eſteem the beſt Collector of Precedents; I have Two Volumes of them by him, which I eſteem the beſt except Raſtall & Coke. But we have a further proof of the legality of theſe Writs, & of the ſettled practice at home of allowing them; becauſe by the Stat. 6th Anne which continues all Proceſſes & Writs after the Demiſe of the Crown, *Writs of Aſſistance are continued among the Reſt.* St. 1 Anne, St. 1, c. 8, § 5.

"It being clear therefore that the Court of Exchequer at home has a power by Law of granting theſe Writs, I think there can be but little doubt, whether this Court as a Court of Exchequer for this Province has this power. By the Statute of the 7th & 8th W. 3d, it is enacted 'that all the Officers for collecting and managing his Majeſty's Revenue, and inſpecting the Plantation Trade in any of the ſaid Plantations, ſhall have the ſame powers &c. as are provided for the Officers of the Revenue in England; alſo to enter Houſes, or Warehouſes, to ſearch for and ſeize any ſuch Goods, & that the *like Aſſiſtance* ſhall be given to the ſaid Officers as is the Cuſtom in England.' Stat. 7 & 8 W. 3, c. 23, § 6.

"Now what is the Aſſiſtance which the Officers of the Revenue are to have here, which is like that they have in England? Writs of Aſſiſtance under the Seal of his Majeſty's Court of Exchequer at home will not run here. They muſt therefore be under the Seal of this Court. For by the law of this Province 2 W. 3d Ch. 3 'there ſhall 'be a Superior Court &c. over the whole Province &c. who ſhall have 'cognizance of all pleas &c. & generally of all other matters, as fully '& [amply] to all intents & purpoſes as the Courts of King's Bench, 'Common Pleas & *Exchequer* within his Majeſty's Kingdom of England have or ought to have.' Prov. St. 11 W. 3.

"It is true the common privileges of Engliſhmen are taken away in this Caſe, but even their privileges are not ſo in caſes of Crime and fine. 'Tis the neceſſity of the Caſe and the benefit of the Revenue that juſtifies this Writ. Is not the Revenue the ſole ſupport of Fleets & Armies abroad, & Miniſters at home? without which the Nation could neither be preſerved from the Invaſions of her foes, nor the Tumults of her own Subjects. Is not this I ſay infinitely more important, than the impriſonment of Thieves, or even Murderers? yet in theſe Caſes 'tis agreed Houſes may be broke open.

"In fine the power now under conſideration is the ſame with that given by the Law of this Province to Treaſurers towards Collectors, & to them towards the ſubject. A Collector may when he pleaſes diſtrain my goods and Chattels, and in want of them arreſt my perſon, and throw me instantly into Goal. What! ſhall my property be wreſted from me! — ſhall my Liberty be deſtroyed by a Collector, for a debt, unadjudged, without the common Indulgence and Lenity of the Law? So it is eſtabliſhed, and the neceſſity of having public taxes effectually and ſpeedily collected is of infinitely greater moment to the whole, than the Liberty of any Individual."

 "*Thacher.*

1761.

Thacher's argument.

"*Thacher.* In obedience to the Order of this Court I have ſearched with a good deal of attention all the antient Reports of Precedents, Fitz. N. Brev. & the Register, but have not found any ſuch Writ as this Petition prays. In the latter indeed I have found Two Writs which bear the Title of Brev. Aſſistentice, but theſe are only to give poſſeſſion of Houſes &c. in caſes of Injunctions & Sequeſtration in Chancery. By the Act of Parliament any private Perſon as well as Cuſtom Houſe Officer may take a Sheriff or Conſtable & go into any Shop &c. & ſeize &c. (here Mr Thacher quoted an Authority from Strange which intended to ſhew that Writs of Aſſiſtance were only temporary things.)

"The moſt material queſtion is whether the practice of the Exchequer is good ground for this Court. But this Court has upon a ſolemn Argument, which laſted a whole day, renounc'd the Chance of [Chancery] Juriſdiction which the Exchequer has in Caſes where either party is the King's Debtor.

"In England all Informations of uncuſtomed or prohibited Goods are in the Exchequer, ſo that the Cuſtom Houſe Officers are the Officers of that Court under the Eye & Direction of the Barons & ſo accountable for any wanton exerciſe of power.

"The Writ now prayed for is not returnable. If the Seizures were ſo, before your Honors, and this Court ſhould enquire into them you'd often find a wanton exerciſe of power. At home they ſeize at their peril, even with probable Cauſe."

Otis's argument.

The extended ſketch of *Otis's* argument expreſſes his legal poſitions no better than *Adams's* original notes, reprinted in the text, and has been twice printed already, once in 2 Minot's Hiſt. Maſs. 91–99, and again, with little alteration, in 2 John Adams's Works, 523–525. *Vid. ſupra*, 478, 479. It is therefore omitted here. The Keith MS. is evidently from a more perfect copy; but the variations are trifling. The moſt important one is in the punctuation of the following paſſage, which is thus in the Keith MS.: "I have taken more pains in this cauſe than I ever will take again. Although my engaging in this & another popular Cauſe has raiſed much Reſentment, yet I think I can ſincerely declare that I cheerfully ſubmit myſelf to every odious name for Conſcience ſake." In the works of *Minot* and *Adams* there is a comma after "again," and a period after "Reſentment," followed by "But." "Another popular cauſe" was doubtleſs the controverſy between *the Province & Paxton*, *poſt*, Appendix, II.

Cur. adv. vult.

The report in the Keith MS. concludes thus: "The Court ſuſpended the abſolute determination of the matter." This accords with *Hutchinſon's* accounts. *Ante*, 415, note.

E. Otis's Quotations from Coke on Magna Carta, cap. xxix.

"NULLUS liber homo capiatur, vel impriſonetur, aut diſſeiſietur de libero tenemento ſuo, vel libertatibus, vel liberis conſuetudinibus ſuis, aut utlagetur, aut exuletur, aut aliquo modo deſtruatur, nec ſuper eum ibimus, nec ſuper eum mittemus, niſi per legale judicium parium ſuorum, vel per legem terræ. Nulli vendemus, nulli negabimus, aut differemus juſtitiam, vel rectum." 2 Inſt. 45.

"This is a beneficial Law, and is conſtrued benignly," &c. p. 47.

"[Per judicium parium ſuorum.]" "And it extendeth to the King's ſuit in caſe of treaſon or felony, or of miſpriſion of treaſon or felony, or being acceſſory to felony before, or after, and not to any other inferior offence. Alſo it extendeth to the trial itſelf, whereby he is to be convicted: but a Nobleman is to be indicted of treaſon or felony, or of miſpriſion, or being acceſſary to in caſe of felony, by an inqueſt under the degree of nobility: the number of Noblemen that are to be triers are, 12 or more.*" p. 49.

* *i. e.* Tr. pr Pares.

"The ill ſucceſs hereof," [The St. of 11 H. 7, c. 3, authorizing Juſtices, "(without any finding or preſentment by the verdict of twelve men) by their diſcretions to hear and determine all offences and contempts,"] "and the fearful end of theſe two oppreſſors," [Empſon and Dudley] "ſhould deter others from committing the like, and ſhould admoniſh Parliaments, that inſtead of this ordinary and precious trial *Per legem terrœ*, they bring not in abſolute and partial trials by diſcretion." p. 51.

"If Treaſon or Felony be done, and one hath juſt cauſe of ſuſpicion, this is a good cauſe and warrant in Law for him to arreſt any man, but he muſt ſhew in certainty the cauſe of his ſuſpicion: and whether the ſuſpicion be juſt or lawful, ſhall be determined by the Juſtices in an Action of falſe impriſonment brought by the party grieved, or upon a *Habeas corpus*, &c." p. 52.

"If an affray be made to the breach of the King's peace, any man may by a Warrant in Law reſtrain any of the offenders, to the end the

1761. the King's peace may be kept, but after the affray ended, they cannot be arrested without an express Warrant." p. 52.

"The like Writ" [of habeas corpus] "is to be granted out of the Chancery, either in the time of the Term (as in the King's Bench) or in the Vacation; for the Court of Chancery is *officina justiciæ*, and is ever open, and never adjourned, so as the Subject being wrongfully imprisoned, may have justice for the liberty of his person as well in the Vacation time, as in the Term." p. 53.

"Now it may be demanded, if a man be taken, or committed to prison *contra legem terræ*, against the Law of the land, what remedy hath the party grieved? To this it is answered, First, that every Act of Parliament made against any injury, mischief, or grievance doth either expressly, or impliedly give a remedy to the party wronged, or grieved: as in many of the Chapters of this great Charter appeareth; and therefore he may have an action grounded upon this great Charter." p. 55.

"[Nulli negabimus, aut differemus, &c.]" "These words have been excellently expounded by latter Acts of Parliament, that by no means common right, or Common Law should be disturbed or delayed, no, though it be commanded under the Great Seal, or Privy Seal, order, writ, letters, message, or commandment whatsoever, either from the King, or any other, and that the Justices shall proceed, as if no such writs, letters, order, message, or other commandment were come to them. *Judicium redditum per defaltam affirmatur, non obstante breve Regis de prorogatione judicii.*"

"That the Common Laws of the Realm should by no means be delayed, for the Law is the surest sanctuary, that a man can take, and the strongest fortress to protect the weakest of all; *lex est tutissima cassis*, and *sub clypeo legis nemo decipitur:* but the King may stay his own suite, as a *capias pro fine*, for the King may respit his fine and the like.

"All Protections that are not legal, which appear not in the Register, nor warranted by our books, are expressly against this branch, *nulli differemus:* As a Protection under the Great Seal granted to any man, directed to the Sheriffs, &c. and commanding them, that they shall not arrest him, during a certain time at any other man's suit, which hath words in it, *per prærogativam nostram, quam nolumus esse arguendam;* yet such Protections have been argued by the Judges, according to their oath and duty, and adjudged to be void." p. 56.

"[Justitiam vel rectum.]" "It is called Right, because it is the best birth-right the Subject hath, for thereby his goods, lands, wife, children, his body, life, honor, and estimation are protected from injury and wrong: *major hæreditas venit unicuique nostrum a jure, & legibus, quam a parentibus.*" p. 56.

NOTE. In the margin of *James Otis's* copy of Lord *Coke's* Second Institute, (6th ed. London 1681,) now owned by Mr. *George Frisbie Hoar,*

1761.

Hoar, of Worcefter, the mark ☞ is frequently written, especially in the margin of the twenty-ninth chapter of Magna Charta, and the commentary thereon, as fhown above. Remembering alfo *Otis's* reference, as reported by *Quincy*, to "29 M." (*ante*, 56,) it can hardly be doubted that the paffages thus indicated, or fome of them, were cited in the argument upon the Writs of Affiftance, though fome of them were alfo referred to in the argument for opening the Courts in 1765. *Ante*, 205–207; 2 John Adams's Works, 158, 159, & notes.

The reference in the margin to "Trial per Pares" is apparently in *Otis*'s hand; and the words "this ordinary and precious trial *Per legem terræ*," and "Action of falfe imprifonment," are underfcored with ink. This paragraph about trial by jury was a favorite with the patriot lawyers of that time. Compare *Adams*, *arguendo*, in *Advocate General* v. *Hancock*, *ante*, 460.

There is alfo a mark in the margin of the paffage referred to in *Thacher's* argument, (*ante*, 53, 54,) "The Exchequer is an ancient Court of Record for the King's affairs, touching his rights and revenues of his Crown," &c. 2 Inft. 551.

1761.

F. Contemporaneous Notices in the Boston Gazette.

Monday, November 23. Report of second hearing and decision.

"BOSTON, *November* 23. Wednesday last, a Hearing was had before the Hon. the Superior Court "of Judicature then sitting in this County, upon a Petition "of the Officers of the Customs for a Writ of Assistance — "As this was a Matter in which the Liberty of the People "was most nearly interested the whole Day and Evening "was spent in the Argument. The Gentlemen in favour "of the Petition alledged, that such Writs by Law issued "from the Court of Exchequer at home; and that by an "Act of this Province, the Superior Court is vested with "the whole Power and Jurisdiction of the Exchequer; and "from thence it was inferr'd, that the Superior Court might "lawfully grant the Petition.

"The Arguments on the other Side were enforced with "such Strength of Reason, as did great Honour to the "Gentlemen concerned; and nothing could have induced "one to believe they were not conclusive, but the Judgment of the Court *immediately* given in Favour of the "Petition. (1)

"It is probable that very *urgent* Necessity for this Writ "was set forth in the Petition, as some *private* Hints had "been given that the King's Officers were set at Defiance — An Assertion which no *unbiassed* man will believe "to be true, who is either acquainted with the Character "of the Body of Merchants in this Town, or knows the "*powerful* influence under which the King's Officers are "*protected.*

"It is worth observing, that the Power of the Exchequer "had

(1) Quincy's Report, *ante*, 57, *acc.*

"had never been exercifed by the Superior Court, for near "Sixty Years after the Act of this Province invefting them "with fuch Power had been in Force — The Writ, which "was the firft Inftance of their exercifing that Power now "granted, was never afked for, or if afked, was conftantly "deny'd for this long Courfe of Years, until *Charles Pax-* "*ton*, Efq; whofe Regard for the Liberty and *Property* of "the Subject, as well as the *Revenue of the King*, is well "known, (2) apply'd for it in 1754 — It was granted by the "Court in 1756, (3) *fub filentio*, and continued till the De- "mife of the late King — Upon this new Application, it is "now revived, and no doubt will be of *eminent* ufe to the "prefent Generation at leaft; otherwife it is not to be pre- "fumed the Court would have allowed it — it will never be "looked upon in an *indifferent* Light; and therefore if it "lives to Pofterity, it will afford to them one ftriking Char- "acteriftic, at leaft of the *prefent Times*, according as *they* "fhall find the *Effects* of it to be, when it may arrive to "*more perfect maturity*, whether good or bad."

The above report is the only notice in the Bofton Gazette during this year, of proceedings in court concerning the Writs of Affiftance. The italics are in the original.

December 7.

In the Gazette of December 7th 1761 "A FAIR TRADER" fays: "WRITS OF ASSISTANCE are now eftablifhed and granted to the Officers of the Cuftoms, who were tho't by many Perfons, to have had full Power enough over us before." And on the 21ft of December the leading article, which is not figned, fays: "Let us then all lend a helping hand to this good work — not only cuftom houfe

Dec. 21.

(2) *Vid. ante*, 421, note; *Province of Maffachufetts Bay* v. *Paxton*, *poft*, Appendix II. Governor *Bernard*, on the 17th of May 1764, wrote: "When I firft came to this Government, feizures were much more frequent than they have been for two or three years paft. They were all made by one officer only — Mr. *Paxton*, the Surveyor of the Port." 3 Bernard Papers, 216.

(3) At Auguft term 1755, *ante*, 407.

1761. house officers but others — let ALL apply for writs of assistance — for *it shall be lawful for* ANY PERSON *having a writ of assistance from the exchequer* — these are the words of the act — and *there is an exchequer in this province, to all intents and purposes* — a court that can exercise as many of the powers of the exchequer as they please."

1762. January 4. The first article in the Gazette of January 4th 1762 repeats with such clearness and power the very grounds taken by the counsel against the writ, as almost to compel the inference that it was from the pen of one of them; and at that time *James Otis* was a frequent contributor, both in his own name, and anonymously. No further reason is necessary for printing the whole article.

"*To the* PRINTERS.

Statement of Argument against the Writs.

"SINCE the advancement of so great a lawyer as the Hon. Mr. H–TCH–NS–N to the *first J—st—s* seat, (4) "it would be deem'd the highest impertinence for any "one to express the least surprize, that the Superior Court "of this province, should after *solemn hearing*, adjudge "themselves authoriz'd to grant *such* a writ, as the WRIT "OF ASSISTANCE; or even to doubt, whether *by law*, "they have power so to do: I hope however, I may say "without offence, especially as I am inform'd that this "writ is not yet given out, (5) that I heartily wish it never "may —

"It seems necessary to preface all our objections against "such a power being given to the custom-house officers, "with

(4) *Vid. ante*, 410, 411. And add, to the references there given, Hutchinson to John Remington, March 27, 1767, 26 Mass. Archives, 272; Judge *Trowbridge*, April 19, 1775, quoted in Eliot's Biog. Dict. 274, note.

(5) It had actually been issued to *Paxton* a month before, (*ante*, 418,) but had perhaps not yet been used.

"with a formal declaration againſt an *illicit* trade; for to "bear any *ſpirited* teſtimony againſt their abuſe of power, "and eſpecially to offer ſuch abuſe as the ſtrongeſt reaſon "why they ought not to be truſted with more, has been "repreſented by theſe very perſons and THEIR PATRONS, as "if we had *combin'd* to break thro' all the *juſt* reſtraints of "the laws of trade, and to force a free port.—I do there-"fore *from principle* declare againſt an illicit trade; I would "have it *totally* ſuppreſſ'd, with this proviſo only, that it "may have the ſame fate in the other governments; other-"wiſe all the world will judge it unequitable: it is becauſe "*we only* are ſeverely dealt with, that we complain of un-"reaſonable treatment; and the writ of aſſiſtance, being a "further degree of ſeverity will give us ſtill further reaſon "to complain— 1762.

"BUT it is not trade only that will be affected by this "new ſeverity: every houſholder in this province, will "neceſſarily become *leſs ſecure* than he was before this writ "had any exiſtence among us; for by it, *a cuſtom houſe* "*officer* OR ANY OTHER PERSON *has a power given him*, *with* "*the aſſiſtance of a peace officer*, TO ENTER FORCEABLY *into a* "DWELLING HOUSE, *and rifle every part of it where he ſhall* "PLEASE *to ſuſpect uncuſtomed goods are lodgd*!—Will any "man put ſo great a value on his freehold, after ſuch a "power commences as he did before?—every man in this "province, will be liable to be inſulted, by a *petty officer*, "and threatned to have his houſe *ranſack'd*, unleſs he will "comply with his unreaſonable and *impudent* demands: Will "any one then under *ſuch* circumſtance, ever again boaſt "of *britiſh* honor or *britiſh* privilege?—I expect that "ſome *little leering* tool of power will tell us, that the pub-"lick is now amuſ'd with *mere chimeras* of an overheated "brain; (6) but I deſire that men of underſtanding, and "morals,

---

(6) The very expreſſion uſed by Otis at the firſt argument—"This wanton exerciſe of this power is not a chimerical ſuggeſtion of a heated brain," *ante*, 475, note 28.

1762. "morals, would only recollect an inftance of this fort; "when a late comptroller of this port, by virtue of his "*writ of affiftance*, FORCEABLY enter'd into and rummag'd "the houfe of a *magiftrate* of this town; and what render'd "the infolence intollerable, was, that he did not pretend a "fufpicion of contraband goods as a reafon for his conduct, "but it was only becaufe the honeft magiftrate had a day "before taken the liberty to execute a good and wholefome "law of this province againft the comptroller. — (7)

"IT is granted that upon *fome occafions*, even a *brittifh* "freeholder's houfe may be forceably opened; but as this "violence is upon a prefumption of his having forfeited his "fecurity, it ought never to be done, and it never is done, "but in cafes of the moft urgent neceffity and importance; (8) "and this neceffity and importance always is, and always "ought to be determin'd by *adequate* and *proper* judges: "Shall fo tender a point as this is, be left to the difcretion "of ANY perfon, to whomfoever this writ may be given! "fhall the *jealoufies* and mere *imaginations* of a cuftom "houfe officer, as *imperious* perhaps as injudicious, be "accounted a fufficient reafon for his breaking into a free-"man's house! what if it fhall appear, after he has put a "family which has a right to the King's peace, to the "utmoft confufion and terror; what, if it fhould appear, "that there was no juft grounds of fufpicion; what repara-"tion will he make? is it enough to fay, that damages may "be recover'd againft him in the law? I hope indeed this "will always be the cafe; — but are we *perpetually* to be "expof'd to outrages of this kind, & to be told for our *only* "confolation, that we muft be *perpetually* feeking to the "courts of law for redrefs? Is not this vexation *itfelf* to "a man of a well difpofed mind? and befides, may we not "be infolently treated by our *petty tyrants* in *fome* ways, for "which the law prefcribes no redrefs? and if this fhould be "the

(7) *Cafe of Walley & Ware*, *Otis*, *arguendo*, *ante*, 476, note 29.
(8) S. P. *Otis*, *arguendo*, *ante*, 471.

1762.

"the cafe, what man will hereafter think his rights and "privileges worth contending for, or even worth *enjoying*.

"THE people of this province formerly upon a *particular* "*occafion* afferted the rights of *englifhmen;* and they did it "with a *fober*, *manly* fpirit: they were *then* in an infulting "manner afked 'whether englifh rights were to follow "'them to the ends of the earth' (9) — we are *now* told, "that the rights we contend for 'do not belong to the "'Englifh' — thefe writs, it is faid, 'are frequently iffued "'from the exchequer at home, and executed, and the "'people do not complain of it — and why fhould we de-"'fire more freedom than they have in the mother coun-"'try'—fuch is the *palliating* language of the great *patrons* "of this writ — and who claims more liberty than belongs "to us as *Britifh* fubjects? we defire no fecurities but "fuch as are deriv'd to us from the *britifh* conftitution, "which is our glory — no laws but what are agreeable to "the *true fpirit* of the *britifh* laws, to which we always "have, and I hope always fhall yield a chearful obe-"dience (10) — thefe rights and fecurities, we have with "other *britifh* fubjects glorioufly defended againft *foreign* "invafions, and I hope in God we fhall always have fpirit "enough to defend them againft all *other* invafions. — Is "there then any *exprefs* act of parliament authorizing the "exchequer to iffue fuch writs? for if there is not *plain* "*law* for fuch a power, the practice of one court *againft* "*law*, or which is the fame thing, *without law*, can never "be deem'd a *good* precedent for another, allowing there is "no reafon *to doubt*, the one is *legally* vefted with all the "power and jurifdiction of the other: but if ALL this be "matter of *uncertainty*, ought it not then forever to be de-"termin'd

(9) By the Judges prefiding at the trial of *John Wife* and other inhabitants of Ipfwich, in 1687, for denying the validity of a tax affeffed by *Andros* and his Council without an affembly. Felt's Hift. Ipfwich, 124. Wafhburn's Jud. Hift. Mafs. 106.

(10) Compare the accounts of *Bernard*, *Hutchinfon*, and Chief Juftice *Marfhall*, *ante*, 430, 434–437, notes.

1762. "termin'd in favor of common right and liberty? and would "not every wiſe man ſo determine it? (11)

"BUT admitting *there is ſuch* a practice at home, and "that it is not diſputed, even at this time, when there "is ſo warm a ſenſe of liberty there; it may neverthelеſs "be an Infringement upon the conſtitution: and let it be "obſerv'd, there may be at ſome times a neceſſity of con-"ceeding to meaſures there, which *bear hard* upon liberty; "which meaſures ought not to be drawn into precedent "here, becauſe there is not, nor can be ſuch neceſſity for "them here; and to take ſuch meaſures, without any neceſ-"ſity at all, would be as violent an infraction on our liber-"ties, as if there was no pretence at all to law or precedent. "It is idle then, to tell us we ought to be content under "the ſame reſtrictions which they are under at home, even "to the *weakning of our beſt ſecurities*, when it is tolerated "then only *thro' neceſſity*, and there is no neceſſity for it "here.—In *England* ſomething may be ſaid for granting "theſe writs, tho' I am far from ſaying that anything can "juſtify it. In *England* the revenue and the ſupport of "government, in ſome meaſure, depend upon the cuſtoms; "but is this the caſe here? are any remittances made from "the officers here? has the king's revenue, or the revenue "of the province ever received the addition of a farthing, "from all the collections, and all the ſeizures that have "been made and forfeited, excepting what has been remit-"ted by the late worthy collector *Mr. B—r—ns*? (12)—I "aſſert nothing: but if no benefit accrues to the publick, "either here or at home, from all the monies that are "receiv'd *for the uſe of the publick*, Is not this PECULATION? "and

(11) Compare Otis's arguments, in February—"Better to obſerve the principles of law than any one precedent" (*ante*, 473)—and in November—"It is worthy conſideration whether this writ was conſti-tutional even in England, and I think it plainly appears it was not," *ante*, 55. See alſo Thacher's argument, *ante*, 52.

(12) Compare *Bernard's* and *Paxton's* accounts of *Barons*, *ante*, 425, 426, note.

1762.

"and what reaſon can there be, that a *free people* ſhould be "expoſ'd to all the inſult and abuſe, to the riſque and even "the *fatal conſequences*, which may ariſe from the *execution* "of a writ of aſſiſtance, ONLY TO PUT FORTUNES INTO "PRIVATE POCKETS.

"I deſire it may be further conſider'd, that the cuſtom "houſe officers at home, are under certain *checks* and *reſtric-* "*tions*, which they cannot be under here; and therefore the "writ of aſſiſtance ought to be look'd upon as a *different* "*thing* there, from what it is here. (13) In *England* the "exchequer has the power of controuling them in *every* "*reſpect*; and even of *inflicting corporal puniſhment upon* "*them for mal-conduct*, of which there have been inſtances; "they are the proper officers of that court, and are ac- "countable to it as often as it ſhall call them to account, "and they do in fact account to it for money receiv'd, and "for their BEHAVIOR, once every week — ſo that the people "there have a ſhort and eaſy method of redreſs, in caſe of "injury receiv'd from them: but is it ſo here? Do the "officers of the cuſtoms here account with the Superior "Court, or lodge monies received into the hands of that "court; or are they as officers under any ſort of check "from it? — Will they *concede* to ſuch powers in the Su- "perior Court? or does this court, notwithſtanding *theſe* "are powers *belonging* to the exchequer — notwithſtanding "it is *ſaid to be veſted with* ALL THE POWERS *belonging to* "*the exchequer* — and, further, notwithſtanding this *very* "*writ of aſſiſtance* is to be granted AS a power belonging to "the exchequer, will the Superior Court itſelf, aſſume the "power of calling theſe officers to account, and puniſh "them for miſbehavior? It would be a ſmall conſolation, "if we could have one inſtance: Have we not ſeen already, "ONE of thoſe officers, and he an *inferior* one too, REFUS- "ING to account to *any power* in the province, for monies "receiv'd by him *by virtue of his office*, belonging to the "province,

(13) Compare *Thacher's* argument, *ante*, 56.

1762. "province, and which we are aſſured by the JOINT DECLA-"RATION of the three branches of the legiſlature is UNJUSTLY "as well as *illegally* detain'd by him? (14) Does not every "one then ſee that a writ of aſſiſtance in the hands of a "cuſtom houſe officer here, is in reallity a *greater* power & "more to be dreaded, than it is in England? *greater* be-"cauſe UNCONTROUL'D — and can a community be ſafe "with an uncontroul'd power lodg'd in the hands of *ſuch* "officers, ſome of whom have given abundant proofs of the "danger there is in truſting them with ANY?" (15)

---

(14) *Province* v. *Paxton*, *poſt*, appendix II.

(15) There is alſo a communication upon the extent of the duty of aſſiſting cuſtom houſe officers in executing Writs of Aſſiſtance, occupying a column in the Gazette of February 22d, 1862. See alſo "Journal of the Times" in Boſton Evening Poſt of June 26, 1769.

G. Subfequent Action of the General Court. 1762.

AT the next feffion of the General Court, on the 22d of February 1762, the following bill was introduced and paffed to be engroffed in the Council:

Propofed Act.

"An Act for the better enabling the Officers of his "Majefty's Cuftoms to carry the Acts of Trade into Ex-"ecution.

"Whereas it is the Defire of this Court, that the Of-"ficers of his Majefty's Cuftoms in this Province may be "affifted in the due Execution of their Office, for the "fecuring his Majefty's Dues, and for the preventing of "Fraud:

"Be it enacted by the Governour, Council and Houfe "of Reprefentatives, That upon Application of any of the "Officers of his Majefty's Cuftoms in this Province, im-"powred by Commiffion to feife upon Oath made to the "Superiour Court of Judicature, Court of Affize, and Gen-"eral Goal Delivery, or to the Court of General Seffions of "the Peace, or to the Inferiour Court of Common Pleas, "or to either of the Juftices of faid Courts, or to any one "of his Majefty's Juftices of the Peace of the County, that "he has had Information of the Breach of any of the Acts "of Trade; and that he verily believes or knows fuch "Information to be true; it fhall be lawful in every fuch "Cafe, for fuch Court or Juftice, to whom Application may "be made as aforefaid, upon reducing fuch Oath to Writ-"ing, with the Name of the Perfon [Informing and the "place] informed againft, and not otherwife, to iffue a Writ "or Warrant of Affiftance, which Writ or Warrant of "Affiftance fhall be in the Form following and no other, "Viz[t].

" fs.

1762. "   ss. To the Sheriff and Coroner of the County "of   and to their respective deputies; and to the "respective Constables of the Town of   in said "County — Greeting.

"Whereas A. B.   of his Majesty's Cus- "toms, hath this Day made Complaint on Oath, That "(setting forth the Complaint and Oath with the name "of the Person complained of) You and every of You "in his Majesty's Name, upon Sight thereof, are strictly "Commanded to be aiding and assisting to the said A. B. "in the due Execution of his Office relating to the In- "formation aforesaid. Hereof fail Not at your Peril, and "make Return of this Warrant and of your Doings there- "on unto myself in seven Days from the Date hereof. "Dated at B. the   Day of   In the "Year of his Majesty's Reign: Anno Domini

"And be it further enacted, That it shall be lawful for "any Person or Persons authorized by Writ or Warrant "of Assistance, in matter and Form as aforesaid, and not "otherwise, in the Daytime to enter and go into any "House, Shop, Cellar, Warehouse, or other Place; and "in Case of Resistance, to break open Doors, Chests, "Trunks and other Packages, them to seize and from "thence to bring any Kind of Goods or Merchandize "whatsoever prohibited and unaccustomed there found and "them secure. And all his Majesty's good Subjects are "required to be aiding and assisting in the due Execution "of said Writ or Warrant of Assistance, and all such shall "hereby be defended and saved harmless."

The bill was also passed through all its stages by the House, with the amendment inclosed in brackets in the third paragraph, (*supra*, 495,) and was returned to the Council on the 6th of March, and there passed on the same day.(1) After the bill had been sent up from the House, the

(1) 66 Mass. Archives, 191. Journal H. R. 1761–2, pp. 271, 278, 292, 294.

1762.

the Governor ſent a meſſage to the Houſe that he had ſigned certain bills, of which this was not one; and the Houſe thereupon ſent a meſſage to the Council by *James Otis* to inquire if they had paſſed on this bill, and the Council returned a meſſage to acquaint the Houſe that the Council had paſſed it to be enacted.(2)

Opinion of the Judges.

At a Council held on the 6th of March 1762, "His Excellency informed the Council that he had a Bill laid before him for his conſent intituled an Act for the better enabling the Officers of his Majeſty's Cuſtoms to carry the Acts of Trade into Execution which appeared to him to be repugnant and contrary to the Laws of the Realm and particularly to the Act of Parliament of the 7th and 8th of William the Third Chap: 22, in purſuance of which Act the Judges of the Superior Court heretofore granted Writs of Aſſiſtance to the Officers of the Cuſtom Houſe, Wherefore he thought proper in Council to take the opinion of the Judges upon this Queſtion,

"Whether if this Bill ſhould be enacted, The Superior Court as a Court of Exchequer could (conſiſtently with ſuch Act) grant a Writ of Aſſiſtance in purſuance of the Act of Parliament of the 7th and 8th of William the Third in the ſame manner as if ſuch Bill was not enacted.

"The Judges having the Queſtion in Writing given to them retired into the Lobby, and ſoon after returning, unanimouſly declared their opinion,

"That if this Bill ſhould paſs into a Law the Superiour Court would be reſtrained from granting a Writ of Aſſiſtance in the manner they have heretofore done and in the manner ſuch Writs of Aſſiſtance are granted by the Court of Exchequer in England."(3)

Governor's diſapproval.

On the 6th of March the Governor prorogued the General

---

(2) 24 General Court Rec. 316, 317.
(3) Council Rec. 1762, fol. 111.

63

1762. eral Court, after making a speech to the two Houſes, in which he gave theſe reaſons for refuſing to ſign this bill:

"I have had a Bill laid before me, which I have not "Power to paſs to be enacted, I mean the Bill Intituled "'An Act for the better enabling the Officers of his Maj-"eſty's Cuſtoms, to carry the Acts of Trade into Execution;' "which is so plainly repugnant and contrary to the laws "of England, and particularly to the Act of Parliament of "the ſeventh and eighth of King William the Third, Chap-"ter twenty-ſecond, that if I could overlook, it is impoſſi-"ble it ſhould eſcape the Penetration of the Lords of Trade: "In such Caſe, if I was to tranſmit this Bill as paſſed here, "it would have no other Effect than to give a Proof of my "Ignorance of my Buſineſs, and your Inattention to the "Conditions upon which we are intruſted with the Power "of Legiſlation." (4)

Hutchinſon's account. (4) Journal H. R. 1761–2, p. 299. The Chief Juſtice wrote the ſame day to Mr. Bollan, the agent of the Province in England: "This Veſſel tarrying longer than expected gives opportunity of acquainting you that troubleſome ſeſſion of the General Court is at an end. The Governor for the ſake of peace complied, I think, farther than he would otherwiſe inclined to have done with the oppoſers of government & found by experience the truth of Sir R. Walpole's ſaying that one expedient makes neceſſary a great many more and to-day they preſented him a bill reſtraining the Superior Court from iſſuing writs of aſſiſtance except upon ſpecial information to a Cuſtom houſe officer oath being firſt made, the informer mentioned & the perſon ſuppoſed to own the goods & the place where they were ſuſpected to be concealed. You will not imagine it poſſible for him to have ſigned ſuch a bill and after requiring ſuch of the Juſtices of the Superior Court as were in town to give their opinion upon ſome points he refuſed it." 26 Maſs. Archives, 8.

Bernard's account. On the 13th of April, the Governor wrote to the Lords of Trade as follows: "I ſhall in this aquaint your Lordſhips with my rejecting a Bill of a very popular conſtruction & my reaſons for & manner of doing it. The Bill, of which I here incloſe a Copy, was the laſt Effort of the Confederacy againſt the Cuſtomhouſe & Laws of Trade. The intention of it was to take away from the Officers the writ of Aſſiſtance granted in purſuance of the Act of Will. 3; & ſubſtitute in the room of it another Writt which would have been wholly inefficacious. This was covered with all the Art which the thing was capable of: but I was too

too well acquainted with the Subject to be deceived in it. I had not the leaſt doubt, upon the firſt reading of it, of rejecting the bill. Nevertheleſs as it was very popular; & I knew that the negativing of it would occaſion a clamour, I gave it a more ſolemn condemnation than it deserved; the manner of which will appear from the enclosed Copy of the Act of Council. This anticipated all objections & reduced the popular cry to a murmur only, which ſoon ceaſed, & I believe there is now a total end to this troubleſome Altercation about the Cuſtom houſe Officers." 2 Bernard Papers, 58. See alſo Bernard to John Pownall, April 25, and to Lord Barrington, May 1, 1762, Ib. 186, 188. 1762.

H. Writs of Aſſiſtance in other Colonies.

WRITS OF ASSISTANCE do not appear to have been granted in any of the Colonies except Maſſachuſetts and New Hampſhire, until after the paſſage of the St. of 7 G. 3, c. 46, and even then they were refuſed almoſt everywhere. (1)

1. *New Hampſhire.*

1762. New Hampshire.

At May term 1762 in Rockingham County of the Superior Court of Judicature of the Province of New Hampſhire.

"Upon the motion of the Hon'ble John Temple, "Esqr., Surveyor General of his Majeſty's Cuſtoms, &c. "Deſiring that Writs of Aſſiſtants might Iſſue from this "Court (to the Collector of his Majeſty's Cuſtoms) for "that part of the port of Piſcataqua that is within this "Province — It is conſidered that ſuch a Writ iſſue ac-"cording to the ſaid motion when applyed for by the "ſaid Collector." (2)

2. *Connecticut.*

---

(1) Hutchinſon to Jackſon, May 1, 1765, 26 Maſs. Archives, 138. Opinion of Attorney General De Grey, Auguſt 20, 1768, *ante*, 453. Chief Juſtice Trumbull to W. S. Johnſon, June 14, 1769, *infra*, 503. John Adams to Calkoens, October 4, 1780, 7 John Adams's Works, 267. "We are well informed, that the officers of the cuſtoms applied the laſt year to the chief juſtice or bench of judges, in ſeveral of the colonies, for granting them writs of aſſiſtance, but that thoſe juſtices from a tender regard to the conſtitution, and the rights of American freeholders, did actually refuſe a compliance with thoſe demands." "Journal of the Times," of April 29, 1769, in Boſton Evening Poſt, of June 26, 1769.

(2) The writer is indebted to the kindneſs of the Honorable Samuel D. Bell,

1768. Connecticut.

2. *Connecticut.*

No application to the Superior Court of Connecticut for Writs of Aſſiſtance appears to have been made until after the paſſage of the St. of 7 G. 3, c. 46, when in March 1768

"Upon the Petition of Duncan Stewart, Collector, and Thomas Moffat, Comptroller, of his Majeſty's Cuſtoms for the Port of New London, Eſquires, requeſting this Court to grant them Writs of Aſſiſtance purſuant to the ſpirit and true meaning of the Act of Parliament therein referred to — And no information being made by ſaid Petitioners, or otherwiſe, of any ſpecial occaſion for ſaid Writ — This Court is of Opinion that it is needful to conſider on the purport of ſaid Acts, and the manner and form of granting ſuch Writs of Aſſiſtance, according to the uſage of his Majeſty's Court of Exchequer: Therefore this Court will further conſider and adviſe thereon." (4)

"An

D. Bell, Chief Juſtice of New Hampſhire, for a copy of this record, to which his attention was firſt directed by a notice dated "Province of New Hampſhire, July 15, 1762," and publiſhed in the Boſton Gazette of July 26, 1762.

(4) Stuart's Life of Trumbull, 79. This "court record," as Mr. *Stuart* calls it, "muſt have been a private memorandum, or looſe file, which he found perhaps among Gov. *Trumbull's* MSS., for it does not appear on the records proper," as the writer has been informed by Mr. *J. Hammond Trumbull*, to whom he is indebted for the copy (*infra*, 504,) of the ſubſequent motion, and other facts relating to Writs of Aſſiſtance in Connecticut.

On the 3d of March 1768, *Hutchinſon* wrote to *Jackſon*: "The Commiſſioners ſhewed me a letter from ſome of their Officers in Connecticut, who by direction had applied to the Superior Court for Writs of Aſſiſtance agreeable to the late Act of Parliament. The Officers ſay they were refuſed & that the Chief Juſtice gave as a reaſon that the Court was of opinion ſuch writs were unconſtitutional. The Officers are ordered to make a more formal application & to obtain the Anſwer of the Court in writing." 26 Maſs. Archives, 296. "It is ſaid the grand Penſioner, always ready with his Council, has adviſed the C—m——rs to remonſtrate Home againſt the Civil Authority of Connecticut, for declining to iſſue Writs of Aſſiſtance for a General Search of contraband Goods, in the baſe unconſtitutional

Manner

1769. A ſimilar application was made at April term 1769 at Norwich, ſupported by the opinion of Attorney General *De Grey*;

Manner they have been granted in another Province. Perhaps the ſame Advice may be given relative to the Chief J—ſt—ce of Philadelphia, who we hear has alſo acted in a like worthy Manner upon a ſingular Demand." Boſton Gazette of Auguſt 15, 1768.

Immediately after the application in the text, Governor *Pitkin* wrote to *William Samuel Johnſon*, then an agent of the Colony in England, aſking him to "Tranſmit an Account Relative to Writs of Aſſiſtants iſſued under the Seal of his Majeſty's Court of Exchequer: in what Manner application is made in order to obtain them, and whether general Warrants are iſſued &c &c." Pitkin to Johnſon, March 11, 1768, 2 Trunbull MSS. 169, in Maſs. Hiſt. Soc. Lib. *Johnſon* replied: "I have made all the enquiry I could, ſince I received your Letter, concerning Writs of Aſſiſtance to Cuſtom Houſe Officers, but cannot yet perfectly ſatisfie myſelf with reſpect to them. It is ſurpriſing how little Attertion Gentlemen here pay, & how ſlender Intelligence they can give out, relative to things not Immediately within their own departments. It ſeem'd to be clearly the Opinion of ſeveral Lawyers, that I ſpoke with upon the ſubject, that they were not Iſſued but in particular Caſes, and upon Information on Oath, not in general Terms, nor to be made uſe of as general Warrants, at the Diſcretion of the Officer, which appeared to me to be the only legal and reaſonable Method. But upon application to the Clerks of the Excheqr. for Copies of the uſual Writs Iſſued here in Caſes of this Nature, they have furniſh'd us with the encloſed, which you will ſee are very general, and not groundedupon any particular Fact, or Information, & they add, that all the addtional Inſtruction, beſide what the Writs expreſs & direct, is, that the King's Officer, take unto him a Peace Officer, if he breaks open any Houſe or place. I am not ſatisfied however that this ought to be the Proceedure in Connecticut; nevertheleſs I tho't it expedient to forward these Copies to you, as ſoon as I could, but shall continue to make farther enquiry into this matter, and if anything material Occurs, it shal be immediately communicated to you." Johnſon to Pitkin, July 23, 1768, Johnſon's letters in ſame Collection, 97, 98.

Roger Sherman also wrote to *Johnſon*, informing him of the refuſal to grant the writs. 6 Bancroft's Hiſt. U. S. 279. And *Jonſon* replied on the 28th of September: "I can add nothing material to what, you will ſee, I have ſaid to his Honr. the Govr. upon the Subject of the Writ applied for by the Cuſtom Houſe Officers. It ſeems it is in Practice here, tho' how it can have exiſted, ſo long as it has, I am at a loſs to Determine. It is certainly of a dangerous Nature. The Revenue Laws have

De Grey; (5) and renewed at May term at Hartford, in the following form: 1769.

"Colony

---

have all of them, I think, too much of the Arbitrary in them, & too ftrongly tend to Defpotifm. You juftly Object, that the officer might as well be Authorized by his Commiffion as by fuch a Writ, to which they Anfwer that he has fuch Authority, & that the ufe of the Writ, & the Attendance of the Civil Officer is only to preferve the Peace, which the Revenue Officer has not the Authority to Command, sho'd any difturbance happen. The Intention of this Provifion is therefore, plainly to bring the Common Law in Aid of the Revenue Laws, & to give the latter, all that Countenance & Sanction, which may be derived from the former." Letters & Papers 1761–1776, fol. 83, in Mafs. Hift. Soc. Lib. See alfo Johnfon to Trumbull, September 29, 1769, Stuart's Life of Trumbull, 80.

In May 1768, an attempt made in the legiflature of Connecticut to remove Trumbull, who was alfo Lieutenant Governor, from the office of Chief Juftice, on the ground of the importance of feparating the judiciary from the other branches of government, was defeated, "upon mature deliberation of the whole matter; the affair of general warrants lying in the fituation they are now in, and danger of difficulties from many quarters, jealoufies and uneafinefs of the people, and the like." Connecticut Courant, December 1768.

(5) *Ante*, 453. The writer of the "Journal of the Times," under date of April 29, 1769, fays: "The C—l——r of the port of New-London in Connecticut, has lately applied a fecond time to the fuperiour court there for fuch writs; at the fame time laying a letter before them, which he had received from one of the crown lawyers in England in anfwer to one wrote upon the fubject, in which letter a great compliment was paid to the chief juftice of the Maffachufetts, for the proof he had given of a right underftanding of the law, and of his zeal for his Majefty's fervice, by fo readily granting thofe writs, upon the application made by the cuftom-houfe officers; and his example was recommended as worthy of their imitation. The court did not however think proper to show a like complaifance, but chofe to refer this requeft, to the confideration of their general affembly at the approaching feffion." Bofton Evening Poft of June 26, 1769.

"At April 1769 term laft at Norwich, Mr. Stewart," the Collector, as we learn from Chief Juftice *Trumbull*, "made further application to the Superior Court for fuch Writs; and produced Forms of fuch from the Board of Commiffioners as they judged proper for us to give, with *the Cafe* per Mr. *De Grey*. To which the Court replied, that they would be further advifed, and as the Seffions of the General Affembly was near, they fhould afk their advice and direction. Accordingly the matter

1769. " Colony of Connecticut
" Hartford County ss. May 23d, A.D. 1769.

" To the Honourable Jonathan Trumbull Esqr Chief " Justice: Robert Walker, Matthew Griswold, Eliphalet " Dyer, and Roger Sherman, Esquires, Assistant Justices of " his Majesty's Superior Court of Judicature within for " said Colony:

" May it please your Honours.

" At the request of David Lisle Esqr Solicitor of his " Majesty's American Customs, signified to me by letter of " the 9th instant, I am now to desire and move your Hon- " ors that a final and judicial determination be had, con- " cerning the issuing of Writs of Assistants to the Officers " of his Majesty's Customs within the said Colony, in con- " sequence of their motion heretofore made for that pur- " pose.

" THOMAS SEYMOUR,
" Attorney for Our Lord the King,
" within and for the County of Hartford." (6)

3. *Rhode*

ter was fully laid before them. They appointed a Committee to consider the letters &c. laid before the Assembly. Within their province fell this matter, and they advised that the Assembly take no notice of it; that it properly belonged to the Superior Court; that, *as individuals*, not as members of the Assembly, they advised the Court *not to grant* such Warrants, which seemed to be the universal opinion." Trumbull to Johnson, June 14, 1769, Stuart's Life of Trumbull, 80, 81.

(6) " Since this," Chief Justice *Trumbull* continues, " Mr. *Seymour*, as Attorney for the King, by direction of the Board of Commissioners, has made application to me for a Judicial Determination on the Matter. I have given him no answer, nor do I intend giving any till the Next Term, which now soon comes on.

" I have taken care to find what the Courts in the other Colonies have done, and find no such Writs have been given by any of the Courts except in Massachusetts and New Hampshire, where they were given as soon as asked for. I believe the Courts in all the other Colonies will be as well united, and as firm in this Matter, as in anything that has yet happened between us and Great Britain.

" I have never yet seen any Act of Parliament authorizing the Court of

3. *Rhode Iſland.*

1769.

Probably refuſed in Rhode Iſland.

An examination of the records and dockets of the Supreme Court of Judicature of the Colony of Rhode Iſland

---

of Exchequer in giving ſuch Writs as they give, but conceive they have crept into uſe by the inattention of the people, and the bad practices of deſigning men. We are directed to give ſuch writs as the Court of Exchequer are enabled by Act of Parliament to give, which are very different, as I conceive, from ſuch Writs as they do give. Our Court will on all occaſions of complaint grant ſuch Warrants as may be neceſſary for promoting his Majeſty's ſervice, and at the ſame time conſiſtent with the liberty and privilege of the ſubject, and made returnable to the court; but further than that we dare not go, and they muſt not expect we ſhall." Trumbull to Johnſon, June [July ?] 14, 1769, *ub. ſup.*

Johnſon, in a letter dated "Weſtminſter, Octo[r] 16th, 1769," acknowledging the receipt of a letter from *Trumbull* of July 14th, wrote: "The Intelligence, you have favour'd me with, of the Steps which have been taken relative to Writs of Aſſiſtance, is very obliging, as well as uſeful to the purpoſe you mention. It gives me pleaſure to find that it is ſo probable that the Courts of the other Colonies will be agreed with you in this important point. Union in this, as in everything elſe, is of the laſt Importance. If an United Stand is made upon this occaſion, I think it extremely probable that this capital Point will be carryed without much difficulty; & it will be a very great fatisfaction, & not a little redound to their Honour, that the Sup[r] Court of Connecticut have taken the lead in a matter of ſo much Conſequence to the Liberty, the Property, and the Security, of the Subject. The Example of the Courts of the Maſſachuſetts Bay and N: Hampſhire ought not to Influence the Courts in the other Colonies. It is eaſy to Account for their Conduct. But of them it is moſt Candid to ſay that they were ſurpriſed into this Injudicious Step, & to ſuppoſe that they wiſh it were now *Res Integra* & to do again, that they might Unite with their Brethren throughout the Continent in making a neceſſary & noble Stand againſt ſo dangerous an Encroachment upon the Rights of a free People." Johnſon's Letters, 217, 218.

Although we have no record of the ſubſequent action of the court, yet we can hardly fail to infer from the letters above quoted that the writs were ultimately refuſed; eſpecially when we remember that the Chief Juſtice and two of his aſſociates, *Griſwold* and *Dyer*, were among the aſſiſtants who had left the Council Chamber in 1765 to avoid witneſſing the taking of the oath to execute the Stamp Act by Governor *Fitch;* Stuart's Life of Trumbull, 91, 92; and that a third, *Roger Sherman*, told *John Adams* a few years later, that "he read Mr. Otis's

 Rights

1769. Island 1761–1769, which seem to be quite complete, discloses no trace of Writs of Assistance; and the only papers upon the subject are among the files of March term 1769, and consist of the opinion of Attorney General *De Grey* (printed *ante*, 452–454) and of a letter from the Solicitor of the Board of Customs in Boston to the Attorney General of Rhode Island, desiring him to move the Superior Court for Writs of Assistance to the officers of the customs there. (7)

4. *New York.*

Rights &c. in 1764, and thought that he conceded away the rights of America," and "thought the reverse of the declaratory act was true, namely, that the Parliament of Great Britain had authority to make laws for America in no case whatever." 2 John Adams's Works, 343.

(7) This letter, which is in a different hand from the signature, and seems to have been a circular prepared by order of the Commissioners of Customs in Boston to be transmitted to all the Colonies, (*ante*, 455; *infra*, 510,) is as follows:

"Sir

"I am directed by the Comissioners of His Majestys Customs to "transmit you the Form of a Writ of Assistants to the Officers of the "Customs, as issued by the superior Court here; likewise blank Forms "of the Writ, and a copy of the Opinion of the Attorney General in "England in relation thereto; and I am to desire the Favour of you "to move the superior Court of your Province that Writs of Assistants "may be issued to the Officers undermentioned, and from time to time "to such Officers as the Board may direct to apply for the same, by "their Solicitor. I am, Sir,

"Your most humble servant

"D. Lisle, Solicitor to the American Customs

"Boston March 16th 1769

"Charles Dudley Esqr Collector

"John Nicholl Esqr Comptr

"Nicholas Lechmere Esqr Searcher.

"Mr. Attorney General of Rhode Island."

The following letter from the Chief Justice of Rhode Island to Chief Justice *Trumbull* (2 Trumbull MSS. 222, in Mass. Hist. Soc. Lib.) shows that the Writs were not granted immediately; and, taken in connection with the state of feeling in Rhode Island (*ante* 436, 437) and the want of any evidence of any action of the Court upon the subject, makes it probable that none were ever issued.

"South Kingston Aug. 7th 1769

"Sir

"Judge *Russell* did me the Honor to transmitt me your Letter to him "of

4. *New York.* 1768.

" Thurſday the Twenty eighth day of April, 1768.
" Preſent
" The Honōble Daniel Horſmanden Eſq.r Chief Juſtice.
" The Honōble David Jones Eſquire ſecond Juſtice.
" The Honōble William Smith Eſquire third Juſtice."

" On the application of Andrew Elliot Eſquire Collector " and Lambert Moore Eſquire Comptroller of his Majeſty's " Cuſtoms of the Port of New York, for Writts of Aſſiſt- " ants to themſelves and the other Officers of the ſaid Cuſ- " toms,

Granted in New York.

" of the 14th June laſt reſpecting Writs of Aſſiſtants to the Cuſtom " Houſe Officers. As I was then but juſt nominated in the Court, had " not seen M.r *De Greys* State of the Caſe, nor had any opportunity of " converſing with any One of my Brethren; I did not return your " Honor an Anſwer. And indeed Sir I remain juſt in the ſame Situa- " tion, without having had an Opportunity of Information in any One " Point; ſo that it is impoſſible for me to ſay what will ~~likely~~ be the " Determination of the Court, eſpecially as there are ſeveral new Mem- " bers with whom I never converſed on the Subject. The Caſe hereto- " fore in the year 1767 was moved in our Court, who then put of the " Determination, making the ſame Excuſe as you did in Connecticutt: " had it been then determined I am very ſure it would have paſſed in " the Negative.

" Should it be found on Examination that the Writ ought to be " granted, I think there can't be much in the Objection that it may be " miſuſed & the Offenders eſcape with Impunity; to ſuppoſe a Court " authoriſed to grant a Writ, and not have Power to puniſh the abuſe " of it, to me appears a ſolecïſm.

" M.r *Trumbull* who did me the Favor of yours from M.r *Ruſſell* told " me that Col.o *Dyer* was bound on a Journey to the Weſtward, & " that he intended to take the Opinion of the Judges there; As I think " with you 'that Union of Sentiment & Practice of the Court of each " Colony is needful on this Occaſion' I beg the Favor of you to let me " know the Opinion of the Judges in the weſtern Colonies, as well as " thoſe of your Court. Our next Term will be at Newport the firſt " Monday in September.

" I am with great Reſpect
" Sir your moſt hble & obedient Servant
" J. A. Helme.

" The Honble Jonathan Trumbull Esq"

1768. "toms, agreeable to an Act of Parliament made in the "Seventh Year of his present Majesty's Reign: It is "ordered by the Court that Writts of Assistants issue to "the Officers of his Majesty's said Customs severally, ac-"cording to the directions of the said Act." (8)

5. *New Jersey.*

Probably not granted in New Jersey.

Even the St. of 7 G. 3, c. 46, did not remove the difficulties in the way of granting Writs of Assistance in New Jersey; (9) and as the records of the court there, which are in quite a perfect state, contain no evidence of any writs having been issued (10), it seems likely that those difficulties were not overcome. One of the earliest statutes of the State of New Jersey, passed during the Revolutionary War, shows that the subject must have attracted some attention in that State. (11)

6. *Pennsylvania.*

---

(8) Minute Book 1766–69, fol. 453, in the office of the County Clerk in New York City. This is the only known evidence of the issuing of Writs of Assistance in New York. It was after the passage of St. 7 G. 3, and the particular form in which the writs were issued does not appear.

(9) Governor Bernard to Lieutenant Governor Franklin, March 24, 1768, quoted *ante*, 451.

(10) The writer is indebted for this information to the courtesy of Chancellor *Green* of New Jersey, who has kindly examined the records.

(11) By St. of June 24, 1782, c. 317, entitled "an Act for preventing an illieit Trade and Intercourse between the Subjects of this State and the Enemy," § 18, it was enacted, "that it shall and may be lawful for any judge of the Court of Common Pleas in any County of this State, and he is hereby authorised and required, upon Application to him made, and due and satisfactory Cause of Suspicion shewn, on Oath or Affirmation, which Oath or Affirmation shall be taken in Writing and subscribed, as in case of stolen Goods, that Goods, Wares, or Merchandize, liable to Seizure by Virtue of this Act, are concealed or deposited in any Dwelling-house or other Building whatoever, within such County, to grant a Warrant, directed to the Sheriff or any of the Coroners of such County, who are hereby respectively required to pay Obedience to such Warrant, and to make Search for, and to seize and secure such Goods, Wares or Merchandize; and in case of Refusal to permit such Search, or if Opposition be made thereto to break open Doors and Locks for

1768.

6. *Pennſylvania.*

Probably refuſed in Pennſylvania.

It would ſeem that in Pennſylvania Writs of Aſſiſtance were refuſed, even after the paſſage of the St. of 7 G. 3, c. 46. Chief Juſtice *Allen* was at firſt oppoſed to iſſuing them. (12) And ſome examination of the files and records of the Court has not diſcloſed any ſigns of his having changed his opinion.

7. *Maryland.*

No evidence in Maryland.

Nothing has been diſcovered upon the ſubjects of Writs of Aſſiſtance in this Province. But as early as 1698 an application was made to the Governor and Council by an officer of the cuſtoms for a "Warrant of Aſſiſtance." (13)

8. *Virginia.*

---

for the Purpoſe aforeſaid. PROVIDED ALWAYS, That no ſuch Search ſhall be made before Sun-riſing, nor after Sun-ſetting. AND PROVIDED ALSO, that no Perſon ſhall be hereby authorized to enter any Houſe or other Building as aforeſaid, other than the Sheriff or Coroner, and two reſpectable Freeholders not being the Informers, or intereſted in the Seizure, unleſs Oppoſition be made by an armed Force."

(12) Boſton Gazette of Auguſt 15, 768, quoted *ante*, 502, note. Opinion of Attorney General De Grey, *ante*, 454. He had been oppoſed to the Stamp Act. 5 Bancroft's Hiſt. U. S. 182.

(13) The writer's firſt knowledge of this was acquired from an "Index to the Calendar of Maryland State Papers, compiled under direction of John Henry Alexander, Esq. L.L. D.," Baltimore, 1861, p. 5. The record referred to in that calendar is as follows:

"March 30, 1698. It being preſented to his Excellency and this Board by David Kennedy Eſquire his Majeſty's Collector of the Diſtrict of Pocomoke that his Majeſty's Service is much prejudiced for want of a Warrant of Aſſiſtance to empower him to preſs Men and Horſes for that whilſt he is a Going to a Juſtice of the Peace perhaps Ten or Twelve Miles from the Place where he has Occaſion for Aſſiſtance the Traders may take Liberty to run what Goods they pleaſe in the Interim," &c. This petition was "referred to his Majeſty's Lawyers to conſult and make report what ſort of Warrant ſhall be granted." But no report appears. 10 Maryland Council Rec. fol. 17.

The writer is indebted to the politeneſs of Mr. *Alexander* for a copy of this record, as well as for the information that no trace of Writs of Aſſiſtance in later times has been found in Maryland.

1769

Special writs granted in Virginia.

8. *Virginia.*

In Virginia, after the paſſage of St. 7, G. 3, c. 46, the Supreme Court of Juſtice refuſed to grant general Writs of Aſſiſtance, but granted ſpecial Writs. (14)

9. *Other Colonies.*

Writs of Aſſiſtance refuſed elſewhere.

The only evidence, attainable at preſent, of proceedings in the other Colonies tends to ſhow that Writs of Aſſiſtance were not granted in any that afterwards became part of the United States. (15)

---

(14) This appears by the following correſpondence, preſerved in the State Paper Office in London, for copies of which the writer is indebted to the kindneſs of Mr. *Bancroft*.

On the 15th of May 1769 *John Randolph*, Attorney General of Virginia, wrote to the Commiſſioners of the Cuſtoms at Boſton : " Upon receipt of your favor of 21ſt March, incloſing the form of a Writ of Aſſiſtants, and the opinion of the Attorney General, shewing the legality of the ſame, I immediately laid them before our Supreme Court of Juſtice, which was then ſitting; and moved that a ſimilar Writ might be granted to thoſe Officers of the Cuſtoms, whoſe Names you mentioned in your Letter. The Gentlemen of our Bar very ſtrenuouſly oppoſed the Motion, and inſiſted that the Writ ſent was by no means conformable to the Act of Parliament ; that its direction was too general, and ought to be regulated by the 32d clauſe of the 14 Car. II. ; that the Act gives no authority to enter houſes etc. in the night time ; and that the Writ ought not to be a ſtanding one, but granted from time to time, as the information of the Officer to the Supreme Court, on oath, may render neceſſary. Theſe obſervations at length prevailed, and the Court directed me to prepare a Writ agreeable to the words of the Act of Parliament, which was accordingly done and approved of, a copy of which I thought proper to tranſmit to you."

Lord *Botetourt*, in a letter to the Earl of *Hillſborough*, dated " Williamſburg, May 16, 1769," incloſed a copy of the above letter, and added : " I was upon the Bench when he made the motion, and concurred with my Brethren in directing him to draw a Writ exactly conformable to the Acts of Parliament which relate to that matter and are in force in this Colony ; and it is with great pleaſure I can aſſure your Lordſhip that the Bench of Counſellors are always of opinion to make the Law the rule of their conduct, however diſagreeable the letter of it may be to them in their ſeveral capacities."

(15) " To the everlaſting Honor of the great and worthy *'Squire Graſpall,*

Graſpall, that Man of *Truth and Juſtice*, we are well informed that every Province in America, except Maſſachuſetts-Bay and Halifax, have refuſed to grant General Warrants or Writs of Aſſiſtants to the Order of the Commiſſioners; even the little Colonies of Georgia and the Florida's have abſolutely refuſed it." Boſton Gazette of September 11, 1769. This ſquib is evidently aimed at *Hutchinſon*, in alluſion to his granting Writs of Aſſiſtance and his plurality of offices. *Vid. ante*, 418, 426, note 10. If its ſtatements could be relied on as ſtrictly accurate, they would ſeem to indicate that in New Hampſhire (*ſupra*, 502) the application had not been renewed ſince the paſſage of St. 7 G. 3, or, if renewed, that the writs had been granted in a modified form; and that in New York the Writs iſſued "according to the directions of the ſaid Act," (*supra*, 508,) were ſpecial, as in Virginia, *supra*, 510, note. 1769.

I. Were the Writs of Affiftance legal?

A REPORT of the controverfy upon the Writs of Affiftance would be incomplete without an examination of the legal correctnefs of the decifion of *Hutchinfon* and his affociates. Such an examination naturally refolves itfelf into four queftions.

1ft. Did Acts of the Parliament of Great Britain bind the Colonies?

2d. Were thofe Acts of Parliament, which provided for Writs of Affiftance, void for unconftitutionality?

3d. Did thofe Acts, properly conftrued, authorize the iffuing of general Writs of Affiftance?

4th. Had the Superior Court of Judicature of the Province the powers of the Englifh Court of Exchequer in this refpect?

I. The infeparablenefs of taxation and reprefentation, and the diftinction between external and internal taxes, were familiar to the law of England before the difcovery of America.

In the reign of Edward 3 Irifh nobles were fometimes fummoned to the Englifh Parliament — "an excellent prefident to be followed," fays Lord *Coke*, "whenever any Act of Parliament fhall be made in England concerning the ftate of Ireland." (1) In 1441 Chief Juftice *Fortefcue* held, that an act of the Irifh Parliament, forfeiting offices in Ireland held by abfentees, vacated an office previoufly expreffly granted by the King to one or his deputy; and faid that an Englifh ftatute granting a tax would not bind the Irifh, unlefs approved by their Parliament. For this laft pofition the counfel for the lofing party fuggefted the reafon

(1) 4 Inft. 350. Bro. Ab. Parliament, 84.

reaſon, that they were not repreſented in Parliament. (2) In 1486 the ſame doctrine and the ſame reaſon were laid down

Taxation and repreſentation.

---

(2) *Pilkington's caſe*, 20 H. 6, 8. This was *ſcire facias* to repeal letters patent of the King, granting an office in Ireland to *A.*, which he had previouſly granted to *John Pilkington* to occupy by himſelf or his deputy. *A.* pleaded "that the ſaid land of Ireland is and always has been a land ſeparated and ſevered from the Kingdom of England, and ruled and governed by the cuſtoms and laws of the ſame land; and that the Lords of that ſame land, who are the King's Council, have uſed from time to time in the abſence of the King to elect a Juſtice, who, ſo elected, ſhall have power to pardon and puniſh all felonies, treaſons &c. *to aſſemble a Parliament &c. and by advice of their Lords and Commonalty to make ſtatutes;* and further how a Parliament was ſummoned," at which it was ordained, that every one who held any office in Ireland ſhould before a certain day occupy it by himſelf, or forfeit it; and that the plaintiff occupied the ſaid office by a deputy until that day, ſo that the office became void, and was afterwards granted to the defendant by the ſaid letters patent, which he prayed might be made effectual. This plea was demurred to, but adjudged good.

Pilkington's caſe.

Sir *John Forteſcue*, C. J. K. B., after ſhowing that "this preſcription was not in any of the perſons of Ireland, but in the King himſelf," under whom the defendant as well as the plaintiff claimed, added, "the land of Ireland is ſevered from the Kingdom of England; *for if a tenth or fifteenth be granted here, that ſhall not bind thoſe of Ireland, even if the King ſhall ſend that ſtatute into Ireland under his great ſeal, unleſs they will in their Parliament approve it; but if they will allow it, then it ſhall be held there that they ſhall be bound by it;* and ſo this preſcription is good; ſo that the letters patents ſhould be adjudged effectual." Upon the delivery of this opinion, Serjeant *Portington*, for the plaintiff, ſaid that it was very true "that a tenth granted in the Parliament here shall not bind thoſe of Ireland, *becauſe they have no commandment with us by Writ to come to Parliament:* but this is no proof that the land is ſevered from England, for a tenth granted shall not bind thoſe of Wales, or of the County Palatine of Cheſter, and yet they are not ſevered from this Kingdom."

The Chief Juſtice's brother, Sir *Henry Forteſcue*, had previouſly been C. J. K. B. in Ireland; the plaintiff's counſel, Serjeants *Yelverton* and *Portington*, were both ſoon after raiſed to the bench; and Serjeant *Markham*, the defendant's counſel, ſucceeded Chief Juſtice *Forteſcue* as C. J. K. B. in England. 4 Foſs's Judges of England, 309, 310, 354, 379, 442, 462.

It will be obſerved that the Chief Juſtice's ſtatement as to the power of the Engliſh Parliament was merely *obiter dictum;* for the caſe only concerned

External and internal taxes.

down by all the Judges of England, limited however to internal as oppofed to external legiflation. (3)

Lord

---

concerned the power of the Irish Parliament to legiflate where the English Parliament had not.

The only other judge who appears to have faid anything was *Ayfcoghe* (a Judge of the Common Bench — Ib. 282), who feems to have refted his opinion upon the rule of pleading, that the plaintiff, having by demurrer admitted a prefcription, could not object to the validity of that prefcription; "for when he has not denied the prefcription, we muft underftand that fuch cuftom is in the land of Ireland, becaufe we shall not be fkilled to take cognizance here what is the law there, except only upon the allegation of the party." This treating the law of Ireland as a foreign law, to be pleaded and proved as a fact, indicates an opinion that the two Iflands were governed by diftinct laws. See *Palfrey* v. *Portfmouth, Saco & Portland Railroad*, 4 Allen, 56, 57.

Cafe of Waterford Merchants.

(3) *Cafe of the Merchants of Waterford*, 2 Ric. 3, 11, 12. Certain Merchants of Waterford in Ireland, who had shipped merchandife there to be carried to Flanders, but whofe fhip had been driven by ftrefs of weather into Calais (then an Englifh port), and there informed againft by the Treafurer of Calais, and feized for a violation of St. 15 H. 6, c. 8, applied to the King in Council for reftitution, and fhowed a royal licenfe to carry merchandife from Ireland whitherfoever they would.

"And upon that matter were two queftions: 1st. If corporate towns in Ireland and others dwelling in Ireland were bound by a ftatute made in England; 2d. If the King could give a licenfe againft the ftatute, and efpecially when it was now ordained by the ftatute that the informer should have one half and the King the other. And for the folution of thefe queftions all the Juftices were affembled in the Exchequer Chamber.

"And there as to the firft queftion it was faid, that in the land of Ireland they have a Parliament of their own, and every kind of Court as in England, and by the fame Parliament they make laws and change laws, *and they are not bound by a ftatute in England, becaufe they have here no Knights in Parliament; but this is to be underftood of affecting their lands and things on land only, for their perfons are fubjects of the King, and as fubjects are bound as to doing anything outfide their land contrary to ftatute*, like the inhabitants in Calais, Gascoigne, Guienne, &c. while they were fubjects."

"And as to the fecond queftion, the King can well enough give a licence with a claufe of *non-obftante*," "fo far as it touches the King, but not fo far as it touches a party;" and that there was a difficulty in

pardoning

Lord *Coke* declared in the Houſe of Commons in 1627 that "the lord may tax his villein high or low, but it is againſt the franchiſes of the land, for freemen to be taxed, but by their conſent in Parliament." (4) Lord *Hale* is ſaid to have been of opinion that "no acts here can bind the Iriſh

Coke.

Hale.

---

pardoning after an action brought or ſeizure made, in which the informer had an intereſt.

It is evident that no final decree was then entered; for upon the death of Richard 3 and the acceſſion of Henry 7 the petitioners renewed their bill; and after notice to the Treaſurer of Calais, the caſe was reheard, and ſeems to have been diſpoſed of upon the ground previously indicated, that the informer had acquired an intereſt which the King could not releaſe. *S. C.* 1 H. 7, 1.

In the courſe of this ſecond hearing "*Huſſey*, C. J. ſaid that the ſtatutes made in England ſhould bind thoſe of Ireland. Which," the reporter adds, "was not much denied by the other Juſtices, although ſome of them were of a contrary opinion the laſt term in his abſence. Then he ſaid they muſt ſee how the ſtatutes and their licence could be together," and proceeded to do ſo. 1 H. 7, 2, 3. *Huſſey's* ſtatement has ſometimes been underſtood as an aſſertion that all Engliſh ſtatutes bind Ireland, and ſo the reporter may have underſtood it; but "the ſtatutes" would ſeem rather to apply to the particular ſtatutes in queſtion, which had been held at the previous hearing by a majority of the Judges, at leaſt, to be binding on the Iriſh. That Lord *Coke* did not conſider the firſt opinion as ſhaken by the laſt is ſhown by his repeatedly quoting it with approval. *Calvin's caſe*, 7 Rep. 22 *b*. *Parliament in Ireland*, 12 Rep. 111. And ſee Jenk. Cent. 164.

In explanation of the opinion "as to the ſecond queſtion," it ſhould be remembered that the power of the King to diſpenſe with penal ſtatutes was recognized to ſome extent by law, until the paſſage of the Bill of Rights in 1688. See *Caſe of Non-obſtante*, 12 Rep. 18; Co. Lit. 120 *a*, & Hargrave's notes; St. 1 W. & M. St. 2, c. 2, § 12; 3 Hallam's Conſt. Hist. Eng. (7th ed.) 60, 104; Amos's notes to Fortescue de Laudibus, c. 9.

(4) 2 Parl. Hist. 237. Lord *Mansfield's* ſtatement in the Houſe of Lords in 1766, that a doubt thrown out in the Houſe of Commons in 1621, "whether Parliament had anything to do with America," "was immediately anſwered, I believe, by *Coke*," is ſhown, by refering to the Journals of the Houſe, to have been unwarranted, in ſo far as he attempted to vouch in the authority of his greater predeceſſor. 16 Parl. Hiſt. 176. 1 Commons Journals, 591, 592.

Mansfield's miſſtatement of Coke.

Blackſtone. Iriſh in point of ſubſidies." (5) Even Sir *William Blackſtone*, in the debate on the repeal of the Stamp Act, is reported to have "declared, Tory as he was, that Parliament had no right to impoſe internal taxes." (6) And Lord *Camden*, in his firſt ſpeech in the Houſe of Lords, ſaid that the Act of 1766, declaring the right of the Britiſh Parliament to make laws to bind the American Colonies in all caſes whatſoever was "illegal, abſolutely illegal, contrary to the fundamental laws of nature, contrary to the fundamental laws of this Conſtitution;" (7) and, nine years later, ſpeaking "not only as a ſtateſman, politician and philoſopher, but as a common lawyer," told the houſe, "You have no right to tax America." (8)

Camden.

Power of Parliament.

Yet *Coke* agreed with the uniform current of Engliſh authority, in holding that an Act of Parliament bound Ireland or the Colonies, if expreſſly named or neceſſarily included therein. (9) And *Camden*, in the winter of 1767–8, ſaid

(5) MS. on the Prerogative of the Crown, quoted by Lord *Camden* in the Houſe of Lords in the Debate on the Repeal of the Stamp Act. 16 Parl. Hist. 169, 170.

(6) 2 Walpole's Memoirs of George 3, 279.

(7) 16 Parl. Hist. 168, 169, 170, 177. 5 Bancroft's Hiſt. U. S. 403. This ſpeech was reprinted from the Political Regiſter of October 3, 1767, in the Boſton Gazette of January 18, 1768, and was read a few days earlier in the Maſſachuſetts Houſe of Repreſentatives by *Otis*, who "triumphed upon it moſt immoderately." Bernard to Jackſon, January 16, 1768, 6 Bernard Papers, 67.

Quincy's report of Camden.

(8) Quincy's Life of Quincy, 329. It was on this occaſion that Lord *Camden* "imagined, that a power reſulting from a truſt, arbitrarily exerciſed, may be lawfully reſiſted; whether the power is lodged in a collective body, or ſingle perſon;" and cited with approval the ſaying of *Selden*, that to reſiſt tyranny was the cuſtom of England, and the cuſtom of England was the law of the land. Ib. 330, 332. The notes then taken by *Joſiah Quincy, Jr.* were in the opinion of *Benjamin Franklin*, who was alſo preſent, "by much the beſt account preſerved of that day's debate." Ib. 492. *Quincy's* journal is alſo the earlieſt evidence we have of *Camden's* prophecy to *Franklin* in 1758 of American Independence, and was evidently copied by *Gordon*. Ib. 269, 270. 1 Gordon's Hiſt. U. S. 136.

(9) *Orork's caſe*, 1 And. 263. *Earl of Derby's caſe*, 2 And. 116. *Calvin's*

faid in the Houfe of Lords that "though he had been clearly of opinion that Parliament had no fuch right, yet fince it had been declared by Parliament, he did not think himfelf, or any man elfe, at liberty to call it in queftion." (10) The reafon of this is to be found in that principle of the Englifh law, which attributes to Parliament the fupreme legiflative authority and the ultimate power of deciding what accords with the Conftitution. (11) In England, as has been truly faid by Lord *Brougham*, though it founds to American ears like a paradox, "things may be legal and yet unconftitutional." (12)

Under the Colony Charter, Maffachufetts conftantly afferted her right of exemption from Parliamentary taxation, upon the ground of not being reprefented in Parliament. (13) And

Maffachufetts Colony.

Calvin's cafe, 7 Rep. 17 *b*, 22 *b*. *Parliament in Ireland*, 12 Rep. 111. 4 Inft. 201. *Procefs into Wales*, Vaugh. 400. *Crow* v. *Ramfey*, 2 Ventr. 5. 1 Chalmers Opinions, 195, 197, 201. *Campbell* v. *Hall*, Cowp. 204. 1 Bl. Com. 101, 106. Barrington on Sts. (5th ed.) 160, 166, & notes. Stokes Law of the Colonies, 4, 28, 29. 1 Chit. Com. & Manuf. 638. Dwarris on Sts. (2d ed.) 527, 906. Clark's Colonial Law, 10, 11. *Quincy*, who heard Lord *Mansfield* deliver his opinion in *Campbell* v. *Hall*, only fays in his journal, "He was perfpicuous and eloquent." Quincy's Life of Quincy, 252.

(10) William Samuel Johnfon from London to Roger Sherman, September 28, 1768, Letters & Papers 1761–1776, fol. 83, in Mafs. Hift. Soc. Lib. See alfo Camden to Grafton, September 4, 1768, in Grafton's Autobiography, and 5 Campbell's Lives of the Chancellors, 280, 281; Quincy's Life of Quincy, 329.

(11) 4 Inft. 36. Bac. Max. 19, 4 Bacon's Works, (ed. 1824) 63. 1 Bl. Com. 9, 89–91, 160–162, 164. Woodeson's Elem. lect. 3, p. 48. *Stockdale* v. *Hanfard*, 11 A. & E. 108, 109, and 2 P. & D. 105, 106. 1 Kent Com. 448.

(12) *Wenfleydale Peerage*, 5 H. L. Cas. 979.

(13) In 1641 the Government of the Colony declined to folicit favors from Parliament, "for this confideration, that if we fhould put ourfelves under the protection of the Parliament, we muft then be fubject to all fuch laws as they should make, or at leaft fuch as they might impofe upon us; in which courfe, though they should intend our good, yet it might prove very prejudicial to us." 2 Winthrop's Hift. N. E. 25. And fee Ib. 42, 182, 183. *Edward Winflow*, the agent fent to England

Earlieft pofition of Maffachufetts.

And upon this theory ſeveral acts were paſſed by the General Court to carry into effect the Acts of Trade and Navigation. (14)

Province of Maſſachuſetts.

Under the Province Charter the ſubjection to the authority of Parliament ſeems to have been leſs diſputed on grounds of legal right. The firſt ſtatute of the Province was "an act ſetting forth general priveledges," one of which was that no tax ſhould be impoſed or levied on perſons or eſtates, "on any colour or pretence whatſoever, but by the act and conſent of the Governour, Council and

---

England in 1646 to plead for the judicial and legislative rights of the Colony, argued that "if the Parliaments of England should impoſe laws upon us, having no burgeſſes in their Houſe of Commons, nor capable of a ſummons by reaſon of the vast distance of the ocean, being three thouſand miles from London, then wee should lose the libertie and freedome of English indeed." 3 Maſs. Col. Rec. 96, 97. Winslow's New England's Salamander Diſcovered, 23 Maſs. Hiſt. Coll. 137, 138. In 1661 the General Court declared, "Wee conceive any impoſition prejudiciall to the country contrary to any juſt lawe of ours, not repugnant to the lawes of England, to be an infringement of our right." 4 Maſs. Col. Rec. pt. ii. 25.

Acts of Trade.

(14) Maſs. Col. St. May, 1663, 4 Maſs. Col. Rec. pt. ii. 86, 87. Letter of General Court to Royal Commiſſioners, May 11, 1665, Ib. 202. Col. St. October, 1677, 5 Ib. 155. In 1678 the General Court, in anſwer to the objections of the Lords of Trade and the Attorney and Solicitor General, wrote "That for the Acts paſſed in Parliament for incouraging trade and navigation, wee humbly conceive, according to the usuall ſayings of the learned in the lawe, that the lawes of England are bounded within the fower ſeas, and doe not reach Amerrica; the ſubjects of his Majeſtie here not being repreſented in Parliament; ſo wee have not looked at ourſelves to be impeded in our trade by them, nor yett wee abated in our relative allegiance to his majeſtie. However, ſo ſoone as wee underſtood his Majeſties pleaſure, that those Acts ſhould be obſerved by his Majeſties ſubjects of the Maſſachuſets, which could not be without invading the liberties and propperties of the ſubject, untill the Generall Court made provision therein by a law, which they did in October 1677," &c. Ib. 200. And they committed the enforcement of the Acts of Trade to the Governor and Council; and ordered him to take the required oath to execute them, and the Acts "to be published in the market place in Boſton by beate of drum." Ib. 236, 262, 337.

and Reprefentatives of the People, affembled in General Court."(15) But this act was difallowed by the King, under the power reserved to him in the new Charter. (16) Three years later Parliament expreffly extended the Acts of Trade to the American Colonies, and declared all laws, by-laws, ufages or cuftoms, repugnant to thofe or any future acts which fhould relate to and mention the Colonies, to be illegal and void. (17) And the lawful authority of all Acts of Parliament, which concerned the Colonies and in terms applied to them, was acknowledged in the Provincial Courts of law, and expreffly admitted in the addreffes of the General Court of Maffachufetts Bay to the Governor in 1757 and 1761; and in matters of external commerce, at leaft, was not ferioufly difputed until after the paffage of the Stamp Act. (18)

The oppofite pofition, if taken in the argument upon the Writs of Affiftance, would have been too ftriking to have been omitted in the contemporary reports. Yet none of them contain anything which could bear that conftruction, except a single expreffion in *Quincy's* Report. (19) And

---

(15) Prov. St. 4 W. & M. (1692); Prov. Laws, (ed. 1699), 1; Anc. Chart. 214.

(16) 2 Hutchinfon's Hift. Mafs. 64, 65.

(17) St. 7 & 8 W. 3, c. 22, § 6. This act was published here by the Governor. Copies of Council Rec. in Office of Secretary of Commonwealth, 1696, fol. 409.

(18) *Ante*, 200, 442–444. 3 Hutchinfon's Hift. Mafs. 65 & note, 92, 164, 463. 2 Marshall's Life of Washington, 74–79. Franklin's Examination before the Houfe of Commons in 1766, 4 Franklin's Works, 169, 170, 196; 16 Parl. Hift. 170, 176. *Hutchinfon* in the fame year went fo far as to pretend that all Acts of Parliament, "except fuch as apparently were confined to the Realm," were law here. *Ante*, 443, 444. On the other hand, the magiftrates of one county in Virginia held that the Stamp Act was not binding there. 5 Bancroft's Hift. U. S. 426, 427. And in South Carolina, with characteriftic originality, a grand jury, by direction of one of the judges. is faid to have prefented parliamentary jurisdiction as a nuifance. Chalmers, Letter to Lord Mansfield in 1780, a copy of which is in the poffeffion of Mr. *Sparks*.

(19) *Ante*, 50.

And the elaborate argument printed in the Bofton Gazette (20) immediately after the decifion, as well as the later publifhed writings of *Otis* and *Thacher*, (21) affert in the moft explicit terms the rightful authority of Parliament to legiflate for the Colonies. (22)

Were unconftitutional Acts of Parliament void?

II. But *Otis*, while he recognized the jurisdiction of Parliament over the Colonies, denied that it was the final arbiter of the juftice and conftitutionality of its own acts; and relying upon words of the greateft Englifh lawyers, and putting out of fight the circumftances under which they

---

(20) *Ante*, 488–494.

(21) Vindication of Conduct of Houfe of Reprefentatives (1762) 15, 20, 32. Rights of British Colonies (1764) 49, 60, 66, 93, 109. Bradford's Mafs. State Papers, 23–25. Remarks on Defence of Halifax Libel (1765) 22, 25. Sentiments of a British American (1765) 5. Confiderations in behalf of the Colonists (1765) 9, 36. Bernard to Shelburne, December 24, 1766, *ante*, 449; 6 Bancroft's Hift. U. S. 38, 39. *Otis* in 1764 even went fo far as to fay, "There is no foundation for the diftinction fome make in England between an internal and external tax on the Colonies." Rights of British Colonies, 63.

Quincy's notes to Blackftone.

(22) It is not propofed to purfue the political hiftory of the queftion. Yet it may be mentioned as a curiosity, that in *Quincy's* copy of the first volume of Blackftone's Commentaries (3d ed. Oxford 1768), in the poffeffion of his fon the Honorable *Jofiah Quincy*, are marginal notes in his handwriting, in which "*Qu.*" is written opposite every affertion of the power of Parliament to legiflate for Ireland or the Colonies. 1 Bl. Com. 103–108. Againft *Blackftone's* statement that "the Statute 6 Geo. 3, c. 12, expreffly declares the power of Parliament to make ftatutes to bind the Colonies in all cafes whatfoever" (1 Bl. Com. 109) *Quincy* writes, "The American Colonies expreffly declared the contrary. (See the Journals of the feveral Affemblies on the Continent.) How is the controverfy to be decided?" In the Houfe of Lords in 1766 Lord *Mansfield* had faid of the fame difpute, "It is only affertion againft affertion." 5 Bancroft's Hift. U. S. 449. *Quincy's* question finds an anfwer in a note of Mr. Justice *Coleridge* to the fame page of *Blackftone*. "It is hardly neceffary to ftate that the American Colonies, who had united to the number of thirteen States, in their opposition to the mother country, fucceeded in eftablishing their independence, and were recognized as a feparate independent nation by a treaty of peace, executed on the 3d of September 1783." 1 Bl. Com. (15th ed.) 109.

they were uttered, contended that the validity of ftatutes muft be judged by the Courts of Juftice; and thus fore-fhadowed the principle of American Conftitutional Law, that it is the duty of the judiciary to declare unconftitutional ftatutes void.

Coke.

His main reliance was the well known ftatement of Lord *Coke* in *Dr. Bonham's cafe* — "It appeareth in our books, that in many cafes the common law will control Acts of Parliament and adjudge them to be utterly void; for where an Act of Parliament is againft common right and reafon or repugnant or impoffible to be performed, the common law will control it and adjudge it to be void." (23) *Otis* feems alfo

---

Bonham's cafe.

(23) 8 Rep. 118 *a*, quoted by *Otis*, *ante*, 474. *Dr. Bonham's cafe*, (fo far as is material to exhibit this point,) was an action of falfe imprisonment, brought against the prefident and cenfors of the College of Phyficians in London, for committing the plaintiff to jail for practising medicine in London without their licenfe. The defendants juftified, on the ground that it was granted in their charter, and fince confirmed by Act of Parliament, that no one should practice medicine in London without licenfe from them, under penalty of 100*s.* for each month, one half to the King, and one half to the College: and it was moreover granted that they should have the fupervifion of all phyficians practifing in London, and the punishment of them for malpractice, and the fcrutiny of all medicines: "fo that the punishment of the fame physicians fo delinquent in the premifes might be by fine and imprifonment, and other fuitable manner." *Coke*, C. J., *Warburton* & *Daniel*, JJ., gave judgment for the plaintiff upon two points: 1st. That the defendants had no power to commit the plaintiff for the caufe alleged. 2d. That if they had fuch power, they had not purfued it. 116 *b*, 117 *a*, 121 *a*. The 2d point need not be further noticed here.

Of the first point "the caufe and reafon shortly was" that the claufe giving the power to fine and imprifon did not apply to thofe practifing without licenfe, but only to thofe who were guilty of malpractice. "And that was made manifeft by five reafons, which were called *vividæ rationes*, becaufe they had their vigor and life from the letters patent and the act itfelf," "by conftruction, and conferring all the parts of them together." 117 *a*. "And all thefe reafons were proved by two grounds or maxims in law: 1. *Generalis claufula non porrigitur ad ea quæ fpecialiter funt comprebenfa.*" 118 *b*. "2. *Verba pofteriora propter certudinem addita ad priora quæ certitudine indigent funt referenda.*" 119 *a*.

The fourth of the reafons thus derived from the whole context, and fupported

alſo to have had in mind the equally familiar *dictum* of Lord *Hobart* — "Even an Act of Parliament made againſt natural

Hobart.

ſupported by legal maxims for reſtraining the application of general words, was this: "The cenſors cannot be judges, ministers, and parties; judges to give ſentence or judgment; ministers to make ſummons; and parties to have the moiety of the forfeiture, *quia aliquis non debet eſſe judex in propria cauſa, imo iniquum eſt aliquem ſuæ rei eſſe judicem;* and one cannot be judge and attorney for any of the parties." "And it appears in our books, that in many caſes, the common law will control Acts of Parliament, and ſometimes adjudge them to be utterly void: for when an Act of Parliament is against common right and reaſon, or repugnant, or impoſſible to be performed, the common law will control it, and adjudge such Act to be void." 118 *a*. And see *S. C.* 2 Brownl. 265.

Coke's defence.

When this paſſage was made one of the points of attack against him, *Coke* called the King's attention to the fact (which had been omitted in the questions drawn up by his enemies, Lord Chancellor *Elleſmere* and Sir *Francis Bacon*) that the words of his report did "not import any new opinion, but only a relation of ſuch authorities of law, as had been adjudged and reſolved in ancient and former times, and were cited in the argument of *Bonham's caſe;*" "and therefore the beginning is, It appeareth in our books, etc. And ſo it may be explained, as it was truly intended." 6 Bacon's Works, (ed. 1824) 400, 405, 407. One of the authorities thus referred to was the remark of *Herle*, *C. J.*, in *Tregor* v. *Vaughan*, 8 E. 3, 30, that "ſome statutes are made against law and right, which they that made them, perceiving, would not put them in execution." The others are either caſes in which a limited construction had been given to general words in order to avoid an abſurdity; or inſtances of rejecting repugnant or unfavorable provisions, as in other English and American caſes. *Caſe of Alton Woods*, 1 Rep. 47. *Cromwell's caſe*, 4 Rep. 13. Jenk. Cent. 196, pl. 4. *Riddle* v. *White*, Gwillim's Tithe Caſes, 1387. *United States* v. *Cantril*, 4 Cranch, 167. *Sullivan* v. *Robbins*, 3 Gray, 476. *Campbell's caſe*, 2 Bland, 232. *Cheezem* v. *State*, 2 Ind. 149.

Coke's later ſtatements.

In a later caſe *Coke* is reported to have ſaid "that *Forteſcue* and *Littleton* and all others agreed, that the law conſists of three parts: First, Common Law: Secondly, Statute Law, which corrects, abridges, and explains the common law: The third, Custom, which takes away the common law: But the common law corrects, allows, and diſallows, both statute law and cuſtom; for if there be repugnancy in statute, or unreaſonableneſs in custom, the common law diſallows and rejects it, as it appears by Dr. *Bonham's caſe*," &c. *Rowles* v. *Maſon*, 2 Brownl. 197,

ural equity, as to make a man judge in his own cafe, is void in itfelf: for *jura naturæ funt immutabilia*, and they are *leges*

197, 198. In his first Inftitute he repeats the same claffification, adding, "The common law hath no controler in any part of it, but the High Court of Parliament." Co. Lit. 115 *b*. Again he fays, in a paffage which feems to have been cited by *Otis*, (*ante*, 56) "the fureft construction of a statute is by the rule and reafon of the common law." Co. Lit. 272 *b*. S. P. *Harbert's Cafe*, 3 Rep. 13 *b*. And in his fecond Inftitute, in commenting on the 12th chapter of Magna Charta, declaring that affizes should "not be taken except in their own counties," and on the apparently repugnant decifion that "if a man be diffeifed of a commote or lordship marcher in Wales, holden of the King *in capite*," the affize should be taken in an adjoining county in England, he fays, "the reafon is notable, for the Lord Marcher, though he had *jura regalia*, yet could not he doe juftice in his owne cafe." "Hereby it appeareth (that I may obferve it once for all) that the beft expofitors of this and all other ftatutes are our bookes and ufe or experience." 2 Inft. 25.

The fame rules of conftruction have prevailed ever fince. Acts of Parliament are always to be construed according to the common law and natural right, even if it should be neceffary for this purpofe to adopt what would otherwife be a forced construction. *Fulmerfton* v. *Steward*, Plow. 109. *Sheffield* v. *Ratcliffe*, Hob. 346. *Williams* v. *Pritchard*, 4 T. R. 3. *The King* v. *Inhabitants of Cumberland*, 6 T. R. 194. Dwarris on Sts. (2d ed.) 484, 623. The rule has been thus expreffed by one of the most exact of modern English judges: "The rule by which we are to be guided in construing Acts of Parliament is to look at the precife words, and to construe them in their ordinary fenfe, unlefs it would lead to any abfurdity or manifest injustice; and if it should, fo to vary and modify them as to avoid that which it certainly could not have been the intention of the legiflature fhould be done." *Parke*, B., in *Perry* v. *Skinner*, 2 M. & W. 476.

Confirmed by other English and

For an example of American opinion upon this subject, it is fufficient to quote from Chief Justice *Marfhall* the following "principles in the expofition of statutes:" "An Act of Congrefs ought never to be conftrued to violate the Law of Nations if any other poffible construction remains, and confequently can never be construed to violate neutral rights, or to affect neutral commerce, further than is warranted by the Law of Nations as understood in this country." "Every part of the statute is to be confidered, and the intention of the legiflature to be extracted from the whole;" and "where great inconvenience will refult from a particular construction, that construction is to be avoided, unlefs the meaning of the legiflature be plain, in which cafe it must be obeyed."

American authorities.

Holt.

leges legum." (24) Lord *Holt* is reported to have ſaid, "What my Lord *Coke* ſays in *Dr. Bonham's caſe* in his 8

---

obeyed." *Murray* v. *The Charming Betsey*, 2 Cranch, 118. *United States* v. *Fiſher*, Ib. 386.

Conſtruction of Conſtitution.

The ſame doctrine has been applied to the construction of a written conſtitution. Chief Juſtice *Parſons*, and his aſſociates (and afterwards in turn ſucceſſors) Justices *Sewall* and *Parker*, in an opinion given to the Maſſachuſetts Houſe of Repreſentatives in 1811, ſaid: "The natural import of the words of any legiſlative act, according to the common uſe of them, when applied to the ſubject-matter of the act, is to be conſidered as expreſſing the intention of the legiſlature; unless the intention, ſo reſulting from the ordinary import of the words, be repugnant to ſound, acknowledged principles of national policy. And if that intention be repugnant to ſuch principles of national policy, then the import of the words ought to be enlarged or reſtrained, ſo that it may comport with thoſe principles; unleſs the intention of the legiſlature be clearly and manifestly repugnant to them. For although it is not to be preſumed that a legiſlature will violate principles of public policy, yet an intention of the legiſlature, repugnant to thoſe principles, clearly, manifestly and constitutionally expreſſed, must have the force of law." *Opinion of Juſtices*, 7 Maſs. 524, 525.

Thus by weighing *Coke's* words, and comparing them with his own statements and later authorities, they are relieved from the miſconstruction, which has occaſioned modern commentators either, like Chancellor *Kent*, to praiſe a boldneſs which *Coke* never aſſumed, or, like Lord *Campbell*, to ſneer at what they would not take the trouble to understand. 1 Kent Com. (6th ed.) 448. 2 Campbell's Lives of the Chancellors, 248, note. 1 Campbell's Lives of the Chief Justices, 290.

Day *v.* Savadge.

(24) *Day* v. *Savadge*, Hob. 87. The diſpute there was upon the liability of a freeman of London to pay wharfage to the city, and the queſtion was whether this ſhould be tried by certificate of the mayor and aldermen according to the cuſtoms of London (which had been confirmed by Act of Parliament) or by a jury. The very paragraph which contains the *dictum* quoted in the text shows that there was another ſufficient reaſon for ordering a trial by jury. That paragraph, which concludes the opinion, is thus: "By that that hath been ſaid it appears, that though in pleading it were confeſſed that the cuſtome of certificate of the customes of London is confirmed by Parliament, yet it made no change in this caſe, both becauſe it is none of the customes intended, and becauſe even an Act of Parliament, made againſt naturall equitie, as to make a man judge in his owne caſe, is void in it ſelfe, for *Jura naturæ ſunt immutabilia*, and they are *leges legum.*" *Bracton*,

8 Rep. is far from any extravagancy, for it is a very reafonable and true faying, That if an Act of Parliament fhould ordain that the fame perfon fhould be party and judge, or what is the fame thing, judge in his own caufe, it would be a void Act of Parliament." (25)

The

Bracton, with more accuracy, wrote, "*Jura enim naturalia dicuntur immutabilia, quia non possunt ex toto abrogari vel auferri, poterit tamen eis derogari vel detrahi in fpecie vel in parte.*" Lib. 1, c. 5, § 8. Bracton.

(25) *City of London* v. *Wood*, 12 Mod. 687. Approved by *Wilde*, J., in *Commonwealth* v. *Worcefter*, 3 Pick. 472, and by *Metcalf*, J., in *Williams* v. *Robinfon*, 6 Cufh. 335, 336.

Nemo debet effe judex in fua propria caufa has always been a fundamental maxim of the common law. *Chancellor of Oxford's cafe*, 8 H. 6, 18; Bro. Ab. Patent, 15. Lit. § 212. Co. Lit. 141 *a*. *Derby's cafe*, 12 Rep. 114; 4 Inst. 213. 2 Rol. Ab. Judges, A. *Hesketh* v. *Braddock*, 3 Bur. 1858. *The Queen* v. *Juftices of Hertfordfhire*, 6 Q. B. 753. *Dimes* v. *Grand Junction Canal*, 3 H. L. Cas. 759. *Egerton* v. *Brownlow*, 4 H. L. Cas. 240. *Pearce* v. *Atwood*, 13 Mafs. 340, 341. *Commonwealth* v. *McLane*, 4 Gray, 427. *Hufh* v. *Sherman*, 2 Allen, 597. *Wafhington Ins. Co.* v. *Price*, Hopk. Ch. 1. *Peck* v. *Freeholders of Effex*, Spencer, 475; 1 Zab. 657. Governor *Winthrop*, when accufed before the General Court of Maffachufetts in 1645 for acts done by him as a magiftrate, "coming in with the reft of the magiftrates, placed himfelf beneath within the bar and fo fat uncovered." 2 Winthrop's Hift. N. E. 224. And fo did Lord *Holt* upon the trial in 1693 of a fuit brought by the Crown to teft his right as C. J. K. B. to appoint the chief clerk for enrolling pleas in that court. *Bridgman* v. *Holt*, Show. P. C. 111. Yet an interefted judge may act if no other has jurifdiction of the matter. *Anon.* cited 8 H. 6, 19 *b*, and Bro. Ab. Judges, 6. *Great Charte* v. *Kennington*, 2 Stra. 1173; Bur. Set. Cas. 194. *The Queen* v. *Great Weftern Railway*, 13 Q. B. 327. *Ranger* v. *Great Weftern Railway*, 5 H. L. Cas. 88. *Commonwealth* v. *Ryan*, 5 Mafs. 92. *Hill* v. *Wells*, 6 Pick. 109. *Commonwealth* v. *Emery*, 11 Cush. 411. *In re Leefe*, 2 Barb. Ch. 39. Or if he is expreflly authorized by ftatute. *The King* v. *Juftices of Effex*, 5 M. & S. 513. *Commonwealth* v. *Worcefter*, 3 Pick. 472. *Commonwealth* v. *Reed*, 1 Gray, 474, 475. And an interefted judge may do formal acts neceffary to bring the cafe before the proper tribunal. *The King* v. *Yarpole*, 4 T. R. 71. *Dimes* v. *Grand Junction Canal*, 3 H. L. Cas. 787. *Jeffries* v. *Sewall*, 2 John Adams's Works, 138, 139. *Richardfon* v. *Bofton*, 1 Curt. C. C. 251. *Buckingham* v. *Davis*, 9 Maryland, 329. *Heydenfeldt* v. *Towns*, 27 Alab. 430. But if a judge caufes a fuit in which he is interefted to be brought

No man a judge in his own caufe.

Other English authorities.

The law was laid down in the same way, on the authority of the above cases, in Bacon's Abridgment, first published in 1735; in Viner's Abridgment, published 1741–51, from which *Otis* quoted it; and in Comyn's Digest, published 1762–7, but written more than twenty years before. And there are older authorities to the same effect. So that at the time of *Otis's* agreement his position appeared to be supported by some of the highest authorities in the English law. (26) The

---

brought before him, his judgment therein will be void, although he is sole judge of the court. *Mayor of Hereford's case*, cited 7 Mod. 1; 2 Ld. Raym. 766; & 1 Salk. 201, 396. *Richardson* v. *Welcome*, 6 Cush. 332. Judge *Rolle* was of opinion that even consent of parties would not give jurisdiction to an interested judge, "because it is against natural reason." *Smith* v. *Hancock*, Style, 138. But it is now well settled that the objection of interest may be waived, unless it is made by constitution or statute an absolute disqualification. *Regina* v. *Cheltenham Commissioners*, 1 Q. B. 475. *Kent* v. *Charlestown*, 2 Gray, 281. *Tolland* v. *County Commissioners*, 13 Gray, 13. *Sigourney* v. *Sibley*, 21 Pick. 106. *Paddock* v. *Wells*, 2 Barb. Ch. 335. *Oakley* v. *Aspinwall*, 3 Comst. 547.

(26) Bac. Ab. Statutes, A. Vin. Ab. Statutes, E. 6, pl. 15; *ante*, 51. Com. Dig. Parliament, R. 27. Story's Miscellaneous Writings, 125–133. Doct. & Stud. lib. 1, cc. 2, 6. 1 Finch, c. 6. Noy's Max. 19. *John Milton*, in his Defence of the People of England, appealed to "that fundamental maxim in our law, by which nothing is to be counted a law, that is contrary to the law of God, or of reason." 6 Milton's Prose Works, (ed. 1851) 204.

Blackstone.

Even Sir *William Blackstone* in his Commentaries, first published in 1765, admitted "that the rule is generally laid down that acts of parliament contrary to reason are void;" adding, however, "but if the parliament will positively enact a thing to be done which is unreasonable, I know of no power that can control it." 1 Bl. Com. 91. And so the law was stated in the editions published during his life, the eighth and last of which was published in 1778. In the posthumous editions his statement is thus modified: "I know of no power in the ordinary forms of the Constitution, that is vested with authority to control it;" and the qualifying words appear in the corrections for the press made in his own handwriting in the margin of a copy of the eighth edition, now owned by Mr. *Francis E. Parker* of Boston. Perhaps the American Revolution forced itself more distinctly upon the notice of the learned commentator between 1778 and his death in 1780.

Opposite the statements of the power of the Parliament in 1 Bl. Com. 49, 97,

The ſame doctrine was repeatedly aſſerted by *Otis*, (27) and was a favorite in the Colonies before the Revolution. (28) There are later *dicta* of many eminent judges to

American authorities.

97, 161, 189, *Quincy* in his copy wrote "Qu," and references to Vattel's Law of Nations, Bk. 1, c. 3, pp. 15–19, and Furneaux's Letter to Blackſtone, 81, 83. And at *Blackſtone's* ſtatement, "It muſt be owned that Mr. *Locke* and other theoretical writers have held that 'there remains ſtill inherent in the People a ſupreme power to remove or alter the legiſlature, when they find the legiſlative act contrary to the truſt repoſed in them; for when ſuch truſt is abuſed, it is thereby forfeited, and devolves to thoſe who gave it.' But *however juſt* this concluſion may be *in theory*, we *cannot adopt it*, nor argue from it, under any diſpenſation of government at preſent actually exiſting." — 1 Bl. Com. 161, 162 — the words here printed in italics are underlined by *Quincy*, who adds in the margin, "*Tamen quære* whether a concluſion can be juſt in theory, that will not bear adoption in practice." This very paſſage affords another inſtance of *Blackſtone's* careful reviſion of his work. In the ſixth and ſubſequent editions the word "practically" is inſerted before the word "adopt"; and for the words "argue from it" are ſubſtituted "take any legal ſteps for carrying it into execution."

Quincy's notes to Blackſtone.

(27) *Jeffries* v. *Sewall*, 2 John Adams's Works, 139. Rights of the Britiſh Colonies, 41, 61, 62, 71, 72, 73, 109, 110.

(28) In the controverſy of Maſſachuſetts with the other Confederated Colonies of New England in 1653 upon the right of the Confederation to make offenſive war, all parties agreed that any acts or orders manifeſtly unjuſt or againſt the law of *God* were not binding. 10 Plym. Col. Rec. 215–223; 2 Hazard Hiſt. Coll. 270–283. In 1688 "the men of Maſſachuſetts did much quote Lord *Coke*." Lambert MS. quoted in 2 Bancroft's Hiſt. U. S. 428. And in 1765, *Hutchinſon*, ſpeaking of the oppoſition to the Stamp Act, said, "The prevailing reaſon at this time is, that the Act of Parliament is againſt Magna Charta, and the natural Rights of Engliſhmen, and therefore, according to Lord *Coke*, null and void." "Summary of the Diſorders in the Massachuſetts Province proceeding from an Apprehenſion that the Act of Parliament called the Stamp Act deprives the People of their natural Rights," 26 Maſs. Archives, 180, 183. And ſee Hutchinſon to Jackſon, September 12, 1765, quoted *ante*, 441; Arguments of *Adams* and *Otis* on the Memorial of Boston to the Governor and Council, *ante*, 200, 201, 205, 206; 2 John Adams's Works, 158, 159 note. Even the Judges appointed by the Royal Governor do not ſeem to have been prepared to deny this principle. *John Cushing*, one of the aſſociate Juſtices, in a letter to Chief Juſtice *Hutchinſon*, dated "In a hurry, Feb[y]. 7, 1766," upon the queſtion whether the Courts ſhould be opened without ſtamps, wrote,

Maſſachuſetts.

to the effect that a statute may be void as exceeding the just limits of legislative power; (29) but it is believed there is

wrote, "Its true It is said an Act of Parliament against natural Equity is void. It will be disputed whether this is such an Act. It seems to me the main Question here is whether an Act which cannot be carried into execution should stop the Course of Justice, and that the Judges are more confined than with respect to an obsolete Act. If we admit evidence unstamped *ex necessitate* Q. if it can be said we do wrong." 25 Mass. Archives, 55. And in 1776, after the Governor had left, and the Council and House of Representatives had assumed the government, *John Adams*, in answering a letter of congratulation upon his own appointment as Chief Justice of Massachusetts, from *William Cushing*, his senior associate, and who upon *Adams's* declination became Chief Justice in his stead, and afterwards a Justice of the Supreme Court of the United States, wrote, "You have my hearty concurrence in telling the jury the nullity of acts of parliament." 9 John Adams's Works, 390, 391, & note.

Virginia.

In a case before the General Court of Virginia in 1772, *George Mason*, as reported by *Thomas Jefferson*, argued that the provision of the statute of that Colony of 1682, that "all Indians which shall hereafter be sold by our neighboring Indians, or any other trafiqueing with us as for slaves, are hereby adjudged, deemed and taken to be slaves," was "originally void, because contrary to natural right and justice," citing *Coke* and *Hobart*, *ubi sup.* The only authority cited on the other side was 1 Bl. Com. 91. As the court held that the act of 1682 had been repealed by a subsequent statute, it became unnecessary to decide the question. 2 Hening's Sts. at Large, 491. *Robin* v. *Hardaway*, Jefferson R. 114, 118, 123. And in the Debates on the adoption of the Constitution of the United States, *Patrick Henry* said that the Virginia Judges had opposed unconstitutional acts of the legislature. 4 Elliott's Deb. (2d ed.) 325. *Et vid. sup.* 519, note.

Modern cases.

(29) *Ellsworth*, in 3 Madison Deb. 1400; 5 Elliot's Debates, 462. *Chase*, J. in *Calder* v. *Bull*, 3 Dall. 388. *Marshall*, C. J. and *Johnson*, J. in *Fletcher* v. *Peck*, 6 Cranch, 135, 136, 143. *Thompson*, J. in *Ogden* v. *Saunders*, 12 Wheat. 304. *Story*, J. in *Wilkinson* v. *Leland*, 2 Pet. 657, 658. *Ham* v. *M'Claws*, 1 Bay, 95. 5 Dane Ab. 248. *Parker*, C. J. in *Foster* v. *Essex Bank*, 16 Mass. 270, 271, and *Ross's case*, 2 Pick. 169. *Richardson*, C. J. in *Opinion of Justices*, 4 N. H. 566. *Prentiss*, J. in *Lyman* v. *Mower*, 2 Verm. 519. *Redfield*, C. J. in *Hatch* v. *Vermont Central Railroad*, 25 Verm. 66. *Hosmer*, C. J. in *Goshen* v. *Stonington*, 4 Conn. 225. *Spencer*, C. J. in *Bradshaw* v. *Rogers*, 20 Johns. 106. *Walworth*, C. in *Varick* v. *Smith*, 5 Paige, 159, and *Cochran* v. *Van Surlay*, 20 Wend. 373. *Bronson*, C. J. in *Taylor*

is no inftance, except one cafe in South Carolina (30), in which an act of the legiflature has been fet afide by the courts, except for conflict with fome written conftitutional provifion. (31)

Under a written Conftitution.

The reduction of the fundamental principles of government in the American States to the form of written conftitutions, eftablifhed by the people themfelves, and beyond the control of their reprefentatives, neceffarily obliged the judicial department, in cafe of a conflict between a conftitutional provifion and a legiflative act, to obey the Conftitution as the fundamental law and difregard the ftatute. This duty was recognized, and unconftitutional acts fet afide, by courts of juftice, even before the adoption of the Conftitution of the United States. (32) Since the ratification of that

---

Taylor v. *Porter*, 4 *Hill*, 144, 145. *Jewett*, J. in *Powers* v. *Bergen*, 2 Selden, 367. *Bland*, C. in *Campbell's case*, 2 Bland, 231, 232.

South Carolina.

(30) In 1792 the Superior Court of South Carolina held that an act paffed by the legislature of the Colony in 1712, which took away the freehold of one man and vefted it in another, was "againft common right, as well as againft Magna Charta," and "therefore *ipfo facto* void." *Bowman* v. *Middleton*, 1 Bay, 252.

Power of legiflature.

(31) It was faid by Chief Juftice *Parfons*, and repeated by Chief Juftice *Shaw*, that "the legiflature may make all laws not repugnant to the Conftitution." *Stoughton* v. *Baker*, 4 Mafs. 529. *Commonwealth* v. *Alger*, 7 Cufh. 101. And fee *Opinion of Juftices*, 7 Mafs. 525; *Patterfon*, J. in *Vanhorne* v. *Dorrance*, 3 Dall. 308; *Iredell*, J. in *Calder* v. *Bull*, 3 Dall. 398, 399; *Wafhington*, J. in *Beach* v. *Woodhull*, Pet. C. C. 6; *Baldwin*, J. in *Bennett* v. *Boggs*, Bald. 74; 1 Kent Com. 448; Verplanck, Senator, in *Cochran* v. *Van Surlay*, 20 Wend. 382; *Bronfon*, J. in *People* v. *Fifher*, 24 Wend. 220; *Cowen*, J. in *Butler* v. *Palmer*, 1 Hill N. Y. 329, 330; *Gibfon*, C. J. in *Harvey* v. *Thomas*, 10 Watts, 66, 67; *Rogers*, J. in *Commonwealth* v. *M'Clofkey*, 2 Rawle, 374; *Hufton*, J. in *Braddee* v. *Brownfield*, 2 W. & S. 285.

Before U. S. Conftitution.

(32) The very few reports which have been preferved of the judicial decifions of that period afford two fuch examples. In 1786 the Judges of the Superior Court of the State of Rhode Island refufed to act under a ftatute of the General Affembly, which provided for the trial of an offence upon information before the Judges without a jury, contrary to the Constitution of the State as embodied in the Royal Charter of Charles 2. *Trevett* v. *Weeden*, reported by James M. Varnum, Providence,

that Conſtitution the power of the courts to declare unconſtitutional ſtatutes void has become too well ſettled to require an accumulation of authorities. (33) But as the office of the judiciary is to decide particular caſes, and not to iſſue general edicts, only ſo much of a ſtatute is to be declared void as is repugnant to the Conſtitution and covers the caſe before the court, unleſs the conſtitutional and unconſtitutional proviſions are ſo interwoven as to convince the court that the legiſlature would not have paſſed the one without the other. (34)

III. The St. of 13 & 14 Car. 2, c. 11, § 5, declared that it ſhould be lawful for any perſon "authorized by writ of aſſiſtance under the ſeal of his Majeſty's Court of Exchequer" to take an officer and go into any houſe or ſhop and ſeize and bring out uncuſtomed goods. This ſtatute, in which the name firſt appeared as applied to this proceſs, (35) did not define what it was, but aſſumed it to be already

---

Providence, 1787; 2 Chandler's Crim. Trials, 279 *& ſeq.* And in 1787 the Judges of the Superior Court of North Carolina ſet aſide an act of that State, which deprived a citizen of his property without trial by jury, in violation of the State Conſtitution of 1776. *Den* v. *Singleton*, Martin N. C. 49.

(33) Federaliſt, No. 78. *Vanhorne* v. *Dorrance*, 2 Dall. 308. *Cooper* v. *Telfair*, 4 Dall. 19. *Marbury* v. *Madiſon*, 1 Cranch, 177–180. 1 Wilſon's Works, 461, 462. 3 Story on Conſt. U. S. §§ 1570, 1608. 1 Kent Com. 449–454.

(34) *Bank of Hamilton* v. *Dudley*, 2 Pet. 526. *Commonwealth* v. *Knox*, 6 Maſs. 77. *Wellington, petitioner*, 16 Pick. 95–97. *Commonwealth* v. *Kimball*, 24 Pick. 361. *Norris* v. *Boſton*, 4 Met. 288. *Fiſher* v. *McGirr*, 1 Gray, 21. *Warren* v. *Mayor & Aldermen of Charleſtown*, 2 Gray, 98, 99. *Jones* v. *Robbins*, 8 Gray, 338, 339.

(35) The diſcuſſions on either ſide of the ocean diſcloſed no earlier trace of it. And none was found when in 1785 Lord *Mansfield* poſtponed the argument of a caſe for the purpoſe of a ſearch. *Cooper* v. *Boot*, 4 Doug. 347.

It would ſeem that the writ of aſſiſtance may have been framed in analogy to the warrants iſſued under the act of the ſame year, which provided that "for the better diſcovering of printing in corners without licenſe, one or more meſſengers of his Majeſties chamber, by warrant under

already known. The only proceſs, mentioned in any earlier ſtatute or law book, to which the name could be referred, would ſeem to be the warrant mentioned in St. 12 Car. 2, c. 19, (confirmed by St. 13 Car. 2, St. 1, c. 7, and ſubſequent ſtatutes,) which could only iſſue upon information on oath, and authorized the entry of a houſe for one month only after the offence, and by which, "if the information upon which any houſe is ſearched ſhould prove to be falſe," the informer was made liable in full coſts and damages to the party injured. (36)

As general warrants were not authorized by the common law, (37) *Otis* argued that the writ of aſſiſtance mentioned

under his Majeſties ſign manual, or under the hand of one or more of his Majeſties principal Secretaries of State, or the Maſter and Wardens of the Company of Stationers, or any one of them, ſhall have power and authority with a conſtable to take unto them ſuch aſſiſtance as they ſhall think needful, and at what time they ſhall think fit, to ſearch all houſes and ſhops where they ſhall know, or upon ſome probable cauſe ſuſpect any books or papers to be printed," &c., and to ſeize any unlicenſed books, "together with the ſeveral offendors," and bring them before Juſtices of the Peace. St. 13 & 14 Car. 2, c. 33, § 15. That ſtatute expired in the ſame reign in which it was framed, and ſimilar warrants for the ſeizure of papers were held illegal in 1765. *Entick* v. *Carrington*, 19 Howell's State Trials, 1029, 1070; 2 Wils. 292.

(36) Theſe proviſions of Sts. 12 Car. 2, c. 19, and 13 & 14 Car. 2, c. 11, § 5, are copied *ante*, 397, note.

(37) Impeachment of Lord C. J. *Scroggs*, 8 Howell's State Trials, 191, 193, 200. 1 Hale P. C. 580. 2 Hale P. C. 113, 114, 150. 2 Hawk. c. 13, § 10, cited by Otis, *ante*, 53. Authorities cited *infra*, *note* 42. 15 Parl. Hiſt. 1402; 16 Ib. 6–15, 207–209. 4 Bl. Com. 291. 2 Gabbett's Crim. Law, 156, 158.

Lord *Coke* even doubted whether any ſearch warrants for ſtolen goods were legal; but his doubt was diſregarded in practice, and overruled by later authorities. 4 Inſt. 176, 177. 2 Hale P. C. 113, 149. *Entick* v. *Carrington*, 19 Howell's State Trials, 1067; 2 Wils. 291.

The Act of 1 Jac. 1, c. 19, "for the well garbling of ſpices," provided that all ſpices and drugs in London or the liberties thereof ſhould be "ſufficiently cleaned, ſevered, garbled and divided, and afterwards ſealed up by the garbler thereunto appointed," or his deputy, before ſale. The meaning of "garble" in this ſtatute ſeems to have been directly

tioned in St. 13 & 14 Car. 2, muſt be ſpecial, according to St. 12 Car. 2. This ſeems to have been conſidered at the time of the argument and afterwards the moſt important point; (38) and upon the ordinary rules of interpreting ſtatutes *in pari materia* together, and according to the rule and reaſon of the common law, the concluſion of *Otis* ſeems inevitable. If the writ of aſſiſtance contemplated by the Sts. of Charles 2 was general to ſearch all houſes and iſſued without oath, it is a little remarkable that Lord *Hale*, neither in diſcuſſing general warrants, nor in ſpeaking of theſe very ſtatutes, gives any hint of ſuch a departure from the principles of the common law. (39)

It muſt be admitted that in practice general writs of aſſiſtance were commonly uſed in England. (40) But they do not ſeem to have been the ſubject of judicial remark there before the argument in Maſſachuſetts, after which Lord *Mansfield* took every opportunity to aſſert that general writs

---

directly oppoſite to that in which it is now commonly uſed; for Lord *Coke* ſays, "To garble, ſignifieth in our legall underſtanding to ſever and divide the good and ſufficient from the bad and inſufficient." 4 Inſt. 264. The St. of 1 Jac. 1, c. 19, § 3, authorized the ſaid garbler of ſpices and his "deputy or deputies, aſſignee or aſſignees," at all times "in the daytime to enter into any ſhops, warehouſes or cellars within the ſaid city or liberties thereof," and ſearch for, ſeize and garble ſpices and drugs "there ungarbled, which have been accuſtomed to be garbled." And *Coke* says, "This had been implyed if it had not been expreſſed" —which ſeems hardly conſiſtent in principle with his opinion about ſearch warrants for ſtolen goods.

(38) 3 Hutchinſon's Hiſt. Maſs. 94. *Ante*, 435, 438, 467, 471, 472, 475, 490, 501–505 notes, 510, 511.

(39) 2 Hale P. C. 116. Treatiſe concerning the Cuſtoms, in Hargrave's Law Tracts, 210, 223, 224, 225.

(40) *Breve aſſiſten' pro Officiar' Cuſtum', temp. Jac.* 2, Brown's Exch. Pract. 358; *ante*, 398, note. Sir *Robert Walpole* and Sir *Philip Yorke* in the Houſe of Commons in 1733, 8 Parl. Hiſt. 1280, 1289. *Gridley, arguendo, ante*, 480. *Opinion of Judges, ante*, 497. Hutchinſon's Hiſtory and Correſpondence, quoted *ante*, 414, 415 note, 455. Dickinſon's Farmer's Letters, (Boſton ed. 1768) 50, 51. Opinion of De Grey, A. G., *ante*, 453. Johnſon's and Trumbull's Letters, *ante*, 502, 505, note.

writs of aſſiſtance were expreſſly authorized by ſtatute, (41) which was certainly not the fact. And the practice was no more uniform nor better eſtabliſhed than that which was allowed

---

(41) In delivering his opinion upon the invalidity of general warrants, he is reported by *Burrow* to have ſaid, "There are many caſes where particular Acts of Parliament have given authority to apprehend under general warrants, as in the caſe of writs of aſſiſtance," &c. *Money* v. *Leach*, 3 Bur. 1766; 19 Howell's State Trials, 1026, 1027. Sir *William Blackſtone's* report of the ſame caſe ſpeaks only of the form in uſe, omits all mention of the ſtatute, and puts the ſentence thus: "The words of the writs of aſſiſtance in the cuſtoms and exciſe are equally general; yet a probable ſuſpicion will juſtify acting under them." 1 W. Bl. 561.

The laſt clauſe of this ſentence muſt be miſreported; for it was well ſettled law that a perſon ſearching under a writ of aſſiſtance and finding nothing was not juſtified. *Legliſe* v. *Champante*, 2 Stra. 819, evidently the authority intended by *Otis*, *ante*, 471. *Shipley* v. *Redmain*, before Lord *Camden*, quoted by *Plomer*, *arguendo*, in *Cooper* v. *Boot*, 4 Doug. 347. *Bruce* v. *Rawlins*, 3 Wils. 63. By Lord C. J. *De Grey*, in *Boſtock* v. *Saunders*, 2 W. Bl. 914; 3 Wils. 434. By Lord *Mansfield*, in *Cooper* v. *Boot*, 4 Doug. 343; 3 Esp. R. 138. In the Common Bench in 1773, Lord C. J. *De Grey*, *Gould*, *Blackſtone*, & *Nares*, JJ. held that the ſame rule applied to an exciſe officer acting under St. 10 G. 1, c. 10, § 13, which provided that if any officer ſhould ſuſpect goods to be concealed with intent to defraud, "upon oath made to the Commiſſioners of Exciſe, ſetting forth the grounds of his ſuſpicion, it ſhall be lawful for them to authorize the officer to enter the houſe by day or night, and if by night with a peace officer, and ſeize and carry away ſuch goods." *Boſtock* v. *Saunders*, 2 W. Bl. 912; 3 Wils. 434. An oppoſite deciſion was made in the King's Bench twelve years later by Lord *Mansfield*, *Buller*, *Aſhurſt*, & *Willes*, JJ. *Cooper* v. *Boot*, 4 Doug. 339; 3 Esp. R. 135.

Lord *Mansfield*, in delivering his opinion in the laſt caſe, ſaid, "The caſe of the writ of aſſiſtance is not applicable. There there is no warrant, and all is left to the diſcretion of the officer; beſides, which is very material, there is a poſitive clauſe in the ſtatute of Charles 2, which makes the whole depend on the actual finding of goods." "That however is a politic prevention to avoid abuſe; but on this point we give no opinion." And he ſaid that to hold the officer liable if no goods were found "would be adding to the ſtatute a clauſe which the legiſlature, with the ſtatute of Charles 2 before their eyes, have purpoſely avoided." 4 Doug. 348, 349; 3 Esp. R. 146. The opinion given by *De Grey* as Attorney allowed no force, either by Lord *Camden*, or by Lord *Mansfield* and his aſſociates, in the matter of general warrants. (42) But Lord *Camden*, who led the way in that matter, had not yet been raiſed to the Bench.

It is hard to imagine that the ſame Houſe of Commons which condemned general warrants in 1766 (43) intended to authorize general writs of aſſiſtance in 1767. (44) Even after the paſſage of the St. of 7 G. 3, ſome of the American courts refuſed to iſſue anything but ſpecial writs of aſſiſtance; (45) and attempts were made to limit them by

---

Attorney General in 1768 was to the same effect. *Ante*, 454. But the "poſitive clause," which Lord *Mansfield* thought ſo "very material," was not in St. 13 & 14 Car. 2, c. 11, but in St. 12 Car. 2, c. 19, § 4; and there ſeems to be no good reaſon for holding that ſection to apply to writs of aſſiſtance under 13 & 14 Car. 2, which would not alſo make applicable the other proviſions of St. 12 Car. 2. Both ſtatutes were quoted as applicable to writs of aſſiſtance by *Gould*, J. in *Bruce* v. *Rawlins*, 3 Wils. 63.

Mr. Juſtice *Buller*, according to the report in *Douglas*, ſaid, "In the Exchequer, officers are never permitted to be aſked what their information is"—or, as more fully reported by *Eſpinaſſe*, "It has been reſolved by a majority of all the Judges, that the officer is not obliged to declare the grounds of his ſuſpicion, leſt accidents ſhould happen to him." 4 Doug. 343; 3 Eſp. R. 138. The uſe of the word "reſolved," inſtead of "held" or "determined," the giving of the ſame reaſon as *Hutchinſon* in his account of the matter (*ante*, 415 note), and the want of printed reports of any ſuch adjudication, ſuggeſt the poſſibility that upon receiving *Hutchinſon's* inquiries while the queſtion was pending before him, an auricular opinion of the English Judges was obtained by the miniſtry.

(42) *Wilkes* v. *Wood*, Lofft, 18; 19 Howell's State Trials, 1076, 1167. *Huckle* v. *Money*, 2 Wils. 207; 19 Howell's State Trials, 1405. *Money* v. *Leach*, 3 Bur. 1692, 1742, 1767; 19 Howell's State Trials, 1002, 1027; 1 W. Bl. 561, 562. *Entick* v. *Carrington*, 19 Howell's State Trials, 1068, 1071; 2 Wils. 292. 1 Cavendish Debates, 122–124. Lord *Denman*, C. J. in *Stockdale* v. *Hanſard*, 9 A. & E. 155, and 2 P. & D. 145.

(43) 16 Parl. Hiſt. 207, 209.

(44) St. 7 G. 3, c. 46, *ante*, 452.

(45) In Connecticut, *ante*, 501, 504, 505, notes: Rhode Iſland, *ante*, 506,

by ftatute. (46) But in England the practice of iffuing general writs of affiftance continued until 1817, when a limit was impofed upon their ufe by an order of the Board of Cuftoms, providing that no writ of affiftance fhould in future be delivered to any officer of the cuftoms, unlefs he fhould previoufly make oath before a magiftrate of his belief and grounds of belief that fmuggled goods were lodged in a certain houfe. (47) And thus the reafonablenefs of the pofition of the Colonies was finally vindicated in the mother country.

In Maffachufetts, the General Court recognized and applied the principles of the common law on the fubject of general warrants, even in time of war, not allowing general warrants to iffue even for the arreft of deferters in the Old French War, (48) or to fearch for the arms of difaffected perfons at the beginning of the War of the Revolution. (49) Thofe principles were confirmed in 1780 by the Declaration

---

506, note: Pennfylvania, *ante*, 454, 502, note: Virginia, *ante*, 510, note: Other Colonies, *ante*, 500, 511, notes.

John Dickinfon, in the 9th of his Farmer's Letters, commenting on the St. of 7 G. 3, wrote, "I am well aware that writs of this kind may be granted at home, under the feal of the Court of Exchequer. But I know alfo, that the greateft afferters of the rights of Englifhmen have always ftrenuoufly contended that fuch a power was dangerous to freedom, and exprefly contrary to the common law, which ever regarded a man's house as his caftle, or a place of perfect fecurity. If fuch power was in the leaft degree dangerous there, it muft be utterly deftructive to liberty here. For the people there have two fecurities againft the undue exercife of this power by the Crown, which are wanting with us, if the late act takes place," to wit, independent judges to try an action againft the offenders, and redrefs in Parliament. Farmer's Letters, (Bofton ed. 1768,) 50, 51. See alfo Bofton Gazette of September 5, 1768, quoted *ante*, 452.

(46) In Maffachufetts in 1762, *ante*, 495. In New Jerfey in 1782, *ante*, 508, note.

(47) 1 Chit. Com. & Manuf. 790, 791. Wildman's General Orders of the Cuftoms, 358.

(48) Prov. St. 31 & 32 G. 2, c. 1, (1758) Mafs. Temp. Laws, pp. 355, 356.

(49) St. 1776, c. 7, Acts of Mafs. Colony 1775–1780, p. 33.

tion of Rights, prefixed to the Conſtitution of Maſſachuſetts, as follows: "Every ſubject has a right to be ſecure from all unreaſonable ſearches and ſeizures of his perſon, his houſes, his papers and all his poſſeſſions. All warrants therefore are contrary to this right, if the cauſe or foundation of them be not previouſly ſupported by oath or affirmation; and if the order in the warrant to a civil officer to make ſearch in ſuſpected places, or to arreſt one or more ſuſpected perſons, or to ſeize their property, be not accompanied with a ſpecial deſignation of the perſons or objects of ſearch, arreſt, or ſeizure; and no warrant ought to be iſſued but in caſes, and with the formalities, preſcribed by the laws." And the ſubſtance of this article was incorporated into one of the earlieſt amendments of the Conſtitution of the United States. (50)

IV. The only queſtion remaining is, whether the Superior Court of Judicature of the Province had in this matter the powers of the Court of Exchequer in England.

Upon this point *Gridley's* argument ſeems hard to meet. The Act of Parliament of 13 & 14 Car. 2, c. 11, § 5, one of the Acts of Trade, empowered "any perſon authorized by writ of aſſiſtance under the ſeal of his Majeſty's Court of Exchequer," to enter with a peace officer houſes, &c. The General Court of the Colony afterwards provided for the ſtrict obſervation of thoſe acts. (51) And the Engliſh St. of 7 & 8 W. 3, c. 22, § 6, provided "that the like aſſiſtance ſhall be given" to officers of the cuſtoms in the American Colonies, "as by the ſaid" Act of Car. 2 "is provided for the officers in England." By the Province Charter "the great and general court or aſſembly"

---

(50) Declaration of Rights, art. 14. U. S. Conſtitution, amendment 4. And ſee *Sanford* v. *Nichols*, 13 Maſs. 289; *Commonwealth* v. *Dana*, 2 Met. 334–336; *Stone* v. *Dana*, 5 Met. 101, 102; *Commonwealth* v. *Lottery Tickets*, 5 Cuſh. 370; *Fiſher* v. *McGirr*, 1 Gray, 29, 30; *Robinſon* v. *Richardſon*, 13 Gray, 456, 457; *Grumon* v. *Raymond*, 1 Conn. 43; *Sailly* v. *Smith*, 11 Johns. 503; U. S. St. 1799, c. 110, § 68, 1 U. S. Sts. at Large, 677, 678; 7 Dane Ab. 246.

(51) Maſs. Col. Sts. *ante*, 518, note 14; Anc. Chart. 721. 1 Hutchinſon's Hiſt. Maſs. 290. Hutchinſon's Collections, 521.

bly" was veſted with power "to erect and conſtitute judicatories or courts of record, or other courts," to try all crimes and civil actions; reſerving the probate juriſdiction to the Governor and Council, and the juriſdiction in admiralty to Judges to be commiſſioned by the King. And under the power thus conferred, the General Court of the Province, by the firſt Judiciary Act which obtained the King's approval, eſtabliſhed a Superior Court of Judicature, and beſtowed upon it all the juriſdiction which "the Courts of King's Bench, Common Bench and Exchequer within his Majeſty's Kingdom of England have or ought to have." (52)

In ſupport of the argument that the Superior Court had not the powers of the Court of Exchequer, much reliance was placed upon their refuſal to entertain juriſdiction of a bill in equity.(53) But no Court of the Province could well have aſſumed, on any pretence, a general equity juriſdiction, in the face of the opinions repeatedly expreſſed by the Engliſh Government upon that ſubject. (54)

Whether

---

(52) Prov. St. 11 W. 3 (1699), Anc. Chart. 331.

(53) *McNeal* v. *Brideoak*, *ante*, 53, 470.

(54) In England, before Lord *Bacon's* impeachment and conviction for corruption, (which, Lord *Hale* ſays, "gave ſuch a diſcredit and brand" to his decrees, "that they were eaſily ſet aſide, and made way in the Parliament of 3 Car. for the like attempts againſt decrees made by other Chancellors," and which was juſt before the granting of the Charter to the Maſſachuſetts Company,) decrees in chancery were not reviſed by the Houſe of Lords ſitting judicially, but by legiſlative act of both Houſes of Parliament. Hale's Juriſdiction of the Houſe of Lords, 193–195; Nottingham MSS. quoted in Hargrave's Pref. cliii. note.

Chancery juriſdiction in the Maſſachuſetts Colony.

Under the Maſſachuſetts Colony Charter the General Court exerciſed an extenſive chancery juriſdiction, as appears by the following examples: Redemption of land from mortgage, *Hues* v. *Rogers*, 4 Maſs. Col. Rec. pt. ii. 292. Charitable truſt, *Caſe of Roxbury Free School*, 4 Ib. pt. ii. 434, 435, 441, 455–458; 5 Ib. 5, 6, 22. Specific performance by executor of teſtator's contract, *Shoare* v. *Boſworth*, 5 Ib. 36. Sequeſtration of lands, *Patch* v. *Patch*, 5 Ib. 39. Miſtake, *Mavericke* v. *Phillips*, 4 Ib. pt. i. 187; *Groſs* v. *Collecot*, 5 Ib. 150, 247, 273. Fraud, *Thatcher* v. *Thatcher*, 5 Ib. 245, which was referred to the county

court,

Whether the authority of the Court of Exchequer in matters of revenue was a part of its jurisdiction in equity does

---

court, with power to compel a discovery. In some cases, the want of remedy at law is assigned as the ground of jurisdiction in equity. *Dedham* v. *Natick Indians*, 4 Ib. pt. ii. 49; *Sears* v. *How*, 5 Ib. 379. A considerable equity jurisdiction was conferred on the county courts. Sts. 1671, 4 Ib. pt. ii. 488; 1682, 5 Ib. 375; 1685, 5 Ib. 477; Anc. Chart. 52, 93, 94, 148. And see Washburn's Jud. Hist. Mass. 28, 34; Plym. Col. Laws of 1672 and 1685 (ed. 1836) 260, 296. After the repeal of the Massachusetts Colony Charter, the President, or Governor, and Council exercised similar jurisdiction. *Hadley* v. *Hopkins Academy*, 14 Pick. 264, 265. Washburn's Jud. Hist. Mass. 98.

Chancery jurisdiction in the Province.

Immediately after the Province Charter, the General Court attempted to establish a Court of Chancery; but the act was disallowed by the King in Council. Prov. Sts. 4 & 5 W. & M. (1692–3) Anc. Chart. 222, 274. Rec. 1699, fol. 256. 2 Hutchinson's Hist. Mass. 31. 4 Dane Ab. 518. 6 Ib. 405. *Charles River Bridge* v. *Warren Bridge*, 7 Pick. 368. In 1704 Attorney General *Northey* gave an opinion to Queen *Anne* that the Province Charter conferred no authority on the General Court to establish such a court. 2 Chalmers' Opinions, 182, 183. But *Ryder* and *Strange*, as Attorney and Solicitor General, in 1738 gave an opinion that the colonial assembly could establish a Court of Exchequer in South Carolina. 2 Ib. 170. The condition of Chancery jurisdiction in the Province of Massachusetts Bay is thus expressed in "the opinion of a great lawyer in the Colonies," quoted by Governor *Pownall*, whose term of office intervened between the decision of *McNeal* v. *Brideoak*, *ubi supra*, and the argument upon the Writs of Assistance. "There is no Court of Chancery in the charter governments of New England, nor any court vested with power to determine causes in equity, save only that the justices of the inferior court and the justices of the superior court respectively have power to give relief on mortgages, bonds, and other penalties contained in deeds. In all other chancery and equitable matters, both the Crown and the subject are without redress. This introduced a practice of petitioning the legislative courts for relief, and prompted those courts to interpose their authority. These petitions becoming numerous, in order to give the greater despatch to such business, the legislative courts transacted such business by orders or resolves, without the solemnity of passing acts for such purposes; and have further extended this power by resolves and orders beyond what a Court of Chancery ever attempted to decree, even to the suspending of public laws; which orders or resolves are not sent home for the royal assent." Administration of the Colonies, (3d ed.) 81, 82. The jurisdiction mentioned by Governor *Pownall* was conferred by Prov. Sts. 10 W.

does not appear to have been determined when the caſe of the Writs of Aſſiſtance came up. But the opinion ſeems to have ſince prevailed in England, that the revenue juriſdiction of that Court was ſtrictly a common law juriſdiction, although ſome of its incidental proceedings might take the form of proceſſes in equity. (55) And the writs of aſſiſtance to officers of the cuſtoms certainly ſeem to bear a cloſer analogy to the common law writs of aid, which always iſſued from the Exchequer, than to the writs of aſſiſtance out of Chancery to take poſſeſſion of lands. (56)

Yet it is evident that the exerciſe of the juriſdiction of the Exchequer by the Superior Court was conſidered by both parties

W. 3; 12 Anne; 5 G. 1; 8 G. 2; Anc. Chart. 325, 326, 401, 402, 424, 501. And ſee 4 Dane Ab. 243; 6 Ib. 398; 7 Ib. 516, 518; 2 Amer. Juriſt, 361, 362; Waſhburn's Jud. Hiſt. Maſs. 158, 167. Governor *Bernard*, in his anſwer on the 5th of September 1763, to the "Queries propoſed by the Lords Commiſſioners of Trade and Plantations," for a copy of which, taken from the MSS. in the King's Library, the writer is indebted to Mr. *George Bancroft*, ſays: "It might have been made a queſtion whether the Governor of this Province has not the power of Chancellor delivered to him with the Great Seal, as well as other Royal Governors; but it is impracticable to ſet up ſuch a claim now, after a non-uſage of 70 years, and after ſeveral Governors have, in effect, disclaimed it, by conſenting to bills for eſtablishing a Court of Chancery, which have been diſallowed at home. A Court of Chancery is very much wanted here, many cauſes of conſequence frequently happening, in which no redreſs is to be had for want of a Court of Equity. I am inclined to think that if a complainant in a matter of equity ariſing within this Province ſhould file his bill in the Court of Chancery in England, ſuggeſting there was no Provincial Court in which he could be relieved, that the bill would be retained, in the ſame manner as I ſuppoſe a libel in the high Court of Admiralty would be admitted, if there was no inferior court of Admiralty in the Province, unleſs it was uſed only to enforce the neceſſity of eſtablishing a Provincial Court of Equity."

(55) *Eyre*, C. B., in *Cawthorne* v. *Campbell*, 1 Anſt. 208. Lord *Redeſdale*, in *Wall* v. *Attorney General*, 11 Price, 696 & *ſeq.* *Rogers* v. *Maule*, 3 Y. & Col. Exch. 77, 79. *Attorney General* v. *Holling*, 15 M. & W. 697; 8 Beav. 288, note.

(56) *Ante*, 395, 396.

parties to be very doubtful. No inftance was fhown in which this Court had exercifed any of the powers of the Exchequer, which might not have been exercifed by the King's Bench or Common Bench; and it certainly did not poffefs all the powers of that Court even in matters of revenue. (57) And this objection feems to have been thought the only one worthy of notice in England. (58)

A careful examination of the fubject compels the conclufion that the decifion of *Hutchinfon* and his affociates has been too ftrongly condemned as illegal: and that there was at leaft reafonable ground for holding, as matter of mere law, that the Britifh Parliament had power to bind the Colonies; that even a ftatute contrary to the Conftitution could not be declared void by the judicial Courts; that by the Englifh ftatutes, as practically conftrued by the Courts in England, Writs of Affiftance might be general in form; that the Superior Court of Judicature of the Province had the power of the Englifh Court of Exchequer; and that the Writs of Affiftance prayed for, though contrary to the fpirit of the Englifh Conftitution, could hardly be refufed by a Provincial Court, before general warrants had been condemned in England, and before the Revolution had actually begun in America. The remedy adopted by the Colonies was to throw off the yoke of Parliament; to confer on the judiciary the power to declare unconftitutional ftatutes void; to declare general warrants unconftitutional in exprefs terms; and thus to put an end here to general Writs of Affiftance.

---

(57) *Ante*, 52, 471, 482, 486, 488, 493.

(58) Opinion of *De Grey*, A. G., in 1768, *ante*, 452, 453. And fee Adams to Tudor, Auguft 6, 1818, 10 John Adams's Works, 342. Governor *Pownall* was too well acquainted with the Government and laws of the Province, to have fuggefted in 1766, "the creating in America, by Act of Parliament, Courts of Exchequer for the exprefs purpofes of the Crown's revenue," if it was clear that fuch a Court already exifted here. Adminiftration of the Colonies, (3d ed.) App. iii. 44.

APPENDIX II.

Gray, Treasurer of the Province of Massachusetts Bay, *vs.* Paxton. (1)

Gray *v.* Paxton. Rec. 1761, fol. 235.

A resolve of the General Court, authorizing "H. G., the Province Treasurer," to demand and sue for money due to the Province, does not authorize him to sue therefor in his own name.

ASSUMPSIT. "Harrison Gray, of Boston in the County of Suffolk, Treasurer and Receiver General of the Province of the Massachusetts Bay," sued "Charles Paxton

---

(1) The case of the Writs of Assistance, though the most important, was not the only one which excited the feeling of the people against the officers of the customs. There were also several suits at common law, growing out of forfeitures in the Court of Admiralty, to the best known of which *Paxton* was a party. The statements of this dispute in some histories are confused and inaccurate by reason of omitting to notice the fact that two actions were brought against *Paxton*, the first in the name of the Treasurer, the second in the name of the Province.

The controversy arose thus: The Act of Parliament of 6 G. 2, c. 13, imposed a duty on all foreign rum, molasses, or sugar imported into the Colonies, to be recovered in any Court of Admiralty or Court of Record, "one third part thereof for the use of his Majesty, his heirs and successors, to be applied for the support of the Government of the Colony or Plantation where the same shall be recovered," one third to the Governor, and the other to the informer.

Petition of Merchants to the General Court.

On the 17th of December 1760 a petition to secure the rights of the Province in this respect was presented to the General Court, signed by all the merchants who a few weeks later signed the remonstrance against the Writs of Assistance, (*ante*, 412,) except "Nat Wheelwright," "Joseph Scott," "Jam[s] Warden," "James Pitts," "John Winniett," and "Sam[l] Gridley." A comparison of the two petitions shows that "John Lowell" (*ante*, 413,) should have been printed "John Powell." The petition to the General Court also bears the names

1761. GRAY v. PAXTON. Declaration.

Paxton of ſaid Boſton Eſquire" "for that whereas the ſaid Charles at ſaid Boſton on the firſt day of March Inſtant was Indebted

---

names of "John Amory" and "Benj[a] Hallowell." 44 Maſs. Archives, 446. In the Boſton Gazette of September 4, 1769, *James Otis* published a depoſition, given (as he ſaid) by *Paxton* on the 28th of February 1761 before Judge *Ruſſell*, teſtifying "that *Benjamin Barons* Esq: Collector of his Majeſty's Cuſtoms for the port of Boſton, entered into a Confederacy with the following perſons, viz. *Benjamin Hallowell*, ſenior, who for ſome years paſt hath publicly profeſſed himſelf an enemy to the Court of Vice-Admiralty in this Province, and hath declared the ſame to be a Nuiſance, and ought to be laid aſide, or words to that purpoſe; and that *James Otis*, jun[r] Eſq: who reſigned his commiſſion of Advocate General, and immediately thereafter appeared advocate for the meeting hereafter to be mentioned; and ſundry other perſons who are ſuppoſed to have been concerned in carrying on an illicit trade."

Hearing before Houſe and Council.

The Houſe of Repreſentatives on the 19th of December 1760 ordered that the "Petitioners are allowed to be heard upon the Floor by their Council," and "the Regiſter of Vice Admiralty, and any other Person or Perſons belonging to that Court, who may be affected by the conſequence of this application, may attend (if they ſee cauſe) at that time." A hearing was had accordingly, at which *Otis* appeared as counſel for the petitioners, and a committee appointed by the Houſe "to take the petition and all the papers in the caſe under conſideration, and report what they judge proper for this court to act thereon." To this committee the Council, after a hearing on the 26th, joined others. Journal H. R. 1760, pp. 107, 122, 238. 3 Hutchinſon's Hiſt. Maſs. 89.

Report of Committee.

The committee reported that in ſix caſes of ſeizures of goods there had been paid "for procuring information, £282. 6. 8;" "charged as paid to lawyers more than legal fees, £56. 12;" for "condemnation dues at 5 per cent, £79. 8. 3¾;" "receiving and paying, at 3 per cent, £47. 11. 1¼;" and "marſhal's cuſtody of the goods at 3s. per day beſides ſtorage, £18. 3;" making the "amount of illegal charges £484. 1. 11;" that all theſe expenſes were charged upon the ſhare of the Province, the effect of which was to leave it in one caſe "five ſhillings and eight pence farthing," in another "thirty-eight ſhillings and eight pence," and in the other four nothing whatever; and that the amount due to the Province as aforeſaid (after deducting £8. 12. for lawful fees of the Judge of Admiralty) was £475. 9. 11. Journal H. R. 1761, pp. 180, 181, 239–241. Copy of Report on file in Court of Common Pleas.

The

Indebted to the ſaid Province in the ſum of Three hundred & fifty ſeven pounds one ſhilling and eight pence lawfull money

---

The papers on file in the Court of Common Pleas ſhow that *Paxton* was acting as marſhal in January 1756; and that the decrees in the five earlieſt caſes were made in 1753, 1756, and 1759 by *George Cradock* as Deputy Judge, and in the ſixth in 1760 by *Chambers Ruſſell* as Judge of the Court of Vice Admiralty. *Vid. ante*, 233, 426 & 427 notes; Washburn's Jud. Hiſt. Maſs. 184. It was cuſtomary for the Judges of that and other Courts of civil law in the Colonies to appoint Deputies. 1 Doug. Hiſt. N. A. 484. Governor Pownall's Meſſage, *poſt* Appendix III.

Reſolve of the General Court.

The Houſe of Repreſentatives, upon the recommendation of their committee, on the 13th of January, 1761, "Reſolved that Harriſon Gray, Eſq. the Province Treaſurer, be and hereby is impowered and directed to demand and receive the aforeſaid ſum of 475£ 9s. 11d of the reſpective perſons from whom it ſhall appear to be due; and in caſe of their refuſing or neglecting payment for the ſpace of one month after demand, to bring an action or actions at common law for recovery of ſaid ſum, to the uſe of his Majeſty, to be applied to the ſupport of this Government as this Court ſhall hereafter direct." Journal H. R. 1761, p. 181. *Hutchinſon* ſays, "Oppoſition however was made in Council; and it was plainly ſhewn that no ſuch action could lie. The Superior Court having all the powers within the Province of the Court of King's Bench in England, might put a ſtop to the proceedings of the Court of Admiralty, whenever it took cognizance of a cauſe not within its juriſdiction, by a writ of prohibition; but in this caſe juriſdiction had been expreſſly given by an Act of Parliament to the Court of Admiralty. The Province might have appeared by an attorney, and have taken exceptions to the decree, and, if the exceptions had not prevailed, might have brought an appeal to the High Court of Admiralty in England; but the opportunity was wilfully ſlipped, and there was now no remedy. It was ſaid, however, that the people were diſſatisfied, and that it would not be believed that there was no remedy, unleſs there was a trial: and a majority of the Council concurred with the Houſe." 3 Hutchinſon's Hiſt. Maſs. 90. Upon the power of the Superior Court of Judicature to iſſue a writ of prohibition to the Court of Vice-Admiralty, ſee Dummer's Defence of the New England Charters (Boſton ed. 1745) 26–29; *Scollay* v. *Dunn*, *ante*, 74.

Action of the Governor.

The Governor, in a meſſage to the Houſe on the 16th of January, objected "that this money is part of His Majeſty's Revenue, granted to him by Act of Parliament," and therefore muſt be ſued for by his Attorney General, though, when recovered, to be received by the Treaſurer; and that the propoſed Reſolve "would amount to altering an Act

1761. GRAY v. PAXTON.

money for ſo much lawfull money before that time had & received by the ſaid Charles to & for the uſe of the Province aforeſaid, and the ſaid Charles being ſo Indebted then and there promiſed the ſaid Province to pay the ſame on demand yet the ſaid Charles tho' often requeſted has not paid the ſame ſum but neglects it. To the damage of the ſaid Harriſon Gray in his ſaid capacity the ſum of Three hundred and ſixty Pounds." Writ dated March 18th 1761, and returnable at July term 1761 of the Inferior Court of Common Pleas. (2)

Plea in abatement.

And the ſaid Charles comes & defends &c. & prays Judgment of the Writ aforeſaid & that the ſame may be abated. For 1st. The Plaintiff herein ſues in an Indebitatus aſſumpſit, And yet has not in his Declaration ſhewed that the ſaid Charles was ever indebted to the Plaintiff or ever promiſed him to pay him anything or broke any Promiſe, Contract or Agreement with or to the Plaintiff. 2[ndly]. According to the Plaintiff's own ſhewing the money alledged to be received by the ſaid Charles was to the Uſe of the Province of the Maſſachuſetts Bay, & the Debt & Promiſe grounded thereon were to the ſaid Province, And the right of

---

Act of Parliament," and therefore refuſed his aſſent. The Houſe on the 27th replied, "We are far from apprehending that a reſolve of this Court can alter an Act of Parliament. We are quite ſenſible that if an Act of this Court should obtain the royal ſanction, it cannot do it. Every Act made by the General Court or Aſſembly of this Province is voidable; becauſe the ſame may be diſallowed by His Majeſty: Every Act we make repugnant to an Act of Parliament extending to the Plantations is (*ipſo facto*) null and void," and that they held the King's Prerogative as ſacred as the People's liberties; but that this money was the Province's, not the King's, and the form of the grant by Parliament was the ſame as that uſed in Provincial Revenue Acts, which had been always approved by the King. The Governor, after another proteſt, on the 31st of January finally approved the reſolve. Even *Hutchinſon* ſays, "this objection from the Governor was really of no weight." "But he hoped to prevent Mr. Otis from carrying on the ſuit." Journal H. R. 1761, pp. 241–247. 3 Hutchinſon's Hiſt. Maſs. 90, 91. 2 Minot's Hiſt. Maſs. 80–86.

(2) Writ on file in Court of Common Pleas.

1761.

GRAY *v.* PAXTON.

of action accruing on the Breach of such Promise was to the said Province & not to the Plaintiff according to his own Shewing. 3dly. The Plaintiff has not in his Declaration shewed or alledged any Matter or Cause Sufficient to intitle him to bring forward as he doth this Action & maintain the same. All these things the Defendant is ready to verify, Wherefore he prays Judgment that this Writ be abated & for costs." (3)

In Inferior Court plea in abatement overruled and verdict and judgment for plaintiff.

This plea was overruled by the Inferior Court. (4) The defendant then pleaded the general issue, which was joined by the plaintiff (5) and submitted to the jury, who returned a verdict for the plaintiff of £357. 1. 8. and costs, (6) upon which judgment was rendered. (7) The defendant appealed, and at August term 1761 of the Superior Court "the parties appeared and being fully heard upon the plea in abatement (8), it is considered by the Court that the writ abate

(3) Plea in abatement on back of writ. Rec. 1761, fol. 235.

(4) Rec. 1761, fol. 235.

(5) Pleadings indorsed on writ.

(6) Verdict on file.

Governor Bernard's report of the decision.

(7) Rec. 1761, fol. 235. Governor *Bernard* in a letter to the Lords of Trade of August 6th 1761, speaks of this action as "being one of the first fruits of Mr. Barrons's confederacy, in which I had a principal share of trouble, it being particularly designed by some of Mr. Barrons's friends, to involve me in a dispute with the General Court, which however I prevented." "This cause is determined against Mr. Paxton in the Inferior Court, & he has appealed against that determination to the Superior Court. If judgement should be given against Mr. Paxton in this Court also, these two points will be settled: 1. That Money paid in pursuance of a decree of the Court of Admiralty having jurisdiction in the case, and unappealed from, may be recovered in a Court of Common Law by other persons for other uses, notwithstanding such decree. 2. That money given by Act of Parliament to His Majesty for the use of the Province can be recovered by the Provincial Treasurer *ex officio*, without the intervention of the King's Attorney or any person acting by authority under His Majesty." 2 Bernard Papers, 46. As to *Barons*, *vid. ante*, 425 note, 492, and his Petition to the General Court, January 16, 1762, in Boston Evening Post, June 11, 1770.

(8) In *John Adams's* Diary, immediately after his account of the

Writs

1761.

GRAY *v.* PAXTON.

In Superior Court writ abated and judgment for defendant.

abate and that the judgment of the Inferior Court aforesaid be reversed (9) and that the said Charles Paxton recover against

---

Adams's report of the argument.

Writs of Assistance, are the following unfinished notes of the argument, which are not published in his Works, and are now printed by permission of Mr. *Charles Francis Adams:*

"*Gray* v. *Paxton.* Otis drew a writ *vs.* Paxton for Money had & "recd to the use of the Province. Prat pleaded in abatement, "That, altho the suit was brot in Grays name, altho Gray was Plan-"tiff, yet no promise was alledged to have been made to Gray. The "Deft is alleged to be indebted to the Province, for money re'd to the "Provinces use, and to have promised to pay it to the Province, yet "the Province is not Plaintiff. It is *Gray* v. *Paxton*, but it should have "been *the Province of the Massachusetts Bay* v. *Paxton.* The Treasu-"rer and Receiver General has not a Right *ex Officio*, to demand, sue "for and recover all Monies that are due to the Province. No more "than a Nobleman's steward has to sue for and recover the demands "of the Nobleman: No more than the Cashier of the Bank of Eng-"land has to sue for and recover all Monies due to the Bank of Eng-"land. A steward may sue, but not in his own Name; he must sue "in the Name of his Master. The Cashier may sue, but not in his own "Name; he must sue in the Name of the Govr & Company of ye Bank "of England. A corporate body is one Person in Law and may sue or "be sued. And there is an Instance, before the Court this term, in "your own Dockett, of a suit brot by a Town, *the Town of Dorchester* vs. "*A B* &c. There is a special Law of this Province, which impowers."

Dorchester Proprietors *v.* Man.

The case here referred to is doubtless "the Proprietors of the common and undivided lands in Dorchester, now in Stoughton, who sue by James Foster, Richard Hall, and Joseph Hewin a Committee for that purpose," *v.* Joseph Man. *Man v. Dorchester Proprietors*, Rec. 1761, fol. 232. The files of the Superior Court in that case have not been found. Those of the Inferior Court show that *Thacher* was counsel for the defendant and *Prat* for the plaintiff. The provincial statute alluded to is probably the act of 11 W. 3 (1699), which authorizes every town treasurer "to demand and receive all debts, rents and dues belonging or owing to such town, or the poor thereof, and to sue for and recover the same by due process in the law." Anc. Chart. 341.

(9) The decision that the action should have been brought in the name of the Province, and not of *Harrison Gray*, its Treasurer, was doubtless correct. *Bainbridge* v. *Downie*, 6 Mass. 258. *Irish* v. *Webster*, 5 Greenl. 171. *State* v. *Boies*, 2 Fairf. 474. *Hodgson* v. *Dexter*, 1 Cranch, 363. *Dugan* v. *United States*, 3 Wheat. 180.

againſt the ſaid Harriſon Gray, Treaſurer and receiver as aforeſaid coſts taxed at £4. 6. 9." (10)

1761.

GRAY *v.* PAXTON.

" Excon iſſued 7th Dec. 1761."

---

(10) Rec. 1761, fol. 235. On the 27th of Auguſt 1761 Governor Bernard wrote to the Lords of Trade thus: "*Gray* agt *Paxton.* This cauſe was determined without a jury, by a plea of abatement to the writ, which the Court determined in favor of the defendant. The point upon which it turned was that the Treaſurer could not ſue for the money *ex officio;* and there was no order of the General Court to enable him. There has been an order made ſince the bringing this writ; and it is expected that a new writ will be brought in purſuance of that order; and then will ariſe another queſtion, whether an order of the General Court can enable a perſon not authorized by his office to ſue for money given to the King by Act of Parliament. My reaſons for the negative your Lordships will ſee in the Votes of Jany 1761, pa. 246." 2 Bernard Papers, 51.

Governor Bernard's report of the final deciſion.

This ſtatement is not quite accurate; for the reſolve "made ſince the bringing this writ," to wit on the 15th of April 1761, was ſubſtantially in the ſame terms as the reſolve of January 13th. *Ante*, 543 note. *Poſt*, 548 note.

On the 22d of July 1761, *John Pownall* wrote to Governor *Bernard*, "The fees and charges of proceedings in Admiralty courts are become ſo shamefully exorbitant, as to be matter of notice to Government, and have been in one or two caſes pretty ſeverely cenſured by the Council." 9 Bernard Papers, 221.

Exorbitant fees in Admiralty.

On the 17th of May 1764, Governor *Bernard* wrote, it would ſeem to Lord *Egremont*, "When I first came to this government, ſeizures were much more frequent than they have been for two or three years paſt. They were all made by one officer only (Mr. *Paxton* the ſurveyor of the port) and wholly by means of private intelligencers, who were never diſcovered. To encourage theſe, It has been uſual to allow the proſecutor a ſum of money, about ten or fifteen per cent. of the value of the ſeizure, to pay for private intelligence, upon no other voucher than his own oath that he had engaged to pay that ſum to the intelligencer. This, with the conſent of all parties, was inſerted in the proſecutor's bill of charges, and allowed by the Judge. There was no danger that this would be uſed to the King's detriment: for as the Governor paid as much as the King, it muſt be ſuppoſed that he would take care that the ſums allowed should be neither exorbitant nor unneceſſary." 3 Bernard Papers, 216. This laſt ſtatement can hardly be called anything but a wilful falſehood; for it was the charging of all theſe expenſes on the share which belonged to the King for the uſe of the Province, which occaſioned the ſuit reported in the text. *Ante*, 542, note.

Governor Bernard's falſehood.

Province v. Paxton. Rec. 1762, fol. 303.

Judges and jurors are not disqualified by their intereſt as inhabitants of the Province from ſitting in a civil action brought by the Province to recover money due to it.

The General Court may authorize the Province Treaſurer to ſue in behalf of the Province for money granted by Act of Parliament to the King for the ſupport of the Province.

Money paid under a decree of the Court of Vice-Admiralty cannot be recovered back by an action at common law.

Province of Massachusetts Bay *vs.* Paxton.

ON the 21ſt of September, 1761, a new action was brought in the name of "the Province of the Maſſachuſetts Bay in New England, which ſues by Harriſon Gray of Boſton in the County of Suffolk Eſq[r] Treaſurer and Receiver General of the ſame Province, who by an Order of the Great and General Court of ſaid Province held at ſaid Boſton on the twenty-fifth day of March A. D. 1761, (1) is ſpecially impowered to ſue on the behalf of ſaid Province," returnable at October term of the Inferior Court, in which the plaintiff declared in aſſumpſit "for that whereas the ſaid Charles of ſaid Boſton on the firſt day of September laſt was Indebted to the ſaid Province in the ſum of Three hundred and fifty-ſeven pounds three ſhillings and eight pence lawful money for ſo much lawful money before that time had and received by the ſaid Charles to and for the uſe of the Province aforeſaid, and the ſaid Charles being ſo Indebted then and there promiſed the ſaid Province to pay the ſame on demand, yet the ſaid Charles though often requeſted has not paid the ſame ſum, but neglects it, to the damage of the ſaid Province, as they ſay by the ſaid Harriſon Gray who ſues as aforeſaid the ſum of Three hundred and ſixty pounds." (2)

"And the ſaid Charles by Benjamin Prat his Attorney comes and ſays that this Honourable Court ought not to take cognizance

(1) This reſolve was in fact paſſed on the 15th of April, 1761, and was preciſely like that of January 13th, 1761, (*ante*, 543, note,) except in extending the authority to any ſucceſſor of the preſent Treaſurer, and in not requiring any delay, after demand and refuſal, before bringing ſuit. Journal H. R. 1761, p. 339. 23 General Court Rec. 732.

(2) Rec. 1762, fol. 303. Copy of Writ on file.

1761.

PROVINCE v. PAXTON.

cognizance of this cauſe, nor he in this Court be held to anſwer therein. For that all the Judges of this Honourable Court and all the Jurors there Returned for the Trial of all Causes there to be tried by a Jury are Inhabitants within ſaid Province and directly Intereſted in the Event of this Suit. And this he is ready to verify, wherefore he prays Judgment whether this is a Court competent to hear and try this Cauſe, and that he may not be held here to anſwer therein. (3)

Plea to the Juriſdiction.

"Which plea if overruled the ſaid Charles reſerving to himſelf the benefit thereof in any Courts to which this Cauſe may be carried, and alſo reſerving to himſelf all Exceptions to the Plaintiff's Appearance defends &c[a] and prays Judgment of the Plaintiff's Writ aforeſaid, becauſe he ſays there is no Law, Letter of Attorney, or any other Act or Thing ſufficient in Law to warrant the plaintiff in ſuing by the ſaid Harriſon Gray Eſq[r] or to enable him here to appear and proſecute the ſame Action as he there did and in and by the Writ and Declaration aforeſaid is ſuppoſed. And this the ſaid Charles is ready to verify, wherefore he prays Judgment that this Writ be abated and for Coſts.

Plea to the plaintiff's right to ſue.

"Saving which if overruled and reſerving the benefit thereof and all Exceptions the ſaid Charles ſays he never promiſed the ſaid Province in manner and form as ſaid Province declares and thereof puts &c[a] " (4)

General iſſue.

The Court overruled the pleas in abatement, and continued the caſe for trial to January term 1762, when "the caſe after a full hearing was committed to the Jury who were ſworn according to Law to try the ſame, who Returned their Verdict thereon upon Oath, that is to ſay, they find for the Plaintiff the ſum ſued for." Judgment was rendered accordingly,

Trial, verdict, and judgment for the plaintiff in Inferior Court.

(3) "Jurymen and Judges, belonging to this Province, ſat in the caſe of *Gray* and *Paxton*, though intereſted, for the neceſſity." *John Adams*, in Diary of November 5, 1762, 2 John Adams's Works, 138. *Et vid. ante*, 531, note, for ſimilar caſes.

(4) Pleas, and Copy of Record of Inferior Court, on file.

1762. PROVINCE v. PAXTON.

ingly, and the defendant appealed to the Superior Court, (5) and on the 27th of January entered into a recognizance in the ſum of Ten Pounds with *Samuel Quincy* and *Pelham Winſlow* as ſureties to proſecute his appeal with effect. (6)

Paxton's petition for the appointment of a Special Juſtice.

Paxton then preſented a petition to the Governor and Council, repreſenting "That your Petitioner was ſued at the laſt October Court by ſaid Province, for three hundred fifty ſeven pounds three ſhillings and eight pence, and Whereas ſaid action is to be tried at the Superiour Court now holden at Boſton, and the pretended cauſe of Action aroſe on Matters Adjudged in the Court of Admiralty by His Honour Judge Ruſſell; your Petitioner imagines that He cannot with propriety ſet by means whereof there will be only four Judges and ſo the Court may be equally divided which will be attended with very great inconvenience as there are ſeveral points of Laws of much Importance to be ſettled in ſaid cauſe, and which cannot be concluſively done without a Majority of the Court. Wherefore your Petitioner prays Your Excellency and Honors would appoint a ſpecial Juſtice to ſit in ſaid cauſe, in the place of His Honor Judge Ruſſell, ſo that there may be a full Court: and Whereas your Petitioner hath in ſaid Action pleaded to the Juriſdiction of the Court, he prays he may not by this petition be underſtood to give up ſaid plea, or any others; the right of which he expreſſly begs leave to reſerve. And as in Duty bound &c[a]." (7)

Timothy Ruggles appointed a Special Juſtice.

The Governor and Council accordingly iſſued a Commiſſion to *Timothy Ruggles*, (8) reciting the firſt ſection of the Province

---

(5) Copy of Record of Inferior Court, Verdict and Bill of Coſts, on file.

(6) Recognizance on file.

(7) 44 Maſs. Archives, 454. It was uſual to appoint ſpecial juſtices to ſit in particular caſes. Washburn's Judicial Hiſt. Maſs. 155–158.

Adams's account of Ruggles.

(8) *John Adams* relates that *Ruggles*, when Chief Juſtice of the Worceſter Court of Common Pleas, in May, 1761, upon hearing of the election of *James Otis* into the Houſe of Repreſentatives, ſaid: "Out of this election will ariſe a damned faction, which will ſhake this Province to its foundation." Adams to Tudor, March 29, 1817, 10 John Adams's Works, 248.

1762.
PROVINCE v. PAXTON.

Province Act of 11 William 3, which eftablifhed the Superior Court of Judicature, and proceeding thus: —

"We therefore repofing efpecial Truft and Confidence in your Loyalty, Prudence and Ability have affigned conftituted and appointed and do by thefe Prefents affign constitute and appoint you the faid Timothy Ruggles to be a Juftice of our Superior Court of Judicature &c[a] for the tryal of a Caufe depending on an Appeal in the faid Court now holden at Bofton in and for the County of Suffolk between Charles Paxton Efq: Appellant and [the Province of the Maffachufetts Bay in New England, which fues by (9)] Harrifon Gray Efq[r]. Treafurer and Receiver General of the Province aforefaid Appellee, in the room of Chambers Ruffell Efq[r] one of the ftanding Juftices of our faid Court who declines to fit as Judge in the faid Caufe being interefted in the Event thereof. And we do hereby Authorize and impower You to have, ufe, exercife and execute all and fingular the Powers, Authorities, and Jurifdictions to Juftices of our faid Court belonging or in any wife appertaining fo far as it relates to the faid Cafe; and with other our Juftices of the faid Court (or any of them fo as to make a Quorum of faid Court) to hear and determine faid Cafe and Matter, and to give Judgment therein and award Execution thereupon, and to do that which to Juftice therein appertains according to Law." (10)

In Superior Court, pleas in abatement overruled.

At February term 1762 of the Superior Court, "both parties appeared, and the pleas in abatement (as on file) having been argued and overruled, The cafe after a full hearing was committed to a Jury fworn according to Law to try the fame, who returned their verdict therein upon oath,

---

(9) The words in brackets are interlined both in the original commission and in the copy in the Book of Commiffions, 1756–1767, fol. 262, in the office of the Secretary of the Commonwealth.

(10) The original commiffion, dated February 23, 1762, is on file with the papers in the cafe, and bears a certificate of *Hutchinfon* as Lieutenant Governor that *Ruggles* qualified under it on the 25th of February.

1762. PROVINCE v. PAXTON.

Verdict and judgment for defendant.

oath, that is to ſay, they find for the appellant reverſion of the former judgment and coſts. It's therefore Conſidered by the Court that the former judgment be reverſed, and that the ſaid Charles Paxton recover againſt the Province of the Maſſachuſetts Bay who ſued by Harriſon Gray Eſq. Treaſurer thereof, Coſts taxed at £6. 1. 0." (11)

Bernard's account.

(11) Rec. 1762, fol. 203. Verdict and bill of coſts on file. On the 1ſt of March, 1762, Governor *Bernard* wrote: The cauſe of Mr. *Gray* agst. *Paxton* has been heard in the Superior Court when purſuant to the direction of all the Judges the jury found a verdict for the defendant." 2 Bernard Papers, 81. S. P. February 27, 1762, Ib. 19.

Hutchinson's report.

Hutchinſon's report is more particular: "When the cauſe came upon trial, it was very feebly ſupported, by shewing that the charges ought not to have been allowed by the Court of Admiralty; and by repreſenting that Court as not congenial with the ſpirit of the English Conſtitution, for which reaſon no indulgent conſtruction ought to be allowed to their proceedings. The Court ſummed up the cauſe to the jury, ſo as to shew that the action had not been ſupported; and cautioned them againſt departing from the rules of law, and conſequently from their oaths, in compliance with popular prejudices; and, contrary to the prevailing expectation, they found coſts for the defendant." He then refers to the acknowledgment, by the two houſes, of the authority of Acts of Parliament, (*ante*, 544, note,) and adds: "Juries were diſpoſed to receive the law from the Court, and could not eaſily be induced to depart from their oaths." 3 Hutchinſon's Hiſt. Maſs. 91, 92. As to the jurors' oath, *vid. poſt*, note to *Erving* v. *Cradock*.

Adams's comments.

"Who is it that has always given his opinion in favor of prerogative and revenue, in every caſe in which they have been brought in queſtion, without one exception? Who is it that has endeavored to bias ſimple juries, by an argument as warm and vehement as thoſe of the bar, in a caſe where the Province was contending againſt a cuſtom-houſe officer? And what were the other means employed in that cauſe againſt the reſolutions of the General Aſſembly?" John Adams's Diary, December 30, 1765, 2 John Adams's Works, 170.

But there can be no doubt that the Judges of the Superior Court rightly held the decree in Admiralty to be concluſive. *Gelſton* v. *Hoyt*, 3 Wheat. 318. *Baxter* v. *New England Marine Ins. Co.*, 6 Maſs. 277. *Whitney* v. *Walsh*, 1 Cush. 29.

Erving vs. Cradock.

Erving v. Cradock. Rec. 1761, fol. 230.

The owner of a ship and cargo, seized for breach of the revenue laws, and libelled in the Court of Vice-Admiralty, compounded with the Government officers, by leave of that Court, by paying half the value of the property; and then sued the collector in trespass for the seizure. The jury, against the express instructions of the Superior Court, returned a verdict for the plaintiff; and the Court gave judgment upon it.

TRESPASS by John Erving against George Cradock, "for that the said George on the twenty-sixth day of April last, with force and arms at said Boston took the said John's Brigantine called the Sarah, his Tackle, Apparrell, Gunns, Boat, and two barrels and an half of Gunpowder belonging to her, and his Cargoe on board her, viz, forty reels of Cable Yarn, one bale of Canvas, eighty five bundles of Russia Duck, four hundred and fifty nine bars of Steel, two hampers of Stone ware, two cases of Geneva, one bundle of Brushes, one case of painted Canvas, one box of China ware, one case of striped Holland, all of the value of one thousand pounds Sterling, and carried them away, and detained them untill the said John made a fine by five hundred and fifty five pounds, four shillings, and four pence Sterling, with the said George for having the delivery of the said Brigantine, Tackle, Apparrell, Gunns, Boat, and Cargoe, contrary to the King's peace, and to the Damage of the said John, as he saith the Sum of a thousand Pounds." Writ dated March 24th, 1761, and returnable at July term 1761 of the Court of Common Pleas.

The defendant pleaded the general issue, the plaintiff joined issue (1) and obtained a verdict, (2) upon which the court of common pleas rendered judgment, and the defendant appealed to the Superior Court, in which at August term

(1) Writ and plea on file in the Court of Common Pleas.

Governor Bernard's statement.

(2) "This is an action brought by the hon'ble *John Erving*, Esq[r] one of the Council against M[r] *Cradock*, heretofore and now temporary Collector of this Port. This case is this: M[r] *Cradock* about 16 months ago, as Collector, seized a Vessel of M[r] *Erving's* charged with contraband trade & libelled her in the Court of Admiralty. M[r] *Erving*

1761. ERVING v. CRADOCK.

term 1761 "the parties Appeared, and the Case, after a full hearing was committed to a Jury Sworn according to Law to try the Same, who returned their Verdict therein upon Oath, that is to say they find for the Appellee Seven hundred and forty pounds lawfull Money, damage and cost. It

---

Erving appeared personally in Court & prayed leave to compound, which being agreed to by the Governor & Collector as well as the King's Advocate, was allowed by the Court at one half of the value, which upon appraisement was ascertained at above £500 sterling. This sum Mr *Erving* paid into Court; & it was equally divided between the King, the Governor & the Collector. Mr *Cradock* remitted the King's share to the Commissioners of the Customs; the Governor received his third, & Mr *Cradock* his own. And now Mr *Erving* has brought his action against Mr *Cradock* for damages accrued to him by means of this seizure; and in the Inferior Court has got a verdict." Governor Bernard to Lords of Trade, August 6, 1761, 2 Bernard Papers, 46, 47.

Papers on file.

This statement is fully supported by the papers on file in this case in the Court of Common Pleas, which consist of the writ, pleadings, and officer's return; the clearance of the vessel at Port Kirkwall in the Orkneys on the 31st of December, 1759; two invoices of the cargo; Governor *Pownall's* certificate, dated December 20, 1759, of Cradock's having taken the oaths of office as Collector on the 18th of December; the depositions of the master and one of the sailors to their voyage from Amsterdam to the Orkneys and thence to Boston, and the seizure of the vessel on the 26th of April, 1760, by *William Sheaffe*, and the unloading of the cargo by orders of *Cradock;* copies of the information filed by *Prat* as Advocate General in the Court of Vice-Admiralty on the 3d of May, 1760, and of the order thereon; a subpœna to *Sheaffe* to appear as a witness in the Inferior Court on the 23d of July, 1761; and a copy of the decree of that Court approving the composition between the parties, by which *Erving* was to forfeit one half of the vessel and goods and to pay all the costs, and the value of the half forfeited was to be paid to the King, the Governor and the informer, in equal thirds.

Master's deposition.

The master gave this account of the conversation between the parties to this action after the arrival of the vessel: "My owner said she should not be unloaded, for that she had not broke bulk or committed any breach of trade, and that if he did unload her he must answer the consequence and stand to all damadges. The Collector then answered that there was something of value hid clandestinely on board, and that he was very poor and expected to get Two Thousand pounds sterling for his share. My owner then told him that he would be very much disapointed,

It is therefore confidered by the Court that the faid John Erving recover againft the faid George Cradock, the Sum of Seven hundred and forty pounds lawfull Money of the Province

---

apointed, for that the whole Veffell and Cargo would not amount to half that Sum."

Governor Bernard's letters.

Governor *Bernard*, in his letter to the Lords of Trade of Auguft 6, 1761, after ftating the cafes of *Gray* v. *Paxton* and *Erving* v. *Cradock*, (as quoted *ante*, 545, 553, 554, notes,) and defcribing the three actions brought by *Barons* in his own name to recover damages for his fufpenfion, (*ante*, 425, note,) added: "I ftate to your Lordships only the actions that are now brought. But it is generally underftood that M^r. *Ervings* is only a leading action to a great many others; and that if he meets with fuccefs, every one that has had goods condemned, or been allowed to compound for them at their own requeft, will bring actions againft the officer who feized them. Your Lordships will perceive that thefe actions have an immediate tendency to deftroy the Court of Admiralty and with it the Cuftom houfe, which cannot fubsift without that Court. Indeed the intention is made no fecret of: In the two cafes above mentioned that were tried in the Inferior Court, the chief fubject of the harangues of the council for the plaintiff (and fome of the Judges too) were on the expediency of difcouraging a Court immediately fubject to the King and independant of the Province and which determined property without a jury; and on a neceffity of putting a ftop to the practices of the Cuftom houfe officers, for that the people would no longer bear having their trade kept under reftrictions, which their neighbours (meaning Rhode Ifland) were entirely free from. And one gentleman, who has had a considerable hand in promoting thefe difturbances, has been fo candid as to own to me, that it was their intention to work them up to fuch a pitch as should make it neceffary for the miniftry to interfere and procure them juftice (as they call it) in repealing or qualifying the Molaffes Act, and in obliging the Neighbouring Provinces to obferve the fame reftraints which this is to be kept under. In regard to both thefe points, if they were follicited in another manner, there would be much to be faid in their behalf." 2 Bernard Papers, 48, 49.

"The pretence for this action is, that the feizure was illegal and a trefpafs, and that the payment of M^r. *Erving* was not voluntary, but extorted by violence and *durefs*. Upon this shadow of reafon, two of the Judges of the Inferior Court, M^r. *Watts* and M^r. *Wells*, directed the jury to find a verdict for the plaintiff, and give him for damages every farthing he was out of pocket; and faid they muft put a ftop to thefe proceedings of the Cuftom houfe officers; if they did not there would be tumults and bloodshed; for the people would bear with them no

1761. ERVING v. CRADOCK.

Province (3) damage and costs taxed at £ ." The defendant appealed to the King in Council; but on the 25th of March 1762, the plaintiff acknowledged on the record that he had received of the defendant "full satisfaction of this Judgment." (4)

---

no longer. The jury accordingly gave the plaintiff near £600 sterling damages." Bernard to Pownall, August 28, 1761, Ib. 9.

Judges of the Inferior Court.

Samuel Watts and *Samuel Welles*, the Judges here mentioned, as well as *John Erving*, the plaintiff, were members of the committee of the General Court on the petition of the merchants against *Paxton*, and Judge *Watts* made the report. *Ante*, 542, note. Journal H. R. 1761, p. 238.

(3) One fourth less, or £555, sterling. Prov. St. 23 G. 2, c. 5, Mass. Perpet. Laws (ed. 1759) 340; Anc. Chart. 779. *Infra*, note 4.

Governor Bernard's report of proceedings in Superior Court.

(4) Rec. 1761, fol. 230. The files of this case in the Superior Court have not been found. But the letters of Governor *Bernard* contain a full account of the proceedings subsequent to the appeal from the judgment of the Inferior Court.

"*Erving* v. *Cradock*. This action came before a jury in the Superior Court. Upon the summing up the evidence the judges were all of opinion that tho' Mr Cradock might by means of some irregularity in the seizing of the ship have been guilty of a trespass (which however was neither proved nor admitted) yet it was wholly purged by the composition confirmed by the Court of Admiralty, the decrees of which were of equal force with a judgement at common law. It was urged by the Chief Justice that the Court of Admiralty was part of the Constitution of the Province, it being expressly provided for by the Charter. The whole Bench directed the jury, as strongly as they could, to find for the defendant. Nevertheless they found for the plaintiff and gave upwards of £550 sterling in damages, being all he said he was out of pocket. This was no surprise to those that were acquainted with the violence with which these proceedings are carried on. It was remarkable that Mr. Erving, according to the Usage of these Courts, spoke a great deal for himself, when he had admitted everything necessary to prove that he had incurred a forfeiture and declared he only acquiesced only in expectation that a time should come when he should have his *revenge;* a word he used several times to express the purpose of his conduct. He declared after the verdict that he should be supported by the principal merchants of London against any representations the Governor could make.

Appeal to the King in Council.

"Mr. Cradock will take care to enter an appeal to the King in due time: as he will nevertheless be subject to execution, care will be taken to prevent his being sent to gaol before orders come from England. They now begin to talk of bringing more actions against Custom house officers who have made seizures and have had them condemned

demned or compounded in Court for them. A Cuſtom houſe officer has no chance with a jury, let his cauſe be what it will. And it will depend upon the vigorous meaſures that shall be taken at home for the defence of the officers, whether there be any Cuſtom houſe here at all." Bernard to Lords of Trade, Auguſt 2, 1761, 2 Bernard Papers, 51, 52. To the ſame effect is his letter of the next day to Governor *Pownall*, Ib. 10.

Releaſe of judgment.

On the 27th of February 1762 Governor *Bernard* wrote to Lord *Barrington*, that he apprehended this cauſe would "ſoon be ended by the plaintiff's diſcharging his judgment to prevent his anſwering in appeal. So that the King's authority is now triumphant in every inſtance." 2 Bernard Papers, 29. Attorney General *Trowbridge* and Mr. *Auchmuty* were retained by the Governor to proſecute the appeal, and were paid "out of the King's share" of ſeizures, upon an order of Governor *Bernard* and Surveyor General *Lechmere* of October 19, 1761; Boſton Gazette, June 11, Auguſt 27, and September 3, 1861. And after *Erving* had acknowledged ſatisfaction of his judgment, *Trowbridge*, on the demand of *Temple*, *Lechmere's* ſucceſſor, (*ante*, 428, note 17,) on the 4th of May 1762 refunded part of the fees.

Counſel in the caſe.

Hutchinſon's report of a ſimilar caſe.

The circumſtances of a caſe reported by *Hutchinſon* correſpond ſo nearly with thoſe of *Erving* v. *Cradock*, as to leave little doubt of its being the ſame. He ſays, "The Court imagined their opinion upon what was a mere matter of law, would have the ſame influence with the jury as formerly in a like caſe," evidently *Province* v. *Paxton*, *ante*, 552. "The Judges could have no doubt that the decree of the Court of Admiralty, where it had juriſdiction, could not be traverſed and annulled in a court of common law; but the jury notwithſtanding gave their verdict for the plaintiff. As it was a perſonal action, and the value more than 300*l*. ſterling, an appeal clearly lies by charter to the King in Council. It was claimed, and granted." 3 Hutchinſon's Hiſt. Maſs. 161. The entry of 1766 in the margin of the page is of no weight to diſprove the identity of the caſe; for on the ſame page *Hutchinſon* ſtates the decree of the Court of Admiralty in the caſe of the *Freemaſon*, which was in 1763; and on the next page, as having occurred "juſt after theſe," the admiſſion by *Cockle* at Salem of veſſels from Anguilla, which was in 1764. *Ante*, 390, 423. The queſtion whether *Hutchinſon*, in this place, is ſpeaking of 1761 or 1766 is rendered intereſting by the fact that he ſpeaks of theſe caſes as having occurred "while the minds of the people of every rank and order, in all parts of the Province, were more or leſs diſturbed with apprehenſions of taxes by authority of Parliament." Compare *John Adams's* Preface of 1819 to Novanglus, 4 John Adams's Works, 6; 4 Bancroft's Hiſt. U. S. 370.

The fact that judgment was thus rendered on a verdict found against the expreſs inſtructions of the judges, in a civil action of great moment to the Government, show how much deference was paid to the verdict of a jury in the Province of Maſſachuſetts Bay. And this caſe is not a ſolitary inſtance. In

Goodſpeed *v.* Gay.

In 1763 in an action of trover brought againſt a military officer for recruiting a man who was claimed as a ſlave, the plaintiff recovered a verdict, upon which judgment was rendered, "although," Governor *Bernard* wrote, "upon the tryal the Judges told the jury that there was no evidence againſt the defendant, not the leaſt pretence to charge him in ſuch an action." *Goodſpeed* v. *Gay*, Rec. 1763, fol. 47. Governor Bernard to General Amherſt, May 14, 1763, 2 Bernard Papers, 305. This explanation deprives that caſe of any authority upon the queſtion of maintaining trover for a negro. *Vid. ante*, 98–102, note.

Otis *v.* Robinſon.

In 1770, in giving an account of the action of *James Otis* againſt *John Robinſon*, one of the Commiſſioners of the Cuſtoms, for aſſault and battery (Tudor's Life of Otis, 365, 503; Rec. 1772, fol. 109.) *Hutchinſon*, after mentioning the verdict of £2000 for the plaintiff in the Inferior Court, and the defendant's appeal to the Superior Court, wrote, "I hope that a better jury will not give exorbitant damages. If they should, there will be no remedy but by an Appeal to the King in Council." 25 Maſs. Archives, 438. The Chief Juſtice evidently meant here no remedy of any value; for the ſtatutes of the Province clearly

Reviews.

allowed as of right a review in this as in other ordinary civil cauſes, although they would not allow it of judgments upon informations for the forfeiture of goods. Prov. Sts. 13 W. 3; 24 G. 2; 30 G. 2; Anc. Chart. 368, 574, 611. The review of an action at law was introduced here very early. In 1639 it is ſpoken of as already exiſting. 1 Maſs. Col. Rec. 275. It was at firſt called a "bill of review," and doubtleſs derived its origin from the analogous remedy in chancery. St. 1642, 2 Ib. 11. *Sewall, J.*, in *Burrell* v. *Burrell*, 10 Maſs. 222. Bacon's Ordinances of 1619, 1 Sand. Ord. Ch. 109. *Elliott* v. *Balcom*, 11 Gray, 286, and authorities cited. 6 Dane Ab. c. 189. Rev. Sts. c. 99. Gen. Sts. c. 146, §§ 19–38. See alſo Plym. Col. Laws (ed. 1672) 12; (ed. 1836) 254; Nantucket St. of 1672, Hough's Nantucket Papers, 43; 1

New Trials.

Doug. Hiſt. N. A. 518. New trials did not come into uſe in England until after the ſettlement of the Maſſachusetts Colony. *Slade's* caſe, Style, 138. *Wood* v. *Gunston*, Style, 466. *Wheeler* v. *Honour*, 1 Sid. 58. *The Queen* v. *Helston*, 10 Mod. 202. *Witham* v. *Lewis*, 1 Wils. 55. *Bright* v. *Eynon*, 1 Bur. 394, 395. And though recognized as poſſible, they ſeem to have been very rarely ordered by the Courts of the Province. *Angier* v. *Jackson*, *ante*, 83, 85.

Right of jury in Maſſachuſetts Colony.

In the Colony of Maſſachusetts, the right of the jury to determine the law was never denied in criminal caſes; but was for forty years alternately recognized and diſallowed in civil actions. Lechmere's Plain Dealing (1641) 23 Maſs. Hiſt. Coll. 85. Body of Liberties, arts. 29, 30, 31, 70, 76, 77, 28 Ib. 221, 228, 229. Sts. 1642, 2 Maſs. Col. Rec. 21; 1657, 3 Ib. 424, 425, & 4 Ib. pt. i., 290, 291. Maſs. Col. Laws, (ed. 1660) 47, 48, 77, 78; (ed. 1672) 86, 87, 152. Washburn's Jud. Hiſt. Maſs. 45.

By art. 31 of the Body of Liberties, the jury had "liberty to give a

non-

non-liquet;" and this power was sometimes exercised. *Cleves* v. *Jocelin* (1641) 2 Winthrop's Hist. N. E. 257. *Hall* v. *Louden* (1649) and *Boidon* v. *Pratt* (1650) in Middlesex County Court Rec. But this term, derived from the Roman law, and unknown to the law of England, (Bacon's Reading on the Statute of Uses, 4 Bacon's Works, ed. 1824, p. 184,) occasioned so much doubt and confusion in practice, that the provision was repealed by the St. of 1657, *ub. sup.*, in which the right and duty of the jury to decide the case when they could were very strongly asserted.

Non-liquet.

In the early times of the Massachusetts Colony, if the Court and jury did not agree, the case was brought to the General Court. But this practice occasioned difficulties and disputes between the two houses; and they, according to the custom of the time, consulted the elders, whose advice was "that the magistrates may be, by expresse law, directed to accept the juries verdict and to grant judgment accordingly, unlesse they shall judge the juries verdict to be evidently contrary to law and evidence, in which case, that they may bee impowered by law to cause the jurie to answer for their default in the same court, before a jurie of twenty-four persons chosen by the freemen, or otherwise to bee liable to bee served by the party aggrieved with a writ of attainder out of the same court, or otherwise as this honoured court may see more aptly and amply to provide. It being the great liberty of an English subject to be tryed by his peers, before whom he hath free and full libertie to plead law for his indempnitie and safety." Hutchinson's Coll. 436, 439. The General Court did not adopt this suggestion in criminal cases; but in May 1672 passed an act requiring all judges in civil cases, after having "used all reasonable endeavours for clearing the case to the jury by declaring the law, and comparing the matter of fact therewith," to accept and render judgment upon every verdict, "unless upon corruption or error in the jury giving in their verdict contrary to law and evidence the party cast shall in open court attaint the jury," in which case a trial should be had by a jury of twenty-four, upon whose verdict judgment should be rendered. Mass. Col. St. 1672, Mass. Col. Laws (Suppl. to ed. 1672) 171, 172; 4 Mass. Col. Rec. pt. ii., 508, 509; Anc. Chart. 147. Under this statute, if the judges did not approve of the verdict of a petit jury, they sent them out again; but if the jury persisted, the judges were obliged to record the verdict. *Greene* v. *Baker*, Rec. 1680, fol. 114. Attaints were brought so often, that another statute was passed to check and regulate them, after which they became less frequent. Rec. 1672—85, *passim*. St. 1684, 5 Mass. Col. Rec. 449; Anc. Chart. 147.

Verdicts made conclusive, subject to attaint.

The law of attaints in England in civil cases was very like that of Massachusetts. A verdict against the instructions of the Judges, if affirmed by the jury of attaint, was final. Lit. § 514. Co. Lit. 217 *b*, 294 *b*. *Chevin & Paramour's case*, Dyer, 201 *a*. 301, *a*, *b*. 1 Rol. Ab. 180. Vin. Ab. Attaint, A. Com. Dig. Attaint, B. And, although the petit jury

Attaints in England.

jury could not be attainted for not considering evidence ruled out by the Court, the authorities are not agreed upon the question whether following the instructions of the Court would excuse them from an attaint. *Heydon* v. *Ibgrave*, Dyer, 129 *b.* *The Queen* v. *Ingersoll*, Cro. Eliz. 308, 309. *Needler* v. *Bishop of Winchester*, Hob. 227. *Bushell's case*, Vaugh. 145, 148, 150, & T. Jon. 17. *Chichester* v. *Philips*, T. Raym. 405. *Groenvelt* v. *Burwell*, 1 Ld. Raym. 470. *Bridgman* v. *Holt*, Show. P. C. 123. According to the weight of authority, no attaint lay in a criminal case. Co. Lit. 294 *b.* *Floyd & Barker's case*, 12 Rep. 23. *Bushell's case*, Vaugh. 146, & T. Jon. 16. Lord *Holt* in *Groenvelt* v. *Burwell*, 1 Ld. Raym. 469, & 12 Mod. 391. 1 Hawk. c. 72, § 5. Bac. Ab. Juries, M. Trials per Pais, 274. 1 Chit. Crim. Law, 530. Lord *Mansfield*, in 4 Doug. 115. Lord *Camden*, in 17 Parl. Hist. 731. *Commonwealth* v. *Anthes*, 5 Gray, 202, 291. 2 Hale P. C. 310, *contra.*

Attaints obsolete.

Attaints were apparently obsolete, both in England and in this country, before the American Revolution. Gilb. C. P. 128. Bac. Ab. Juries, M. 1. 3 Bl. Com. 389, 405. Barrington on Sts. (5th ed.) 74, 103. Hargrave's note to Co. Lit. 155 *b.* *Witham* v. *Lewis*, 1 Wils. 55. *Eichorn* v. *Lemaitre*, 2 Wils. 369. *Bright* v. *Eynon*, 1 Bur. 393. *Tyssen* v. *Clarke*, 2 W. Bl. 942. *Angier* v. *Jackson*, *ante*, 85. Pownall's Administration of the Colonies (3d ed.) Appendix, § 3, p. 44. 6 Dane Ab. 230, 244. *Shaw*, C. J., in *Commonwealth* v. *Anthes*, 5 Gray, 198, 202.

Oaths of jurors in Massachusetts.

The prescribed forms of oath, in the Colony and Province of Massachusetts, seem to have referred the jury to the established law, rather than to that laid down by the Court in the particular case. In the Massachusetts Colony the ordinary oath of the petit jury required them to return a verdict "according to the evidence given you, and the laws of this jurisdiction." The grand jury's oath was similar. The "Oath of Life and Death" in Massachusetts, and all the oaths of petit juries in the Plymouth Colony, were simply "according to your evidence." 3 Mass. Col. Rec. 48. Mass. Col. Laws (ed. 1660) 86; (ed. 1672) 107. Plym. Col. Laws (ed. 1685) 73. By one of the earliest acts of the Province these forms were somewhat modified. The grand jurors' oath was put into substantially its present shape, (*ante*, 268, note); one form was prescribed for petit jurors in all criminal cases, being the same used in England (2 Hale P. C. 293) ending "according to your evidence;" and the "Jurors oath in civil causes," in this form: "You swear that in all causes betwixt party and party that shall be committed unto you, you will give a true verdict therein according to law, and the evidence given you." Prov. Sts. 4 W. & M., p. 60. In some objections forwarded to England against the acts of this session, (for a copy of which from the State Paper Office in London, the writer is indebted to Mr. *Henry T. Parker*,) it was suggested "whether the words 'according to law' in the juryman's oath be not to spare, confounding the court and jury together." New England Board of Trade, 7 Original Papers, 15. Yet the act was confirmed by the King. Mass. Prov. Laws, (London ed. 1724) p. 28; (Boston ed. 1726,) p. 27.

Opinions of Holt and Somers.

It would have been ftrange, indeed, if the doubt suggefted had been allowed any force in England under a King who had appointed, as his higheft Judges in law and equity, *Holt* and *Somers*, of whom the firft in 1697 declared from the bench that "in all cafes and in all actions the jury may give a general or fpecial verdict, as well in caufes criminal as civil, and the Court ought to receive it, if pertinent to the point in iffue, for if the jury doubt they may refer themfelves to the Court, but are not bound fo to do;" and in 1704 fubmitted the criminality of an alleged libel to the jury; and the other had previoufly written, "The office and power of these juries is *judicial;* they only are the judges from whofe fentence the indicted are to expect life or death; upon their integrity and underftanding the lives of all that are brought into judgment do ultimately depend; from their verdict there lies no appeal; by finding guilty or not guilty, they do complicately refolve both law and fact. As it hath been the law, fo it hath always been the cuftom and practice of thefe juries, upon all general iffues, pleaded in cafes civil as well as criminal, to judge both of the law and the fact." 3 Salk. 373, pl. 6. *Tutchin's cafe*, 14 Howell's State Trials, 1128, 1129. Effay on Grand Juries, 9, 10.

Earlier English authorities.

It is hard to refift the temptation of paufing to weigh and compare the earlier ftatements and opinions of *Glanville*, *Bracton*, *Fleta*, *Britton*, *Fortescue*, *Littleton*, *Coke*, *Bacon*, *Milton*, *Sidney*, *Hale*, *Vaughan*, and the Judges who tried the *Seven Bishops*, with thofe of Chief Juftice *Bromley* and Sir *Nicholas Hare*, Juftice *Clerk*, Lord Commiffioner *Keble* and Juftice *Jermyn*, Juftice *Berkeley*, Lord *Clarendon*, Chief Juftice *Hyde*, Chief Juftice *Kelyng* and Juftice *Twisden*, Sir *John Howel* as Recorder of London, Chief Juftice *Scroggs*, Chief Juftice *Jeffreys*, and Chief Juftice *Herbert.* But moft of them are familiarly known, and all are eafily acceffible. Glanville, lib. 2, cc. 7, 17, 18; lib. 13, cc. 7, 15. Bracton, lib. 4, c. 19; §§ 3–6. Fleta, lib. 4, c. 9, §§ 1–9. Britton (2d ed.), 130, 136, 219. Fortefcue de Laudibus, c. 26. Lit. § 368. 2 Inst. 426, 427. Hiftory of Henry VII., 9 Bacon's Works (ed. 1824), 483; 5 Ib. 117. Defence of the People of England, 8 Milton's Works (Pick. ed.), 198, 199. Sidney's Difcourfes on Government, c. 3, § 26. 2 Hale's Hift. Com. Law (5th ed.), 141, 147, 155, 156; 2 Hale P. C. 312, 313. *Bushell's cafe*, Vaugh. 150, 153; 6 Howell's State Trials, 1016, 1017, 1021. *Cafe of the Seven Bishops*, 12 Howell's State Trials, 426–430. *Throckmorton's cafe*, 1 Howell's State Trials, 887. *Udall's cafe*, Ib. 1283, 1288. *Lilburne's cafe*, 4 Ib. 1379–1381, 1401. 2 Rufhworth's Hift. Coll. 602, 603, 611. Clarendon's Survey of Hobbes's Leviathan (2d ed.), 93, 126. *Keach's cafe*, 6 Howell's State Trials, 707. *The King* v. *Wagstaffe*, T. Raym. 138, & *Hood's cafe*, J. Kel. 50. *Penn & Mead's cafe*, 6 Howell's State Trials, 959–961. *Scroggs, arg.* in *Bushell's cafe*, Freem. 3, & *jud.* in *Harris's cafe*, 7 Howell's State Trials, 930, & *Carr's cafe*, Ib. 1128. *Jeffreys, arg.* in *Carr's cafe*, Ib. 1115, & *jud.* in *Algernon Sidney's cafe*, 9 Ib. 889, & *Barnardiston's cafe*, Ib. 1349, 1352. *Johnson's cafe*, 11 Ib. 1349, 1350.

Later English opinions.

No other Englifh authorities upon this queftion have been found in the reigns of King *William* III. and Queen *Anne*. But the opinions of later Englifh judges have generally been adverfe to the right of the jury. Sir *John Pratt* in *Galard's case*, cited in 2 Cavendifh Debates, 362, 375. Lord *Raymond*, in *Oneby's case*, 17 Howell's State Trials, 49, 2 Ld Raym. 1493, 1494, 1 Barnard. 17, & 2 Stra. 773; in *Clark's case*, 17 Howell's State Trials, 667 note, 1 Barnard. 305, 4 Doug. 166, 167, & 21 Howell's State Trials, 1036; and in *Francklin's case*, Ib. 1037, 4 Doug. 167, and 17 Howell's State Trials, 672. Lord *Hardwicke*, as Attorney General, Ib. 1669; in the Houfe of Commons, 8 Parl. Hift. 1290; and as Chief Juftice, *the King* v. *Poole*, Cas. temp. Hardw. 28. Chief Juftice *Lee*, in *Owen's case*, 4 Doug. 168, 21 Howell's State Trials, 1038, & 18 Ib. 1228. Chief Juftice *Ryder*, as Attorney General, Ib. 1222; and as Chief Juftice, *Rex* v. *Nutt*, 4 Doug. 168, 21 Howell's State Trials, 1038, and 20 Ib. 837 note. Sir *Michael Fofter*, Fofter's Crown Law, 255, 256. Mr. Juftice *Buller*, at *nisi prius*, in *the Dean of St. Asaph's case*, 21 Howell's State Trials, 945–950. Sir *William Blackftone*, 3 Bl. Com. 378; 4 Ib. 361. Serjeant *Hawkins*, 2 Hawk. c. 22, §§ 21, 22. And, laft and moft important, Lord *Manffield*, as Solicitor General, in *Owen's case*, 18 Howell's State Trials, 1223; and as Chief Juftice, in *Shebbeare's case*, 4 Doug. 169, & 21 Howell's State Trials, 1038; in *Miller's case*, 20 Ib. 893, 895; in *Woodfall's case*, Ib. 901, 912, 918, 5 Bur. 2667, & Lofft, 778; and in *the Dean of St. Asaph's case*, best reported *nom. the King* v. *Shipley*, 4 Doug. 73, also in 21 Howell's State Trials, 956, and lefs fully 3 T. R. 428 note. If *Erskine's* great argument for the defendant in that cafe could be thought to have been influenced by the interefts of his client, fuch a view would add weight to Mr. *Bearcroft's* exprefs admiffion, in his argument for the Crown, of the right of the jury to take upon themfelves, if they pleafed, the decifion of every queftion of law involved in the general iffue, and to his refufal to adopt the fuggeftion of Lord *Mansfield* to fay "power" instead of "right." 4 Doug. 94 note. And Mr. Juftice *Willes*, who diffented from Lord *Mansfield* on this point, faid that Mr. *Bearcroft* expreffed "the fentiments of the greater part of Weftminfter Hall." 4 Doug. 173, 175. It is worthy of remark that the earlier decisions of Lord *Mansfield* and his affociates were made without argument of this queftion. By Lord *Mansfield*, C. J. & *Willes*, J., 4 Doug. 169, 174; 21 Howell's State Trials., 1038, 1039. And in *Horne's Trial* for a libel in faying that the Americans, "preferring death to flavery, were for that reafon only inhumanly murdered by the King's troops at or near Lexington and Concord in the Province of Maffachufetts on the 19th of April," 1775, Lord *Mansfield* himself fubmitted to the jury the criminality of the alleged libel. 20 Howell's State Trials, 653, 759. See also *Almon's case*, Ib. 836, 838; Serjeant *Glynn*, *Thurlow*, A. G., *Wedderburn*, S. G., *Dunning & Burke*, 2 Cavendifh Debates, 99-104, 125, 126, 145, 369, 373, 374.

Lord Manffield.

It

It is not proposed to do more than refer to well known authorities upon this subject. But there is one, ("undoubtedly the first common lawyer in England," as *Quincy* justly called him — Quincy's Life of Quincy, 329,) who should not be omitted in an investigation of American constitutional law from an ante-Revolutionary point of view, and who, upon a question affecting the liberty of the subject, outweighs all those cited in the last paragraph. Lord *Camden*, whether as counsel for the defendant, as attorney general, or upon the bench, uniformly maintained the doctrine that the jury in criminal cases were judges of the law as well as the fact. *Owen's case*, 18 Howell's State Trials, 1227. *Hensey's case*, 19 Ib. 1355, 1356. By *Erskine*, *arguendo*, 21 Ib. 928, 1012, & 4 Doug. 152. Pettingal on Juries, 122, cited 21 Howell's State Trials, 853. 2 Cavendish Debates, 125, 142. By Lord *Camden*, 29 Parl. Hist. 1408. In the House of Lords, in 1770, upon Lord *Mansfield's* leaving with the clerk the opinion in *Woodfall's case*, Lord *Camden* said that he considered it as a challenge directed personally to himself, which he accepted; and declared himself ready to maintain that Lord *Mansfield's* doctrine was not the law of England; and put to him questions in writing, framed with a view to ascertain how far the opinion denied the right of the jury to decide the law in cases of libel, which Lord *Mansfield* evaded answering. 16 Parl. Hist. 1321. 2 Cavendish Debates, 352, note. 4 Walpole's Memoirs of George III., 216, 220, 221. Lord *Chatham*, as usual, concurred with Lord *Camden*, and opposed Lord *Mansfield*. 16 Parl. Hist. 1305. Lord *Camden* retained the same opinion to the end of his life. In his last speech in the House of Lords, in the debates on Fox's Libel Bill in 1792, he declared that "the jury had an undoubted right to form their verdict themselves according to their consciences, applying the law to the fact; if it were otherwise, the first principle of the law of England would be defeated and overthrown. If the twelve judges were to assert the contrary again and again, he would deny it utterly, because every Englishman was to be tried by his country; and who was his country but his twelve peers, sworn to condemn or acquit according to their consciences? If the opposite doctrine were to obtain, trial by jury would be a nominal trial, a mere form; for, in fact, the Judge, and not the jury, would try the man. He would contend for the truth of this argument to the latest hour of his life *manibus pedibusque*. With regard to the Judge stating to the jury what the law was upon each particular case, it was his undoubted duty so to do; but having done so, the jury were to take both law and fact into their consideration, and to exercise their discretion and discharge their consciences." 29 Parl. Hist. 1536. See also, Ib. 729, 1408; and 1 Lord Brougham's Statesmen of George III. 3d series (ed. 1853), 216, 217.

Lord Camden.

In the Province of Massachusetts, and for many years after the adoption of the State Constitution, trials by jury were held before the whole bench, and the Judges expressed their several opinions or doubts to the jury; and on a review in the same Court before a new jury, each dissenting

Practice in Province of Massachusetts.

ſenting Judge reargued the caſe. *Province* v. *Paxton*, *ante*, 552 note. *Erving* v. *Cradock*, *supra*, 555, 556, notes. *Bromfield* v. *Little*, *ante*, 108. *Pateshall* v. *Apthorp*, *ante*, 185, 186. *Richardson's case*, 3 Hutchinſon's Hiſt. Maſs. 286. *Trial of British Soldiers*, (ed. 1770), 178, 197, 207 ; (ed. 1824), 122, 136, 143. *Commonwealth* v. *Boston*, 2 Monthly Anthology, 99. *Shaw*, C. J. in 9 Pick. 569, 570.

Hutchinſon. *Hutchinson* nowhere appears to have aſſerted that the jury were bound to take the law from the Court. In *the Province* v. *Paxton* he ſays that the Court "cautioned the jury againſt departing from the rules of law, and conſequently from their oaths." *Ante*, 552, note. Their oaths, it will be remembered, referred them to the law, not to the inſtructions of the Judges. *Supra*, 560. The moſt that is reported in other trials at which *Hutchinson* preſided is that the Judges "imagined," or "ſuppoſed it was proper," that the jury should be influenced by their opinion in matter of law. *Supra*, 557. *Trial of Warren & others*, *ante*, 249. In an action brought to recover land claimed under a will, and tried before the whole Court in 1767, an objection that the will gave the demandant no title, and therefore should not be admitted, was unanimouſly overruled, as "the firſt of the kind ever made" and "ſubverſive of the hitherto uninterrupted courſe of practice"; and "the Court ſaid, the will ſhould go in as evidence to the jury, who, upon finding the ſpecial matter, would bring the point of law properly before the Court." *Gibbs* v. *Gibbs*, *ante*, 251, 252. But the Court do not appear to have ſaid what could be done if the jury should insist on returning a general verdict for the tenant.

Trowbridge. Soon after the appointment of *Trowbridge*, a learned crown lawyer, who had been Attorney General of the Province, and was better acquainted than the other Judges with the recent Engliſh text books and decisions, the rulings of the Superior Court of Judicature tended to limit the right of the jury. In a civil action for libel in 1767, *Lynde*, *Cushing*, *Oliver* and *Trowbridge*, JJ., refuſed to allow *John Adams* to argue to the jury whether the words were actionable or not. *Cotton* v. *Nye*, Rec. 1767, fol. 228 ; 2 John Adams's Works, 207. Among Judge *Trowbridge's* MSS. is a memorandum, in his own handwriting, indorsed "Jurors to take the law from the Court," containing references to 2 Hawk. c. 22, §§ 21, 22, and Plow. 114, 231, 259, 496. And upon

Trial of British Soldiers. the trial of the British Soldiers in December, 1770, he instructed the jury accordingly, relying on *Hawkins*, Lord *Raymond*, and *Foster*. *Trial of British Soldiers*, (ed. 1770), 186 ; (ed. 1824), 127. *Josiah Quincy*, *Jr.*, in opening the defence, had taken the ſame ground. Ib. (ed. 1770), 69, 136, 143, 144 ; (ed. 1824), 44, 45, 86, 92. But *John Adams*, aſſociated with *Quincy*, leſs carried away by zeal for his client, argued the law at length to the jury, and appealed, for the rules of law which muſt govern the caſe, only to the authorities which he cited. Ib. (ed. 1770), 149, 155, 156, 160 ; (ed. 1824), 96, 104, 105, 110 ; 1 Gordon's Hiſt. U. S. 291, 296. The real danger there was that the jury would

would not be restrained by any rules of law from convicting the prisoners; and the counsel for the Crown did not dispute the principles of law upon which the defendants relied. Paine's Argument on the *Trial of the Soldiers*, (ed. 1824), 118. 2 John Adams's Works, 236. And see Ib. 317. It is also to be remarked that those soldiers who were convicted against the instructions of the Judges were branded in the hand by order of the Court. Rec. 1770, fol. 55. Boston Gazette of December 17, 1770. Among Judge Trowbridge's MSS., under the head of "New Tryals in Criminal Cases," is this collection of authorities: *Rex* v. *Davis*, 1 Show. 336. *Regina* v. *Clarke*, 1 Stra. 106. *Rex* v. *Walthamstow & Wilts*, 1 Stra. 101. *Dr. Salmon's case*, 1 Stra. 104. *Regina* v. *Bewdley*, 1 P. W. 212. *Rex* v. *Marchant*, 2 Keb. 403. *Rex* v. *Hannis*, 2 Keb. 765. *Rex* v. *Bowden*, 1 Keb. 124. *Regina* v. *Banks*, 6 Mod. 245. *Anon.* 3 Salk. 362. *Rex* v. *Simmons*, 1 Wils. 329. *Rex* v. *Smith*, 2 Show. 165, & T. Jon. 163. *Rex* v. *Read*, 1 Lev. 9. *Rex* v. *Jackson*, 1 Lev. 124. To which Judge *Trowbridge* adds, "In the case of ye *King* agst *Jackson* it seems to be agreed by ye whole Crt that a new Tryal could not be had in a Capital Case." And the statements of *Hutchinson* and *Bernard*, concerning the *Trial of the Soldiers* and the previous conviction of *Richardson* for murder in the same year, show that when a jury convicted against the instructions of the Court, the only remedy was supposed to be to respite the prisoner until a pardon could be obtained from the King. 3 Hutchinson's Hist. Mass. 286, 287, 328. Hutchinson to Gage, April 22, 1770, 25 Mass. Archives, 387. Bernard to Hutchinson, July 15, 1770, 8 Bernard Papers, 109. Hutchinson's Letters, November 26, December 3, 5 & 6, 1770, 27 Mass. Archives, 58, 63, 64, 65, 67. *Richardson's case*, Rec. 1772, fol. 15.

That *John Adams* did not consider the *Case of the British Soldiers* as conclusive against the right of the jury to decide the law in favor of any man notwithstanding the instructions of the Court, even in a civil action, is clearly shown in his own notes of an argument made by him immediately afterwards. In an action to recover a balance of account, tried in the Inferior Court, *Adams* says, "the jury found a verdict for the sum sued for. *Kent* moved it should be rejected. I denied the power of the Court to reject it, and said if he would move for a new tryal, that would not be without a precedent in the Superior Court, tho' it would be in an Inferior Court." MS. note by *John Adams* of *Wright & Gill* v. *Mein*, January term 1771, in the possession of Mr. *Charles Francis Adams*. Then follows this collection of authorities, apparently noted as they were found: St. Westm. 2, c. 30. Barrington on Sts. (2d. ed.) 74, 103, [5th ed. 100, 136]. Lord *Mansfield* in *Baldwin's case*, Junius to Ld. M. [Letter of November 14, 1770]. 3 Bl. Com. 378. 5 Bac. Ab. 285, 286, 292, "relating to general and special verdict," [Verdict, C., D]. 1 Inst. 228 *a*. Lit. § 368. *Rawlyns' case*, 4 Rep. 53 *b*. *Oneby's case*, 2 Ld Raym. 1490, 1494. Foster, 255. 1 Trials per Pais

John Adams.

Pais, 283. *Bright* v. *Eynon*, 1 Bur. 393. *Argent* v. *Darrell*, Cas. temp. Holt, 702. *Aſh* v. *Aſh*, Ib. 701. *Gay* v. *Cross*, Ib. 703. *Buſhell's case*, Vaugh. 147. [*Anon.*] 1 Salk. 405. [S. C. *Wright* v. *Crump*,] Farr. [7 Mod.] 2. *Fitzjames* v. *Moys*, 1 Sid. 133. *Graves* v. *Short*, Cro Eliz. 616. Cunningham Law Dict. Attaint, 3. Gilb. C. P. 128. 1 Bl. Com. 63. Lord *Camden's* Questions to Lord *Mansfield* in the Houſe of Lords, [*ante*, 563]. 4 Bl. Com. 354, 431. *Baker's case*, 5 Rep. 104. At the end of all which *Adams* adds: "*Mem.* Everything that is ſaid by the Court to the jury, is uniformly ſtyled in our books a direction. So the Court give a charge to the grand jury to preſent a particular offence, &c. But the queſtion is whether the jury are bound, in point of conſcience or of law, to obſerve that direction and find according to it? Are they ſubject to any penalty, or fine or impriſonment if they find contrary to that direction? No man will ſay that they are." In the Superior Court, on appeal, at February term 1771, the plaintiff filed a new declaration, and obtained an increaſed verdict, upon which judgment was rendered, although the defendant moved for a new trial. *Mein* v. *Wright*, Rec. 1771, fol. 210, and papers on file.

It is manifeſt from the coincidence in date that the discussion in *John Adams's* Diary, from which the following extract is taken, was part of his preparation for the argument of this caſe: "The oath of a juror, in England, is to determine cauſes 'according to your evidence.' In this Province, 'according to law and the evidence given you.' It will be readily agreed that the words of the oath, at home, imply all that is expreſſed by the words of the oath here; and whenever a general verdict is found, it aſſuredly determines both the fact and the law. It was never yet diſputed or doubted that a general verdict, given under the direction of the Court in point of law, was a legal determination of the iſſue. Therefore the jury have a power of deciding an iſſue upon a general verdict. And if they have, is it not an abſurdity to ſuppoſe that the law would oblige them to find a verdict according to the direction of the Court, againſt their own opinion, judgment and conſcience? It has already been admitted to be moſt adviſable for the jury to find a ſpecial verdict, where they are in doubt of the law. But this is not often the caſe; a thouſand caſes occur in which the jury would have no doubt of the law, to one in which they should be at a loſs. The general rules of law and common regulations of ſociety, under which ordinary tranſactions arrange themſelves, are well enough known to ordinary jurors. The great principles of the Conſtitution are intimately known; they are ſenſibly felt by every Briton; it is ſcarcely extravagant to ſay they are drawn in and imbibed with the nurſe's milk and firſt air. Now, should the melancholy caſe ariſe that the Judges should give their opinion to the jury againſt one of theſe fundamental principles, is a juror obliged to give his verdict generally, according to this direction, or even to find the fact ſpecially, and ſubmit the law to the Court? Every man, of any feeling

feeling or confcience, will anfwer, no. It is not only his right, but his duty, in that cafe, to find the verdict according to his own beft underftanding, judgment, and confcience, though in direct oppofition to the direction of the Court. A religious cafe might be put, of a direction againft a divine law. The English law obliges no man to decide a caufe upon oath againft his own judgment, nor does it oblige any man to take any opinion upon truft, or to pin his faith on the fleeve of any mere man." 2 John Adams's Works, 254, 255.

This was when he was in the height of his practice at the bar, the first conftitutional lawyer of the Province, and only four years before he was appointed by the Revolutionary Government, upon the removal of *Trowbridge* and his colleagues, Chief Juftice of Maffachufetts. 3 Ib. 23, note. By refigning that office without ever having taken his feat, he laid aside the opportunity of carrying out himfelf on the bench the principles which he had uniformly maintained at the bar.

Law of Maffachufetts in civil cafes.

But thefe principles were fuppofed to be the law of Maffachufetts long after the adoption of the State Conftitution. Even in civil cafes, the right of the jury to decide the law feems to have been recognized until since the beginning of the prefent century. *Stickney* v. *Atwood*, (1784) 6 Dane Ab. 251. Sullivan on Land Titles (1801), 343. *Coffin* v. *Coffin*, (1808) 4 Mafs. 25. St. 1807, c. 140, § 15. But the power of the Court to grant new trials, which appears to have been in familiar ufe before the beginning of the regular feries of reports, has prevented the rendering of judgments on verdicts againft the directions of the Court in civil cafes. *Brown* v. *Swan*, 1 Mafs. 202. *Cogswell* v. *Brown*, 1 Mafs. 237. St. 1804, c. 105, § 6. *Bryant* v. *Commonwealth Ins. Co.* 13 Pick. 550. *Coffin* v. *Phenix Ins. Co.* 15 Pick. 295. *Cunningham* v. *Magoun*, 18 Pick. 15. *Miller* v. *Baker*, 20 Pick. 289. And it has recently been determined that if the evidence introduced by the plaintiff in a civil action "is fuch that the Court would fet aside any number of verdicts rendered upon it, *toties quoties*, then the caufe should be taken from the jury, by instructing them to find a verdict for the defendant." *Denny* v. *Williams*, 5 Allen, 5. And fee *Steinmetz* v. *Currey*, 1 Dall. 234; *Chandler* v. *Van Roeder*, 24 How. 226, 227.

In criminal cafes.

In criminal cafes, the right of the jury to decide the law was repeatedly recognized and affirmed, and never denied, in Maffachufetts, until 1846, since which it has been difallowed. *Theophilus Parsons*, in Mafs. Debates on U. S. Constitution in 1788, (ed. 1856) 194, 195; 2 Elliott's Debates, (2d ed.) 94. Pamphlet Trials of *Bowen* (1816) 51, 52, 56, and *Phillips* (1817) 17. *Parker*, C. J., Mr. *Dutton*, and *Jackson*, J. in Debates in Mafs. Convention of 1820, (ed. 1853) 540–542. *Commonwealth* v. *Blanding*, (1825) 3 Pick. 305. Pamphlet Trials (1828) of *Lyman*, 60, and *Child*, 90. *Commonwealth* v. *Knapp*, (1830) 10 Pick. 496. *Bryant* v. *Commonwealth Ins. Co.* (1833) 13 Pick. 550, 551. Pamphlet Trial of *Snelling*, (1833) 75. *Commonwealth* v. *Kneeland*, (1835) 20 Pick. 208, 227; Review of, by Cofmopolite, 25. *Commonwealth*

wealth v. *Porter*, (1846) 10 Met. 263. *Commonwealth* v. *Abbott*, (1847) 13 Met. 123. St. 1855, c. 152. *Commonwealth* v. *Anthes*, (1857) 5 Gray, 185. *Commonwealth* v. *Martin*, (1857) 5 Gray, 303, note. *Commonwealth* v. *Lawrence*, (1857) 9 Gray, 135. *Commonwealth* v. *Rock*, (1857) 10 Gray, 5.

Maine. Vermont.

In Maine, the law is eftablifhed in favor of the right of the jury in criminal cafes. *State* v. *Snow*, (1841) 18 Maine, 346. And in Vermont, *State* v. *Williams*, (1829) 2 Verm. 488, 489. *State* v. *Croteau*, (1849) 23 Verm. 14. *State* v. *McDonnell*, (1860) 32 Verm. 531. In New Hampshire, it once was, but has fince been decided otherwife. Pamphlet Trials of *Farmer* (1821) 68, and *Blaifdell* (1822) 54. *Pierce* v. *State*, (1843) 13 N. H. 536. So in Rhode Island, the earlieft laws recognized the right; but the modern decifions are adverfe to it. 1 R. I. Col. Rec. (1647) 203, 404. *Dorr's Trial*, (1844) (Pitman's ed.) 121, 122, 131. *State* v. *Smith*, (1859) 6 R. I. 34. In Connecticut, the right of the jury to decide the law has been acknowledged fince the Revolution, even in civil cafes, and feems to be ftill in criminal cafes. *Witter* v. *Brewfter*, (1788) Kirby, 423. 2 Swift's Dig. (1823) 412.

New Hampshire. Rhode Ifland. Connecticut.

New York.

In the Province of New York, the right was repeatedly afferted by counfel in criminal cafes, and not denied by the Court. *Bayard's Trial*, (1702) 14 Howell's State Trials, 502, 503, 505. *Zenger's Trial*, (1735) 17 Ib. 706, 722, 723. See also Remarks on Zenger's Trial by "two eminent lawyers in one of our Colonies in America." Ib. 726, 731. The Supreme Court of the State of New York in 1804 was equally divided upon the queftion, *Kent & Thompson*, JJ. affirming the right, and *Lewis*, C. J. & *Livingston*, J. denying it. *People* v. *Crofwell*, 3 Johns. Cas. 337. The queftion does not appear to have been since argued before the fame Court or the Court of Errors or Court of Appeals in that State. But the right of the jury was repeatedly affirmed in 1825 by *Walworth*, J. (afterwards Chancellor). *People* v. *Thayers*, 1 Parker C. C. 598. *People* v. *Videto*, Ib. 604. It has lately been denied by fome Judges of the local Supreme Courts. *People* v. *Pine*, (1848) 2 Barb. 568. *People* v. *Finnegan*, (1848) 1 Parker C. C. 152, 153. *Carpenter* v. *People*, (1850) 8 Barb. 611. *Safford* v. *People*, (1854) 1 Parker C. C. 480. In New Jerfey, the right was affirmed by early ftatutes. Weft New Jerfey Laws of 1676, cc. 19, 22; 1681, cc. 6, 7, 10; (Leaming & Spicer's ed.) pp. 396, 397, 398, 428, 429. See alfo Dickinfon's Farmer's Letters, (Boston ed. 1768) 51.

New Jerfey.

Pennfylvania.

In Pennfylvania, before the Revolution, the right of the jury to decide the law for themfelves appears, from the notes of Prefidents *Shippen* and *Reed* (1 Dall. 30), to have been admitted, even in civil cafes. *Albertson's lessee* v. *Robertson*, (1764) 1 Dall. 9. *Boehm* v. *Engle*, (1767) Ib. 16. *Proprietary's lessee* v. *Ralston*, (1773) Ib. 19. *Anon.* (1773) Ib. 20. And in 1784 *M'Kean*, C. J. began his charge in a civil cafe by telling the jury that as the counfel "have quoted many cafes, but have not appealed to the Court for their opinion on the different points of law, the jury muft take the whole together, and form their own judgment upon

upon the subject." *Wilcox* v. *Henry*, Ib. 71. This report had been revised by the Chief Justice. Ib. pref. iii. The only American Judge between the Revolution and the year 1800, who is known to have denied the right of the jury to decide the law in a criminal case, was a Judge of a Court of Common Pleas in Pennsylvania. *Addison's* Charges to Grand Juries, (1792) 53. *Pennsylvania* v. *Bell*, (1793) Addison R. 160, 161. *Pennsylvania* v. *M'Fall*, (1794) Ib. 257. He was afterwards impeached by the House of Representatives, and removed by the Senate, and disqualified to hold any judicial office in the State, for interfering with the rights of an associate in charging the grand and petit juries. *Addison's Trial*, Lancaster, 1803. And the right of the jury in criminal cases was then generally recognized in Pennsylvania, as is shown by the testimony of her most eminent lawyers upon the trial of Judge Chase in 1804. Testimony of *William Lewis* and *Edward Tilghman*, 1 Chase's Trial, (Smith & Lloyd's ed.) 131–135, 148; Ib. (Evans's ed.) 20, 21, 27. And it seems to be still in that State. *John Read*, *arguendo*, in *Hanway's Trial*, (1851). *Guffy* v. *Commonwealth*, (1853) 2 Grant, 68.

In Virginia, the right of the jury in criminal cases seems to be admitted, though the early authorities are stronger than the later ones. *Maury* v. *Collector of Hanover*, (1763) Wirt's Life of Patrick Henry, 27, 28. Statements of *Hay* and *Nicholas*, 1 Chase's Trial (Smith & Lloyd's ed.) 175, 176; Ib. (Evans's ed.) 36, 92. *Dance's case*, (1817) 5 Munf. 363. *Davenport* v. *Commonwealth*, (1829) 1 Leigh, 596. *Leigh*, as *amicus curiæ*, in *Garth* v. *Commonwealth*, (1831) 3 Leigh, 770, 777. 6 Amer. Jurist, (1831) 243. *Doss* v. *Commonwealth*, (1844) 1 Grattan, 559. *Delaplane* v. *Crenshaw*, (1860) 15 Grattan, 482. Also in South Carolina. *State* v. *Allen*, (1822) 1 McCord, 529. And in Tennessee. *Mitchell* v. *State*, (1833) 5 Yerger, 346, *McGowan* v. *State*, (1836) 9 Yerger, 195. *Nelson* v. *State*, (1852) 2 Swan, 486, 487.

Virginia.

South Carolina.

Tennessee.

But it is believed to have been denied in every other Southern State in which the question has arisen, except where, as in Georgia and Arkansas, it had been established by express enactment. Constitution of Georgia of 1777, arts. 41–43, Watk. Dig. 14. Georgia Penal Code of 1833, div. 14, § 16, Prince's Dig. 660. *Holder* v. *State*, (1848) 5 Georgia, 444, 445. *Ricks* v. *State*, (1855) 16 Georgia, 603–605. *McPherson* v. *State*, (1857) 22 Georgia, 484, 485. Rev. Sts. of Arkansas, c. 85, § 25. *Patterson* v. *State*, (1846) 2 English, 60. *Sandford* v. *State*, (1850) 6 English, 331. It was early denied in Maryland. Judge *Winchester* and *Luther Martin*, (1804) 1 Chase's Trial, (Smith & Lloyd's ed.) 297; 2 Ib. 150, 151; Ib. (Evans's ed.) 106*, 182, 183. And even after the Constitution of that State in 1851 had expressly declared that "in trial of all criminal cases the jury shall be judges of the law as well as the fact," the Court of Appeals decided that the jury had no right to judge of the constitutionality of a statute. *Franklin* v. *State*, (1858) 12 Maryland, 246, 249. The right of the jury to decide the law is de-

Georgia.

Arkansas.

Maryland.

North Carolina. Alabama. Miffiffippi. Kentucky. Miffouri. Texas.

nied in North Carolina. *State* v. *Peace*, (1854) 1 Jones N. C. 251. In Alabama. *Pierson* v. *State*, (1847) 12 Alab. 153, 154, and *Batre* v. *State*, (1850) 18 Ib. 123, 124, modifying the earlier opinion in *State* v. *Jones*, (1843) 5 Ib. 672–674. In Miffiffippi. *Williams* v. *State*, (1856) 32 Mifs. 389. In Kentucky. *Montee* v. *Commonwealth*, (1830) 3 J. J. Marfh. 149, 150. *Commonwealth* v. *Van Tuyl*, (1858) 1 Met. Ky. 5. In Miffouri. *Hardy* v. *State*, (1842) 7 Miffouri, 607. And in Texas. *Nels* v. *State*, (1847) 2 Tex. 282.

Ohio. Indiana.

It has alfo been denied in Ohio. *Montgomery* v. *State*, (1842) 11 Ohio, 427. *Robbins* v. *State*, (1857) 8 Ohio State R. 166, 167. In Indiana, the right was firft denied, then affirmed, again denied, and finally eftablifhed by an amendment of the Conftitution. *Townsend* v. *State*, (1828) 2 Blackf. 151. *Armstrong* v. *State*, (1836) 4 Blackf. 247. *Carter* v. *State*, (1851) 2 Ind. 619. *Williams* v. *State*, (1858) 10 Ind. 503.

Power of the Legiflature.

The authority of the Legiflature to confer this right upon the jury (if they did not have it before) was recognized by the whole Supreme Court of New York in *People* v. *Croswell*, 3 Johns. Cas. 413; afferted by *Jackson*, *Dewey* and *Thomas*, JJ. of the Supreme Court of Maffachufetts, and denied by *Shaw*, C. J., *Metcalf*, *Bigelow* and *Merrick*, JJ., of the same Court. Debates in Mafs. Convention of 1820 (ed. 1853) 542. *Commonwealth* v. *Anthes*, 5 Gray, 222, 236, 250, 251, 303.

U.S. Supreme Court.

Georgia *v.* Brailsford.

There can be no better evidence of the recognition in the laft century of the right of the jury to decide the law, even in civil cafes, than the unanimous decifion of the Supreme Court of the United States, as declared by Chief Juftice *Jay* in 1794 in a civil caufe of great importance, to which a State was a party, and which was therefore tried at the bar of the Supreme Court. *Georgia* v. *Brailsford*, 3 Dall. 4. The authenticity of the report of that cafe is hardly open to queftion. It had probably been fubmitted to Chief Juftice *Jay* himfelf; for there is no reafon to doubt that Mr. *Dallas* kept up the practice, which he had eftablished in his firft volume, of fubmitting each cafe, before printing, to "the examination of the prefiding judge of the Court in which it was determined." 1 Dall. pref. iii. And the report was quoted by *Alexander Hamilton*, within ten years after the decifion, in a criminal trial of great importance and intereft, and its accuracy not difputed. *People* v. *Crofwell*, 3 Johns. Cas. 347, 358. "Speeches at full length" in that cafe, published in New York in 1804, pp. 11, 49, 77.

Cabot *v.* Bingham.

Another cafe, not ufually referred to upon this fubject, which came before the Supreme Court of the United States in 1795, prefents fo curious an analogy to the cafes of the *Province* v. *Paxton*, *ante*, 548, and *Erving* v. *Cradock*, *supra*, 553, as to be worthy of being here ftated. In an action for money had and received, the defendant contended that he received the money as agent of the United States at Martinique, for the fale, purfuant to a decree in admiralty there, of a neutral veffel, captured and sent in to that ifland during the Revolutionary War, by an American privateer

privateer owned by the plaintiffs. The jury, under the inſtructions of the Circuit Court, returned a verdict for the plaintiffs, and the defendant ſued out a writ of error. *Cabot* v. *Bingham*, 7 Dane Ab. 655 *& seq.*; 3 Dall. 19; Printed Caſe of the Daniſh Brig the Hope. Mr. *Dane* ſays that the common law courts in Maſſachuſetts had previouſly been in the practice of trying the queſtion of prize or no prize, when it aroſe incidentally; contrary to the practice in England and in other States. 7 Dane Ab. 645, 646, 659, 660. In the Supreme Court of the United States, *Iredell*, J., in giving his opinion in favor of the juriſdiction of the Court below, ſaid: "It will not be ſufficient to remark that the Court might charge the jury to find for the defendant; becauſe, though the jury will generally reſpect the ſentiments of the Court on points of law, they are not bound to deliver a verdict conformably to them." 3 Dall. 33. Neither of the Judges expreſſed any doubt of this, but the Court was equally divided on the queſtion of jurisdiction.

The extent of the rights and duties of juries in this reſpect has not ſince come before the Supreme Court of the United States. But individual Judges of that Court, before and after the caſes juſt cited, repeatedly affirmed the right of the jury to judge of the law in criminal caſes. *Iredell & Wilson*, JJ. in *Henfield's Trial*, (1793) Wharton's State Trials, 87, 88. 2 Wilſon's Works, 372. *Chase*, J. (1800) in *Trial of Fries*, 196; of *Callender*, Wharton's State Trials, 634, 709, 710, 713 & seq.; and on his own trial, (1804) (Smith & Lloyd's ed.) 34, 35, (Evans's ed.) Appendix, 44, 45. *Marshall*, C. J. in 1 *Burr's Trial*, (1807) 470; 2 Ib. 444, 445, 448. *Duvall*, J. in *Trial of Hodges*, (1815). *Baldwin*, J. (1830) in *United States* v. *Wilson & Porter*, Bald. 99, 108. See alſo *Talmadge*, J. in *Trial of Smith & Ogden*, (1806) 236, 237; *Cases under the Embargo Laws*, 3 Bradford's Hist. Maſs. 108, & *Lyman's Trial*, 41. And this right does not ſeem to have been denied by any Judge of the Supreme Court of the United States before 1835, except upon queſtions of the conſtitutionality of ſtatutes, of which an exception was made by *Patterson*, J. in *United States* v. *Lyon*, (1798) Wharton's State Trials, 336, by *Chase*, J. in *Callender's Trial*, *ub. sup.* and by *Baldwin*, J. in *United States* v. *Shive*, Bald. 512 — a diſtinction which can hardly be maintained. See *Theophilus Parsons* in Convention of 1788, *ub. sup.*; *Shaw*, C. J. in *Commonwealth* v. *Anthes*, 5 Gray, 188–192; *Curtis*, J. in *United States* v. *Morris*, 1 Curt. C. C. 59; *ante*, 529. But the more recent opinions of ſome Judges of the Court deny the right of the jury to decide the law adverſely to the inſtructions of the Judge in any caſe whatever. *Story*, J. in *United States* v. *Battiste*, (1835) 2 Sumner, 243; *Curtis*, J. in *United States* v. *Morris*, (1851) 1 Curt. C. C. 49–63; and ſundry unreported caſes.

Other opinions of U. S. Judges.

It is worthy of notice how the history of this queſtion after the English Revolution of 1688 repeated itſelf in America nearly a century later. The great conſtitutional lawyers and judges of either Revolutionary period

Conclusion.

period—*Somers* and *Holt*; *Adams*, *Jay*, *Wilson*, *Iredell*, *Chase*, *Marshall*, *Hamilton*, *Parsons* and *Kent*—with one voice maintained the right of the jury upon the general iſſue to judge of the law as well as the fact. But they had hardly paſſed away, or fifty years elapsed ſince either Revolution, when the courts of the new government began to aſſert as much control over the conſciences of the jury, as had been claimed by the moſt arbitrary Judges of the Monarch whom that Revolution had overthrown. The analogy recalls the motto from *Grotius*, placed by Mr. *Dallas* upon the title-page of his reports: *Atque eo magis necessaria est hæc opera, quod et nostro sæculo non desunt, et olim non defuerunt, qui hanc juris partem ita contemnerent, quasi nihil ejus præter inane nomen existeret.*

APPENDIX III.

Governor Pownall's Meſſage to the Council upon the Juriſdiction of Judges of Probate.

1760.

Governor's Meſſage upon Judges of Probate.

PROVINCE OF THE MASSACHUSETTS BAY.

Probate Rec. Lib. I. fol. I.

At a Court of Probate held by the Governor, with the Council or Aſſiſtants at the Council Chamber in Boſton on the 9th day of February A. D. 1760.

His Excellency having been pleaſed to lay before the Court ſundry matters to be by them conſidered, the ſame were referred to a Committee and are as follows, viz.:

GENTLEMEN, — By the Royal Charter granted to His Majeſty's Province the Maſſachuſetts Bay, it is Eſtabliſhed and Ordained "That the Governor of ſaid Province or Territory for the Time being, with the Council or Assistants, may Do, Execute or Perform all that is neceſſary for the Probate of Wills and Granting of Adminiſtrations for, touching or concerning any Intereſts or Eſtate which any Perſon or Perſons ſhall have within our ſaid Province or Territory" — with Liberty to the Subject of Appeal to His Majeſty.

The Governor with the Council or Aſſiſtants is thus Conſtituted a Court of Juſtice of ſuch Ample Juriſdiction and important Powers as ſeem not to have been hitherto ſufficiently attended to; And to this Inattention it muſt be Imputed that the Idea of the nature of the Court and the Laws

1760. Laws of Practice which it ought to adopt should so long remain Vague and Indeterminate, And the Court itself still exist without a Seal, Records and Rules or even the Common Formalities of a Judicial Court.

In order to Establish These necessary Points and form some Regular Plan of Conduct it should be observed That This Court and this Only is immediately Constituted by Charter antecedent to all Provincial Law.

The matter subjected to its Judgment is all Estates and Interests in this Province so far as they are connected with the Probate of Wills or the Granting Administration.

The Jurisdiction Granted is the Execution of this Probate of Wills or Granting Administration with all that is necessary thereto.

These things under the old Charter were cognizable in the County Court; and in England, so far as concerned Personal Estate, in the Spiritual Court only.

As the business of this Court was never the Object of Common Law; And as its Proceedings for the most Part are in matters Executory and cannot admit of Tryals and Processes according to the Methods of the Common Law, *it cannot be a Common Law Court.*

As it is a Judiciary of Laymen and cannot execute its Decrees by Excommunication and Ecclesiastical Censures *it cannot be* deemed *a Spiritual or Ecclesiastical Court.*

It therefore follows that it is A CIVIL LAW COURT. This Idea will not only point out to us what ought to be the Rules or Practice of this Court; but from this alone can its present method of administration be accounted for.

No Common Law Court has a power of Substitution; No Law of the Province establishes the Court of the County Judges of Probates, Though many Laws recognize them as Constituted. This power of Substitution or Delegation is Incidental to every Civil Law Judge, and this Incidental Right is specially mentioned in the Charter by the words *all that is necessary* thereto.

The Wisdom therefore of our Predecessors has from this Idea, understanding the Power they were Vested with by said

ſaid Grant of a Civil Law Juriſdiction, Delegated or Substituted Judges of Probates in the ſeveral Counties who are thereby by Inferior Civil Law Courts for Distinct Peculiars, and ſubſiſt by a Delegation of Power to Judge in the firſt Inſtance from whom lies an appeal to the Governor with the Council or Aſſiſtants as the Superior Court of the Province for ſuch matters.

All Civil Law Courts in England (whether they be called Spiritual or merely Civil) are controulable by the King's Bench ; but the State and Relation of theſe Delegates of the Supream Power in the Province exempt them from receiving Prohibitions and Mandamus from the Common Law Superior Court.

An appeal to his Majeſty in Council does, in this Caſe as in all others ſpecifyed by the Charter, lye from their Decrees, and there alone the Grievance can be redreſſed. But in the mean while in all ſuch Caſes wherein an Inhibition or Mandamus would iſſue in England there ſeems to be by the preſent indeterminate method of Practice of this Superior Civil Law Court, a defect of Juſtice. And yet the Proper and conſtitutional Remedy does by Charter lye within their Juriſdiction.

The Proviſion made by the Laws of this Province reſpecting Inſolvents Estates and other matters which impower the Judge of Probate to Execute theſe matters —— Theſe matters being the Subject matter of Chancery and Appeal lying to the Governor with the Council or Aſſiſtants —— The Governor with the Council or Aſſiſtants Acts in ſuch Caſe as a Civil Law Court Remedial or a Court of Chancery.

This Court Therefore being a Civil Law Court having Juriſdiction in thoſe matters wherein the Spiritual or Eccleſiaſtical Courts and the Court of Chancery in England exerciſe Juriſdiction, The Civil Law ſo far as it hath been adopted or recognized as authority in either the Eccleſiaſtical Courts or the Court of Chancery and ſo far as it hath been eſtabliſhed by Law in England ought to be the Law and Rules of this Court, ſo far as the Circumſtances and

1760. and Laws of this Province will admit of ſuch Reception.

The Civil Law is the Baſis of the Practice of the Eccleſiaſtical Courts in England, but they have admitted alſo of ſome of the Papal and other Decretals, the Canons, &c: and have alſo incorporated therewith Acts of Parliament and Reſolutions of Comon Law Courts by which they have been controuled. Their is the Rule of Practice in that Court in England. And therefore ſo far as this Superior Civil Law Court acts in matters wherein that Court exerciſes Juriſdiction it may receive ſaid Rule as the rule of its Practice; Though the Civil Law alone ſhould ſtill be the Basis of its Practice ſo far as the Circumſtances and Laws of the Province will admit.

In the ſame Manner where the Objects or Matters are matters cognizable by Chancery and come under the Juriſdiction of this Court; the Civil Law with ſuch alterations and additions as has been made in that Caſe by the Common and Statute Law of England ſhould, ſo far forth as ſaid Law extends hither or is received as the Common Law of the Country, be the Baſis of the Rules and Practice of the Civil Law Court; as Chancery is itſelf in great meaſure in its proceedings, Examination of Evidence, Hearings and Determinations, a Civil Law Court and regulated by the Forms and the Rules of ſuch.

This Point being preciſely Determined, the Rules and Laws of theſe Courts are Fixed and Known, Things taken up by the Wiſdom of the Courts and Eſtabliſhed by the Experience of Ages.

There is one matter further which deſerves very ſerious Conſideration as to this Court of Governor with the Council or Aſſiſtants, the conſidering of which in this Light will relieve it of very great difficulties and embaraſſment — It is concerning a matter not subject to its Juriſdiction by Charter but ſubjected to it by a Law of this Province.

By an Act of this Province, Confirmed by their Majeſty's William and Mary Aug[t] 22, 1695, "all Controverſies concerning Marriage and Divorce are to be heard and Determined

termined in a Court of Civil Law, in which Courts Queſtions of Divorce are Determinable ſo far forth as Marriage by the Law of the Province is eſteemed a Civil Contract, ſo far may it be Determined in ſaid Court. 1760.

Divorce in the genuine and original Senſe of that Word was Diſſolutio Vinculi Matrimonii. It ſuppoſed the Exiſtence and real Validity of the Marriage, and from thence Determined the Contract and abſolved the Parties from the Civil Covenant. In this Senſe of the Word the Civil Law Courts uſed to Divorce, and reſcind this Kind of Contract as they did others, either for Fraud and groſs Circumvention in entering into the Contract or for Eſſential Contraventions Subſequent to it.

When the See of Rome took this Power out of the hands of these Lay Courts, It gave to the Spiritual Court Power only to Judge whether the Marriage was originally Valid according to Canon Law, and if not, to paſs Sentence of Nullity, as void ab Initio: And alſo for certain Cauſes (when the Perſon were actually under the Tyes of Matrimony) to order the Parties to live Separate, till both parties ſhould agree to come together again as before, and improperly called theſe, which were Controverſies of Marriage, Sentences of Divorce, Whereas the real Power of Divorce a Vinculo the Pope reſerved in his own hands.

And thus Matters continued to the Reformation, when Henry the 8th, Vindicating to himſelf the Legal Power of the Supremacy, The Power of the See of Rome being by act of Parliament aboliſhed in England, Henry referred this Power to Parliament, and there alone it rests in England. If the Law of this Province Veſts this Power in the Governor and Council as a Civil Law Court in the Case of a Civil Contract, and this Law be confirmed, The Caſe of Divorces in this Province are freed of all Difficulty. If not, The Doubt then remains whether this Power lies with the Legiſlature of this Province or only with the Parliament of Great Brittain. I have ſaid in the Caſe of a Civil Contract, becauſe a Doubt may ariſe whether if the Parties be Married by a Miniſter ordained by a Biſhop

 of

1760. of the Church of England or Ireland, whether it be a Civil Contract or not.

The Committee having reported upon the matters aforesaid — The following Orders were made thereon viz$^{t.}$

Whereas in and by the Royal Charter granted to this Province by King William and Queen Mary it is eftablifhed and ordained that the Governor for the time being, with the Council or Affiftants, may do, execute or perform all that is neceffary for the Probate of Wills and granting of Adminiftrations for, touching or concerning any Interest or Eftate which any Perfon or Perfons fhall have within faid Province; and whereas the Laws of this Province have made provifion to Appeals from the Decrees and other Proceedings of the Judges of Probate, to the Governor and Council — To the end therefore that all proceedings had in confequence of any fuch appeals and other matters tranfacted by the Governor with the Council or Affiftants as the Supreme Court of Probate, may be kept Seperate and apart from their Tranfactions relative to matters of any other Nature or kind.

Ordered, that there be a Regifter appointed for this Court, to enter all Determinations and Proceedings therein (whether upon Appeals or otherwise) relating to Probate of Wills, granting Adminiftrations or Guardianfhips and Settlements of Eftates, in a Book to be provided for that purpofe only; who fhall give out attefted Copies of all fuch Determinations and Proceedings, as occafion may require, and fhall be Sworn for the faithful Difcharge of his Truft.

Ordered likewife, that there be a Seal provided and appropriated to the ufe of this Court. Alfo

Refolved, that the Supreme Court of Probate be ftatedly held twice in each year, for tranfacting the Affairs cognizable therein — Viz$^{t.}$: on the Second Wednefday in the May Seffion of the General Court, and on the Second Wednefday of the Seffion of the fame Court, next following the firft day of November annually.

Upon a Queftion being moved relating to Appeals from the Judges of Probate — Refolved

Resolved by this Court, that no Judges of Probate ought to admit of Appeals, unless the same be claimed, Bond given, and Reasons of Appeal filed, in Time and manner as the Law directs; and that upon the Appellants failing to comply with the Directions of the Law in any or either of those Particulars, such Judges ought to carry their respective Orders and Decrees (from which such Appeal was or shall be claimed) into execution. 1760.

His Excellency having observed that there still remained to be considered these two Points namely (1st.) What Rules or orders are to be observed by the Court in its Judicial Capacity, (2nd.) In what method the exercise of its Jurisdiction may be carried into Execution, — Said matters were referred to the Same Committee as before, to consider and report thereon.

APPENDIX IV.

Quincy on the Impeachment of Public Officers.*

Messieurs Edes & Gill,

Please to insert the following.

'*If to differ ever hereafter with an upstart Minister, is to be construed as a* Crimen laesæ Majestatis ; *if the Giant* Prerogative *is to be let loose, and stalk about, to create* unusual *Terrors, and inflict* unpractised *Punishments; if the fiercest Thunderbolts of Jupiter are to be launched by a low Miscreant against the slightest Offence, and even against Innocence itself; if the favourite Motto of the* North, *the* Nemo me impune lacessit, *is to be adopted as the future rule of Government in our once happier Land, we may then boast as much as we please of our invaluable Liberties, purchased with the Blood of our heroic Ancestors ; — but let us watch them narrowly, lest, before we are aware, they should depend upon too slight a Thread.*'

READER ! Make thine own Comment — Permit me alſo to make my own Application. If the preceding Quotation excite Sentiments in thy Mind, different from thoſe Senſations which affect my Breaſt, I will not pluck out thine Eyes, or tear out thy Heart. My Creed will not condemn thee, neither will thy Faith obtain my Salvation. Theoretic Opinions are of but little Conſequence to Mankind : It is the practical Deportment which is of Importance to the Community. For let a Man's Thoughts in Religion and Politicks, be what they may, they are of inconſiderable Moment to his Fellow-men : but when once the Principles of a Man prompt

---

* Published in the Boston Gazette, Jan. 4, 1768.

prompt him to proſtitute his Office, or neglect the ſacred Duties of his Station, the State has an undoubted Right to demand the Infliction of due Puniſhment, and it is incumbent upon every Individual of Society to forward a rigourous Execution of Justice. And when it happens, that any one Man has obtained, *by a general Amaſſment of Power*, ſuch an unlimited Sway, in the State, as to be able, with Impunity, *to condemn the Innocent as a Judge, and destroy the Constitution as a Statesman*, deplorable indeed is the Fate of that Nation. But there is Hope, that the Caſe is not deſperate, unleſs this rapacious Graſper of Sovereignty, elated with a Plentitude of Power, has had the Effrontry to make an open Avowal of his Designs, and Hardineſs ſufficient to proclaim his Reſolution to fulfill their Accomplishment. When ſuch is the Object, ſuch the Determination, ſuch the Boldneſs of only one single Tyrant, irremediable, indeed, in all human Probability, is the Malady of the Common-wealth. For when deſpotic Views of this complection are form'd and executed, 't is Demonstration, that the Minds of the People are ſunk in Submiſſion; and should ſome dauntleſs Champion of the Cauſe of Freedom, providentially ariſe for their Defence, they would fly, like a timid Herd, and leave the virtuous Hero to be ſacrific'd as a Victim. Never indeed was there a Wolf of the State, who did not think the People were but Sheep: — Strange Infatuation of Mankind! They bow the Knee to the Image, they themſelves have form'd, and tremble before the Bugbear of their own Creation.— Strip yon gorgeous Monarch of his Regalia, take from that deſpotic Tyrant, the Powers with which a deſpiſed Rabble have invested him; — the *one* sinks, a weak, puſilanimous Mortal, the *other* hides, a wretched, contemptible and execrated Monster.

It is almost incredible, that one, who had enjoy'd the Felicity of living under a British Government, should be endued with ſo inſatiable a "*Lust of Power*" as to wiſh the Subversion of it's Constitution. — It is equally incredible, that any Man, who knew the characteristic Bravery of Freemen, ſhould dare make the Attempt. — *Quid non mortalia Pectora*

Pectora cogis Imperii sacra Fames? An exorbitant Thirst of Dominion, united with a defperate Mind, will do Wonders. Restlefs Ambition will be unwearied in the Race for the Prize of Power; an intrepid Spirit will, at all Hazards, win the Palm. With a Wifh to Command, and Ability to Execute, Conqueft is inevitable.—The Thirst of Rule renders the Plan of Empire obvious to the Afpirer; a Determination to accomplifh, facilitates the Progrefs of Attainment.—Happy for Americans, their wife and venerable Ancestors, confcious of the predominant Vices of Mankind, have been eminently careful in guarding every Avenue, where it was probable, the ambitious and intrepid Enemy would labour to enter, by Stratagem and Force, in order to destroy that noble Fabrick, the complicated Work of Heroes, Saints and Ages, the *British Constitution.*

A short Attention to the following Extracts will abundantly convince every intelligent Mind, that, while the first Principles of our Constitution, the Fundamentals of all our Liberties, are adher'd to, no Subject, however great and powerful, is beyond the Reach of a strict Examination into his Conduct, or out of Danger of a Scourge for his Crimes.

"A Peer of the Realm may be Impeached *in Parliament* by Articles exhibited at the Suit of the King, by the Attorney General, as against the Earl of Bristol. Rush. 249.

By Articles exhibited by another Peer. Rush. 254.

So *the Commons* may *by Parol*, charge a Peer before the King and Lords. Seld. Jud. Parl. 24. (3 Vol. 2. p. 1596. 1598, 9.)

Or a Commoner. Vide Seld. 3 Vol. 2. p. 1598, 9.

So before the Lords at a Conference. Seld. Jud. Parl. 30, 31, 32. (3 Vol. 2. p. 1598, 1599.)

The Right of Impeachment by the Commons was allowed by the Lords, 20 June 1701.

In the Proceedings upon an Impeachment, by the Commons, a Member stands with others at the Bar of the Lords, there, in the Name of all the Commons of England, impeaches fuch an one, and acquaints the Houfe, that

that the Commons in due Time will exhibit Articles against him, and maintain them. Lords Journ. 1. 15. Ap. 1751, 1701.

Though the Commons impeach only for a particular Grievance, they may afterwards exhibit other Articles against him. Seld. Jud. Parl. 21. (3 Vol. 2. p. 1595.)

And the Delivery of ſuch Articles is not neceſſary till the Party appears. Seld. Jud. Parl. 23. (3 Vol. 2. p. 1596.)

If Articles are not exhibited against the Lords impeached, the Lords, by Meſſage, remind the Commons of it. Lords Journ. 5 May 1701. 15 May 1701. 4 June 1701.

But the Commons are Judges of the proper Time for exhibiting them. 31 May 1701. Yet the Lords *claimed* a Power to limit the Time. 4 June 1701.

Articles of impeachment need not purſue the ſtrict Forms of Law. Seld. Jud. Parl. 22, 27. (3 Vol. 2. p. 1595, 7.)

Where an Impeachment is for a capital Offence, he ſhall be committed to Cuſtody. Seld. Jud. Parl. 97. (3 Vol. 2. p. 1624.)

Yet the Commitment will ſometimes be omitted, at the Diſcretion of the Lords, Raym. 382.

And when an Impeachment is for High Treaſon, generally, without ſpecial Matter, it is uſually omitted. It was omitted in the Caſe of Ld. Clarendon, though the Commons complained of it. Life of Clar. 251 & 302.

After Anſwer by a Lord impeached, a Copy is made, and ſent to the Commons. Lords Journ. 14. 24.

After Anſwer, the Commons join Iſſue by Replication. 23 May 1701.

And may conſider whether they will reply or not. Seld. Jud. Parl. 199. (3 Vol. 2. p. 1628.)

Causes for Impeachment.

The Duke of Norfolk was Impeached for High Treaſon. 28 H. 6. Art. 1, 2, 3. Seld. Jud. Parl. 27. 3 Vol. 2. p. 1597.

For High Treaſon in ſubverting the fundamental Laws, and introducing arbitrary Power. Lord Finch, Sir Robert Berkley,

Berkley, Lord Strafford. 2 Rush. 606. 3 Rush. 1365. (Vid. Rush. Pt. 3. Vol. 1. 136.)

Michael de la Pool was Impeached, 10 R. 2. That he excited the King to act against the Advice of Parliament. Seld. Jud. Parl. 25. (3 Vol. 2. p. 1596.)

The Spencers, *that they gave bad Counsel to the King.* 4 Inst. 54.

Michael de la Pool was Impeached, that he, being Chancellor, acted contrary to his Duty. Seld. Jud. Parl. 26. (3 Vol. 2. p. 1596.)

The Duke of Buckingham was Impeached for a Plurality of Offices. 2 Car. Rush. 306.

The Earl of Oxford for exercising incompatible Offices. 8 May 1701.

So Lord Halifax. 9 June 1701.

The Spencers, Father and Son, were Impeached, for that they prevented the great Men of the Realm from giving their Counsel to the King, except in their Presence. 4 Inst. 53.

That they put good Magistrates out of Office, and advanced bad. 4 Inst. 53.

Lord Finch was impeached for threatening the other Judges to subscribe to his Opinion. Art. 4. 5. 6. Vide Rush. Part. 3. Vol. 1. 137.

For delivering Opinions which he knew to be contrary to Law. Art. 7. Vid. Rush. Pt. 3. Vol. 1. 137.

Is the Sword of Justice become pointless, that the Wicked go unpunish'd? Why is the Sabre of the Law sheathed, when the exhorbitant Crimes of the *peerless Man* demand the arm of the Executioner? — Woe unto the Land, when the Greatness of the Criminal shall dismay his Accusers, and his Authority shall make *the righteous Man* to tremble; when the enormous Power of Guilt shall exalt itself above the Judgment-Seat, and bid Defiance to the Tribunal of Justice!

PRO LEGE.

A

TABLE

OF THE

PRINCIPAL MATTERS

Contained in this Volume.

www.ingramcontent.com/pod-product-compliance
Lightning Source LLC
LaVergne TN
LVHW021104110826
845150LV00001B/163

* 9 7 8 1 4 2 5 5 6 5 4 1 1 *